Critical Writings

F. T. MARINETTI

Critical Writings

EDITED BY GÜNTER BERGHAUS

Translated by Doug Thompson

FARRAR, STRAUS AND GIROUX

NEW YORK

Farrar, Straus and Giroux
19 Union Square West, New York 10003

Copyright © 2006 by Luce Marinetti, Vittoria Marinetti Piazzoni, and Ala Marinetti Clerici
Translation, compilation, editorial work, foreword, preface, and introduction
copyright © 2006 by Farrar, Straus and Giroux, LLC
All rights reserved
Distributed in Canada by Douglas & McIntyre Ltd.
Printed in the United States of America
First edition, 2006

Library of Congress Cataloging-in-Publication Data
Marinetti, Filippo Tommaso, 1876–1944
   [Selections. English 2006]
   Critical writings / F. T. Marinetti ; edited by Günter Berghaus ; translated by Doug
Thompson.
      p.   cm.
   Includes bibliographical references and index.
   ISBN-13: 978-0-374-26083-5 (hardcover : alk. paper)
   ISBN-10: 0-374-26083-4 (hardcover : alk. paper)
   1. Futurism (Literary movement)—Italy.   2. Italian literature—20th century—History
and criticism.   I. Berghaus, Günter, 1953–   II. Title.

PQ4088M29813 2006
858'.91209—dc22

                                                                                2005024282

Designed by Debbie Glasserman

www.fsgbooks.com

1   3   5   7   9   10   8   6   4   2

CONTENTS

EDITOR'S FOREWORD

The idea of publishing a new translation of F. T. Marinetti's critical writings goes back to the year 2001, when Luce Marinetti informed me that Farrar, Straus and Giroux intended to reissue its edition of her father's book *F. T. Marinetti: Selected Writings*, which had been first published in 1972. Soon afterward, I had the occasion to speak to Roger Straus and to tell him that as a university professor who had been teaching Futurism for fifteen years, I very much hoped that he was going to publish more than just a reprint of the Flint-Coppotelli edition, which was now some thirty years old and no longer meeting the needs of a new generation of students and scholars.

Since the 1970s, Futurism has become a standard subject in university courses of art history, Italian studies, comparative literature, drama, and so on. However, most students lack the necessary linguistic skills to use the Mondadori edition of Marinetti's collected writings, and only a small number of texts has become available in English translation. Flint's edition was a pioneering one in the Anglo-Saxon world, but since its publication, more than two thousand books have been published on Futurism and have caused a considerable shift of emphasis in what is being taught in seminars dedicated to the Futurist movement. R. W. Flint's *F. T. Marinetti: Selected Writings* and Umbro Apollonio's *Futurist Manifestos* are currently the two most widely used text collections of Futurist manifestos, but unfortunately both omit a large number of writings that are now considered to be central to our understanding of Futurism, such as political manifestos and reflections on

Futurist theater and action art. Both books have been out of print for many years and, as I suggested to Roger Straus, it was the right time to replace them with an expanded edition of Marinetti's critical writings.

During my next visit to Rome, I discussed the matter again with Luce Marinetti, who fully supported my suggestion and proposed me to Mr. Straus as a suitable editor for such an undertaking. I compiled a list of writings that I felt should go into the new edition. However, these texts would have amounted to two substantial volumes, which in the current climate in the publishing world was deemed unfeasible. For a while I reflected on the possibility of compiling a volume of writings that had been excluded from the Flint-Coppotelli edition, but as quite a few texts in that collection were incomplete, and the translations did not always capture the meaning or flavor of the original, I decided to present a new list to the publisher. It included all manifestos generally considered to be fundamental for an understanding of Marinetti's aesthetic concepts—among them literature, theater, cinema, radio—plus a selection of critical writings from the early and middle period of the Futurist movement. Unfortunately, a representative sample of texts from the pre-Futurist period, 1884–1908, had to be omitted, and the number of proposed writings from the 1920s and '30s was reduced from twenty-five to eleven. Some manifestos, which carried Marinetti's signature but were essentially the work of other writers and artists, also had to be sacrificed.

Initially it had been suggested that I should function as both editor and translator of the edition. Although my command of the English and Italian languages is quite good, neither is my native tongue. Furthermore, I am not a philologist but a theater scholar, writer, and director. I therefore began a search for a suitable translator, one who was familiar with the Italian literature and culture of the early twentieth century, had an interest in the avant-garde, and—last but not least—had the time to turn some 200,000 words of highly complex prose into English. I am glad to say that my collaboration with Doug Thompson, who had recently retired from his professorial chair at Hull University, has been excellent, and his experience as a translator, as well as his extensive knowledge of twentieth-century Italian literature and politics, has been a great asset in this endeavor.

I have attempted to enhance comprehension of the texts by adding notes to sentences containing references to concepts, names, and subject matter unlikely to be generally known to a twenty-first-century public. In several cases I also had to explain neologisms or expressions that had assumed a specific meaning in Futurist circles. For example, the terms *passatismo* (traditionalism) and *passatista* (traditionalist), originally coined by Enrico Annibale Butti, took on a new dimension in Marinetti's writings, when he directed venomous attacks on a culture that rated the achievements of previous centuries above modern developments. We translated this term, variously, as clinging to the past, traditionalism, or fogydom. *Amore* (love) or *sentimento* (feeling) are not usually, in Marinetti's essays, neutral descriptions of the sensations of the heart, but instead relate to an insincere, hollow, overblown display of emotion. They do not refer to true, deep feelings, but to a gushy, mawkish, romantic, tear-jerking emotionalism, for which, again, we have used a variety of expressions in our translations. Some technical terms, used over and over again by Marinetti, had to be rendered in a consistent fashion. The choice of words we finally settled on was not always the most obvious, but it was the most appropriate one in this context—for instance, *parole in libertà* (Words-in-Freedom), *fisicofollia* (Body Madness), *sintesi* (minidramas), *interpenetrazione* (intermingling), *sinottico* (multichanneled), *moltiplicato* (extended), *eccitatorio* (Board of Initiatives). This means that some familiar titles of manifestos have been altered to reflect this choice of terminology, for example *Dynamic, Multichanneled Recitation* (rather than *Dynamic and Synoptic Declamation*), *Extended Man and the Kingdom of the Machine* (rather than *Multiplied Man and the Reign of the Machine*), and *A Futurist Theater of Essential Brevity* (rather than *Futurist Synthetic Theater*).

In the annotations the reader will find quite a few references to my own publications on Futurism. This is not intended as self-aggrandizement, nor as a deprecation of other scholars' writings on the subjects. As this collection of essays and manifestos is, in the first instance, aimed at a public unfamiliar with Italian, any references to critical literature in a non-English language are unlikely to be of much use to the reader. So, at a time when some 98 percent of studies concerned with F. T. Marinetti or Futurism are only available in Italian, my own modest contributions assume a rather disproportionate significance to the English or American reader. Critical literature and editions repeatedly referred to in the Notes have been listed in the short Bibliography at the back of the volume.

As far as Marinetti's own publications are concerned, we have used as our basic text Luciano de Maria's edition, *Teoria e invenzione futurista,* cited in both the first and the second editions. In some cases, the meaning of a text could only be clarified by having recourse to French versions of the essays and manifestos. Other editions regularly referred to were those of Luigi Scrivo (*Sintesi del futurismo,* 1968), Giovanni Lista

(*Futurisme: Manifestes, proclamations, documents*, 1973, and *Marinetti et le futurisme*, 1977), and Luciano Caruso (*Manifesti, proclami, interventi e documenti teorici del futurismo*, 1980). In my estimate, the editions mentioned above still omit some 60 to 70 percent of Marinetti's critical writings. A number of these can be found in the Beinecke Library of Yale University and the Getty Center in Los Angeles. Unfortunately, the famous *Libroni*, Marinetti's paste-up volumes of newspaper clippings, were sold to the Agnelli family and have not been made available for my research. I can only hope that one day this invaluable collection of ephemeral writings will be accessible again, and scholars will be spared time-consuming and laborious visits to dozens of Italian libraries in order to find an article or essay Marinetti published in the periodical press of the time.

In July 1941 the magazine of the Italian Writers' Union, *Autori e scrittori*, announced the establishment of an editorial board charged with the task of publishing a complete critical edition of Marinetti's writings. This undertaking, seen to be on a par with comparable commissions for the collected works of Pascoli, Carducci, D'Annunzio, and Pirandello, was described as being "eagerly awaited in Italy and abroad." Sixty years later we are still waiting for the first volume to appear in print. I am grateful to Luce Marinetti and Roger Straus for bringing this modest English-language anthology more speedily into the world. And last but not least, I congratulate Doug Thompson for completing his Herculean task within a rather tight time schedule.

GÜNTER BERGHAUS

JUNE 2004

TRANSLATOR'S PREFACE

As a translator, my primary concern is what Marinetti did with language. Behind the swaggering, iconoclastic, far-reaching revolution in the literary and plastic arts that Marinetti set in motion almost single-handedly toward the end of the first decade of the twentieth century, then stoked furiously for the rest of his life, there lies an enormous contradiction—and not a little irony! Although demanding entirely new modes of expression in keeping with the violence of his favored subject matter—"Up to now, literature has extolled a contemplative stillness, rapture, and reverie. We intend to glorify aggressive action, a restive wakefulness, life at the double, the slap and the punching fist . . . Art, indeed, can be nothing but violence, cruelty, and injustice" (*The Foundation and Manifesto of Futurism*)—whether in words, paint, or stone, his own expository writing frequently displays all the worst rhetorical excesses of the Italian post-Unificatory tradition, which he sought to destroy.

No other significant Italian writer, at any time, has made use of emphatics quite as much as Marinetti. At times the pages of his manifestos bristle with forests of exclamation marks or are punctured by a profusion of suspension points, inviting, one supposes, either admiration or reflection. Yet, where every utterance demands our special attention, the demand soon becomes tedious and loses its force. In keeping with the tradition he deplored, his sentences are often seemingly interminable, piling up clause upon clause, phrase upon phrase, repeating identical words or phrases or syntactical structures, seeking effect more than clarity, driven by passion rather more than by mind. "Let's leave wisdom behind as if it were some hideous shell," he cries,

> and cast ourselves, like fruit, flushed with pride, into the immense, twisting jaws of the wind! . . . Let's become food for the Unknown, not out of desperation, but simply to fill up the deep wells of the Absurd to the very brim! (*The Foundation and Manifesto of Futurism*)

In his *Technical Manifesto of Futurist Literature* of 1912, he called for the abolition of syntax, of punctuation, of adjectivals and adverbials, of conjunctions; a veritable apocalypse to set language free in order to express speed, dynamism, war, the undaunted, striving spirit, child of the Will. Yet he seems not to have had sufficient faith in a language purged of its traditional markers and procedures to entrust his revolutionary vision of unreason to it.

As a language, English has always been uncomfortable with such melodramatic extremes of passion and with the rhetorical devices Marinetti employed to give voice to them. However, no matter how wide the temperamental gulf separating modern English from Marinetti's Italian, in seeking to convey his meanings and something of the flavor of his means, the translator must perforce settle for a more or less inelegant hybrid, striving for a balance which eschews the most absurd and—at this distance in time—frankly laughable extremes of the medium without distorting its message out of all recognition.

When Marinetti did attempt to put his apocalyptic language into practice—in his poetry and fictional prose—he sought to communicate impressions of all five senses through the association of ideas that an accumulation of assumed collocates would conjure in the receiving mind, "bending back the contours of ordinary language and rational syntax," as George Steiner puts it in speaking of Heidegger. It was Hesiod who perhaps first suggested that Chaos lies outside grammar; but Marinetti, like Columbus, wishes to ply his craft beyond the boundaries of the already known world. His use of *Words-in-Freedom*—free-style word arrangements that do not adhere to conventional rules of grammar, orthography, or typography—has essentially the same purpose as Dante's or Milton's use of the epic simile, conveying meaning along a slender chain of sense that dangles from the known, at one end, to penetrate the obscure or unknown, at the other. For Marinetti, it is a fecundating Chaos which supposedly conveys its meanings through suggestion (in reality, autosuggestion) at the level of subliminal understanding in the individual being, re-creating the world anew out of chance proximities and encounters. The experience is both terrifying and exhilarating, for by cutting the moorings of grammar, syntax, and commonly recognized lexical combinations, Marinetti leaves us hanging by a thread, no longer reassured by the collective experience and knowledge which grammar and syntax imply, but entirely alone, clutching at whatever flies by, desperately trying, often failing, to make sense of it. Marinetti believes that by revisiting Chaos mankind may yet find new powers and attain new dimensions, which will enable him to better understand and perhaps eventually to dominate and rise above the essential irrationality of existence. One senses that he would have embraced wholeheartedly latter-day theories of black holes and antimatter; like the Jehovah of the Flood, like Euripides, he seeks to destroy everything and begin all over again.

Despite Marinetti's somewhat disingenuous denial of Futurism's at least partial dependence on Nietzsche, Nietzsche too sought to break free of the bonds of inherited discourse so as to arrive, along uncharted paths, at insights that were wholly new. Rooted in apocalypse and Chaos, Marinetti's linguistic discarding goes far beyond that of the philosopher (whose Zarathustra, it will be remembered, opted rather for "dancing the vision"), representing perhaps the ultimate reach of decadent Romanticism. Theoretically, Futurism was, as Mark Ford suggests, "a means of obliterating the past"; in practice, the futures it brought forth came from exploration, extension, and intensification of what already existed in the different art forms it influenced so profoundly. Originality *ex novo* is pure fantasy. It is rediscovery of what was lost or neglected, rather than obliteration, which energizes and leads to renewal. Marinetti and his associates, through their radical questioning and practical stripping down of linguistic and other forms, revealed untried, exciting new pathways to artistic creation, and this was their considerable achievement.

There have always been attempts at stretching—at times even to breaking point—the commonly recognized links between language and experience, and these, as Steiner observes, "lead either to autism and the silence of unreason or . . . to poetry." And this really is the crux of the matter so far as the translator of the "creatively revolutionary"—as opposed to the "expository"—Marinetti is concerned. Because the association of ideas sparked off by *Words-in-Freedom* is to a greater or lesser extent dependent on the individual's own association of particular words with particular circumstances, the possibilities of a communicative contract between writer and reader are much reduced, and thus the "meaning" as perceived by the one may bear very little resemblance, if any, to that perceived by the other. With grammatical and syntactical signposts all removed, almost every word becomes a crossroads at which only intuition can suggest the right way, and when that fails, only the blind leap is left. And this is the translator's problem with this particular Marinetti: there is often too little common ground and thus, inevitably, the translator sometimes finds himself in the unfamiliar situation of having to "invent" meaning, out of desperation, to fill the "silence." For Marinetti, it must be stressed, this by no means represents a negative impasse, for his words thus, supposedly, take on the role of wellspring of creation, and the poem—if there is to be one—is ultimately made by the translator (bearing in mind that every attentive reader is also a translator). Ironically, it was this creative process (and perhaps the limitations of his habitual subject matter) which stunted Marinetti's own poetic growth and the quality of his output. Of course, for the reader who wants to know what Marinetti really meant, these extreme practices of his represent a veritable cul-de-sac.

DOUG THOMPSON
AUGUST 2004

INTRODUCTION

F. T. Marinetti (1876–1944):
A Life Between Art and Politics

Filippo Tommaso Marinetti was born in Alexandria, Egypt, as the second son of the Piedmontese lawyer Enrico Marinetti and Amalia Grolli, daughter of a literary professor from Milan. His family had come to Egypt in 1865, invited by Ismail Pasha to act as legal advisers to foreign companies and individuals (more than 100,000 at the time) participating in the extensive modernization program initiated by the Khedive. Young Filippo Tommaso received his education at an international *collège* run by French Jesuits. From an early age he was a prolific writer of poetry, written exclusively in French, which was like a second mother tongue to him. In order to see his works published, he founded a magazine, *Le Papyrus: Revue bi-mensuelle littéraire, artistique, fantaisiste et mondaine*. In 1894 Marinetti was sent to Paris to take his baccalaureate at the Sorbonne. Soon afterward he moved to Italy, where, in accordance with his father's wishes, he studied law. In 1899 he was awarded a doctorate, but he never set up a lawyer's office and instead pursued his interests in poetry, music, and drama.

During his student years, Marinetti collaborated on a number of literary journals and used his contacts on the Parisian art scene to have some of his verses published in respected literary magazines such as *La Plume, La Nouvelle Revue, Mercure de France, La Vogue, Vers et Prose,* and *Gil Blas*. As a critic he took an active role in the literary debates of his time and published a large number of essays and polemical articles. Marinetti's writings from this period demonstrate his deeply felt conviction that the great advances of modern civilization also ought to be reflected in the art and literature of his time. Many of these latest developments he had had occasion to study in Paris; but at the turn of the century, Italy too was catching up with other major European countries. The agrarian character of the young nation was undergoing a rapid and profound transformation and giving way to industrial capitalism, especially in the north. Milan became a city of banks, department stores, theaters, cinemas, and music-halls. Traditional buildings were demolished to allow large arterial roads to be cut through the urban center. Streets were illuminated with powerful arc lamps; modern traffic with buses, trams, bicycles, and automobiles was replacing the horse-drawn cart and coach; houses were fitted with sanitary services unknown anywhere else on the peninsula. In short: the lifestyle of a modern metropolis began to emerge in Italy, too.

However, despite this "Arrival of the Future," Italy's cultural world remained firmly rooted in the nineteenth century. Instead of reflecting a country transformed by steam engines, automobiles, airplanes, electricity, and telephones, artists remained in their ivory towers standing aloof from the experience of the modern world. Marinetti judged the Italian poets of his time to be "unsophisticated, absolutely unaffected by the modern spirit and contemptuous of the heaving research that animates the soul of our century."[1] And his friend Carlo Carrà found that the artistic creations of these years were "dominated by works that had no other scope than that of satisfying the frivolous and corrupt taste of society."[2] Consequently, a group of bohemian artists and writers, who used to congregate at Milan's Caffè Savini, sought to resuscitate the dormant cultural life of their home country and declared war on the cultural establishment. Together they developed a new artistic philosophy, which was designed to galvanize into action a country that, in their view, was steeped in traditionalism and festering with decaying institutions. They proclaimed the cultural bankruptcy of a nation that clung to the past and ignored the great advances of the modern world. They ridiculed the ossified cultural and political institutions, the servile respect paid to an intellectual and artistic cult of the glorious Italian past. Instead, they sought nothing less than to revolutionize life and society in all their diverse aspects: moral, artistic, cultural, social, economic, and political.

Marinetti was a leading member of this group and in 1908 attempted to set up a new artistic movement, which he intended to name Elettricismo or Dinamismo. He was certainly qualified to function as the leader of such an enterprise. He was an established writer, critic, and publisher who had achieved literary success with his collections of poems, notoriety with his play *Le Roi Bombance*, and popular fame with many public appearances as an agitator and reciter of poetry. As collaborator of *Anthologie-Revue*, *La Plume*, *La Revue blanche*, *La Revue d'art dramatique*, and *La Vogue*, and as editor of a successful international magazine, *Poesia*, he possessed excellent connections in Italy and abroad. With the help of the Egyptian Pasha Mohammed El Rachi, a business friend of his late father and a shareholder of *Le Figaro*, he managed to place a foundation manifesto, which he had previously circulated as a broadsheet and issued in several Italian newspapers, on the front page of *Le Figaro*. In the months that followed, *The Foundation and Manifesto of Futurism* caused a tremendous stir and set the somnolent and stultified cultural scene in Italy ablaze. It rang in a new era in the history of modernist art and literature and set the tone for the operational tactics to be adopted by other avant-garde movements in the early twentieth century.

THE FUTURIST FUSION OF ART, LIFE, AND POLITICS

From 1909 to 1912 Marinetti and his followers published no fewer than thirty manifestos that outlined their artistic concepts and ideas. However, their aims could hardly be achieved by conventional art and literature alone. The publication of a theoretical statement, the performance of a play, or the exhibition of a painting, however controversial and polemical it may seem, remained an act of intellectual discourse. The true transformation of art into life could only be achieved through entering the public arena in a direct and combative manner. This is where Futurist politics and action art (*art-action*, or "introducing the fist into the struggle for art")[3] came into play. Futurism sought to bridge the gap between art and life and to bring aesthetic innovation into the real world. Life was to be changed through art, and art was to become a form of life. The Futurist project of innovation attempted to obliterate the contemplative, intellectual concept of culture and aimed at a total and permanent revolution in all spheres of human existence. What was later called "Futurist Re-fashioning of the Universe" was aimed at a transformation of humankind in all its physiological and psychological aspects, of the social and political conditions prevailing in the modern metropolis.

Marinetti's studies of law had provided him with a sound knowledge of modern political theories. But he also took a lively interest in the practical politics of his country, particularly those of radical and subversive groups. Together with his friends the anarchist poets Gian Pietro Lucini and Umberto Notari, he frequented various libertarian circles in

Lombardy. He visited meetings held by the Socialist Party and the trade unions; he became friendly with some leading members of the Revolutionary Syndicalist movement. Consequently, Marinetti was invited to recite his poetry in their meeting halls and to give lectures on art and politics (as an example, I have included in this collection the speech *The Necessity and Beauty of Violence*, document 11). It was Marinetti's firm belief that artists, with their superior creativity, intuition, and vitality, had an important contribution to make to the process of social and political renewal. From developing a program of revolutionary change in art and life it was a natural and logical step to become engaged in the political struggles of the times.

Marinetti was brought up in a partly African, partly French environment (see the biographical text *Self-Portrait*, document 1), but despite (or possibly because of) this cosmopolitan upbringing, he possessed a patriotic love of Italy. He confessed his great admiration for Francesco Crispi, one of the leading architects of the Italian nation, and lent his wholehearted support to the irredentists, who sought to liberate the *terre irredente*, or "unredeemed territories," still occupied by Austria. However, Marinetti never became a champion of Enrico Corradini and the conservative Nationalists, but instead supported the revolutionary nationalism of the anarcho-syndicalist movement. Syndicalists and anarchists sought to distinguish between their concept of a "just war," which moved humanity closer to freedom and justice, and the Nationalists' militarism and warmongering in the service of the capitalist class. They propagated the theory that just as there was a class conflict between proletariat and bourgeoisie, a battle for hegemony was fought between the proletarian and the bourgeois nations. From this premise they arrived at the myth of a revolutionary war designed to rally the Italians against the bourgeois states that controlled the wealth of the world. They advocated proletarian support for Italy's war with Turkey (1911) and entry into the First World War, saying that war "will give us Italians a sense of our strength as a nation" and will serve as "a means of rekindling the class struggle and pave the way for revolution."[4]

Marinetti adopted many of the anarcho-syndicalist views and amalgamated them with the lessons he had learned from Nietzsche, Sorel, and Bergson. It was from these ideas that he developed his concept of "war, the sole cleanser of the world," which runs as a pervasive thread through his work. In many of his writings and speeches he propagated a concept of *élan vital* and "healthy violence" that required destruction in order to construct a new world. Just as he believed in the "destructive gesture of libertarians," he promulgated the "healing force of war" as a fundamental principle of progress (see documents 3, 11, and 38–40).

Viewed from the vantage point of the twenty-first century, and knowing, as we do, the horrific outcome of militant nationalist propaganda, we often find it difficult to understand why so many starry-eyed artists and writers across Europe supported the Great War.[5] But without the experience of the mass slaughter of the First World War and the millions of dead soldiers and civilians in the Second, many intellectuals in the early twentieth century took a favorable attitude toward war and saw it as an exhilarating sporting event or a cleansing process beneficial for a healthy organism. A whole generation of Italian writers greeted the outbreak of war in 1914 as the fulfillment of their past dreams. The grandiose metaphors of *guerra come festa*, of war as a mystical, orgiastic experience of the Darwinian-Nietzschean principle of life as struggle, finally appeared to have become reality. The Futurists went to the front in the Lombard Battalion of Volunteer Cyclists and Automobilists, "dancing and singing," as they had predicted in *The Battles of Trieste*.[6] However, their first experience of a bombardment shocked them, and this festive mood changed rapidly. In December 1915 the battalion was disbanded and the Futurists returned to Milan. In summer 1916 most of them were under arms again, but this time the "heroic spectacle of battle"[7] had fatal consequences for the architect Antonio Sant'Elia (who was killed on August 10) and the artist Umberto Boccioni (who died after falling from his horse on August 17).

Marinetti's active service at the front did not in the least resemble that of a common soldier. He was allowed to move in and out of the war zone more or less as it pleased him. Giovanni Antonucci rightly called him an "itinerant ambassador,"[8] who employed this freedom to travel up and down the peninsula, giving lectures or making one of his many personal appearances as a *reduce dal fronte* at performances of the Futurist Theater of Essential Brevity.[9] Marinetti periodically engaged in frontline combat, but for him, his Futurist activities were a form of combat too, albeit on the home front rather than in the trenches. He therefore made every attempt to strengthen the "forcefully patriotic, antineutralist and anti-German Theater of Essential Brevity"[10] and to organize public events in support of the war effort.

THE FUTURIST POLITICAL PARTY AND THE BEGINNINGS OF THE FASCIST MOVEMENT

During the First World War, some six million Italians were called up for military service, and about four million of them were involved in frontline combat. The myth of war as propagated by the Interventionists did not fall on fertile ground among the nonintellectual population. The majority of them had little enthusiasm for the war they had been forced to fight, and as hostilities dragged on, this aversion spread against the whole political and military establishment, which was held responsible for the barbarous and senseless killing at the front. To represent their interests, the National Association of War Victims (Associazione Nazionale fra Mutilati ed Invalidi di Guerra, or ANMIG) was founded (April 29, 1917) and became the target of politicians from the Left and Right (see note 5 to document 53).

On November 11, 1918, the armistice was signed. The return of millions of ex-servicemen to civilian life caused chaos and social strife, which gave rise to a political movement of war veterans. Its most radical wing was formed by the Arditi (the "daring ones"), who had belonged to the assault troops in the Italian army. Among them were many Futurists, who organized themselves into a political party, the Fasci Politici Futuristi.[11] Their first political manifesto had been elaborated by Marinetti on the basis of his earlier "Futurist Political Program" of October 1913. They possessed their own organ, *Roma futurista*, which propagated the party's left-wing, revolutionary politics. In the summer of 1918, they joined forces with Benito Mussolini and participated in the founding of the Fasci di Combattimento in Milan's Piazza San Sepolcro (March 23, 1919). Many Arditi cells pledged their allegiance to the new association, and in recognition of their backing several prominent Ardito-Futurists were elected into the Fascist leadership at both a regional and a national level.

The early history of the Fascist movement was characterized by terrorist attacks and violent activities, often carried out with the connivance of the police and condoned by conservative politicians, as long as they were directed against the Socialist Party (PSI). However, Futurist opposition to the reformist PSI, which they considered to be a reactionary force in the country, did not necessarily imply opposition to socialist politics. In fact, quite a number of socialists (although not members of the official Socialist Party) were members of the Futurist Political Party. And when Antonio Gramsci founded a *radical* socialist party, the Partito Comunista Italiana, in 1921, he had the active support of many Futurists. It was therefore only a question of time before Marinetti and Mussolini would be at loggerheads over this issue. After the assembly in Piazza San Sepolcro, Marinetti voiced his concern over "the rather reactionary tendency of the rally to act against socialism. We have to prepare an Italian revolution against the vile government, the monarchical order, the Vatican, the parliament."[12] Furthermore, during the anti-Bissolati demonstrations in January 1919, Marinetti observed: "He [Mussolini] is a megalomaniac who will little by little become a reactionary."[13]

Consequently, the Arditi and Futurists proved to be less reliable in their antisocialist activities than the Fascists. On May 26, 1919, General Enrico Caviglia ordered the territorial army "to take measures to forbid the sale and reading in the barracks of the Bolshevik [*sic!*] newspaper *L'ardito*." And on July 30, 1919, a police report disclosed a rift between Mussolini and the Arditi and on August 6, 1919, informed the Minister of War that Carli, Vecchi, and Ambrosini had rescinded their cooperation with Mussolini's Fascio and were instead orientating toward the socialist movement.[14] For the time being, the Futurists and Fascists continued their coalition, but behind a facade of mutual friendship, Marinetti was deeply suspicious of Mussolini's intentions and disagreed with him over the question of how much support was to be given to the working-class organizations in their attempt to overcome the serious economic crisis that was plaguing Italy after the war. Were they to cooperate only with other combatants' organizations such as the Proletarian League, or also with the trade unions? And how were they to relate to the Socialist Party?

Before these issues could be resolved, the two leaders had to face the challenge of the imminent elections of November 1919. At the first congress of the Fasci di Combattimento in Florence in October 1919, Marinetti sought to sway the delegates toward a left-wing, Futurist position (see his speech in document 62). He described the atmosphere at the gathering as "totally Futurist, everybody talks about Futurism and is possessed by Futurist ideas."[15] In the crucial meeting of the Central Committee in Milan on October 16–18, the Futurist line triumphed over the conservative position. Even Mussolini declared himself a supporter of the Futurist wing. He and Marinetti prepared the ground for the election campaign and they spoke together at several election rallies.[16]

As it turned out, the elections were a disaster. The Fascist ticket failed abysmally, receiving only 4,657 votes (or 1.72 percent) from the 270,000 electors registered in Milan. Mussolini's reaction is well known: he finally broke with his left-wing past, rid himself of uncomfortable allies such as the Ardito-Futurists and revolutionary Interventionists, and prepared his conquest of the conservative establishment. The Futurists realized how dangerous the pact with the Fascists had been and how it had marred their reputation among the working class and other leftist sections of the population. In 1920 Marinetti decided to part company with the Fascists. He prepared a resignation statement for the next congress in Milan (March 23–25, 1920) in which he accused the Fasci of having estranged themselves from the laboring masses and of offering insufficient support to the proletarian demands for social justice and economic improvement. Furthermore, he censured them for possessing a reactionary law-and-order mentality and for offering far too little opposition to the clerics and monarchists. He was also highly critical of Mussolini's personality cult, of the way he ran the Fascist movement, and of the political views he expressed in his newspaper, *Il popolo d'Italia*. If his diary entries are to be trusted, one-third of the congress supported his views. But Mussolini vindicated himself and won over the majority of the delegates. Marinetti's reaction to the situation was clear and unequivocal. He summed up his feelings about the political development of the Fasci: "We have not come down as victors from the battlefield in order to march toward Reaction!"[17] On May 29 he handed in his resignation from the Central Committee and quit the Fasci di Combattimento.

Artists who had previously lent their support to the Futurist-Fascist alliance were now highly critical of Mussolini's conduct, his increasingly conservative attitudes, and his campaign for a "return to order." Many of them aligned themselves with a new political force: the Communist Party of Italy (PCI), founded on January 21, 1921. Because of the enlightened protector role played by Antonio Gramsci and some local party secretaries of a Gramscian conviction, a communist brand of Futurism came into existence. Unfortunately, the anti-intellectual stance of the majority of the PCI leaders prevented the party from developing a progressive cultural policy and from supporting a lively artistic practice within its local branches. Too many of its functionaries were unwilling to maintain a constructive dialogue with rebellious artists and could not accept their individualism and unorthodox lifestyles. Given this hostile attitude toward all avant-garde arts (not only of bourgeois but also of Soviet origin), few left-wing Futurists were able to make the PCI their political home. Some of them became engaged in anti-Fascist groups such as the Guardie Rosse, the Arditi del Popolo, or the Arditi Rossi. But as they were unable to establish an effective united front against the regime, many of these organizations were dissolved, their members being imprisoned or forced into exile.[18]

RETURN TO AN ARTISTIC AGENDA AND
ACCOMMODATION WITH MUSSOLINI'S REGIME

During the First World War, cultural life in Italy had largely lain dormant. Most members of the Futurist movement were serving at the

front and could only occasionally assemble for group activities. Therefore, there were no major exhibitions and only a few theater performances, usually as benefits for the Red Cross. In August 1918 Mario
Carli painted a gloomy picture of the state of affairs when he wrote to
Marinetti: "If one of us doesn't do something quickly and redirect
Italy's attention toward this intellectual movement, which is the most
important of this century, Futurism will founder in the silence of a general lack of interest."[19] However, in the chaos and strife that followed
the armistice, the time had not yet come for relaunching Futurism as
an artistic movement. Consequently, Marinetti decided to move into
the political arena and to establish Futurism as a political force, in its
own right, in the country.

But as the elections of November 1919 revealed, their program
failed to convince the Italian people, and many Futurists were subsequently seized by a "spiritual crisis." Marinetti recovered from the election fatigue in the arms of his new girlfriend, Beny (Benedetta Cappa,
later to become his wife), and focused once again on art and literary activities. During the first postwar months he had found that "the immense burden imposed on me by the Futurist Political Party does not
prevent me entirely from returning to my artistic work."[20] But in 1920
he complained about "the feverish political and social upheavals which
obstruct any publishing activities and artistic initiatives."[21] The newspaper *Roma futurista*, founded in 1918, was the official organ of the
Futurist Political Party and, as of 1919, of the Association of Italian
Arditi. At the end of 1919, Marinetti decided to turn the political newspaper into an artistic journal. He proposed Giacomo Balla as co-editor
and discussed with him a "Surprise Program for 1920," which was published in issue 53 of January 4, 1920. In this leading article they declared: "The Futurist artists, tired out for a long time, after four years
of war, have returned to their impassioned creative work." Giuseppe
Bottai, chief editor on the paper, was not particularly enthusiastic
about the new direction which Marinetti was proposing and wanted to
have at least the front page dedicated to political news. He prepared a
long article in the old manner for the next number and, as he described
in a letter to Mario Carli, had to face Marinetti's wrath: "Marinetti en-
raged himself for two hours: No politics, no politics! Politics, what a
f—— up!"[22]

The hectic activities of the years 1920–24 (exhibitions, theater tours,
concerts, publications, openings of nightclubs and cabarets) were designed to relaunch Futurism with a new membership and a new
artistic direction. And indeed, against all expectations, a "second wave"

of Futurism rose like the phoenix from its ashes, attracted a whole phalanx of young artists, and initiated a series of innovative artistic developments in Italy. Mussolini's crackdown on left-wing parties and organizations and eventually his silencing of all openly anti-Fascist voices in Italy compelled Marinetti to rethink his position and to reconsider that of Futurism in a State run by a Fascist dictator. His literary creations of 1921–22 indicate a deep disillusionment with his former friends who were deserting him for the Fascist Party (PNF) and a disappointment with Mussolini's political machinations. Marinetti's decision in 1920 to leave the Fasci di Combattimento showed that he was fully aware of Mussolini's volte-face and the reactionary politics his remodeled Fascist association was pursuing. Although his own political maneuvers also revealed a high degree of opportunism, they did not attain the same level of success. After Mussolini's March on Rome in October 1922, Marinetti realized that a brand of Fascism that was very different from that they had supported in 1919 had become a political reality. Marinetti rightly feared that Futurism was going to be increasingly marginalized in an Italy governed by a Fascist dictator. He had to think about his own and his movement's survival, and as he could not ignore or circumvent the new realities, he had to seek an accommodation with the new situation.

Therefore, in the 1923 *Manifesto to the Fascist Government*, he agreed to let Mussolini run the political operations of the country and to reserve autonomy for Futurism in the field of art. The official line he adopted after 1923 was that Futurism operates in "the unlimited domain of pure fantasy" and only "intervenes in the political battle in the hours of grave danger for the Nation."[23] The Futurist Congress of 1924 and the honors bestowed on Marinetti were a clear sign that the movement was ready to enter into a dialogue with the Fascist regime and to find a modus vivendi with the predominantly conservative artistic establishment. Within the Fascist leadership there were still people who had not entirely renounced the "Spirit of 1919" and were willing to grant Futurism a position (albeit a small one) in the cultural landscape of the new Italy, as a kind of semi-official avant-garde of the regime. But all attempts at finding official recognition of Futurism as the official art of the Fascist State were thwarted by the reactionary cultural bureaucracy.

Consequently, the Futurist movement underwent a major restructuring process. Militant anti-Fascists left while pro-Fascist members increased in number and significance. It is, however, essential to distinguish between the Futurist leadership (overwhelmingly pro-Fascist in the 1919 sense of the word, and also willing to come to some form of arrangement with the regime) and the mass of followers (a very heterogeneous mixture of pro-Fascists, a-Fascists, and anti-Fascists). The proliferation of Futurist groups and artists affiliated with the movement (estimated to be more than one thousand in the late 1920s and early 1930s)[24] made it impossible for Marinetti to keep a check on them or to control their activities from his headquarters. In fact, it is to his credit that he never attempted to impose a monolithic ideology on the movement and maintained amicable relationships even with "independent Futurists" who were opposed to his politics.

FUTURIST SURVIVAL TACTICS IN THE DEVELOPED FASCIST STATE
Italian Fascism was an imperfect and inefficient system whose totalitarian claims were never fulfilled in its actual practice. Control of the people and of the country's institutions was merely achieved to a limited degree, usually only in those areas that were regarded as essential for the status quo. Despite the outward form of an authoritarian regime and personal dictatorship, Italian Fascism never developed into a totalitarian State like Nazi Germany. Furthermore, the cultural policies of Fascism lacked ideological and aesthetic definition and allowed divergent groups to coexist and to fight one another's lines of action. Consequently, there was no mass exodus into exile as after Hitler's seizure of power. Even "internal exile," which was common in Nazi Germany,[25] was rarely a necessity in Mussolini's Italy.

After 1925, the relationship between Futurism and Fascism was highly contradictory and determined by reasons of exigency as well as idealist sentiments. Artists who wanted to make a living from their profession had to pay at least lip service to the ideological dictates of the regime. If they managed to "pull a few strings" and rekindle the ties and connections with former friends and acquaintances who now sat in positions of power, they were usually able to gain a contract, an exhibition space, a subsidy, or a commission. Political motivations rarely played a role in this; opportunism, nepotism, and careerism were often far more decisive factors. Without these channels of influence and the protection of high-ranking bureaucrats, Futurism would have been annihilated by conservative critics and party functionaries.

For the regime, too close a connection with the Futurist *enfants terribles* would have brought them into disrepute. Mussolini's artistic policy (if ever there was one) was characterized by a "return to order" and a pragmatic use of modernism. Futurism could sometimes play a useful role in propagating the government's modernist image and was there-

fore allowed to represent the "modern" Italy at international exhibitions
and literary conventions; but it was never allowed to occupy more than
a marginal position in the cultural landscape at home. Some of the
leading artists—Marinetti, Prampolini, Settimelli, Carli, Fillìa, Tato—
were given certain privileges, mainly to integrate the movement into
the system and to defuse their potential disruptiveness. But even as
such a tamed organization Futurism never enjoyed the same favors
that were offered to Novecento artists. Corrado Govoni gave a good
impression of this ambivalent attitude of the *gerarchi* toward the Futurists when he wrote: "They pet Marinetti up to a certain point, and
as stealthily as possible (it's best not to compromise oneself too much),
and then they refuse recognition to Futurism and massacre the Futurists."[26] Futurists continued to be troublesome and vexing individuals
and were—to use Enzo Benedetto's apt phrase—as welcome in the
Fascist temples of art as dogs in a church.[27] The clamor of their public
appearances, the rhetoric of their publications, and, most of all, their
polemics and protests were like grit in the wheels of a smoothly running State machinery and were hence frowned upon by the Fascist cultural establishment.

In view of this opposition and the often hostile reactions he incurred,
it was something of a personal success for Marinetti to be admitted to
the Italian Academy and to become Secretary of the Writers' and Journalists' Union. But despite these positions of influence and his access
to high-ranking functionaries, including the Duce himself, his ability
to assist fellow Futurists in their fight for survival was strictly limited.
The conservative, if not reactionary, tastes of the Fascist bureaucrats
increasingly stifled the artistic life of the country and left little room
for maneuver on the fringes of official policy. Under the changed
circumstances of the advanced Fascist State, artists were increasingly
controlled and regimented by an ultra-conservative Fascist bureaucracy. Therefore, Marinetti's *movimento futurista* remained, especially
for young artists, about the only open forum of debate and experimentation they could find in Italy. For them it was an important organization "not because it was a shop where you could do good business, but
because it provided us with the oxygen to breathe, it pumped air into
our brains, it gave us a space to live."[28]

After 1937, the Ministry of Popular Culture made it emphatically
clear that the last vestiges of "liberalism" and "plurality," which for a
while had offered a minimal platform for Futurists and other mod-
ernists, had been shed once and for all. Inspired by the Nazi system of
totalitarianism, the Fascist bureaucrats sought to impose tight control

on cultural life down to the last village of the peninsula. Right-wing hard-liners occupied nearly all important positions in the cultural hierarchy and from then on dominated what passed for artistic debate in the country. After the "Degenerate Art" exhibition in Munich in 1937, they began a concerted attack on Futurism, portrayed as "a caricature of art and a dishonor to the intellect."[29] Marinetti was in the forefront of the small group of intellectuals who fought against the concept of degenerate art, against the burning of books, against political censorship, and similar measures designed to restrict artistic freedom and civil liberties, which gained him the reputation of being "anti-Fascist." We know from Yvon de Begnac's diary that Marinetti intervened with the Duce to prevent Nazi-style anti-Semitism in Italy[30] and that the Jewish community was grateful for his support.[31] He vehemently opposed the repression of intellectual freedom and organized meetings of writers and theater people to protect against the new censorship measures.[32] In a last *serata* at the Teatro delle Arti in Rome, on December 3, 1938, Marinetti defended an innovative, forward-looking, animated contemporary art. He was admired for this, by some, as "a man with guts, who is dynamic and coherent, a passionate comrade, capable of throwing himself into the battle and sacrificing himself for the cause of modern art."[33] But the support he received from other artists made little impression on the Fascists. In January 1939, they shut down the Futurist paper *Artecrazia*,[34] which was eventually replaced with *Mediterraneo futurista*, a periodical that was totally subservient to the regime. The following years were nothing but an epilogue of the Futurist movement. The few remaining active members spun out what Marinetti, without a hint of irony, called the "archaeological classicism of the avant-garde."[35] Clearly, Futurism had lost its innovative force, and it fittingly came to an end with Marinetti's death on December 2, 1944.

Critical Writings

THE PRE-FUTURIST YEARS
(1876–1908)

Marinetti was born in Alexandria, Egypt, and received an education based on the arts and humanities at a French college. He became entirely bilingual and from an early age was a prolific writer of poetry. In order to see his works published, he founded a magazine, *Le Papyrus*. The twenty-one issues that appeared between February 1894 and January 1895 also contained his first essays on literary questions, new artistic trends, and political issues. In 1895, Marinetti's father decided that his son should study law at an Italian university and sent him to Pavia. After a transfer to Genoa, Filippo Tommaso graduated, on July 14, 1899, with a thesis titled "The Role of the Crown in Parliamentary Government."

Marinetti's commitment to his legal studies was rather halfhearted. He spent most of his time pursuing his true calling, poetry, and published his works in respected literary magazines in France. At that time, Symbolism, inaugurated in 1886 with the publication of Jean Moréas's manifesto in *Le Figaro*, was the most influential school of literature, and Marinetti converted wholeheartedly to its aesthetics. He also served as a kind of literary agent, getting young French poets published in Italy and placing recent Italian writing in French magazines and anthologies. His name appeared as collaborator in a number of literary magazines, and from 1898 on he functioned as editor in charge of *Anthologie-Revue de France et d'Italie*. As a result of his activities as a "literary manager," Marinetti became a major force on the Italian literary scene. In 1899 he published an anthology of contemporary Italian poets and voiced his own views on recent Italian literature in essays for *La Vogue*. As he rightly observed: "Italian poetry has changed very little since Leopardi. To the eye of the observer, it appears most unsophisticated, absolutely unaffected by the modern spirit and contemptuous of the heaving research that animates the soul of our century." This lack of a "modern spirit" he sought to change, both as a writer and as a cultural organizer.

Marinetti made a considerable impact with his first poetry collections, *La Conquête des étoiles* (1902) and *Destruction* (1904); his play *Le Roi Bombance* (1905); and his journalistic essays on literary and theatrical matters. He was also a talented musician and served as a regular reviewer of musical concerts and opera productions. At the same time, he made many public appearances as a reciter of French and Italian poetry.

1

∽

Self-Portrait

I had a strange, colorful, uproarious sort of life. I started off with rose
and black, a blossoming, healthy little tot in the arms and between the
carbon-coke breasts, of my Sudanese nurse. Which maybe explains my
somewhat *blackish* concept of love and my open antipathy toward
milk-and-honey politics and diplomacy.

My father's Piedmontese tenacity was passed on to me in the blood.
It is to him that I owe the great strength of his willful, domineering,
sanguine temperament, but fortunately, I have not inherited his dense
tangle of spiritual arguments, nor his fantastic memory which made him,
in his time, the greatest civil law lawyer in Alexandria.[1]

> *On certain evenings, down there in the witchery of Africa,*
> *They would take us onto your dark, deserted beaches,*
> *A doleful flock of boarders*
> *Who crept along, placid and slow, watched over*
> *By our priests, strict and black . . . Little blots*
> *Of ink we were against the immaterial*
> *Silks of a divine, oriental sky.*

My mother,[2] who was entirely composed of the most delicate, musical
poetry of affectionate tears and tenderness, was Milanese. Though born
in Alexandria, I feel myself bound to Milan's forest of chimneys and its
ancient Cathedral.

> *O Cathedral of Milan! I have terrified you*
> *Brushing with my seagull's wings*
> *Against the monstrous, steep slopes*
> *Of your age-old cliffs . . .*
> *You say, I am a Milanese in too great a hurry.*

When I was six, I was often severely scolded when I was caught red-handed, spraying passersby from our balcony.

They weren't exactly passing by; rather were these solemn Arab merchants standing around, extending their lengthy, ceremonious greetings, with their backs arching their salaams, beneath their many-colored turbans, avidly bargaining for Parisian bed linen and chests of fruit with Jewish brokers and camel drivers.

On one side, my father's house in Alexandria looked out onto a busy street, and on the other onto a huge walled garden that was filled with palm trees, fans gently waving against the foamy blue laughter of the African sea.

I lived out my days on a tiny wooden balcony in a dreamy sort of closeness with some fat turtledoves which, perched up among the date palms, just a couple of meters from me, cooed away melodiously, perhaps preparing my ears for their future sensitivity to sounds.

When the noise of the merchants talking disturbed my friends, the doves, I would turn on the tap of my childish liquid scorn, down among them.

For a long time, at the French Jesuit College of St. Francis Xavier,[3] all I ever learned was how to play soccer, and to fight with any of my classmates who said anything against Italy. Many times my terrified mother would find me covered in blood as a result of these furious games.

I was just fourteen when Father Bufferne, my Humanities teacher, solemnly announced one day in class that a description of mine, of the dawn, was far superior to any of those written by Chateaubriand, and predicted my glory as a very great poet.

I evinced a mad passion for Mary, a sweet fourteen-year-old girl who was a pupil at a nuns' school next to my college. From the Levant, with her large liquorice eyes, her camelia cheeks, her fleshy, sensual lips, slinky, tender, all woman already, sly and full of malice. To kiss her, I climbed onto the shoulders of my Arab servant every day, and after having cut myself on the sharp glass shards on a wall top, I would wait among the branches of a fig tree, until she could slip away without the nuns noticing. But sometimes, up in the fig tree, there would be chameleons with me, drinking in the heat of the afternoon. Trying to get a better look at one of them one day, I lost my balance and fell, dislocating my shoulder.

My love for Mary was all mixed up with a terrible crisis I was in over mysticism.[4] From being fourteen to when I was sixteen, I was

> . . . *the adolescent*
> *who submitted the stirrings of his feeble body*
> *to the voluptuous embrace of the Evening,*
> *to the scent of incense and sweetened hosts,*
> *when the Month of Mary*
> *came to visit us in the parlor,*
> *like a perfumed lady,*
> *more beautiful than the sisters of my friends!*

But the religious constraints of my teachers, the Jesuits, rather than supporting my mystical urges, cut them down. I was expelled from the college for having brought in some of Zola's novels.[5] I got myself into debt for the first time in my life in order to set up my first journal, *Le Papyrus*, which was brimful of Romantic poetry and anticlerical invectives against the Jesuits.[6] However, I found myself in the impossible situation of not being able to continue my classical studies in Alexandria, much to the fury of my father, who felt compelled to pack me off to Paris.[7]

Alone in Paris. At eighteen years of age. Evenings in the Latin Quarter, with all the ladies of easy virtue at my disposal. And all the usual student upsets. A disastrous examination in mathematics, but a triumphant one in philosophy, on the theories of Stuart Mill.[8] I arrived in Milan a *bachelier ès lettres*, with a French culture, though incontrovertibly Italian—and that despite all the temptations of Paris.

While I was reading for my degree in law at the University of Genoa,[9] one of my poems written in Free Verse, "Les Vieux Marins," which had been published in the *Anthologie-Revue*,[10] was awarded a prize by Catulle Mendès and Gustave Kahn, the directors of Sarah Bernhardt's *Samedis populaires*, and was then gloriously recited by the great actress herself, in her own theater.

With the little money allowed me by my father, sworn enemy of all my literature, I dashed off to Paris. My entry into the literary circles there represented the acclaimed rise of a new, young, great poet: the doors of the publishing houses were open to me, editors and journals were entirely deferential.

My literary campaign throughout Italy then began to unfold, promoting both French Symbolism and Decadentism, with endless lectures in which I introduced Baudelaire, Mallarmé, Verlaine, Rimbaud, Laforgue, Gustave Kahn, Claudel, Paul Fort, Verhaeren, and Jammes to Italy.[11] The establishment and development of the international revue *Poesia*[12] then followed, a teeming hothouse in which our best young poets germinated and burst into flower: Cavacchioli, Paolo Buzzi, Govoni, Palazzeschi, Gian Pietro Lucini, and Luciano Folgore.[13] Thus it was that in 1905 Futurism was born.[14]

I was the much-acclaimed author of *La Conquête des étoiles* (Conquest of the Stars),[15] a poem far from the realistic; nevertheless I followed all the disturbances and ideological developments of the Italian socialist movement very closely, and these crystallized into my tragedy *Le Roi Bombance* (King Guzzle).[16] This fat-bellied king of mine stormed onto the Parisian stage, already bearing the scandal of Futurism in his symbols and grotesque actions.[17] For a whole month, Paris was violently shaken by the revolutionary truculence of this work and by the arguments raging back and forth about the *Futurist Manifesto*, which appeared in *Le Figaro*, as well as about my sword gash, dealt me in a duel with the novelist Charles-Henri Hirsch.[18] The Parisian papers dubbed me "The Caffeine of Europe"![19]

The text translated here is taken from the chapter "Alessandria d'Egitto," in *Marinetti e il futurismo* (1929). It is based on "Autoritratto" in *Scatole d'amore in conserva* (1927), which itself is taken from the autobiographical sketch "Il delizio pericolo," in *Come si seducono le donne* (1920) and *Racconte-Novelle: Periodico quindicinnale* (December 15, 1920). It was reprinted with some evocative illustrations by Prampolini in *Novella: Rivista mensile di novelle italiane e straniere e di varietà* in January 1925 and excerpted in *L'impero*, February 3–4, 1925, under the title "Caffeina dell'Europa." Two more evocations of Marinetti's early life can be found in the poetic autobiographies *La grande Milano tradizionale e futurista* and *Una sensibilità italiana nata in Egitto*, both written between 1943 and 1944.

THE FOUNDATION OF FUTURISM
(1909)

In 1908 Marinetti devised a political and cultural program that could serve as the basis for a new artistic school, which he intended to call Elettricismo or Dinamismo. In October 1908 he drafted a manifesto in which he explained his principal aims and objectives. The final version was read to his friend Paolo Buzzi on December 20 and was ready for publication on December 24, 1908. It was sent out to a large number of luminaries in the literary and art world, who were invited to comment or even join the movement. But then an unforeseen event took place: 200,000 people were killed in an earthquake in Sicily. Marinetti realized that this was hardly an opportune moment for startling the world with a literary manifesto, so he delayed publication until he could be sure he would get front-page coverage for his incendiary appeal to lay waste to cultural traditions and institutions. Several Italian newspapers published the manifesto in early February 1909 or reported on its content. Toward the middle of February, Marinetti traveled to Paris, where in the Grand Hôtel he composed the introductory paragraphs and submitted the full text to the editors of the prestigious newspaper *Le Figaro*.

Reaction to the controversial manifesto was lively, ranging from enthusiasm to qualified acceptance to total derision. The journal *Poesia*—now carrying the subtitle "Mouthpiece of Futurism"—contained in the April–June 1909 issue an extensive collection of responses from individuals and newspapers. Needless to say, most of those selected were positive, thus skewing the picture, which otherwise would have included a large number of critical and skeptical voices. Marinetti's plan to publish a two-volume anthology of responses to the foundation manifesto never came to fruition. But he had the manifesto printed in a variety of formats and a large number of copies. His apartment on the via Senato, where he and his friends had discussed the foundation of a new literary school, became the headquarters of the movement, soon to include a fine-arts section, a branch for musicians, and one for "women's activities" (*azione femminile*). An inheritance from his father made it possible for Marinetti to employ a secretary and two clerks and to have bundles of his manifestos shipped to the farthest corners of the globe.

Marinetti was the first to conduct American-style advertising campaigns for a cultural product. There is no doubt that, by the end of 1909, large sections of

Italian society—and not only the cultured elite—had become aware of the Futurist movement. Marinetti gladly accepted the epithets *Caffeina d'Europa* and *Poeta Pink*, the latter echoing the name of a popular medicine that was advertised thus: "The Pink Pill is to the weak organism what water is to the withering flower. The Pink Pill gives rich and pure blood and slams the door shut on illness. It immediately restores vitality to the exhausted organs and is the best remedy for anemia, sclerosis, general fatigue, and nervous exhaustion." Some derided him for his "impudent careerism and intolerable exhibitionism" (Vaccari, *Vita e tumulti,* 185); others adopted his "art of hype" and forged a new relationship between art and society.

Among the general populace, Futurism raised a great deal of interest but also consternation and confusion. Consequently, several newspapers sought enlightenment from Marinetti and requested interviews, which the author all too willingly granted. Marinetti seized upon the general interest in his new school to issue a second manifesto, which described his own, and his collaborators', journey into the future. The metaphorical language still bore close resemblance to his pre-Futurist poetry, but he also established a new creative genre: "the art of generating manifestos" (*l'arte di fare manifesti*).

2

The Foundation and Manifesto of Futurism

My friends and I had stayed up all night,[1] sitting beneath the lamps of a mosque, whose star-studded, filigreed brass domes resembled our souls, all aglow with the concentrated brilliance of an electric heart. For many hours, we'd been trailing our age-old indolence back and forth over richly adorned, oriental carpets,[2] debating at the uttermost boundaries of logic and filling up masses of paper with our frenetic writings.

Immense pride filled our hearts, for we felt that at that hour we alone were vigilant and unbending, like magnificent beacons or guards in forward positions, facing an army of hostile stars, which watched us closely from their celestial encampments. Alone we were, with the stokers working feverishly at the infernal fires of great liners; alone with the black specters that rake through the red-hot bellies of locomotives, hurtling along at breakneck speed; alone with the floundering drunks, with the uncertain beating of our wings, along the city walls.

Suddenly we were startled by the terrifying clatter of huge, double-decker trams jolting by,[3] all ablaze with different-colored lights, as if they were villages in festive celebration, which the River Po, in full spate, suddenly shakes and uproots to sweep them away down to the sea, over the falls and through the whirlpools of a mighty flood.

Then the silence became more somber. Yet even while we were listening to the tedious, mumbled prayers of an ancient canal and the creaking bones of dilapidated palaces on their tiresome stretches of soggy lawn,[4] we caught the sudden roar of ravening motorcars, right there beneath our windows.

"Come on! Let's go!" I said. "Come on, my lads, let's get out of here! At long last, all the myths and mystical ideals are behind us. We're about to witness the birth of a Centaur and soon we shall witness the flight of the very first Angels! . . . We shall have to shake the gates of life itself to test their locks and hinges! . . . Let's be off! See there, the Earth's very first dawn! Nothing can equal the splendor of the sun's red sword slicing through our millennial darkness, for the very first time!"

We approached the three panting beasts to stroke their burning breasts, full of loving admiration. I stretched myself out on my car like a corpse on its bier, but immediately I was revived as the steering wheel, like a guillotine blade, menaced my belly.

A furious gust of madness tore us out of ourselves and hurled us along roads as deep and plunging as the beds of torrents. Every now and then a feeble light, flickering behind some windowpane, made us mistrust the calculations of our all-too-fallible eyes. I cried out: "The scent, nothing but the scent! That's all an animal needs!"

And we, like young lions, chased after Death, whose black pelt was dotted with pale crosses, as he sped away across the vast, violet-tinted sky, vital and throbbing.[5]

And yet we had no idealized Lover whose sublime being rose up into the skies; no cruel Queen to whom we might offer up our corpses, contorted like Byzantine rings! Nothing at all worth dying for, other than the desire to divest ourselves finally of the courage that weighed us down!

But we sped on, squashing beneath our scorching tires the snarling guard dogs at the doorsteps of their houses, like crumpled collars under a hot iron. Death, tamed by this time, went past me at each bend, only to offer me his willing paw; and sometimes he would lie down, his teeth grinding, eyeing me with his soft, gentle look from every puddle in the road.

"Let's leave wisdom behind as if it were some hideous shell, and cast ourselves, like fruit, flushed with pride, into the immense, twisting jaws of the wind! . . . Let's become food for the Unknown, not out of desperation, but simply to fill up the deep wells of the Absurd to the very brim!"

I had hardly got these words out of my mouth when I swung the car right around sharply, with all the crazy irrationality of a dog trying to bite its own tail. Then suddenly a pair of cyclists came toward me, gesticulating that I was on the wrong side, dithering about in front of me like two different lines of thought, both persuasive but for all that, quite contradictory. Their stupid uncertainty was in my way . . . How ridiculous! What a nuisance! . . . I braked hard and to my disgust the wheels left the ground and I flew into a ditch . . .

O mother of a ditch, brimful with muddy water! Fine repair shop of a ditch! How I relished your strength-giving sludge that reminded me so much of the saintly black breast of my Sudanese nurse[6] . . . When I got myself up—soaked, filthy, foul-smelling rag that I was—from beneath my overturned car, I had a wonderful sense of my heart being pierced by the red-hot sword of joy![7]

A crowd of fishermen, with their lines, and some gouty old naturalists were already milling around this wondrous spectacle. Patiently, meticulously, they set up tall trestles and laid out huge iron-mesh nets to fish out my car, as if it were a great shark that had been washed up and stranded. Slowly the car's frame emerged, leaving its heavy, sober bodywork at the bottom of the ditch as well as its soft, comfortable upholstery, as though they were merely scales.

They thought it was dead, that gorgeous shark of mine, but a caress was all it needed to revive it, and there it was, back from the dead, darting along with its powerful fins!

So, with my face covered in repair-shop grime—a fine mixture of metallic flakes, profuse sweat, and pale-blue soot—with my arms all bruised and bandaged, yet quite undaunted, I dictated our foremost desires to all men on Earth who are truly alive:

THE FUTURIST MANIFESTO

1. We want to sing about the love of danger, about the use of energy and recklessness as common, daily practice.
2. Courage, boldness, and rebellion will be essential elements in our poetry.
3. Up to now, literature has extolled a contemplative stillness, rapture, and reverie. We intend to glorify aggressive action, a restive wakefulness, life at the double, the slap and the punching fist.
4. We believe that this wonderful world has been further enriched by a new beauty, the beauty of speed. A racing car, its bonnet decked out with exhaust pipes like serpents with galvanic breath . . . a roaring motorcar, which seems to race on like machine-gun fire, is more beautiful than the Winged Victory of Samothrace.[8]
5. We wish to sing the praises of the man behind the steering wheel, whose sleek shaft traverses the Earth, which itself is hurtling at breakneck speed along the racetrack of its orbit.

6. The poet will have to do all in his power, passionately, flamboyantly, and with generosity of spirit, to increase the delirious fervor of the primordial elements.

7. There is no longer any beauty except the struggle. Any work of art that lacks a sense of aggression can never be a masterpiece. Poetry must be thought of as a violent assault upon the forces of the unknown with the intention of making them prostrate themselves at the feet of mankind.

8. We stand upon the furthest promontory of the ages! . . . Why should we be looking back over our shoulders, if what we desire is to smash down the mysterious doors of the Impossible? Time and Space died yesterday.[9] We are already living in the realms of the Absolute, for we have already created infinite, omnipresent speed.

9. We wish to glorify war—the sole cleanser of the world[10]—militarism, patriotism, the destructive act of the libertarian,[11] beautiful ideas worth dying for, and scorn for women.[12]

10. We wish to destroy museums, libraries, academies of any sort, and fight against moralism, feminism,[13] and every kind of materialistic, self-serving cowardice.

11. We shall sing of the great multitudes[14] who are roused up by work, by pleasure, or by rebellion; of the many-hued, many-voiced tides of revolution in our modern capitals; of the pulsating, nightly ardor of arsenals and shipyards, ablaze with their violent electric moons; of railway stations, voraciously devouring smoke-belching serpents; of workshops hanging from the clouds by their twisted threads of smoke; of bridges which, like giant gymnasts, bestride the rivers, flashing in the sunlight like gleaming knives; of intrepid steamships that sniff out the horizon; of broad-breasted locomotives, champing on their wheels like enormous steel horses, bridled with pipes; and of the lissome flight of the airplane, whose propeller flutters like a flag in the wind, seeming to applaud, like a crowd excited.

It is from Italy that we hurl at the whole world this utterly violent, inflammatory manifesto of ours, with which today we are founding "Futurism," because we wish to free our country from the stinking canker of its professors, archaeologists, tour guides, and antiquarians.

For far too long has Italy been a marketplace for junk dealers. We want to free our country from the endless number of museums that everywhere cover her like countless graveyards. Museums, graveyards! . . . They're the same thing, really, because of their grim profusion of corpses that no one remembers. Museums. They're just public flophouses, where things sleep on forever, alongside other loathsome or nameless things! Museums: ridiculous abattoirs for painters and sculptors, who are furiously stabbing one another to death with colors and lines, all along the walls where they vie for space.

Sure, people may go there on pilgrimage about once a year, just as they do to the cemetery on All Souls Day—I'll grant you that! And yes, once a year a wreath of flowers is laid at the feet of the *Gioconda*[15]— I'll grant you that too! But what I won't allow is that all our miseries, our fragile courage, or our sickly anxieties get marched daily around these museums. Why should we want to poison ourselves? Why should we want to rot?

What on earth is there to be discovered in an old painting other than the labored contortions of the artist, trying to break down the insuperable barriers which prevent him from giving full expression to his artistic dream? . . . Admiring an old painting is just like pouring our purest feelings into a funerary urn, instead of projecting them far and wide, in violent outbursts of creation and of action.

Do you really want to waste all your best energies in this unending, futile veneration for the past, from which you emerge fatally exhausted, diminished, trampled down?

Make no mistake, I'm convinced that for an artist to go every day to museums and libraries and academies (the cemeteries of wasted effort, calvaries of crucified dreams, records of impulses cut short! . . .) is every bit as harmful as the prolonged overprotectiveness of parents for certain young people who get carried away by their talent and ambition. For those who are dying anyway, for the invalids, for the prisoners—who cares? The admirable past may be a balm to their worries, since for them the future is a closed book . . . but we, the powerful young Futurists, don't want to have anything to do with it, the past!

So let them come, the happy-go-lucky fire raisers with their blackened fingers! Here they come! Here they are! . . . Come on then! Set fire to the library shelves! . . . Divert the canals so they can flood the museums! . . . Oh, what a pleasure it is to see those revered old canvases, washed out and tattered, drifting away in the water! . . . Grab your picks and your axes and your hammers and then demolish, pitilessly demolish, all venerated cities![16]

The oldest among us are thirty; so we have at least ten years in which to complete our task. When we reach forty, other, younger, and more courageous men will very likely toss us into the trash can, like useless manuscripts. And that's what we want!

Our successors will rise up against us, from far away, from every part of the world, dancing on the winged cadenzas of their first songs, flexing their hooked, predatory claws, sniffing like dogs at the doors of our academies, at the delicious scent of our decaying minds, already destined for the catacombs of libraries.

But we won't be there . . . Eventually, they will find us, on a winter's night, in a humble shed, far away in the country, with an incessant rain drumming upon it, and they'll see us huddling anxiously together beside our airplanes, warming our hands around the flickering flames of our present-day books, which burn away beneath our images as they are taking flight.

They will rant and rave around us, gasping in outrage and fury, and then—frustrated by our proud, unwavering boldness—they will hurl themselves upon us to kill us, driven by a hatred made all the more implacable because their hearts overflow with love and admiration for us.

Strong, healthy Injustice will flash dazzlingly in their eyes. Art, indeed, can be nothing but violence,[17] cruelty, and injustice.

The oldest among us are only thirty. And yet we have squandered fortunes, a thousand fortunes of strength, love, daring, cleverness, and of naked willpower. We have tossed them aside impatiently, in anger, without thinking of the cost, without a moment's hesitation, without ever resting, gasping for breath . . . Just look at us! We're not exhausted yet! Our hearts feel no weariness, for they feed on fire, on hatred and on speed! . . . Does that surprise you? . . . That's logical enough, I suppose, as you don't even remember having lived! Standing tall on the roof of the world, yet again we fling our challenge at the stars!

Do you have any objections? . . . All right! Sure, we know what they are . . . We have understood! . . . Our sharp, duplicitous intelligence tells us that we are the sum total and the extension of our forebears. — Well, maybe! . . . Be that as it may! . . . But what does it matter? We want nothing to do with it! . . . Woe betide anybody whom we catch repeating these infamous words of ours.

Look around you!

Standing tall on the roof of the world, yet once again, we hurl our defiance at the stars! . . .

This manifesto first appeared in the form of a two-page leaflet under the heading "The International Magazine, *Poesia*, has founded a new literary school with the name 'Futurism.' " It was sent out to a large

number of newspapers and journals, some of which printed it in full (*Gazzetta di Emilia* [Bologna], February 5; *Gazzetta di Mantova*, February 9; *L'arena* [Verona], February 9–10; *La tavola rotonda* [Naples], February 14), others in excerpts (*Il pungolo* [Naples], February 6; *Monsignor Perrelli* [Naples], February 6; *Il mattino* [Naples], February 8–9; *La vita del giorno* [Trieste], February 10; *Gazzetta di Venezia*, February 13; *Il giorno* [Naples], February 16–17). Other Italian newspapers reported on its content. The famous French version in *Le Figaro* of February 20, 1909, consisting of introduction and manifesto, had a few passages changed or shortened. The French text with the "censored" passages reinstated was published as a four-page leaflet and was widely distributed across Europe and the Americas. Excerpts appeared in dozens of newspapers and magazines, translated into English, German, Spanish, Russian, Czech, and other languages. Our translation here follows the complete, "official" version in *Poesia* 5, nos. 1–2 (February–March 1909).

3

Futurism: An Interview with
Mr. Marinetti in Comœdia

After the sensation caused by the Futurist Manifesto, published recently in *Le Figaro*, and commented on in these pages by our chief editor, we thought that now, in the very moment that *King Guzzle*, a satirical tragedy by the leader of the school, is being rehearsed at the Marigny Theater,[1] it would be interesting and highly topical if we were to ask Signor Marinetti to explain certain points in his program.

"I am very pleased," the editor of *Poesia* replied very kindly, "to have the opportunity you are offering me to clarify a number of points in our recent manifesto, which may have seemed obscure or incomplete. In general, there has been little or no comprehension of how, in our thinking, we can reconcile the glorification of patriotism and the exaltation of the anarchists' acts of destruction. Without getting bogged down in long, tedious digressions of a more or less philosophical nature, you will acknowledge, as I do, that these two apparently contradictory ideas, the collective and the individual, are, in fact, closely related. Does not the development of the collective depend on the exertions and initiatives of individuals? Similarly, the prosperity of a nation derives from antagonism toward, and imitation of, the multiple elements of which it is composed. In the same way, the industrial and military competition that emerges between peoples is a necessary element in the progress of mankind. A strong nation can contain, at one and the same time, masses of people intoxicated by patriotic enthusiasm and reactionaries who are panic-stricken by revolt! There we have two different directions for the same instinctive courage, strength, and energy.

"Is not the anarchist's act of destruction a good yet absurd reminder of the ideal of an impossible justice, a barrier against the invasive impertinence of the triumphant and dominant classes? Personally, I prefer the bomb of a Vaillant[2] to the groveling of the bourgeoisie, who are nowhere to be seen when things get dangerous; or to the useless egotism of the peasant, who maims himself to avoid serving his country."

—There is, however, a flagrant contradiction between your Futurist ideals and your glorification of war, which would constitute rather a return to a barbaric age.

"Yes, but it's a question of health, which takes precedence over everything else. Is not the life of nations, when all's said and done, just like that of the individual who only rids himself of infections and excess of blood by having recourse to the bathtub and to bloodletting?"

Then Marinetti adds, smiling at the paradox: "I believe that a people has to pursue a continuous hygiene of heroism and every century take a glorious shower of blood."

—War is not enough for you, however. You also teach that museums and libraries should be burned down.

"Well, that is just a violent image of our desire to get right away from enchantment with the past, from the despotism of pedantic academies, which stifles intellectual initiative and the creative power of the young.

"Isn't it symptomatic that today, unfortunately, it is an indisputable fact that the public is turning away from all creative endeavor, that it is only interested in erudite works and documentation, and—like a cowardly, easily satisfied gentleman of leisure—considers every new conquest to be reckless and unnecessary? I want to contest this fetish of an admirable past which seems to me all the more dangerous in that it bears heavily on genius, with all the weight of its venerable dust."

—How do you explain the hostile reception given to your manifesto by a good many of those young literary men whose aspirations you have defended, and whose efforts and daring works you have glorified in Italy, both in your countless lectures and in the pages of your journal, *Poesia*?

"This animosity doesn't surprise me at all. It justifies the eruption of Futurism, in the sense that it shows just how far the virus of routine, of imitation and pedantry has infected a large number of thinking and working young people."

—Some people think very badly of you for having talked a great deal about "scorn for women." Are you not afraid of bringing upon yourself the ferocious attacks of the more exquisite half of the human race because of this?

"I have perhaps been far too concise, and I'll try and clarify our ideas on this point, immediately. We wish to protest against the narrowness of inspiration to which imaginative literature is being increasingly subjected. With noble but all-too-rare exceptions, poems and novels actually seem no longer able to deal with anything other than women and love. It's an obsessive leitmotif, a depressing literary fixation. Truly, is woman the only starting point for, and the only purpose of, our intellectual development, the unique driving force of our sensibilities?

"We desire a serious reduction, in the contemporary mind, of that exaggerated importance, which our snobbishness and complicitous sense of chivalry have encouraged a usurping feminism to assume. This movement is triumphant in the France of today, thanks to a magnificent elite of intellectual women who daily demonstrate their admirable talents and their irresistible charm. However, feminism is harmful and even ridiculous in Italy and everywhere else, where it is limited to being merely an outlet for petty ambitions and oratorical aspirations.

"In short, we want to combat the tyranny of sentimental love, which, above all in the Latin countries, undermines and saps the strength of creative minds and of men of action. We wish to replace the idealized profile of Don Juan with that of Napoleon, with that of Andrée and of Wilbur Wright,[3] in the imagination, and, in general, to root out the evils of twenty years of vain obsession with amorous adventures and adultery.

"We wish to spur young people toward the most impertinent of intellectual vandalisms, so that they live with a taste for madness, a craving for danger, and a hatred for all those who counsel caution.

"We wish to prepare the way for a generation of strong, muscular poets who know how to develop their courageous bodies, every bit as much as their vibrant spirits.

"These poets, bursting with pride, are in a hurry to bring down academic chairs and proctors, and to progress against the tide, amid the dusty mass of tattered old ideas and lame opinions.

"Glorification of instinct and flair in the human animal, the cultivation of divining intuition, wild, ruthless individualism, contempt for ancient, exploitative wisdom, giving free rein to our emotional and physical impulses, daily heroism of body and spirit. These are the things that we desire."

L.C. [La Cocherie]

This interview was first published in the French theater magazine *Comœdia* on March 26, 1909. It was reprinted under the title "The First Victories of Futurism: Interview with M. Marinetti by a Journalist of *Comœdia*" in *Poesia* 5, nos. 3–6 (April–July 1909), and used again by way of introduction to the play *Poupées électriques* (1909).

4

✌️

Second Futurist Proclamation: Let's Kill Off the Moonlight

1

"Hey there! You Hell-raising poets, Futurist brothers-in-arms! . . . Hey! Paolo Buzzi, Palazzeschi, Cavacchioli, Govoni, Altomare, Folgore, Boccioni, Carrà, Russolo, Balla, Severini, Pratella, D'Alba, Mazza![1] Let's get the hell out of Paralysis, let's raze Goutville to the ground, and lay the great military Railroad up the slopes of Gorisankar, the roof of the World!"[2]

We were all leaving the city,[3] with measured, sprightly steps that seemingly wanted to dance, looking everywhere for obstacles to overcome. All around, as well as deep within us, the ancient, powerfully intoxicating European sun was reeling among the wine-colored clouds . . . And it beat down on our faces with its great crimson-flaming torch before splitting asunder and spewing itself out into infinity.

Swirls of vexing dust; a blinding mixture of sulfur, potassium, and silicates perceived through the immense windows of the Ideal! . . . Fusion of a new solar globe that will soon blaze forth for all to see!

"Cowards!" I shouted, turning around to face the people of Paralysis, huddled together beneath us, looking like a huge mass of restive shells, already in place for our cannons of the future.

"Gutless scum! Gutless! . . . What are you howling about, like cats being skinned alive? . . . Are you scared we're going to set a light to your miserable little hovels? . . . Well, we aren't just yet! . . . After all, we'll have to keep ourselves warm somehow next winter! . . . For the moment, we're happy enough just blowing up all the old traditions, like broken-down bridges! . . . War, you say? . . . Well, yes, exactly; that's our one hope, our raison d'être, our sole desire! . . . Yes, war! . . . Against your lot, because you're not dying off quickly enough; and war, too, against all the other deadbeats that get in our way!

"Yes, our very sinews insist on war and scorn for women, for we fear their supplicating arms being wrapped around our legs, the morning of our setting forth! . . . What claim do women have on us, or for that matter, any of the stay-at-homes, the cripples, the sick, and all the caution-mongers? Rather than have their timid little lives torn apart by their dismal little anxieties, by their restless nights and fearful nightmares, we prefer a violent death; and we glorify it as the only one fitting for man, beast of prey that he is.[4]

"We want our children to follow their whims untrammeled, brutally opposing the old and jeering at everything that has been consecrated by time!

"I suppose this scandalizes you? Makes you boo and hiss me?[5] . . . Speak a bit louder! . . . I didn't hear what was wrong! Louder! What? Ambitious, you say? . . . You bet we are! Yes, we're ambitious, because we don't want to rub up against your filthy hides, foul-smelling, mud-colored herd that you are, shuffling along the time-worn furrows of this Earth! . . . Yet 'ambitious' isn't quite the right word! What we really are is young artillerymen on the rampage . . . And however much you don't like it, you're going to have to get used to the roar of our cannon! What's that you say? . . . We're crazy?[6] . . . Fantastic! You've said it at last, just what I expected! . . . Oh yes, just the right expression! . . . But take care how you use this immense treasure of a word, and get back in line damned quick, so as to hide it in your deepest vaults! With that word between your fingers and on your lips, you'll go on living for another twenty centuries . . . As far as I'm concerned, I'm telling you, the world is weighed down with wisdom! . . .

"And that's why we, today, are preaching a methodical, everyday heroism, a taste for wholehearted recklessness, a habitual passion, total abandonment to delirium . . .

"We preach the plunge into the darkness of death beneath the blank, staring eye of the Ideal . . . And we ourselves shall set an example, resigning ourselves to the wild Seamstress of Battles, who, when she has sewn us into our fine scarlet uniforms, glowing in the sunlight, will anoint our hair—already combed by gunfire—with flames . . . In just the same way as a heavy summer's evening smears a dazzling dance of fireflies over the fields.

"Men have to recharge their nerves every day with reckless pride! . . .

They have to stake their lives on a single throw of the dice, without keeping a close eye on the cheating croupier or the way the dice are running, standing with their heads bowed on the vast green carpet of war, hatching under the brooding heat of the sun. Don't you see that it's a fundamental necessity for the soul to give the body a baptism of flame, to launch it like a fireship against the enemy, the eternal enemy who, if he doesn't exist already, we have to invent!? . . .

"Look down there, at all those millions of stalks of corn arranged in their battle lines . . . Spirited soldiery with sharpened bayonets, those cornstalks which glorify the strength that is in the bread that is changed into blood, to spurt forth to the highest heaven. Blood, you should know, has neither value nor splendor unless it is liberated from its imprisonment in the arteries, by iron or by fire! And we shall teach all the *armed* soldiers on Earth how their blood should be spilled . . . But first of all we have to clean out the great barracks where you insects are swarming! . . . It won't take long . . . but for the time being, you lice can go back once more, for tonight anyway, to your filthy beds of tradition which we no longer wish to sleep in!"

As I was turning away from them, I realized, from the pain in my back, that I had been dragging those semicorpses along for ages in the great black net of my words, with their ludicrous, fishlike glint, all heaped up beneath the last wave of light which the evening was driving toward the broad reef of my brow.

2

The city of Paralysis, with its henhouse squawking, with futile pride in its broken columns, with its pompous domes spawning their paltry little statues, with its farcical cigarette smoke curling away over feeble little ramparts that would not withstand even a puff of wind . . . fades at our backs bobbing along in time with the rhythm of our swift steps.

In front of me but still a few kilometers away, the Lunatic Asylum suddenly came into view, high up on a fine, rounded hilltop that seemed to be trotting along like a young colt.

"Brothers," I said, "let's take our rest one final time before we set about building the great Futurist Railroad!"

We lay down, swathed in the immense madness of the Milky Way, in the shadow of the Palace of the Living, and suddenly the crashing of the great squared hammers of time and space fell silent . . . but Paolo Buzzi couldn't sleep, for his weary body flinched continuously at the pricks of the poisonous stars that assailed us from all sides.

"Comrade!" he murmured. "Chase those bees away that are buzzing around the crimson rose of my will!"

Then he fell asleep in the visionary shadow of that Palace brimful of fantasy, from which rose the slow, soothing, all-embracing melody of eternal joy.

Enrico Cavacchioli was dozing and dreaming aloud: "I can feel my twenty-year-old body getting younger and younger! . . . I'm going back, more and more at a child's pace, toward my cradle . . . Soon, I shall be reentering my mother's womb! . . . So I can do whatever I like! . . . I want some precious trinkets to smash . . . Towns to flatten, swarms of people to devastate! . . . I want to tame the winds and keep them on a leash . . . I want a pack of winds, fleet-footed hounds, to hunt the puffed-up, whiskery clouds."

The sound of my sleeping comrades' breathing was like the sleep of a mighty sea along a shore. But the bounding energy of the dawn was already spilling over from the mountains, so generously had the night poured out its perfumes and its glorious dews, all about us. Paolo Buzzi, rudely wakened by that tide of delirium, was writhing about, as if seized by the anguish of a nightmare.

"Can you hear the Earth's sighing? . . . The Earth is twisting in torment at this terrifying light! . . . Too many suns were bent over her pallid sickbed! We must let her sleep! Let her sleep some more! Forever! . . . Give me some clouds, heaps of clouds, to cover her eyes and sobbing mouth!"

At these words, the Sun proffered us its shimmering, red wheel of fire from the far horizon.

"Get up, Paolo!" I shouted. "Take hold of that wheel! . . . I proclaim you driver of the world! . . . And yet, I fear, alas! We shall not be adequate to the great task of the Futurist Railroad! Our hearts are still attached to all this useless junk: peacocks' tails, strutting weathercocks, prissy perfumed kerchiefs! . . . Nor have we yet driven the baleful ants of wisdom from our brains . . . What we need is madmen! . . . Let's go and set them free!"

We drew close to the walls that were bathed in the sun's gaiety, skirting round a sinister valley in which thirty grating metal cranes were lifting trolleys full of steaming linen, the useless laundry of the Pure, washed clean already of all the filth of logic.

A couple of psychiatrists appeared, uncompromising, at the doorway of the building. All I had in my hands was a gleaming motorcar headlight and it was with its bright brass casing that I brought about their deaths.

Mad men and women, coatless, half-naked, burst out through the wide-open doors in their thousands, torrents of them, so as to make the Earth's wrinkled face young again and give it back some color.

Immediately, some of them wanted to wield the shining belfries, as if they were ivory clubs; others started playing at hoops with some of the cupolas . . . The women were combing their long cloud tresses with the sharp teeth of a constellation of stars.

"O you mad people, our dearly beloved brothers, follow me! . . . We shall build the Railroad along the tops of all the mountains, as far as the sea! How many of you are there? . . . Three thousand? . . . It's not enough! Besides, boredom and monotony will soon cut short your thrusting forward . . . Let's run and see what the wild animals think, in their menageries at the gates of the Capital. Of all beings, they are the most alive, the least rooted, the least vegetative of all! Let's go! . . . To Goutville! To Goutville! . . ."

And so we left, an awesome surge from a huge sluice gate.

This army of madness hurled itself from plain to plain, streamed through the valleys, rose rapidly to the hilltops, with the irresistible, free-flowing power of a liquid passing between enormous connecting vats, and finally, in a hail of cries, with bodies and fists beating against the walls of Goutville, made them boom like a bell.

After knocking out, killing, or trampling over its keepers, this remonstrating tide flooded the immense, slimy corridor of the menagerie, whose cages, full of dancing pelts, swayed in the steam from the animals' piss and rocked more gently than cages of canaries in the arms of the madmen.

The reign of the lions rejuvenated the Capital. Their wild manes and the enormous strength of their arched backs sculpted the facades. Their torrenting power, gouging out a path, turned the streets into innumerable tunnels with their roof blown away. All the dead wood of the inhabitants of Goutville was burned in their houses, which, full of screaming branches, shook under the sudden hailstorm of dismay that struck their rooftops.

With sudden dashes and clownlike antics, the madmen leaped onto the beautiful lions, which, quite unconcerned, didn't even feel them, while those bizarre cavaliers, for their part, reveled in the gentle taps of the tails that continually knocked them down. All of a sudden the beasts halted, the madmen fell silent before the walls that shook no more.

"The old folks are dead! . . . The young have fled! . . . And that's how it should be! . . . Quick now! Pull up the lightning conductors and the statues! . . . Plunder the caskets brimful of gold! . . . Ingots and coins! . . .

All the precious metals will be melted down, for the great military Railroad! . . ."

We rushed outside, with the madmen waving their arms about, the madwomen all disheveled, with the lions, tigers, and panthers ridden bareback by cavaliers tensed, twisted, and delirious in their exhilaration.

Goutville was now nothing more than a huge vat, full of red wine eddying with froth, that oozed ceaselessly from its gates, whose draw-bridges had become pulsating, echoing funnels . . .

We crossed the ruins of Europe out into Asia, scattering the terror-stricken hordes of Goutville and Paralysis far and wide, like a sower spreading seed with the wide sweep of his arm.

3

By midnight we had almost reached the sky, and stood on the Persian Plateau, sublime altar of the world, whose terraces harbor populous cities. In endlessly stretching lines along the Railtrack we slaved over crucibles of barites, aluminum, and manganese which, every now and then, terrified the clouds with their blinding flash. And in a circle, the majestic troop of lions watched over us, with their tails erect and their manes ruffled by the wind, and they pierced the deep, black sky with their clear, sonorous roaring.

But gradually, the warm, bright smile of the moon spread out from the ragged clouds. And when she finally appeared, all dripping with the intoxicating milk of the acacias,[7] the madmen felt their hearts leave their breasts and rise up to the surface of the liquid night.

All at once, a shrill cry split the air; a sound growing louder, and everyone rushed forward . . . It was one of the madmen, very young, with innocent eyes, who had been struck down along the Track.

His corpse was taken up at once. In his hands he held a sensuous white flower, whose pistil wagged like a woman's tongue. Some wanted to touch it, which would have been dreadful, since quickly and easily as a dawn spreading out over the sea, a sighing foliage rose miraculously out of an earth rippling with unexpected waves.

Out of the swirling blue grasslands emerged the streaming heads of an infinite number of female swimmers, thrusting upward, opening their mouths and eyes, still full of water, with a gasp. Then, in a delirious flood of perfumes, we saw a fabulous forest growing all about us, its drooping foliage seeming exhausted by a breeze that was too lethargic. A bitter sweetness rippled all about it . . . The little birds drank in the sweet-scented shade with long warblings of pleasure, and every now and then they burst into laughter in their nooks and crannies, playing hide-and-seek like lively, mischievous children. A blissful sleep was gradually overcoming the army of madmen, who began to howl in terror.

Instinctively, the beasts rushed to their aid. Three times, tensed like coiled springs, in curving leaps of explosive anger, the tigers charged at the invisible phantoms that seethed in the depths of that forest of delights . . . At last, a breach was made; a deluge of torn greenery, whose long groans awakened the distant, loquacious echoes hidden in the mountains. Yet while we were all struggling to free our limbs from the last clinging lianas, we suddenly felt the sensual Moon, the Moon with her lovely warm thighs, languidly settling herself upon our weary backs.

Then, in the airy emptiness of the high plateaus, we heard a cry: "Let us kill the moonlight!"

Some ran to the cascades nearby. Gigantic wheels were set up and the turbines transformed the rushing waters into electric pulses that clambered up along wires, up high poles till they reached globes that were buzzing and glowing.

And so it was that three hundred electric moons, with their rays like dazzling white chalk, snuffed out the green, antique queen of all loves.[8]

And the military Railroad was built. A spectacular Railroad, following the highest mountain chains, and along which our fierce locomotives were soon hurtling, bristling with shrill cries, away from one summit to the next, hurling themselves down the steepest gradients, then climbing up again in search of hungry chasms, of absurdly impossible bends, of impossibly zigzagging roads . . . All around, from far off, boundless hatred marked our horizon, thick with the fleeing hordes from Goutville and Paralysis, which we tipped out into Hindustan.

4

Relentless pursuit . . . Look! We've already crossed the Ganges! At last, our gasping breath drove the sluggish clouds with their enfolding hostility before us, and on the horizon we caught sight of the greenish dance of the Indian Ocean, upon which the sun placed a fantastic golden muzzle . . . Stretched out over the Gulf of Oman and the Bay of Bengal, it was treacherously planning an invasion of the land.

At the very end of the Cormorin Peninsula,[9] encircled by heaps of bleached bones, stood a colossal, emaciated Ass whose back, gray like parchment, was sagging under the delightful weight of the Moon . . . This was the learned Ass, whose prolix member has been much exaggerated in literature. From time immemorial he has been braying out his asthmatic resentment against the haze on the horizon, where three great vessels advance motionlessly, their sail-spars looking like X-rayed spinal columns.

All at once the enormous herd of wild beasts ridden by the madmen thrust forward numberless muzzles out upon the surging waves, and from beneath their swirling manes they called on the Ocean to come to our aid. And the Ocean responded to the appeal, arching his immense back and violently shaking the promontories, before making his leap. For a long time he tried out his strength, swaying his haunches and bending his booming belly down between his immense, powerful legs. Then with a great heaving of his loins, the Ocean was able to lift his own great mass and overflow the jagged shoreline . . . Now the formidable invasion commenced.

We were marching through the vast encirclement of restless waves, great gouts of white foam that rolled and plunged, showering the backs of the lions . . . and these, ranged in a semicircle about us, with their fangs, their hissing froth and their roaring, seemed an extension of the waters. Sometimes, from high up in the hills, we would watch the Ocean gradually swelling out its monstrous form, like an immense whale that drives itself forward with a million fins. And it was we who led it thus right up to the chain of the Himalayas, and like a fan, the swarming hordes in flight, which we wanted to smash against the sides of Gorisankar, opened up to it.[10]

"Make haste, brothers! . . . Do you really want the wild animals to overtake us? We must stay in the front ranks despite our ponderous steps sticking in the mud . . . To Hell with these clammy hands of ours and these feet that drag roots in their wake! . . . My God! We're no better than poor wandering trees! What we need is wings! . . . So let us make ourselves some airplanes."

"They've got to be blue!" the madmen shouted, "blue so the enemy can't see them and so that we merge into the blue of the sky which, whenever there's a wind, flies over the mountain tops like a huge flag."

And from the ancient pagodas, the madmen seized the blue robes that were worn to the glory of the Buddhas,[11] to build their flying machines.

We cut out our Futurist airplanes from the buff-colored sailcloth of boats. Some of them had stabilizing wings and, being fitted with engines, soared like bloody vultures that took wriggling calves up into the sky.

Look at this, for example. My multicellular biplane with its tail rudder: 100 horsepower, 8 cylinders, 80 kilograms . . . Between my feet I have a small machine gun I can fire by pressing a steel button . . .

And we're off, intoxicated by our skillful maneuvers, in exhilarating flight, sputtering, weightless, and pitched like a song inviting drinking and dancing.

"Hurrah! At last we're worthy to command the great army of mad-men and beasts we unleashed! . . . Hurrah! We're in command of our rearguard: the Ocean with its encircling host of foaming cavalry! . . . Forward, mad men and women, lions, tigers, and panthers! Forward, you squadrons of waves! . . . By turns, our airplanes will be war ban-ners and passionate lovers for you! Delightful lovers who swim, with arms wide apart, through the rippling foliage, or who dally awhile on the seesaw breeze! . . . But look up there, to your right, at those sky-blue shuttles . . . It's the madmen rocking their monoplanes back and forth in the south wind's hammock! . . . In the meantime, I sit like a weaver at his loom, warping and wefting a silky cerulean sky! . . . Oh, how many fresh valleys, how many craggy mountains, below us! . . . How many flocks of rose-tinted sheep, scattered over the slopes of the green hills that offer themselves to the sunset! . . . O my soul, how you loved them! . . . But no. No! Enough of that! You will never again take pleasure in that kind of insipidity! . . . The reeds from which at one time we used to make our shepherds' pipes provide the cannon for this plane! . . . Nostalgia! Triumphal ecstasy! . . . Soon we shall have caught up with the inhabitants of Goutville and Paralysis, since we are flying so swiftly, despite the gusting headwinds . . . What does the anemome-ter say? . . . The wind in our faces is coming at a hundred kilometers an hour! . . . So what? I climb to two thousand meters, to fly over the plateau . . . And look! Just look at the hordes! . . . There, just there in front of us, now beneath us already! . . . See, down there, directly be-low us, in all that expanse of greenery, the tumultuous madness of that torrent of humanity still pressing on doggedly, trying to escape! . . . What's this noise? . . . It's the trees that come crashing down! Wonder-ful! The enemy hordes are already pressed hard up against the high walls of Gorisankar! . . . And we shall do battle with them! . . . Can you hear? Can you hear our engines, how they applaud? . . . Hey there, great Indian Ocean, join us in our battle!"

The Ocean followed us unerringly, flattening the walls of the vener-ated cities and casting down their illustrious towers that seemed like ancient knights with clanging armor, toppled from the marble saddles of their temples.

"At last! At last! So here you are, standing before us, great seething mass of people from Goutville and Paralysis, vile leprosy defiling these beautiful mountain slopes . . . We are flying fast against you, flanked by the galloping lions, our brothers, and at our backs our friend, the menacing Ocean, which follows on our heels to deter any defectors! . . . A precaution only, for we do not fear you! . . . Yet your numbers are infinite! . . . And we could use up all our ammunition, growing old in the slaughter! . . . Let me adjust my sights! . . . Raising to eight hundred meters! . . . Ready! . . . Fire! . . . Oh what ecstasy, playing skittles with Death! . . . And that's something you cannot take away from us! . . . What, retreating yet again? We shall soon have overrun this plateau! . . . My plane races along on its wheels, slipping along on its skids and rises in flight once more! . . . I'm heading into the wind! . . . Well done, you madmen! . . . On with your massacre! . . . Just look! I'm switching off the ignition and quietly gliding down, perfectly balanced, to touch down where the fighting is fiercest!

"See the furious coupling of war, this enormous vulva inflamed by the lusts of courage, this shapeless vulva that splits wide open to offer itself more easily in the terrible spasm of imminent victory! Ours is the victory . . . I'm sure of it, for the mad are already hurling their hearts at the sky, like bombs! . . . I raise my sights to a hundred meters! . . . Ready! . . . Fire! . . . And our blood? . . . Oh yes! The blood of all of us, in gushes, to put back some color into the ailing sunrises of the Earth! . . . Yes, we shall know how to warm you in our passionate arms, poor wretched Sun, doddering, shivering, and trembling on the summit of Gorisankar! . . ."

According to a statement in Marinetti's memoirs ("Il bosco di Provenza ove nacque il manifesto 'Uccidiamo il Chiaro di Luna,'" *La grande Milano*, pp. 227–29), this allegorical fable, rich in allusions to classical mythology, was inspired by the Provençal bard Frédéric Mistral, and was conceived on one of Marinetti's many journeys between Milan and Paris. The text was first published, in French, as *Tuons le clair de lune!* in *Poesia*, August–October 1909. Both the French and Italian texts were issued as two eighteen-page pamphlets, with a title that translates as *The International Review, "Poesia," Publishes This Proclamation of War in Response to the Insults with Which the Old Europe Has Gratified Triumphant Futurism*. It then appeared in Paolo Buzzi's *Aeroplani. Canti alati, col. II° Proclama futurista di F. T. Marinetti*, published in 1909 by the Edizioni di "Poesia." In 1911 a new edition with the title *Uccidiamo il chiaro di luna!* was issued by what was now called Edizioni futuriste di "Poesia." This was reprinted in the collections *I manifesti del futurismo* (1914 and 1919).

5

Preface to Mafarka the Futurist

Great Conflagrationary Poets!
My Brother Futurists!
Gian Pietro Lucini, Paolo Buzzi, Federico de Maria, Enrico Cavacchioli, Corrado Govoni, Libero Altomare, Aldo Palazzeschi![1]

Here is the great, explosive novel I promised you.[2] Like our souls, it is polyphonic; it is, at the same time, a lyric poem, an epic, an adventure novel, and a drama.

I am the only man who has dared write such a masterpiece, and it will be my own hand that will destroy it, when the growing splendor of the world has equaled it with its own and rendered it superfluous.

In spite of what the inhabitants of Goutville and Paralysis may say about it, this work of mine unfurls an immortal banner in the winds of glory, on the topmost peak of human thought; and my creator's pride is well pleased.

Don't think of justifying it; watch it, rather, bounding and exploding like a well-primed grenade over the shattered heads of our contemporaries, then dance, whirling in a warlike reel, splashing about in the quagmire of their imbecility, taking no heed of their monotonous driveling.

When I told them, "Scorn for women!" they all hurled their feeble abuse at me, like a pack of brothel keepers, infuriated by a police raid! But don't think I'm casting doubts on the animal worth of women, but rather on the sentimental importance that is attributed to them.[3]

My battle is against the gluttonous heart, that yielding up of lips, half-opened, to drink in a nostalgia for the twilight, the yearnings excited by hair weighed down by stars that are too high,[4] *the color of disaster . . . I wish to vanquish the tyranny of love, obsession with having only one woman, that monstrous romantic moonshine that washes over the brothel's facade!*

I roared at them, "Let's glorify war!" and from that day on, the crazed, icy hand of dread has mauled their spleens, groping around their insides between their cramped bellies and their brittle ribs.

Is there any painter capable of evoking on canvas the yellowy-green pallor flushing their cheeks as they bumble around, mumbling their ritual incantations about the wisdom of nations and universal disarmament?

From time to time, they throw their arms around one another's necks, catching their breath before hurling themselves en masse against us, the Enemy to be destroyed, to be destroyed at all costs!

They are a grotesque breed and utterly illogical, these worshipers of Peace! . . . They'll never get it into their heads that war is the world's sole cleanser! Am I not, at very least, something of a barbarian for these false devotees of progress—these people who, to avoid resembling the Ancient Romans, have quite readily given up the habit of the daily bath?

But let's not waste time worrying about the fatal silting up of their minds, from which the sea is forever receding. Instead, let's have a laugh at the way their cowardly inertia can still flare up in a sudden frenzy, in the hope of frightening us. Some of them hurl themselves against us, unbuttoning their starched collars and rolling up their sleeves, trying desperately to look fierce. Others don their provincial-style Sunday best to register their solemn disapproval of us. But their stupid pomposity barely touches the habitual indifference of the populace, and, it has to be said, the less foolish among them sit back on their heels, in silence, with their snouts stuck in their tankards of ignorance.

My brother Futurists! Look at each other's faces . . . and I know well enough that you in no way resemble that despicable crew! . . . So, can you then resign yourselves—you of all people—to remaining the miserable slaves and children of the cunt? And do you too, then, wish to strangle the bellowing Future and the unpredictable destiny of mankind?

In the name of the human Pride we revere, I tell you that the hour is at hand when men of broad vision, with minds of steel, will become prodigious in their siring, simply by bringing their boundless wills into play, those wills of giants whose doings are beyond question . . . And what I am telling you is this, that the human spirit is an untried womb . . . And it is we who are impregnating it for the first time![5]

Mafarka's Discourse on Futurism[6]

"Mafarka! Mafarka!"

Mafarka woke with a start in the streaming lava of an African sunset.

He had slept for a long time in the inaccessible hollow of a rock, at the end of an inlet that communicated with the sea by means of a narrow channel. He was surrounded by the seething, scarlet torrent of crashing waves, stirred up by a madness, by a pent-up fury, churning away beneath huge, inert boulders that weighed down heavily upon them.

Out at sea, the unbridled running of the storm.

"Mafarka! . . . Mafarka! . . . Master! . . . O Lord! . . ."

He sprang to his feet.

"Who is it calling me, down there, beyond the headland? . . . Who calls me, among the harsh cries of the waves?"

A sailing ship, all ebony and crimson, entered the channel. Another three came on behind, pitching and tossing without making much headway. They were filled to the gunwales with black sailors, like vats stuffed with grapes and carted along a rutted, potholed street.

Bunches of human beings, a thousand gesticulating arms . . . a melee of clashing voices and crashing waves in the bubbling red vat of the gulf. The sailors were all shouting at once, as though demented, to make their voices heard above the booming voice of the sea . . .

"Master! . . . We, your brothers, your children, your companions in battle, have come to offer you . . . but no, what are we saying? To beg of you to accept supreme command! . . ."

Mafarka, standing upright and still, gave his answer, spitting into the sea: "Pah! Ugh! . . . Get the hell out of it, you sons of a bitch, you lily-livered slaves! . . . I haven't got time to waste messing about with dumb animals and cowards! . . . Don't you have any ideas of your own, any will of your own . . . You people I've always seen skittering about me with the absorbed solemnity of busy turkeys? . . . Just sort out your own problems! . . . Personally, I don't give a damn anymore about your shabby little lives, with all their insipidities, their infirmities and degenerative diseases . . . You are people doomed to early decrepitude and death! . . . What I desire is to reach beyond myself, creating eternal

youth out of a strength that comes entirely from within! . . . But what's
the point of my telling you this? . . . For, make no mistake, you're
wrong, coming here and disturbing me in my solitude! And I won't forgive you for it . . . You compel me to hurl my spirit into the sea like a
cat fastened up in a sack! . . . What do you want? . . . Is it my strength
and my genius? . . . Oh! Abdullah! You really could have spared me this
task! . . . You, yes you, my brother in arms . . . You, the valorous young
captain I loved above all others! . . . Do you really not know who I
am? . . . Do you really think I can be bothered listening to your en-
treaties and taking your advice? . . . What have you got running in your
veins? . . . What are you made of, that you needed to throw yourself
upon me, like a child clinging to his mother's skirts? . . . What sort of a
heart do you have, not having felt the desire to kill me and take my
place? . . . Is life so long, then, that you're willing to waste half of it at
my knee? . . . To tell you the truth, I fled because I feared getting old
with a paltry little scepter in my hands! . . . I was afraid of all the compromises age forces on us and loss of nerve in the future . . . I felt jealousy and envy for you, yes, for you and your triumphant youth that
sooner or later would leave me behind.[7]

"Are you telling me I should take up the scepter again? . . . I'd rather
have a shepherd's crook! . . . A fine occupation that, and just right for a
hero like me, keeping watch over the soldiers' fodder![8] . . . After the
victory, what use would my presence be? . . . If the Arabs were to be
my soldiers, I'd be proud to concede it . . . But that they should become my flock . . . oh, what a sad fate that would be! The very idea of it
would be enough to corrupt them and me to the core, for all time! . . .
My words are not to be taken lightly, Abdullah! . . . I have weighed
their desperate courage with a detached mind! . . . And that's why I
have left the fruits of victory to those slow, calculating souls, who revel
in anguish! . . .

"I know I'll be accused of abandoning you defenseless to your enemies, after having made use of you to establish my own fame . . . Certainly not for pride's sake, especially since I have given back to you the
crown you had lost! . . . Now having had the pleasure of it . . . what
shall I say? . . . I'd had enough of it the moment it was done! . . .

"Could it be, Abdullah! that in order to stamp my will on the lives of
my people, you would like me to imitate the ridiculous tattooist, who
carefully draws symbolic figures on the skin, then patiently pricks out
their outline, using a tiny piece of tortoiseshell with serrated teeth? . . .
Or do you really expect me to give up my days, expending all my energies, beating out crude laws with a pitiless hammer? . . . Well, no thank

you! I am neither tattooist nor engraver! . . . All I care about is blood spurting out under the relentless blows of my axe. I'm quite incapable of inserting the pigments of my finely ground, then watered-down ideas, into the incision, with a tiny brush . . .

"I do not have the cautious wisdom of the bookkeeper[9] . . . I'm perfectly capable of seizing power, but only to cede it at once, into scrupulous hands . . . My fighter's grip would crumble your crown into dust . . . And I have no wish to waste my time in thwarting conspiracies and unmasking traitors! . . ."

A voice then cried out:

"O Master! Lord! . . . There are no longer any traitors left, and you have no more enemies! The Bubassa partisans are all dead . . . And even Sabattan!"

"That I know! . . . for I killed him myself, in fact, on the bridge of the sailing ship, where he came to challenge me for the last time!"

"All glory to you, Mafarka! . . . Glory to your invincible strength! . . . We call upon your all-powerful arm!"

"And what would you do with it, now that the war is over! . . . Besides, you could tell everyone that I've now become a builder of mechanical birds! . . . You think that's funny? . . . Clearly, you don't understand! . . . I am creating and giving birth to my son, a gigantic, invincible bird, who has enormous, flexible wings, made to embrace the stars.[10]

"No power will be able to withstand him . . . neither the shock of the storm nor the slashes of lightning! . . . He is down there at the far end of the gulf and you can see him . . . In the thirty days I have been toiling, I have never once doubted that I would create a son wholly worthy of my spirit . . . Infinity is his! . . . Do you think such a miracle is not possible? That's because you have no faith in your power as men! . . . You must needs have the joy and the will to give yourselves up entirely to the marvelous, as a suicide gives himself up to the sea! . . . With my own hands I have carved him, my son, from the wood of a young oak! . . . And I have discovered a formula that transforms vegetal fibers into living flesh and sturdy muscle! . . . My son's face is well proportioned and full of strength, but no one, as yet, has had the chance to admire him . . . I work at him with my chisel during the night, by the light of the stars!

"During the day, I cover him over with tiger skins so that the workers don't sully him with their brutish eyes . . . The smiths of Milmillah, under my instruction, are building a great cage of iron and oak to protect my child from the ravages of the wind. There are two thousand of

them, whipped out of their villages and obedient to my every word . . .
The weavers of Lagahourso, in the meantime, are preparing a lightweight yet hard-wearing material that will clothe the huge webbed wings
of my child. It is a canvas that is indestructible, woven from date-palm
fibers, and it is being variously colored, out in the sun, with tints of
gold, blood and rust."

He moved with great flying steps over the topmost points of the
rocks. His body seemed free of all human weight and ungainliness, so
that sometimes he could be seen gliding high and free above the flapping of the sails and the unceasing cries of the sailors, like a colossal
eagle protecting its offspring.

And Abdullah, hoisting himself up the mainmast of his own boat,
cried: "Mafarka! Mafarka! . . . We offer you all our strength, and our
arms are ready to serve you in this heaven-sent task!"

"No! No! I thank you, inhabitants of Tel-el-Kibir! . . . But it is you,
Abdullah, who are destined to command the city! . . . Besides, it is not
subjects I want, but slaves!"

Suddenly there was a great clap of thunder over the sea. The lightning, like a giant with his head down between his clasped hands and
with legs of gold, flashed through the air and leaped, all electric and
violet-hued, from a cloud trampoline and dived straight into the sea. The
herd of waves, like buffaloes with horns of vapor, galloped beyond the
opening to the channel into the open sea to inspect the spoils of ships
and men, all crammed into the cove, which rightfully was their domain.

"Away, Abdullah, away you go! . . . Do you not see the storm? . . .
Waiting to ambush you, out there . . . There is nothing I can do to save
you! . . . And it will be impossible for you to climb these slippery walls."

Mafarka's booming voice rang through the air in response to the
thunder.

And while he was speaking, he went on walking over the steep, high
rocks, and his mouth, it also full of the storm, hurled violent words, so
as to cut like hatchets through the squall.

"Away with you! . . . I have no wish to see you sink in this gorge!"

And Abdullah answered: "No! No! What do we care about the storm
or about death? . . . We wish to gaze one last time upon your face! . . .
We desire that our eyes, already doomed to die, drink in your passionate image!"

Then Mafarka drew himself up to his full height, calling yet again:
"Allah! Allah! Thanks be unto Thee! . . . For I see that my teachings are
at last bearing glorious fruit! . . . Yes! Oh yes, my brothers, I open my
arms to you and press you all to my heart . . . You are at last worthy to

hear the mysterious word of my religion![11] . . . I teach you to despise death, to nourish yourselves on danger, to risk your lives, as you are doing, for an idea, for a glimpse, for the extraordinary!

"Your eyes are brighter and clearer than ever before! . . . Now, your ears can hear the voice of the Sun and the sighs of the stars, while the storm unleashes itself upon you with its great whips of foam lashing the waves. I teach you to press your wills from your muscles, from your mouths, like the crimson breath of a furnace, like a supernatural power, so that it dominates, transforms and raises up wood and granite and all the metals!

"For that is how I now release my still youthful and powerful will from my own body, although it is already worn out with too many fruitless endeavors . . . This is how I shall infuse my will into the new body of my progeny. He will have all the strength of beauty unspoiled by the sight of death! I shall breathe my spirit into him through a kiss: I shall dwell in his heart, in his lungs and behind the windows of his eyes: I shall stand looking out from the scarlet terrace of his lips . . . He is more beautiful than all the men and all the women on Earth! His colossal stature stands twenty cubits high, while his all-powerful arms can move two wings that are bigger than the tents of the Bedouin and the roofs of your dwellings, for an entire day . . . And you should know that I have fathered my son without recourse to any vulva! . . . Do you not understand what I am saying? . . . Listen to me, then . . . One evening, all of a sudden, I found myself wondering: Is there really any need for gnomes, scurrying about on my chest like seamen on a deck, to lift my arms? . . . And is there really some captain on the quarterdeck of my brow to open my eyes as if they were two compasses? To both of these questions my unerring spirit replied: Most certainly not! And from that I came to the conclusion that it is entirely possible to create an immortal giant with unfailing wings, out of one's own flesh, without the collaboration and foul-smelling involvement of a woman's uterus!

"You must believe in the absolute, defining power of the will, which you have to cultivate and strengthen by subjecting yourselves to a harsh discipline, until such time as it bursts forth from our nerve centers and soars beyond the limits of our muscles with unimaginable speed and force.

"Our will must go out from us so as to take possession of matter and change it according to our whim. In that way we can mold everything around us and endlessly regenerate the face of the earth[12] . . . Soon, if you appeal to your wills, you too will create offspring, without need of any vulva.

"It is in this way that I have killed love, and in its place I have set the sublime will of heroism! . . . To experience this new ecstasy, you have to hone the pleasure of whatever task you undertake till it becomes painful, and through this, gradually redouble your effort, while forever shifting your goal further off. You must turn the regrets that you feel for emotions destroyed, in this process, into an exquisite delirium. You must take in the earth's languid, soporific, and melancholy landscapes, and all its sunsets and all its moonlit scenes, with equally implacable gaze . . . You must prepare yourself for, and cultivate every kind of danger, so as to experience the intense pleasure of thwarting them . . .

"This is the new Sensuality that will liberate the world from Love, once I have established the religion of the manifest Will and everyday Heroism as the norm.

"But where is your will? . . . Where is your heroism? It is not that you lack courage! . . . Indeed, for a long time you stroked the flanks of Death! . . . But your desire was not strong enough . . . and precisely for this reason She did not deem you worthy of her bed, glistening with worms! . . . Do you still not understand? . . . What dumb beasts you are! . . . You can have no hope of me instilling in you the principles of my philosophy, you puff and blow like zumhara players do,[13] swelling out their cheeks further and further! This is my thought, compressed like my fist . . . Just as there are countless fragments of organic matter whirling around the Sun, which receive its light and remain attached to it by indestructible chains, as well as by filial loyalty, each one of us, in like manner, receives an endless flow of light from the universe and is enriched by memories and sensations, throughout his pilgrimage, owing to the infinite number of transformations our immortal matter undergoes! . . .

"Our spirit, which is the highest manifestation of ordered, living matter, accompanies that same matter in all its changes, preserving in its new forms all the sensations of its past, the subtle vibrations of energies previously expended . . . The individual divinity and continuity of the determining, all-powerful spirit has to be able to express itself so as to change the world! . . . This is the only true religion!

"Let us make every single moment of our lives shine out, through the acts of our tempestuous wills, moving from risk to further risk, forever courting Death, which, with her rough kiss, will make the fragments of our mindful beings eternal, in all their beauty!

"In precisely this way, future lives will be embellished, and in their new, living forms, they will experience the concentrated joy of our extraordinary lives.

"I glorify violent Death, which is the crown of youth, Death which gathers us in whenever we are worthy of her immortalizing voluptuousness! . . . Woe betide any man who lets his body grow old and his spirit wither!"[14]

On hearing these words, the son of Muktar rose up, gigantic, on the bowsprit of one of the ships, and sang out these words: "I believe in you, Mafarka! . . . And in a moment, you will see me die in the triumphant splendor of my youth!"

And so saying, from high up on the heaving prow, he hurled himself, arms flung wide, upon a pointed rock on which he remained half impaled, squirming and covered in blood, like the tunny fish that a storm nails to the reef.

A great roaring responded to his last, heart-rending gasps.

"Silence!" Mafarka cried. "I raise my voice, for not even death itself has the right to interrupt me."

He stood tall against the wind that beat against him from all sides, with the violence of a crowd that raises up its tyrant or its liberator on a hundred arms. And his voice rose above the creaking of the masts and the boards and above the flakes of scudding foam that the wind, threshing tirelessly, flailed about the threshing floor of that tragic gulf.

"Think upon my tempered spirit, my agile, quivering sinews beneath my insatiable, clear-sighted will! My metallic brain sees everywhere precise angles in rigorous geometrical systems . . . Future days lie there before me, fixed, straight, and parallel, like the military roads clearly mapped out by the armies of my desires . . . And my youthful past is abolished, abolished! . . . Oh yes, I too had nights of love in which it pleased me to blind myself in the cool arms of some young virgin . . . And I would bury my head between her scented breasts so as to lose sight of the many different regrets piling up like clouds on the horizon![15] . . . Oh yes! Love, women . . . all of that can momentarily blot out the sky and fill up the well of space! . . . but I have erased these things from my memory! And yet there were indeed sweet, shady places in my country, where the light, at dusk, was pleasant and intimate . . . The stars were so familiar that you might have wanted to hold out your hand to them, full of seed, as if they were silvery sparrows. And the night was so indulgent to my lack of courage. Between the arms of a woman I would sense the memory of my daytime failings brushing against my feet, reaching my heart, groping for my relaxed yet restless nerves, while my imagination made delicious, golden leaps toward my soaring, fugitive sensations . . . All of this is life's poison! . . . At that time, I savored and suffered everything: living and desiring, dreaming and attending to my sufferings in the shadows! . . . Poetry! Poetry! . . . Sublime putrefaction[16] of the spirit! At last, here I am as I wanted to be, dedicated to my own death and ready to give birth to the God that all carry deep within them! . . . My death is a condition of my life! . . . Better that it is so! . . . Oh, the delirium of cracking oneself like an eggshell out of which will come the perfect new being! . . . balancing between life and death![17] Make haste to weigh up my days! . . . I hold my destiny in the palm of my hand, like the neck of a faithful steed, ready to bear me wherever soars the eagle of my desires."

The waves beat out the rhythm of Mafarka's words like a landslide crashing down upon the rocks. With the rhythm of each of those utterances, bellowed into the wind, it seemed as though the waves hurled corpses in their thousands into the jaws of the cliffs.

The boats bobbed furiously, buffeting the swarming shadows of the seamen who clung to the masts like gadflies to the hooves of a tumbled horse.

Mafarka cried out to them:

"I bid you farewell and give you my blessing! . . . Take them! And the kiss of your lord and your king! . . . Go! I command you! . . . But beware! . . . Beware! . . . Mind how you go! Weigh anchors quickly! . . . Take good care, Abdullah! Give the order at once that each of the boats moves away alone along the channel, spreading their foresails to take advantage of the current! . . . Pull in your oars! . . . otherwise you will smash them! . . . Don't use your topsails or else the wind passing over the rocks will capsize you in the heavy swell! . . . Depart! Away! One by one skimming lightly over the billow! . . . You crewmen, spread yourselves evenly, two to the stem and two at the stern! . . . Yes! Yes! Well done, Abdullah! . . . Like that! And those who are still left alive announce to the city of Tel-el-Kibir that soon Mafarka will pass on his spirit into the mouth of his son, Gazurmah, the invincible lord of space, the giant with immense, orange-colored wings."

When he had uttered these words, the lowing herd of sea buffaloes scaled the cliffs, with a fearful uproar of heaving backs and horns of spray, overturning all the boats buffeting each other in the creek. Only two of them got away, with hoisted sails, along the narrow channel, as if they were thieves . . .

"Goodbye! Goodbye, my brothers! . . . May Death hold you in his violet lips and suck out your blood, and may his caress bruise your bodies and his kiss ecstatically flay the flesh from your bones! . . . Take your pleasure, take your pleasure then, Abdullah! Take your pleasure my friend amid the harsh grating of useless, splintered oars, amid the smashing of masts and the great lacerating laughter of hysterical sails, burning with the desire to be naked . . . naked and dripping with a lover's sweat, between Death's scything arms!"

Mafarka ran first to one place then to another, along the tops of the rocks, urging on to the delirium of dying all those lives that were writhing in ecstasy upon the quivering body of the great black Goddess.

"Die!" he cried out; "Die of pleasure, flesh of man! . . . die in ecstasy!"

His voice was hoarse and sobbing like that of the man who, through the power of his caresses, urges the flesh of his adored lover toward a terrifying climax, saying to her, "Feel your pleasure, my love! Feel it all over your body! In your breasts and in your little pink mouths! . . . You are tortured with pleasure, are you not? . . . Oh, then suffer yet more torture!"

Down below, the two surviving boats were scudding, black, dancing, sublime in the welter of the storm, and their waterlines, white with foam, were grinning above the ebony waves, like the mouths of negroes.

Mafarka the Futurist: An African Novel **was first published in French by Sansot in early 1910 (although the title page gives 1909 as its date), and in the same year in an Italian translation by Marinetti's secretary, Decio Cinti.**

6

c✧ↄ

We Renounce Our Symbolist Masters,
the Last of All Lovers of the Moonlight

We have sacrificed everything for the success of this Futurist concept
of life. To such a degree that today, after having loved them intensely,
we hate the glorious forefathers of our intellects, the great Symbolist
geniuses, Edgar Poe, Baudelaire, Mallarmé, and Verlaine.[1] Today we
feel nothing but contempt for them for having swum in the river of
time, continually looking back over their shoulders toward the distant
blue wellspring of the past, toward the "ciel antérieur où fleurit la
beauté."[2]

For those geniuses, there was no poetry without nostalgia, without
evocation of times that were dead and gone, without the mists of history and legend.

We detest them, the Symbolist masters, we who have dared to step
naked from the river of time and who create—despite our better judgment and with our bodies grazed and scraped on the rocks of our steep
ascent—new springs of heroism that sing, new torrents that deck the
mountain in scarlet.

We are red and we love red: eyes and cheeks reddened by the glare
of the locomotive's firebox, and we love and sing the ever-growing triumph of the machine which they stupidly denounced.

Our Symbolist fathers had a passion that we think was ridiculous—
the passion for things eternal, the desire for the immortal, imperishable masterpiece.

We, however, consider that there is nothing more base or abject
than having one's eyes fixed on the immortal when creating a work of

art, more abject and base than the calculated, usurious concept of the Christian paradise, which should repay us for the virtues we exercised on Earth one million percent.

One should simply create, precisely because creating has no use or value, is without recompense, is ignored, despised, is—in a word—heroic.

To the poetry of nostalgic memory, we oppose that of feverish expectation. Against tears of beauty, shed over the tomb, we set the finely chiseled features of the pilot, the chauffeur, and the aviator.

Instead of the concept of the immortal, the imperishable, in art, we propose that of continuous becoming, the evanescent, the transitory, and the ephemeral.

Thus, we shall transform the *nevermore* of Edgar Poe[3] into intense joy, and we shall teach how to love the beauty of an emotion or a sensation *inasmuch as it is unique and destined to disappear irrevocably.*

History, in our eyes, can be nothing but a falsifier, or at best a miserable little stamp collector or a collector of medals and of counterfeit coins.

The past is necessarily inferior to the future. And that's how we want it to be. How could we possibly see any virtue at all in our most dangerous enemy, the past, that gloomy mentor and abominable tutor?

This is why we renounce the obsessive splendors of the centuries that are gone forever and why we cooperate with triumphant machines, which keep the earth enclosed in their net of speed.

We connive with the Machine to destroy the poetry of far-off times, of faraway places and of solitude in the wild, the poignant nostalgia of parting, and in their place we set the tragic lyricism of speed in all places, at all times.

Indeed, our Futurist sensibility is no longer moved by the dark mystery of an unexplored valley or of a mountain gorge which, against our wills, we imagine. Instead, they are traversed by an elegant ribbon of white road where, all of a sudden, coughing and spluttering, an automobile comes to a halt, gleaming with progress and full of civilized voices—like the corner of a boulevard set down in the middle of nowhere.

Every pine wood madly in love with the moonlight has a Futurist road crossing it from one side to the other.

The day of simple, tearful moaning, in lengthy soliloquies, is over. With us, the day of the rootless man begins, of extended man who fuses with iron, who feeds upon electricity and understands nothing beyond the desire for danger and day-to-day heroism.[4]

That's enough to give you an idea how much we despise those who defend the aesthetics of Nature,[5] stupid anachronism that it is.

Multicolored billboards in the green meadows, iron bridges which chain the hills together, surgical trains that cut through the blue belly of the mountains, huge turbines, new muscles of the earth, may you be praised by the Futurist poets, since it is you who are destroying the old morbid sensibilities and the billing and cooing of the earth!

With these sorts of passions and innovatory impulses, how do you expect us to accept the concept of art which is current in contemporary Italy? For far too long Italy has been subjected to the enervating influence of Gabriele D'Annunzio, the little brother of the great French Symbolists, who, like them, is full of nostalgia and fawning over the naked body of a woman.

We must fight against Gabriele D'Annunzio at all costs,[6] because it is he, with his great talent, who has distilled the four intellectual poisons that we want to destroy once and for all. First, the sickly, nostalgic poetry of memory and of faraway places; second, a romantic sentimentalism, dripping with moonlight, which is elevated into the fatalistic ideal of Woman-Beauty; third, an obsession with the erotic, with the adulterous triangle, the spice of incest and the titillation of what Christians call sinfulness; fourth, an academic passion for the past, a mania for antiquity and for collecting things.

In the same way, we turn our backs on the tremulous, pastoral sentimentalism of Pascoli, who, in spite of his undoubted genius, will nevertheless stand condemned because of the influence his cowardly humility has had.[7]

And finally, we are very happy to have to partake no longer of the disgusting milky coffee of the sacristan, dished up by our despicable Fogazzaro.[8]

We accept none but the enlightened work of four or five great precursors of Futurism. I am alluding to Émile Zola; Walt Whitman; Rosny-Aîné, the author of *Bilateral* and *The Red Wave*; Paul Adam, the author of *Trust*; Gustave Kahn, the creator of Free Verse; and Verhaeren, the glorifier of machines and of tentacular cities.[9]

Futurist lyricism,[10] which is essentially fluid, ever-changing, just like the pictorial dynamism of the Futurist painters, Boccioni, Carrà, Russolo, Balla, and Severini, expresses our "I" with increasing speed, that "I" which is created through endless inspiration.[11] Futurist lyricism,[12] a perpetual dynamism of thought, an uninterrupted flow of images and sounds, can alone express the ephemeral, unstable, symphonic universe which takes shape in us and with us.

It is the total realization of the dynamic nature of our flexible minds; the complete "I," sung, painted, and sculptured, yet never fixed, in its perpetual becoming; a succession of lyrical states which precludes all the Parnassian ideas about reciprocal outwardness and extension.[13] This is the great strophe that has been orchestrated by Futurist Free Verse.

Against abstract art, which is static and formalistic,[14] we set an art of continuous movement, of aggressive struggle, and of speed.

To the imperious assertions of a dogmatic intellectualism, we reply by shouting, "We want to destroy Museums and Libraries! . . . Do you have any objections? Enough! Enough of that! We are well aware of what our lovely, lying intelligence tells us! We don't want to hear it!"[15]

All glory to the poetic spirit, the faculty which Edgar Poe calls "the most exalted of all—since those truths which to us were of the most enduring importance could only be reached by that analogy which speaks in proof-tones to the imagination alone, and to the unaided reason bears no weight" (Edgar Poe, *The Colloquy of Monos and Una*).[16]

Against a skeptical, pessimistic determinism, we therefore set the cult of creative intuition, freedom of inspiration, and a self-induced optimism. Against a nostalgic, sentimental, or erotic moonlight, we finally exalt an unjust and cruel heroism such as will tame the all-conquering zeal of the motor.

This manifesto was first published in French in *Le Futurisme* (1911) and with a few variations in *Guerra sola igiene del mondo* (1915). It also appeared in *L'Italia futurista* of August 5, 1917.

THE FUTURIST POLITICAL
PROGRAM (1909–13)

As Marinetti emphasized in his essay *Futurism's First Battles* (document 25), it dawned on him at a very early stage that Futurism could only attain its proclaimed aim of total renewal of Italian society if it was to go beyond the publication of manifestos, books, and artworks and "take to the street, lay siege to the theaters, introduce the fist into the battle for art."

In the crisis of the Left, which fell between the acceptance of the Socialist Party into the established political system and the emergence of the Communist Party as a new magnet for the revolutionary forces, there existed in Italy a plethora of subversive groups and associations in all major and most minor cities. The constant shifts and changes in the membership of these federations suggest a considerable overlap of recruits and shared ideology between the groups, which were all dissatisfied with the existing system of parliamentary democracy, the corrupt government, and the leadership of Giovanni Giolitti. It was within this medley of radicals and subversives of the extreme Left that Marinetti centered his political engagement. The Futurist project of liberating Italy from the cumbersome forces of the past, and of leading humankind into a golden future, could not be achieved by a handful of artists and intellectuals alone. Marinetti had to seek allies in the political arena and take the concept of a revolutionary "art-in-action" into the midst of the sociopolitical revolutionaries, whose *beaux gestes libertaires* he had praised in his first Futurist manifesto.

Marinetti's negotiations would have foundered at once had he not approached his potential allies with a sufficiently developed political program. It is worth remembering that Marinetti had a doctorate in law, gained with a thesis on the role of the crown in parliamentary government, and that his professional studies had provided him with a sound knowledge of modern political theory.

Marinetti's political writings began with an analysis of the deeper causes of the unrest that shook Milan in 1898 (*Les Émeutes milanaises de mai 1898*), and reveal his sympathies with the socialists and his interest in the social problems of the underdeveloped southern regions of Italy. In 1908 Marinetti became involved in the irredentist struggle for the restitution of Austrian territories considered to be Italian. His engagements in Trieste ended with his arrest, but subsequently he published the essay "Trieste, Our Beautiful Powderkeg," in which he affirmed his commitment to the irredentist cause.

In 1909 the common people of Milan became familiar with Futurism not only through the many posters announcing the foundation of this new artistic movement but also through the election leaflets and the Futurist political manifesto posted up in the streets. There is no information available as to how the Italian electorate responded to this proclamation. But we know that Marinetti planned to stand in the local elections in Piedmont, with an anarcho-syndicalist program of a nationalistic bent. It is possible that the project of a Union of Revolutionary Forces, of May 1910, and the lectures titled "The Necessity and Beauty of Violence" of June–July 1910, belonged in this context and were organized to stimulate the debate on Futurism as a political movement.

Over the next few years the Futurists engaged actively and consistently in the political battles of the period. The flier outlining the Futurist political program (*Third Futurist Political Manifesto*, document 13), of which 100,000 copies were distributed during the 1913 elections, gave rise to the suspicion that Marinetti intended to stand against Leonida Bissolati (1857–1920), the reformist Socialist leader who cooperated with the bourgeois government and was expelled from the PSI in 1912. In two interviews with *Giornale d'Italia* and *L'avvenire di Messina*, Marinetti replied, rather cautiously, that for the time being his artistic activities forbade him to consider the offers he had received for a political candidacy, but that in the near future he intended to enter the formal political arena.

7

ooloo

First Futurist Political Manifesto

In the *First Manifesto of Futurism*, published in *Le Figaro* on February 20, 1909, which is to say about two years before the foundation of the Italian Nationalist Association[1] and three or so years before the Libyan War, we proclaimed ourselves to be *Futurist Nationalists*, by which we meant antitraditionalists.[2] We glorified patriotism, the army, and war. We initiated an anticlerical, anti-Socialist campaign to prepare the way for an Italy that was greater, stronger, more advanced, and more receptive to the New, an Italy liberated from her illustrious past and thus fit to create for herself a tremendous future.

For the purpose of reviving opposition to the Triple Alliance and reviving irredentism, we launched the Futurist Movement in Trieste,[3] where we had the honor of holding the first of our Futurist *serate*[4] (at the Rossetti Theater on January 12, 1910).[5]

We ended our second Futurist *serata* (at the Teatro Lirico in Milan, on February 15, 1910)[6] with the cry: "Long live war, the sole cleanser of the world! Long live Asinari di Bernezzo![7] Down with Austria!"

These cries, hurled at an audience of four thousand and echoed by a great number of students, earned us—in that moment of pacifism and indifference—a storm of jeering whistles, the insults and smears of the conventionalists.

But we had already released the following manifesto throughout the whole of Italy:

Futurist Voters!

We Futurists, whose sole political program is one of national pride, energy, and expansion, denounce before the whole country the irrevocable shame which a possible clerical victory would bring upon us.

We Futurists call on all the talented young people of Italy to engage in a struggle to the bitter end against candidates who have any truck with the traditionalists and with the priests.

We Futurists want a national representation which, freed from mummies and from every sort of pacifist cowardice, will be ready to extricate us from any snare and to respond to any offense whatsoever.

THE FUTURISTS

This manifesto was published with the title *Elettori futuristi!* as a small flier and a large poster during the General Elections of March 7 and 14, 1909. It also appeared as *Manifesto politico dei futuristi* in *La democrazia* (Lecce) on March 13, 1909. The text translated here follows *Guerra sola igiene del mondo* (1915).

8

Our Common Enemies

We Futurists, who are we?[1] A close-knit group of minds and hands decidedly in revolt, but with our feet on the ground. No fraternity has ever before gathered together life's natural aristocracies and democracies in such a determined, logical manner. Don't be shocked by the seeming contradictions of the written word! You can be sure, brothers, that the Futurist Manifesto has been spelled out for the benefit of a single, immense phalanx of souls, that of the strong and the exploited. Which of you would not feel the urge to march beneath our banner against the dull yet arrogant hegemony of the mediocre? If a Latin *idea* (and by this we don't mean *a word*) has circled the earth, it is a sign that eternal human force has yet again caught fire; it is a sign that in this land of ours, of the oppressed and of oppressors, the eternal, dynamic phenomenon of rebellion has found recruits even in the magnificent antithesis of its opposing idealistic currents. Opposing, yet directed toward a single end, that of the redemption of our race and of art.

In the glorious obscurity of your multiple labors, you live by the brightest ray of faith and by that same token renew yourselves to carry out daily your physical tasks. You feel so powerfully the enormous weight of the social machine that is crushing you, that catapult of sordid egoism, of the most unjust cruelty, of insatiable social cannibalism.

We live upon the airy heights of the gigantic human mountain and seek to pour forth our flooding emotions in a song that longs for the stars. We are well aware of the noxious black fogs exhaling from the hell in which you live your tormented lives, because the same gigantic, brute force prevents us from flying to the empyrean[2] and touching the stars with our brows. We feel and we think with you, and our song, just for one moment, forgets its Impossible Paradises, to fall into the rhythm of that Infernal Reality.

Brothers, we are but a single army that has lost its way, in the dark wood of the Universe, as we journey from its summit to its very depths. Our enemy is one and the same: crows, vultures, wolves, sheep, asps— the tragicomedy of eternal zoological symbols! Is it indeed necessary to rehearse their banal, doom-laden names: clericalism, moralism, commercialism, academicism, pedantry, pacifism, and mediocrity? They laugh in the face of a like-sounding word, which will destroy them all.

In this sad family with its common yet disparate ends, *Futurism* is the only member that has the right to be alive today; it lives and will go on living beyond the shameful deaths of all the rest.

Brother heroes, let us recognize each other once and for all in the light of our glowing torches! We desire a Fatherland, we desire a great and strong Fatherland. So then? When you feel yourselves aroused at your best by your wonderful ideal, do you not instinctively dream of holding a gun in your hands? Doesn't any one of you feel himself to be a soldier in a battle that is approaching? Can you really be sure that your offspring will not one day condemn you for having raised them by ignoring, by scorning the greatest of all Aesthetics, that of frenzied battalions, armed to the teeth? I am telling you that war, any war at all, is made with guns, and that all our enemies are at the gates, that every kind of zeal is needed, that all forms of heroism compel us in these hours of immense psychological upheaval, in our desperate wait for war. We are all unsettled and maybe even fearful cowards. We have to convert the great hatred we have accrued into a great love, into great heroism. If rivers of blood run healthily through this dumbfounded, anemic world, we shall be the first Archangels of Health. Never forget it!

The opposite wings of politics and literature, beating with frantic intensity, will yet again sweep away the smoke-filled skies of human sacrifice. Trade unionists all, whether of manual labor or of the intellect, of life and of art, destroyers and creators together, realistic or idealistic anarchists, heroes of all strengths and of all beauties, let us go forward dancing, propelled by the same superhuman intoxication, toward the common apotheosis of the Future!

The essay was published in the anarcho-syndicalist journal *La demolizione*, March 16, 1910.

9

War, the Sole Cleanser of the World

And now you find me ready to explain to you what it is that cleanly separates Futurism from the concept of anarchy.[1]

Anarchy, turning its back on the infinite principle of human evolution, suspends its curving leap only at the absolute ideal of universal peace, at a ludicrous paradise composed of warm embraces, under rustling palm leaves, out in the country.

We Futurists, on the other hand, affirm the continuous perfection and endless progress of humankind, both physiological and intellectual, as absolute principles of Futurism.

We consider the hypothesis of the friendly unification of peoples to be outmoded and utterly dispensable, and we see for the world only one form of purgation, and that is war.[2]

The distant goal of anarchy, a sweet affection, sister to cowardice, seems to us like a horrible cancer that disposes peoples to great sufferings.

What's more, the anarchists are content to attack the political, legal, and economic branches of the social tree, but we want something more . . . We want to dig out its deepest roots and burn them, those which are planted in the mind of man. These go by the names of desire for minimum effort; cowardly quietism; love of whatever is ancient and old, of whatever is sickly and corrupted; horror of the new; scorn for youth; veneration of time, of accumulated years, for the dead and the dying; an instinctive need for restricted order, for laws, chains, obstacles, for police stations, for morality, for chastity; fear of unrestricted freedom.

Have you ever witnessed a gathering of young, revolutionary anarchists? There can be no more depressing sight. You will become aware, in fact, of an urgent desire in every one of those red, impetuous souls, to deprive themselves immediately of their independence and their initiative and to hand over the governance of their assembly to the oldest person among them. Or rather, to the greatest opportunist, to the most prudent, in fact, to the one who, having already gained a little power and a bit of authority, will have a fatal interest in maintaining the status quo, in quelling violence by opposing all adventurous instincts, taking risks, and heroism.

This new chairman, though guiding the general discussion with apparent fairness, will lead it by the nose to the trough of his own personal interest.

Do you revolutionary spirits still seriously believe in the usefulness of such gatherings?

If indeed you do, then be content with choosing a chairman or, better still, a regulator of debates, and elect the youngest among you to this position, the one who is least known, least important, and make sure that his role is limited to choosing the next person to speak and, with stopwatch in hand, allotting an equal length of time to each.

But what sets an even wider gap between the Futurist and the anarchistic points of view is the great problem of love, the great tyranny of sentimentalism and lust, from which we wish to liberate mankind.

This manifesto appeared first in French in the collection *Le Futurisme* **(1911) and was translated into Italian in the booklet** *Guerra sola igiene del mondo* **(1915). Later, it was reprinted, with a few minor textual variations, in the collections** *I manifesti del futurismo* **(1919) and** *Futurismo e fascismo* **(1924), and a large section of it was incorporated into the chapter "Technocratic Government" in** *Democrazia futurista* **(1919).**

10

⚮

Against Sentimentalized Love
and Parliamentarianism

Our hatred, to be precise, for the tyranny of love, we summed up in the laconic expression "scorn for women."[1]

We scorn woman when conceived as the only ideal, the divine receptacle of love,[2] woman as poison, woman as the tragic plaything, fragile woman, haunting and irresistible, whose voice, weighed down with destiny, and whose dreamlike mane of hair extend into the forest and are continued there in the foliage bathed in moonlight.

We despise that horrible, heavy Love[3] that impedes the march of men, preventing them from going beyond their own humanity, doubling themselves, overcoming themselves so as to become what we term *extended man*.

We despise that horrible, heavy Love, that immense leash with which the sun keeps the valiant earth chained in its orbit, when certainly it would prefer to leap wherever chance took it, to take its chance with the stars.

We are convinced that love—sentimentalism and lust—is the least natural thing in the world. All that's natural and important in it is the coitus, whose goal is the futurism of the species.

Love—romantic obsession and sensual pleasure—is nothing but the invention of poets, who made a present of it to mankind . . . And poets will retract it as one takes back a manuscript from the hands of a publisher who has shown that he is incapable of publishing it decently.

In this attempt to free ourselves, the suffragettes are our best allies in that the more rights and powers they can secure for women, the more will their urge to love be impoverished, to such an extent that they will cease to be the focal point of sentimental passion or of lust.[4]

The sexual life will be reduced simply to the function of preserving the species, which will be an enormous gain for the growing stature of mankind.

So far as the claimed inferiority of woman is concerned, we think that if her body and spirit had experienced an upbringing identical to that of the spirit and body of man, over very many generations, it might perhaps have been possible to speak of equality between the two sexes.

What is certain, however, is that in her present state of servitude, both intellectual and erotic, woman, finding herself in an absolute state of inferiority from the point of view of intelligence and character, can only be a mediocre legislative instrument.[5]

And precisely for this reason, we most fervently defend the right of suffragettes while at the same time pitying their childish enthusiasm for the ridiculous, miserable little right to vote.

Indeed, we are certain that they will zealously seize hold of it and will thus help us, even without meaning to, to destroy that great crap heap of corruption and banality to which parliamentarianism has by this time been reduced.

Parliamentarianism has become more or less everywhere a disreputable form of government.[6] It did yield some positive results in the past. It created, for example, the illusory sense of participation of the majority of people in government. I say illusory, because it demonstrated that the people cannot nor ever will be represented by delegates they don't know how to choose.

The people thus remain forever outside government. Yet, on the other hand, it is precisely to parliamentarianism that the people owe their very existence.

The pride of the masses has been increased by the electoral regime. The stature of the individual has been raised by the idea of representation. This idea, however, has utterly falsified the evaluation of people's intelligence by exaggerating beyond measure the value of eloquence. This uncomfortable fact gets worse with each day that passes.

It is for this reason that I foresee the aggressive entry of women into parliament, with some pleasure. Where could we find a more effective, more excitable dynamite?

Almost all European parliaments are nothing more than noisy henhouses, stalls, or sewers.

Their overriding principles are: first, corrupting cash and shrewd handouts for the purpose of gaining a seat in parliament; second, eloquent verbosity, grandiose falsification of ideas, the triumph of high-sounding phrases, negro drumtalk, and the flapping of windmills.

Through the parliamentary system, these grotesque features hand over absolute power to a horde of lawyers.

As you well know, lawyers are just the same in every country. They are people who are intimately bound up with everything that is despicable, futile . . . They are spirits who see only the minute, day-to-day facts and are utterly incapable of stimulating great universal ideas, of understanding either the clashes and fusion of races or the soaring of the bright, flaming ideal and its effects on individuals and whole peoples. They are litigation merchants, prostituted brains, emporia of subtle ideas and polished syllogisms.

As a result of parliamentarianism, an entire nation is at the mercy of those manufacturers of justice who, using the malleable metal of the law, carefully lay traps for the foolish.

So let's be quick and grant women the right to vote. After all, this is the absolute, logical conclusion of the idea of democracy and universal suffrage as it was conceived by Jean Jacques Rousseau and the other harbingers of the French Revolution.

Let women hasten, with lightning rapidity, to put this complete bestialization of politics to the test.

We, who profoundly despise career politicians, are happy to leave parliamentarianism to the spiteful claws of women, because the noble task of finally killing it off is indeed left to them.

Oh! Don't misunderstand me, I am taking great care to avoid irony; I speak now with the utmost seriousness.

Woman, as she has been shaped by our contemporary society, can do no other than cause the principle of corruption, which is inseparable from that of the franchise, to burgeon most gloriously.

Those who oppose the legitimate rights of the suffragettes do so in defense of reasons which are absolutely personal. What they are defending so fiercely is their monopoly on useless, noxious eloquence, which will very soon be taken away from them by the women. And this, when all is said and done, does not interest us in the slightest. We have far bigger mines to lay among the ruins.

It is very apparent that a government composed of women or one supported by women would drag us fatally down the road of pacifism and Tolstoyan cowardice,[7] to the triumph of clericalism and moralizing cant . . .

Maybe! Probably! And I don't like it! . . .

Moreover, we shall experience a war of the sexes, doubtless organized by the great capitalist conglomerates, characterized by all-night reveling and by regulation wages for women workers. Maybe there are a few misogynist humorists who are already dreaming of a St. Bartholomew's Night[8] for women.

But you'll be supposing that I'm amusing myself dishing out these outlandish paradoxes . . . but just remember that there's nothing more paradoxical and outlandish than reality, and that one should have very little belief in the logical probabilities of history.

The history of peoples is largely a question of chance, a bit reckless, hardly ever clear-cut, like a girl who's a bit featherbrained, only remembering the things her father taught her at the new year or when she's been left by her lover. But sadly, it's still a bit too wise and not disorganized quite enough, this fledgling history of the world. So women should get mixed up in it as much as they did earlier on, as men really are saturated in their age-old wisdoms. These are not paradoxes, I swear to you, but a sort of groping around in the night of the future.

You will admit, for example, that the victory of feminism, and particularly the influence of women in politics, will end up destroying the family principle. And that could be easily demonstrated. But, scared stiff, you would surely rebel against it, adducing all kinds of ingenious arguments against me, because there's absolutely no way that you want the family to be touched. "All rights, all freedoms, should be granted to women, you proclaim, but the family will be preserved! . . ."

Well, permit me a little skeptical smile, and let me tell you that if the family, which stifles all vital energies, is to disappear, then we'll have to try and get along without it.

It goes without saying that if nowadays women dream of gaining political rights, it's because, without being really aware of it, they have a deep conviction that as mothers, brides, and lovers, they form a closed circle and are simply totally deprived of any positive role in society.

Doubtless you will have experienced the departure of a Blériot,[9] spluttering and still held back by the mechanics, amid the terrific wind smacks of the propeller as it begins to turn.

Well then, I tell you, that in the presence of such an exhilarating spectacle, we strong Futurists have suddenly felt ourselves detached from women who have become, all of a sudden, too earthbound, or, perhaps more precisely, have become symbols of an earth that we must needs leave behind.

We've even dreamt of one day being able to create our own mechanical son,[10] fruit of pure will, synthesis of all the laws the discovery of which science is about to hurl down upon us.

This text was first published in French under the title "Le Mépris de la femme" as Chapter 6 of the collection *Le Futurisme* (1911), and in Italian in *Guerra sola igiene del mondo* (1915). Subsequent editions in *I manifesti del futurismo* (1919) and *Futurismo e fascismo* (1924) omitted the first two paragraphs. In *Futurismo e fascismo*, the text of this manifesto is dated June 1910.

11

✑

The Necessity and Beauty of Violence

I

The principles we Futurists pursue are love of progress, of freedom, and of danger, together with the promotion of courage and everyday heroism.[1]

Our great enemies are traditionalism, modesty, and cowardice.

From a clear love of danger, from habitual courage and from everyday heroism spring precisely—and naturally—an urgent need for and recognition of the beauty of violence.[2]

All of this is entirely free of any political agenda; something you'll not be very used to. I am revealing my thoughts to you in this very straightforward manner so that in them you will easily recognize a proposal for action.

I am well aware of the reservations you have built up against us Futurists, as a result of the more or less entertaining gossip of mercenary newspapers, those emasculated custodians of Italian mediocrity and enemies of any sort of novelty.

Maybe you don't yet have any clear notion of what we are and what we stand for . . .

Just imagine, in the doleful, stagnating republic of letters and arts, a group of young men who are utterly rebellious and destructive, who are fed up with adoring the past, sick of academic pedantry, bursting with the desire for fearless originality, and positively gasping for a life that is free, full of adventure, vitality, and a habitual heroism, and who want to liberate the Italian spirit from that heap of prejudices, banalities, deference, and veneration that we call *traditionalism*.

We see ourselves as the destructive nitric acid that it would be well to throw over all political parties, as they are in a state of putrefaction.

In our Futurist Manifesto, published in *Le Figaro*, in Paris, we extolled Patriotism, War—the sole cleanser of the world—the destructive acts of the anarchists, and the beautiful ideas worth dying for,[3] gloriously opposed to the ugly ideas for which we live.

Certainly, these principles and these words have never, until now, had any contact with each other.

You have been accustomed to thinking of patriotism and war as being totally opposed to anarchism, which caused so many lives to erupt, in the struggle for greater freedom.

I declare that these two apparent opposites, the collective and the individual, are closely bound together. Is not the development of the collective, in reality, the result of the efforts and initiatives of many individuals?[4] This is how the prosperity of a nation is shaped, out of the antagonisms and the conformities of the multiple organisms of which it is made.

In the same way, the industrial and military rivalries that develop between different nations are a necessary factor in human progress.

A strong nation can contain, at one and the same time, droves of people intoxicated with patriotic enthusiasm and the wholly insensitive, thirsting for rebellion! They represent two different outlets for the selfsame instincts of courage, power, and energy.[5]

Do not the destructive acts of the anarchist perhaps represent an absurd yet beautiful hankering after the ideal of a justice that can never be realized?

Are they not perhaps a barrier erected to oppose the invasive arrogance of the dominant, victorious classes? Speaking personally, I much prefer the anarchist's bomb to the cringing attitude of the bourgeois, who hides away in a moment of danger, or to the vile egoism of the peasant, who deliberately injures himself rather than serve his country.

As far as praising war is concerned, it certainly does not represent— as some have claimed—a contradiction in our ideals, nor does it imply any regression to a barbaric age. To anyone who makes that sort of accusation against us, our response is that important questions of health and of moral health ought, of necessity, to be resolved precisely by having recourse to war, in preference to all other solutions. Is not the life of the nation rather like that of the individual, who fights against infection and high blood pressure by means of the shower and the bloodletting? Peoples too, in our view, have to follow a constant, healthy regime of heroism, and indulge themselves with glorious bloodbaths!

And the consequences? You will tell me . . . We know them well enough! We know that a period of misery inevitably follows a war, whatever its outcome. Quite a short period, however, when the war has been won, and not as long as one would think, when it has been lost.

Yes, but don't we have such periods of misery—and without the light of any glory—as a result of a simple crisis in the stock market or the dirty game of stockjobbing? Away with you! Out with this sort of self-interest! . . . Will you then accept no other ideals than those of your own comfort and a quiet life?

To your shame, you have learned from Giolitti (before the war) and from Bissolati (after the war) the absurd, unfortunate recipe for a self-centered, mercenary, and cautious peace.[6]

We, on the other hand, support and promote the dual preparation for war and revolution, under the auspices of a more intense patriotism, in the divine name of Italy, inscribed across our skies in the red fumes of a new Italian courage.

We believe that only a love of danger and heroism can purify and regenerate our nation.

Those among you who are more loyal to tradition will object that that sort of intellectual program will inevitably remain at the level of utopianism and vain paradox.

Arturo Labriola[7] censured in us Futurist poets and painters our tendency to mix art and politics, so as to defend our national pride and encourage the expanding working-class movement.

Arturo Labriola seems to me to have succumbed, not unnaturally, to a prejudice, given the historical novelty of our attitude.

Indeed, try and answer my question:

From the moment we realized we owe the fearful state of corruption, opportunism, and easygoing commercial cynicism into which the Italian parliamentary system has gradually sunk, to several generations of politicians, we poets and artists (by virtue of what I would say is a total absence of any profitable market) have been the only ones to keep alive the flame of an absolute selflessness, in the blinding light of an ideal of unattainable beauty, and have we not, therefore, we who write verse or paint pictures or compose music, without any hope of adequate remuneration, have we not perhaps the right to teach selflessness? And why should it not be granted to us to chase the merchants from the temple[8] and to offer our strength and our hearts to Italy, in the name of art?

Do you maybe think we are incapable of practical politics because of our excessive imagination? Certainly, regardless of all our artistic shortcomings, we shall do no worse than our predecessors. And besides, we believe that history awaits us. Doubtless you will have observed that in the unfolding of human events, a period of idealistic, self-sacrificing violence is inevitably followed by one of self-centered, avaricious mercantilism, such as that in which we now find ourselves.

Now, we wish to revive the bold, passionate endeavor of the race that knew how to bring about Italian independence, and we shall do it without the exciting stimuli of unfurling flags and military bands, we poets and artists; without having recourse to new political systems, and spreading only the fire of an inextinguishable enthusiasm throughout this Italy, which must not fall into ironic or skeptical hands, only electrifying this Italy, which belongs to its combatants, with an implacable courage.

You will tell me, in obedience to the teachings of Georges Sorel,[9] that nothing is more harmful to the interests of the revolutionary proletariat than intellectuals. And you'll be right, for in this present day intellectualism and culture are synonymous with egotistical ambition and a backward-looking obscurantism.

But we artists are not intellectuals of that sort. Above all else, we are fast-beating hearts, bundles of electrified nerves, instinctive beings who are ruled only by a divine, intoxicating intuition, and we believe ourselves to be, or indeed are, all ablaze with the proverbial sacred flame.

Without stopping, we have passed through the catacombs of pedantic erudition. We know enough to walk without stumbling, and we won't stumble, we wouldn't even if we were less cultured, for we have the sure instincts of youth.

To youth, we grant all the rights and the authority which we refuse, wishing to snatch them violently from the old, the dying, and the dead.

Futurism therefore proclaims the necessary intervention of artists in public affairs, so as to turn government into a selfless art, at last, in place of what it is now, robbery become a pedantic science.

But I can already hear you mumbling about our technical inexperience. What of it? Away with you! . . . Don't forget that the Italian race is only capable of producing great artists and great poets, whom it should not be entirely impossible to instruct quickly, after a few months' observation of parliamentary mechanisms.

I believe that parliamentarianism, a political institution that is both unsound and frail, is inevitably destined to perish. I believe that Italian politics is destined to plunge into its final agony, unless it agrees to substitute artists—creative talents—for the lawyer class, whose talent is for long-windedness and obfuscation, which has monopolized it until now, demonstrating beyond all measure its specific function, that of exploiting skillfully and of selling its knowledge and its words.

Therefore, it is especially from these habitual practices of the lawyers that we wish to liberate Italian political life. And it is for this reason that we vigorously oppose the people's lawyers, and generally every sort of intermediary, such as brokers and middlemen, all the great cooks of universal happiness,[10] and most particularly the enemies of all violence, the ignoble masters of low diplomacy, whom we deem to be harmful to and obstacles to the rise of a greater freedom.

Their presence has by now become ridiculous, laughable, in the midst of this violent, inflexible life of ours, which is intoxicated by a frenzied ambition, and over which there towers the new, terrible god of danger.

The dark forces of Nature, ensnared in the nets and traps of chemical and mechanical formulas, and therefore enslaved by mankind, wreak a terrible revenge, leaping at our throats, with all the impetuous savagery of mad dogs.

But you know all about this, you who labor in the arsenals, you stokers on ocean liners, you submariners, you steelworkers and laborers at the gasworks!

II

It seems pointless[11] to me to demonstrate how, by virtue of the lightning development of science and the marvelous conquest of speed, both on the earth and in the sky, with life having become ever more tragic and the ideal of an idyllic rural serenity having departed forever, the human heart must now become ever more accustomed to imminent danger, so that future generations can be revitalized by real love of just such danger.

Human progress increasingly demands the chancer's spirit, the bloodhound's tenacity, the aviator's fearless intuition, the medium's sensibilities, and the poet's foresight.

The psychic complexity of the world is significantly increased through the accumulation of experience furnished by history and the continuously corrosive skepticism and irony employed by international journalism.

The restlessness and instability of nations have become so marked as to upset all calculations of historical probability.

I could also tell you about the wear and tear that has affected all the spurious old formulas which had an influence on the movement of peoples, all the recipes and panaceas for immediate and certain happiness. By now we are deeply convinced that everything is becoming ever more complex, that every ideological simplification, whether revelatory or administrative in character, is an illusion, and that an absolute order, whether of a political or a social nature, is absurd.

We have come to the point where it is necessary to accept, within and outside ourselves, the coexistence of the most contradictory elements.

No one's power or will could persuade the people ever to give up the freedoms they have won. To do so would be like wanting to be diligent servants, just when the railway networks have made the world smaller and offered it, like a plaything, to be passed around and looked at, to every single citizen.

These individual freedoms, which proliferate as they develop toward a possible and desirable anarchy, must coexist with the principle of authority. This latter, the better to safeguard single liberties, has a tendency to destroy them.

There is, then, coexistence, yet at the same time, a healthy struggle between opposing principles, as with the different elements which make up the blood of man. By the same token, Italy must always maintain within herself a dual passion for either a possible proletarian revolution or an even more likely patriotic war.

Between the people—synonymous with increasing liberty—and the government—synonymous with decreasing authority—there exists, to some extent, the same friendly and antagonistic relationship that is to be found between the owner and the tenants of a house.

There is, in fact, a certain similarity between a revolution against a government that is guilty of tyranny or of incompetence, and the sudden move of a tenant, when his landlord refuses to make the necessary repairs to prevent rain and wind getting in, or give protection against lightning, or when he was unable to protect his own tenants from thieves in the night.

In this last case, just as the tenant breaks his contract, so the people make a revolution.

Every Italian must clearly understand the fusing together of these two ideas, of revolution and war, destroying completely the stupid, cowardly rhetoric which enfolds them in horror, by exalting in and around themselves the idea of struggle and disregard for life, which alone can elevate man, by giving maximum splendor and value to every moment that he lives.

As it happens, I think that saving Ferrer's life was not important—a life ended magnificently with a vigil and a heroic death.[12] What did matter was to prevent, at all costs, the infamous triumph of clerical conservatism.

The education system is shamefully poisoned by Christian morality, with the stupid pardoning of offenses degenerating into systematized cowardice and working tirelessly toward the emasculation of the race.

The only thing that is taught in Italy today is unquestioning obedience and fear of physical pain; and in this we see the trembling collusion of Italian mothers, who are certainly not equipped to create warriors or, indeed, revolutionaries.

Wherever we go, we Futurists emphasize, with our words and our example, the need for vigorous propaganda in favor of personal courage. We desire that a spirit of revolt and war should circulate, like surging blood, among Italian youth.

The State, whose origins were violent, can only be strengthened by this rushing, red ferment which, by ensuring the flexibility of its administrative arteries, maintains a sense of responsibility at the head and in the centers of control.

The concept of cyclical historical evolution, by means of which, in the dreams of many shortsighted imperialists, we are destined to return to a form of tyrannical government and an uncomplaining popular slavery, we now believe to be utterly childish.

We, for our part, present the future evolution of mankind as an oscillating, irregular movement, like one of those picturesque wooden wheels bearing buckets and turned by a blindfolded animal, which in the East are used for extracting water from a river to irrigate their gardens. Because of the primitive construction of the wheels and the buckets, the water that is extracted is full of sand, and this continually raises the level of the soil in such a way that the apparatus itself has to be raised continually, ad infinitum.

As history unfolds with the selfsame water of events, there will be an unfailing, ever-increasing quantity of the fine sand of freedom.

For this reason, we can no longer conceive of the authority of the State as a check on a people's desire for freedom. To the contrary, we believe that the revolutionary spirit of the people must act as a check on the authority of the State and its conservative spirit, that symptom of old age and steadily encroaching paralysis.

Is not violence perhaps synonymous with the youth of a people? Order, pacifism, moderation, the diplomatic and reformist spirit, are these not perhaps representative of the gradual blocking of the arteries, old age, and death?

It is only by means of violence that the idea of justice, which is now in tatters, can be restored. However, it will not be that seemingly inevitable justice in which might is always right, but a justice which is more healthy and sound, predicated on the rights of the most courageous, the least self-centered, those of the heroic citizen.

It is precisely in this way that I can immediately satisfy those of you who are most tormented by a desire for dogmatic clarity, by establishing, as the only moral yardstick, that the good is whatever develops and increases the physical, intellectual, and instinctive activities of mankind, urging the fulfillment of man's most splendid being, while the bad is everything that erodes and interrupts the development of these activities.

Just as a Tithonian pacifism and fear of war[13] have brought about our grievous political enslavement, so too the horror of violence and the stupid propaganda against the duel—residue of courage and not of barbarism[14]—have turned the Italian citizen into a ridiculous marionette, one who is ill-used by pettifogging lawyers and whose response to a beating is legal proceedings or blackmail.

Here, for example, is a truth to be shouted from the rooftops: any man who surprises his own lover or the mother of his children in the arms of a seducer must kill them both. The dilemma is, in fact, quite simple: if the man who is betrayed were to respect the life of his adversary, he would no longer respect his own. By not killing, he would increase his own reasons for dying.

In Sicily, a land that is fortunately rich in violence, though for all that no less civilized, adultery is extremely rare, precisely because the custom of the personal vendetta is prevalent.

And here we touch on one of those facile conflicts between a regulating authority and the freedom of the individual, which latter must always prevail in the final analysis, by virtue of that law which moves us ever closer to anarchy, and which governs mankind.

The principle of juridical sanctions in the question of offenses against the person, for example, destroys that most important sense of one's physiological dignity, which is closely linked with that of the psyche, and channels all human activities toward exploitative stratagems such as usury, meanness, and the tyrannical divinity of lucre.

We have thus fallen, by taking a different route, into the muddy pool of our contemporary Italian life, whose sides are guarded by the dense scrub of police laws and by the hedges of bureaucracy, which inevitably wear down and tear to pieces every deep-seated human instinct and all legitimate revolt.

Who will free us from them? When shall we finally surface from the muddy waters? Ah! If only we could tear our hearts from our breasts, to save those at least, and hurl them far away, clear of the thorns, like some object that is dear to us.

Over the pools, the great birds of prey laugh harshly, with the monotonous beating of their wings.[15] Leaden clouds. Far off, the most ironical smile of the most declining of suns.

The dispirited night of a millenarian tedium and skepticism. The much-loved, ideal stars are no longer in the sky. Where have they fled? How can we call them back to Italy's zenith? Their names are warlike patriotism, revolution, everyday heroism. Maybe they lie sleeping on the tragic hills of Calatafimi![16] Perhaps they are dead forever! What does it matter? Let us not weep. We have to rebuild them, hammering with our wills on the Julian Alps,[17] those white anvils, the spurting rays of our nerve ends! . . . We have to forge those burning stars anew, to fling them back into the Italian sky! . . .

This facile, discouraging, and destructive irony is, in fact, a third serious vice, which is profoundly Italian. From it stems a disastrous refusal of all innovation and all healthy, stimulating optimism. This is the tragic, blithely accepted poison that is unfortunately polluting the best part of Italy, by which I mean the people of the South, who have the richest constructive imaginations and an ingenious talent for reading the future. It is this irony, which is composed of Epicureanism,[18] caustic wit, and thoughtlessness that, one flame-colored sunset several years ago, at the gates of the Monumental Cemetery of Milan,[19] stupidly accompanied the return of a mass of revolutionaries who had escorted the ill-omened coffin of a worker killed in a serious clash with the army, with the cheerful rhythms of carousing and dancing.[20]

I too had accompanied that black tide of humanity, its angry faces churning, and upon which the coffin bobbed, like a funereal dinghy, to which the stooped bearers curiously gave legs. Overhead, red flags were flying with the flaming movement and breath of an equal number of enormous bellows. Flaming torches, like rags of bloody poverty; reformist speakers leaning forward with their harpoons to spear the slippery octopus of equivocation; speeches of stomach-churning moderation, such as might cause the stars to fall, out of boredom, or the moon from disgust, like gleaming spit!

We were truly drowning in a flood of stupidly paternalistic counsel, and it was wholly fitting that after such a grubby comedy, the crowd should go back to the city, to lunch,[21] with the rhythmic steps of a dance, singing the workers' anthem, to escort a second coffin—not of a dead worker this time, but of the Revolution! . . .

III

To arrive at this longed-for social and political renewal of our Country,[22] we must necessarily overcome certain obstacles which, at first sight, seem insurmountable, since we bear them within us, in the shape of characteristic elements of our race.

I want to talk about *the self-centeredness of clerical utilitarianism*, about *hypersensuality*, and about biting, destructive *irony*.

I call *self-centeredness* that intellectual habit which makes every judgment subject to considerations, feelings, and prejudices that are entirely personal. I call *self-centeredness* that indifference, or rather that scorn which every Italian harbors against pure ideas, opposing them only when they are upheld by an enemy, having regard to them only when they are upheld by a friend.

We have to fight against this very serious fault, above all by radically transforming our putrid educational system, which is meant only to reward the base prostitution of the plodding, idiotic pupils who, through licking the vanity of some professor or other, day after day, end up absorbing his pompous and dogmatic imbecility.

We Futurists, who yield up to youth all rights and all authority, would prefer that in schools those students should be encouraged and rewarded who, from their earliest years, demonstrate that they have ideas of their own and a distinctive viewpoint when judging men and books.

Untrammeled intuition, which is a capacity for having and creating new ideas, is what we wish to promote! And it is for this reason that we would exile all priests from schools, for they, being no longer able to implant faith in this irreligious day and age, content themselves by softening and debasing pupils' spirits, bringing into being that phenomenon of *idiotic, timid utilitarianism*, which goes by the name of Clericalism.

Italians! We have to intensify and everywhere kindle all-out war against clericalism, a political party which, being no longer grounded in mysticism and yet having lost all hope of temporal power, through our children is threatening our future greatness.

Priestly utilitarianism, fear of life, this is the mire in which our nation is wallowing, covering itself with the slime of sloth and *hypersensuality*.

This other Italian—indeed, Latin—vice, is manifested in a thousand different ways, and most of all in the tyranny of sentimentalism, which scythes through the energies of men of action, because of their obsession with conquering women, because of the romantic ideal of fidelity and the infamous tendency toward a fatal, enervating lust.[23]

This inauspicious tendency must be opposed, both in schools and outside, by means of a continuous, well-planned development of physically demanding sports, of fencing, swimming, and especially gymnastics. The latter must follow the methods of the Swede, Ling, being freed from the old style of acrobatics and parade-ground exercises.[24] It must be a rationalized gymnastics aimed at developing the thorax, expanding the lungs, setting the heart beating, controlling the intestines, stimulating blood circulation, increasing the number of blood corpuscles, strengthening the sinews, and toning the muscles, to shape a human body that is beautiful, slender, strong, and resilient, which can think, desire, and knock down men, ideas, and things with equal ease.

We Futurists, being thoroughly convinced of the influence that Art exercises on all the activities of a people, wish to purge it of sentimentalism, of the D'Annunzian obsession with sex,[25] and of Don Juanism, creating instead an art that glorifies individual strength and freedom, the victories of science, and man's increasing dominion over the dark forces of nature.

In short, in the imaginations of our young people, we want to replace the tiresome Don Juan with dynamic, imposing figures such as Napoleon, Crispi, Ferrer, and Blériot.[26]

We know for a fact that a licentious romanticism exaggerates the importance of women in our lives; for while Italian women—who are utterly inferior to the women of Germanic origins—are delightful dispensers of passionate caresses, they are absolutely incapable of understanding and supporting a man engaged in heroic, unselfish struggle.

Italian women, though the sweetest of mothers, cultivate cowardice in their own sons, when they aren't simply dominated by priests or by the constant desire for excessive luxuries—they become almost invincible enemies and an insurmountable barrier, in all the great conflagrations of war and revolution.

Our excessive sensuality generates not only this exaggerated importance of women, who are nothing but voluptuousness and encumbrance, but, as a consequence, an obsession with ostentatious luxury and domestic comforts.

Alas! Sometimes, our preoccupation with a good dinner, or a woman's feathery hat, or a fine carpet to show off to our guests, sometimes—as I said—a preoccupation of this sort is all that is necessary to turn an Italian politician away from his selfless course or to interrupt some heroic, self-sacrificing project.

It is for this reason that we Futurists believe that marriage is one of the greatest dangers confronting our exaltation of courage and intellectual freedom.

And this is why we preach the need for celibacy for great men of pure ideas and action.

To our great disappointment, we have recently seen a man of the highest, most explosive ideals succumb to just such an enervating atmosphere of conjugal serenity, and thus, totally renouncing all courageous actions, sink skeptically into a comfortable armchair—highly cultured among his too-much-loved, friendly, but useless books—to greet our explosive enthusiasm with the most facile of smiles and a discouraging, destructive irony. [. . .]²⁷

Irony! What irony! The old Italian irony! . . . This is our enemy, which we must destroy, which we must trample down, with our zeal, with our courage, with our optimism, even if they aren't quite real!

Workers! Be on your guard against the irony of skepticism and egoism, for it will melt your heart in the moment that it is justly roused and create in you that shameful *fear of the call to arms*!

In the ten years I have lived in Milan, studying the ebb and flow of Italian socialism, day after day, carefully reading every meeting like a very interesting, sad book, how often have I blushed, as an Italian . . . And I say it again, *as an Italian*, seeing huge masses of workers, stirred by the most legitimate demands and by a magnificent desire for greater liberty; huge masses of people, I say, suddenly seized by the most absurd collective fear, on hearing the four impertinent notes of the police trumpets!

A herd in flight . . . Backs bent and foolish legs pounding, before the ragged, undisciplined trot of a cavalry that is unable to gallop on the paving stones.

It goes without saying, the speakers who, in the reformist way, tinted the crowd pink rather than red, had disappeared . . . Where had they gone? And why? Doubtless because of some sudden revolution of their bowels! . . .

But a red vision presents itself to my mind, a vision which comforts my Futurist blood . . .

I see a smoky sunset in the capital, along a street glistening with rain and already dappled and trembling with reflections . . .

In the great network of tram lines and telephone wires, a thousand angry lights snap at the flesh of the shadows! . . . The famished pallor of the houses! . . . Dark, cantankerous outlines! . . . Down there, in the side streets, where all the lamps were shattered, darkness, tremendous darkness, rolled down from who knows which ruined heaven!

At the end of a street, a dense crowd, jet black . . .

That crowd is made up of your women and children; their arms are linked together, like an African jungle by night; all fitted together like bricks in a wall!

You men will form up in front of your womenfolk, in that tragic jungle of rock and iron, beneath the round electric fruit trees, blown up, milky white, intensely white, and you will calmly load your rifles for those ferocious beasts, the policemen.

Then suddenly, mockingly, the trumpet notes will sound again, fateful razor slash across the hushed throat of the silence . . .

And then, the shouted command: "Forward!"

But I also hear derisory, awe-inspiring laughter, answering that trumpet call, and the throng, petrified by courage, cry out: "Italians do not run away! Out of a sublime love of danger, we accept the bloody struggle beneath the glittering stars of Italy, which will not permit us not to turn back!"

I see an immense tangle of red, an angry fray of rearing horses, beneath a hail of tiles. Let the slaughter come! . . . We shall celebrate together, workers of Italy, if we survive . . . We shall celebrate, since nothing else will happen; nothing else but the salutary incision of the scalpel in the gigantic boil of fear and the Italian habit of leading a mundane and colorless life.

For in place of the propaganda of cowardice, we counter with that of courage and an everyday heroism . . .

And in place of the money swamp, we counter—let it be, let it be!—with an aesthetic of violence and blood!

This speech was given at the Chamber of Labor, in Naples, on June 26, 1910, and on July 30 at the Sala d'arte moderna, in Milan. On June 28, 1911, Marinetti repeated his talk in Parma, following the interdiction against the *serata* in the Teatro Reinach and the workers' invitation to speak in their meeting hall (see document 25, *Futurism's First Battles*). The original text, preserved under the title "L'amore del pericolo e l'eroismo quotidiano" in the Beinecke Rare Books and Manuscript Library, was partly printed in *La giovane Italia* on July 10, 1910, and *L'internazionale* on July 16, 1910, and another section in the Neapolitan journal *La propaganda*, on July 16–17, 1910. An updated version, with several paragraphs eliminated and new ones added, appeared in *L'ardito* on June 15, 22, and 29, 1919, and was reprinted in Chapter 23 of *Democrazia futurista* (1919).

12

∽

Second Futurist Political Manifesto

Our openly warlike and fiercely patriotic attitude was the main cause of the hostility and libelous reports that were systematically lavished on us by the Italian press.

With millions of copies of manifestos, books, and leaflets in all languages, with many a punch and a slap, with more than eight hundred lectures, exhibitions, and concerts, we impressed on the whole world, and particularly Europe, the predominance of the creative and innovative Italian genius over those of all other races.

We have thus had the glory of bringing Italian art to a position of prominence in world art, which has been overtaken and left behind by us.

At the outbreak of the Libyan War (1911),[1] we published this other manifesto:

We Futurists who, for more than two years, amid the disapproving whistles of the citizens of Goutville and Paralysis, have been glorifying a love of danger and violence, patriotism and war, the sole cleanser of the world, are happy to be experiencing, at last, Italy's great Futurist hour, while that filthy pack of pacifists writhes in agony, holed up, by this time, in the deep cellars of their comical palace at The Hague.[2]

To our great satisfaction, we have recently doled out many a good beating, in streets and in squares, to the most rabid adversaries of war, shouting these our unshakable principles in their faces:

1. Every individual and our entire people must be given total freedom, other than the freedom to be cowards.
2. Let it be declared that the word ITALY must take absolute precedence over the word LIBERTY.
3. The tiresome memory of the greatness of Ancient Rome must be
   eradicated by an Italian greatness that is a hundred times more
   impressive.

For us today, Italy has the form and the power of a beautiful dreadnought,[3] with its squadron of torpedo boat islands. Proud of feeling
the warlike fervor that is animating the whole country, to be the equal
to our own, we urge the Italian government, which has at last become Futurist, to magnify our national ambitions, pouring scorn on
the stupid accusations of piracy and proclaiming the birth of PAN-
ITALIANISM.

Futurist poets, painters, sculptors, and musicians of Italy! While
ever the war lasts, leave aside your verses, your brushes, your chisels,
and your orchestras! The blood-red vocation of our genius has begun!
The only things we can admire today are the immense symphonies of
shrapnel and the bizarre sculptures that our inspirational artillery is
creating among the enemy masses.

**The full text, as given here, appeared first in *Guerra sola igiene del
mondo* (1915). The included manifesto was dated October 11, 1911,
and was published in broadsheet form under the titles *Per la guerra
sola igiene del mondo* and *Tripoli italiana* and in the Milanese weekly *La
grande Italia* on October 15, 1911. A second edition of the 1915 text
contains this line at the bottom: "The Futurist movement in the fields
of literature, painting, and music is currently suspended, owing to the
poet Marinetti's absence in the theater of war." In *Futurismo e fascismo*
(1924), the text is called *Manifesto a Tripoli italiana*.**

13

✑

Third Futurist Political Manifesto

Futurist Political Program

Futurist Electors![1] With your vote you should attempt to realize the following program:

Italy, absolute and sovereign. The word ITALY must predominate over the word LIBERTY.

All freedoms must prevail other than those of being cowardly, pacifist, or anti-Italian.

A bigger fleet and a bigger army; a people proud to be Italian, in favor of war, the sole cleanser of the world, and of an Italy that is intensively agrarian, industrialized, and commercialized.

Economic protection and patriotic education for the proletariat.

A foreign policy that is self-interested, shrewd, and aggressive—colonial expansion—free trade.

Irredentism—Pan-Italianism—the supremacy of Italy.

Anticlericalism and antisocialism.

A cult of progress and speed, of sport, of physical strength, of fearless courage, of heroism, and of danger, against any obsession with culture, classical education, the museum, the library, and archaeological remains. The suppression of Academies and Conservatories.

Many practical schools for commerce, industry, and agriculture. Many institutes for physical education. Gymnastics in schools every day. Supremacy of gymnastics over books.

A minimal number of teachers, very few lawyers, very few doctors, a great many agriculturalists, engineers, chemists, mechanics, and businessmen.

Stripping away of the authority of the dead, the old, and the opportunists, to the benefit of audacious youth.

Against monumentalization and the meddling of government in matters of art.

Ruthless modernization of antiquated cities (Rome, Venice, Florence, and so on).

Abolition of industries owned by foreigners, which are both humiliating and unreliable.

THIS PROGRAM WILL TRIUMPH OVER:

The clerical-moderate-liberal program	The democratic-republican-socialistic program
Monarchy and Vatican	Republic
Hatred and disparagement of the people	Popular sovereignty
Traditional, ceremonial patriotism	International pacifism
Occasional militarism	Antimilitarism
Clericalism	Anticlericalism
Narrow-minded protectionism or halfhearted support for free trade	Self-interested free trade
The cult of ancestry and skepticism	Mediocrity and skepticism
Premature senility and moralism	Premature senility and moralism
Opportunism and unscrupulous greed	Opportunism and unscrupulous greed

Repressiveness	Demagoguery
The cult of museums, ruins, and monuments	The cult of museums, ruins, and monuments
Foreign ownership of industry	Foreign ownership of industry
Obsession with culture	A culture of political rallies
Academicism	Positivistic rationalism
The ideal of an Italy of past glories, bigoted and gout-ridden	The ideal of a petty-bourgeois, little Italy that is miserly and sentimental
Quietist reign of the belly	Gluttonous indifference
Black cowardice	Red cowardice
Obsession with the past	Obsession with the past

MILAN, OCTOBER 11, 1913
FOR THE DIRECTORIAL COMMITTEE OF THE FUTURIST MOVEMENT:
MARINETTI—BOCCIONI—CARRÀ—RUSSOLO

The "Futurist Political Program" appeared first in *Lacerba* on October 11, 1913, where it served as a countermanifesto to Papini's essay "Let's Give a Damn About Politics" (*Lacerba*, October 1, 1913). It was distributed as a quarto flier by the Direzione del movimento futurista in Milan and as an octavo flier by the Direzione della sezione futurista siciliana in Messina. Reprints can be found in *Guerra sola igiene del mondo* (1915) and various other Futurist anthologies.

THE FUTURIST COMBAT IN THE
ARTISTIC ARENA (1910–15)

The period from 1910 to 1915 represented the "heroic" years of the Futurist movement, that is, the period when it established itself within the Italian cultural landscape and exercised considerable influence in other countries as well. Marinetti's foundation manifesto had offered an apt formulation of the zeitgeist and had given inspiration to a new generation of writers and artists eager to overhaul the cultural institutions in their own countries. All over the Italian peninsula, young artists formed Futurist groups and networks, held exhibitions, published books and magazines, organized theater performances, and so on.

Marinetti wrote a whole series of new manifestos that outlined his views on art and culture. The other members of the movement also published a number of proclamations that explained the Futurist aesthetics in a range of artistic media and developed new perspectives in their respective disciplines (painting, sculpture, music, architecture, and so on). Marinetti made sure that the thirty-five manifestos that came from their pens in the years 1909 to 1915 were modeled on his own writings and that all had a similar tone and format. Some colleagues resented the interventions of the *piccolo Kaiser* (as Palazzeschi called Marinetti) and asked whether the movement they had joined was called Futurism or Marinettism, but the leader made it quite clear, in his controversy with the French painter Delmarle, that "Futurism is not a *petty religion* or a *school*, but rather a great movement of intellectual energy and heroism" (see document 19, page 104). Nonetheless, personal and aesthetic divergences kept several talented sympathizers out of the movement and forced others to quit, thus leading to the first schisms and the emergence of independent futurisms.

Marinetti's international background guaranteed that his patriotism was never an inward-looking, narrow-minded nationalism. Given his close connection with the French literary scene, many of his writings were also published in French and had an international readership in mind. Several manifestos were specifically geared toward the modernization of cultural traditions in countries other than Italy, and the first touring exhibition, in 1912, did much to propagate the ideas and concepts of Futurism among artists not only in Europe but also in the Americas and the Far East.

Marinetti's creative writings of this period included the "African" novel *Mafarka the Futurist* (1910), the war poem *The Battle of Tripoli* (1912), and the "prophetic" novel *The Pope's Airplane* (1912). One can observe in these creations a gradual abandonment of his Free Verse aesthetics of the late-Symbolist years and a move toward a freer treatment of language and of the graphic organization of the printed page. Nonetheless, in 1912 he was seized by a "creative crisis," as he confessed to Palazzeschi in June of that year. He saw himself forced to admit that Futurist literature—just like Futurist drama, music, and painting—was still too much entrenched in aesthetic principles that harked back to a previous era. Out of this realization arose a new literary program, which he outlined in two manifestos, and the new technique of "Words-in-Freedom," presented in *Lacerba* as poetic realizations of his new concepts. Some of these were later issued in collected form under the title *Zang Tumb Tumb*.

14

∽

Against Academic Teachers

In our struggle against the professorial passion for the past, we violently reject Nietzsche's ideals and doctrines.

I have no choice but to show how utterly mistaken the critics are in labeling us Neo-Nietzscheans.[1] Indeed, all you have to do is peruse the constructive part of the great German philosopher's work to be convinced that his Superman,[2] whose origins lie in the philosophical culture of Greek tragedy, presumes, in his creator, an enthusiastic return to paganism and mythology. Nietzsche, despite his urge toward the future, will continue to be seen as one of the fiercest defenders of the beauty and greatness of the past.

He is a traditionalist who walks upon the peaks of the Thessalian mountains, but alas! terribly encumbered by the longest ancient Greek texts.

His Superman is a product of the Greek imagination, spawned from the three great stinking corpses of Apollo, Mars, and Bacchus. He is a mixture of elegant Beauty, the warrior's strength, and Dionysian ecstasy, which are manifested in the greatest classical art. We are opposed to this Greek Superman, begat from the dust of libraries, and against him we set the Man who is extended by his own labors, the enemy of books, friend of personal experience, pupil of the Machine, relentless cultivator of his own will, clear in the flash of his own inspiration, endowed with the feline power of scenting out, with the ability to make split-second judgments, possessing those instincts typical of the wild—intuition, cunning, and boldness.

The children of this present generation, who live out their lives between cosmopolitanism, the tide of trade unionism, and the flights of aviators, are like preliminary sketches of the extended man we are preparing.

So as to give our attention to him, we abandoned Nietzsche one December evening, leaving him on the doorstep of a library, which swallowed him in its swinging doors into a comforting, erudite warmth.

I very much doubt that Nietzsche would have vomited, as we did, whenever we read these abominable principles, written with the chalk of imbecility upon the facades of Museums, Academies, Libraries, and Universities:

YOU WILL NO LONGER THINK!
YOU WILL NO LONGER PAINT!
YOU WILL NO LONGER CONSTRUCT!
NO ONE WILL EVER SURPASS THE OLD MASTERS!
ALL ORIGINALITY IS FORBIDDEN!
AWAY WITH FOLLY AND ECCENTRICITIES! YOU MUST IMITATE, IMITATE, AND IMITATE AGAIN!
TO ATTAIN TO THE ARTISTIC PARADISE, YOU HAVE TO IMITATE THE LIVES OF OUR SAINTS.

But we took no heed of the wise counsels that Nietzsche wished to give us and we watched in horror, as our Italian youth slipped down into the great sewers of intellectualism.

That night, we slept, and at dawn we clambered up to the portals of the Academies, Museums, Libraries, and Universities, to write this inscription—which is also an answer to Nietzsche's classical Superman—upon them, in the heroic charcoal of the workshop:

TO THE EARTHQUAKE
THEIR ONLY ALLY
THE FUTURISTS DEDICATE
THESE RUINS OF ROME AND ATHENS

That day their old, erudite walls were shaken by our unexpected shouts:

"Shame on those who allow themselves to be seduced by the demon of admiration! Shame on anyone who admires and

imitates the past! Shame on those who prostitute their own genius!!"

You must fight ferociously against these three relentless enemies and corrupters of Art! Imitation, Prudence, and Lucre, which can be summed up in the one word: "cowardice."

Cowardice in the face of admirable examples and formulas that have been learned. Cowardice in the face of a need for love, on the one hand, and the fear of poverty, on the other, which menace the necessarily heroic life of the artist!

Poets, painters, sculptors, musicians, you must fight, fight whether within or beyond your selves, as you fought this morning in leaving your beds, against the rule of inertia and somnolence. As the world has need of nothing but heroism, then excuse—as we do—the bloody act of indiscipline carried out by the Palermo student Lidonni, who, regardless of the law, avenged himself on a tyrannical teacher.[3]

Traditionalist teachers were entirely to blame for this death. Traditionalist teachers, whose wish it is to drown the irrepressible energies of young Italians in their stinking, subterranean sewers.

When, oh when, will they leave off emasculating those spirits which must create the future? When will they cease teaching the brutalizing adoration of a past, which cannot be surpassed, to children whom they seek to reduce to plodding little courtiers?

Let's get moving and make everything all over again! —To do so, we have to go against the tide.

Soon the moment will come when we shall no longer be content with defending our ideas with slaps and punches; we shall then have to go on the offensive in the name of thought, the artistic offensive, the literary offensive, against glorified *scabs* and tyrannical teachers.[4]

However, the faintheartedness of our enemies will most likely deprive us of the luxury of killing them.

These are by no means paradoxes, believe you me! At all costs, we have to drag Italy out of this crisis of traditionalist cowardice.

What would you say, for example, about that Futurist plan to introduce a mainline course in risk-taking and physical danger into all our schools? Regardless of their own wishes, the pupils would be subjected to the necessity of continually confronting a series of dangers, each one more fearsome than the last, skillfully arranged and always unforeseen, such as fires, drowning, the collapse of a ceiling or other like disasters . . .

Now courage is absolutely the prime subject because, as far as the great Futurist hope is concerned, all authority, all rights, and all powers will be violently torn from the hands of the dead and the dying and given to young people between twenty and forty years of age.

Just now, while we are waiting for the war with Austria, which we cry out for, there is nothing we find more interesting on this earth than the fine, casual-seeming deaths of airmen, which are happening all the time.

Blériot was right to voice his opinion: "More and more corpses yet will be necessary in the name of progress!"[5]

The only time we care about blood is when it spurts from the arteries; anything else is cowardice.

I have to add that for all these very good reasons, magistrates don't care for us at all. The police keep an eye on us,[6] priests draw back when we pass by, and the Socialists loathe us intensely.

This hatred and scorn we reciprocate, for we despise them all as the worthless representatives of pure, unworldly ideas such as Justice, Divinity, Equality, and Liberty.

Since these pure, absolute ideas, more than any others, are susceptible to corruption, they can in no way be controlled by the conventionalists.

This manifesto was first published as a one-page broadsheet in May 1910. The title, *Contro i professori*, was changed in Chapter 9 of the collection *Le Futurisme* (1911) into "Ce qui nous sépare de Nietzsche." The Italian text was reprinted in *Guerra sola igiene del mondo* (1915), *I manifesti del futurismo* (1919), and *Futurismo e fascismo* (1924).

15

ᥫᨆ

Extended Man and the Kingdom of the Machine

The foregoing[1] will have prepared you for understanding one of our chief Futurist endeavors, namely the abolition in literature of the seemingly unquestionable fusion of the dual concepts of *Woman* and *Beauty*. The effect of this has been to reduce romanticism to a kind of heroic assault, launched by a warlike, lyrical male on a tower that is bristling with enemies, gathered about the divine Woman-Beauty.

Novels such as Victor Hugo's *Les Travailleurs de la mer* or Flaubert's *Salammbô* can explain my idea. What we're looking at is a dominant leitmotif that is threadbare and tedious, and of which we wish to rid literature and art as a whole.[2] That's why we are developing and proclaiming a great new idea that is circulating in contemporary life, namely the idea of mechanical beauty. Thus we are promoting love of the machine—that love we first saw lighting up the faces of engine drivers, scorched and filthy with coal dust though they were. Have you ever watched an engine driver lovingly washing the great powerful body of his engine? He uses the same little acts of tenderness and close familiarity as the lover when caressing his beloved.

We know for certain that during the great French rail strike,[3] the organizers of that subversion did not manage to persuade even one single engine driver to sabotage his locomotive.

And to me that seems absolutely natural. How on earth could one of these men have injured or destroyed his great, faithful, devoted friend, whose heart was ever giving and courageous, his beautiful engine of steel that had so often glistened sensuously beneath the lubricating caress of his hand?

Not an image, this, but rather a reality, almost, that we shall easily be able to put to the test in a few years' time.

You will undoubtedly have heard the comments that car owners and car workshop managers habitually make: "Motorcars, they say, are truly mysterious . . . They have their foibles, they do unexpected things; they seem to have personalities, souls and wills of their own. You have to stroke them, treat them respectfully, never mishandle them nor overtire them. If you follow this advice, this machine made of cast iron and steel, this motor constructed according to precise calculations, will give you not only its due, but double and triple, considerably more and a whole lot better than the calculations of its creator, its father, ever dreamed of!"

Well then, I see in these words a great, important revelation, promising the not-too-distant discovery of the laws of a true sensitivity in machines![4]

We have therefore to prepare for the imminent, inevitable identification of man with his motorcar, so as to facilitate and perfect an unending exchange of intuitions, rhythms, instincts, and metallic discipline, absolutely unknown to the majority and only guessed at by the brightest spirits.

There can be no doubt that, in admitting Lamarck's transformist hypothesis,[5] it has to be acknowledged that we aspire to the creation of a nonhuman species in which moral anguish, goodness, affection, and love, the singular corrosive poisons of vital energy, the only off-switches of our powerful, physiological electricity, will be abolished.

We believe in the possibility of an incalculable number of human transformations, and we are not joking when we declare that in human flesh wings lie dormant.

The day when it will be possible for man to externalize his will so that, like a huge invisible arm, it can extend beyond him, then his Dream and his Desire, which today are merely idle words, will rule supreme over conquered Space and Time.

This nonhuman, mechanical species, built for constant speed, will quite naturally be cruel, omniscient, and warlike.

It will possess the most unusual organs; organs adapted to the needs of an environment in which there are continuous clashes.

Even now we can predict a development of the external protrusion of the sternum, resembling a prow, which will have great significance, given that man, in the future, will become an increasingly better aviator.

Indeed, a similar development can be seen in the strongest fliers among birds.

You will easily understand these apparently paradoxical hypotheses if you think of the externalized will that is continually in play during spiritualist séances.[6]

What's more, it's certain, and you can observe it easily enough yourself, that today, ever more frequently, one comes across people from the lower classes who, though utterly devoid of any culture or education whatsoever, are nonetheless gifted with what I call the "great mechanical intuition" or "a nose for things metallic."

And that's because those workmen have already had the experience of an education in machinery and, in a certain sense, have identified closely with it.

In order to prepare for the formation of the nonhuman, mechanical species of extended man, through the externalization of his will, it is very important that the need for affection, which man feels in his veins and which cannot yet be destroyed, be greatly reduced.

The man of the future will reduce his own heart to its proper function of blood distribution. The heart, by some means or other, must become a sort of stomach of the brain, which is fed systematically, so that the spirit can embark on action.

Today, one encounters men who go through life more or less without love, in a beautiful, steel-toned frame of mind. We have to find ways of ensuring that these exemplary beings continue to increase in number. These dynamic beings do not have any sweet lover to see at night, but instead lovingly prefer, every morning, the perfect start-up of their workshops.

What's more, we are convinced that art and literature exercise a determining influence over all classes in society, even over the most ignorant, who by some mysterious process of infiltration absorb them.

We can thus either promote or retard the movement of humanity toward this form of life that is free of sentimentalism and lust. In spite of our skeptical determinism that we have to kill off each day, we believe in the value of artistic propaganda against panegyrics favoring Don Juans and ludicrous cuckolds.

These two words must be purged entirely of their meaning in life, in art, and in the collective imagination.

Does not the ridicule poured upon the cuckold perhaps contribute to the exaltation of the Don Juan? And the exaltation of Don Juan contributes to making the cuckold seem ever more ridiculous?

Freeing ourselves from these two motifs we shall also free ourselves

from the great obsessive phenomenon of jealousy, which is nothing but
a by-product of a vanity that springs from Don Juanism.

The whole enormous business of romantic love is thus reduced to
the single purpose of preservation of the species, and physical arousal
is at last freed from all its titillating mystery, from relish for the sala-
cious and from all the vanity of Don Juanism; it becomes merely bodily function, like eating and drinking.

The *extended man* we dream of will never experience the tragedy of
old age!

But it is for this reason that young men of this present age, at long
last sick and tired of erotic books, of the twofold drug of sentimentalism and lust, and being at last made immune to the sickness of Love,
will have to learn to systematically purge themselves of all heartaches.
This they can do through daily eradication of their emotions and seeking
endless sexual amusement in rapid, casual encounters with women.

This frank optimism of ours is thus diametrically opposed to the
pessimism of Schopenhauer, that bitter philosopher who so often proffered the tantalizing revolver of philosophy to kill off, in ourselves, the
deep-seated sickness of Love with a capital L.[7]

And it is precisely with this revolver that we shall so gladly target the
great Romantic Moonlight.[8]

Although this text was written in May 1910, it was first published in
***Guerra sola igiene del mondo* in 1915 and reprinted, in a slightly short-**
ened version, in *I manifesti del futurismo* (1919) and *Futurismo e fascismo*
(1924).

16

⁓

Lecture to the English on Futurism

So as to give you some idea of what we represent, I'll tell you straight-away what we think of you.[1]

I shall express myself with total frankness, refraining absolutely from flattery toward you, that all-too-common practice of international speakers who crush foreign audiences with their encomiums to then stuff them full of all sorts of banalities.

One of our young humorists has said that every good Futurist should be discourteous twenty times a day. So I'm going to be discourteous with you, bravely confessing all the ill we think of you English, after telling you what we like about you.

Well, I want you to know that we admire the unremitting, warlike patriotism that sets you apart. We admire your national pride that guides your great muscular race with courage. We admire your power-ful individualism which yet does not prevent you from opening your arms wide to welcome individualists from other countries, whether they be libertarians or anarchists.

But it's not only your great love of liberty we admire. What distin-guishes you from all other peoples is the fact where there is so much pacifist cant and evangelical funk, you nurture an unbridled passion for struggle in all its forms, from boxing—at its most simple, brutal, and swift—to the roaring monstrous mouths of your cannon, crouched in their rotating steel turrets on the bridges of your dreadnoughts,[2] when they catch the distant, tantalizing scent of enemy squadrons.

You are perfectly aware that there is nothing more damaging for the blood of men than the pardoning of offenses. You know too that periods of prolonged peace, which are fatal to the Latin races, are equally poisonous for the Anglo-Saxon race . . . However, I promised you discourtesies, and here they are:

In some ways, you are victims of your own traditionalism, which takes on something of a medieval hue. In spite of yourselves, the stench of musty archives and the jangling of chains still abide, embarrassments in your otherwise precise, confident, forward march.

And you will confess that such a thing is rather strange in a race of explorers and colonizers, whose huge ocean liners have, without any doubt, caused the world to shrink.

More than anything else, I reproach you for the unhealthy obsession you have with aristocracy. Nobody in England will admit to being *bourgeois*. Indeed, every Englishman registers scorn for his neighbor precisely by calling him *bourgeois*.

You have a mania for always appearing *chic*. This love of the *chic* causes you to be forever turning your backs on the impulsive leap, the heart's violence, the explosive outburst, screams, and even tears.

The English want to remain ice cold at all costs, whatever the situation, whether at the bedside of someone deeply loved, in the presence of death or of joy. Because of this love of the *chic*, you never speak about what you are doing, since you make it a rule that you must be ever witty and flippant in your conversation.

When the ladies leave the dinner table, politics are discussed a little, but not very much: after all, that would hardly be *chic*.

All your literary people also have to be socialites, since you are incapable of conceiving a novel that isn't set in the world of high society.

Despite being modern, you still maintain a clear, medieval distinction between master and servant, which is based on an absurd obsession with wealth. It's a common saying here that no man of substance is ever hanged in England . . . And added to this is an equally absurd scorn for the poor. Neither their intellectual strengths nor their genius—if they can lay claim to any—seem to be of the slightest use to you. And yet you are the most voracious devourers of books that I know. However, they are nothing more than one way, among others, of passing the time.

You have neither a fierce, adventuresome love of ideas nor any urge toward the mysteries of the imagination, nor indeed any sense of passion about the future or any thirst for revolution. You are such creatures of habit, in fact, that you firmly believe the old fable that the

Puritans saved England, and that chastity is the most important of a people's virtues. Just call to mind the grim yet absurd condemnation of Oscar Wilde.[3] The intelligentsia of Europe will never forgive you for that. Did you not then proclaim in all your newspapers that there was an immediate need to throw all your windows wide open, for the plague was at an end?

It goes without saying that in this sort of hypocritical, custom-ridden, formalistic atmosphere, your young women are perfectly capable of indulging in the most outrageous sexual games, with an elegantly in-genuous air, so as to prepare themselves carefully for marriage, that amorphous domain of the matrimonial police.

So far as your young men of twenty are concerned, nearly all of them, at some time or other, are homosexual. This perfectly respectable pref-erence of theirs stems from some sort of intensification of camaraderie and friendship, in the realm of athletic sports, before they reach the age of thirty—that age of work and order in which they suddenly return from Sodom to become engaged to some impudent young hussy, quickly registering their severe disapproval of the born invert, the false man, the half woman who makes no attempt to change.

Isn't it still the same as being excessively formalist to declare, as you do, that to know someone properly you have to have broken bread with them, which means having paid close attention to their way of eating?

But how can you judge us Italians from our way of eating, for we al-ways eat hurriedly, with our epigastriums being strangled by love or by the anxieties of social climbing?

That's how you carry out your obsessive desire to keep up appearances at all costs, your meticulous, petty-minded mania for labels, masks, and all kinds of screens, the contrivances of prudishness and moral hypocrisy.

However, I don't want to dwell on it, so I hasten on to condemn what we consider to be your greatest fault of all, a fault that you your-selves have taught Europe and which, in my opinion, is an obstacle to your wonderful, instinctive pragmatism and your science of life moving rapidly.

I want to mention your snobbery, whether it's your passionate, exclu-sive cult of the pure thoroughbred, so far as your aristocracy is con-cerned, or whether it's the creation of a kind of religion of fashion that transforms your illustrious tailors into equally great high priests of bygone religions. I refer also to your dogmatic, imperious rules for liv-ing well and to your sacred tablets of *comme il faut*, by which you de-spise and, with surprisingly little thought, annul the fundamental value of the individual, the moment he infringes the all-important *rules* of snobbery.

All of which causes your life to be singularly artificial and makes you the most contradictory people on earth, so that, for all your intellectual maturity, you can also, at times, look very much like a people still caught up in its formative process.

The love of hygiene was your invention,[4] as was adoration of the muscular and a passionate dedication to all-out effort, which triumph in your fine sporting life. But, unfortunately, you take your intense body worship too far and it becomes a scorn for ideas, and you are enthusiastic only about physical pleasures (and only physical pleasures arouse your enthusiasm). Platonic love is almost nonexistent among you, though that's no bad thing. But you're far too fond of tasty meals, and it is through the brutish religion of food that you calm all your worries and anxieties.

It is from your sensuality that you draw powerful serenity in the face of grief. You should therefore cease giving so much importance to physical pain!

You are thought of as being very religious, although that's nothing but outward show.

You have no interest in the life of the mind, and your race has no real feeling for the mystical. And on this latter point I congratulate you! But at the same time you need the comfort of Protestantism, that maid-of-all-work of your intelligence, which saves you the trouble and effort of thinking for yourselves, without fear and without hope, like a black flag in the darkness.

It's because of your intellectual sloth that you fall on your knees so very often, as well as your liking for good old childish convention.

No one loves the pleasures of the flesh more than you do, and yet in Europe you make a great show of chastity.

You like and generously take in all revolutionaries, but that in no way prevents you from stolidly defending the principles of order! . . . You adore the beautiful flying machines that with their wheels skim the earth, the sea, and the clouds, and yet you carefully preserve even the smallest bit of detritus from the past! . . .

Is this indeed a defect, when all is said and done? You mustn't think that all my observations are criticisms. To contradict oneself is to live and you know how to contradict yourselves with great courage.

But I know besides that you entertain a deep hatred of German clumsiness, and that is sufficient to absolve you entirely.[5]

. . .

So there, I've told you very briefly what we think of England and the English.

And now must I listen to the polite reply that I guess is already taking shape on your lips?

Without doubt, you wish to put a stop to my impoliteness by telling me all the good things you believe about Italy and the Italians . . . Well, no thanks. I don't want to listen to you.

The eulogy you are about to lavish on me can only sadden me, for what you love about our dear peninsula is precisely the object of all our hatred. Indeed, you travel through Italy only to sniff out, in the most meticulous way, all the vestiges of our oppressive past. You are happy, deliriously so, if you have the chance of bringing back home to cherish some miserable little stone that was trampled over by our forebears.

When, oh when, will you rid yourselves of the sluggish ideology of that deplorable man, Ruskin,[6] who—I should like to convince you, once and for all—is utterly ridiculous.

With his morbid dream of the primitive, agrarian life, with his nostalgia for Homeric cheeses and age-old "whirling spindles,"[7] and his hatred of machines, of steam and electricity, with his mania for ancient simplicity, he resembles a man who, after attaining complete physical maturity, still wants to sleep in a cradle and be suckled at his decrepit old nurse's breast, so as to regain the mindlessness of his infancy.

Ruskin would certainly have applauded those traditionalist Venetians who wanted to rebuild their idiotic bell tower of San Marco, as if it were a question of offering a child that had lost its grandma a doll made of cardboard and cloth to take her place.

This speech, given at the Lyceum Club in London, was first published in French in the book *Le Futurisme* (1911); the Italian version appeared in *Guerra sola igiene del mondo* (1915), *I manifesti del futurismo* (1919), and *Futurismo e fascismo* (1924).

17

The Futurist Manifesto Against English Art

F. T. MARINETTI AND C.R.W. NEVINSON[1]

I am an Italian Futurist poet and I love England passionately. I want to cure English art of the worst of all maladies: traditionalism. I thus have every right to speak out loud, without mincing my words, and together with my friend Nevinson, the English Futurist painter, to signal the start of the struggle.

Against

1. the cult of tradition, the conservatism of the academies, the commercial obsession of English painters, the effeminacy of their art and their efforts, which are purely, exclusively decorative.
2. the pessimistic, skeptical, and nostalgic tastes of the English public, which stupidly adores, to the point of ecstasy, everything that is affected, moderate, softened, and mediocre, such as petty reconstructions of things medieval—the graceless Garden Cities, maypoles, Morris dances, Fairy stories, aestheticism, Oscar Wilde, the Pre-Raphaelites, the Neo-primitives,[2] and Paris.[3]
3. a badly focused snobbery that ignores and despises every English attempt at boldness, originality, and invention, and which hurries off to venerate the boldness and originality of foreigners. It should never be forgotten that England had its innovators, such as Shakespeare and Swinburne in poetry; Turner and Constable (who was the very first of the Impressionists and of the School of Barbizon)[4]

in painting; Watt, Stephenson, Darwin,[5] and so on, in the sciences.

4. the false revolutionaries of the New English Art Club,[6] which destroyed the prestige of the Royal Academy and which is now vulgarly hostile to the vanguard movements.

5. the indifference of the King, the State, and the politicians toward art.

6. the English perception of art as an idle pastime, good only for women and girls, while artists are regarded as poor madmen in need of protection and art is seen as a bizarre illness that anyone can talk about.

7. the right of absolutely anyone to discuss and pass judgments where art is concerned.

8. the grotesque, outmoded ideal of the drunken genius who is dirty, unkempt, and classless, given to much drinking, which is synonymous with art; and Chelsea, seen as the Montmartre of London; the sub-Rossettis[7] with long hair beneath their sombreros, and other kinds of traditionalist rubbish.

9. the sentimentalism with which your paintings are loaded to make up for (and here you are plainly mistaken) your lack of tenderness and feeling for life.

10. innovators who are held back by weariness, by well-being, by desperation. Innovators lounging about on their islands or in their oases, who refuse to move forward. Innovators who declare: "Oh yes, we desire what is new, but not what you call new!" The tired old innovators who say: "We admire and follow the Post-Impressionists; but we mustn't venture beyond a certain desirable naïveté (Gauguin, etc.)." These innovators demonstrate not only that they have stopped dead in their tracks, but that they have never understood how art evolves. If in painting and sculpture naïveté, with its deformations and archaisms, has been the goal at all costs, that has been because of the need to break violently free from the academic and the pretty, prior to advancing toward the plastic dynamism of Futurist painting.

11. the mania for immortality. The masterpiece must die with its author. Immortality—so far as art is concerned—is infamy. With their power of construction and their immortality, our forebears in Italian art have enclosed us in a prison of timidity, imitation, and subjugation. They are always with us on their high-backed chairs, these venerable grandfathers of ours, telling us what to do. Their marble brows weigh heavily in the anguish of our youth: "Avoid

motorcars, my children! Wrap up warm! Avoid drafts! Be careful of the lightning!"
12. Enough! Enough! . . . Long live the motorcar! Hurray for the drafts! Hurray for the lightning!

We Desire

1. a strong English art, virile and unsentimentalized.
2. that English artists strengthen their art through a regenerative optimism, with a courageous desire for adventure and a heroic instinct for exploration, with a cult of strength and with moral and physical courage, the strong virtues of the English race.
3. that sport be considered as an essential element in art.
4. to create a great Futurist avant-garde which is the only thing that can save English art, threatened with death as it is, through the traditional conservatism of the academies and the habitual indifference of the public. It will prove a heady alcohol and a relentless goad for creative genius,[8] and maintain a constant preoccupation with keeping the furnaces of invention and art aflame, thereby avoiding the laborious task and expense of clearing the blockages of slag and of continually relighting them.

England, a country that is rich and powerful, will have to uphold, defend, and glorify absolutely its artistic, most revolutionary, and most advanced avant-gardes, if it wishes to save its art from certain death.

This manifesto was published in both Italian and English in *Lacerba*, July 15, 1914. A French edition, entitled "Contre l'art anglais. Manifeste futuriste," appeared as a broadsheet, dated "Londra 11 juin 1914." The English translation, entitled "Vital English Art" and first published in *The Observer* on June 7, 1914, was obviously by Christopher Nevinson, but according to a letter Marinetti wrote to Mario Carli on July 20, 1914, he was the sole author of this manifesto ("mio manifesto contro l'Arte inglese ufficiale, firmato anche dal pittore futurista inglese Nevinson"). The title of the French edition of the manifesto suggests that it was read at the 1914 Futurist exhibition at the Doré Gallery, and again in June 1914 at Cambridge University. Our translation here is based on Marinetti's original Italian text.

18

✑

Futurist Proclamation to the Spaniards

I dreamt about a great people; undoubtedly it was of you Spaniards!

I saw them advancing, from one epoch to the next, conquering the mountains, rising ever higher toward the great light that glows beyond inaccessible peaks.

From on high, at the zenith, in my dreams I contemplated your numberless, heavily laden ships, making long processions like ants over the green meadows of the sea, linking one island with another, like so many ants' nests, heedless of the storms, those terrible footsteps of a god of which you have no fear.[1]

As for you, builders of cities, soldiers, and farmers, you were going at a goodly pace, making progress, yet trailing along behind you a procession of women, children, and treacherous monks.

And it was this rearguard which betrayed you, drawing down upon your army on the march all the sultry atmosphere of Africa, all its ethereal witches and panderers, who hatch their plots in the dark ravines of the Sierra Nevada.[2]

A thousand noxious breezes spied upon your passage and a thousand mellow springtimes, with their vampire wings, lulled you into voluptuous sleep. And at once, the wolves of lust howled deep within their woods. In the slow, rosy breath of evening, the men, with their kisses, crushed the naked women they held in their arms. Maybe they hoped to drive the stars mad with jealousy, the unattainable, far-off stars, lost in the abyss of night! . . . Or maybe the fear of dying spurred them on to repeat their death games, endlessly, upon their love beds![3] —Certainly, the last flames of hell, which were dying down, licked the backs of the men as they labored devotedly upon the lovely, insatiable cunts . . .

And in the meantime, the old Christian sun was dying in a mass of clouds, all streaked with blood, which suddenly exploded, vomiting forth, all red and seething, the French Revolution, that formidable storm of justice.

For a long time, in that deluge of liberty, in which all the paths of authority were at last swept away,[4] you cried out your anguish to those sneaking monks who cautiously circled about your immense wealth.

And there they were, bending over you and mumbling:

"Children, come, come with us into the cathedral of God! . . . It is ancient, yet still solid! Enter into the fold, O little sheep . . . shelter in this fold! Listen to the ever-loving, blessed bells, whose sounds ripple like the rounded flanks of the women of Andalusia. We have covered the altars of the Madonna with violets and roses. The half-light of our chapels is as mysterious as that of the nuptial chamber. The flames of our candles are like the carnations that smile between the teeth of your indolent women . . . Come! You shall have love, perfumes, gold and silks, and you shall even have singing, for the Virgin is indulgent! . . ."

On hearing these words, you took your eyes off the fathomless constellations, and immense fear of the firmaments propelled you into the starved porticoes of the cathedral, beneath the mellifluous sound of the organ, which made you bend the knee absolutely.

And now what do I see? . . . In the impenetrable darkness of the night, the cathedral quakes beneath the anger of a pelting rain. Everywhere, with the utmost difficulty, a suffocating terror raises up enormous slabs of darkness. The tempest, with its desolate cry, accompanies the endless wailing of the organ, and every now and then their mingled sounds are drawn out into a painful clangor. It is the walls of the cloister that are crumbling! . . .

Spaniards! Spaniards! What ever did you expect, held down as you were by fear, with your faces bent low beneath the infectious stench of incense and rotting flowers, in the nave of this cathedral, this foul tomb that cannot save you, Christian livestock, from the deluge, nor lead you to heaven? . . . Arise! Clamber up to your great glass windows still smeared with mystical moonlight, and gaze upon the spectacle of all spectacles! . . .

And behold the sudden uprising wonder, higher even than the ebony-colored *sierras*.[5] Electricity, the sublime, the unique, divine mother of future humanity, her body glowing a vivid silver, Electricity with her thousand flashing, violet-colored arms . . .

See! Just see! . . . how she hurls her diamond thunderbolts from all sides, youthful, dancing, naked, speeding up winding, azure stairways, on the attack, storming the black Cathedral!

There are more than ten thousand of them, trembling, exhausted, throwing themselves into the assault in the rain, striding over the walls, darting here and there, biting into the smoking ironwork of the guttering and, dipping madly, smashing the stained-glass madonnas in the windows.

But you are shaking on your knees like trees uprooted in a flood . . . On your feet! . . . Let the oldest among you make haste to lift the best part of your wealth onto their shoulders. For the others, the younger ones, a task that is much more congenial! . . . Are you the ones in your twenties? Fine, then listen to me! . . .

Brandishing solid gold candelabras, using them like swirling cudgels to smash in the heads of the monks and priests! . . .

Bloody poultices, crimson wadding to stop up the holes in the vaulting and in the broken windows.

A bleeding scaffold of deacons and archdeacons, archbishops and cardinals, stuffed in one after another, with their arms and legs woven together, will hold up the sagging walls of the nave!

But move then, before the triumphant thunderbolts hurl themselves on you to punish you for your age-old sins! . . .

For you are guilty of the crime of living in a trance, in a dream world. You are guilty of never having wanted to live and of having tasted death merely in tiny sips . . . You are guilty of having stifled your own spirits, the desire for, and pride in, conquest, beneath the sad pillows of love, nostalgia, lust, and prayer!

And now break down the fittings of the doors that squeak away on their living hinges! . . . The beautiful land of Spain lies before you, all parched with thirst and pounded by a pitiless sun. She shows you her belly all burnt and shriveled . . . Run, run to her therefore and offer her your aid! . . . Whatever are you waiting for? . . . Ah! I see, there's a ditch in your way—the great medieval moat that defended the Cathedral . . . All right then, fill it up you old men, by throwing in all the riches that are weighing you down! . . . Away they go, everything into it all at once: religious pictures, immortal statues, the guitars that moan away in the moonlight, all the shabby stuff your ancestors revered, precious metals

and woods! . . . The moat is too wide—haven't you anything left with
which to fill it up? . . . Well then, it has to be you! Make the sacrifice!
Down you go one after the other! . . . Your piled-up, decrepit bodies
will prepare the way for the great hope of the world.

And you young men, full of courage, pass over them! . . . Now what's
wrong? . . . Another obstacle? . . . What! It's only a cemetery! . . . Come
on now! Away you go across it! . . . As fast as your legs will carry you, like
a bunch of students on a binge! . . . Trample the lawns, overturn the
crosses and the tombstones! . . . That'll make your ancestors laugh! . . .
They'll be laughing with Futurist joy, happy, crazily happy feeling themselves trampled over by feet that are more powerful than their own!

But what's that you're carrying? . . . Are they hoes? . . . Get rid of
them! . . . They've never dug anything other than graves! . . .

To turn over the earth of the delirious life, you'll be forging new
ones, fusing together the gold and silver of the religious offerings!

At last, at long last, your liberated gaze can move about untrammeled
beneath the vast revolutionary unfurling of the flags of the dawn![6]

The rivers, unconstrained, will show you the way! . . . The rivers
that are finally setting loose their silky green *foulards* of coolness over
the earth from which you have swept away all the clerical rubbish!

For, you Spaniards, be well advised; by pouring down its ruins upon
you, the old Catholic heaven has unwittingly impregnated the aridity
of your great central plateau!

To assuage your thirst during your zealous march, bite your lips until
they bleed—those lips that would still be inclined to pray so as to learn
how to control a slavish Destiny! . . . March forward! . . . You must
break the habit of your aching knees kneeling on the ground, for now
you will not bend them anymore except to crush your former confes-
sors, those quaint-seeming hassocks!

They are suffering agonies—can you not hear them?—beneath
these collapsing stones and the heavy crashing of the landslide which,
together, mark the beat of your steps . . . But woe betide you if you look
back . . . the old black Cathedral may well gradually fall into ruin, with
its mystical windows and its vaulting full of holes, fittingly stopped up
with its stinking poultice of monks and priests!

Futurist Conclusions

The progress of contemporary Spain will not take place without the establishment of agrarian and industrial wealth.

Spaniards! You will undoubtedly achieve this by means of communal and regional autonomy, which are essential, as well as education of the people, to which end the government must each year dedicate 60,000,000 pesetas, drawn from religious and clerical funds.

For this reason you have to eradicate clericalism entirely, with no half measures, as well as destroy Carlism,[7] its natural extension, partner, and defender.

The monarchy,[8] ably defended by Canalejas,[9] is currently engaged in precisely this fine piece of surgery.

If the monarchy fails to complete the task, and if the prime minister or his successors turn out to be weaklings or traitors, then it will be the turn of the Radical-Socialist Republic, led by Lerroux and Iglesias,[10] whose revolutionary hand will cut more deeply, maybe even terminally, into the poisoned flesh of the country.

In the meantime, politicians, men of letters, and artists must work unstintingly, with their books, their speeches, their conferences, and their journals to transform completely the intellectual tenor of Spain.

1. To achieve this, they will have to promote national pride in all its forms;
2. To defend and develop the sense of dignity and the freedoms of the individual;
3. To cultivate and glorify the triumph of science and its everyday heroism;
4. To make a clear-cut distinction between the ideas of nation, a powerful army, and the possibilities of war, on the one hand, from the idea of a reactionary, priest-ridden monarchy, on the other;
5. To fuse the ideas of nation, powerful army, and the possibilities of war, with those of progress and an unfettered proletariat, as well as educating the proletariat to a sense of patriotism;
6. To bring about a transformation—without destroying them—of the quintessential qualities of the Spanish race, by which we mean: a love of danger and struggle, fearless courage, artistic inspiration, a haughty arrogance, and the lithe dexterity that crowned your poets, singers, dancers, your Don Juans, and your matadors, with glory.

All of these abundant energies can be channeled into laboratories and workshops, onto the land, the sea, and the sky, through the endless triumphs of science;

7. To fight against the tyranny of love, the obsession with the ideal woman, the drug of sentimentalism, and the monotonous battles of adultery that exhaust men of twenty-five;

8. To defend Spain from the greatest dangers and from the gravest of all intellectual diseases, that of clinging to the past, by which is meant the methodical, stupid cult of the past, the foul trade in nostalgia for the past.

Be assured, absolutely, O Spaniards, that the former glories of Spain will be *absolutely nothing* in comparison with the Spain that your Futurist hands will one day create.

It is simply a question of will that you have to resolve, by brutally breaking the vicious circle of priests, bullfighters, and singers of serenades in which you still live.

In your country you complain that the youths in your dead cities are free to hurl stones at the precious stone traceries of your Alhambras, at the ancient, inimitable windows of your churches!

How ridiculous! Give sweets to those public-spirited youths, for they are saving you, without intending to, from the most shameful and mischievous of industries, that of exploitation of foreigners.[11]

As for the millionaire tourists, feckless, wide-eyed voyeurs who sniff out the tracks of great men of action, amusing themselves sometimes by putting some ancient warrior's helmet on their thin skulls, you should despise them all, with their small talk full of rubbish and their cash with which they can make you rich! Prevent them from coming to visit this Spain of yours, as they come and visit Rome, Venice, Florence, idealized cemeteries! . . .

I'm well aware that there are those who do their best to dazzle you with the promise of huge profits and who could set you up as experts in the business of trading your glorious past . . . Well, spit on them! Turn your head away.

You Spaniards are fit to be heroic workers, not just guides, ponces, picture copiers, restorers of ancient paintings, stuffy archaeologists, and manufacturers of forged masterpieces.

Take good care you don't draw down on Spain the grotesque caravans of cosmopolitan moneybags, who parade their empty-headed snobbism, their vexing stupidity, their morbid thirst for nostalgia and their roving cocks, instead of using their utmost strength and their wealth to construct the Future!

Your hotels are atrocious, your cathedrals are crumbling . . . So much the better! So much the better! Rejoice in it! Rejoice! What you need is great commercial ports, industrial cities, fertile countryside irrigated by your great rivers which still remain unharnessed.

It's not your ambition, as far as I can tell, to turn Spain into a Baedeker land, a high-class holiday playground, with a thousand museums and a hundred thousand panoramic views and ruins, and to do all this *of your own free will!*

In April 1909 *Prometeo* published a Spanish translation of *The Foundation and Manifesto of Futurism*. A few months later, its translator, Ramón Gómez de la Serna, commissioned from Marinetti a "crushing and scourging proclamation to Spain," which he received in the early autumn of 1910. In issue 19 of *Prometeo*, dated July 1910 but printed much later, Gómez de la Serna announced this new manifesto for the following number, together with a note from Marinetti, saying that the text contained "all my anguished observations, made on a car journey across Spain, centered, for the most part, on the tragic aridity of your central 'tableland,' of Castile." The *Proclama futurista a los españoles* appeared in *Prometeo* 20 (dated August 1910, but published well into the autumn of that year), preceded by an introduction by Gómez de la Serna. It was also printed as a sixteen-page booklet with a small woodcut illustration on the title page and the colophon "Madrid: Prometeo, 1911," and in the volume F. T. Marinetti, *El futurismo*, Valencia: Sempere, [1912?]. It was published in Italian as *Against Traditionalist Spain*, in *I manifesti del futurismo* (1914), and in a revised edition, with a number of stylistic variants, under the title *Futurist Proclamation to the Spaniards*, in *Guerra sola igiene del mondo* (1915).

19

An Open Letter to the Futurist Mac Delmarle

Dear friend,[1]

I was very sorry not to find you in Paris when I was there recently.[2] Most of all, I wanted to tell you that we completely and enthusiastically approve your Futurist manifesto, a battery of surefire ideas aimed at the last remnants of all that is rotten and antiquated in Paris. Montmartre is going down under your blows, with its *cottages*, its *little gardens*, its *little birds*, its Mimi Pinsons,[3] and its mopheaded pain-tasters. We are truly happy to endorse it. Your brave Futurist initiative shows most clearly that Futurism is not a *petty religion* or a *school*, but rather a great movement of intellectual energy and heroism, in which the individual counts for nothing, while the will to destroy and renew is all.[4]

It is as absurd to think of Futurism as being the monopoly of Marinetti, Boccioni, Carrà, Russolo, Severini, Buzzi, Cangiullo, Folgore, Palazzeschi, and so on, as to attribute a monopoly of atmospheric electricity to electric lights and to Mount Etna a monopoly of earthly fire and earthquakes.

Since an illustrious past was crushing Italy and *an infinitely more glorious future* was seething away in her breast, it was precisely here, in Italy, four years ago, that beneath our too-sensuous sky Futurist energy was crying out to be born, to become organized, channeled, to find in us its driving forces, its means of illumination and propagation.

Italy, more than any other country, was in urgent need of Futurism, for it was dying of an obsession with its own past.

The patient invented its own remedy. *We are the doctors the situation demanded*, and the remedy is valid for the sick in all countries.

Our immediate program is one of fierce combat against Italian traditionalism in all its repugnant forms: archaeology, academicism, pedantry, sentimentalism, erotomania, and so on. Therefore, we profess an ultra-violent nationalism, anticlerical and antisocialist, a nationalism opposed to tradition and based on the inexhaustible vigor of Italian blood.

Our Futurist nationalism struggles fiercely against the cult of ancestors which, far from binding our race together, makes it anemic and causes it pitifully to rot away.

But Futurism goes beyond this immediate program, which we have fulfilled (in part) in four years of incessant battle.

Futurism, in its overall program, is an atmosphere of the avant-garde; it is the watchword for all innovators or intellectual sharpshooters of the world; it is love of the new; the impassioned art of speed; the systematic denigration of the antique, the old, the slow, the erudite, and the professorial; it is the strident sound of picks demolishing; it is a new way of seeing the world; a new reason for loving life; the enthusiastic glorification of scientific discoveries and of modern machines; the flag of youth, of strength, and of originality at all costs; it is a huge gob of spittle aimed at all the depressing traditionalists; a steel collar against the habit of backward-looking stiffnecks; an inexhaustible machine gun pointing at the army of the dead, of the gouty and the opportunists, whom we want to strip of their authority and subject to the bold and creative young; it is a stick of dynamite for all venerable ruins.

The word *Futurism* contains the widest possible formula for renewal: one which, being both hygienic and exciting, simplifies doubt, destroys skepticism, and gathers all endeavor into a powerful sense of elation.

All innovatory spirits will gather together beneath the flag of Futurism, because Futurism preaches the need to go ever forward, never to hang back, and because it promotes the destruction of all escape routes offered to the pusillanimous.

Futurism is a man-made optimism opposed to all chronic pessimisms, it is a continuous dynamism, continuous becoming, and tireless will.

Futurism, a wonderful formula for *the conscious rebirth of races*, is therefore not subject to the laws of fashion or to wearing down by time.

These truths appeared sharply to my spirit on the evening of our famous battle at the Costanzi Theater,[5] when, after having put up with the taunts and missiles of five thousand traditionalists (who were more or less the hired mercenaries of the Roman aristocracy) for three hours, we hurled ourselves at them, doling out punches and beatings. The five hundred impromptu Futurists whom we suddenly felt around us that evening, and who helped us to wreck and rearrange, in some measure, the faces of our enemies, fought valiantly, not really to defend us, but merely to ensure the triumph of this *great worldwide energy that is Futurism.*

Dear Delmarle, I have followed your polemic against our friend Severini,[6] who is both a fine fellow and a great Futurist painter. Rest assured that we give little importance to that small personal misunderstanding between you, which, in any case, you can easily mend when you next meet.

Only the explosive ideas of Futurism matter. Futurists can even perish, sometimes, in casting them forth.

This open letter was printed in *Lacerba* on August 15, 1913, following Delmarle's *Manifeste futuriste contre Montmartre,* originally published in *Paris-Journal* (July 13, 1913) and *Comœdia* (July 15, 1913). Marinetti's letter was printed with a number of textual variants in *Guerra sola igiene del mondo* (1915), *I manifesti del futurismo* (1919), and *Democrazia futurista* (1919).

20

Technical Manifesto of Futurist Literature

In an airplane, sitting on the fuel tank, my belly warmed by the head of the pilot, I realized the utter folly of the antique syntax we have inherited from Homer. A furious need to liberate words, dragging them free of the prison of the Latin sentence! Naturally, like all imbeciles, the latter has a wise head, a fat belly, two legs, and two flat feet, but it'll never have a pair of wings. The bare necessities for walking, for running a few short steps and stopping almost at once, gasping for breath!

This is what the spinning propeller told me, as I sped along, two hundred meters above the mighty chimney stacks of Milan. And the propeller went even further: ·

1. **We have to destroy syntax, to scatter nouns at random, even as they come to mind.**
2. **We have to use the verb in the infinitive** so that it adapts itself flexibly to the noun and does not subject it to the "I" of the observing or imagining author. In the infinitive, quite unaided, the verb can capture the continuity of life and the flexibility of the intuition that perceives it.
3. **We have to get rid of adjectives**, so that the unadorned noun retains its essential color. Because the adjective carries a nuancing tendency within itself, its use is thus inconceivable in our dynamic vision, for it implies a pause, a moment of contemplation.
4. **We have to get rid of the adverb**, that old clamp which joins

one word to another. The adverb imposes an irritating unity of tone on a sentence.

5. **Every noun must have its double**, i.e., the noun has to be followed, without the use of conjunctions, by that noun to which it is linked by analogy. For example: man–torpedo boat, woman-bay, crowd-backwash, piazza-funnel, door-tap.

Since the speed of air travel has greatly increased our knowledge of the world, perception through analogy is becoming ever more natural for human beings. Therefore, we have to suppress the "how," the "which," the "thus," the "similar to." Better still, we should fuse the object directly with the image that it evokes, providing a glimpse of the image by means of a single, essential word.

6. **Abolish punctuation as well.** When we have suppressed adjectives, adverbs, and conjunctions it obviously follows that punctuation is also annulled in the continuous variety of a lively style that emerges naturally, without the absurd pauses of commas and periods. To emphasize particular shifts and indicate their direction, we will make use of mathematical signs: $+ - \times : = > <$, and musical notation.

7. Until now writers have given themselves over to direct analogy. For example, they have compared an animal to a man or to another animal, a process which is still, more or less, the equivalent of a kind of photography. (Some authors have described a fox terrier as a very small thoroughbred, for example. Other, more avant-garde writers compared that same trembling fox terrier to a Morse transmitter. I, however, compare it to boiling water. And in this there is **an ever-widening ranking of analogies**, of relations that are increasingly more profound and more solid, however distant their terms may be from each other.)

Analogy is nothing less than the deep love that connects objects that are distant in kind, seemingly different and hostile. Only by means of the widest possible analogies can an orchestral style, which is at one and the same time polychromatic, polyphonic, and polymorphous, embrace the life of matter.

When, in my *Battle of Tripoli*,[1] I compared a trench, bristling with bayonets, to an orchestra, a machine gun to a femme fatale, I intuitively introduced a large part of the universe into a brief episode in African warfare.

"Les images ne sont pas des fleurs à choisir et à cueillir avec parcimonie" (Images are not flowers to choose and to pick in a miserly fashion), as Voltaire said. They are the very lifeblood of poetry. Poetry must be a continuous stream of new images, without which it is nothing more than anemia and greensickness.

The more wide-ranging relations the images contain, the longer they retain their power to amaze. It is necessary—they say—to maintain the reader's sense of wonder. What! Come off it! What we have to guard against, in reality, is a fatal time-wasting, which destroys not only the expressive value of a masterpiece but also its power to amaze. Have not Beethoven and Wagner perhaps already been destroyed for us through our listening to them too frequently and too enthusiastically? In language, we must therefore rid ourselves of everything containing stereotyped images and colorless metaphors, which means just about everything.

8. **There are no categories of images**, noble or crude or commonplace, eccentric or natural. The intuition that perceives them has neither preferences nor preconceptions. An analogical style is thus absolute master of all its material and of its intense life.

9. To reveal the successive movements of an object we have to show the *chain of analogies* it evokes, each one condensed, contained in an essential word.

Here is an expressive example of a chain of analogies which is still masked and weighed down by traditional syntax:

Oh yes, indeed! my little machine gun, you are a bewitching woman, both sinister and divine, at the wheel of an invisible, hundred-horsepower car that roars in outbursts of impatience. Doubtless, before not too long, you will bound into the circle of death, either toward a momentous fall or to a resounding victory! . . . Would you like me to compose madrigals full of grace and color for you? The choice is yours, madam . . . For me you resemble a tribune leaning forward, whose untiring, eloquent tongue touches its encircling, deeply affected audience to the quick . . . In this moment, you are an all-powerful drill that bores a round hole into the adamantine cranium of this stubborn night . . . But you are also a steel-rolling mill, an electric lathe, and what else besides? A huge oxyacetylene torch that burns, cuts through, and then, piece by piece, molds the metallic tips of the latest stars! . . . (*La battaglia di Tripoli*)

In some cases it will be necessary to link images in pairs, like shells strung together, that in their flight fell a whole group of trees.

To encompass and gather together all that which is most fleeting and elusive in materiality, we have to form **tight networks of**

images or analogies that will be hurled into the mysterious ocean of matter. If we disregard the traditional ornamentation, this sentence from my novel *Mafarka the Futurist* is an example of just this sort of tight imagery:

All the bittersweet of his vanished youth brought a lump to his throat, as when from school yards the delighted cries of children are raised toward their masters leaning over the patio balustrades from where the ships can be seen slipping away . . .

And here are three more networks of imagery:

Around the well at Bumeliana, beneath the dense olive trees, three camels, kneeling in the sand, were gurgling contentedly, like ancient stone gutters, the swash of their spittle mingling with the continuous thump of the steam pump that provides the city with its drinking water. Harsh Futurist discords coming from the intense orchestra of the trenches with their snaking fissures and their resonant chambers, amid the comings and goings of bayonets, violin bows that the scarlet rod of sunset enflames ecstatically . . .

It is the sunset director of the orchestra who, with a wide gesture, brings together the flutes of the birds scattered in the trees, and the mournful harps of the insects, and the crunching of stones. It is he who, all at once, silences the tympani of mess tins and of jostling rifles, to permit all the golden stars, standing high, arms wide open, to sing out, full-voiced, upon the stage of the heavens above the muted orchestra. And here is a great lady at the performance . . . in a gapingly low-cut dress, indeed, the desert reveals the melting curves of her huge breasts, rose-tinted, beneath the cascading gems of this exuberant night. (*La battaglia di Tripoli*)

10. Since every sort of order is an inevitable product of cautious intelligence, we have to orchestrate images by arranging them with a **maximum of disorder**.

11. **In literature, eradicate the "I,"** which means all psychology. The man who is damaged beyond redemption by the library and the museum, who is in thrall to a fearful logic and wisdom, offers absolutely nothing that is any longer of any interest. Therefore, we must banish him from literature, letting matter at last take his place, and we must seize its essence with deft strokes of intu-

ition—something that neither physicists nor chemists will ever accomplish.[2]

By means of free-ranging objects and capricious engines[3] catch unawares the breathing, the sensibilities, and the instincts of metals, of stones, of wood, and so on. Replace the psychology of man, by now played out, with the **lyrical obsession for matter**.

But take care not to bestow human feelings on matter; guess rather what its different determining impulses will be, its compressive and its expansive forces, what binds it, what breaks it down, its mass of swarming molecules or its swirling electrons. We are not concerned with producing dramas of humanized matter. It is the solidity of a sheet of steel that interests us for its own sake, by which we mean the incomprehensible, inhuman alliance of its molecules or its electrons, which oppose the penetration of a howitzer, for example. The heat of a piece of iron or wood is now more thrilling for us than the smile or the tears of a woman.

In literature, we want to present the life of the motorcar, this new, instinctive animal whose innate character we shall only know when we are acquainted with the natural proclivities of the different forces that compose it.

Nothing is more interesting to a Futurist poet than the dance of the keys of a mechanical piano. The cinema shows us the dance of an object that divides in two and then joins together again without any human intervention.[4] It shows us the swimmer's jump in reverse, where his feet leave the sea and bounce violently back on the springboard. And finally, it shows us a man racing along at two hundred kilometers an hour. These are all equally movements of matter, outside the laws of intelligence and therefore of an essence that has greater significance.

We need to introduce three elements into literature that have been overlooked until now:

1. **Noise** (demonstration of the dynamism of objects);
2. **Weight** (power of flight of objects);
3. **Smell** (the ability of objects to scatter themselves).[5]

Try and express, for example, the landscape of smells that a dog perceives.[6] Listen to engines and reproduce their conversations.

Matter has always been contemplated by an "I" that was cold, casual, and too preoccupied with itself, full of prejudicial wisdom and human obsessions.

Man tends to soil matter with his youthful joy or the sadness of his old age. Yet it retains an admirable consistency in its impulse toward greater zeal, greater movement, and a greater division of itself. Matter is neither happy nor sad. Its essential features are courage, will, and absolute force. It belongs entirely to the poet-seer, who will know how to free himself from a syntax that is traditional, heavy, restrictive, earthbound, with neither arms nor wings, because it is merely intelligent. Only the poet who is detached from syntax and is in command of Words-in-Freedom will know how to penetrate the essence of matter and destroy the dull hostility that cuts it off from us.

The Latin sentence that has sufficed until now was a pretentious gesture with which arrogant, shortsighted intelligence has striven to contain the manifold, mysterious life of matter. The Latin sentence was thus clearly stillborn.

The deep feelings for life, linked one to another, word after word, in accordance with their illogical coming into being, will provide us with the broad outlines of an **intuitive psychology of matter**. It was all revealed to my spirit, high up in an airplane. Seeing things from a new perspective, no longer frontally or from behind, but straight down beneath me, and thus foreshortened, I was able to break the age-old fetters of logic and the leaden wire of traditional comprehension.[7]

All you Futurist poets[8] who have loved me and followed me thus far, would that you were like me, delirious creators of images, adventurous explorers of analogies. However, your narrow systems of metaphor are sadly weighed down by a leaden logic. I would advise you to lighten them, because by making them exceed all bounds you can hurl them far, spreading them out over a much wider ocean.

Together we shall invent what I call **untrammeled imagination**. We shall arrive, one day, at an art that is even more essential, when we have dared to suppress all the first terms of our analogies so as to give nothing more than the uninterrupted second terms. Because of this, we shall have to renounce being understood. Being understood is not necessary. In any case, we did without it when we were expressing fragments of Futurist sensibility by means of traditional, intellective syntax.

Syntax was a kind of abstract codebook that allowed poets to inform the masses about the color, the musicality, the plasticity, and the architecture of the universe. Syntax was a sort of interpreter or boring tour guide. We have to suppress this go-between so that literature enters directly into the cosmos and becomes one with it.

There can be no doubt whatsoever that my work is clearly distinct from all others by virtue of the tremendous power of analogy. The inexhaustible richness of its images are almost proportionate to the disorder of its logical punctuation. It starts with the first Futurist manifesto, synthesis of a hundred-horsepower engine launched at the craziest speeds on earth.

Why still make use of four boring, exasperating wheels, once we can detach ourselves from the earth? The freeing of words, the spread wings of the imagination, the analogical synthesis of the earth, all embraced at a single glance and gathered in entirely by essential words.

They scream at us: "Your literature will lack beauty! We shall no longer have the symphony of words, their harmonious swaying back and forth, their soothing cadences!" That is understood from the start! And how lucky we are! Indeed, we use all the ugly sounds, all the expressive cries of the violent life that surrounds us. **Bravely, we bring the "ugly" into literature,**[9] **and kill off its ritual pomp wherever we find it.** Away with you! Don't take on these priestly airs, when you are listening to me! You have to spit every day on *the High Altar of Art!* We are entering into the boundless domains of free intuition. After Free Verse, here at last we have **Words-in-Freedom!**[10]

In all of this, there is nothing absolute, nothing systematic. Genius experiences sudden flurries and muddy torrents. Sometimes it demands slow analyses and explanations. No one can suddenly revitalize his own sensibilities. Our dead cells are all mixed up with the living. Art is the need to destroy and scatter oneself, the great jet of heroism that floods the world. Microbes—and let us not forget it—are necessary to the health of the stomach and the intestines.[11] There is also a kind of microbe that is necessary to the health of **art, this extension of the jungle of our veins** that pours forth from our bodies into the infinity of space and time.

Futurist poets! I have taught you to hate libraries and museums, so as to prepare you for **hating intelligence**, and have reawakened divine intuition in you, the characteristic gift of the Latin races. It is through intuition that we shall overcome the seeming hostility that separates our human flesh from the metal of engines.

After the animal kingdom, behold the beginning of the mechanical kingdom.[12] With the knowledge and friendship of matter, of which the scientists can know only the physicochemical reactions, we are preparing for the creation of **mechanical man, one who will have parts**

that can be changed. We shall liberate him from the idea of death, and therefore from death itself, which is the all-embracing definition of logical intelligence.

Answers to objections[13]

I pour scorn on the endless witticisms and ironies, and respond to the skeptical questioning and seemingly more valid objections hurled by the European press against my *Technical Manifesto of Futurist Literature*.

1. Those who have understood what I meant by **hatred of intelligence** have thought they perceived in it the influence of the philosophy of Bergson.[14] Clearly, these people don't know that the first page of my first epic poem, *La Conquête des étoiles*, which was published in 1902, bore these three lines of Dante by way of epigraph:

   > *Insensate strivings of mortality—*
   > *how useless are those* reasonings *of yours*
   > *that* make you beat your wings in downward flight!
   > (*Paradise*, XI, 1–3)

   And this thought of Edgar Poe:

   > The poetic intellect—that intellect which we now feel to have been the most exalted of all—since those truths which to us were of the most enduring importance could only be reached by that *analogy* which speaks in proof-tones to the imagination alone, and to the unaided reason bears no weight.
   > (*The Colloquy of Monos and Una*)

   Long before Bergson, these two creative geniuses were in harmony with my genius, clearly asserting their hatred of groveling, sick, and solitary intelligence, and according all rights to intuitive, prophetic imagination.

2. When I speak about intuition and intelligence, of course, it is not my intention to speak of two domains that are distinct and entirely cut off from each other. All creative spirits have noted, in the course of their creative work, that intuitive features blend with elements of logical intelligence.

It is thus impossible to know exactly the moment at which unconscious inspiration ends and clear-sightedness begins. Sometimes, the latter violently sparks off inspiration; at other times, however, it accompanies it. After several hours of dogged, exhausting labor, the creative spirit is suddenly free of the burden of all obstacles and, in one way or another, becomes prey to a strange spontaneity of conception and execution. The hand that writes seems detached from the body and continues for a long time freed from the brain, which also, somehow detached from the body, having taken flight, looks down from on high, with an awesome clarity of vision, upon the unexpected expression coming from the pen.[15]

In reality, does this overbearing brain passively contemplate or actively direct the flights of fancy that move the hand? It is impossible to be sure. In these moments, all I have been aware of from the physiological point of view has been a great feeling of emptiness in my stomach.

By **intuition**, therefore, what I mean is a kind of thought which is almost entirely intuitive and unconscious. By **intelligence**, I intend a kind of thought that is almost entirely the product of intellect and will.

3. The poetic ideal I dream of, and which would be nothing other than a continuous sequence of second terms in any analogy, has nothing whatsoever to do with allegory. Though allegory, as it happens, is the sequence of second terms of a number of analogies, all *logically* linked together. Sometimes, it is also the second term of a comparison, developed and described in minute detail.

Quite the opposite of this, I aspire to an illogical sequence which is no longer explanatory, but intuitive, in the use of only the second terms of many analogies, all disconnected, one from the other, and very often of opposing meaning, one to another.

4. All stylists, as a breed, have without difficulty seen that the adverb is not just a word that modifies a verb, an adjective, or some other adverb, but is also a musical link that unifies the different sounds in a sentence.

5. I believe it necessary to suppress adjectives and adverbs, because they are, simultaneously and from time to time, the multicolored streamers, the many-toned drapery, the plinths, the parapets and balustrades of the old, traditional sentence.

It is precisely through the judicious use of adjectives and adverbs that the melodious, monotonous rhythm of a sentence is established, as well as the interrogative or emotional raising of its voice and the gradual, restful lapping of its waves upon the shore. With emotions that never alter, the spirit holds its breath, trembles a little, begs to be calmed, and then finally breathes deeply again when the wave of words subsides, punctuated by the slip of shingle and its dying echoes.

Adjectives and adverbs have a triple function: explicative, decorative, and musical, by means of which they indicate the pace either ponderous or light, slow or fast—of the noun as it moves along in the sentence. They are, at times, the walking stick or the crutches of the noun. Their length and their weight regulate the pace of the style, which, as a result, is always under their guardianship, and they thus prevent it from emulating the flight of the imagination.

Writing, for example, "A beautiful young woman walks quickly over the marble paving," the traditional spirit hastens to explain that that woman is young and beautiful, even though the intuition simply posits a beautiful movement. Later, the traditional spirit announces that that woman walks quickly, and finally adds that she walks over a paved marble floor.

This purely explicative process no longer has any raison d'être, as it lacks the unforeseen and imposes itself in advance on all the arabesques, zigzags, and sudden starts of thought. It is thus more or less certain that anyone who does the opposite will not be deceiving himself. Moreover, it is undeniable that by abolishing adjectives and adverbs we shall be giving back to the noun its essential value, total and typical.

Besides, I have absolute faith in the sense of horror I feel for the noun that proceeds, followed by its adjective, as if by a beggar or a puppy dog. On occasions the latter is kept on a leash by some elegant adverb. At times the noun carries an adjective before it and an adverb behind, like the two boards of a sandwich man. These are spectacles that are equally unacceptable.

6. It is precisely for this reason that I have recourse to the arid abstractions of mathematical signs which give quantities by subsuming all explanations, devoid of padding, and avoiding the dangerous obsession with wasting time in all the nooks and crannies of the sentence, with the finicky details of the stonemason, the jeweler, or the bootblack.

7. Words freed from punctuation will radiate out toward one another, their diverse magnetisms will intersect, in proportion to the continuing dynamism of thought. A white space, of varying length, will

show the reader the pauses or rests of the intuition of their differing lengths. Uppercase letters will inform the reader which nouns
contain a dominant analogy.

8. The destruction of the traditional sentence, the abolition of adjectives, adverbs, and punctuation will necessarily bring about the
collapse of the much vaunted stylistic unity, so that the Futurist
poet will at last be able to make use of every kind of onomatopoeia, even the most raucous, that echo the countless number of
sounds made by matter in motion.

All of these flexible intuitions, with which I bring my *Technical
Manifesto of Futurist Literature* to a close, blossomed in my mind,
one after the other, as I was fashioning my new Futurist works, of
which I here present a part of one of my most important pieces:

Battle
Weight + Stench

Noontide three-quarters flutes groans summer-heat **tumbtumb**
alarm Gargaresch crashing crackling march Jingling rucksacks rifles
hoofs nails cannon manes wheels cases Jews unleavened bread
oil-bread dirges trading-shacks whiffs polishing rheum stench cinnamon   mold ebb and flow pepper scuffle filth
swirling orange-trees-in-flower filigree poverty dice chessmen cards
jasmine + nutmeg + rose arabesque mosaic carrion stings shuffling   machine guns = shingle + undertow +
frogs Jingling rucksack rifles cannon metals atmosphere = lead + lava +
300 stinks + 50 sweet-smells paving mattress debris horseshit carrion flickflack piling up camels donkeys **tumb-tuuum** sewer
silvermakers-Souk labyrinth silk blue galabieh crimson orange trees
moucharabieh archways clambering over roadfork small-square
swarming   tannery bootblack gandouras
burnous swarming dripping sweat pouring polychrome wrapping up
protrusions crevices burrows rubble demolition carbolic-acid chalk
licefilth   Jangling rucksacks **tatatatata** hoofs
nails cannon cases lashings uniform-cloth lamb-stench cul-de-sac
leftward funnel rightward crossroads light-and-shade Turkish-bath
frying moss jonquils orange-flower nausea rose-oil-snare ammonia
claws excrement bites dog + 1,000 flies fruits dried fruits carobs
chickpeas pistachios almonds banana-diets date-palms **tumbtumb**

billy goat moldy couscous aromas saffron
tar rotten-egg wet-dog jasmine acacia sandalwood carnations matur-
ing intensity bubbling fermenting tuberose Rotting away scattering anger dying disintegrating pieces crumbs dust heroism
tatatata rifle-fire **pic pac pun pan pan**
tangerine tawny-wool machine guns tree-frogs leper-colony scabs forward rotting-meat filth sweetness sky Jingling rucksack rifles cannons
cases wheels benzoin tobacco incense aniseed village ruins burnt
amber jasmine houses disembowelments abandon terracotta-jar
tumbtumb violets shadows wells donkey-foal corpse crash penis
display garlic bromines aniseed breeze fish
sapling-spruce rosemary groceries palm-trees sand cinnamon Sun
gold balance plates lead sky silk heat padding crimson blue roasting
Sun = volcano + 3,000 flags atmosphere precision bullfight rage
surgery lamps rays scalpel flashing linen
desert clinic × 20,000 arms 20,000 feet 10,000 eyes sights flashing waiting operation sands ships-furnaces Italians Arabs 4,000 meters battalions boilers commands pistons sweat mouths furnaces
For godsake forward oil tatatata ammo-
nia > acacias violets dung roses sand flashing-mirrors everything
on-the-move arithmetic tracks obeying irony enthusiasm
buzzing sewing dunes pillows zigzags
mending feet millstones creaking sand futility machine guns = shingle +
undertow + frogs Vanguard: 200 meters bayonet-charges forward
Arterial-roads bulging heat fermenting hair armpits drum blinding
blondness breathing + rucksack 18 kilograms common sense = seesaw metal moneybox weakness: 3 shudders commands stones anger
enemy magnet lightness glory heroism Vanguards: 100 meters machine
guns rifle-fire explosion violins brass **pim pum pac pac tim tum** machine guns **tataratatarata** Vanguards:
20 meters ant-battalions spider-cavalry ford-roads islands-here-and-
there dispatch-rider-kickstands sands-revolution howitzer-demagogues
cloud-grids rifle-martyrs shrapnel-haloes multiplication addition division howitzer-subtraction grenade-cancellation streaming dripping
landslide blocks avalanche Vanguards: 3 meters
confusion to-ing-and-fro-ing sticking-together peeling-away gashes fire
rooting-out building-yards caving-in blazing panic blinding crushing
going-in emerging running mud-splashes Lives-
races heart-gluttonies bayonet-forkings biting carving-up stinking
dancing leaping anger explosion-dogs howitzer-gymnasts thunder-
trapezes explosion rose joy gut-spurters football-heads scattering-wide

Cannon 149-elephant claws-mahouts heave-ho anger conscripts slowness heaviness center charge rider method monotony trainers distance great-prize parabola × light zang-tumb-tuuum club endless Sea = lacework-emeralds-coolness-extendibility-abandon–weakness battleships-steel-brevity-order battle-Flag (meadows sky-white-hot blood) = Italy strength Italian-pride brothers wives mother sleeplessness newsboy's-cry glory domination coffee war-stories   towers cannon-virility-flights raising range-finder ecstasy **tumb-tumb** 3 seconds **tumbtumb** waves smiles laughter chic chac plaff pluff glugluglugluglu playing-hide-and-seek crystals virgins flesh jewels pearls iodine salts bromine skirts gas liquids boiling 3 seconds   **tumb-tumb** officer whiteness rangefinder crossfire dingalingaling megaphone 4 thousand-meters-high everyone-left enough everybody-still sideslipping-7-degrees rising glowing   hurtling   piercing   immensity   female-blue   deflowering relentlessness corridors cries labyrinth mattresses sighs breakthrough desert bed precision rangefinder monoplane hangar applause   monoplane = balcony-rose-wheel-drumbeat gadfly-drill > Arab-rout ox bloodbath slaughterhouse wounds refuge oasis humidity fan coolness   siesta creeping germination attempt expansion-of-vegetation I-shall-be-greener-tomorrow lets-stay-wet store-this-drop-of-water you-have-to-climb-up-3-centimeters-to-get over-20-grams-of-sand-and-3,000-grams-of-darkness milky-way-coconut-palm stars-coconuts milk dripping juice delight

The manifesto and its supplement, originally printed as four-page leaflets in French and Italian and dated May 11, 1912, and August 11, 1912, respectively, served as an introduction to the collection *I poeti futuristi* (Milan: Edizioni futuriste di "Poesia," 1912), although its theoretical position superseded the *vers libres* presented in that volume. Our translation follows the latter edition.

21

Destruction of Syntax—Untrammeled
Imagination—Words-in-Freedom

FUTURIST SENSIBILITY

My *Technical Manifesto of Futurist Literature* (May 11, 1912), in which
I invented *essentialist lyricism, Untrammeled Imagination,* and *Words-in-Freedom,* is concerned exclusively with poetic inspiration.

Philosophy, the exact sciences, politics, journalism, teaching, and
business, also seeking precise forms of expression, will still have to
make use of syntax and punctuation. And indeed, I am compelled to
make use of them myself so as to make my concept clear to you.

Futurism is based on the complete renewal of human sensibility
brought about by the great discoveries made by science. Anyone who
today uses the telegraph, the telephone, and the gramophone, the
train, the bicycle, the motorcycle, the automobile, the ocean liner, the
airship, the airplane, the film theater, the great daily newspaper (which
synthesizes the daily events of the whole world), fails to recognize that
these different forms of communication, of transport and information,
have a far-reaching effect on their psyche.

An ordinary man can be transported by a day's train journey from a
godforsaken little town, on whose deserted squares the sun, the dust,
and the wind silently amuse themselves, to a great capital city, bristling
with lights, action, and noise . . . The inhabitant of a mountain village
can each day follow with trembling anxiety the newspaper reports on
the Chinese in revolt,[1] the London and New York suffragettes, Dr. Carrel's experiments,[2] and the heroic sleighs of the polar explorers.[3] The

faint-hearted, stay-at-home citizen of any provincial town can indulge himself with the headiness of danger at the cinema, watching a big-game hunt in the Congo. He can admire Japanese athletes, Negro boxers, indefatigable American eccentrics, the most fashionable Parisian women, just by spending a dime at the music-hall. And when finally he is lying down in his bourgeois bed, he can enjoy himself listening to the costly, far-off voice of a Caruso or a Burzio.[4]

These possibilities, which have become commonplace, arouse no curiosity among superficial souls, who are utterly incapable of getting to the bottom of any new event, *like the Arabs who looked on indifferently at the first airplanes in the skies over Tripoli.*[5] For the sharp observer, however, these possibilities also represent modifications to our sensibilities, since they have created the following significant circumstances:

1. Increase in the pace of life which, today, has a quicker rhythm. A balancing act between the physical, intellectual, and emotional upon the tightrope of speed, stretched between two opposite magnetic poles. Multiple and simultaneous consciousnesses in the same individual.
2. A horror of anything old or well known. Love of the new, the unforeseen.
3. A horror of the quiet life, love of danger, and identification with everyday heroism.
4. Destruction of a sense of the *hereafter* and an increased value of the individual who wants to live his life (*vivre sa vie*), as Bonnot[6] put it.
5. Manifold increase in, and removal of, all limitations set on human ambitions and desires.
6. Precise knowledge of all those things that each one of us feels to be inaccessible and unattainable.
7. Semi-equality between man and woman, and less of an imbalance in their social rights.
8. A reduction in the value of love (whether as sentimentalism or lust), brought about by the greater sexual freedom and accessibility of women and by a universal increase in female luxuries. Let me explain: Nowadays women care more for luxuries than for love. A visit to a great dressmaking salon in the company of an obese and gouty banker friend, who pays her bills, is the perfect substitute for the most passionate of love trysts with an adored younger man. The woman finds all the mysteries of love in her choice of an

extravagant gown, in the latest fashion, something that her friends do not yet possess. A man cannot love a woman unless she has these luxuries. The lover has lost all status, while Love has lost its absolute value. An intriguing question but one which I am content merely to skim over.

9. A rethinking of the idea of patriotism, which nowadays has become the heroic idealization of the commercial, industrial, and artistic solidarity of an entire people.

10. A rethinking of the perception of war, which has become the bloody yet necessary test of a people's strength.

11. Business pursued with passion, art, and idealism. A new awareness of financial matters.

12. Man greatly extended by machines. A new awareness of machines, a fusion of the instincts with what the engine gives us and with its harnessed power.[7]

13. Sport pursued with passion, art, and idealism. The concept and love of achieving "records."

14. A new sensibility created by tourism, ocean liners, and great hotels (the annual mix of different races). Passion for cities. Abolition of distances. Derision for the *divine green silence* and for the ineffable landscape.

15. The Earth grown smaller through speed. A new awareness of the World. Let me explain: A human being successively acquires awareness of his home, his neighborhood, his town, his region, his continent. Today he possesses a sense of what the world is. He has a despicable need for knowledge about his ancestors, but also a constant desire to know what his contemporaries, in every part of the world, are up to. And as a consequence, the individual has a need to communicate with all the peoples of the world. And as a further consequence, he needs to feel himself the center, judge, and driving force of the infinite, whether explored or not. An immense expansion of our sense of humanity and an urgent need to determine, at every moment, our relations with the whole of mankind.

16. Nausea at the curved line, the spiral, and the *tourniquet*. Love of the straight line and of the tunnel. The speed of trains and automobiles, which look down from on high at cities and countryside, familiarize us with foreshortened perspectives and visual syntheses. A horror of slowness, of minutiae, of analyses and detailed explanations. Love of speed, abridgment, and synopsis: "Tell me everything, quickly, *in a couple of words!*"

17. Love of profundity and essence in all operations of the spirit.

These are some of the elements of the new Futurist sensibility that have generated our pictorial dynamism,[8] our antigraceful music[9] devoid of rhythmic framework, our Art of Noise,[10] and our Words-in-Freedom.[11]

WORDS-IN-FREEDOM

Discarding all the stupid definitions and all the confused verbalisms of the professors, I am telling you that *lyricism* is that most rare *capacity for inebriating oneself with life* and *inebriating life with our selves*. The ability to transform the muddy waters of life that envelop and flow through us, into wine. The ability to paint the world with those very specific colors of our ever-changing selves.

Now, just suppose that a friend of yours, who has this very gift of lyricism, finds himself in an area of intensified life (revolution, war, shipwreck, earthquake, etc.) and then comes, immediately after, to relate his impressions to you. Do you know what this deeply affected, lyrical friend of yours will do instinctively? . . .

He will begin by brutally destroying syntax as he talks. He won't waste time building sentences. He won't give a damn about punctuation and finding adjectives. He will ignore linguistic subtleties and nuances, and in his haste he will breathlessly fling his visual, auditory, and olfactory impressions at your nerve ends, precisely as they strike him. The vehemence of his emotional steam will burst the conduits of the sentence, the valves of punctuation, and the adjustable bolts of adjectivization. Handfuls of essential words in no conventional acceptable order. The sole purpose of the narrator is to convey all the vibrations of his being.

If this narrator, who has a gift for lyricism, also has a mind full of all kinds of ideas, he will quite inadvertently connect his sensations with the entire universe either known or intuited by him. And in order to convey the exact value and the proportions of the life he has lived, he will hurl huge networks of analogies at the world. He will thus convey life's analogical bedrock, telegraphically, that is, with the same economical rapidity that the telegraph imposes on reporters and war correspondents in their summary reports. This need for brevity corresponds not only to the laws of speed that govern us, but also to the relationships that the poet and his audiences have had over many centuries. Indeed, between the poet and his audience the same relations apply that exist between two old friends. These latter can explain themselves in half a word, with a gesture, a glance. This is why the poet's imagination has to be able to make connections between things that have no apparent connection, *without using conductor wires*, but rather condensed *Words-in-Freedom*.

THE DEATH OF FREE VERSE[12]

There have been a thousand reasons for the existence of Free Verse, but now it is its destiny to be replaced by Words-in-Freedom.[13]

As poetry and sensibility have evolved, two irremediable defects of Free Verse have become apparent:

1. Free Verse fatally urges the poet toward facile, sonorous effects, transparent tricks with mirrors, monotonous cadences, a ridiculous clanging of bells and the predictable ripostes of internal and external echoes.
2. Free Verse artificially channels the flow of lyrical emotion between the great walls of syntax and the locks of grammar. Free, intuitive inspiration, which is directed straight at the intuition of the ideal reader, thus finds itself pent up and distributed, like drinking water, to slake the thirst of all obstinate, finicky intellects.

When I speak of destroying the channels of syntax, I am being neither categorical nor systematic. In the Words-in-Freedom, imbued with my unrestrained lyricism, you will still find, here and there, traces of normal syntax and even some grammatically logical sentences. This imbalance between precision and freedom is inevitable and natural, given that poetry is, in reality, a superior life, one that is more compressed and intense than that which we live from day to day—and reflecting this, it is made up of elements that are intensely alive and some which struggle finally with death.

There is no need, therefore, to worry overmuch about these latter aspects. But we must avoid, at all costs, rhetorical flourishes and commonplaces expressed telegraphically.

UNTRAMMELED IMAGINATION

What I mean by "untrammeled imagination" is the absolute freedom of images or analogies, expressed by means of Words-in-Freedom, unencumbered by syntactical conductors or by punctuation.

> Until now writers have given themselves over to direct analogy. For example, they have compared an animal to a man or to another animal, a process which is still, more or less, the equivalent of a kind of photography. (Some authors have described a fox terrier as a very small thoroughbred, for example. Other, more avant-garde writers compared that same trembling fox terrier to a Morse transmitter. I, however, compare it to boiling water. And in this there is an *ever-widening*

ranking of analogies, of relations that are increasingly more profound and more solid, however distant their terms may be from each other.)

Analogy is nothing less than the deep love that connects objects that are distant in kind, seemingly different and hostile. Only by means of the widest possible analogies can an orchestral style, which is at one and the same time polychromatic, polyphonic, and polymorphous, embrace the life of matter.

When, in my *Battle of Tripoli,* I compared a trench, bristling with bayonets, to an orchestra, a machine gun to a femme fatale, I intuitively introduced a large part of the universe into a brief episode in African warfare.

Images are not flowers to choose and to pick in a miserly fashion, as Voltaire said. They are the very lifeblood of poetry. Poetry must be a continuous stream of new images, without which it is nothing more than anemia and greensickness.

The more wide-ranging relations the images contain, the longer they retain their power to amaze . . . (Technical Manifesto of Futurist Literature)

The untrammeled imagination and Words-in-Freedom take us right into the essence of matter. By discovering new analogies between things that are distant from, and seemingly opposed to, each other, we shall appreciate them ever more deeply. Instead of *humanizing* the animal, the vegetal, and the mineral (an outmoded system) we shall be able to *animalize, vegetalize, mineralize, electrify or liquefy style,* causing it to live something of the same life as matter itself.[14] For example, in order to render the life of a blade of grass, I say: "I shall be greener tomorrow." Through Words-in-Freedom we shall have: **Condensed metaphors.—Telegraphic images.—The sum total of all vibrations.—Nuclei of thoughts.—Open or closed fans of movement.—Glimpses of analogies.—Balance sheets of color.—The dimensions, weights, measurements, and speed of sensations.— The plunge of the essential word into the waters of sensibility, without the concentric circles that the word produces.—Repose of intuition.—Movements in double, triple, quadruple, and quintuple times.—The analytical and explanatory masts that support the bundle of intuitive wires.**

DEATH OF THE LITERARY "I"; MATTER AND MOLECULAR LIFE[15]

My *Technical Manifesto of Futurist Literature* fought against the obsession with the "I," which the poets have described, sung about, analyzed, and spewed up until the present day. To get rid of this obsessive "I," we must abandon the habit of humanizing nature by attributing human passions and concerns to animals, plants, water, stone, and clouds. Instead, we have to express the infinitesimally small things that surround us, the imperceptible, the invisible, the whiz of atoms, Brownian motion,[16] all the enthusiastic hypotheses and all the domains explored by the dark-field microscope. I'll explain what I mean: I want to introduce the infinite life of molecules into poetry, not really as scientific document but as intuitive element that must be merged, in the work of art, with the spectacle and drama of the infinitely huge, for it is this fusion that represents the total synthesis of life itself.

In order to give some assistance to the intuition of my ideal reader, I make use of italics for all those Words-in-Freedom that express the infinitesimally small and molecular life.

THE SIGNAL ADJECTIVE, BEACON ADJECTIVE, OR ATMOSPHERIC ADJECTIVE

We usually suppress the qualifying adjective wherever we find it, for it presupposes a pause in intuition or an overdetailed definition of the noun. None of this is intended categorically. We are dealing with a tendency. We need to use the adjective as little as possible and in a manner that is absolutely different from how it has been used hitherto. We have to think of adjectives as being like railway signals or traffic signals of style, which regulate the tempo, the slowing down, and the stops in the flow of the analogies. So we shall be able to assemble even as many as twenty of these signal adjectives.[17]

I use the term signal adjective, beacon adjective, or atmospheric adjective for adjectives, which are separated from the noun, which are isolated in parentheses, which have become a kind of absolute noun, and are thus more comprehensive and more powerful than the normal one.

The signal adjective or beacon adjective, suspended on high in the transparent cage of the parenthesis, projects its rotating light far and wide.

The outline of this adjective frays at the edges and is scattered all about, illuminating, impregnating, and enveloping a whole area of Words-in-Freedom. If, for example, in an agglomeration of Words-in-Freedom that describes a sea voyage, I place the following signal adjectives in parentheses: (calm blue methodical regular-in-its-habits), not only is the sea *calm blue methodical regular-in-its-habits*, but the ship, its engines, its passengers, what I am doing, and my very spirit are *calm blue methodical and regular-in-their-habits*.

THE VERB IN THE INFINITIVE

In this case, too, my statements are not categorical. I maintain, however, that in a lyricism which is pugnacious and dynamic, the verb in the infinitive will be indispensable since, being round as a wheel and, like the wheel, adaptable to all carriages in the train of analogies, it constitutes the very speed of the style.

The verb in the infinitive, by its very nature, disallows the existence of the sentence and prevents the style from coming to a halt and settling down at a given point. While **the verb in the infinitive is round** and smooth-running like a wheel, the other moods and tenses of the verb are triangular or square or oval.

ONOMATOPOEIA AND MATHEMATICAL SIGNS

When I said that "we must spit every day on the *Altar of Art*,"[18] I urged the Futurists to free lyricism from a solemn atmosphere, full of penitence and incense, that is habitually called Art with a capital *A*. This Art with a capital *A* is in fact the clericalism of the creative spirit.[19] And it was for this reason that I encouraged the Futurists to destroy and mock the garlands and palms and haloes, the precious cornices, stoles, and embellishments, all the historical garb and Romantic bric-a-brac that make up a great part of the poetry produced up to now. In its place I proposed a swift lyricism, brutal and immediate, a lyricism which to all our predecessors would have seemed antipoetical, a telegraphic lyricism that bears not the slightest hint of books but, as much as possible, the taste of life. And stemming from this is the courageous introduction of onomatopoeic arrangements to render all the noises and sounds—even the most raucous—of modern life.

Onomatopoeia, which has the effect of enlivening lyricism with rough, raw elements of reality, was used in poetry (from Aristophanes to Pascoli) more or less timidly. We Futurists are initiating a bold and continuous use of onomatopoeia. It doesn't have to be systematic. For example, my "Adrianopolis Siege-Orchestra" and my "Battle Weight + Stench"[20] required a lot of onomatopoeic arrangements. Ever with the intention of providing the highest number of vibrations and a deeper synthesis of life, we are abolishing all stylistic links, all the polished clasps with which traditional poets connect the images in their sentences. Instead, we make use of the briefest or anonymous mathematical and musical signs, and between brackets we place indicators such as: (quickly) (more quickly) (slowing down) (two time) to regulate the speed of the style. These brackets can also cut a word or an onomatopoeic arrangement in two.

TYPOGRAPHICAL REVOLUTION[21]

I am initiating a typographical revolution, directed against the beastly, nauseating concept of the book[22] of verse, in the traditional, D'Annunzian manner, against the handmade paper of the seventeenth century, decorated with galleys, Minervas, and Apollos, with initial letters in red with fancy squiggles, vegetables, mythic missal ribbons, epigraphs, and Roman numerals. The book must be the Futurist expression of our Futurist thought. And this is not all. My revolution is directed against the so-called typographical harmony of the page, which contradicts the ebb and flow, the leaps and bounds of style that surge over the page. We shall therefore use *three or four different colors of ink* on a single page, and should we think it necessary, as many as twenty different typographical characters. For example: italic for a series of like or swift sensations, *bold Roman characters* for violent onomatopoeias, and so on. With this typographical revolution and this multicolored variety of characters, my purpose is to double the expressive power of words.[23]

I am at war with the precious, ornamental aesthetics of Mallarmé and his quest for the rare word, for the unique, irreplaceable, elegant, evocative, and exquisite adjective. I don't want to evoke an idea or a sensation with these traditionalist charms or affectations, I want to seize them roughly and hurl them straight in the reader's face.

Moreover, with this typographical revolution, I am at war with Mallarmé's static ideal,[24] for it allows me to impose on words (already free, dynamic and torpedolike) every kind of speed—that of the stars, the clouds, the airplanes, the trains, the waves, the explosives, the flecks of sea spray, the molecules, and the atoms.

And in this way, I achieve the fourth principle of my *Foundation and Manifesto of Futurism* (February 20, 1909): "We assert that the magnificence of the world is enriched with a new beauty, the beauty of speed."

MULTILINEAR LYRICISM[25]

Furthermore, I have devised a *multilinear lyricism* with which I succeed in obtaining that lyrical simultaneity that obsesses the Futurist painters as well; *multilinear lyricism*, by means of which I am convinced I obtain the most complex lyrical simultaneities.

The poet hastily sets down on several parallel lines a number of strings of colors, sounds, smells, noises, weights, thicknesses, and analogies. One of these lines will, for example, be olfactory, another musical, and yet another pictorial.

Let's just suppose that the string of pictorial analogies dominates other strings of sensations and analogies. In this case, it will be printed in larger characters than those of the second and third lines (one of which contains, for example, the string of musical sensations and analogies, while the other has that of olfactory sensations and analogies).

On a page containing many batches of sensations and analogies, each one of which is made up of three or four lines, the series of pictorial sensations and analogies (printed in large characters) will take the first line of the first batch and will continue (always with the same size characters) as first line of all subsequent batches.

The series of musical sensations and analogies (second line), being less important than the chain of pictorial sensations and analogies (first line), but more important than that of the olfactory sensations and analogies (third line) will be printed in characters that are not as big as those of the first line, though bigger than those in the third line.

Example, taken from the description of a bridge built by the Bulgarians and destroyed by the Turks under a hail of bullets:

CHOPPING RED RED STREAKED SHAKING ENDLESS
hurrrraaaaaah   hurrrraaaaah
victory   victory   joy   joy   revenge   massacre   on and on
tatatatatatatatatatatatatatatatatata
THE END   DESPERATION   LOST NOTHING TO BE DONE
   ABOUT IT   USELESS
immerse yourself   coolness   spread out   open up   going soft   spread out
boom bangbang   whoosh   whoosh   frrrrr
horse-shit   piss   bidet   smell of ammonia   smell of typography

SUNLIGHT   REPEATEDLY   20,000   SHOTS   A   MINUTE
ughghghghghghahahahah
joy   joy   joy   joy   again   again   revenge
tatatatatatatatatatatatatata
START AGAIN   USELESS   USELESS   WE HAVEN'T THE
   EQUIPMENT
you want   to swim   fiber   2 millimeters
whoosh   whoosh   whoosh   splatsplat   glughhh
ammonia smell   smell of a mature woman   armpits   like tubers   corpse

None of these most significant, conclusive innovations will look *new* to that herd of provincial critics, stuffed full—as they are—with Nordic culture, and who admire, as a matter of course, anything that comes from our past or from abroad, and happily dismiss the creative genius that is exploding under their very noses in Italy.

The caution and ignorance of the ostrich in a revolution. These critics will fall over themselves to attribute Words-in-Freedom, the beacon adjective, and multilinear lyricism to Mallarmé, Verlaine, or maybe even to Dante Alighieri, yet they'll deny they were invented by the Italian Futurists. These disparaging super-imbeciles should understand, once and for all, that Italians, in this day and age, are a race of innovative artists. If, for the moment, genius and creativity spring only from the Futurist group, that is owing to the fact that, with a network of violence and heroism, we have established about ourselves an insurmountable barrier against their epidemic of imbecility.

For quite some time past, their slimy tongues would have tired our wandering feet, if our journal had been called LACERBEN (*Halbmonatsschrift für Kultur und die Künste*)[26] and if our names had been: Buzzinsky, Folgorinescu, Carratzaski, Jean Papin, So-Fi-kio, Boccionoff, François B. Pratellin, Mazza-bey, Govonyndsen, Roussoleaux, Palatzewsky, Ballah-ben-Room, Severinson, Don Francisco Cangiulleiros, Arturo d'Albaceras, Dynams Correnterbury, Liberus d'Hautmer, Mancelle-Frontin, Van den Kaväcchiolberg, Efféten von Mähawrynettkëns.[27]—And they would say: "Why isn't anyone translating these foreign geniuses, so that we can get to know them? Our poor country! I'm going to go and study in Germany for a couple of years."

FREE EXPRESSIVE ORTHOGRAPHY

The historical necessity of free expressive orthography is demonstrated by the successive revolutions that have continued to free the lyrical power of the human race from shackles and from regulations.

1. Indeed, poets began by channeling their lyrical intoxication into a series of equal breaths with emphases, echoes, chimes, or predetermined rhymes at fixed distances (**traditional prosody**). Poets later varied these different breaths, measured out originally by the lungs of their predecessors, in more liberal ways.
2. Later still, poets felt that different moments of their lyrical rapture should create appropriate pauses of widely varying and unforeseen lengths, with total freedom with regard to accentuation. So they arrived at **Free Verse**, a form that nonetheless always preserved the syntactical order of their words, so that the lyrical enchantment could pour down into the spirit of the listener, through the logical channel of the syntax.

3. Today, we no longer desire that the lyrical rapture arranges words syntactically prior to hurling them forth with pauses we have invented, besides which, we have **Words-in-Freedom**. Moreover, our lyrical intensity must be free to dismantle and remake words, cutting them in half, extending and reinforcing their centers or their extremities, increasing or reducing the number of their vowels and consonants. In this way, we shall have the *new orthography* that I call *freely expressive*. This instinctive transformation of words is in keeping with our natural tendency toward onomatopoeia. It little matters if the modified word becomes ambiguous. It will blend with the onomatopoeic orchestration or compendium of noises, and will soon give us the opportunity of reaching a *psychic onomatopoeic orchestration*, the resonant yet abstract expression of an emotion or of pure thought. But some complain that my *Words-in-Freedom*, my untrammeled imagination, require a special sort of recitation, otherwise they run the risk of not being understood. Although I don't give a damn whether the masses understand it or not, my response is that the number of Futurist speech-makers is fast increasing,[28] and indeed, even the traditional, much loved poem also requires a special kind of recitation if it is to be fully appreciated.

This text, dated May 11, 1913, was first published in *Lacerba* on June 15, 1913, with addenda on November 15, 1913, and reprinted in various anthologies of Futurist manifestos. A French version was presented as a lecture entitled "Imagination sans fils et les mots en liberté," at the opening of a Boccioni exhibition at the Galerie Boëtie in Paris (June 22, 1913). The translation here has been arranged in the manner in which it was printed in *I manifesti del futurismo* (1914), but including the addenda from *Lacerba* of November 15, 1913.

22

⁓

Down with the Tango and Parsifal!

A circular letter to some cosmopolitan women friends
who give tango tea-dances and who Parsifalize themselves

A year ago I responded to an investigation being carried out by *Gil Blas*, exposing the weakening, poisoning effects of the tango. This epidemic of swaying back and forth is gradually spreading worldwide,[1] and is threatening to infect all races, turning them into jelly. And so, once again, we see that we have to hurl ourselves against the imbecility of fashion and head off this sheeplike current of snobbism.

Monotony of seductive, swaying hips, between the flashing eyes and Spanish daggers of de Musset, Hugo, and Gautier;[2] industrialized packaging of Baudelaire; *Fleurs du mal* swaying in the taverns of Jean Lorrain to be picked by impotent "voyeurs" such as Huysmans or by inverts like Oscar Wilde.[3] The last manic yearnings of a sentimental, decadent, paralyzing Romanticism for the cardboard cut-out femme fatale.

Ungainliness of the English and German tangos, mechanized desires, and jerking by bones and evening suits that do not know how to express their sensibilities. Copied from the Parisian and Italian tangos, mollusks in pairs, wild felinity of the Argentine race, only to arrive at a stupidly domesticated, drugged, and tarted-up version of it.[4]

Possessing a woman isn't rubbing yourself up against her but penetrating her. Barbarian!

One knee between her thighs? Come on, you need two! Barbarian!

Fine, yes, we are barbarians! Down with the tango and its cadenced swoons. Are you really convinced there's a lot of pleasure to be had, gazing into each other's mouths and ecstatically examining each other's teeth, like a pair of hallucinating dentists? Jerk . . . Swoop . . . So, do

you really find pleasure in desperately bending over each other, uncork-
ing your love lusts, each in turn, without ever quite getting there? . . .
or staring at the toes of your shoes, like hypnotized cobblers? . . . O
dearest heart, do you really take a size 35? . . . What lovely shoes you're
wearing, my dreamchild! . . . And you toooo! . . .⁵

Tristan and Isolde, holding back their suffering, so as to excite King
Marke. Love in dribbles. Sexual anguish in miniature. Candy floss of
desire. Lechery in public. Delirium tremens. Delirious hands and feet.
Miming coitus for the camera lens. A masturbated waltz. God help us!
Away with these niceties of the skin! Let's have the brutality of violent
possession and the fine fury of a muscular dance that's uplifting and invigorating.

Tango, the rolling and pitching of sailing ships that have dropped
their anchors in the uttermost depths of idiocy. Tango, the rolling and
pitching of sailing ships awash with tenderness and lunar silliness.
Tango, tango, tossing about enough to make you vomit. Tango, the
slowly unfolding funeral of dead sex! We're not talking about religion,
that's for sure, nor morals, nor modesty! These three words have no
meaning for us! We shout out *To Hell with the tango!* For the sake of
our Health, our Strength, our Will, and our Virility.

If the tango is bad enough, *Parsifal* is even worse, as it inoculates the
dancers, swaying to and fro, bored and listless, with an incurable musical neurasthenia.⁶

How can we avoid *Parsifal*, with its downpours, its puddles, and its
floods of mystical tears? *Parsifal* is a systematic devaluation of life! A
factory cooperative of sadness and despair. Tuneless stretching and
straining for weak stomachs. Poor digestion and heavy breathing of
forty-year-old virgins. Whining of flabby and constipated old priests.
Wholesaling and retailing of bad consciences and a stylish effeminacy
for snobs. Blood deficiency, feebleness of the loins, hysteria, anemia,
and greensickness. Prostration, brutalization, and violation of Mankind.
Ridiculous scraping of failed, mutilated notes. Snoring of drunken
organs sprawling in the vomit of foul-tasting leitmotifs. False tears
and pearls flaunted by a Mary Magdalene with a plunging neckline
more suited to Maxim's.⁷ Polyphonic pus from Amfortas's festering
scabs. Worn-out wailings of the Knights of the Holy Grail. Nonsensical Satanism of Kundry⁸ . . . Antediluvianism! Antediluvianism! . . .
Enough of it!⁹

Kings and queens of snobbism, be aware that you owe absolute obedience to us, to the Futurists, the living innovators! So leave the corpse
of Wagner, the innovator of fifty years back, to the bestial lusts of his

devotees. His work has already been surpassed by Debussy,[10] by Strauss, and by our own Futurist, Pratella, and counts for nothing! You helped us defend him when he needed it. We will teach you to love and defend something living, dear, sheeplike slaves of snobbism.

And what's more, you're forgetting *the ultimate argument, the only one that's likely to persuade you*; adoring Wagner and *Parsifal* nowadays, when the latter is playing everywhere, but especially in the provinces . . . and giving tea-tango dances like all the fine bourgeoisie the world over. Time to move on! These things **are no longer chic!**

You're no longer *à la mode*. Come on! Get a move on! Abandon the limp dance and the moaning organs, and follow the Futurists! We have other pleasures to offer you, and much more fashionable . . . Because—and I'll say it again—the Tango and *Parsifal* ARE NO LONGER CHIC!

This letter was first published as a two-page leaflet, dated January 11, 1914, and in *Lacerba* on January 15, 1914. A French broadsheet version, entitled *A bas le Tango et* Parsifal! *Lettre futuriste circulaire à quelques amies cosmopolites qui donnent des thès-tango et se parsifalisent* (Milan: Direction du Mouvement Futuriste), is dated January 11, 1914. The Italian text was reprinted with a few textual variations in *I manifesti del futurismo* (1919).

23

⚶

Geometrical and Mechanical Splendor
and Sensitivity Toward Numbers

GEOMETRICAL AND MECHANICAL SPLENDOR IN WORDS-IN-FREEDOM
We have already attended to the grotesque funeral of conventional
Beauty (Romantic, Symbolist, and Decadent), whose chief characteristics were memory, nostalgia, the mists of legend gathered through re-
moteness in time, fascination with the exotic produced by distance in
space, the picturesque, the imprecise, the pastoral, solitude in the
wilderness, every kind of disorder, shadows at twilight, decay, weariness, the ragged vestiges of bygone days, crumbling ruins, mildew, a
taste for putrefaction, pessimism, tuberculosis, suicide, flirting with
pain, an aesthetic of failure, adoration of death.

Out of the chaos of new, conflicting sensibilities, a new beauty
is born this day, which we Futurists will substitute for what went before and which I name **GEOMETRICAL AND MECHANICAL
SPLENDOR**.

Its essential characteristics are: a healthy forgetfulness, hope, desire,
unbridled strength, speed, light, the will, order, discipline, method; a
feeling for the great city; an aggressive optimism stemming from a passion for sport and the toning of muscles; untrammeled imagination,
being here, there, and everywhere, brevity and simultaneity derived
from tourism, business, and journalism; a passion for success, a pioneering instinct for breaking records, the enthusiastic emulation of
electricity and machines; an essential conciseness and compactness;
the sweet precision of machinery and of well-oiled thought; the harmony of energies converging in one victorious path.[1]

My Futurist senses became aware of this *geometrical splendor*, for the first time, on the bridge of a Dreadnought.[2] The speed of the ship, the range of its guns, set high up on the quarterdeck, in that liberating air of a likely war, and that strange vitality of orders transmitted by the admiral, becoming autonomous and dehumanized through the caprice, lack of patience, and failures of steel and copper wire. All of these things radiated *geometrical and mechanical splendor*. I heard the lyrical drive of electricity passing through the armor-plating of its four turrets, descending by way of metal tubes to the powder magazine, drawing its howitzers as far as the breech, as far as its protruding barrels. Raise sights, point, up, flash, automatic recoil, a very personal launching of the shell, impact, crash, stench of rotten eggs, sewer gas, rust, ammonia, and so on. This new drama, which is full of unforeseen Futurist possibilities and geometrical splendor, is for us a hundred thousand times more interesting than human psychology, with its very limited permutations (ambition, love, greed, nostalgia, friendship, betrayal) and its habitual three or four facial impressions.

Great human masses, a sea of protesting arms and faces, can sometimes give us a frisson. But we prefer, by far, that great feeling of solidarity with an obliging motor that is utterly reliable and well regulated. Nothing is more beautiful than a great, humming electric power station that holds water pressure as high as a chain of mountains and electric power as vast as the horizon, compressed into its four distribution columns, bristling with meters, control panels, and shining levers. These panels are our sole models for poetry. Their precursors are gymnasts and tightrope walkers,[3] who in the swelling, relaxation, and pulsating rhythm of their muscles demonstrate the sparkling perfection of precision instruments, and the geometrical splendor that we wish to attain in poetry through our Words-in-Freedom.

1. We are systematically destroying the literary "I"[4] so that it is dispersed throughout the universal flux, and we are coming to the expression of the infinitesimally small and molecular agitation. E.g., the meteoric shifting of molecules in the hole produced by a howitzer (see the final part of "Fort Cheittam-Tépé" in my novel *Zang Tumb Tumb*). Thus the poetry of cosmic forces replaces that of mankind.

   WE ARE ABOLISHING THE AGE-OLD VALUES (romantic, sentimental, and Christian) **OF NARRATIVE**, by virtue of which the importance of a wound, sustained in battle, was greatly exaggerated in comparison with the weapons of destruction, strategic positions, and atmospheric conditions. In *Zang Tumb Tumb* I describe the death by firing squad of a Bulgarian traitor, using only a few Words-in-Freedom, while I greatly extend a discussion between two Turkish generals about the range of their guns and the enemy's cannon. Indeed, I observed in the De Suni battery, at Sidi-Messri, in October 1911,[5] how the bright, insistent volley of a cannon, made red-hot by the sun and by an increased rate of firing, makes the spectacle of mangled, dying human flesh almost negligible.

2. On many occasions I have shown how the noun, worn out by too much contact with, or from the weight of, Decadent, Parnassian[6] adjectives, regains its absolute value and expressive force when it is stripped and isolated. With regard to naked nouns, I distinguish between the **ELEMENTARY NOUN** and the **SYNTHESIS-IN-MOTION NOUN** (or knot of nouns). This distinction, which is by no means absolute, springs from an intuition which is well nigh impossible to identify. Following a flexible, all-inclusive analogy, I see every noun as a **vehicle** or as a belt set in motion by the verb in the infinitive.

3. With the exception of the need for contrasts or a change of rhythm, the different moods and tenses of the verb must be abolished since they turn the verb into a rickety old wheel which adapts to the roughness of the country roads, but is unable to turn quickly on a smooth road. On the other hand, **THE VERB IN THE INFINITIVE IS THE ACTUAL DRIVING FORCE OF THE NEW LYRICISM**, being as smooth-running as the wheels of a train or the propeller of an airplane.

In the forward leap of hope and will, the different moods and tenses of the verb express a prudent yet reassuring pessimism; a narrow, episodic, and casual egotism; an upper and lower limit of strength and weariness, of desire, delusion, and complete rest. The verb in the infinitive expresses optimism itself, total generosity and the delirium of Becoming. When I say "to run," what is the subject of this verb? Everyone and everything, that is, a universal profusion of life that flows around us and of which we are a conscious particle, as, for example, at the end of "Salone d'albergo" (Hotel Lounge) by the free-wording poet Folgore.[7] The verb in the infinitive is the passion of the "I" that gives itself up to the becoming of *all things*, a heroic continuum, unconcerned about the effort and the joy of action. Verb in the infinitive = divinity of action.

4. Using one or more adjectives isolated between parentheses or set beside Words-in-Freedom behind a perpendicular line (or between curly brackets), one can give the sense of the different atmospheres of a story and the tones that govern it. **THESE ATMOSPHERIC-ADJECTIVES OR TONE-ADJECTIVES CANNOT BE REPLACED BY NOUNS.** These are principles arrived at intuitively and difficult to demonstrate.[8] However, I believe that by isolating, for example, the noun "cruelty" (or, in the description of a massacre, placing it between curly brackets), one will be imbued with a cruel frame of mind that is fixed and firm in sharp outline. However, if I place the adjective "cruel" in parentheses or between curly brackets, I turn it into an atmospheric-adjective or tone-adjective that will envelop the entire description of the massacre without arresting the flow of the Words-in-Freedom.

5. Despite the deftest contortions, the syntactical sentence always implied a scientific, photographic outlook that was absolutely contrary to the laws that govern the emotions. **BY USING WORDS-IN-FREEDOM THIS PERSPECTIVE IS DESTROYED** and we arrive naturally at a many-sided emotional perspective (e.g. *Uomo* + *montagna* + *vallata* ["Man + Mountain + Valley"] by the free-word poet Boccioni).[9]

6. With Words-in-Freedom, we sometimes **CREATE SYNOPTIC TABLES OF LYRICAL VALUES**, which make it possible for us, when reading, to follow many different currents of intersecting or parallel sense impressions at the same time. These synoptic tables must not be thought of as an end in themselves but as a means of increasing the expressive lyrical force. We have therefore to avoid attempting pictorial effects, or amusing ourselves by playing around with intersecting lines or unusual typographical distortions.

In Words-in-Freedom we must totally eradicate everything that does not aspire to express the fleeting, mysterious Futurist sensibility by means of this most innovative geometrical and mechanical splendor. The free-wording poet Cangiullo in "Fumatori IIᵃ" (Second-Class Smokers Carriage) was very successful in suggesting the long, monotonous flights of fancy and the outward spreading of smoke-boredom experienced on a long train journey, with this **TYPOGRAPHICALLY DESIGNED IMAGE**:[10]

In their continuous attempts at expression through maximum force and depth, Words-in-Freedom are naturally transformed into **AUTO-ILLUSTRATIONS** by means of freely expressive orthographical and typographical forms, the synoptic tables of lyrical values, and typographically shaped analogies, as for example the typographically designed balloon in my *Zang Tumb Tumb*.[11] As soon as this higher form of expression is achieved, Words-in-Freedom go back to their normal, habitual flow. Moreover, the synoptic tables of values are the foundations of criticism using Words-in-Freedom (see, for example, "Bilancio 1910–1913" [Balance Sheet 1910–1913] by the free-wording poet Carrà).[12]

7. **FREELY EXPRESSIVE ORTHOGRAPHY AND TYPOGRAPHY ALSO HAVE THE FUNCTION OF RENDERING THE FACIAL EXPRESSIONS AND OTHER GESTURES OF THE NARRATOR.**

In this way, Words-in-Freedom arrive at making use of (and expressing perfectly) all those qualities of communicative effusiveness and casual brilliance that are characteristic of the southern races. This energy stemming from a variety of tones, from vocal and facial expressions, hitherto to be found only among the most moving tenors or brilliant conversationalists, find their natural expression in the various sizes of typographical characters that reproduce facial grimaces and the incisive, clear-cut power of our gestures. Thus, Words-in-Freedom become the lyrical, transfiguring extension of our animal magnetism.

ABSTRACT ONOMATOPOEIA AND SENSITIVITY TOWARD NUMBERS

8. Our growing love for matter, the will to penetrate it and to know its vibrations, the physical bonds that tie us to machines, urge us to **THE USE OF ONOMATOPOEIA.**

Sound, which results from the rubbing together or the collision of solids, liquids, or gases at speed, requires that onomatopoeia, the reproduction of sound, be one of the most dynamic elements in poetry. And as such, onomatopoeia can take the place of the verb in the infinitive, particularly if it is set against one or more other onomatopoeias. (E.g., the onomatopoeic *tatatata* of machine guns opposing the *urrrraaaah* of the Turks, at the end of the "Ponte" [Bridge] chapter in my *Zang Tumb Tumb*.)

The brevity of the onomatopoeic words in this case allows us the use of the most versatile interweaving of diverse rhythms. These would lose part of their speed if they were to be expressed more abstractly, with more detailed development, that is, without the mediation of onomatopoeia. There are different sorts of onomatopoeia.

(a) **ONOMATOPOEIA THAT IS DIRECT, IMITATIVE, EL-EMENTARY, AND REALISTIC,** which serves to enrich poetry with a brutal reality and stops it becoming too abstract and arty. (E.g., *pic pac pum*, rifle-fire.) In my "Contrabbando di guerra" (War Contraband), in *Zang Tumb Tumb*, the screeching onomatopoeia *ssiiiiii* reproduces the whistle of a tugboat on the river Meuse and is followed by the muted *ffiiiiiffiiiiii*, echoing from the farther bank. These two instances of onomatopoeia meant I didn't have to describe the width of the river, for that is, in fact, defined by the contrast between the two consonants *s* and *f*.

(b) **ONOMATOPOEIA THAT IS INDIRECT, COMPLEX, AND ANALOGICAL.** E.g., in my poem "Dune,"[13] the onomatopoeic *dum-dum-dum-dum* expresses the revolving sound of the African sun and the great orange mass of the sky, creating a relationship between sensations of weight, heat, color, scent, and sound. Another example is the onomatopoeic *stridionla stridionla stridionlaire*, which is repeated in the first canto of my epic poem, *La Conquête des étoiles*,[14] which establishes an analogy between the clashing of great swords and the angry surging of the waves, before the onset of a great battle of waters in a storm.

(c) **ABSTRACT ONOMATOPOEIA** is the expression through sound of the most complex and mysterious of our sensibilities, even though we are not conscious of them. (E.g., in my poem "Dune," the abstract onomatopoeia *ran ran ran* corresponds to no sound in nature or machinery, but expresses rather a state of mind.)

(d) **PSYCHIC ONOMATOPOEIC ARRANGEMENT**—that is, the fusion of two or three abstract onomatopoeic elements.

9. My love of precision and concentrated brevity have naturally given me a taste for numbers, which live and breathe on the page like living beings in our new **NUMERICAL SENSIBILITY**. For example, instead of saying, as would more or less all traditional writers, "a deep, far-reaching tolling of bells" (an imprecise and therefore ineffectual observation), or else, as would an intelligent countryman, "you can hear this bell from such and such a village or such and such another" (a more precise and therefore more effective observation), with intuitive precision, I seize on the powerful sound of the reverberation, and establish its extent by writing, "bell tolling extent 20 square kilometers." I thereby suggest a whole vibrant horizon and a number of distant beings who are listening to the same bells. I escape from the imprecise, the banal, and take hold of reality through an act of will, which subjugates and transforms, in an original manner, the sound of the vibrating metal.

The mathematical symbols $+ - \times =$ can bring about some wonderful syntheses and, in the abstract simplicity of their impersonal mechanisms, they contribute to the creation of geometrical and mechanical splendor. For example, it would have required at least a whole page of description to portray this vast, complex panorama of battle that I have instead conveyed through this supreme lyrical equation: "horizon = gimlet   most piercing some sun + 5 triangular shadows (1 kilometer to one side) + 3 diamond shapes of rosy light + 5 bits of hills + 30 columns of smoke + 23 blazes."

I use the $\times$ to convey pauses for searching thoughts. Thus I eliminate the question mark which fixed its air of doubt too arbitrarily on only one aspect of consciousness. With the mathematical $\times$, the pause for doubt is immediately extended over the entire assembly of Words-in-Freedom.

In the same intuitive way, among the Words-in-Freedom, I introduce numbers that have no direct meaning or value but that (being directed by their sounds and by the eye toward our numerical sensibilities) express the varying mystical intensities of matter and the unfailing reactions of our sensibilities.

Critical Writings

I create some real theorems or lyrical equations, introducing numbers that are chosen intuitively and placed in the very center of a word, with a certain number of $+ - \times =$. I articulate the thickness, the prominence, and the volume of the things that the word must express. The arrangement $+ - + - + + \times$, for example, serves the purpose of communicating the changes and the increase in speed of a motorcar. The arrangement $+ + + + +$ has the purpose of bundling similar (equal) sensations together. (E.g., "the fecal stench of dysentery + the honeylike smell of plague sweat + the stink of ammonia etc.," in "Treno di soldati ammalati" [A Trainload of Sick Soldiers] in my *Zang Tumb Tumb*.)

Thus for Mallarmé's "ciel antérieur où fleurit la beauté,"[15] we substitute geometrical and mechanical splendor and the numerical sensibility of Words-in-Freedom.

This manifesto appeared in two installments in *Lacerba*, March 15, and April 1, 1914. The French edition has a colophon, "Milan Direction du Mouvement Futuriste 11 Mars 1914," and a four-page leaflet of the Italian edition is dated March 18, 1914. The manifesto was reprinted many times and exercised profound influence, not only on the mechanical art of the second wave of Futurism, in the 1920s, but also outside Italy. In *Spagna veloce e toro futurista* (1931) the manifesto is entitled "Geometric Splendor and the Aesthetics of the Machine." The last reprint I am aware of was in Maria Goretti's *Poesia della macchina* (Rome: Edizioni futuriste della "Poesia," 1942). The text translated here follows *I manifesti del futurismo* (1919).

24

༄

On the Subject of Futurism:
An Interview with La diana

Interviewer: Many people have already exclaimed, and others have often repeated it, that Futurism is not to be taken seriously.

And that's why the Futurist serate, which should be the most tranquil and peaceful of discussions, from which truth should clearly emerge, frequently degenerate into the most uncouth demonstrations of the ignorant and illiterate, for whom only the vilest of epithets are fitting.

The Futurists relish the struggle, it being their first principle. What is certain, however, is that they do not care for the base, abusive hostility of a brainless, pig-headed public, of a drunken mob incapable of either reason or reflection, or indeed, of thinking! Their reply to the mob—and in this they are surely right!—is a kick up the backside. They think of these people, who interrupt their serate, in the same way as those stupid dogs that snarl at sprightly thoroughbreds, out of a poisonous envy, and treat them in exactly the same way.

They love war, which stimulates all latent energies. They desire action, which represents life. They are against dreaming, in which all desires sleep and even the strongest organisms rot, thought becomes fossilized, and the will is destroyed.

"The Futurist *serate*," F. T. *Marinetti wrote to me in one of his most recent letters,* "mean precisely **the violent incursion of life into art**. Artists, **alive** at last, and no longer up in their ivory towers, despising aestheticism, asking to participate, like workmen or soldiers, in the progress of the world."

This, in few words, is the essence of Futurism. Yet I am tempted to quote further bits from other of his letters. The public and the critics should put aside the somewhat uncivilized, discourteous attitudes they reserve for all that pertains to Futurism, and view it with all that calm and serenity which are the foremost, essential qualities of the judge.

"Futurism," *F. T. Marinetti tells me,* "which was begun six years ago by me and my friends, Boccioni, Carrà, and Russolo, sought to modernize art, to snatch it away from the museums and libraries, to liberate it from the professors and the opportunists, to enrich it with **vigorous action**."

Thus Futurism is not fighting for an old, amateurish, revolutionary ideal with no practical goals, as is, unfortunately, the journal Lacerba, *which, mistakenly, the majority think of as Marinetti's mouthpiece.*[1]

"*Lacerba*, which was born traditionalist, with these ridiculous, revolutionary attitudes (**individualism, egoism, intellectual anarchy**), became Futurist for twenty or so issues as a result of our efforts, but then went back to being traditionalist and ineffectual, as it is now. I'll explain what I mean. Nothing is more absurd than battling against Germanism in order to defend Latin culture. (And this happens through the collaboration of traditionalists like Prezzolini,[2] who, after having been a systematic denigrator of Italy, of the army, of war and irredentism, writes articles **like those of Salvemini**[3] **and against the Libyan war, to attack Austria instead**.) We oppose Germanism as we have always opposed it, in that it represents cultural, academic, and archaeological obsessiveness.

"And Germanism must be opposed in order to defend **the imaginative spontaneity of Italian creative genius**, which has everything to fear from libraries, museums, and professors. Our allies Papini and Soffici,[4] who were attracted a couple of years ago by the instinctive, purely creative, forward drive of my great Futurist friends, Boccioni,

Carrà, Russolo, Buzzi, Pratella, and Govoni, left the stifling atmosphere of *La voce* behind, for a while, to join us. But their Futurism was not in their blood, it was still crammed full of an undigested culture, which revealed itself in the shape of a dilettantish sort of revolutionism, destroying for the sake of destroying, in writing today, "We Don't Give a Damn about Politics," then the day after tomorrow, "War against Austria!,"[5] and in stuffing an article full of obscenities (a boorishness that has always been typical of Tuscany **and which has nothing in common with Futurism**, which is exact in its expression, as in my much maligned *Mafarka the Futurist* and my *King Guzzle*)."[6]

So here, dear critics, with your double-thick lenses and fine-tuned sensibilities, here is the best, the most authoritative proof that Futurism, which was born and grew healthy and strong in the minds of strong young men, is not concerned with trivialities nor with the delirium of sick minds! And if you tell me that Marinetti himself sometimes uses foul language in his disgusting dithyrambs, recited between the stage and "the gods" in every Futurist serata, I shall simply observe that in such cases, he is severely provoked by a public that deserves no better treatment.

"We fight ferociously against the critics, useless intermediaries or dangerous exploiters that they are, **and not against the public** whom we wish to improve, to raise to a comprehension of life that is more elevated and profound, more powerful and succinct, more original and forthright. The public have often misunderstood us. That is only natural, considering the superficial nonsense of the common clichés and professorial idiocies that pass for ideas among them. We are not pessimistic, however. The public will understand us, but it will take time and, especially, boundless energy. This latter we possess. The mobs that have hissed us, shown their contempt and showered us with vegetables, have also—much against their wills—admired our artists' courageous, selfless, heroic struggle to reinvigorate, rejuvenate, and quicken the genius of the Italian people. The great mass of new ideas that we have developed is rolling about in the mud and over rocks, shoved and soiled by the hands of innumerable unheeding urchins. And these latter, making fun of the strange colors which cover that huge, unexpected toy, are involuntarily affected by its glowing, magnetic content . . .

"To everyone we say: Let's get a move on, ever more quickly, let's not hold back, let's not dream, let us exclude all who are skeptical. Let us work for the people of Italy, to free them from the cult of the past, and to fashion with them an Italy that is more brilliant, more heroic, and more passionate about what is modern. **For Italy above all else**, for we are all too aware of the limitations of our own strengths, which are appropriate to the development of our race within the geographical confines that destiny has allotted us. The impact of Futurism on the world at large will occur through the example and the travails of an Italy which has become Futurist!"

This is what the traditionalists would call a program. But F. T. Marinetti shies away from all limitations and the channeling of action.

"We believe, with Bergson," *he says*, "that 'la vie déborde l'intelligence,'⁷ which is to say that it overflows, swamps and suffocates the infinitesimally small faculty of intelligence. One cannot intuit even the immediate future other than by involving oneself *totally* in the living of one's life. From this stems our violent, besetting love of action. We are the Futurists of **tomorrow**, not of **the day after tomorrow**. We do have some notion of where we are going, but we systematically banish these visions from our brain, since they are almost always unhealthy and almost invariably the product of a depressed frame of mind. We mistrust them, for they lead to intellectual anarchy, to absolute egoism and individualism, which is equal to the **negation of all endeavor** and tempering action. We prefer being accused of **functionalism** rather than of being prophets of pessimism, harbingers of the great Nothingness. Our intense focusing on the present is preparing the way for a Tomorrow which will emanate directly from us.⁸

"Bold, continuous progress; abolition of the authority of the dead and the old, of the sluggards, of the cowards, of the velvet-tongued, the delicate, the effeminate, the nostalgics and the weak. Life intensified. Daily heroism. Let's experience all dangers and all struggles. Let's dirty our hands by digging trenches, be ready for combat, for punches, for the rifle.

"Solidarity of the innovators; utter recklessness directed at endless progress; heroic selflessness aimed at giving the world more light, more freedom, and more novelty. These are our marching and battle orders, so as not to turn back but to move forever forward, **more powerful, more profound, more complex, more succinct, and at an ever-increasing speed**.

"Encompassing every possible act of daring, yet banishing that dreamed-of future from our minds, for it can sap all energy from our today and from our tomorrow!"

This text was published in the first issue (January 1915) of the Neapolitan magazine *La diana*, an influential cultural review published from 1915 to 1917 and open to contributions from Vociani, Metaphysics, Futurists, Dadaists, and so on. It also published many works of the French avant-garde. I have omitted here the first part of the introduction by the interviewer, Carlo Albertini.

BIRTH OF A FUTURIST THEATER
(1910–17)

In the broad spectrum of Futurist activities, one area always assumed a special significance: theater. Marinetti explained the main reason for this when he wrote, "Ninety percent of all Italians go to the theater, while a mere 10 percent read books and journals." Another reason was surely that Marinetti, as well as several other members of the group, were active playwrights and were deeply dissatisfied with the state of Italian theater. They had seen their plays performed in substandard productions according to aesthetic principles that had nothing whatsoever in common with Futurism. They therefore had a personal interest in seeing companies develop artistic ambitions rather than being driven purely by commercial considerations.

At the beginning of the twentieth century, Italian theater was an industry that operated along capitalist principles. Plays were never produced by a theater owner but by impresarios, who stood at the helm of the companies and to whom a playhouse would be let for a limited period. These actor-managers toured with their troupes from city to city and presented productions that were entirely geared toward the prevailing tastes of middle-class audiences. Impresarios were dependent on immediate box office returns and never invested a great deal of money in a new "season." Their repertoire consisted of assembly-line productions, put together within a week or two (and often less than that), and often repeated for years on end. There were no directors or scenic designers involved, as we know them nowadays. Whatever the play, it had to fit into one of the generic sets most companies had at their disposal, usually consisting of a couple of painted backdrops, executed in a vague and stereotypical fashion, to represent a "classical," "medieval," or "modern" setting.

When these companies arrived in town, they became a social attraction not because of a new play but because of a star actor or actress. He or she was loved by the crowds and celebrated in the salons of the bourgeoisie. The play or the playwright served no other function than to furnish these *mattatori* with a framework in which they could exhibit their craft and their physical assets. And as they displayed the latest fashions on stage, they also acted as "models" and arbiters of taste. At a time when a play was considered nothing but a vehicle for an actor, it was not the performer who adapted to the role, but the role was adapted to the star. Texts were often changed beyond recognition; passages that did not demand the presence of the star on stage were cut; subsidiary roles the company could not afford to cast were eliminated; scenes that did not offer maximum opportunity for the display of the protagonist's artistry were rewritten. And if the play lacked scope for the soloist, then interpolations were made to guarantee the applause of the audience. If an author had occasion to see his play on stage, he would have had difficulty recognizing it as his own.

But most of the audience did not go the theater to see a play; they went to watch a "virtuoso" performance, a dazzling display of vocal and gestural brilliance. What was considered "great acting" at the time, we would probably regard today as extremely stilted, rhetorical, or melodramatic. It was acting according to formula, using a limited range of routine tricks, to which the soloist would add his or her personal bravura numbers.

Naturally, such a system did not provide a healthy context for a dramatic literature of any artistic merit. The development of the first "art theaters" in Europe had not had any lasting repercussions in Italy. The long-delayed reform of the theater could not be brought about by uneducated, nomadic actors and commercially minded theater directors. It had to come from innovators in the wider cultural field who took an interest in the theater and had enough competence to identify ways of improving the outdated system. Marinetti was one of them, and his sustained onslaught eventually showed positive results.

25

✑

Futurism's First Battles

I have to tell you that we are far too excited by our Futurist ideas to dress them up in diplomatic language and elegant attire. I shall therefore be inordinately assertive in this book, all the more because I truly detest suggestive hints and academic eloquence. Indeed, the fierce battle we are waging daily against everything and everybody in Italy has notably increased our habitual violence. Circumstances dictate that we use brutal measures. This dangerous course of action doesn't allow for any mawkish sentiments. We are strong enough to scornfully brush aside the smokescreen sent up by the skeptics of our time. We are not allowed to use arms, and this forces us to do what we can with stones and ignoble hammers, with brooms and umbrellas to smite and prostrate the vast throng of our enemies: the Traditionalists.[1]

On October 11, 1908, having worked for six years at my international journal, *Poesia*,[2] attempting to free Italian lyric genius from its traditional, commercial shackles that threatened to kill it off, I suddenly sensed that articles, poems, and polemic were no longer enough. The approach had to be totally different; we had to go out into the streets, lay siege to the theaters, and introduce the fist into the struggle for art.

My poet friends Paolo Buzzi, Corrado Govoni, Enrico Cavacchioli, Armando Mazza, and Luciano Folgore helped me search for the right watchword. For a moment, I hesitated between the words "Dynamism" and "Futurism." My Italian blood, however, surged the more strongly when my lips proclaimed aloud the freshly invented word "Futurism."[3]

It was the *new formula, art-as-action,* and a guiding rule for mental health. It was a youthful, regenerative banner that was antitraditional, optimistic, heroic, and dynamic, to be raised above the ruins of an obsessive concern with the past (a static state of mind, traditionalist, academic, pessimistic, pacifist, nostalgic, decorative, and aesthetic).

On February 20, 1909, I published the famous *Futurist Manifesto* in *Le Figaro.* It was the burning fuse of our great rebellion against the cult of the past, the tyranny of academies, and the base venality which are together crushing the life out of contemporary literature. Everyone knows about the storms of polemic and the violent rush of insulting remarks and enthusiastic applause which greeted that manifesto.

I have to say, however, that very many of those who insulted us had no understanding whatsoever of the lyrical and somewhat prophetic violence of that great revolutionary proclamation.

As luck would have it, the young intuited with their blood what they had not understood with their minds.

It was, in fact, to the blood of the Italian race that we had appealed, and it answered us precisely with 22,000 enthusiastic followers gathered by us in one month.[4] Almost all of these were young people between twenty and thirty years of age! And I can tell you here and now, with legitimate pride, that all the students of Italy were almost always with us!

Our movement went on expanding by the day, winning over all literary and artistic communities the world over.—The Futurist painters Boccioni, Carrà, Russolo, Balla, and Severini united with the Futurist poets and, not long after that, we had the joy of launching Balilla Pratella's *Manifesto of Futurist Music,* which was a fine cry of revolt against the Conservatories, against the tyranny of Publishers, and against the stupidly conventional, profit-driven organization of the melodrama in Italy.[5]

Our ever-growing influence soon showed itself in unexpected ways, even in the writings of our opponents. Indeed, the Italian newspapers devoted lengthy polemical articles to the wholly Futurist conception of Gabriele D'Annunzio's latest novel, and he, in an explanatory interview, plagiarized our clearly stated scorn for women as being essential to the existence of the hero in our times.[6]

Gabriele D'Annunzio followed us at a distance, as a convinced traditionalist, without, of course, ever having the guts to turn his back on his countless following of erotomaniacs and stylish archaeologists. We, however, were anything but satisfied at providing one of the most revered writers in contemporary Italy with such a distinctive image. It wasn't sufficient to see ourselves being courageously defended by a great sculptor such as Vincenzo Gemito and by an esteemed novelist such as Luigi Capuana, who publicly regretted in the Italian press that, because of their advancing years, they were not able to come and fight at our side, with fists and heavy punches, against the old, degenerate Italy that was rotten and corrupt.[7]

And it was precisely with fists and heavy punches that we fought in the theaters of the great Italian cities.

After the great Futurist victory in Trieste, won at the Rossetti Theater,[8] we were immediately in the limelight at the Teatro Lirico in Milan, before an audience of four thousand people, which we did not spare from the most insolent and most cruel truths.[9]

I had a few great young poets about me. With me, in verse and in prose, they denounced the truly ignominious state in which our intellectual life was struggling, the opportunism and the mediocrity that presided over our foreign policy, and the urgent need to raise our national dignity at all costs, for without it neither art nor literature are possible.

The *serata* had been organized by us in honor of General Asinari di Bernezzo, who had been unjustly retired for making far too Futurist a speech against Austria, to his troops. Therefore, disregarding the gale of interruptions, I had an ode in praise of his most noble act recited in its entirety.[10]

That ode, which was full of insults against the cowardice of the government and the monarchy, raised a tremendous uproar. I then addressed myself to the public in the stalls—the conservatives, the priests, and the out-and-out pacifists—and then to those up in the gallery, where the mass of workers from the Labor Exchange were roaring like the menacing waters of a sluice.[11]

All of a sudden, one of those men dared to cry out, "Down with this country!" and it was then that with the full power of my lungs I let out my cry of "Long live war, the world's only cleanser! Down with Austria!" This cry, repeated persistently, unleashed a battle throughout the whole building, which immediately divided into two camps.

The theater personnel came up onto the stage, putting on their official cummerbunds,[12] but we went on with our violent demonstration against the Triple Alliance,[13] amid the frenetic cheering of the students.

The police invaded the stage and I was arrested, but released not long after.

That memorable *serata* had powerful repercussions in the German and Austrian press. The Vienna papers had no hesitation in angrily demanding solemn reparations of the Italian government, which were not conceded.

The third Futurist *serata*, held in Turin, was a magnificent battle.[14]

On the stage of the largest theater in the city, three painters of tremendous talent appeared, together with me and some other poets. Boccioni, Russolo, and Carrà commented on and loudly defended their *Manifesto of Futurist Painting*, which was no less violent and revolutionary than that of the poets.

At the reading of this manifesto, which was in open revolt against academic art, museums, the realm of professors, archaeologists, and secondhand and antique dealers, a hitherto unheard-of rumpus broke out in the hall, where more than three thousand people thronged, the great majority of them being artists. The students of the Albertine Academy[15] cheered the Futurists with great gusto, while other sections of the audience wanted to make them shut up. But it wasn't very long before the great hall became a veritable battlefield: punches and beatings with sticks; countless brawls and scuffles in the stalls and up in the gallery; police intervention, arrests, women fainting amid the indescribable clamor and uproar of the mob.

There then followed other tumultuous *serate*—in Naples, Venice, Padua.[16] Everywhere, they split the audience into two camps, the free and the slaves, the living and the dying, the builders of the future and the stuffers of corpses.

Our words brutally unmasked souls, leaving no room for half-measures.

In every one of these theaters, within a short time we saw courage increase, as well as the number of men who were truly young at heart, but also mummies bizarrely stirring into life, drawn by our words from their ancient tombs.

One evening, when the battle raged more violently than ever, the Traditionalists having organized some resistance, we were pelted for more than an hour with every kind of missile. But as usual, we remained impassive, standing tall and smiling.

When we performed at the Mercadante Theatre, in Naples, 160 policemen stood watching onstage, behind us, not lifting a finger, because the Chief of Police had ordered them to let us be conveniently slaughtered by the conservative, priest-ridden audience.[17]

All of a sudden, among the parabolas of potatoes and rotten fruit, I managed to catch an orange that had been thrown at me. I peeled it as calm as could be and proceeded to eat it slowly, segment by segment.

Then a miracle occurred. A strange good humor took hold of those dear Neapolitans, and gradually, as my bitterest enemies gave themselves up to applause, the fortunes of the evening turned in our favor.

Naturally, I lost no time in thanking the bellowing herd (whose admiration was suddenly stopped in its tracks) by heaping further insulting truths upon them; with the result that they waited for us outside the theater entrance, to cheer us and lead us in a triumphal procession all over the city.

After each of these boisterous *serate*, we usually divided among us the task of proselytizing, and each one of us went off with his own particular abrasive, polemical strengths into the circles and clubs and even into the streets—in fact, into every corner of the city. Every day, we held several meetings, never letting up, never resting, for the task we have taken upon ourselves demands almost superhuman strength.

[...][18]

Everywhere, in Milan, in Padua, in Ferrara, and in other provincial cities,[19] our presence unleashed storms of enthusiasm and hatred. But what we refer to as the Futurist Revolution of Parma has remained especially memorable.

The police had forbidden the Futurist *serata* that we had planned in a theater in Parma.[20] Fifty Futurist students, led by the young, courageous Caprilli, Talamassi, Copertini, Burco, and Jori,[21] had been expelled from the university by their bigoted, terrified teachers. These flagrant injustices caused a great deal of upset.

Ten thousand people, split into two camps, for and against Futurism, rioted in the streets, surrounding me and my friends—Futurist poets, painters, musicians, and students.

The soldiers, infantrymen, and fusiliers tried in vain to quell this incipient revolution, and while this was happening, I had absolutely no desire to get up and speak. However, a few days after, I had the following text distributed throughout the whole of Parma.[22]

Futurist Letter to the Citizens of Parma

If I did not respond immediately to your demand of *Speech, Marinetti, speech!* made by countless voices, it was because we Futurists are not in the habit of taking or obeying orders from anyone.

And what's more, as you were laying siege to the Marchesi café,[23] showering us with applause and curses, we were quietly sipping our cups of tea, thinking that we wouldn't be able to be heard with all that din.

There were more than ten thousand of you, all dressed up in your holiday best, yet so beautifully ruffled by the electricity of Futurism, so intoxicated by the light of spring in your own city, which a few hours earlier had emerged reborn out of a relentless downpour of rain.[24]

We couldn't forget that above all else we were artists, thirsty for new sensations and for brilliant aesthetic disputes. Unmindful already of the police ban that prevented us from proclaiming Futurism in a theater, we gave ourselves up to the pleasure of painting and singing in there, smoking the endless cigarettes of creative nights.

All of one mind, Boccioni, Carrà, Russolo, and I felt pleasure at having our unflinching backs crushed by this swarm of people (and dotted here and there, the red of the carabinieri's uniforms) who were shaking their fists and seething with rage below balconies, sagging beneath hordes of people.

Amid the tossing green foliage[25] of a battalion of running fusiliers and the bridling of the cavalry along the street which had no sidewalk, the vehement whistles of the police suddenly ripped the gaily colored silk of the sky with so much force that a couple of shining Italian rainbows fell from it onto the panting chests of two of their officers.

If we hadn't been totally captivated by that sort of spectacle, and if my voice had been able to control your deafening whirlpool, foaming beneath a hail of flying fists, I would have shouted out that Futurism glorifies just that, violence and courage, it defends and exalts youth in art and in life, against the measureless armies of the dead, the dying, the opportunists, and the cowardly. I would have shouted that Futurism teaches everyday heroism, an intense love of life, disdain for the past and for the dead, progress in all its different forms, endless freedom, and Italian pride.

Be wholly alive, be free of all nostalgia, despise anything that was, and, leaving your ancestors behind, construct an even greater Italy of the future!

Anybody among you who shouted "Down with Futurism!" was unconsciously complying with that miserable brood of bigoted, terrified little professors who exclude from their university our bold young friends Caprilli, Talamassi, Copertini, Provinciali, Burco, and Jori, who are only guilty of Futurism, a sublime new offense.

For the honor of Parma and of Italy, from the stage of the Reinach

Theater we shall soon[26] be loudly condemning this abuse of power by those sad men who gnaw away at ancient scrolls and young skulls.[27]

That being the case, we shall doubtless have the joy of admiring, for a second time, your magnificent, explosive violence!

The text translated here is taken from *Guerra sola igiene del mondo* (1915), but most of it had previously appeared in French as an introduction to *Le Futurisme* (1911), explaining to people outside Italy the militant rationale behind the *serate*, which more than anything else had brought notoriety to the Futurist movement in 1910–11.

26

The Battles of Trieste

Our train is moving toward Trieste, the red powder keg of Italy.[1]

Oh, what feelings of rage we have, we Futurist poets, bearers of explosive ideas, destroyers of the old Italy, pent up in this compartment like eagles in a cage . . . But our spirits rush on in the darkness, ahead of the train, which tries hard to keep up with us.

The day is not far off when, perforce, people will have to recognize, on our piled-up corpses, the agonizing sincerity of our program and the tragic seriousness of our violence. This, however, will not stop us from being happy, wildly happy, this evening, if for no other reason than to scoff at the slowness of the clapped-out train that is carrying us, creaking throughout the whole length of its black frame, clacking its rattling teeth, dragging its iron slippers and stretching itself out in all the stations, like a drunkard in the wine haze of every tavern: Treviglio, Brescia, Verona . . .

—Away with misery and seriousness!

—We shall go dancing and singing to the war.

—Here's Vicenza . . . This fog stinks of old bigots!

—Well, in fact, we're passing over the snuff-ridden, moldering spirit of Senator Fogazzaro[2] . . . How disgusting!

Hundreds of electric lamps stretch away before us, to right and to left . . . Our luminous Futurist phlegm, spat into the filthy night.

At dawn, the border:[3] tragic stony ravines, the likely theater of future battles.[4] Each one of us is already silently deciding upon his combat position.

Cormons, Miramar[5] . . . and here is the Adriatic, an immense gray flag unfurled, beating rapidly and waiting anxiously for the sun to transform it into the triumphant tricolore of Italy.

Trieste at last! . . . A flurry of excited cries, a lightning outburst of hurrahs! All our friends have come to wait for us. A hundred eager hands are held out toward us . . . A hundred excited, enraptured glances search feverishly among us for the one invisible god: the uplifting Italian standard!

At seven in the evening, behind the curtain at the Rossetti Theater, we are bickering about the tricolor borders of a poem with the Austrian Chief of Police, who preens himself with his decorations, while a roaring, torrentlike crowd floods into the galleries.

When, at last, we show ourselves at the footlights, the whole population of Trieste is before us . . . all of them, with the burning youth of its pugnacious males and the glitter of Parisian elegance, which makes the litheness of its women so distinctive.

Outside, a tide of thousands clamored violently, hemmed in between the vile cordons of policemen.

Are there any professors, any pedants or invalids in the auditorium? Not that we can see . . . Silence of the Assize Court when sentence is passed, or rather, silence of the submarine depths, where I fling forth the sentences of my speech, like torpedoes against the ancient Roman galleys which pitch invisibly upon the heaving and surging of the crowd.

Speech to the People of Trieste

Friends, or enemies perhaps![6]

I shall not be talking to you today about the essential ideals of Futurism, but rather about its practical, directly utilitarian point of view.

Have you ever thought about the vast army of dead geniuses, who are now practically unknown, yet who constrict the small battalion of living geniuses, on all sides, crushing them relentlessly?

We only think about dead geniuses, we work and we spend only for them. Everything is granted them, all things are offered, everything is easy for them. Streets are leveled, doors are thrown wide open. Everywhere they go in triumph, throughout our cities, they come into our houses, and with the stench of their tombs they pollute our spring air.

Oh yes! The tombs march against us! The ominous seepage from the cemeteries . . . The dead take possession of the living!

Cemeteries? What am I saying? Italy shouldn't be called the Land of the Dead but rather the *Bank of the Dead!* . . . No, don't laugh; I'm speaking the terrible truth.

It is only the dead who are well paid. The living receive nothing but derision, insults, false accusations, and they go hungry!

The young are the most downtrodden. And it is for the young especially that we strive, for they are the most alive of the living.

Obviously, the money that is spent on art in Italy doesn't end up in the pockets of the dead, but rather in the well-sewn-up pockets of their sextons! . . . I mean, of course, the traditionalist publishers, the professors, the scholars, and the useless critics, whose base venality and disparaging envy we violently oppose.

Under the reign of these exploiters of the past, every day a poet of genius is killed off, through hurling upon him the paper mummy of a poet who died five hundred years ago. The publishers bin the manuscripts of a famished genius in order to lavish their money on sumptuous editions of masterpieces which are well known to all and which have been reprinted a hundred thousand times already. American millionaires, urged on by these self-advertising money grubbers, come to Italy to squander fabulous sums in buying works that often have no more value than that of their illustrious grime accumulated over centuries.

The cold, anemic, soporific music of our grandfathers is inflicted on the public, while many young musicians wait in vain, in the anguish of an exhausting misery, for someone to deign to notice that even a living musician can have a bit of talent.

And when we are not faced with the formidable army of dead geniuses, we have to contend with that army—not quite so strong though equally vast—of illustrious old dotards.

And as if that were not enough, we have to defend ourselves, day and night, against the cunning assaults of the opportunists, of the narrow-minded and venal attitudes which abound in the world of art. And against these different legions of mummies, corpses, sextons, and grave robbers, we declare implacable war.

The cult of the past and the commercialization of the arts—these are the two terrible plagues that are devastating our country.

In our struggle, as a matter of course, we hold in contempt every sort of obedience, of docility and imitation. We despise all sedentary tastes and every kind of foot-dragging caution. We fight against majorities corrupted by power and spit on current and traditional opinions, just as we deride all moral and philosophical commonplaces.

In the field of literature, we advance the ideal of a great and strong scientific literature which, set free from every sort of classical claptrap, from every sort of erudite purism, will extol the most recent discoveries, the new intoxication with speed and the heavenly life of the aviator.

Our poetry is essentially and unreservedly a poetry in revolt against established forms. We have to destroy the rail tracks of verse, to blow up the bridges to what has already been said, and set in motion the loco-motives of our inspiration, along a path entirely determined by chance, toward the limitless fields of the New and the Future! Far better a sen-sational journey that ends in disaster than a monotonous trail trudged every day! For far too long now we have put up with the stationmasters of poetry, the ticket inspectors of the metrical sleeping car, and the senseless punctuality of prosodic timetables.

In politics, we are as distant from internationalist, antipatriotic social-ism—a tawdry exaltation of the rights of the belly—as we are from timid, clerical fogydom, symbolized by carpet slippers and bed warmers.

All liberties and all progress within the great circle of the Nation!

We revere patriotism and militarism, our song is war, sole cleanser of the world, proud flame of enthusiasm and generosity, noble baptism of heroism, without which peoples would stagnate in self-centered tor-por, in their economic ambitions, in their poverty of mind and will.

We despise and fight against the tyranny of love, which, especially among Latin peoples, scythes down the energies of men of action. We fight against a rancid sentimentalism, an obsession with adultery and the conquest of women in the novel, the theater, and in life.

All these burning, dynamic ideas of ours annoy and exasperate the public; but we Futurists are pleased about that because our only fear is the easy approbation and insipid praises of the mediocre.

We are certain that nothing is easier and, at the same time, more despicable than pleasing the public, by flattering their uncouth, con-ventional tastes. Therefore we seek pleasure only in our great Futurist ideal, and of a hostile public we ask nothing more than to be booed!

This speech was greeted with a tremendous outburst of applause . . . The keels of the past crumble in the slapping groundswell of these ex-cited hands.

And here's Armando Mazza,[7] with his huge athletic body, coming forward like a wrestler. His booming voice crashes against the theater's walls and seems to cover the whole world with our primordial Futurist wills. In reality, the mummified sages, the custodians of good sense, and all those who carry their armchairs on their backs, as do tortoises their shells, feel themselves crushed beneath the feet of that giant who, in a loud voice, calls on all firebrands to revolt.

Down with the museums! Let's rebury the dead! Let us glorify violence! Long live war! Death to the pacifists! Away with the torpid majorities! All glory to the wild beasts! . . . Red hot punches too in the trembling chests of the Traditionalists, the flayed shrubs, warped by lava, on the flanks of a volcano!

Then the Futurist poets, one after the other,[8] and with the same devil-may-care attitude of students on the razzle, pour out in torrents the red wine of their sublime poetry, into three thousand invisible goblets, held out enthusiastically to receive it.

But all of a sudden, a great din breaks out and sets off an infernal stampede.

They're howling at the scandal; hands of drowning spectators grip tight hold of their seats; others desperately clasp their round, bald heads, as if they were seizing hold of the world to save it. Lifeless eyes search anxiously for crucifixes that are nowhere to be seen. The raging of the throng increases; it's the great uprising of the mummies. Not one of them is Italian; they're all Austrian, or else *lickspittles*. But in the end, powerful youth prevails. All the men are on their feet, and with their fists, with the exploding of their voices, they force the dead to lie down in their tombs.

The gust of enthusiasm urges us outside and carries us through the streets of Trieste.

We go into the Café Milano, a furnace that releases burning brands of delirious cheers upon us! Around the great, fraternal table, flushed cheeks, fire in the voices, poetry and patriotism fermenting vermilion . . . Armando Mazza is prevailed upon to recite the famous Manifesto for a third time. There's an abundance of alcohol, flowing freely, and it sets people's minds on fire. A young man stands up, his eyes electrified with creative intelligence, and proclaims his Futurist faith, his ardent support for our movement in rebellion against the past . . . Everyone listens to him intently and he, overtaken by frenzied inspiration, lets fly a thousand contradictory ideas, like so many rockets shooting out, without a break, from their launcher. This man is the stout Triestine poet Mario Cavedali.

We leave the Café Milano to take our fiery Italian souls into the nighttime lair of the Austrian officers, the Eden.

However, there we find lots of Hungarians who, with their actions and dances, are accompanying a wild imbroglio of gypsy violins. They greet us warmly, extolling the liberation of Hungary and Trieste and—willing martyrs of patriotism—they shimmy to the sonorous hammering of a tzambal and the wild bowing of violins.[9]

Joy, madness, and war!

In a corner, a few Austrian officers reveal the same jaundiced color as their flag.

When we leave, a frenzied, studentlike, devil-may-care intoxication infects our boisterous column.

We Futurists have no hesitation in proclaiming the death of wisdom, the ignominy of the word "prudence" . . . God help anyone who is incapable of a bold hooliganism! God help anyone who, every night, does not feel himself to be the absolute lord of the city, swollen with indignation at those who are sleeping!

In a long Indian file, at first we walk rapidly and then we break into a run, forming noisy, mocking chains around the foul-looking faces of the policemen, those walking urinals.

So, still running, we arrive at the San Carlo Quay. A great yacht rides at anchor, with its three tall masts piercing the clouds . . . How far up do they go, those masts? We simply have to know! . . . up and up! . . . Who could stop us following their sharp leap away into the sky? What does it matter if the yacht is swaying, if the rigging is whining in the fearsome breath of the *bora*?[10] . . . And we clamber up by the mainmast, looking for the nests of the stars . . . From up there, we shall maybe make out on the horizon the lights of the awe-inspiring naval squadron of Admiral Bettolo.[11]

We set off then toward Servola,[12] whose whitish clouds of smoke, down there, are like huge pillars constructed to bear the reddening vaults of the night . . . Happy as schoolboys let loose, we surge around the sooty bellies of the foundries, which give birth to great walls of sparks . . . Cries of victory burst from our breasts . . . At last, the craziest of Futurist images becomes a reality: see these fiery buildings on the march, disemboweling themselves and spilling their innards of topaz and rubies on the ground!

And so we witness the fusion of the new, Futurist sun, which is deeper in color, more fantastic, and hotter than the old one of yesterday. So intently do we watch its immense incandescent flow in monstrous chimneys, gigantic windlasses, all plumed in smoke, that we don't even hear the screeching flight of the trains passing beneath our feet, those scurrying iron mice . . .

Oh! How envious we are of the houses crouched on the hills around, attentive houses whose eyes are lit up each night by the intoxicating jewels of fire. How we envy the clouds with their faces warmed and the sea's horizon furrowed by long, scarlet reflections!

In Trieste, young people never sleep. Theirs is a healthy insomnia, which made us devour the great Futurist feast offered us by our friends and wittily served in inverse order:

Coffee
Sweet memories on ice
Marmalade of dead glories
Mummy roast with professorial liver
Archaeological salad
Goulash of the past, with explosive peas, served in a history sauce
Dead Sea fish
Clotted blood soup
Entrée of demolition
Vermouth.

Everywhere, in the sumptuous halls of the Filarmonica, in the intellectual salons and fashionable meeting places, the ladies vied with each other in presenting us with gifts and exquisite courtesies. They had been fascinated rather than alarmed by the incendiary force of our Futurist determination.

We left the city reluctantly, our eyes already turned toward new battlefields. Trieste accompanied us to our train and their hundred most illustrious sons, who ran behind our wagon, applauded us with lusty shouts of *Long live Italy! Long live Futurism!*

The text appeared in Marinetti's compilation *Rapporto sulla vittoria del Futurismo a Trieste*, published as an introduction to Aldo Palazzeschi's *L'incendiario* (1910). It was reprinted, in a revised form, in *Guerra sola igiene del mondo* (1915) and in a highly condensed manner in *L'Italia futurista*, March 18, 1917.

27

⌘

The Battles of Venice

Against Traditionalist Venice

We turn our backs on the ancient Venice, worn out and brought to ruin by centuries of pleasure seeking, although once even we loved that city and took it to our hearts, in a great, nostalgic dream.[1]

We reject the Venice of foreigners, this marketplace of fake antique dealers, this magnet for universal snobbism and imbecility, this bed worn out by endless droves of lovers, this bath adorned with jewels for cosmopolitan whores, immense sewer of traditionalism.

We wish to cure and begin the healing process of this putrescent city, this magnificent carbuncle from the past. We want to bring the Venetian people back to life, to ennoble them, fallen as they are from their former greatness, stupefied by a sickening spinelessness and humiliated by their habitual, shady little businesses.

We wish to prepare for the birth of an industrial and military Venice which can dominate the Adriatic, this great Italian lake.[2]

We rush to fill in its stinking little canals, with the rubble of its crumbling, pockmarked palaces.

We'll set fire to the gondolas, rocking chairs for cretins, and we'll raise up to the skies the imposing geometry of metal bridges and factories plumed with smoke, so as to abolish the drooping curves of its ancient architecture.

Let the reign of divine Electric Light begin at last, to liberate Venice from the whorish moonlight of its furnished bedrooms.

. . .

On July 8, 1910,[3] 800,000 leaflets containing this manifesto were hurled by the Futurist poets and painters from the top of the Clock Tower onto the crowds returning from the Lido.[4] Thus began the campaign which, for three years, the Futurists waged against traditionalist Venice.

The following speech against the Venetians, extemporized by Marinetti at the Fenice Theater,[5] provoked a terrible battle. The Futurists were whistled at while the traditionalists were beaten up.

The Futurist painters Boccioni, Russolo, and Carrà punctuated this speech with many resounding slaps. The fists of the Futurist poet Armando Mazza, who is also an athlete, stay fixed in the memory.

A Futurist Speech by Marinetti to the Venetians

Venetians!

Whenever we shouted, "Let's kill off the moonlight!"[6] we were always thinking of you, the rotten old Venice tarnished with Romanticism.

But now the sound of our voices is amplified, and we add on a higher note, "Let us liberate the world from the tyranny of sentimentalism. We've had more than enough of amorous adventures, of lechery, of sentimentalism and nostalgia!"

Why do you persist, Venice, in offering us veiled women at every shadowy bend of your canals?

Enough! We've had enough! O Venice, old procuress that you are, stop whispering obscene invitations to visitors from all over the Earth, for behind your heavy mantilla of mosaics you still persist in providing exhausting romantic nights, querulous serenades, and fearful muggings.

O Venice! I, too, once loved the luxuriating shadows of your Grand Canal, awash with the choicest debaucheries, and the feverish pallor of your beauties, who slip away from their balconies, down stairways festooned with lanterns, through lightly falling rain and rays of moonlight, amid the clashing of swords in combat . . .

But that's enough! All this absurd, abominable, irritating nonsense is just too nauseating! What we want now is that the electric streetlamps, with their thousand stabbing points, slice into and violently tear apart your mysterious darkness, which is so bewitching and persuasive!

Your Grand Canal, when widened and deepened, must inevitably become a great commercial port. Once your canals have finally been filled in, trains and trams will be hurtling along the great streets built over them, bringing stacks of merchandise to a discerning public, which is rich, and busily employed by industrialists and businessmen! . . .

There's no use howling against the presumed ugliness of the loco-motives, trams, motorcars, and bicycles, which for us represent the opening lines of our great Futurist aesthetic. They're always good for flattening a few filthy, grotesque, Nordic professors, sporting their lit-tle Tyrolean hats.

But you love to fawn on foreigners, and your servility is despicable!

Venetians! Venetians! Why do you still desire to be ever the faithful slaves of the past, the filthy gatekeepers of the biggest brothel in his-tory, nurses in the most wretched hospital in the world, in which souls are languishing, mortally corrupted by the syphilis of sentimentalism?

Oh! I'm not short of images if I seek to define your smug, foolish in-ertia, like that of some great man's son or the husband of some famous singer! Now, might I not now, perhaps, think of your gondoliers as gravediggers, bent on rhythmically scooping out graves in a flooded cemetery?

But nothing offends you, since your humility knows no bounds.

Besides, it's well known that you are wisely preoccupied with en-riching the Association of Great Hotels, and that for precisely this rea-son you insist on rotting without stirring yourselves!

And yet at one time you were invincible warriors and artists of ge-nius, you were bold navigators, clever industrialists, and tireless mer-chants[7] . . . And now you have become hotel waiters, guides, pimps, antique dealers, swindlers, forgers of old paintings, plagiarizing and im-itative painters. Have you therefore forgotten how, above all else, to be Italians, and that this word, in the language of history, means "builders of the future"?

Now then! Don't try and defend yourselves by blaming it all on the debilitating effects of the sirocco![8] It was this hot, warlike wind which swelled the sails of the heroes at Lepanto![9] This very same African wind will suddenly, at some infernal noontide, speed up the dull labors of the corrosive waters that are undermining your venerable city.

Oh, how we shall dance on that day! Oh, how we shall cheer on the lagoons, to urge them to destruction! And what an immense roundelay we shall dance around the illustrious ruins! We shall all be wildly happy, we, the last rebellious students in a world that is far too prudent!

In just this way, O Venetians, did we sing and dance and laugh, wit-nessing the death throes of Philae,[10] which ended like a doddery old mouse behind the Dam of Aswan,[11] that immense trap for electric cables, in which the Futurist genius of England imprisons the fleeing, sacred waters of the Nile!

Come on, raise your heads, at least, and shout that I'm a barbarian, incapable of appreciating the divine poetry which laps against your enchanted islands!

Away with you! There's no reason for you to be proud of it! . . .

Liberate Torcello, Burano, the Isle of the Dead,[12] from all the sickly literature and all of that inflated Romantic flim-flam with which the poets, poisoned by the fevers of Venice, have veiled them. Then, laughing like me, you will be able to think of those islands as piles of shit that the mammoths dropped, here and there, when they forded your prehistoric lagoons.

But instead, you stupidly gaze out upon them, content to rot in your filthy waters, so as to endlessly enrich the Association of Great Hotels, which carefully prepares luxurious nights for everyone who is anyone, on this planet.

To be sure, it's no small achievement, getting them sexually aroused. Even though your guest be an Emperor,[13] he still has to travel, for quite some time, through the filth of this enormous sewer full of fabled relics; his gondoliers have to plow with their oars through several kilometers of liquefied shit, with its divine scent of latrines, passing close to boats filled with the choicest garbage, past suspicious-looking bags floating by, to be able to reach his destination, as a real Emperor should, very pleased with himself and with his imperial scepter!

So that, O Venetians, has been your glory, up to now!

Shame on you! Shame on you! You should throw yourselves down, one on top of the other, like sandbags, to make a dike at the outer limits of the Lagoon, while we prepare a great, strong, industrial, commercial, and military Venice on the Adriatic, our great Italian lake!

Marinetti described the battles of Venice in *Le Futurisme* (1911), *Guerra sola igiene del mondo* (1915), *I manifesti del futurismo* (1914 and 1919), *Futurismo e fascismo* (1924), and *Marinetti e il futurismo* (1929). The first section, "Against Traditionalist Venice," was initially part of Marinetti's speech accompanying the distribution of a broadsheet against past-loving Rome (see document 28), and was then called "Advice to the Venetians." The version translated here was published as a leaflet by Marinetti's journal *Poesia*, dated April 27, 1910, and was also signed by Boccioni, Carrà, and Russolo. A French version, with five caricatures

by André Warnot, was published by the French journal *Comœdia* on June 17, 1910. The section here titled "A Futurist Speech by Marinetti to the Venetians" was also published in French as a four-page leaflet by the journal *Poesia* and in *Les Tendences nouvelles* 9 (1911) and was responded to by ten French writers in the following number.

28

The Battles of Rome

Against Traditionalist Rome

Single-handedly, Ruskin's influence has determined the obsessive cult of our past throughout Europe, and has completely misled Europe about the character of contemporary Italy.[1]

Indeed, they are hardly aware of the tremendous industrial and commercial development taking place in Lombardy and Liguria.

Milan! Genoa! . . . This is where the new, revitalized Italy lies! Here are the cities that we love! It is cities such as these that lift our Italian pride! We have great centers which are aflame day and night, breathing their huge fires all over the open countryside. We have soaked with our sweat a whole forest of immense mill chimneys, whose capitals of stretching smoke hold up our sky, which wishes to be seen as nothing but a vast factory ceiling.

We no longer heed the charming counsels of the bountiful Italian sun, that young procurer with the seductive smile, who would even now like to lead our race, like a whore, to sing and dance and drink in her bower. We have a countryside that is washed, watered, and served by countless canals, diligent servants with shiny, geometric elbows.

We have valleys which are scooped and torn apart by endless, unsleeping trains. All through our beautiful Lombard and Ligurian nights, our metalworks achieve gigantic proportions, their iron voices booming, their white glow immense.

All our mountains are now lit up, assailed by a host of electric moons, hurriedly, busily bustling about, noisy and disheveled.

These are the things we love about our country! But foreigners, alas! give their love only to those cities which we think of as the three suppurating sores of our peninsula, Florence, Rome, and Venice.

Florence is a huge, exquisite piece of medieval parchment which has fallen into the loveliest countryside in the world. If you enter among the ancient pages of its streets, you become confused by swarming colonies of literary woodworms, whose continuous laughter gnaws away at ancient miniatures depicting warfare. Gentlemen guides, coffee-house geniuses, professional acerbics, garrulous, insolent cabbies, and experts on old paintings—that's the people of Florence!

Rome languishes among its pestilential ruins, with the six-monthly circulation of its blood which foreign gold pumps slowly around its arteries of great hotels.

Just think, Rome, whose shops close down after the Americans have left, could be reduced to poverty even at the merest suspicion of a case of cholera!

The tourist industry. That is what we are fighting against, remorselessly. It is a disgusting trade which transforms two-thirds of the Roman people into likely allies of our enemies of tomorrow, enemies whom our hoteliers will have accommodated most attentively but not lovingly robbed anywhere near enough!

It is inevitable that on the outbreak of war, Rome will only be able to contribute a contingent of lazy opportunists and inveterate pacifists.

I entered Rome, one evening, in a speedy, sixty-horsepower car, and leaving the St. Sebastian Gate behind me, I was just about to reach a point between the Aqueduct of Nero and the Botanical Gardens.

I was going at full speed, with the steering wheel pointing directly at the Arch of Constantine.

With my Futurist devil-may-care attitude, I completely failed to notice a lump of stone, on the darkened road, that had rolled down from the Neronian ruins . . . At least, I saw it too late, and anyway, I was moving too fast! . . . A violent crash . . . and my radiator was shattered! . . .

It was sort of symbolic, like a warning, or rather a punishment sent from the dead, distant centuries . . . And I shouted at the Romans, as loudly as my lungs would allow, "Every man for himself! You should fence off the ancient Roman ruins! They're more contagious and death-dealing than any plague or cholera! You should dig a deep ditch and construct a great circular wall to shut all those vindictive, mean-minded

remains of Roman walls in an impenetrable enclosure . . . And then,
go and stretch your bodies out, a fair way off, out in the country, to preserve you from the very worst of the "malarias"—that which comes
from the tombs along the Appian Way!"[2]

But the Romans answer me with an ironic smile, sweetened with archaeological dust and gross gluttony. They go on living the lives of
dusty mice, contented, proud to eat the crumbs of sweetmeats that the
"misses" chew with strong teeth, while they purse their red lips and
open wide their blue eyes between the immense surviving legs of the
headless Colosseum![3] . . .

The Divine Comedy *Is a Fleapit of Commentators*[4]

Futurism will countenance neither laws nor codes nor magistrates nor
policemen nor pimps nor moralizing eunuchs. Futurism is a flail with
which we daily bloody the faces of the cowards of Italy. Futurism is a
crackling stick of dynamite beneath the ruins of the past.

Flail or dynamite!

But that's not enough! We are imposing something very different on
the world! We want to create the contagion of courage, and we've already done so. On many occasions, we have seen our enemies suddenly hold out their arms to us, praising us with the selfsame lips that
had booed us.

Those half-dead people, infected by an epidemic of cowardice, were
impressed by the fiery intoxication of our heroism. It could be they saw
shining in our eyes the glorious passion we nourish for Art.

To Art, which in fact merits and demands the sacrifice of the very best
of us, we give our absolute, unequivocal love, without the solace of any
disgraceful hope of immortality, the dream of mercenary souls, which
is as despicable in its way as the calculated Christian Paradise.

We want the work of art to be cremated with the body of its maker.
Does not the work of art which survives the dead Genius perhaps infect the living Genius with nostalgia, with caution, and with a terrifying knowledge?

Who can deny that the *Divine Comedy* is nowadays nothing but a
filthy fleapit of commentators?[5] What's the point of venturing onto the
battlefield of thought when the fight is over, to count the dead, to study
the fine wounds, to gather up the shattered weapons and the booty left
behind, beneath the ponderous flight of the learned crows and the
flapping of their papery wings?

Futurism is a great mass of shining metal that we have rooted out, with our own hands, from deep within a volcano, and which, with our own hands, we have raised up to the sky.

And now we are walking closely, with our arms raised, holding it in our burnt hands, up along a rough path, and we are breathing in unison, not watching to see whether any of us outstrips the others by virtue of their more powerful muscles and the strength of their tireless lungs. What does it matter if our footprints are continually being wiped out by those who come after us? The only thing that enthuses us is the desire not to let that great, fiery mass, which we wish to bear to the loftiest peak of human thought, fall to the ground, so that the world may have greater thirst for novelty, more fires of violence, more light of heroism, and more love of freedom!

The Battle at the Teatro Costanzi, March 9, 1913

The Roman traditionalists, who had listened in silence to the orchestra's performance of Balilla Pratella's *Futurist Music* at the Futurist Five o'clock Tea[6] in the Costanzi Theater on February 21, 1913, were so angered by it that they vowed they would be revenged, returning en masse to the Futurist *serata* of March 9. This latter turned into a bloody battle and proved to be yet another victory for Futurism.[7]

The Futurists Marinetti, Boccioni, Palazzeschi, Russolo, Balla, Folgore, Cavacchioli, and Auro d'Alba, as they stood at the footlights to defend the *Free Verses* of Paolo Buzzi and the *Futurist Music* of Balilla Pratella (conducted by the impassive composer himself, amid the missiles hurled by the six thousand traditionalists), presented a wonderfully heroic spectacle.

When the poet Marinetti and the painter Boccioni gave the signal for the battle to commence, by flattening the papal bootlicker and his friends with their cudgels,[8] the Futurists found they were not alone. Five hundred young men—painters, poets, musicians—hurled themselves into the fray to defend them, crying *Long live Futurism!*

Rome is in an uproar. Polemics on Buzzi's *Free Verses* and Russolo's *Art of Noise* intermingle, in drawing rooms and clubs, at the Aragno[9] and in via Mercede,[10] where the newsboys are shouting out "Futurist *Lacerba!*" and a huge crowd argues animatedly in front of the canvases of the Futurist painter Balla, which are on show at the Lux bookshop.[11]

Eighty Italian and foreign artists, among whom were numbered the sculptors Zanelli,[12] Mestrovich,[13] and Prini[14] and the painters Carena[15] and Pieretto Bianco,[16] offered the Futurists Marinetti, Boccioni, and Balla a sumptuous banquet, to glorify their heroic behavior at the Costanzi. Boccioni, Balla, and Marinetti replied to the very many enthusiastic toasts, and the latter introduced the poems of a new Futurist poet, Dinamo Correnti,[17] by reciting them.

In *Il resto del Carlino*, Arturo Labriola[18] foresees true musical genius in Balilla Pratella. Giuseppe Sergi, the sociologist,[19] praises the exhibition of Futurist painters to high heaven in one of his critical studies.

In the *Giornale d'Italia*, Bellonci[20] reprimands the Roman public like this: "My dear readers, recognize in yourselves that Futurism which you deride, and do not lose sight of the fact that hidden behind the agendas and the actions, there are men of true genius in this group of Marinetti's, lively poets such as Buzzi and Palazzeschi, Govoni, Folgore and Marinetti himself; and extremely able painters, such as Boccioni and Balla, as well as a born musician."

The first part of this text, "Against Traditionalist Rome," was distributed in a street action in Rome in June 1910, and published, in French, in Chapter 3 of the collection *Le Futurisme* (1911). An Italian version appeared in *Guerra sola igiene del mondo* (1915), in the journal *L'Italia futurista* (May 13, 1917), and in the collection *I manifesti del futurismo* (1919), where the title was altered to "Against Florence and Rome, the Festering Carbuncles of our Peninsula." Marinetti's speech accompanying the distribution of the broadsheet contained a last section, "Advice to the Venetians," that was not included in the text of the flier, but was turned into a separate publication, *Marinetti, Boccioni, Carrà, Russolo contro Venezia passatista, 27 Aprile 1910* (see p. 168). The second part, "The *Divine Comedy* Is a Fleapit of Commentators," was given as a lecture at a matinee performance at the Costanzi Theater, in Rome, on February 21, 1913. The text was published in *Guerra sola igiene del mondo* (1915), in the journal *L'Italia futurista* (April 22, 1917), and in the collection *I manifesti del futurismo* (1919). The third part, "The Battle at the Teatro Costanzi, March 9, 1913," is taken from *Marinetti e il futurismo* (1929).

29

The Battle of Florence

GREAT FUTURIST *SERATA* AT THE VERDI THEATER,

DECEMBER 12, 1913

A condensed (physical and spiritual) report on the battle

MARINETTI'S SPEECH[1]
I have the impression I am down below the Turkish fortresses in the Dardanelles,[2] and I can see your munitions diminishing though they never hit us . . . (*Shouts, terrible uproar, an endless rain of missiles*)

Your frantic joy gives me pleasure, since it signals yet another triumph for our heroic movement. Certainly, for more than fifty years, such profusion of youthful life has never been seen in this ancient stronghold of tradition! (*Shouts, trumpets, boos*)

Your energy, your fury, are wonderful signs that this Florentine race has not yet been entirely suffocated by libraries and professors, that its reawakening is close at hand! (*Shouts, a hail of macaroni, carrots, tomatoes, potatoes, and onions*)

I think this game has gone on too long. We shall wait until there is at least an intermittent silence. We shall ask those who support us to make their presence felt by the crowd, violently if needs be, so that you listen to us, and boo us only after you hear what we have to say. We are introducing ideas with which you are unfamiliar. (*Shouts of "Yes! yes! yes!" . . . Stink bombs land on the stage. A man faints in the scuffling of carabinieri, police, and stewards.*) These choking, stinking missiles demonstrate that traditionalism defends itself as best it can! . . . (*Enthusiastic applause, insults, scuffles, laughter*)

We are just a handful of trainers in a cage of roaring, yet terrified, wild beasts. (*Applause*)

Tomorrow, you'll leave this place, bearing with you, despite your-selves, an admiration you won't be able to repress. You already admire our heroic nonchalance! You find us detached, tireless in our efforts to liberate Italian art from its past and to promote the creative genius of our race. (*Infernal uproar, all kinds of missiles*) You are six thousand mediocrities against eight artists whose incredible genius you cannot deny! You will not make us turn back, no matter what you throw at us! (*From all sides there are shouts of "Madhouse! Madhouse!"*) I prefer our madhouse to your Pantheon! (*Applause, boos, trumpet blasts, insults, scuffles, and missiles*) And now I hand over to my friend, Soffici. [. . .]³

MARINETTI'S SPEECH (CONTINUED)

We want an Italy that is sovereign and absolute! . . . What I mean is that if the monarchy, which currently encapsulates our national pow-ers, were some day or other to harm, reduce, or corrode the strength of the Nation, we should come out ferociously against it. (*Endless ap-plause and boos*)

The word "Italy" must prevail over the word "freedom."⁴ The word "freedom," which had an absolute value of violence and regeneration on the lips of Garibaldi and Mazzini,⁵ has become an idiotic, worn-out word in the mouths of the anti-Libyans Turati and Bissolati.⁶ (*Applause. Ten minutes of pandemonium*) In contrast, the word "Italy" today attains its deepest radiance, its maximum, most dynamic and combative importance!

As far as we are concerned, internationalism simply means masking egotistical, fearful preoccupations with skin and guts behind empty words. Internationalism also signifies being absorbed or crushed by some foreign nationalism! (*Applause, shouts, fisticuffs down in the stalls*)

Every kind of freedom and progress, by all means, but within the ideal orbit of a Nation which becomes ever more Futurist!

Every kind of freedom, yes, except the freedom to be cowards! . . . (*Boccioni, pointing at those nearest to him, cries, in a loud voice: "Like you!" Shouts, swearing, applause*) A Nation which is fiercely anticlerical and antisocialist. (*Widespread shouts, applause, and a waving of hand-kerchiefs*) The socialists should be assured that we representatives of a new, artistic, Italian youthfulness will fight with all possible means, and giving no quarter, against their vile assaults on the political, mili-tary, and colonial prestige of Italy. (*An isolated cry of "Down with the war!," violently interrupted by opposing and patriotic cries*)

The ranks of the Futurists are growing daily. The socialists should be aware, therefore, that their attempts to discourage the Nation and disrupt its wonderful progress will be systematically opposed by us, using every kind of violence. We are Futurist nationalists and therefore fiercely opposed to that other great, ever-present danger of clericalism, with all its layers of reactionary moralizing, police repression, antediluvian academicism, and self-interested pacifism or commercialism.

Just now, we are going through a critical period of political turmoil, exacerbated by the natural exhaustion which follows any war.[7] (*Roars, handclaps, whistles*)

Italy must catch her breath, after her magnificent, patriotic effort. We shall therefore not allow the skeptics (and there are many in Italy) and the pacifist cowards or those without balls, whichever they are, to exploit this moment of Italian weariness, to reduce our military strength and the increased standing of Italy in the Mediterranean.

It's for these reasons that I consider all anti-Libyan socialists, republicans, and radicals to be miserable scum. Equally scum are the liberals and conservatives who are not able to defend themselves and duly glorify the colonization of Libya.[8] (*Cries of "Long Live Libya! Up with the war!"*)

I was in Libya at the start of the war,[9] and I paid particular attention to its agriculture. A few days ago, my total optimism has been vindicated by the resolute statement made by the American consul in Tripoli, which predicted tremendous future prosperity for that land, so gloriously conquered by Italian blood. (*Cries of "Up with Libya! Up with the Army!"*)

Every endeavor, therefore, and all necessary money, brutality, and blood for the vigorous, practical completion of this Libyan exploit. This completion is today the colonial Futurism of Italy. I end with the cry "Libya Forever!"

(*Shouts. Cries of "Libya Forever!" Applause. Indescribable confusion. Arguments, scuffles, fisticuffs, punches, slaps, invasion by the carabinieri!*)

Marinetti's speech at the Verdi Theater in Florence was printed in *Lacerba* of December 15, 1913.

30

The Exploiters of Futurism

We insist that we have in no way been involved in the invention, execution, and distribution of a film that is going around Italy, arousing people's curiosity by virtue of its ably wrought title, *Mondo Baldoria* (Reveling World), "the first Futurist film."[1] Some fragments of Pathé News, in which we figured, were incorporated in the film in such a way as to make people think the film was ours. We scornfully reject any responsibility for all the shameful theatrical forgeries and foolishness, both written and painted, that many people, in bad faith and with the sole aim of financial gain,[2] pass off as Futurist events.

A *serata*[3] or a lecture cannot be called a Futurist *serata* or lecture unless it is based on the following six fundamental principles (elaborated in the first twenty-two Futurist manifestos):

1. THE SYSTEMATIC DEMOLITION OF AN EXCESSIVE ADHERENCE TO THE PAST (tradition and mercantilism)
2. WORDS-IN-FREEDOM
3. DYNAMISM IN THE PLASTIC ARTS
4. MULTITONAL MUSIC WITHOUT RHYTHMIC REGULARITY
5. THE ART OF NOISE
6. THE FUTURIST POLITICAL PROGRAM (ANTITRADITIONALIST NATIONALISM)

We shall always regard as SHAMEFUL EXPLOITERS OF FUTUR-ISM all those who publicly declare themselves to be Futurists yet do not defend these principles.

The manner of delivery in Futurist lectures must be given over in part to Free Verse and in part to Words-in-Freedom, so that the irresistible liberation of lyricism from prosody and syntax will be amply demonstrated. Free Verse and Words-in-Freedom must characterize poets belonging to the Directorate of the Futurist Movement.

Counterfeits are greatly on the increase now that Futurism, famous throughout the world, has become a profitable label. Every day we receive the most outlandish proposals, expressed with an enthusiasm that disgusts us, from people who, having at one time insulted, reviled, and derided us, would today like to promote Futurism for their own financial gain.

The mercenary attitude that drives these people, and the dull-witted nature of their tardy admiration, characterize them as the enemies of Futurism whom we should fear most, for Futurism is essentially a heroic altruism and prophetic instinct. Having speculated on the cult of the past, these traditionalists in disguise would now like to speculate on the enthusiasm of the Futurists. We therefore want to put our young, faithful, and tenacious followers on their guard against all that, as they live isolated in small provincial centers and cannot be entirely familiar with the works and principles of Futurism, which may seem contradictory and somewhat muddled to them.

Futurism, as an antitraditionalist tendency, which is both renovator and stimulus of the Italian genius, is extremely broad, has an infinite number of gradations, and embraces a huge variety of temperaments which are more or less Futurist.

We urge our real friends not to let themselves be fooled by the unavoidable proposals of *serate*, which the new speculators on Futurism are making to them, in the same way they make them to us, albeit fruitlessly. Their sole purpose is financial gain and prostituting Futurism in some great theatrical shindig.[4]

Futurist *serate* should explode at the right time, when some new statement can wait no longer, as was the case recently at the University of Bologna,[5] and requires vehement promotion, a violent defense concluding logically in punches, slaps, and a kick in the teeth of the conventionalists, actions for which, so far, we hold the patent.

Real Futurist *serate* were fierce battles from which we always emerged victorious, having routed thousands of conventionalists as we nonchalantly smoked our cigarettes between two protective walls of admirers, who had turned up by chance. These latest Futurists don't have any of our sense of strategy or of the solidarity of a battalion that is well drawn up. Without us, they run the risk of causing reversals that will be harmful to the Movement.

Only those Futurists who, even if very young and unknown, have shown they possess a Futurist creative power, a combative spirit, physical strength, and an enthusiastic belief in the Futurist manifestos and in us, the inventors of Futurism, are, or will be, admitted to the Directorate, and will remain in it.

This text was published as a broadsheet, with a note: "All newspapers which publish this article in its entirety and provide us with a reference copy of it shall be sent a copy of *Zang Tumb Tumb*, first book of Words-in-Freedom by F. T. Marinetti." It also appeared in *Lacerba* on April 1, 1914.

31

Manifesto of Futurist Playwrights: The Pleasures of Being Booed

Of all the literary genres upon which Futurism can have most immediate influence, it is undoubtedly the drama. Therefore, we want dramatic Art to cease being what it is today, namely, a wretched product of a theater industry, subject to the popular amusement and pleasure business. We have to sweep away all of the foul prejudices that weigh so heavily on playwrights, actors, and audiences alike.

1. First of all, we Futurists instruct authors **to despise the public**, and especially those habitués of opening nights, whose psychology we can sum up like this: rivalry between women's hats and dresses; the vanity associated with expensive seats that gets transformed into intellectual pride; boxes and stalls occupied by the aging rich, whose attitudes are naturally dismissive and whose digestion[1] is so appalling it makes any kind of mental effort impossible.

   The public, which varies from month to month, from city to city, and from district to district, and which is subject to political and social trends, to the whims of fashion, to wet weather, to hot spells or cold spells, to the last thing read in the afternoon, and which, sadly, nowadays desires nothing more than being left to digest their dinners pleasurably at the theater, has absolutely nothing to say by way of critical approval or disapproval of a work of art.

   The author may try his damnedest to entice the spectators away from their mediocrity, as one pulls a shipwrecked man toward the shore. He needs to take care, though, not to let himself be grasped by their fearful hands, for he would go to the bottom with them, to the sound of clapping hands.

2. Moreover, we express our **horror of instant success**, which usually crowns works that are mediocre and banal. The plays that enthuse an entire audience, without intermediaries, without explanations, are works which are more or less well constructed, but which are absolutely devoid of innovation and therefore of creative genius.

3. Playwrights should have no other concern than that of an **absolute, innovative originality**. Any work for the theater that starts out from a commonplace or draws its conception, its plot, or some part of its development from other works of art, is utterly despicable.

4. The leitmotifs of love and the adulterous triangle, having already been much overused, must be banished entirely from the theater.

   Love and the adulterous triangle must have only a secondary value on stage, as episodes or additional features; i.e., they must have the same value they now have in real life, thanks to the great efforts of the Futurists.

5. Since dramatic art, like all the other arts, can have no other purpose than that of snatching the soul of the audience from its base, day-to-day reality and exalting it in an atmosphere of dazzling intellectual intoxication, we despise all of those works whose aim is merely to stir the emotions and make people weep, through the inevitably pathetic scene of a mother whose son is dead or that of a girl who cannot marry the man she loves, and other banalities of that sort.

6. In art, and most especially in the theater, we **loathe every sort of historical reconstruction**, whether its interest stems from the figure of an illustrious hero or heroine (Nero, Julius Caesar, Napoleon, or Francesca da Rimini[2]) or from a fascination with the pointless lavishness of costumes or scenery from the past.

   Modern theater must reflect something of the great Futurist dream that arises out of our daily lives, accentuated by speed on the ground, at sea, and in the air, and dominated by steam and electricity. We have to introduce into the theater a sense of the rule of the Machine, the great tremors that stir the crowds, the new currents of ideas, and the great discoveries of science, which have totally transformed our sensibilities and mentalities as men of the twentieth century.

7. Dramatic art should not take psychological snapshots, but tend rather toward **a synthesis of life at its most typical** and most significant.

8. Drama cannot exist without poetry, which is to say, without spiritual excitement and compression.

Regular rhythms must, however, be excluded. The Futurist writer will thus make use of **Free Verse**,[3] the unpredictable orchestration of images and sounds, which will range from the simplest tones when dealing, for example, with the entrance of a servant or the closing of a door, to the rhythm of the passions, set in cadenced or even sometimes chaotic verses, when dealing with the announcement of a people's victory or the glorious death of an airman.

9. We need to destroy the obsession with financial reward among writers, for it is greed for monetary gain that has propelled into the theater writers whose only gifts are those of the critic or the social chronicler.

10. We want actors to be completely subordinate to the authority of writers, and to rescue them from thralldom to a public that urges them, fatally, to look for facile effects, thus distancing them from any profound interpretation whatsoever. It is for this reason that we must abolish the grotesque custom of applauding and booing, which may well serve as a barometer of parliamentary eloquence but certainly not of the value of a work of art.

11. While we are waiting for this to happen, let us remind authors and actors of **the pleasures of being booed**.

Everything that is booed is not necessarily either beautiful or new. But everything that is immediately applauded is certainly not superior to the average intelligence and is thus something that is mediocre, banal, spewed up again, or overdigested.

In affirming these Futurist convictions, I am happy in the knowledge that my own genius, frequently whistled at by audiences in France and Italy,[4] will never be buried beneath applause that is too heavy, like any old Rostand![5] . . .

A first version of this manifesto was published as a flier with the title *Manifesto dei drammaturghi futuristi* and was dated October 11, 1910. It was reprinted in the Turin theater journal *Il nuovo teatro*, nos. 5–6 (December 25, 1910–January 5, 1911), under the title *Conclusioni futuriste sul teatro*. Another flier, again entitled *Manifesto dei drammaturghi futuristi*, carries the date January 11, 1911. In *Guerra sola igiene del mondo* (1915) it is called *La voluttà d'esser fischiati*. A first French version, *Manifeste des auteurs dramatiques futuristes*, appeared as a flier, dated April 22, 1911. It was reprinted under the title *La Volupté d'être sifflé* in *Le Futurisme* (1911). The manifesto was not signed, as the title suggests, by Futurist playwrights, but by thirteen poets, five painters, and one musician, some of whom had never written a play in their life.

32

The Variety Theater

We feel a deep contempt for the theater of today (poetic, prose, and musical) because it wavers between historical reconstructions (pastiche or plagiarism) and photographic reproductions of our daily lives. These make for a theater that is finicky, slow, analytical, and watered down—in fact, entirely worthy of the age of the oil lamp. Instead, we delight in visiting the Variety Theater (or music-hall, café-concert, or hippodrome),[1] which in this day and age offers the only theatrical entertainment worthy of a true Futurist spirit.

FUTURISM PROMOTES THE VARIETY THEATER because:

1. Fortunately, the Variety Theater, born like us into the age of electricity, is without traditions, masters, or dogmas, and it feeds on the rapidly passing events of the moment.
2. The Variety Theater is pure action and sets out to distract and amuse, using comic effects, erotic suggestion, or startling imagination.
3. Authors, actors, and stagehands, in the Variety Theater, have only one raison d'être, one means of triumph, that of endlessly inventing new ways of causing amazement. From which it follows that it is absolutely impossible for them to fall into stagnation or to repeat themselves. As a result, there is fierce competition of mind and muscle to beat all records for agility, speed, and strength, for complexity and elegance.

4. The Variety Theater is unique, at present, in making use of film,[2] which enriches it with innumerable, otherwise unattainable visions and displays (battles, riots, races, motorcar and airplane races, journeys, ocean liners, the wonders of the city, the countryside, the oceans, the skies).

5. The Variety Theater, offering, as it does, a lucrative showcase for numerous inventive artists, quite naturally generates what I call the "Futurist Marvel,"[3] produced by modern gadgetry. And here are just a few of these wondrous inventions: 1. powerful caricatures; 2. the very depths of absurdity; 3. delightful, unsurpassable ironies; 4. all-embracing, definitive symbols; 5. cascades of uncontrollable laughter; 6. well-conceived analogies between human beings, the animal kingdom, the plant world, and the world of machines; 7. glimpses of revealing cynicism; 8. intricate interplay of witty sayings, puns, and riddles, which have the effect of airing the brain in an enjoyable manner; 9. the whole gamut of laughter and smiles to calm the nerves; 10. the whole gamut of silliness, idiocy, gawkiness, and absurdities, which drive intelligence imperceptibly to the edge of madness; 11. all the new meanings of light, sound, noise, and words, with their mysterious and inexplicable extensions into the least known parts of our sensibilities; 12. the piling up of events that are raced through in an instant, and of stage characters bundled off, from right to left, in a couple of minutes ("and now let's take a glance at the Balkans": King Nicholas, Enver-Bey, Daneff, Venizelos,[4] arms akimbo then slaps between Serbs and Bulgarians, a *couplet*, then everything vanishes); 13. instructive satirical pantomime; 14. caricatures of grief and nostalgia, strongly imprinted upon our sensibilities through gestures that are exaggerated by their spasmodic, hesitant, and wearying slowness; grave words made ridiculous by comic body language, bizarre disguises, twisted words, grimaces, and buffoonery.

6. The Variety Theater of today is a melting pot of the many elements of a new sensibility in the making. In it one finds an ironic decomposition of all the tired old stereotypes—the Beautiful, the Great, the Solemn, the Religious, the Ferocious, the Seductive, and the Terrifying, as well as abstract sketches of the new prototypes that will take their places.

The Variety Theater is thus a synthesis of everything that humankind has hitherto instinctively refined to lift its spirits, by laughing at material and moral anguish. What's more, it is the bubbling fusion of all laughter, all smiles, all guffaws, all contortions, and all grimaces of future humanity. In it we have a taste of the happiness that will shake humankind a hundred years from now, of their poetry, their pictures, their philosophy, and the forward leap of their architecture.

7. The Variety Theater offers the healthiest of all the kinds of entertainment, by virtue of the dynamism of its form and color (simultaneous movement of jugglers, ballerinas, gymnasts, multicolored riding troupes, dancers *en point*, whirling around like spinning tops). With the rhythm of its quick, exhilarating dances, the Variety Theater inevitably drags the most sluggish souls out of their torpor and forces them to run and to leap.

8. The Variety Theater is the only one that closely involves the audience. The latter does not sit there unmoving, like some stupid voyeur, but noisily participates in the action. It sings along with the actors, beats time with the orchestra, and communicates through spontaneous witticisms and bizarre exchanges with the actors, who themselves lark about with the musicians.

   The Variety Theater makes use of cigar and cigarette smoke to fuse together the atmosphere in the auditorium with that on stage. And because the audience collaborates with the actors' imagination in this way, the action takes place on stage, in the boxes and in the stalls, all at the same time. It continues after the show is over, among the hordes of admirers, the sybaritic dandies who crowd around the exit to squabble over the starlets. Then comes the final double victory: a posh dinner, and then to bed with her.

9. The Variety Theater is an instructive schooling in sincerity for the male, since it plays up his predatory instincts as well as tearing away all the woman's veils, all her words, her sighs, her romantic sobs that deform her and conceal her true qualities. Instead, it emphasizes all the admirable, instinctive qualities in a woman, her particular strengths—her grasp of things, her seductiveness, her fickleness, and her resilience.

10. The Variety Theater is a school for heroism on account of its attempts to beat difficult records and to surpass all previous efforts, which create on stage a strong, healthy sense of danger (e.g., death-defying leaps, looping the loop on bicycles, in a motorcar, or on horseback).

11. The Variety Theater is a school for subtlety, complexity, and mental synthesis for its clowns, its conjurors, its mind readers, its geniuses

with mental arithmetic, its goofy actors,[5] its imitators and parodists, its musical wizards, and its American eccentrics,[6] those whose pregnant fantasies give birth to the most unlikely objects and devices.

12. The Variety Theater is the only school to recommend to quick-witted adolescents and youngsters because it rapidly and incisively explains the most abstruse problems and the most complex political events. For example: a year ago, at the Folies-Bergère, two dancers presented the discussions, which went backward and forward, between Cambon and Kiderlen-Wächter on the questions of Morocco and the Congo,[7] with a meaningful, symbolic dance that was worth at least three years' study of foreign affairs. The two dancers, facing the audience with their arms tightly linked so that they stood side by side, made territorial concessions by jumping backward and forward, to left and to right, never letting go of each other, with neither of them ever losing sight of his goal, which was that of cheating each other in turn. They gave an impression of extreme courtesy, considered flexibility, anger, diffidence, obstinacy, precision—all in a matchless, diplomatic manner.

Furthermore, the Variety Theater sheds much light on the most important rules of life:

(a) the need for complication and varied rhythms;
(b) the inevitability of lies and contradictions (e.g., two-faced English dancers: a little shepherdess and a nasty soldier);
(c) the supreme power of the organized will and its diverse effects on human powers;
(d) the synthesis of speed + transformations (e.g., Fregoli).[8]

13. The Variety Theater systematically devalues idealized love and its romantic obsessions, by repeating endlessly, with the mechanical monotony of everyday routine, the tedious yearnings of passion. In bizarre fashion, it mechanizes sentiment, it healthily devalues and tramples upon obsession with sexual possession, it reduces lust to its natural function of coitus, ridding it of all its mystique, its depressing anguish, and its unwholesome idealism.

In contrast, the Variety Theater gives meaning to, and a taste for, casual love affairs that are ironical, without commitment. Open-air café-concert performances on the terraces of casinos offer a very entertaining battle between a consumptive moonlight, tormented by endless desperation, and the electric light that flashes frenziedly over imitation jewels, painted flesh, highly colored petticoats, velvets, sequins, and the false, cherry-colored lips. Of course, in the end, it is the lively electric light that triumphs, while the feeble, faltering moonlight is defeated.[9]

14. The Variety Theater is naturally antiacademic, primitive, and naive, and thus carries more significance because of the unexpectedness of its revelations and the simplicity of its means (e.g., the chanteuses' habitual round of the stage, at the end of each *couplet*, like wild animals in a cage).

15. The Variety Theater destroys the Solemn, the Sacred, the Serious, and the Sublime in Art with a capital *A*. It assists in the Futurist destruction of immortal masterpieces, by plagiarizing them, parodying them, treating them casually, without formal presentation and without any apologies, just like any other ordinary turn. And so, we support unconditionally a forty-minute performance of *Parsifal*, which is currently in preparation for a great music-hall in London.[10]

16. The Variety Theater destroys all our preconceived notions about perspective, proportion, time, and space (e.g., a tiny porch and gate, thirty centimeters high, stands on its own in the middle of the stage, and through it certain eccentric Americans pass back and forth, opening and closing the gate in all seriousness, as if they had no choice).

17. The Variety Theater provides us with all the greatest records achieved to date: the fastest speed and the finest acrobatic and balancing feats of the Japanese, the greatest muscular frenzy of the negroes, the highest development of intelligence in animals (horses, elephants, seals, dogs, and tamed birds), the finest melodic inspiration of the Gulf of Naples and of the steppes of Russia, the very essence of the Parisian spirit, the greatest comparative strengths of the different races (boxing and wrestling), the most freakish of human anatomies, and the greatest beauties among women.

18. While the theater we have at present highlights the inner life, erudite cogitations, libraries, museums, boring struggles with conscience, and the stupid analyses of feelings, in short—both the reality and the word are foul—*psychology*, the Variety Theater exalts action, heroism, the open-air life, skill, the authority of instinct and intuition. In opposition to psychology it offers what I call *body-madness*.

19. And finally, the Variety Theater offers every country that does not have one great capital city (such as Italy), a brilliant digest of Paris,

the city generally regarded as the unique, bewitching abode of ultrarefined luxury and pleasure.

FUTURISM WANTS TO TRANSFORM THE VARIETY THEATER INTO THE THEATER OF AMAZEMENT, OF RECORD-SETTING, AND OF BODY-MADNESS

1. It is absolutely necessary to eradicate all logic from shows in the Variety Theater, to exaggerate their extravagant expenditure, in all sorts of strange ways, to multiply the number of contrarieties in them, and to make the improbable and the absurd reign supreme on the stage. For example: Have the chanteuses paint their bare necks and chests, their arms, and especially their hair in all of those colors which, up to now, have been spurned as means of seduction. Green hair, violet arms, sky-blue neck and chest, orange-tinted chignons, and so on; or else interrupt a song only to make it go on in the form of a revolutionary speech; or again, pepper a romantic song with insults and swear words and so on.

2. Prevent any set of traditions from becoming established in the Variety Theater. So we have to fight against and eliminate Parisian-style *revues*,[11] which are as stupid and tedious as Greek tragedy, with their masters of ceremonies of both sexes taking on the role of the ancient chorus, with their processions of political personages and events underscored with witty maxims, with their regular sequences of extremely tedious numbers. In fact, the Variety Theater must not be what it unfortunately almost always continues to be today—a more or less humorous sort of newspaper.[12]

3. Introduce the element of surprise and the need for action among the audience in the stalls, the boxes, and the gallery. Here are some random suggestions: spread a strong glue on some of the seats so that their occupants, whether male or female, are stuck there, to the amusement of everyone else (of course, evening suits and dresses that are damaged will naturally be paid for by the management, on the way out); sell the same seat to ten different people, causing obstruction, bickering, and wrangling; offer free tickets to men or women who are known to be a bit off their heads, irascible, or eccentric, and who are likely to provoke a scene with their obscene gestures, their nipping of women's bottoms, or other objectionable behavior; sprinkle itching powder or sneezing powder all over the seats, making people scratch or sneeze, and so on.

4. Corrupt all classical art on stage—for example, putting on all the Greek, French, and Italian tragedies in a single evening, condensing them and mixing them up comically. Liven up the works of Beethoven, Wagner, Bach, Bellini, and Chopin by inserting Neapolitan songs. Put Zacconi, Duse, and Mayol, or Sarah Bernhardt and Fregoli,[13] on stage together. Play one of Beethoven's symphonies backward, starting on the final note. Reduce the whole of Shakespeare to a single act. Do the same thing with the most respected actors. Get actors to perform *Hernani*[14] in sacks, with only their heads showing. Soap the boards on the stage to make the actors slip and slither about in the most tragic moments.

5. Make full and frequent use of the American type of eccentric, with their grotesque looks, their terrifying dynamism, their vulgar expressions, their enormous savagery, their novel waistcoats, and their huge trousers, roomy as a ship's hold, out of which will come— together with a thousand other things—the great Futurist merriment that must rejuvenate the face of the world.

Now, don't you forget it, we Futurists are YOUNG ARTILLERY-MEN OUT ON A SPREE, as we proclaimed in our manifesto *Let's Kill Off the Moonlight*, fire + fire + light against the moonlight and open warfare against all the old firmaments, every night   great   cities   ablaze   with   neon   signs   enormous negro's face (30m. high + 150m. the height of the building = 180m.) open shut open shut a golden eye 3m. high. **SMOKE SMOKE MANOLI SMOKE MANOLI CIG-ARETTES**   woman in a blouse (50m. + 150m. the height of the building = 170m.) squeezing releasing bust violet rosy lilac sky-blue   froth of electric light in a glass of champagne (30m.) fizzing evaporating in a shadowy mouth   luminous ads fading dying beneath a persistent black hand coming to life again going on stretching on into the night endeavor of a human day   courage + folly never dying nor stopping nor sleeping   neon signs = formation and disintegration of mineral and vegetal center of the earth   blood circulation in the ferrous facades of Futurist houses lighting up turning red (joy anger upward upward still farther soon even stronger still) hardly at all sentimental nostalgic negative pessimistic shadows besiege the city   brilliant reawakening of the streets which during the day channel the smoky swarming of the workaday world

two horses (30 meters high) roll golden balls around with
their   hoofs   **GIOCONDA   LAXATIVE   SALTS**
crisscrossing **trrrr trrrrr** Elevated **trrrr trrrrr** overhead **beepbeepbeeping whisssstling** ambulance sirens + electric
pumps   transformation of streets into gorgeous corridors leading urging logical necessity the crowd toward trepidation +
hilarity + the din of the music-hall   **FOLIES-
BERGÈRE   EMPIRE   CREME-ECLIPSE** tubes of mercury
red red red deep blue deep blue violet   enormous golden
letter-eels fire crimson diamond Futurist challenge to the tearful night
stars put to rout warmth enthusiasm faith conviction
will penetration of a neon sign into the building opposite **yellow slaps**
in the face for that dozing gouty old fogy in bookworms' slippers Three
mirrors are looking at him   the sign dives into the
three reddish-golden chasms opening closing opening closing of the
depths of three billion kilometers   horror going out going
out soon hat cane stairs taxi jostling crowds **kee-kee-kee** here we
are   dazzling promenade   Swaying of the
panther-ladies of easy virtue in the tropics of popular music
curvaceous warm smell of music-hall gaiety = tireless
ventilator of the world's Futurist mind.

**This manifesto was published in a number of editions. A first broad-
sheet version is entitled *Il teatro di varietà: Manifesto futurista*, and is
dated September 29, 1913. A French edition appeared simultaneously
and carried the title *Le Music-Hall: Manifeste futuriste*. The Italian version
appeared in *Lacerba* on October 1, 1913, and was reprinted in various
collections. On November 21, 1913, the *Daily Mail* published the *Lacerba*
version in an abridged form under the title *The Meaning of the Music-
Hall. By the Only Intelligible Futurist F. T. Marinetti*. A complete English
translation by D. Neville Lees was issued by Gordon Craig in *The Mask 6*,
no. 3 (January 1914). A later, four-page leaflet, probably from the end
of 1913, contains some textual variations, which I have included in our
translation here.**

33

Dynamic, Multichanneled Recitation

Awaiting the pleasurable honor of returning to the front,[1] we Futurists are actively renewing and quickening the spirit of our race, making it more manly.

The range of our activities is increasing steadily. A great Futurist exhibition of Balla's in Rome.[2] A lecture by Boccioni on Futurist painting at the Fine Arts Institute in Naples.[3] Boccioni's manifesto aimed at our Painters in the South.[4] A lecture by Boccioni on Futurist painting, in Mantua.[5] A lecture-cum-recitation on the topic of Words-in-Freedom by Marinetti, Cangiullo, Jannelli, and Bruno Corra at the Fine Arts Institute in Naples.[6] Francesco Cangiullo editing a section called "Pages on Futurism" in *Vela latina*.[7] Eight Futurist *serate* on the Art of Noise and the Sound Machines by Luigi Russolo and Ugo Piatti at Marinetti's house.[8]

I have offered politicians the only possible solution to the financial crisis—namely, the gradual, judicious selling off of our artistic patrimony in order to increase the military, industrial, commercial, and agricultural strength of Italy a hundredfold, and crush our hated, eternal enemy Austria, once and for all.[9]

Yesterday, Settimelli, Bruno Corra, Remo Chiti, Francesco Cangiullo, Boccioni, and I were urging a Florentine audience to war through our forcefully patriotic, antineutralist, anti-German Theater of Essential Brevity.[10] Today, I wish to free intellectuals from the age-old, static, pacifist, and nostalgic type of recitation and create a new, dynamic, synoptic,[11] and warlike form of recitation.

My indisputable world leadership in reciting Free Verse and Words-in-Freedom has made it all too clear to me how inferior recitation is, in the way it has been understood until now. This traditional sort of recitation, even when supported by the most wonderful vocal organs and by the strongest of temperaments, always inevitably ends up being a monotonous series of high and low points, a hodgepodge of gestures, which time and time again wash over the inveterate stupidity of lecture audiences in floods of boredom.[12]

I've been amusing myself far too long, seducing them and stirring up their emotions more effectively than any other reciter in Europe. I've done this by ushering the most astonishing images into their dull minds, caressing them with studied modulations of my voice, with velvety softness and brutality until, cowed by my look or mesmerized by one of my smiles, they have felt the effeminate urge to applaud that which they neither understood nor appreciated.

I've had plenty of experience of the effeminacy of crowds and their virginal vulnerability when hammering Futurist Free Verse into them. Well-rehearsed tricks of facial expression and gesture served the early forms[13] of Futurist lyricism most admirably, that lyricism which, by making use of all the tendencies of Symbolism and Decadentism,[14] represented, in a certain sense, the most poignant and complete humanization of the universe.

The chief characteristic of the traditional speaker of verse is that he doesn't move around, even though the excessive movement of the upper part of his body gives the impression that he's a puppet in the hands of a puppet master, performing at a fair.

In the new Futurist lyricism, which expresses geometrical splendors, our literary "I" is burnt up and destroys itself in the superior vibrancy of the cosmos,[15] so that the one who recites must also disappear, in a manner of speaking, in the dynamic, multichanneled revelation of the Words-in-Freedom.

Futurist recitation must engage the legs as well as the arms. This sort of lyrical gymnastics will compel poets to whine less and be more forceful and more positive.

The speaker's hands must manipulate a variety of noisy instruments. That'll put an end to them rowing around haphazardly in the muddy minds of their audience. There'll be no more flailing around by the conductor, as he stresses the phrasing, nor any more populist, more or less ritual gestures, nor the languid actions of the prostitute as she moves her hands over the body of her worn-out client. Caressing hands, lace-making hands, hands which supplicate, nostalgic or senti-mental hands—all of that will disappear with the absolute dynamism of the reciter.

The Futurist speaker of verses must therefore:

1. Wear self-effacing clothes (maybe an evening suit), avoiding clothes that may suggest particular situations. No flowers in buttonholes, no gloves.
2. Dehumanize his voice completely, removing all modulations or nu-ancing, as a matter of course.
3. Dehumanize the face entirely, shunning all expression as well as all movement of the eyes.
4. Make his voice metallic, liquefied, vegetalized, be turned to stone and electrified, fusing it with the very vibrations of matter itself, ex-pressed by means of Words-in-Freedom.
5. Gesticulate geometrically, thus making his arms entirely rigid like railway signals or lighthouse beams to point out the direction of the movement of forces or of pistons or wheels, to express the dynamic nature of Words-in-Freedom.
6. Gesticulate as if drawing or surveying, so as to create syntheses of cubes, cones, spirals, ellipses, etc., in the air.
7. Make use of a range of elementary instruments such as hammers, trowels, motor horns, drums, tambourines, saws, and electric bells, so as to produce, precisely and without the slightest difficulty, a va-riety of simple or abstract onomatopoeias and different onomato-poeic harmonies.

    These various instruments, in certain orchestral compilations of Words-in-Freedom, can behave as if in an orchestra, each one be-ing played by a particular individual.
8. Employ the services of other speakers who are of either equal or in-ferior status, mingling or alternating his voice with theirs.
9. Move around between different points in the hall, more or less quickly, running or walking slowly, thus making his body move-ments reflect the enunciation of the Words-in-Freedom. Every part of the poem will therefore have its own specific radiance and the audience, though following the speaker as if he were a magnet, will not be passively subjected to the lyric force, but through look-ing around at the different points of the hall, will share in the dy-namism of the Futurist poem.
10. Finish off the performance with two, three, or four blackboards

arranged around the hall, on which he must rapidly sketch theorems, equations, and synoptic tables of lyrical values.

11. In his recitations he must be inventive, tirelessly creative:

a) deciding instinctively, at every moment, the point at which the tone-adjective and the atmospheric adjective have to be spoken and repeated.[16] Since there aren't any precise indicators in the Words-in-Freedom, he must follow his own inclinations, taking the greatest care to attain maximum geometrical splendor and numerical sensibility. In this way, he will work closely with the author who uses Words-in-Freedom, intuitively laying down new laws and creating novel and unforeseen horizons in the Words-in-Freedom that he interprets.

b) With all the cool detachment of an engineer or a mechanic, explaining and clarifying the synoptic tables and the equations of lyrical values that establish clear, more or less geographical zones (between the most obscure and complex parts of the Words-in-Freedom), and occasional concessions to the reader's comprehension.

c) By imitating engines and their rhythms, in everything and for everything (without bothering about understanding), when reciting these most obscure and complex parts and especially all of the onomatopoeic harmonies.

The first "Dynamic and Multichanneled Recitation" took place on March 29, 1914, at the permanent Futurist Exhibition, 125 via del Tritone, in Rome.[17]

PIEDIGROTTA

Words-in-Freedom by the Futurist Free-worder,
FRANCESCO CANGIULLO

performed by {**MARINETTI**
                {**CANGIULLO**

with the assistance of

those most celebrated dwarf artists

$\left\{ \begin{array}{l} \text{Miss TOFA } (\textbf{\textit{Sprovieri}}) \\ \text{Mr PUTIPÙ (Balla)} \\ \text{Mr TRICCABBALLACCHE (Radiante)} \\ \text{Mr SCETAVAIASSE (Depero)} \\ \text{Mr FISCHIATORE (Sironi)} \end{array} \right.$

who will appear in their patented onomatopoeic creations

FINAL CHORUS FOR SIX VOICES

Before the performance begins, MARINETTI will explain the artistic value of onomatopoeic artists, the Gentlemen

TOFA-PUTIPÙ-TRICCABBALLACCHE-SCETAVAIASSE-FISCHIATORE

I began by explaining to the audience the artistic and symbolic value of the various onomatopoeic instruments. In the *tofa*, which is a large seashell that Neapolitan street urchins blow to make a dark blue, tragicomic moaning sound, I find a biting satire of that particular mythology, with all its sirens, tritons, and conch shells, which populates the antiquated Bay of Naples.[18]

The **putipù** (an orange-colored noise), sometimes called a *caccavella* or a *pernacchiatore*, is a small box made of tin or terracotta, covered with hide, and into which a reed is placed, which resonates comically if a wet hand is rubbed over it. It represents the ferocious irony with which a young and healthy race rebukes and fights against the nostalgic poisons of the Moonlight.

The **scetavaiasse** (a rose-and-green-colored sound), whose bow is a wooden saw that has little bells all over it and bits of tin, is a good-natured parody of the violin as expression of the inner life and of anguished feelings. Facetiously, it pokes fun at musical virtuosity—Paganini, Kubelik,[19] the angelic viola players of Benozzo Gozzoli,[20] classical music, the halls of the conservatories, which are full of boredom and depressing gloom.

The **triccabballacche** (a red noise) is a sort of wooden lyre whose cords are made of extremely fine wooden rods, which are tipped with square hammers, also made of wood. They are played like cymbals, by opening and closing the raised hands which hold the two verticals.

They are a satire on the processions of Greco-Roman priests and lyre players found on the friezes of old-fashioned buildings.

Then I recited *Piedigrotta*, in a dynamic fashion—**wonderful, overpowering Words-in-Freedom, sprung from the most exhilarating, most original genius of Francesco Cangiullo, a great Futurist performer of Words-in-Freedom, the most important writer in Naples and the greatest humorist in all Italy**. From time to time the author leaped to the piano while alternating with me in the recitation of his Words-in-Freedom. The hall was lit by red lamps that redoubled the dynamic effects of the *piedigrottesque* backcloth, painted by Balla. The audience greeted the appearance of the procession of dwarves with frenzied applause, as they circled around me while I recited, all arrayed in their tissue-paper hats.

The gaily colored vessel that the painter Balla carried on his head was greatly admired.[21] Very much in evidence, in a corner, was a bile-green-colored still life of three Crocean philosophers,[22] a tasteful, funereal contrast with the brightly lit atmosphere of Futurism. Those people who believe in a joyous, optimistic, and divinely carefree art carried the doubters with them. The audience accompanied with their gestures and their voices the marvelous uproar that broke out from time to time during my performance, and this resulted in a most obvious and effective fusion with the onomatopoeic instruments.

The second dynamic, multichanneled performance I did myself in London on April 28, 1914, at the Doré Galleries.

I recited several passages from my *Zang Tumb Tumb: Adrianopoli* in a dynamic and multichanneled fashion. On the table, arranged in front of me, I had a telephone, some boards, and the right sort of hammers so that I could act out the orders of the Turkish general and the sounds of rifle and machine-gun fire.

At three different points in the room, three blackboards had been set up, and these I approached, each in their turn, either walking or running, so as to make rapid chalk sketches of some analogy or other. My audience, continually turning so as to follow all of my movements, was utterly enthralled, their bodies alight with emotion at the violent effects of the battle described by my Words-in-Freedom.[23]

In a room some distance away, two great drums were set, and with these the painter Nevinson,[24] who was assisting me, produced the thunder of canon, when I telephoned him to do so.[25]

The growing interest of the English audience turned into frenzied enthusiasm when I arrived at the peak of the dynamic performance, alternating the Bulgarian song "Sciumi Maritza"[26] with my dazzling images and the rumble of my onomatopoeic artillery.

The first Italian edition of this manifesto appeared in Francesco Cangiullo's brochure *Piedigrotta* (1916), where it is dated March 11, 1916. However, a letter Marinetti sent to Cangiullo in April 1914 shows that the text of the manifesto, except the introductory paragraphs, was already written and typeset shortly after the first performance of *Piedigrotta* on March 29, 1914.

34

こ*o*

A Futurist Theater of Essential Brevity

(A-technical—Dynamic—Simultaneous—Autonomous—
A-logical—Unreal)

F. T. MARINETTI, EMILIO SETTIMELLI, BRUNO CORRA

While waiting for the start of our great, much-called-for war, we Futurists alternate our violent antineutralist action in the piazzas and universities[1] with our artistic activities, thereby preparing Italian sensibilities
for the great hour of supreme Danger. Italy must be fearless, relentless,
flexible, and swift as a swordsman, shrugging off blows like a boxer, impassive when hearing of a victory that has cost fifty thousand lives, or
when hearing about a defeat.

Italy has no need of books or magazines to learn how to come to a
lightning decision, how to hurl herself into battle, how to maintain all-
out effort and absorb every possible misfortune. These are of interest
and concern to a mere minority. To a greater or lesser extent they are
tedious, they are obstacles and slow things down; they can only
dampen enthusiasm, cut short our forward dash, and poison the minds
of a people at war with doubts. War, which is an intensified form of Futurism, compels us to march and not to fester[2] in libraries and reading
rooms. **We believe, therefore, that today it is only through the
theater that we can instill a warlike spirit in Italians.** As it happens, 90 percent of all Italians go to the theater, while a mere 10 percent read books and journals. So what is called for is a **Futurist theater**,
one that is totally opposed to the conventional theater of the past, which
still spins out its depressing, boring, funereal fare on the somnolent stages
of Italy.

It is pointless to belabor our protests against the theater of the past,
which was utterly nauseating and has already been dumped by tradi-

tionalist audiences, we condemn all contemporary theater for being prolix, analytical, full of textbook psychology, explicatory, watered down, finicky, static, as full of prohibitions as a police station, divided into cells like a monastery, musty like an old, uninhabited house. For the most part, it is pacifist and neutralist, quite the opposite of the ferocious, overwhelming, and unifying momentum of war.

We are creating a Futurist Theater that will be:

COMPRESSED[3]

that is, very short, squeezing into a few minutes, a few words and a few gestures, innumerable situations, sensibilities, ideas, sensations, facts, and symbols.

The writers who wanted to revitalize the theater (Ibsen, Maeterlinck, Andreyev, Paul Claudel, Bernard Shaw) never thought of freeing themselves from a technique characterized by prolixity, detailed analysis, and lengthy exposition, and of creating a truly pithy form of theater. Seeing the works of these authors, an audience has precisely the same attitude as a group of bystanders, mildly indulging their fear and their pity, as they watch the lingering agony of a horse that has collapsed on the pavement. The sighs and applause that break out at the end relieve the audience's stomachs of all the undigested time they have swallowed. Each act reminds you of having to wait patiently, in some antechamber, for a minister to receive you (*coup de théâtre*: a kiss, a shot, a word that reveals all, etc.). All of this traditional or semi-Futuristic theater, instead of concentrating action and ideas into the smallest number of words and gestures, totally destroyed the notion of multiplicity of locations (always a source of great interest and dynamism) by shoving lots of landscapes, piazzas, and streets into the one sausage of a single room.[4] With the result that this kind of theater is entirely static.

We are certain that by being brief, it is possible to arrive mechanically at a theater that is entirely new, and perfectly in harmony with our lightning-fast yet pithy Futurist sensibilities. Our acts might even be *instantaneous*, lasting but a few seconds.[5] Because of this essential brevity, this compression, the theater will be able to fend off, and even overcome, competition from the *cinema*.

A-TECHNICAL

Traditional drama, more than any other literary form, compels genius to become deformed, to be diminished. This medium, much more than the opera or the novel, is constrained *by technical requirements*: **1.** it discards all concepts which do not conform with public taste; **2.** having identified an idea for a play (that is easily expressed in a few pages), it dilutes it, waters it down into two, three, or four acts; **3.** it surrounds the character who most interests us with a lot of people who have no significance whatsoever—caricatures, bizarre characters, and other pains in the neck; **4.** it constructs each act in such a way that it lasts somewhere between one-half and three-quarters of an hour; **5.** the acts are crafted as if (a) one should begin with seven or eight pages that are utterly irrelevant; (b) one should introduce only a tenth of the main idea in the first act, half in the second, and two-fifths in the third; (c) one should design the acts in ascending order, so that each act is merely a preparation for the finale; (d) one should always make the first act *a bit tedious*, provided the second is *entertaining* and the third is *entirely absorbing*; **6.** it never fails to shore up every *essential* line with around a hundred or more insignificant lines, *by way of preparation*; **7.** it uses at least a full page to explain, with great precision, the significance of an entrance or an exit; **8.** it systematically applies *the rule of superficial variety* to the entire work, to the acts, the scenes, the lines, for example, by making one act take place in the daytime, one in the evening, and another at dead of night; or by making one act full of pathos, another of anguish, another sublime. When one is forced to make an exchange between two characters longer, the author makes something happen to interrupt it, such as a vase falling, someone going by playing a mandolin . . . or else makes the two characters move about continually, from sitting to standing, from right to left, and at the same time varying the dialogue in such a way that it gives the impression, from one moment to the next, that a bomb is about to explode outside (e.g., the betrayed husband who drags from his wife proof of her deception, when in reality it doesn't until the end of the act; **9.** it pays very close attention to the *plot's verisimilitude*; **10.** it makes sure that the audience *always understands absolutely how and why every action on stage occurs and, above all else, that they know how the protagonists will end up in the final act.*

With our theatrical aesthetics of absolute compression we want to destroy Technique, which from Greek antiquity to today, instead of making things simpler, has become ever more dogmatic, ridiculously logical, meticulous, pedantic, and strangulating. **Therefore**, we maintain:

1. **It is stupid to write a hundred pages when one would suffice**, just because, out of habit and a childish trust in instinct, the audience wants to see the personality of a character emerge from a series of actions, or because the audience needs the illusion that the character himself really does exist, so as to be able to admire

the value of the craftsmanship, while it is reluctant to acknowledge such value if the author hints at it by limiting himself to a few strokes.

2. **It is stupid** not to be in revolt against preconceptions of theatricality, when life itself (which is made up of *actions that are infinitely more awkward, more regulated, and more predictable* than those which are developed in the field of art) is, for the most part, *untheatrical* and even provides, on its side, *endless possibilities for the stage.* **Everything is theatrical when it has value.**

3. **It is stupid** to pander to the primitive desires of the public, which, in the last analysis, wants to see the good character exalted and the bad one defeated.

4. **It is stupid** to worry about verisimilitude (truly absurd, this, since value and genius do not coincide with it at all).

5. **It is stupid** to want to explain a stage action, with all its logic and minutiae, when in life itself it is impossible to grasp an event in its entirety, with all its causes and effects, because reality pulsates around us and assails us with *barrages of unrelated facts that fall into place, each one locked into the next, fused together, knotted together, utterly chaotic.* For example, it is foolish to show a quarrel between two people on stage, *always* in an ordered, logical, and cogent manner, when in our experience of life we almost only ever witness *fragments of an argument* while going about our daily lives as modern men, and we experience them *fleetingly* on a tram, in a café, at a station. Yet they remain cinematically imprinted on our souls as dynamic, fragmented symphonies of gesture, word, sound, and light.

6. **It is stupid** to accept the imposed conventions of *crescendo, exposition, and denouement.*

7. **It is stupid** to let our own genius be weighed down by the millstone of technique, which *everyone* (idiots included), *can learn by continuous study, practice, and patience.*[6]

8. **It is stupid to refuse the daring leap out of the fields already explored into the void of total creation.**

DYNAMIC, SIMULTANEOUS

which means born of improvisation, from a spark of intuition, out of the sensations and revelations of the moment. We believe that a thing has value insofar as it has been improvised (in hours, minutes, seconds) and has not undergone any laborious preparation (over months, years, centuries).

We feel an unquenchable repugnance for drama created in a study, without regard to the theatrical environment in which it is to be presented. **Most of our works have been written in the theater.**[7] The theater itself is for us an inexhaustible source of inspiration: that infectious, magnetic sensation emanating from the gilded, empty theater during a morning's rehearsal, though one's mind is tired; an actor's intonation suggesting the possibility of a paradoxical line of thought to be built upon it; a movement of scenery which sparks off a symphony of light; the voluptuousness of an actress giving rise to an abundance of exciting suggestions.

We were scampering about all over Italy at the head of a heroic battalion of actors, putting on *Electricity* and other Futurist minidramas[8] (alive yesterday but today left behind, condemned by us) which caused nothing less than revolutions in the enclosed spaces of the auditoria. We traveled from the Politeama Garibaldi in Palermo to the Dal Verme Theater in Milan. Our furious massaging of the crowd gave the Italian theaters a facelift, and the audiences' laughter was like the shock of an earthquake. We joined forces with the actors. Then, throughout the sleepless nights of the journey, we talked and talked, each whipping up the inspiration of the others, to the rhythm of tunnels and stations. Our Futurist theater doesn't give a damn for Shakespeare but is very serious about a bit of comic repartee; we fall asleep at a line of Ibsen's, but we get excited at the red and green reflections coming from the stalls. We create an endless dynamism through the intermingling of different times and environments. For example, in contrast to plays such as *Più che l'amore* (More Than Love) where the important actions (e.g., the killing of the gambler) are not seen on stage but are narrated with a total lack of dynamism, or to the first act of *La figlia di Iorio* (Jorio's Daughter),[9] where the actions take place in a single scene without any shifts in time or in place, in the Futurist "compact drama," *Simultaneità* (Simultaneity),[10] there are two environments and many different time levels, which all interact with one another at the same time.

AUTONOMOUS, A-LOGICAL, UNREAL

The Futurist Theater of Essential Brevity will not be subject to logic, it will be in no sense photographic, it will be *autonomous* and will resemble nothing but itself, even though drawing on reality to combine aspects of it in a random manner. Above all, just as for the painter and the composer there exists, strewn all over the external world, a life that is more restricted yet more intense, which is made up of colors, forms, sounds, and noises, so too **for a man gifted with sensitivity to the theater, there** exists a special sort of reality that violently attacks the nerves, and this is composed of that which we call **the world of the theater**.

Futurist theater is born out of the two most vital currents of Futurist sensibility, which are set out in the two manifestos *The Variety Theater* and *Weights, Measures, and Prices of Artistic Genius*, and these are:

1. **Our uncontrollable passion for life in the present, for speed, the fragmentary, the elegant, the complex, the cynical, the muscular, the fleeting, the Futurist; 2.** our most modern, cerebralist[11] **concept of art, according to which no logic, tradition, aesthetic, technique, or opportunity is to be imposed on the genius of the artist, for his only concern must be to create condensed expressions of cerebral energy which will have THE ABSOLUTE VALUE OF NOVELTY.**

Futurist theater will be quite capable of raising its audience's spirits, of making them forget the monotony of their daily lives, by hurling them across **a labyrinth of sensations, full of the most extreme originality and combined in all kinds of unpredictable ways.**

Every evening the **Futurist theater** will provide rigorous training for our race in the rapid, dangerous feats that this Futurist year demands.

CONCLUSIONS:

1. **Eradicate entirely the techniques which are strangling traditional theater.**

2. **Place on the stage all the discoveries (however unrealistic, bizarre, and antitheatrical they might be) that our genius is creating in the subconscious, in the powers of the mind that are poorly defined, in pure abstractions, in pure thought, in genuine fantasy, in its record-setting achievements, and in its physical whimsy.** (E.g., *Vengono* [They Are Coming], the first drama of objects by F. T. Marinetti,[12] a new seam of theatrical sensibility discovered by Futurism.)

3. **Orchestrate the audience's sensibilities like a symphony, probing and reanimating the most sluggish depths of their being, by every possible means. Abolish the barrier of the**

footlights by launching networks of sensation, back and forth, between stage and audience; the action on stage will spill out into the auditorium to involve the spectators.

4. Fraternize, in a friendly manner, with the actors, who are among the few thinkers to have escaped the deforming influence of German-style Kultur.

5. Abolish farce, vaudeville, comic sketches, comedy, drama and tragedy, and in their place create the many different forms of Futurist theater, such as dialogues-in-freedom,[13] simultaneity, interpenetration, short animated poems, dramatized sensations, comic dialogues, negative acts,[14] lines reechoed, nonsense discussions,[15] disintegration of form, scientific spirals,[16] coincidences, display windows,[17] and so on.

6. Through continuous contact, establish an intimate current of cheerfulness, rather than of respect, between us and the mass of spectators, so that we can instill in our audiences the dynamic liveliness of a new, Futurist kind of theater.

These are our *first* pronouncements regarding the theater. Our first eleven minidramas (by Marinetti, Settimelli, Bruno Corra, R. Chiti, Balilla Pratella, and Paolo Buzzi) have been triumphantly staged by Ettore Berti, by Zoncada, and by Petrolini,[18] before huge audiences in Ancona, Bologna, Padua, Naples, Venice, Verona, Florence, and Rome. Soon, in Milan, we shall have a great metal building enlivened by every kind of electromechanical device, whose very presence will permit us to realize our most liberated ideas on stage.[19]

Bruno Corra (Bruno Ginanni Corradini) (1892–1976) started to collaborate with Emilio Settimelli (1891–1954) in 1912 on a series of projects that included literary journals, novels, and plays. In 1913, they became artistic managers of the Compagnia dei Grandi Spettacoli of Gualtiero Tumiati and wrote several minidramas for it. After staging Marinetti's *Elettricità* in Palermo on September 13, 1913, they made plans for setting up a more adventurous and more Futuristically minded theater company. In 1914, this became the troupe directed by Giuseppe Masi and Ettore Berti. The manifesto *A Theater of Essential Brevity* was written to coincide with the premiere of the company in Ancona (February 1, 1915) and to accompany the first printed anthology of plays written for this new genre. It was first issued as a four-page leaflet by the Direzione del Movimento Futurista, dated January 11, 1915, then in the collective volume *Teatro futurista sintetico,* where it is dated February 18, 1915, and in the back of the volume *Elettricità sessuale: Sintesi futurista* (Milan: Facchi, 1920). A number of textual additions were made to the text in *Noi futuristi* (1917), *Dinamo* no. 2 (March 1919), and *I manifesti del futurismo* (1919) and have been included in this translation.

35

⌒

Futurist Dance

(Dance of the Shrapnel—Dance of the Machine Gun—
Dance of the Aviator)

Futurist Manifesto

Dedicated to the Marchesa Luisa Casati[1]

Eight years ago, I wrote, "We shall go to war singing and dancing!"[2] And
that's why today, on the banks of the Vertoibizza,[3] which are thickly strewn
with corpses, beneath a canopy of roaring shells, amid a thousand fires
rapidly fanning out, while snow-white rockets fly too slowly, agonizingly,
wearily, like Lyda Borelli as caricatured by Molinari,[4] I have had a new
vision of Futurist dance.[5]

Dance has always taken its rhythms and its forms from life. The wonders and fears that stirred primitive man, confronted with the incom-
prehensibility and extreme complexity of the universe, are to be found
in their earliest dances, which were perforce sacred dances.[6]

The first Oriental dances, which were permeated by religious awe,
were rhythmic, symbolic pantomimes which naively reproduced the ro-
tary movement of the stars.[7] The "roundel" was born in this way. The
different steps and gestures of the Catholic priest, celebrating mass,
are derived from these earliest dances and bear the same astronomical
symbol.

Cambodian and Javanese dances are distinctive because of their formal elegance and their mathematical regularity. They are slow bas-reliefs in motion.[8]

Arab and Persian dances, on the other hand, are erotic: imperceptible shimmying of the hips accompanied by a rhythmic clapping of hands and beating of drums. Sudden spasmodic starts and hysterical convulsions of the belly dance; the huge, violent leaps of Sudanese dances. They are all variations on a single theme, that of a man sitting cross-legged and a half-naked woman who, with knowing movements, tries to persuade him to make love.[9]

With the glorious Italian ballet dead and buried,[10] stylized forms of primitive dances started up in Europe, refined versions of exotic dances and modernizations of ancient dances.[11] Parisian red pepper + the crest + the shield + the lance + ecstasy before idols that no longer have any meaning + the rippling thighs of Montmartre = traditionalist erotic anachronisms for foreigners.

In Paris before the war, they made the dances from South America more sophisticated: the energetic, anguished Argentine tango, the *zamacueca* from Chile, the Brazilian *maxixe,* and the *santafé* from Paraguay.[12] This latter dance describes the gradual transformation in behavior of an amorous and bold young man toward an attractive and seductive woman whom he, at last, pouncing suddenly, seizes hold of and drags off into a vertiginous waltz.

From an artistic point of view, the Ballets Russes, organized by Diaghilev,[13] is most interesting, for it modernizes popular Russian dances in a wonderful fusion of music and movement, each breaking in upon the other so as to give the spectator a perfect and original expression of the essential strength of the race.

With Nijinsky, for the first time, we see the pure geometry of dance freed from the mimetic and devoid of any sexual excitement. We experience the divinity of muscle in action.[14]

Isadora Duncan creates the Free Dance, without fixed choreography, ignoring muscle and rhythmic unity, to concentrate entirely on the expression of passion, on the passionate creation of the steps themselves. And yet when all is said and done, all she is doing is to intensify, enrich, and modulate, in a thousand different ways, the rhythm of a woman's body that languidly refuses, languidly invokes, languidly accepts, and languidly regrets the male provider of erotic pleasures.

Isadora Duncan, whom I many times had the pleasure of admiring in her free improvisations amid the mother-of-pearl-colored curtains of smoke in her studio, when she danced, carefree, unconstrained, as one speaks, desires, loves, or cries, to any kind of little ditty, such as "Mariette, My Little Mariette," tinkled out on the piano; yet whatever she did, she only managed to convey the most convoluted emotions of a desperate nostalgia, of an agonized sensuousness, or of a childishly feminine gaiety.

There are many points of contact between the art of Isadora Duncan and pictorial Impressionism, just as there are between the art of Nijinsky and the constructions of form and volume in Cézanne.

So, naturally, under the influence of Cubist experiments and especially those of Picasso, a dance of geometric volumes was created, almost independent of the music.[15] Dance became an autonomous art, equal to music. Dance was no longer subject to music, it replaced it.[16]

Valentine de Saint-Point conceived of an abstract and metaphysical dance that should translate pure thought without any sentimentality and without sexual passion. Her *métachorie* is made up of mimed and danced poetry. Unfortunately, they are traditional poems that navigate within the old Greek and medieval sensibilities, abstractions which are danced yet static, arid, cold, and devoid of emotion. Why leave out the invigorating element of facial expression? Why put on a Merovingian helmet and cover one's eyes?[17] The emotions of these dances end up being repetitive, stunted, elementary, and tediously enveloped in the ancient, absurd atmosphere of fearful mythologies that no longer have any meaning for us. A cold geometry of poses that has nothing at all to do with the great, dynamic, instantaneous sensibilities of modern life.[18]

With the most up-to-date of intentions, Dalcroze[19] has created a *rhythmic gymnastics* that is very interesting, but which limits its effects to the toning of muscles and to the portrayal of rural labor.

We Futurists prefer Loïe Fuller[20] and the Negroes' *cakewalk*[21] (making use of electric light and mechanical devices).

We have to go beyond what muscles are capable of and, in the dance, strive toward the ideal of the *body extended* into machine, something we have envisaged for a long time.[22] With our actions, we should imitate the movements of machines; we should pay very close attention to the steering wheel, to wheels, to pistons, and thus prepare the way for the fusion of men and machines, arriving at the metallic character of Futurist dance.

Music is fundamentally and irremediably traditionalist and therefore well-nigh unusable in Futurist dance. Noise, the result of the friction between or the collision of solids, liquids, or gases in swift motion, has become through onomatopoeia one of the most dynamic elements in Futurist poetry. Noise is the language of the new mechanical-human life. Futurist dance will therefore be accompanied by *ordered noises* and by the orchestra of noise instruments invented by Luigi Russolo.

Futurist dance will be

tuneless
rudely ungracious
asymetrical
synthetic
dynamic
Words-in-Freedom[23]

In this Futurist era of ours, while more than twenty million men shape, with their battle lines, a fantastic Milky Way of exploding shrapnel stars that are wrapped about the Earth; while the Machine and High Explosives, working together with war, have increased the power of nations a hundredfold, compelling them to give the very best account of themselves in terms of daring, instinct, and physical resistance; Italian Futurist dance must glorify the heroic man who merges with fast-moving machines and with war, and masters the most Powerful Explosives.[24]

Therefore, I draw the first three Futurist dances from the three instruments of war: shrapnel, the machine gun, and the airplane.[25]

Dance of the Shrapnel

FIRST PART

I wish to represent the fusion of the mountain with the trajectory of the shrapnel. The fusion of human song with the mechanical sound of shrapnel. To present an ideal synthesis of war: a soldier from the Alpine regiment singing,[26] without a care in the world, beneath an unremitting vault of shrapnel shells.

1st movement. Mark out with the feet the *boom-boom* of a shell leaving the mouth of a canon.

2nd movement. With open arms, trace at a moderate speed the whistling trajectory of the shell as it passes over a soldier's head and then explodes

too high above him or somewhere behind him. The dancer will show
a placard with blue lettering: *Short to the right.*

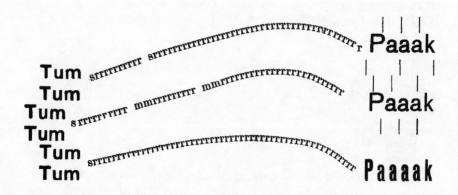

3rd movement. With her open hands (furnished with very long silver
thimbles) raised very high above her head, present the gallant, blissful, silver explosion of the shell with a *paaaak.* The dancer will show
a placard, printed in blue letters: *Long to the left.* Then she will show
another placard with silver lettering: *Don't slip on the ice. Fluid in
the joints.*

4th movement. With her whole body shaking, her hips swaying, and her
arms making swimming motions, present the waves ebbing and flowing and the concentric motions of echoes over the ravines, dales, and
slopes of the mountains. The dancer will show a placard with black lettering: *Water fatigue*; then another with black lettering: *Ration fatigue*;
and yet another in black: *Mules, the mail.*

5th movement. With small, skipping taps of the hands and with the
body in a frozen, ecstatic pose, express the calm and always idyllic indifference of nature and the *tweet-tweet-tweet* of the birds. The dancer
will show a placard whose lettering is haphazard: *300 meters out in the
open.* Then another with red lettering: *15 degrees below zero, 800 meters red violent mellifluous.*

SECOND PART

6th movement. Slow, self-assured, carefree steps of the mountain troops who sing as they march beneath a canopy of continuous, relentless shells. The dancer will light a cigarette, while hidden voices will sing one of many war songs:

The commander of the sixth Alpine regiment
Is starting his cannonade . . .

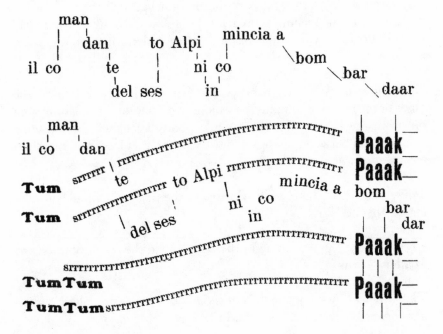

7th movement. The swaying, by which the dancer will continue to express this war song, will be interrupted by the second movement (whistling trajectory of shrapnel).

8th movement. The swaying, with which the dancer will continue to express the war song, will be interrupted by the third movement (explosion of shells high in the air).

9th movement. The swaying will be interrupted by the fourth movement (waves of echoes).

10th movement. The swaying will be interrupted by the fifth movement (the *tweet-tweet-tweet* of the birds in the tranquillity of nature).

Dance of the Machine Gun

I want to present the naked, human quality of the Italian cry of *Savoy!* as it is ripped apart and dies heroically, in shreds, against the mechanistic, geometrical, and inexorable stream of machine-gun fire.

1st movement. With the feet (arms out in front) present the mechanical hammering of the machine gun, rat-at-at-at-at-at-at. With a swift movement the dancer will show a placard, with red lettering: *enemy at 700 meters.*

2nd movement. With her hands cupped (one full of white roses, the other of red) she will imitate the violent and continuous blossoming of fire from the barrels of machine guns. The dancer will have a great white orchid between her lips and she will show a placard with red lettering: *enemy at 500 meters.*

3rd movement. With her arms wide open, she traces the fanlike unfolding hail of shells.

4th movement. Slow turning of the body, while the feet stamp on the wooden boards.

5th movement. Accompany the cry of *Savoooooooy!* with a violent, thrusting, forward movement of the body.

6th movement. On hands and knees, the danseuse will imitate the form of the machine gun, silvery black under its cartridge belt. The arm held in front will violently shake the red-and-white orchid like a gun barrel in the act of firing.

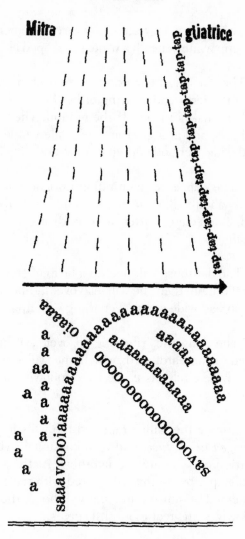

Dance of the Aviator[27]

The danseuse will perform on a brightly colored map (four meters square), on which will be marked, in very large letters, visible to all, the mountains, woods, and rivers, the geometry of the countryside, the great web of city streets, and the sea.

The danseuse must create a continuous billowing of blue veils.[28] On her breast, as if it were a flower, should be a great celluloid propeller which, by its very nature, will gyrate with every movement of her body. Her face will be drip white beneath a white hat shaped like a monoplane.

1st movement. The danseuse, lying on her stomach on the rug map,[29] will imitate with the jerks and swaying of her body the successive attempts an airplane makes to get off the ground. Then she will move forward on all fours, and at a given moment she will leap to her feet, her arms spread wide, her body upright but shuddering all over.

2nd movement. The danseuse, continuing upright, will wave a blue-printed placard about: *300 meters—3 spins of the propeller—climbing.* Then, immediately after, a second placard: *600 meters—avoiding mountain.*

3rd movement. The danseuse will pile up a heap of green cloth to represent a green mountain, then she will leap over it. She will reappear at once, her arms spread wide apart, everything vibrating.

4th movement. The danseuse, vibrating all over, will hold up a great golden sun, made from cardboard, which she will wave about, then quickly run in a wide circle, as if she were following it (frenzied mechanical jerking).

5th movement. Imitate the falling rain and the whistling of the wind, with *noises arranged in advance*, and with continual switching on and off of the electric light, imitate the lightning. At the same time, the danseuse will lift up a frame that is covered with red tissue paper, in the shape of a cloud at sunset, and she will break through it with a nimble leap (slowly, with great mournful surges).

6th movement. The danseuse will wave another frame about, in front of her, covered with dark blue tissue paper, in color and shape like a star-lit night. The danseuse will leap through it. Then she will sprinkle the ground all about her with golden stars (happy, ironic, unselfconscious).

We shall show the audience the amazing costumes, created for these dances, by the great Futurist painter Balla, who has triumphantly staged the first Futurist dance scenario at the Costanzi Theater.[30]

This manifesto of mine does away with all traditional dances, which *must not be revived, nor exhumed, nor renewed.* This does not, however, preclude other ideas about Futurist dance, which our innovative genius will undoubtedly invent.

This text is based on the version that appeared in *L'Italia futurista* of July 8, 1917, reprinted with a different order of the dances and without the illustrations in *Roma futurista* of March 7, 1920. A French translation (*La Danse futuriste. Danse de l'Aviateur—Danse du Shrapnell—Danse de la Mitrailleuse. Danse futuriste*) appeared as a broadsheet in 1920 and was reprinted in *L'Esprit nouveau*, no. 3 (1920).

FUTURISM AND THE GREAT WAR
(1911–17)

Marinetti developed his concept of "war = revolution" early in his career, from a variety of sources, including Georges Sorel on the Left and Enrico Corradini on the Right of the political spectrum. Karl Marx's description of violence as "the midwife of every old society pregnant with a new one" was interpreted in different ways by anarchists and Revolutionary Syndicalists: strike actions, insurrections, revolutions, any form of heroic battle and generative violence was deemed to strengthen the proletariat and assist in the renewal of society. A whole generation of intellectuals, dissatisfied with the corrupt and undemocratic forms of parliamentarianism in Belle Époque Italy, embraced violence in the form of a "rejuvenating war" as a means of creating a new Italy out of the ashes of the past. War was seen as a cleansing process whereby the social body eliminates the unfit and unhealthy, and in particular the pathological and degenerate forms of democracy that only serve the interests of a decrepit and moribund ruling class.

For the Futurists, war also represented life, whereas peace equaled decadence. This was partly a skewed interpretation of the previous two hundred years of Italian history, but also a Social Darwinist view on humankind: aggression, as an anthropological constant, is a necessary precondition of human evolution. What Carrà summed up, in *Guerrapittura*, with the formula "War or revolution—both purifying and invigorating," Marinetti described, in *In This Futurist Year* (document 38), as "demolition work . . . with a view to rebuilding" and as "clear[ing] away the debris [of society] so that we can move a stage further." The idea of armed violence as a purgative medicine, encapsulated in the catchphrase "war—the sole cleanser of the world," was widely shared among intellectuals of the period. The myth of the Great War united writers and artists of often otherwise highly divergent political opinion. But Marinetti's bellicose rhetoric also prompted dissent in socialist and anarchist quarters, as well as among Futurist colleagues such as Renzo Provinciali and Duilio Remondino. Numerous articles were written against Marinetti's warmongering attitude, and whenever he organized a lecture or *serata*, a controversial and often violent reception could be guaranteed.

This section contains texts that are representative of different phases in Marinetti's commitment to war: the revival of irredentism, the Libyan War, the

Interventionist years, and the Great War. In 1908–1909, Marinetti participated in various demonstrations for the completion of Italian unification, with a special focus on the redemption of Trieste from Austrian domination. On October 12, 1911, he arrived in Tripoli as a war correspondent, and observed at close quarters the Turkish-Italian battles, which in a letter to Palazzeschi of January 1912 he described as "the most beautiful aesthetic spectacle of my life." Especially the deployment of airplanes in the conflict made a lasting impression on him. Together with other aspects of the "mechanical orchestra" in this theater of war, they were poetically evoked in a series of articles for *L'Intransigeant* and recited in various Italian theaters in 1912.

In October 1912 Marinetti was at the front again, this time in the First Balkan War (1912–13). He observed the military operation during the Bulgarian-Turkish conflict and the assault on Adrianopolis. The polyphonic spectacle of sounds and smells inspired him to write *Zang Tumb Tumb: Adrianopoli ottobre 1912. Parole in libertà*. Increasingly, Marinetti viewed war as an extension of art by other means, or, as he wrote in the manifesto *In This Futurist Year*, as "an immense Futurist exhibition of aggressive, dynamic canvases." War was seen as a ludic, festive occasion, a gymnastic exercise required to increase the vigor and health of a population. This image of *guerra-festa*, of a jubilant march to the front, "singing and dancing," as he put it in *The Battles of Trieste*, determined Futurist attitudes at the outbreak of the First World War on August 3, 1914.

The Futurists were among the first to demonstrate for Italy's intervention in the European conflict, which eventually took place on May 23, 1915. They enrolled in the Lombard Battalion of Volunteer Cyclists and Automobilists and fought their first battle on October 12, 1915. On December 10, 1915, the unit was disbanded, and for nearly a year the Futurists fought on the "home front" by means of publications, performances, and lectures. In summer 1916 they were again under arms, but this time the engagement had fatal consequences for the architect Antonio Sant'Elia (August 10) and the artist Umberto Boccioni (August 17). Marinetti was posted to an artillery battalion on the Isonzo front, where, on May 14, 1917, he was badly wounded and had to be hospitalized. After a period of convalescence he rejoined the army on September 7, 1917. He served at the front on the river Piave and in the Assa Valley and was involved in the decisive Italian victory at Vittorio Veneto (October 30, 1918). On December 5, 1918, he was officially discharged from the army and could return to Rome, where, during his last stay (August 11–17, 1918), he had set up the Futurist Political Party and its propagandizing journal, *Roma futurista*.

36

✢

Electric War: A Futurist Visionary Hypothesis

Oh, how I envy the men who will be born into my gorgeous peninsula, a century from now, when everything is bursting with energy, shimmering, and harnessed by the new power of electricity!

This obsessive vision of the future seizes my soul in its delicious gusts.

Just look, all along the shoreline, the immense, opaque sea which, no longer at ease, no longer idling like some much-admired courtesan both profligate and treacherous, finally looks as though it has been tamed, has become industrious and productive. The immense, opaque sea, foolishly adored by the poets, labors endlessly by means of its well-tuned, raging storms, to keep countless numbers of iron rafts perpetually in motion, so as to drive two million dynamos, placed along the shore and in a thousand working bays.

Using a network of metal cables, the double strength of the Tyrrhenian and the Adriatic Seas rises up to the crest of the Apennines, to be concentrated in great cages of glass and iron, immense accumulators, enormous nerve centers located here and there along the mountainous spine of Italy.

Pulsing through the muscles, arteries, and nerves of the peninsula, the energy of distant winds and rebellious seas is transformed by the genius of man into many millions of kilowatts, distributed everywhere, without wires and in such fruitful abundance, regulated by the control panels that buzz beneath the hands of the engineers.

These latter dwell in high-tension chambers, where a hundred thousand volts pulsate across the great windows. They sit in front of supply panels and to the left and right of them they have the meters, consoles, control buttons, and switches, and everywhere there is the wonderful flashing of generators.

Those men, at last, have the pleasure of living between iron walls. Their furniture is made of steel and is twenty times lighter and less costly than ours. They are free at last from the states of mind forced on us by a sense of fragility and debilitating softness that, with their rustic ornamentation, wood and fabrics impose upon us. Those men can write in books made from nickel, less than three centimeters thick, which cost next to nothing and yet contain a hundred thousand pages.

Since heat and ventilation are regulated by rapidly acting mechanisms, they can at last feel the fullness and stolid resistance of their wills. Their flesh, losing touch with the continuous wrinkling of the trees, tries to emulate the steel that is all about them.

Those men take off in their monoplanes, their nimble projectiles, to survey the entire radiant distribution of electricity in numberless sectors down on the plain. They take a look at the centers of secondary activities, many-sided hangars from which motor-driven plows continuously burst forth into the countryside, to till, to plow, and to irrigate lands and crops through the use of electricity.

Up there, in their monoplanes, using cordless phones, they control the breathtaking speed of the seed trains which, two or three times a year, cross the plains for a frenetic sowing. —Each wagon has a huge iron arm on its roof which swings horizontally, spreading the fertile seeds everywhere.

And what's more, it is electricity that rapidly takes care of the germination. At last, all of the electricity that the atmosphere above us contains, and all the incalculable amounts of electricity that are in the earth, are being harnessed. That infinite number of lightning conductors and pylons spread endlessly throughout paddy fields and gardens, stroke the taut, convulsive bellies of the clouds with their points, so they can pour forth their stimulating powers right down to the very roots of plants.

The miracle, that great miracle that was dreamed of by the traditionalist poets, is happening all about us.

Everywhere there's abnormal growth of plants, as a direct result of artificial, high-voltage electric power. Both irrigation and drainage are controlled by electricity.

Through electrolysis and the multiple reactions it provokes, electricity everywhere stimulates the assimilation, by plant cells, of the nutritional principles of the soil, and thus directly increases their energy . . . This is why clumps of trees sprout up so marvelously out of the earth and grow with lightning speed, stretching forth their branches, in groves, in great oases . . . Huge, extensive forests climb ever upward, carpeting the mountain sides, obeying our Futurist wishes and lashing the aged, emaciated face, grooved with tears, of the ancient Queen of Love.

From our monoplanes we follow the fantastic growth of these forests toward the moon.

Hurrah! Hurrah for those trains that run so swiftly, down there! Freight trains, for it is only commodities that still move upon the ground. As men have become aerial creatures, they set foot there only very occasionally!

The earth is at last giving up its entire yield. Squeezed by the vast electrical hand of man, it dispenses the full substance of its riches, that fine orange tree promised for so long, to slake our thirst, conquered at last!

Hunger and need have disappeared. Bitter social problems have been obliterated. Financial problems have been reduced to the simple accountancy of production. Freedom for all to make gold and mint their own gleaming coins.

By now, the need for tiring, humiliating labor is finished. At last, intelligence rules everywhere. Physical labor has finally ceased to be servile, for it has but these three purposes: health, pleasure, and perfection. —No longer having to toil in order to acquire food, man has at last conceived the pure notion of endlessly breaking records. His will and his ambition know no bounds. Boundless energy is at work in every soul. People compete with one another in pursuit of the impossible, seeking purification in an atmosphere of speed and danger. All minds become lucid, and all instincts pointed toward the highest splendor, clash with each other in their search for yet more pleasures. Since food is readily available, all can perfect their lives in an endless round of competition. The anarchy of a perpetual striving for perfection.

Not a single one of life's vibrations must be wasted, not one bit of mental energy squandered.

Electrical energy must be acquired endlessly through heat energy or chemical energy.

Out of the discovery of wireless telegraphy, years ago, the function of dielectrics[1] has increased from day to day. All the laws of electricity in rarefied gases have been catalogued.[2] With surprising ease, scientists rule over the docile mass of electrons. The earth, which we already knew to be composed of electrical particles, is regulated like an enormous Ruhmkorff induction coil.[3] The eyes and other human organs are no longer merely sense receivers but real stores of electrical energy.

Unbounded human intelligence reigns everywhere. For a long time now, Tsarism has ceased to exist. Several anarchists, disguised as undertakers, solemnly bore a coffin stuffed with bombs into the imperial palace, and the Tsar was blown sky high with all his persistent medievalism, like the cork of a last bottle of champagne that is way past its best.

Twenty-five great powers govern the world, competing for outlets for a plethora of industrial products. And for this reason, we are at last witnessing the first electrical war.

And we'll put an end to it with good old explosives! We don't as yet know what to do with the rebellion of imprisoned gases that are angrily tossing about beneath the leaden knees of the atmosphere.

On the borders between two peoples, from either side, gigantic pneumatic engines are rolling along their tracks, elephants of steel, bristling with glittering trunks, pointed toward the enemy.

Drinking air, those monsters are easily controlled by operators crouching high up in their all-glass cabins, like elephant drivers. Their small figures are encapsulated in a rubber suit, whose function is to generate the oxygen they need to breathe.

The conscious, sophisticated, electrical potential of those men is able to harness strong, friendly storms to overcome fatigue and lethargy.

All of a sudden, the more skillful of the armies has drastically thinned the atmosphere around its adversary, by means of a violent intake of air by its own thousand pneumatic engines.

And immediately, these latter surge away to right and to left, along their tracks, to make way for locomotives armed with electrical batteries. You can see them pointing toward the frontier like cannon. A few men, who act like masters of primordial forces, control the sights of those batteries that hurl great clusters of writhing lightning bolts into the strata of a new, airless sky that is devoid of all matter.

Can you see them, those writhing knots of thundering serpents spinning away into the blue? They strangle the numberless thrusting chimneys of working cities. They smash the gaping jaws of ports. They swipe the white mountaintops and sweep the bile-colored sea, the howling sea that bores deep and rears madly to tear down coastal cities. Twenty electrical explosions in the sky, an immense glass vacuum tube, have redoubled the courageous aspirations of two rival peoples, with the fullness and splendor of formidable, interplanetary electrical discharges.

Between one battle and the next, sickness is assailed on all sides, confined within the last remaining two or three hospitals, which are now quite superfluous. The weak and the infirm are crushed, crumbled, and pulverized by the fiercely grinding wheels of this intense civilization. The green beard of provincial byways is shaved away by the cruel razors of speed. Radiotherapists, their faces protected by rubber masks, their bodies covered by suits made from lead, rubber, and bismuth, will gaze through spectacles made from salts of lead, upon the piercing yet healing dangers of radium.

Alas! When will they get around to inventing masks and suits to protect us against the deadly infection of idiocy, of that idiocy demonstrated by those of you who naturally disapprove of the cruel sincerity of my assaults upon slavish Italian traditionalism? You say that everyone ought to wash their dirty linen behind closed doors . . . Indeed! Away with you! We are not washerwomen with fussy, delicate hands. This day, with our polluted, lice-ridden linen, we light a bonfire of joy upon the topmost pinnacles of human thought.

We shall spare no one. After having insulted all the foreigners, who adore our past but who despise us as mere serenaders, tour guides, or beggars, we have compelled them to admire us as the most gifted race on Earth.

Mercifully for us, Italy will cease to be the love chamber of the cosmopolitan world.

With this aim in mind, we have taken upon ourselves the propaganda of courage against cowardice of epidemic proportions, the creation of an artificial optimism against a chronic pessimism. Our hatred for Austria; our restless waiting for war; our desire to throttle Pan-Germanism. These things are the natural outcomes of our Futurist theorem! So shut up, you idiots! Against you, like a revolver, we hold up our sundered hearts, gripped between our fingers, our hearts brimful of hatred and daring.

With us, the violent thrust of young gravediggers has its beginning. Enough of tombs! We leave corpses to bury themselves while we enter into the great Futurist City that points its formidable battery of factory chimneys against the ever-encircling army of Death, in our forward march toward the Milky Way![4]

This text was first published in French in *Le Futurisme* (1911) as the second part of Chapter 11 (the first section contains the text of "Birth of a New Futurist Aesthetics"). The Italian version appeared first in *Guerra sola igiene del mondo* (1915) and was reprinted in *L'Italia futurista* on April 29, 1917.

37

⁓

The Futurists, the First Interventionists

MANIFESTO OF ITALIAN PRIDE

In September 1914, while the battle of the Marne was raging and Italy remained completely neutral, we Futurists organized the first two demonstrations against Austria and in favor of the Intervention. At the Dal Verme Theater on September 15, and again in the Cathedral Square and in the Arcade, on the sixteenth, we burnt eleven Austrian flags.[1]

With Boccioni and Armando Mazza I go into Russolo's studio. Yellow green red pink jumble of Futurist noise machines.[2]

Buzzing bursting howling whistling.

The inventor surveys the firing of the blood of the vociferous.

Enough! Lay acids and engines aside! Tonight we'll demonstrate furiously against the Austrians!

The Dal Verme Theater overflowing. Revival of *The Golden Girl of the West*. The theater was like a swarming marketplace, full of Italian voices. Boxes balconies the gallery unleash six thousand applauding hands that sound like three thousand beaks of wild geese gobbling. Cutting short the music of Puccini: scraping arpeggios, puddings groveling violining hysterical nerves and pink candy-floss.[3]

The first act is over. The cretinous garland of singers jostles in front of the curtain, craving applause with beggars' smiles.

Down in his box, Mazza's belly brings forth a tricolored flag of eight square meters. We attach it to a shaft made of two walking sticks lashed together. I lean forward waving it about:

Doooown with Austriaaaa! . . .

From another box up springs Boccioni with an Austrian flag. A Futurist sets fire to it. A blazing fragment drops onto the creamy bosoms in the stalls.

Hoooowls. Fists shaken. Whirlpool. Backwash. 200 500 600 stupefied faces. That's enough! . . . Out! . . . It's the Futurists! . . . Long live Marinetti! . . . Down with Marinetti! . . . Splendid! . . . Out! . . . Bravo! . . . Doooown with Austria! . . . Idiots! . . . Madmen! Madmen! . . . Cowards! . . . Silence . . . (a deluded Puccini dashes to the front of the stage).

No! No! No! What we want is the National Anthem! . . . Down with Puccini! . . .

In the meantime, Mazza, with only one arm—his right—tensed, was holding fast the transparent door of his box which four policemen + two theater managers + three attendants were desperately trying to open.

I cry ouuut: "Down with Austria!" six hundred times with the rhythm and the voice of a mountain cannon.

The following evening there should have been thirty of us. Only eleven turned up. The Victor Emmanuel Arcade was bursting with people.[4] Autumn heat. All the tables were outside. The peaceful pleasures of overfed families savoring their ice creams.

"There aren't enough of us for a demonstration! It's ridiculous!" Boccioni declares.

"No! No! You'll see. It'll all blow up. Come on. Everybody shout out loudly: 'Down with San Giuliano![5] Down with Austria! . . .'"

Immediately a squad of political police hurled themselves upon us. A furious punch-up. Ten twenty fifty students grab hold of me to free me. Kicks, punches, slaps, bites. I force a way through toward the center of the Arcade, a wild boar with frantic fox terriers on its tail.

"Boccioni! Boccioni! Go off to the right! Inside! Get inside! Among the tables! Let's turn them all over!"

Everything collapsing. Everything turned upside down and crashing around. Screams. Elimination of women fainting all over the place. A flying ice cream stall. Insults taunts scuffles. Slap slap sounds of slaps. Pale faces full of fear. Faces turned purple. Noses like taps running red. Raised walking sticks.

My friends pull black-and-yellow flags out of their underwear and set fire to them. Gay bonfires at five seven eight points of the Arcade. Policemen like a hail of missiles. Like torpedo boats we cut through the sea of tables, overturning them to right and to left, creating waves of hysterical mothers and fathers, froth of trampled babies.

Colautti,[6] thickset but towering up on tiptoes, full of passion, grown large with his stick waving in the air, shouts at a couple of portly neutralists:

"There you go! There you go! Eat in peace! Eat up your ice creams!"

And his stick beats down on the table, sending plates glasses fruit and sweets flying in all directions.

The demonstration swells. It spreads.

Three blasts. Flight. Three blasts. Backwash. Whiiiistles. Two hundred policemen. A company of infantrymen arrives at the on-the-double quick. Another one closes off the Arcade's two night exits.

We're trapped. I manage to break free. They catch me again. But I slip through their fingers like a piece of wet soap. Then they have me again, held securely. And off we go to San Fedele,[7] all of us. We meet a platoon of Bersaglieri. Long live the army! . . . Down with Austria! . . .

In the dark courtyard at the police station, I hear Boccioni shouting out. I feel sure we shall have some cowardly kicks in the back, and turning around I knock out a couple of one of the wardens' teeth.

All eleven of us off to San Vittore,[8] in handcuffs.

"Dear Marinetti, you really do deserve the name the Paris newspapers have given you; you really are the caffeine of Europe!

"You're a radiator snaking out your hot tentacular tubing all over the world!"

In the January of 1915, we launched the Futurist Interventionist theatrical roadshows with a manifesto[9] that said:

> Italy has no need of books or magazines to learn how to come to a lightning decision, how to hurl herself into battle, how to maintain all-out effort and absorb every possible misfortune. These are of interest and concern to a mere minority. To a greater or lesser extent they are tedious, they are obstacles and slow things down; they can only dampen enthusiasm, cut short our forward dash, and poison the minds of a people at war with doubts. War, which is an intensified form of Futurism, compels us to march and not to fester in libraries and reading rooms. We believe, therefore, that today it is only through the theater that we can instill a warlike spirit in Italians. As it happens, 90 percent of all Italians go to the theater, while a mere 10 percent read books and journals. So what is called for is a Futurist theater, one that is totally opposed to the conventional theater of the past, which still spins out its depressing, boring, funereal fare on the somnolent stages of Italy.

It will be an all-inclusive theater, yet nontechnical, dynamic, bang up-to-date, its own place, beyond logic, quite unreal.

Then come the Intervention debates in the universities. At Rome University the antineutralist white, red, and green suit,[10] the brainchild of Balla and worn by Cangiullo, is cause of violent scuffles among teachers, students, and janitors who are split for and against war. All of Rome is flooded with Balla's manifesto: *Antineutralist Clothing.*[11]

A few days later, yet another Futurist manifesto, written by Balla and Depero, is launched, with the title *The Futurist Re-fashioning of the Universe.*[12]

A few months later, Benito Mussolini gave up the editorship of *Avanti!* to become involved in the Interventionist movement and assume the leadership of it.

At Rome, on April 12, Marinetti was arrested together with Mussolini and the Futurists Settimelli and Balla during the course of the third great Interventionist demonstration.[13]

I got them to operate on my hernia so that I could set off with the Futurists in the Battalion of Volunteer Cyclists.[14] I then became a member of the Alpine troops,[15] along with Boccioni, Sant'Elia, Russolo, Erba, Funi, Sironi, and other Futurists, in the attack on Dosso Casina. From Dosso Casina I released this *Manifesto of Italian Pride* to the press: [. . .][16]

The Futurists, first into the public squares to insist, with their fists, on our entry into the war, were first onto the battlefields, with many of them killed, wounded, or decorated with honors. Among the most noteworthy, we mention the great Futurist painter and sculptor Umberto Boccioni, who revolutionized modern, plastic art, and who was killed by a fall from his horse at Verona after having fought as a cyclist volunteer, then later as a member of the Alpine corps, at Dosso Casina (Mount Altissimo). Also, Sant'Elia, stupendous architectural genius, today imitated throughout the whole world, who was killed by a bullet through his forehead, leading an attack by his soldiers on the Carso.[17]

He had been wounded three months earlier and decorated with the silver medal in accordance with the following citation:

Under withering enemy rifle fire, he boldly ran forward to take command of a platoon of bombardiers, and although sustaining a head wound, he returned to the line as soon as it was dressed, to encourage and urge on his soldiers by his example and his words, to persist in their defense of the new position they had reached. (Mount Zebio, July 6, 1916)

Sub-lieutenant Giovesi described the death of Sant'Elia to me in the following words:

Illustrious Signor Marinetti,
    To call that death to mind is for me to renew a terrible torment. But I have to carry out my task because the last wish of that good man, Sant'Elia, which he expressed to me on the day prior to his glorious end, with a smile of great enthusiasm on his magnificent face, is for me a sacred duty. I beg you to forgive me for that dear and glorious death if I tell it in this meager, ungrammatical prose.
    "If I should die, dear Giovesi, remember me to the poet Marinetti," and his habitual action of tossing back his long hair accompanied his words. Then, with a cigarette in his mouth, he went on drawing lines, the first outline of a plan for a cemetery for our Brigade, that holy place which, as fortune would have it, was to accommodate him among the very first.

On May 11, 1916, I send from the front to the Florentine paper *L'Italia futurista* the manifesto entitled *The New Ethical Religion of Speed*.[18]

At the battle of Kuk, in June 1917, I am wounded in the groin in the attack on the Case di Zagora.[19]

Gabriele D'Annunzio visits me in the hospital at Udine, bringing me a bunch of red carnations.[20]

The Futurist Marica publishes the manifesto *Let's Increase the Number of Sardinians, the Finest Material for War*.[21]

After Caporetto, the Futurists Marinetti, Mario Carli, and Settimelli found *Roma futurista*, a political newspaper, which they direct from the front.[22] In the meantime, in every Italian city, branches of the Futurist Political Party are founded which, gradually, become Fasci di Combattimento.[23]

This text was first published in *Marinetti e il futurismo* (1929). The first part is virtually identical with a letter Marinetti sent to Francesco Cangiullo from prison in September 1914, printed in Cangiullo's *Le serate futuriste* (Pozzuoli: Tirena, [1930]), pp. 187–90.

38

⌘

In This Futurist Year

We glorify War, sole cleanser of the World
The Foundation and Manifesto of Futurism, *Figaro*, Paris, February 20, 1909

Long live Asinari di Bernezzo![1]
First Futurist *serata*, Teatro Lirico, Milan, February 1910

STUDENTS OF ITALY!
Because an illustrious past was crushing Italy and *an infinitely more glorious future* was surging in her breast, precisely here, in Italy, beneath our too voluptuous sky, Futurist energy needed to be born, six years ago, and had to be organized, channeled, to find in us its generators, its instruments of illumination and propagation. Italy, much more than any other country, had an urgent need of Futurism, since it was dying of an obsessive love for its own past. The invalid invented its own cure. *We are its timely surgeons.* The cure is valid for the sick of all nations.[2]

Our immediate program is one of ferocious combat against Italian traditionalism in whichever of its repugnant forms it appears: archaeology, academicism, senility, quietism, cowardice, pacifism, pessimism, nostalgia, sentimentalism, obsession with eroticism, foreign tourism, etc. Our Nationalism, which is ultraviolent, anticlerical, antisocialist, and antitraditionalist, is rooted in the inexhaustible vigor of Italian blood and is at war with the cult of ancestors which, far from welding the race together, makes it anemic and causes it to rot away. But we shall go beyond this immediate goal, which, during these six years of incessant struggle, has in part already been realized.

Futurism, in its far-reaching aims, has the aura of an avant-garde; it is the watchword of all intellectual innovators and free spirits throughout the world; it is love of the new; the passionate art of speed; the systematic denigration of the antique, the old, the slow, the erudite, and the professorial; it is a new way of seeing the world; a new reason for loving life; the enthusiastic glorification of scientific discoveries and modern machines; the flag of youth, of strength, of originality at all costs; a straitjacket to impede the habit of looking back nostalgically; an inexhaustible machine gun directed at the army of the dead, the gouty, and the opportunists, whom we desire to strip of their authority and subjugate to the audacity of youth and the creators; it is a stick of dynamite set beneath all venerated ruins.

The word "Futurism" contains within it the widest possible formula for renewal, which, being at one and the same time healthy and exhilarating, smoothes away doubts, destroys skepticisms, and unites all exertions into a formidable higher cause. All innovators will come together beneath the banner of Futurism, because Futurism proclaims the need to move continuously forward and because it urges the removal of all compromises with cowardice. Futurism is a man-made optimism opposed to all chronic pessimism; it is a constant dynamism, an endless becoming and an unwearying resolve. Thus, Futurism is not subject to the rules of fashion nor to the attrition of time; it is neither a *petty religion* nor a *school* but rather a great, united movement of intellectual heroisms in which individual pride is nothing while the will to renewal is all.

Many fellow travelers with, or unsatisfactory converts to, Futurism were a cause of ridiculous confusion in Italian minds, between *Futurism* and a kind of amateurish *revolutionism,* whose ingredients are pessimism, intellectual anarchy, an isolating individualism, lack of unity of artistic purpose, and boorishness. Consequently, many people believe that all you have to do to be a Futurist is to be in revolt against everything and everyone, to turn all accepted principles upside down, to contradict oneself systematically every day, to destroy for the sake of destroying, in conclusion, to spew out an endless string of profanities.

We carry out demolition work, yes, but always with a view to rebuilding. We clear away the debris so that we can move a stage further. We consider only absolute sincerity of thought and expression to be Futurist (e.g., *Mafarka the Futurist* and *King Guzzle*).[3] On the other hand, we see as conventionalist any vulgar, facile, and age-old obscenities that some people try to pass off as *Futurist.*

Futurism is: *the strengthening and defense of the Italian spirit* (creation, improvisation), *against cultural obsessions* (museums, libraries). *It is the solidarity of Italian innovators against a mafia of academics, opportunists, plagiarists, commentators, teachers, and hotel keepers. It prepares the ground for innovation. It is the audacity that prefigures Italy's endless progress. It is a heroic disinterestedness intent on giving Italy and the world more courage, light, freedom, innovation, and flexibility. It is the order to march and to fight + batteries of guns at our backs so that we never turn back.*

Futurism is an impassioned attempt at introducing life into art. It opposes the old ideal of the aesthetes, which is static, ornamental, effeminate, elitist, fastidious, and which hates action. In the last thirty years, Europe has been plagued by a revolting socialistic intellectualism that is antipatriotic and internationalist, which separates the body from the spirit and which dreams of a stupid enlargement of the brain. It teaches forgiveness against offenses, proclaiming universal peace and the disappearance of war, whose *horrors* would be replaced by wars of ideas. It was against this intellectualism, which was Germanic in origin, that Futurism hurled itself, exalting instinct, strength, courage, sport, and war.

Artists, alive at last and no longer aloft on the contemptuous heights of aestheticism, desired to collaborate as soldiers and workers in the development of the world. A continuous progress, with the wresting of power from the dead, the old, the slow, the indecisive, the vile, the velvet-tongued, the delicate, the effeminate, and the nostalgic. Day-to-day heroism. Let's experience all dangers and all struggles. Let's dirty our hands digging trenches, yet be ready for the pen, the oar, the rudder, the swipe, the fist, and the rifle.

Some hotfooted spirits, who were nonetheless opposed to practical measures, warned us against pushing Futurism to its logical conclusion, as this, in their view, would mean isolation, the end of our writing and painting activities, especially when considering the public's lack of intelligence, and so on. To this we reply:

1. Futurism is not, nor will it ever be, in any way *prophetic*. Nobody can ever be absolutely sure about how things will turn out. You could be right; but we nonetheless question the *Logic* of your prophecies. We, like Bergson, believe that "la vie déborde l'intelligence,"[4] which is to say that it overflows, swamps, and suffocates the infinitesimally small faculty of intelligence. One cannot intuit even the immediate future other than by involving oneself *totally* in the living of one's life. From this stems our violent, besetting love of action. We are the Futurists of *tomorrow*, not of *the day after tomorrow*. We do have some notion of where we are going, but we systematically banish these visions from our brain, since they are almost always unhealthy and almost invariably the product of a depressed frame of mind. We mistrust them, for they lead to intellec-

tual anarchy, to absolute egoism, which means the negation of all endeavor and every effort at modification. We shall never become prophets of pessimism, proclaimers of the great Nothingness. Our practical, effective Futurism is preparing the way for a Tomorrow dominated by us.[5]

2. We are only fiercely hostile to the critics, who are useless or even dangerous exploiters, but not to the public, whom we wish to advance to a more complete understanding of life. This public has frequently misunderstood us, which is natural enough, given the stupid superficiality of the idiotic things teachers have put into their heads. However, the public will come to understand us; it's all a question of energy, and this we have in plenty.

The crowds who have jeered us have, despite themselves, admired in us the sincere artists that we are, struggling heroically to strengthen, renew, and sharpen Italian genius. The great mass of new ideas that we have formed rolls back and forth in the mud and over the rocks, moved along and contaminated by the carefree hands of the common people. And they, laughing at the strange surface colors of this huge, unforeseen toy, are enthralled by its magnetism and its brilliance. No rhetoric, this: the word "Futurism" alone has miraculously done Italy and the world a great deal of good. Whatever the question, whatever the place, in parliaments, town councils, and in the piazzas, men divide into *traditionalists* and *Futurists*. (Today, in Italy, *traditionalists* is synonymous with *neutralists, pacifists, and eunuchs*, while *Futurists* is synonymous with *violent antineutralists*.)

Among the new Futurists, who are ever on the increase, there are some poor converts who lack daring. Others are very much the opposite, striding over the fine possibilities of tomorrow so as to explore the fascinating impossibilities of the day after. We cry out to all: *Onward! Onward! Into action! Woe betide anyone who stops or lags behind to deny, question, or dream! We war against any ideal of the future that could put an end to our endeavors of today and tomorrow! In Italy, above all,* since here we are aware of our measured strength within the geographical confines of our Nation. Futurism is conquering the world through an Italy that is becoming ever more Futurist.

STUDENTS OF ITALY!

Aggressive, dynamic Futurism is today being fully realized in the great World War that it alone foresaw and glorified before it broke out. **This**

present war is the finest Futurist poem that has materialized up to now. Futurism, to be precise, signaled the outbreak of war in art, through the invention of the Futurist *serata*[6] (the most effective sort of propaganda so far as courage is concerned). Futurism represented the militarization of innovative artists. Today, we are seeing an immense Futurist exhibition of aggressive, dynamic canvases, one we wish to engage in so as to reveal our qualities.

The plastic dynamism of Boccioni, Carrà, Russolo, Balla, and Severini; Balilla Pratella's pluritonal music, devoid of rhythmic structures; Russolo's Art of Noise, the Words-in-Freedom of Marinetti, Buzzi, Folgore, Cangiullo, Govoni, Auro d'Alba, M. Betuda, Dinamo Correnti, and G. Jannelli; the Theater of Essential Brevity, created by Marinetti, Bruno Corra, and Settimelli; together with the Futurist architecture of Sant'Elia, are the natural artistic expressions of this Futurist hour. Bombardments, armored trains, trenches, artillery duels, charges, electric grids, have nothing in common with yesterday's classical styles of poetry, traditional, archaeological, Georgic, nostalgic, or erotic (Baudelaire, Mallarmé, Verlaine, Carducci, Pascoli, D'Annunzio). These passive kinds of poetry are dead and buried. —Today, we are seeing the triumph of Words-in-Freedom, of the lyrical appreciation of all Strengths, without set forms, syntax, punctuation, and minute, ornamental, delicate details. This is the lyricism that seizes hold of the reader, with its synoptic tables of lyrical values, with its aerial sketches of the landscape, its battles between typographical characters, and its onomatopoeic fusillades. Traditionalist poets would like to deride our Words-in-Freedom, by referring to them as *telegraphic lyricism*. We Futurists sing their death telegraphically, and this means we don't have to suffer their stink for very long.

They sigh feebly over the horrors of war, or pompously commemorate dead heroes. They look on war, trembling, just like sheep and oxen, dozing in their pens at night, look upon the far-off, electric breathing of the cities. War, for them, is an elegant conversational poem,[7] a new literary motif, an excuse to evoke Greeks and Romans yet again, in monstrous processions of tercets, among the ruins of their minds. These proponents of pacifism hope, by fighting against Austria and Germany, to kill off War, which they see as a leftover from barbarism. War cannot die, for it is one of the laws of life. Life = aggression. Universal Peace = the decrepitude and death throes of races. War = bloody and necessary trial of a people's strength.

What needs to be killed off and must die is Teutonic traditionalism, which is composed of mindless conformity, pedantic, professorial dullness, obsession with culture, and slavish imitation, with rustic pride, with systematic surveillance, and the idiocy of rules and regulations.

We Futurist Free-Word-smiths, painters, musicians, sound makers, and architects have always seen war as the only inspiration for art, the only purifying morality, the only leaven for the dough of humanity. War alone is capable of renewing, speeding up, and sharpening human intelligence, of ventilating the brain and easing the nerves, of freeing us from our daily cares, of giving a thousand different tastes to life and a modicum of creative talent to the dumb-witted. War is the only rudder to steer us through the new age of the airplane, which we are in the process of creating.

War, which is Futurism intensified, will never kill off war, as the traditionalists would like, but it will kill traditionalism. War is the perfect, culminating synthesis of progress (aggressive speed + violent simplification of all endeavor toward our well-being). War is an immediate demand for courage, exertion, and intelligence, made on everyone. It is an obligatory school of ambition and heroism, of fullness of life and the utmost freedom in one's devotion to the nation.

For a nation that is poor, yet prolific, war is a business, namely the acquisition of the lands that it lacks, by virtue of the superfluity of its blood. On the other hand, the privileged and dominant part of a rich nation realizes, through acquiring great riches, that this is not the point of life. The wretched anxiety of the Parisian and London nights before the war started.[8] The comic-heroic gesturing of young lords who, out of bravado, clambered up onto the roofs of superfast limousines, which were packed with the richest of women, who, with the sweetest of smiles, and dripping jewels, were digesting the most sumptuous of dinners! Over and above this frantic profligacy (women, gowns, champagne, gambling, riding), whether they knew it or not, they were conjuring up the great, explosive, uplifting atmosphere of continuous danger and collective heroism, which is the only thing capable of nourishing and gratifying men's nerves.

After dabbling, in short spells, with art, love, or politics, today they feel the need to risk all in one fell swoop, in the great, conclusive game of war, so as to increase the Nation's power. The Nation = expansion + the multiplication of the "I." Italian patriotism = containing and feeling within itself the whole of Italy and all the Italians of tomorrow.

The War will root out all its enemies: diplomats, professors, philosophers, archaeologists, critics, cultural obsession, Greek, Latin, history, senility, museums, libraries, and the tourist industry. The War will foster gymnastics, sport, schools of practical agriculture, commerce, and industry. The War will rejuvenate Italy, it will enrich her with men of action, it will compel her to live no longer in the past, amid ruins and in a gentle climate, but by virtue of her own national strengths.

STUDENTS OF ITALY!

Today more than ever, the word "Italy" must take precedence over the word "Freedom." All freedoms are ours, with the exception of the right to be cowards, pacifists, and neutralists.[9] Every kind of progress must be sought within the confines of the nation. Let us erase the glory of Rome with the even greater glory of Italy. Let us therefore fight against Germanic culture, not so as to defend the Latin, but rather to oppose both these equally noxious cultures, in defense of the creative Italian genius of today. Against Mommsen[10] and Benedetto Croce,[11] we pit the worldly-wise Italian. Later, we shall settle accounts with antimilitarist pacifists and internationalists, who have converted, in greater or lesser measure, to the War. Away with all debates! All of one mind and en masse against Austria! Our great purgative War is not in the hands of Salandra,[12] but in your own! Desire it and we shall wage it! Start by sweeping out of the universities their old Germanophile janitors (de Lollis,[13] Barzellotti,[14] Benedetto Croce, et al.), whom we have all jeered together!

> This manifesto appeared with a variety of titles. The first edition, a four-page leaflet dated November 29, 1914, is entitled *In quest'anno futurista*. The reprint, in *Guerra sola igiene del mondo* (1915), is called "1915: In quest'anno futurista," and *L'Italia futurista* of May 27 and June 17, 1917, published it as "In quest'anno futurista: 1915." In *Futurismo e fascismo* (1924), this was changed to "Manifesto agli studenti" (Manifesto to the Students).

39

⚜

The Meaning of War for Futurism: Interview with L'avvenire

I saw Marinetti here again, yesterday—as young as ever, as sprightly as ever in everything he does. We talked about Sicily, about his great admiration for the wild, hot, passionate nature of our people and of our sky.

Then, naturally, we talked about war. On behalf of Avvenire, *I asked him for his thoughts.*

"The idea of war brings us joy, it exalts us, and in this we are being quite consistent, for our first public activities in this world began and ended with cries of 'war,'" Marinetti said, with a clear sense of satisfaction. "We alone[1] constantly glorified war because in it we have consistently recognized the one and only inspiration of true and passionate art, the only equalizing and purifying morality, the only leavening for the human race. You see, for the past thirty years, Europe has been infected by a loathsome, philo-socialistic intellectualism, which is both internationalist and antipatriotic, which separates body from spirit and gives a ridiculously exaggerated importance to the mind. It teaches forgiveness for offenses committed, it proclaims universal peace and the abolition of war, whose *horrors* would be replaced by wars of ideas. Futurism hurled itself against this intellectualism, which is Germanic in origin, in praise of instinct, physical strength, courage, every kind of sport, and war.

"We artists, alive at last, no longer aloft on the scornful peaks of aestheticism, wished to participate as soldiers and workmen in the progress of the world. An ongoing progress characterized by wresting away the power of the dead, of the old, the slow, the indecisive, the cowardly, the smooth-tongued, the effeminate, and those who hanker after the past.

"Heroism as an everyday occurrence. Every kind of danger and every kind of struggle. Hands dirty from digging trenches but equally adept with the pen, the rudder, the steering wheel, the chisel, the slap in the face, and the rifle.

"Futurism, then, was the militarization of innovative artists. Futurism marked very precisely the breakthrough of war into art when it created that most effective form of propaganda, the Futurist *serata*.[2] And it was precisely during the very first Futurist *serata* held in Italy, at the Teatro Lirico in Milan, that the cry of "Long live Asinari di Bernezzo" spread through the hall like a call to battle and a demand for war![3]

"Then, in 1911, came our second political manifesto.[4] From that moment, it proved necessary to provide some general direction for the very many young men in Italy, whose hearts throbbed with enthusiasm for Futurism. First, we needed to remove the influence of decadence once and for all, as well as that of a detestable conservatism and clericalism; second, to embed the idea of the nation and war in the concept of progress and freedom. Today, more than ever before, some statements in that manifesto, which at the time seemed ridiculous—such as 'All freedoms are permitted, other than those of being cowards, pacifists, and anti-Italian' or 'The word *Italy* must take precedence over the word *Freedom,*' or again, 'Let us forget the ancient Romans so as to create the great Italians of the future,'[5] or yet again, 'We are fully aware of our strengths measured out along the geographical frontiers of our country'[6]—these statements, as I was saying, are by now a part of the sensibilities of the mass of young Italians."

With the Nationalists, No.

"Well then, in your exaltation of war as a moral factor, as an undeniable fact of life, which is not so detestable after all, aren't you in agreement with nationalism, at least, in a theoretical sense?"

"With nationalism, yes; but with the Nationalists,[7] no," Marinetti quickly added, happily making use of the opportunity to make an important confession. "Look, I was one of the very first members of the nationalist movement in Italy,[8] registering as a member of the organization and taking an active part in the initial promotion of that great idea, which I welcomed with real enthusiasm. However, nationalism, as it is manifested in Italy today, is not and can never be a truly Futurist nationalism which (remaining perforce outside and above all political considerations and interests and needing to keep its distance from all contacts and commitments imposed by the needs of the moment) is of necessity anticlerical and antitraditionalist as well as antidemocratic and antisocialist.

"It should not be forgotten, either, that for a short time, the nationalists showed themselves to be favorable toward Austria and expressed a certain affection for Germany—both of which we always opposed. And even when classical irredentism[9] seemed exhausted and dormant among the Italian people, we Futurists took steps to stimulate and reinforce that national sentiment, supported by those *just aspirations* that are generally recognized today. Unlike the democrats and the socialists, it is not just today that we have become aware of the great threat to mankind posed by Germanic culture, the development of a German sense of identity and Austrian militarism.

"We have always proclaimed the death of Teutonic traditionalism, which is typified by a sheeplike stupidity, academic dullness, obsession with a plagiaristic culture, peasant pride, systematic spying, and a cretinous police force. Then again, frankly, I can't agree with the Nationalists if they want to consolidate the nation around tradition, a mania for monuments, and veneration for ancient ruins. Seeing men who, like Enrico Corradini, are strongly, inspirationally Italian, wasting their time defending Piazza delle Erbe,[10] is truly disheartening. I am with them, however, as brothers-in-arms, when it's a case of spitting in the face or kicking the living daylights out of all those pacifists and socialists who would like to sully, humiliate, and degrade this great word *Italy*. I want to make the point, however, that the Italy of tomorrow must be, and will be, infinitely greater than the archaeological and cultural one the nationalists are hell-bent on cobbling together, restoring, and setting up on pedestals. I mean an Italy that is intensely agrarian, industrialized, and commercialized, powerful and domineering, first among other nations, not because of its past, which is dead and buried, but by virtue of the strength of its creative genius; which means freed from the ridiculous, humiliating, and risky business of foreign tourism. In short, the Italy of Milan, Genoa, and Turin, not that of present-day Rome or Florence or Pisa; an Italy illuminated by electric light and not by *moonlight*; not a 'Baedeker' Italy but an Italy of big business, of huge markets, rich and great in herself, not sustained by the carcasses of her ancestors; an Italy which is less sentimental, with fewer mandolins, fewer ruins, fewer gondolas, fewer . . . Anglo-German maiden ladies between . . . our feet, but with more locomotives, more factory chimneys and electric turbines; an Italy without professors, without archaeologists, with few lawyers, very few doctors, life in the open air, gymnastics, sports, fewer disputations and more punches. Instinct, muscles, fewer armchairs and no slippers! This is the great Italy that our patriotism dreams of because for us Italian Patriotism means containing and feeling in oneself the whole of Italy and the Italians of tomorrow."

The Futurist Mussolini

"With regard to the advantages of war," continues Marinetti, "I could put just one before you and indeed anyone else who is skeptical about or indifferent to our ideas.

"At this moment, our ranks are growing continuously and our legion has now become a huge army which extends all over Europe. To us it seems that right now the world, by which we mean mankind, is cleanly divided and split into two great hosts, the one Futurist, bent on restoring war, asking for war, and achieving it; the other fixed in the past, timid, fearful, indecisive, and cowardly. For the one side, war is the necessary, bloody test of a people's strength, it is the instantaneous imposition of courage, energy, and intelligence on all; it is the compulsory school of ambition and heroism; it is life at its fullest and freedom's zenith—in dedicated service to the nation.

"For the others, for those who look upon it trembling, as do sheep and oxen dozing in their stalls at night, seeing far off the electric pulsing of the city, war will be nothing more than an elegant conversational poem, a new literary motif, a mere pretext for pompously evoking Greeks and Romans in monstrous processions of tercets, among the ruins of their minds.[11]

"By themselves, our verbal propaganda and our immediate, swift actions would never have been able to achieve such rapid, easy progress for our cause. Our arguments, our works of art, our poems would never have brought about so much action and have been so effective.

"This current war is indeed the finest Futurist poem that has appeared until now!"[12]

"Has the number of supporters of your ideas really grown so much?"

"However great the number may be, it would not be sufficiently accurate to demonstrate just how widely our ideas have penetrated public consciousness. There's ample evidence of it all about us. The 'case' of Mussolini is as eloquent a testimony of this as any could be."

"How? In what way?" I ask, not a little taken aback. "Has Mussolini been converted to Futurism?"

"His recent actions, his attitudes and his rebellion are clear demonstration of a Futurist consciousness."[13]

"Well . . . that is your impression rather, based to a greater or lesser degree . . ."

". . . which I deduce from particular facts that are both precise and certain. In the first place, Mussolini was always, like Corridoni, a warm supporter of ours. At all the *serate* we held in Milan, he defended us and enthusiastically championed our cause.[14]

"But apart from this, Mussolini is a Futurist for a further variety of reasons which, as far as I am concerned, are equally undeniable.

"The absolutely lightning speed with which he was converted to the need for war and the virtues of war can be taken as a first point in support of my argument. You must, however, bear in mind the new propaganda system he has adopted—a system which is ours and that we activated.

"He has said that 'at all costs and with all available means' he will finish his work and see through the program that he has imposed.

"Therefore, he personally takes up the fight and does not discount the fist or the pistol shot as forms of argument and the subject of his propaganda. Do you remember his clear, precise statements on this subject?

"But over and above these organizational factors and their outward manifestation, there is within him a more personal Futurism, a tendency which is more deeply rooted. And with this, I am referring to his repeatedly expressed hatred for everything that is outmoded in Italy and which, in his view, should have been eclipsed a long time ago. The arguments he has lately adduced to demonstrate the uselessness, if not the harmfulness of a parliamentary institution such as lifelong membership of the Chamber,[15] are largely our arguments which we have been proclaiming already for . . ."

Toward Montecitorio![16]

"But after all, although Mussolini would indeed be a very important recruit, he is only one . . . As an effect of a conflict that is so widespread and also so serious, I don't have the impression of any compelling reason for self-congratulation . . ."

"But you're ignoring everything else I said; you are not taking into account just how pleasing and beneficial the immediate effects of war will be for us, how it will demonstrate that a country, in order to live and prosper, should only count on its own effective, robust energies.

"Foreign tourism, upon which it is commonly believed the economic prosperity of our people largely depends, necessarily presumes that monuments will be preserved alongside veneration for tradition. It is inconceivable that this industry will not be destroyed and eliminated, revealing itself—as events will demonstrate—to be not only dispensable but downright obstructive and harmful to every other kind of wise and profitable activity.

"War, then, with its violent and cruel realism, will sweep away every other kind of stale traditionalism; and creative genius alone will reassert its secure and solid rights."

Marinetti spoke with his usual fervor, accompanying, indeed illustrating, his words—as southerners do—with broad expressive gestures. He spoke with a touching faith, with a vehemence that trenchantly expressed his invincible conviction—even though our conversation had come down from the artistic and theoretical plain, where it had started, to realities and entered the so-called political field, which is of course brimful of surprises and is always a nasty, brutal business of expedients and compromises.

"Will you therefore be actively committing yourself to political life?" *I wanted to ask this of my courteous guest a bit later, by way of concluding.*

"Ours is certainly a movement of art and artists. We cannot, however, abstract ourselves from political realities that, in large measure, govern all human activities."

"And is it true you are opposed to parliamentarianism?"[17]

"Yes. However, we cannot afford not to aspire to having our own forces in Parliament. We make no secret of this intention and—"

"—you'll try and achieve it very soon."

"Of course. I expect, before long, to organize some real political action by declaring myself a candidate for the usual sort of struggle. I must win a first-class seat[18] with sword in hand. But all of this after the war, after the great war we are waiting for, that we desire and shall fight in. For the moment, let us march—"

"—not molder!"[19]

And there our conversation ended.

. . .

Marinetti! Never so much as in this moment did the life of this Italian seem to me to be worthy of his poem.

GIRAV[20]

This interview appeared in the newspaper *L'avvenire*, published in Messina, on February 23, 1915. The interviewer was the Sicilian Futurist Guglielmo Jannelli Ravidà.

40

Futurism and the Great War

The Great War,[1] which represents the fusion of fervid patriotism, militarism, Garibaldian impulsiveness,[2] revolutionary power, imperialism, and the democratic spirit, renounces all political parties, ridicules all pacifistic diplomatic machinations, crushes and smashes every kind of traditionalism, and revitalizes the world.

The Great War has cleansed and continues to cleanse the world of every kind of medievalism (Tsarism, Kaiserism, and so on).

The Great War is demonstrating the inevitable failure of the notions of methodical preparation, excessive regimentation, and culture.

The Great War is demonstrating the triumph of the concept of intensive and flexible improvisation. Fate is wearied and incensed by a priori arrangement. Improvisation attracts and seduces her.

The Great War is tearing the cemeteries apart with its bombardments; it is overturning all romantic solitariness and plowing it in, with its bombardments; it is decapitating the mountains with its bombardments; it is turning the dead cities upside down with its bombardments, freeing them and stimulating them into new life; it strides over monuments and cathedrals and overturns them; it condemns conservative cities, which insist on living by exploiting their past, to famine; and it is ruining and condemning for all time the perilous, humiliating foreign-owned industries.

The Great War is slaughtering "good taste," effeminate niceties, long-outmoded attitudes, Decadentism and Aestheticism (Baudelaire,

Mallarmé, Oscar Wilde, D'Annunzio), mystical ecstasies, nostalgia, and every sort of sentimentalism about ancient ruins.

The Great War is devaluing love, ridding it of any sense of nobility and reducing it to its natural proportions.

The Great War, with its gigantic, oft-repeated massacres, is humiliating commemorative patriotism, kicking it about, and it will die for want of breath—we hope—beneath the landslide of heroes who are yet to be remembered.

The Great War is inspiring our great generals to make harsh, swift, incisive, daring, and essential pronouncements, which are almost like Words-in-Freedom of war.

The Great War was violently opposed by all the enemies of Futurism: the conservatives, the pacifists, the traditionalists, the priests, the men of order, the erudite, the archaeologists, the critics, the professors, and the lawyers (people such as Barzellotti, Benedetto Croce, Enrico Ferri, Claudio Treves,[3] and so on).

The Great War, with its bombardments, has put out the lamps of the philosophers and made the floor shake beneath the gouty stay-at-homes who think with their feet and would much prefer to misrule Italy from deep within their libraries and their museums.

All the political parties—conservatives, clericals, democrats, traditional nationalists, Interventionist socialists, anarchists, and socialists—are ill at ease with this Great militaristic-revolutionary War.

We Futurists alone are truly in our element in the Great War. We foresaw it, we understand it, and we are party to its confidential secrets . . .

The Great War was already accounted for in *The Foundation and Manifesto of Futurism* (published in *Le Figaro* in Paris on February 20, 1909), something that appeared mad and contradictory at the time but which was merely prophetic.

This essay appeared first in *L'Italia futurista* on July 8, 1917, and was reprinted in the collection *Noi futuristi* of 1917.

FUTURIST ART DURING THE FIRST
WORLD WAR (1916)

Marinetti's last prewar initiative in the artistic domain—the Futurist Theater of Essential Brevity—had to cede place to Interventionist imperatives when the Italian government declared its neutrality in the armed conflict between the European powers. The 1915 tour of the Berti-Masi theater company petered out when audiences became worried about the general call to arms and the lack of food and heating fuel in an exceptionally cold winter. Nonetheless, Marinetti's intention of suspending, or at least limiting, artistic activities during the time of the war effort was not carried out. As the anti-German and patriotic performances of the Annibale Ninchi company in 1916 showed, the Futurists organized further theater performances and exploited them for propagandistic purposes.

Marinetti's military service did not resemble in the least that of a common soldier. He was more or less allowed to wander in and out of the war zone, to travel up and down the peninsula, giving lectures and reciting war poetry, meeting other artists and organizing publishing ventures, or making his many personal appearances as a soldier just returned from the front at Futurist theater performances. He acted more like an itinerant ambassador for the war effort than a frontline combatant. But for Marinetti, of course, his Futurist activities were a form of combat too, albeit on the home front.

The Futurists' experiences in the actual theater of war gave rise to a number of artistic creations that evoked the frontline experiences in the form of Words-in-Freedom, paintings, musical compositions, dances, and so on. However, the general populace, when they found the leisure, time, and money to read books, go to performances, or visit exhibitions, were more interested in entertainment than propaganda. Some Futurists responded to this desire by setting up a Futurist music theater, a circus, or joint ventures with variety stars such as Ettore Petrolini, Luciano Molinari, and Odoardo Spadaro.

From 1916 to 1918, war took its toll on the Futurist ranks, not only because of casualties at the front but also through the lack of new recruits to stand in for members serving in the army. Nonetheless, there were still sufficient activists scattered across the peninsula to publish some thirty periodicals and magazines with a Futurist orientation. Of these, one assumed national importance and clocked up more than just a few issues: *L'Italia futurista*. It appeared from June 1, 1916, to February 11, 1918, and printed political essays, Futurist poetry, and images. One of the editors was Maria Ginanni, who gave a public voice to many female writers and fostered a lively exchange of readers' letters on the relationship between women and Futurism. The paper sold 1,500 copies in Florence alone, which may serve as an indicator that the Futurist circle in this city was not only the biggest but also the most active in Italy. And it was here that another significant initiative arose: the production of the first Futurist film. The Florence group also published a series of books under the imprint Edizioni de "L'Italia futurista," thus complementing the reduced output of Marinetti's Edizioni futuriste di "Poesia."

The other center of Futurist activities during the war was Rome, where Giacomo Balla assembled a number of young and talented artists. They produced several significant manifestos, which have all been translated in Apollonio's anthology. They also attracted the interest and then the collaboration of the Russian impresario Diaghilev, who had set up camp in Rome during the war. In 1916 the Dadaists in Zurich established contact with the Futurists, while Enrico Prampolini's journal *Noi* (1917–25) served as a bridge to other avant-garde groups in Europe. A number of theater productions, exhibitions, and book publications revealed the growing significance of the Roman circle, which was consolidated through the newspaper *Roma futurista* (first issue: September 20, 1918), Marinetti's love affair with (and then marriage to) the Roman painter and writer Benedetta Cappa, and the subsequent move of his headquarters to Piazza Adriana in 1925.

41

cℐ⌀

Birth of a Futurist Aesthetic

I'm sure all sorts of objections have already accumulated in your minds against our destructive, antitraditionalist principles.

Let me take up one of these: "Tell me, which are the works in stone, marble, or bronze that you can set against those unique works bequeathed to us by past centuries?"

My reply is very simple:

1. The masterpieces from the past are nothing but a small selection surviving from an endless number of works which vanished, either because of their poor quality or because of their fragility.

   Therefore, you cannot expect the masterpieces produced over the past fifty years or so to match up to the selected corpus of works created over ten centuries.

2. Besides this, may I also remind you that certain phenomena typical of the modern era, such as international travel, the democratic spirit, and the decline of religion, have ensured that the great, decorative, immortal buildings which at one time expressed regal authority, theocracy, and mysticism, now serve no useful purpose.

Phenomena that are absolutely new—such as the right to strike, equality before the law, the power of majorities, the increasing influence of the masses, the speed of international communications, routine concerns with health and domestic amenities—all of these things, in fact, make the provision of large and airy tenement buildings for the working classes absolutely necessary. The same is true of comfortable trains, tunnels, iron bridges, huge, fast ocean liners, houses carefully sited on hillsides to catch the cool breezes, enormous assembly halls, and bathrooms furnished with everything one needs for the rapid daily care of the body.

In our own times, an aesthetic in tune with utility has no need of royal palaces, those overbearing constructions set on granite foundations which, in the past, towered over poor medieval towns, chaotic jumbles of wretched hovels.

Why on earth would a people in modern times launch the spires of a majestic cathedral toward the skies, making them rise up toward the clouds, clasping the ribs of their vaults like hands in prayer, defending a small cluster of dwellings crouched in their shadows?

What we set against them is a Futurist aesthetic that is already completed and definitive: it is the aesthetic of great locomotives, of winding tunnels, of cruisers, of torpedo boats, monoplanes, and racing cars.

We are creating a new aesthetic of speed. We have virtually destroyed the notion of space and greatly reduced that of time. We are thus preparing the way for ubiquitous, expanded man.[1] We shall arrive, by the same token, at the abolition of years, days, and hours.

Meteorological phenomena are already ahead of us, for the seasons are by now fused together.

The gloomy, annual return of traditional festivals is on the decline, for lack of interest.

Work and recreation are both nocturnal affairs in France, in Italy, in Spain; thus day and night cycles have already been fused into one. It is quite natural that the works of art in which we have expressed this turmoil of life intensified, rolling toward an ideal future, cannot be appreciated or understood by a public that has been shocked by our wild attacks and offended by our violent revolt.

One day they will think better of us. In the meantime, they are beginning to grow weary of those selfsame things that we battle against.

We have induced increasing nausea for what is old, worm-eaten, or moldering. And this is, assuredly, an achievement of vital importance.

In our first manifesto, the following affirmation raised a storm of protest: "A racing car is more beautiful than the Winged Victory of Samothrace."

I'll offer you now an explosive gift that expresses our thoughts even better: "Nothing is more beautiful than the framework of a house being newly built." To a well-built house we prefer the iron skeleton of a house being erected with its girders the color of danger—landing strips for aircraft—with its myriad arms clawing at the sky and combing out the stars and comets, with its aerial platforms, from which the eye can survey the wide expanse of the horizon. We adore that framework, with its rhythm of pulleys and hammers and beating hearts. And occasionally—so be it—the piercing cry and heavy thud of a workman falling, a great splash of blood on the pavement!

The stanchions of a house being built symbolize our burning passion for things coming into being.

Things that are done and finished are cradles of complacency and cowardice—and they sicken us!

Our only love is the immense, moving, passionate structure of a building that we have the skill to complete at any given time, in any given way, in accordance with the ever changing directions of the wind and the weather, our bodies providing the scarlet cement, kneaded by our wills.

You must dread everything tainted with the past. You must look forward to everything belonging to the Future.

Have faith in progress, which is always right, even when it is wrong, for it is movement, life, struggle, and hope.

And avoid taking issue with the pace of Progress. It may be an impostor, traitor, murderer, a thief, or an arsonist, but Progress is nonetheless always right.

But it is from the Far East that the most conspicuous and forceful of Futurist symbols comes to us.

In Japan, they carry on a very strange trade in carbon derived from human bones. All gunpowder factories are working on the production of a new explosive which is deadlier than any other known hitherto. This terrible new compound has carbon from human bones as its principal ingredient, as this has the property of quickly absorbing both gases and liquids. For that precise reason, countless Japanese merchants go rooting about the battlefields of Manchuria, which are thickly strewn with corpses.[2] All over those vast warring landscapes, in great excitement they dig out huge piles of skeletons. A hundred *tsin* (seven kilograms) of human bones fetch 92 kopeks.

However, the Japanese merchants who are in charge of this entirely Futurist trade don't buy skulls because these, it seems, do not possess the necessary qualities. Instead, they collect huge quantities of other bones to send to Japan. To travelers along the Trans-Siberian Railway, the station at Benikou looks, from a distance, like a huge whitish pyramid. Skeletons of heroes will be ground down in mortars, without delay, *by their children or their relatives or their fellow citizens*, to be then brutally vomited out by cannon against enemy armies in distant lands . . .

All glory to the unconquerable ashes of men, who come to life again in the Japanese artillery! My friends, let us applaud this noble example of an ingeniously fabricated violence. Let us also applaud this fine slap in the face for all the stupid cultivators of cemetery gardens.

Quickly! So as to clear the streets, let all the corpses of the beloved and the venerated be stuffed, without delay, down the cannons' throats! Or, better still, let them await the enemy, gently rocking inside beautiful floating torpedoes, proffering their mouths full of deadly kisses.[3]

There will be an ever greater number of corpses. So much the better! The continuous increase of explosive substances will be of enormous value in our spineless world!

Raise high the banner of Futurism! Higher and higher, to exalt the aggressive will of man, without remembrance, and to emphasize yet again the ridiculous vacuity of nostalgic memory, of shortsighted history, and of the past that is dead.

Do we seem too brutal for you? It is because our words are dictated by a new sun, which is certainly not the one that caressed the backs of our easygoing grandfathers, whose slow, measured steps were ever in time with the lazy hours of provincial towns, with their silent, moss-covered streets.

We breathe an atmosphere which to them would have seemed unthinkable. We no longer have time to waste in praying over tombs! And, what's more, how on earth could we make them understand us, with their dull minds, much more in step with the spirit of Homer than with our own?

In the inevitable, impending conflicts between peoples, it will be those who have the deepest awareness of this difference that will be victorious.

The victors will be those who have more genius, more flexibility, more agility, more forgetfulness, who are more Futurist and therefore who are richest.

As for us Italian Futurists, we do not want to see Italy in a position of inferiority on the eve of this forbidding struggle. And it is for this reason that we hurl the ponderous burden of the past, which weighs heavily on her nimble, warlike hull, into the sea.

This text was first published in *Guerra sola igiene del mondo* (1915), by which time Futurism had already established itself and gone beyond its initial phase of radical confrontation with the Italian cultural establishment.

42

The New Ethical Religion of Speed

In my first manifesto of February 20, 1909, I declared that the splendor of the world had been enriched by a new beauty, *the beauty of speed*. Following on from dynamic art, in this Futurist year of our great liberating war, the new ethical religion of speed is born. Christian morality served the purpose of developing man's inner life, but today it no longer has any purpose, since the Divine is utterly finished.

Christian morality protected man's physical self from the excesses of sensuality. It regulated his instincts and gave them a certain balance. *Futurist morality* will protect man from decrepitude brought on by lethargy, nostalgia, fastidiousness, immobility, and custom. Human energies, increased a hundredfold by speed, will command Time and Space.

Mankind began by despising the measured, monotonous rhythm of the great rivers, which was identical to the rhythm of his own gait. He envied the rhythm of torrents, which was like that of galloping horses. Man gained mastery over horses, elephants, and camels to reveal his divine power through an increase in speed. He forged an alliance with more docile animals, captured animals which were rebellious and fed upon those animals which were edible. He extracted electricity and different fuels from the universe, so as to create new allies in the guise of engines. Man made use of fire to shape the metals he had won and made malleable so as to create an ally for himself, in the shape of fuels and electricity. In this way, he established an army of slaves who were hostile and dangerous, yet sufficiently domesticated to carry him swiftly over the earth's horizons.

Tortuous pathways, roads that follow the sluggish rivers, then wind along the uneven backs and bellies of the mountains; these represent the laws of the earth. Never any straight lines; always arabesques and zigzags. Speed at last presents mankind with one of the characteristics of divinity—*the straight line.*

The murky Danube, in its muddy robe, turns its eye on its inner life full of fat, libidinous, fertile fish as it rushes gurgling between implacable, steep-sided mountains, as though along the immense central highway of all the world, a confluence revealed by the swiftly rolling wheels of the constellations. When, finally, will this stolid river permit a motorcar, baying like a crazed fox terrier, to pass along it at breakneck speed? Before long, I hope to see the Danube running in a straight line, at 300 kilometers an hour.

We have to persecute, lash, and torture all those who inveigh against speed.

The guilt of those flophouse cities weighs heavily, where the sun takes up its residence, slows to a standstill, and moves no more. Who can really believe that the sun will be gone this evening? Come on, get a move on! It's not possible! It has settled down here. The piazzas are lakes of stagnant heat. The streets are rivers of languid fire. For the moment, there's no way of getting through them. There's no escape! Flood of sunlight. You would need a frozen boat or a suit of ice to cross that fire. Back into your den! A dictatorship, with police repression of light, which imprisons any rebel who brings a breath of fresh air and speed into town. A sun siege. Woe betide the body that steps out of the house. A clubbing on his head. Dead! Solar guillotines above each door. God help anyone with a thought in his head. Two, three, or four leaden notes fall on him from the ruins of the bell tower. Inside the sultry house, the anger of nostalgic flies. Straining of thighs and of sweat-soaked memories.

Immoral languor of Sunday crowds and Venetian lagoons.

Speed, whose essence is an intuitive synthesis of all forces in motion, is naturally *pure*. *Slowness*, whose essence is the rational analysis of all weariness at rest, is naturally *unclean*. After the destruction of the age-old good and the age-old evil, we are creating a new good, which is speed, and a new evil, which is torpor.

Speed = the synthesis of every kind of courage in action. It is aggressive and warlike.

Torpor = the analysis of every sort of festering caution. It is passive and pacifist.

Speed = scorn for all obstacles, desire for the new and the unexplored. It represents modernity and moral health.

Torpor = stasis, enchantment, immobile admiration of obstacles, nostalgia for things already seen, idealization of weariness and inactivity, distrust of the unexplored. Rancid, romantic concepts of the wild, wandering poet; of the filthy, shock-headed, bespectacled philosopher.

If praying means communicating with the divine, then hurtling along at great speed is a prayer. The sanctity of wheel and rail track. Kneel on the track to pray for divine speed! One must kneel before the spinning gyrocompass,[1] which, at 20,000 revolutions a minute, is the highest mechanical speed attained by man. We must steal from the stars the secret of their stupendous, incredible speed. Let us take part in the great celestial battles and face the star bolts, hurled by invisible cannons. We are pitted against the 1830 Groombridge star,[2] which whirls at 241 kilometers a second; against Arthur, which whirls at 413 kilometers a second. Invisible mathematical gunners. Wars in which the stars are both shells and gunners, striving through speed to flee from a bigger star or to hit a smaller one. Our saints are the innumerable particles that penetrate our atmosphere at an average speed of 42,000 meters per second. Our saints are light and electromagnetic waves of 3×10^{10} meters per second.

The exhilaration of high speeds in a motor car is simply the joy of feeling oneself made one with the one *divinity*. Sportsmen are the first neophytes of this religion. Before long comes the destruction of houses and cities to create huge meeting places for cars and airplanes.

Places inhabited by the divine are trains with restaurant cars for dining at high speed; railway stations, especially those in the American West, where trains speed along at 140 kilometers per hour, taking in the water they need (without stopping) together with the mailbags. Bridges and tunnels. The Place d'Opéra in Paris. The Strand in London. Racing-car circuits. Cinemas. Radio-telegraphic stations. The huge pipes conducting mountain water to snatch electrical power from the atmosphere. The great Parisian couturiers who, through their swift invention of fashions, create a passion for the new and hatred of the déjà-vus. The hypermodern, industrial cities like Milan, which, as the Americans say, have punch (i.e., the clean, precise blow with which the boxer administers his knockout). Battlefields. Machine guns, rifles, cannon, and shells are divine. Mines and mine detectors, blowing up the enemy

BEFORE he does the same to us. Combustion engines and rubber tires are divine. Bicycles and motorcycles are divine. Gasoline is divine. So is religious ecstasy inspired by one hundred horsepower. And the joy of moving from third to fourth gear. The joy of pressing down on the accelerator.[3] The growling pedal of musical speed. Disgusting the people entangled in sleep. The feeling of revulsion I experience when going to bed at night. I pray every night to my little electric lamp, for it has a formidable speed at work within it.

Heroism is a speed that has attained itself, traveling over the biggest of all racetracks.

Patriotism is the directed speed of a nation; war is the necessary testing of an army, the main driving force of a nation.

A motorcar or airplane at high speed permits us to scan and rapidly take in many distant points on Earth, that is, to do the job of analogy by mechanical means. Anyone who travels a lot automatically acquires a certain ability to look at things systematically as he approaches them, to compare one with another and to discover profound similarities between them. Great speed artificially reproduces an artist's intuitive analogy. The ever present, untrammeled imagination = speed.[4] Creative genius = speed.

There is active speed and passive speed; controlling speed (the chauffeur) *and controlled speed* (the motorcar); *speed that models* (writing, sculpturing) and *speed that is modeled* (what is written or sculptured); *there is speed that is borne by different speeds* (a train both pushed and pulled by two locomotives, one in front and the other behind) and *speed that carries other different speeds* (the ocean liner carrying several motorcars capable of different speeds + different men in motion— sailors, engineers, passengers, waiters, cooks, people swimming in the choppy waters of the swimming pools + the water churned by the swimmers + many dogs running or barking + lots of jumping fleas + the potential speeds of many racehorses).

Another example of *speed carrying different speeds* is the motorcar that carries the chauffeur + the speed of his thoughts about the second stage of the journey or the whole of what remains to be covered, while physically the car is still on the first stage. On arrival, the chauffeur in fact experiences the boredom of what he has already seen.

Our life must always be a carrying speed: Thought Speed + Body Speed + Speed of the deck that bears the body + Speed of the element (water or air) that carries the deck (boat or airplane). Detach thought from the mental road so as to place it on the material one. As if with a pencil, imbue a road map with smells (dissemination of the body), thoughts (dissemination of the spirit) = acceleration of speed. Speed destroys the laws of gravity, it makes the values of time and space subjective and therefore turns them into slaves. Kilometers and hours are not equal, they vary in length and duration for the man of speed.

Let us imitate the train and the motorcar, which compel everything that exists along the way to move at the same speed in the opposite direction, and arouse in everything that exists along the way a spirit of contradiction, that is, of life. The speed of the train decrees that the landscape it crosses be divided into two landscapes that rotate in the opposite direction from its own. Every train carries away with it the nostalgic spirit of anyone who watches it passing by. Things that are some distance away—trees, woods, hills, mountains—look fearfully at this rushing forward of things that are flung in the opposite direction to the train. Then they decide to tag along with them, but despondently, and more slowly. Every body moving at speed rocks from side to side and tends to become a pendulum.

Race along race along race along fly fly. Danger danger danger danger to right and to left below and above inside and out scent breathe drink in death. Militarized revolution of gears. Precise concise lyricism.[5] To enjoy more coolness and more life than in rivers and seas, you have to fly in the ice-cold slipstream at full speed.

When I flew for the first time with the aviator Bielovucic,[6] I felt my breast opening up like a great hole into which the vast skyscape was delightfully plunging, smooth, cool, streaming down. Instead of the slow, diluted sensuality of walks in the sun, among flowers, you should prefer the wild, cheek-coloring massage of a frenzied wind. A growing lightness. An infinite sense of pleasure. You skip lightly, nimbly, from your plane. You have shed whatever was weighing down upon you. You have conquered the mugginess of the flight path. You have overcome the law that forces men to creep about.

You have to be continuously altering your speed so that your conscious mind may also take part in it. The absolute beauty of speed is encountered on the double bend, for it pits itself first against the resistance of the ground; second, against the varying atmospheric pressures; and third, against the attraction of the void created by the bend itself. Speed along a straight line is enormous, coarse, and *reckless*. Speed on a bend and after the bend is speed come alive, and *controlled*.

The wonderful drama of zooming along on the racetrack. The car tends toward splitting itself in two. The heaviness of the rear portion, which turns into a cannonball and searches for slopes, ditches, the center of the earth, for fear of new dangers. *Better to perish at once than*

continue to take more risks. No! No! No! All glory be to the Futurist su-
pertrain which, with a mere shrug of the shoulders or touch of the
wheel, will pull the rear end of the vehicle away from the ditch and set
it, once again, upon its straight course. *Close to us*, among us *without
tracks*, motorcars hurtle along, turn back on themselves, they lurch to
this side on the curve of the horizon, flimsy, menaced by all of the
problems set for them by the bends. The double bend conquered at
speed is the supreme manifestation of life. The Victory of the self over
the treacherous intrigues created by our Weight which seeks, through
betrayal, to murder our speed, dragging it down into a pit of immobility. Speed = dissemination + condensation of the "I." All space passed
through by a body is condensed into that same body.

$$\text{Ground speed} \begin{cases} \text{Love of the earth woman; dissemination} \\ \quad \text{throughout the world (horizontal lust)} \\ \text{= motoring along lovingly caressing the} \\ \quad \text{white womanly curves of the roads} \end{cases}$$

$$\text{Air speed} \begin{cases} \text{Hatred of the earth (vertical mysticism)} \\ \text{The upward spiraling self toward the} \\ \quad \text{Nothingness—God = Aviation, the} \\ \quad \text{purgative agility of castor oil} \end{cases}$$

The speedy engagement of a train's wheels with their gnashing
teeth. The wheels draw from the earth all of the sounds that are dormant in matter. Under the pressure of the train, the wheels leap, flash
along in the quick, vibrant snare of the deeply felt moment. Roads traveled by motorcars are slipstreams of globular sounds and spiraling
smells. This one-hundred-horsepower automobile is an extension of
the caverns of Mount Etna.

Roads traveled by cars, as well as railway lines, have a swaying, sup-
ple, forward rush, seeking to wrap themselves speedily about the fin-
ishing post that rises up at some point on the horizon.

Intense pleasure of sitting alone on the dark back seat of a limou-
sine, speeding along between the dancing, glittering *neon signs* of some
capital city by night. That very special pleasure of feeling oneself to be
a speeding body. I am someone who often eats at a railway station between one train and another. My gaze oscillates between the clock
on the wall and my steaming plate. The spinning anxiety-memory-
airscrew pierces my heart. I have to feed it at once with speed. One has
only to believe in the solidity-resistance of speed. The strength and the

complication of thought, the sophistication of desires and of appetites, the paucity of the soil, hunger for honey, spices, meats, and fruits from distant lands—all insist on the Futurist Ethical Religion of Speed.

Speed separates the male cell from the female cell. Speed destroys love, that vice of the sedentary heart, that grievous clotting, that hardening of the arteries which restricts the flow of the life-blood of humanity. Speed increases agility, it increases the circulation of the blood, the railway engines, the motorcars, and the airplanes of the world.

Only speed can kill off the noxious, nostalgic, sentimental, pacifist, and neutralist Moonlight. Italians, be speedy, and you will be strong, optimistic, invincible, immortal!

This manifesto was published in *L'Italia futurista* of June 1, 1916, then reprinted in a broadsheet version, and in *I manifesti del futurismo* (1919). It was issued again, with a few textual variations, in the appropriately named and beautifully designed volume *Lussuria–velocità* (Lust–Speed) in 1921.

43

∽

The Futurist Cinema

The book as a means for conserving and communicating thought is a vehicle that belongs unequivocally to the past. For a long time now it has been destined to disappear, along with cathedrals, towers, crenellated walls, museums, and the ideal of pacifism. The book, static companion of the sedentary, the nostalgic, and the neutralists, can neither amuse nor stimulate the new Futurist generations, who are drunk on revolutionary, warlike dynamism.

The war is increasingly sharpening European sensibilities. Our great cleansing war, which must satisfy *all* our national aspirations, is increasing the revitalizing power of the Italian race a hundredfold. The Futurist cinema that we are preparing—playful deformation of the universe, a-logical, fleeting synthesis of daily life—will become the best school of all for our children. It will be a school for enjoyment, speed, strength, courage, and heroism. Futurist cinema will sharpen and develop sensibilities, it will intensify the creative imagination, and give the conscious mind an overwhelming sense of both simultaneity and omnipresence. In this way the Futurist cinema will play its part in the overall modernization process by putting an end to academic journals (always pedantic), by replacing stage plays (always predictable), and by killing off the book (always tedious and oppressive). The necessity for propaganda will force us every now and then to publish a book. However, we prefer to express ourselves through the cinema, the great graphic designs of Words-in-Freedom, and mobile, illuminated bulletin boards.

With our manifesto *The Futurist Theater of Essential Brevity* and the triumphant tours by the Gualtiero Tumiati, Ettore Berti, Annibale Ninchi, and Luigi Zoncada theater companies, together with two volumes of *The Futurist Theater of Essential Brevity*, which contain eighty theatrical minidramas, we have launched the revolution of the prose theater in Italy.[1] Prior to that, another Futurist manifesto had rehabilitated, glorified, and perfected the variety theater.[2] It therefore makes perfect sense that we should now bring our attempts at livening things up into another area of theater, namely the *cinema*.

At first glance, the cinema, which came into being not many years ago, might seem Futurist already, by which we mean having no past and being free from all tradition. In reality, starting up as *silent theater*, it has inherited all the traditional detritus of the literary theater.[3] We can therefore safely direct all we have said and done with regard to the prose theater at the cinema as well.[4] Our action is both right and necessary in that the cinema, until this moment, *has been and is tending to remain deeply traditionalist*. We, however, see in it the possibility of an art that is supremely Futurist and *a means of expression that is more suited to the multifaceted sensibilities of a Futurist art*.

With the exception of interesting films about travel, hunting, wars, and so on, all that has happened is that conventional dramas, epic dramas, and lightweight dramas have been inflicted on us. The script itself, when it is brief and different, may look like progress, but in reality and in the majority of cases it is nothing more than a trite, pathetic piece of *analysis*. Thus, all the immense *artistic* possibilities of the cinema remain absolutely untapped.

The cinema is an art form in itself. It should therefore never seek to imitate the stage. Because it is essentially a visual medium, it should seek above all to bring about the evolution of the image, to detach itself from reality, from photography, from whatever is thought of as elegant or solemn. Rather, it should become antigraceful,[5] a means of distortion, impressionistic, concise, dynamic, and a vehicle for Words-in-Freedom.[6]

We have to liberate the cinema as a means of expression so as to make it the perfect instrument *of a new art* that is infinitely broader in scope and more versatile than all others currently in existence. We are convinced that only through adapting the cinema will it be possible to achieve that *multifaceted expressiveness* which all modern artistic experiments are seeking. *The Futurist Cinema* is today creating that **polyexpressive symphony** which, a year ago, we announced in our manifesto *Weights, Measures, and Prices of Artistic Genius*. Futurist films will make use of a very wide variety of means of expression, ranging from a slice of real life to a splash of color,[7] from a line to Words-in-Freedom, from chromatic, plastic music to a music of objects. It will be, at one and the same time, picture, architecture, sculpture, Words-in-Freedom, the music of colors, lines, and shapes, a hodgepodge of objects, and reality thrown into chaos. We shall offer new inspiration to the experiments of those painters who seek to push painting beyond the limits of the frame. We shall launch Words-in-Freedom, which break through the boundaries of literature, striding away toward painting, music, and the art of noise, constructing a marvelous bridge between the word and the real object.

Our films will be:

1. **Cinematographic analogies** which make direct use of reality as one of the two elements of the analogy.[8] For example, if we wish to express a state of anxiety in one of our characters, instead of describing him in the various stages of his sadness we shall present an equivalent impression by showing a mountain that is all jagged and pitted.

   Mountains, seas, forests, cities, crowds of people, armies, teams, and airplanes will often be our most formidably expressive words: **The universe will be our vocabulary.**[9]

   For example: We may wish to create a sensation of wild happiness, so we shall show an armchair cover flying playfully around a large coatrack, until they make up their minds to unite. We may want to create a sense of anger, so we shall disintegrate a hot-tempered character into a storm of yellow particles. We may want to show the anguish of a Hero losing his faith in a now defunct, neutralist skepticism, so we'll present him spiritedly haranguing a crowd of people. And then we'll suddenly let Giovanni Giolitti[10] loose on him, to treasonably stuff his mouth with a great forkful of macaroni and drown out his elated words in tomato sauce.

   We shall enliven dialogue by speedily, simultaneously showing every image that is passing through the minds of the characters. For example, when presenting a man saying to his woman, "You're as lovely as a gazelle," we shall show the gazelle. Another example would be if a character says, "I look upon your bright, fresh smile as a traveler, after a long, tiring struggle, contemplates the sea from high up on a mountain," we shall show the traveler, the sea, and the mountain.

   In this way, our characters will be perfectly comprehensible, *just as if they were speaking.*

2. Cinematographic Heroic Poems, Conversations, and Po-etry.[11] We shall flash the images of which they are composed upon the screen.

For example: Giosué Carducci's "Canto dell'amore" (Love Song):

> *On German rocks crouching*
> *like hawks scanning their prey . . .*

We shall show the rocks and the hawks waiting to swoop.

> *From churches endlessly raising*
> *Marble arms above, they pray to their Lord . . .*

> *From convents twixt city and hamlet*
> *Solemnly seated at the sound of bells,* ·
> *Like cuckoos amid sparse branches*
> *Intoning their cares and unexpected joys*

We shall show the churches being gradually transformed into supplicating women, God looking pleased from on high, and then images of convents, cuckoos, and so on.

Another example: Giosué Carducci's "Sogno d'estate" (Summer Dream):

> *Amid your ever clamorous strains of battle, Homer,*
> *It was the noonday heat that crushed me: my head bowed*
> *by Scamander, tho' my heart fled to Tyrrhenian climes*

We shall show Carducci wandering about in a turmoil of Achaeans, nimbly dodging charging horses, paying homage to Homer, then going off for a drink with Ajax to the hostelry called the Red Sca-mander.[12] On his third glass of wine, however, his heart, which can be seen beating, will pop out of his jacket and fly away, like an enormous red balloon, over the Gulf of Rapallo. This is how we shall film the most secret moments of genius.

In these ways, we shall make fun of the work of traditionalist po-ets, transforming their most nostalgically monotonous and whining verse into violent, exciting, and highly exhilarating spectacles, to the greatest benefit of the audience.

3. Simultaneity and Interpenetration of different times and places

on film. We shall show in the one frame and instant, two or three different images, side by side.

4. **Filmed Musical Experiments** (discords, harmonies, symphonies of gestures, actions, colors, lines, and so on).
5. **States of mind dramatized on film.**[13]
6. **Daily exercises aimed at freeing oneself from logic on film.**
7. **Drama of objects transposed onto film.**[14] (Animated objects that are humanized, wearing makeup and clothes, given emotions, civilized, dancing—objects abstracted from their normal environments and placed in an unfamiliar situation which, by way of contrast, highlights their breathtaking construction and nonhuman life.)
8. **Windows**[15] **of ideas, of events, of different types, of objects, etc., on film.**
9. **Amorous encounters, flirtations, brawls, and marriages of grimaces, mimes, etc., on film.** For example: A big nose that imposes silence on a thousand fingers at a convention, by tolling an ear like a bell, while two mustaches, like policemen, arrest a tooth.
10. **Bizarre reconstructions of the human body on film.**
11. **Dramas of disproportions on film**, for example, a man slakes his thirst by taking out a minuscule drinking straw, extending it like an umbilical cord down to a lake, which he then drains in one go.[16]
12. **Potential dramas and strategic plans for feeling on film.**
13. **Plastic, chromatic, or linear equivalents** of men, women, events, thoughts, music, feelings, weights, smells, noises, **on film** (with white lines on black, we shall show the internal and the physical rhythms of a husband who discovers his wife in adultery, and who pursues her lover—the rhythm of his soul and that of his legs).
14. **Words-in-Freedom in motion on film** (synoptic tables of lyrical values—dramas of humanized and animalized letters—dramas of handwriting—typographical dramas—geometrical dramas—numerical sensibilities, etc.).[17]

Picture + sculpture + plastic dynamism + Words-in-Freedom + sound cadences + condensed theater = Futurist Cinema.

In this way we shall dismantle, then re-fashion, the Universe according to our marvelous whims,[18] to increase one hundredfold the power of creative Italian genius and its absolute predominance throughout the world.

This manifesto was published in *L'Italia futurista* on November 15, 1916. A broadsheet version, issued by the Direzione del Movimento

Futurista in Milan, is dated September 11, 1916. The text also appeared in *La rivolta futurista* (Reggio Calabria) on December 1, 1916. It is likely that the manifesto evolved in the summer of 1916, parallel with the making of *Vita futurista*, and that on September 11 only a draft version of it existed. The manifesto was signed by the makers of *Vita futurista*, F. T. Marinetti, Bruno Corra, Emilio Settimelli, Arnaldo Ginna, Giacomo Balla, and Remo Chiti. A slightly different version of the manifesto was contained in the anthologies *Noi futuristi* (1917) and *I manifesti del futurismo* (1919).

44

✍

Some Parts of the Film Futurist Life

I

Projection of the main, innovative principles from the manifesto of Futurist cinema, which was written and distributed in thousands and thousands of copies, by Marinetti, Settimelli, Bruno Corra, A. Ginna, and G. Balla.

"Abolition of the finite, polished, anti-impressionistic, **PHOTO-GRAPHIC** techniques which take away from light and matter every hint of their vibrancy—" "Also the physical surroundings *must* express the state of mind of the character who moves through them."

"Let us free the cinema from its servitude as mere reproducer of reality, from the limitations of motion picture photography, and let us raise it to the level of art, that is, as a means of expression, such as painting, sculpture, architecture, literature, and so on."

"We are beginning to create a new art form, namely **Poly-expressiveness**, a fusion of all the arts, which is born with us, which is absolutely Italian—."

"As a precaution against all facile ironies, let us remember the many real successes of Futurism in the field of lyricism,[1] which we have violently restored to life in less than six years; and in that of painting, which we have strongly influenced and channeled toward a new experimentation. Let us remember that already seven years ago the Futurists were the first to support the notion of the inevitability of the war. At a time when the pacifism engendered by the Triple Alliance[2] reigned supreme, Marinetti, to the amazement and derision of all, shouted out in public (at the Teatro Lirico in Milan) **"War on Austria!"**[3]

II

Presentation of the Futurists Marinetti, Settimelli, B. Corra, Remo Chiti, G. Balla, Arnaldo Ginna.

III

"Futurist Life"[4]

How a Futurist sleeps—played by Marinetti, Settimelli, Corra, and Giulio Spina.

IV

Gymnastics in the morning—fencing, boxing—a Futurist bout with swords between Marinetti and Remo Chiti—an argument, in boxing gloves, between Marinetti and Ungari.

V

A Futurist breakfast—played by Settimelli, Corra, Marinetti, Vènna, Spada, Josia, and Remo Chiti. Also some symbolic old men.

VI

The search for inspiration—drama of objects. Marinetti and Settimelli, taking the necessary precautions, approach certain objects that are strangely lumped together in order to look at them in new ways. Examination of herrings, carrots, and eggplant—**AT LONG LAST understanding** these animals and vegetables, through placing them totally outside their habitual environment. We see completely, for the first time and from all angles, a rubber ball that has fallen on the head of a statue and remained there rather than in the hands of the child who was playing with it. —Acted by Settimelli, Chiti, and Bruno Corra.

A Futurist poetry recitation.

Settimelli reads from his writings. Ungari expresses his feelings with gesture, Chiti his by drawing.

A discussion between a foot, a hammer, and an umbrella. —Utilize the human expressions of the objects, so as to pitch into new fields of artistic sensibility.

VII

A Futurist stroll. Study of new types of walking manners—caricature of a **neutralist walk**, acted out by Marinetti and Balla.

An **Interventionist walk** exemplified by Marinetti—a creditor's walk, exemplified by Balla—a debtor's walk, demonstrated by Settimelli.

A **Futurist march** demonstrated by Marinetti, Settimelli, Balla, Chiti, and so on.

VIII

A **Futurist tea party**—invasion of a traditional tea party—women are enthralled by it—Marinetti speaks amid their enthusiasm.

IX

Futurist Work—pictures distorted both in terms of concepts and execution—Balla falls in love with, and marries, a chair, and a stool is the eventual outcome—performed by Marinetti, Balla, and Settimelli.

This announcement was published in *L'Italia futurista* on October 15, 1916, and in several subsequent issues of the newspaper.

THE POSTWAR POLITICAL BATTLE
(1918–23)

During the First World War the Futurists formed friendships with the elite corps of storm troopers called the Arditi (the Daring Ones). This avant-garde unit was not bound by conventional military discipline and carried out missions that can only be described as death-defying tasks for true daredevils. Several Futurists had volunteered to serve in these units, and Marinetti was a regular guest in their barracks, disseminating propaganda and recruiting new members for his movement. In 1918 this gave rise to Ardito-Futurism as a new ideological phenomenon. Futurism assumed a new direction and reorganized itself as a political association. During the last year of the war, Marinetti drafted a manifesto for the founding of a Futurist Political Party, based on the *Third Futurist Political Manifesto* (document 13) of October 1913. It was published in the last issue of *L'Italia futurista* (February 11, 1918) and stated in its final paragraph: "The Futurist Political Party that we are founding today will be entirely separate from the Futurist Art Movement." In actual fact, there was little left of the "Futurist Art Movement" by 1918, and the party was only kicked into action after the armistice was signed (November 11, 1918). However, during this summer break, Marinetti met Carli and Settimelli in Rome to discuss the foundation of a "paper which binds the Futurists, the Arditi of the Nation, to the Arditi, the Futurists of the army." *Roma futurista: Newspaper of the Futurist Political Party* began its publication on September 20, 1918, but it took until November 30 for a first branch (*fascio*) of the party to be formally constituted.

The Arditi, who were instrumental in the foundation of the Futurist Political Party and its local branches, received, in return for their invaluable support, the assistance of the Futurists, when on January 1, 1919, they founded their own association and on January 19 set up a first cell in Marinetti's apartment in Milan. The Arditi's political program, outlined by the Futurist Mario Carli, resembled in large part the ideas expressed in the *Manifesto of the Futurist Political Party*. Carli also penned a *Manifesto of the Futurist Ardito,* which constituted the Arditi's most comprehensive, most radical, and most Futurist political proclamation.

In 1919 neither the Futurist Political Party nor the Association of Arditi had many members. Their natural recruiting ground was the masses of returning soldiers,

who experienced tremendous difficulties and hardship in their attempts to rein-
tegrate themselves into civilian life. The Ardito-Futurists found an unexpected
supporter of their recruitment drive in Benito Mussolini, who had already shared
a platform with Marinetti in the Interventionist demonstrations of 1915. Mussolini, who had been a representative of the revolutionary wing of the Socialist
Party and then broken with the PSI over the question of Italy's intervention in the
First World War, was in the process of building for himself a new power base in
the combatants' associations. To penetrate this bastion, he needed a thorough
overhaul of his revolutionary credentials. This was the main reason why, in the
summer of 1918, he established contact with the Futurists and the Arditi.
Marinetti's diary makes it very clear that it was Mussolini who first approached
them. In November and December 1918, they joined forces in several victory celebrations, and from then on, Mussolini's paper, *Il popolo d'Italia*, served as a forum
for many Arditi announcements and declarations.

   Many Futurists and Arditi were present at the founding of the Fasci di Combattimento in Piazza San Sepolcro, Milan (March 23, 1919), and took an active part
in their local branches all over Italy. These cells initially possessed a very heterogeneous membership, ranging from anarchists and socialists to nationalists and
monarchists. Mussolini tested the water in various political ponds before deciding
on the direction that was most likely to advance him into a position of power. As
Marinetti's diary notes show (see document 48), he had a shrewd understanding
of Mussolini's character, but nonetheless agreed on a coalition with the Fasci di
Combattimento. In the summer of 1919, they sat together on action committees
of various combatants' organizations, which sought to organize social assistance
for former soldiers. Mussolini tried to give the committees a more political role with
a view to having them run as a political bloc in the elections of November 16,
1919. During those months, Marinetti developed his idea of a Futurist democracy, propagated in many speeches, articles, brochures, and a volume of essays.
These writings give a clear indication that his political sympathies bore closer resemblance to the revolutionary Left than the intransigent Right. And they appear
to have had a significant influence on the Fasci di Combattimento. At their first
congress in Florence, in October 1919, he managed to swing one-third of the
delegates behind his position, but Mussolini was the wilier politician, who in the
long run determined the political future of the Fasci. Marinetti regretted this
"march toward Reaction," which led to the retreat or expulsion of most leftist
members, but it took until May 29, 1920, before he handed in his resignation
from the Central Committee and quit the Fasci di Combattimento.

45

ᴄᴏ

Manifesto of the Futurist Political Party

1. The Futurist Political Party, which we are founding today,[1] wants an Italy that is both strong and free, no longer in servitude to its great Past, to foreigners, who are too much loved, and to priests, who are too much tolerated. We want an Italy that is under no one's control, that is the absolute mistress of all her energies and that is oriented toward her own great future.
2. Italy, sovereign, united, and indivisible. A revolutionary nationalism intent on the freedom, well-being, physical and intellectual improvement, strength, progress, greatness, and pride of all the Italian people.
3. The patriotic education of the proletariat. The fight against illiteracy. Road networks. The construction of new roads and railroads. Obligatory, secular primary schooling that is legally enforced. The abolition of many useless universities and of classical education. Obligatory technical instruction in the workplace. Obligatory and legally enforced gymnastics, sport, and military education in the open air. Schools promoting courage and the Italian spirit.
4. The transformation of Parliament through the equal participation of industrialists, agrarians, engineers, and businessmen in the government of the country. The minimum age limit for deputies to be reduced to twenty-two years. Reduction of the number of lawyer deputies (who are always opportunists) and teacher deputies (who are always ultraconservative). A Parliament that is free of weaklings and scoundrels. Abolition of the Senate.

If this rational and practical Parliament fails to yield positive results, we shall abolish it altogether and bring in a technocratic government without parliament, a government composed of twenty technocrats elected by universal suffrage.

We shall replace the Senate with a Supervisory Assembly made up of twenty young men under the age of thirty, elected by universal suffrage. And instead of a Parliament full of incompetent orators and irrelevant academics, MODERATED by a Senate full of has-beens, we shall have a government of twenty technocrats STIMULATED by an assembly of under-thirty-year-olds.

There would be equal participation of all Italian citizens in government. Equal and direct universal suffrage for all citizens, both men and women, on a broadly based list system, using proportional representation.

5. Substitution of the present rhetorical, quiescent anticlericalism by an actively violent and resolute anticlericalism, so as to rid Italy and Rome of their medieval theocracy, which can find an appropriate country in which to go and slowly wither away.

Our anticlericalism is total and uncompromising and constitutes the basis of our political program. It admits of no half measures nor accommodations, demanding total abolition of the ecclesiastical system.

Our anticlericalism wishes to rid Italy of its churches, its priests, its friars, its nuns, its madonnas, its candles, and its bells.

[Censored]²

The only religion is the Italy of tomorrow. For her we shall fight and maybe even die without caring overmuch what forms of government must necessarily follow the medieval theocracy after its final demise.

6. Abolition of marital permission. Easy divorce. Gradual devaluation of marriage, eventually to be replaced by free love and children reared in State institutions.³

7. Maintenance of the army and the navy in full operational order until the Austro-Hungarian Empire had been dismantled. After which, the reduction of the number of personnel to a bare minimum, while training a large number of officer cadres through a system of rapid instruction. By way of examples, 200,000 men

with 60,000 officers, whose training could be divided into four three-month courses each year. Then, the provision of military and sports education in schools. Preparation for a total mobilization of industry (arms and munitions) to come into effect in the event of war and at the same time as military mobilization takes place. In short, everything ready at minimum cost in the event of war or revolution.

Our war must aim at total victory, which means the dismembering of the Austro-Hungarian Empire, as well as safeguarding our natural boundaries, both land and sea, without which we would not have our hands free for the clearing out, the cleaning up, the renewal, and the expansion of Italy.

Abolition of ceremonial patriotism, of the obsession with monuments, and of every kind of traditionalist State interference in artistic matters.

8. Preparation for the future nationalization of land with the creation of a vast government-owned domain consisting of the property of religious organizations and local authorities, as well as the expropriation of all uncultivated or badly managed lands. High taxation of all inherited property, with limits set on the number of successive heirs.

A taxation system based on direct, progressive taxes with complete verification. Freedom of strike action, of assembly, of association, and of the press. Reform and purging of the police. Abolition of the secret police. Interdiction of army intervention for the purpose of restoring public order.

Cost-free recourse to the law and an elected judiciary. Minimum set wages automatically raised in relation to the cost of living. A legal maximum of eight consecutive hours of work. Parity of remuneration for men and women for equal work. Fair and impartial laws governing individual and collective labor agreements. Transformation of charity work into social welfare and national insurance. Workers' pensions.

Sequestration of two-thirds of all assets gained through war contracts.

9. Establishment of a stock of agricultural land for ex-combatants.[4] We need to acquire a certain amount of landed property in Italy, at prices to be fixed according to special criteria, for distribution— naturally, with due caution and reservations—to ex-combatants or, in cases where they are no longer living, to their surviving families.

Payment for land acquired in this way must be made by the nation as a whole, without distinctions for class, but with progressive distinctions applied with regard to financial circumstances, the funds to come from both voluntary donations and taxes.

Payment for these required lands could be foreclosed within fifty years of the dispossession taking place, so that the Nation's contribution, whether in the form of donations or taxes, would be minimal. Lands expropriated through taxation will revert, if there are any, to the land stock for ex-combatants.

All manual laborers who have served in the armed forces in the war zones must be registered at State expense in the "Workers' National Insurance Fund for Disability and Old Age," to take effect from the first day of their actual service. The State will have to pay their annual contributions for the whole duration of the war. Registration of military combatants in the National Fund will be compulsory and will be the responsibility of the State for the whole period of the military service, but it will afterward become the ongoing responsibility of the individuals concerned for the rest of their lives.

In the case of allowances granted to holders of medals awarded for valor, the amount will be threefold. —The age limit fixed in the regulations will be extended for veterans of the war zone for a period equivalent to that of the duration of the war. —For veterans of the war zone who obtain work in the public sector, their military service and campaigns will be taken into account as far as their age and pension are concerned, with the State, whenever necessary, being responsible for payments into the Pension Fund for the period of their military service. —For the ten years following the war, Public Administrations must alternate open competition with competitions reserved exclusively for veterans of the war zone and disabled war veterans who are physically capable of carrying out the services required.

10. Industrialization and modernization of the moribund cities that are still living in the past.[5] Diminution of the importance of dangerous, unpredictable foreign-owned industries.

Development of the merchant marine and of river traffic. Creation of canalized waterways and the draining of malaria-ridden lands. Realization of the value of all the country's forces and riches. To put a stop to emigration. Nationalization and utilization of all water and all mines. Concession of their potential benefits to local public authorities. Easier finance for industry and cooperatives for agriculture. Consumers' rights.

11. Radical overhaul of the bureaucracy, which today has become an end in itself and a State within the State. And as a result of this, development of regional and municipal autonomy. Devolution of administrative responsibilities and control mechanisms to the regions. The aim is to make every administrative body swift-acting and efficient, and to reduce the number of employees by two-thirds. At the same time, the salaries of Heads of Department must be doubled, the selection procedure must be competitive, and practical experience must be a condition of employment. Departmental Executives to be given direct and consequential responsibility for the improvement and simplification of everything. Cutting out all the dead wood from every administrative body, from the diplomatic service and from all areas of national life. Direct rewards for practical ingenuity and job simplification. Reduction in importance of academic qualifications and encouragement by reward for commercial and industrial initiative. Application of the elective principle for positions of major responsibility. Following the industrial model, simplification of organization in the different branches of the executive.

The Futurist Political Party that we are founding today will be entirely separate from the Futurist Art Movement.[6] This latter will continue in its modernization and strengthening of the creative Italian genius. The Futurist Art Movement, the avant-garde of Italian artistic sensibility, is of course always some way ahead of the slowly changing sensibilities of the people. It is, therefore, an avant-garde that is often misunderstood and often opposed by the majority, who cannot understand its amazing discoveries, the brutal directness of its polemical expression, and the fearless leaps of its intuitions.

The Futurist Political Party, on the other hand, senses present needs and interprets the very frame of mind of the entire race precisely in its purgative revolutionary impulse. All Italians can belong to the Futurist Political Party, men and women of all classes and ages, regardless of whether or not they have any notions whatsoever about art or literature.[7]

This political program signals the birth of the Futurist Political Party, called into being by all those Italians who today are fighting for a more youthful Italy, freed from the millstones of the past and of foreigners.

We shall sustain this political program with the élan and courage that hitherto have characterized the Futurist Movement in the theaters and piazzas. And everyone in Italy and abroad knows what we mean by élan and courage.

This manifesto appeared in the last issue of *L'Italia futurista* (February 11, 1918), that is, during the war and before the Futurist Political Party had actually been founded. Once the party was actually in existence and possessed its own journal, *Roma futurista,* the program was reprinted in its first issue (September 20, 1918) and was also distributed in the form of fliers and posters.

46

※

An Artistic Movement Creates a Political Party

Our Futurist Political Party was born naturally out of the great spiritual current of the Futurist Artistic Movement.[1]

Unique in history, our Party was conceived, desired, and brought into being by a group of artists—poets, painters, musicians, and so on—who, full of genius and courage that they have already demonstrated through their brutal modernization of Italian art, arrived quite logically at a concept of politics utterly devoid of rhetoric, violently Italian, and violently revolutionary, free, dynamic, and armed with tactics that are entirely practical.

Since an illustrious past was crushing Italy and yet *an infinitely more glorious future* was fermenting away in her breast, it was precisely here, in Italy, ten years ago, that beneath our too-sensuous sky Futurist energy was crying out to be born, to become organized, channeled, to find in us its driving forces, its means of illumination and propagation. Italy, more than any other country, was in urgent need of Futurism, for it was dying of an obsession with its own past. The patient invented its own remedy. *We are the doctors the situation demanded,*[2] and the remedy is valid for the sick in all countries.

Our immediate objective was to fight tooth and nail against all the most repugnant forms of Italy's obsession with the past: archaeology, academicism, senility, quietism, cowardice, pacifism, pessimism, nostalgia, sentimentalism, obsession with romantic love, foreign-owned industries, and so on. Our ultraviolent, anticlerical, antisozzialist,[3] and antitraditionalist movement was founded on the inexhaustible vigor of

Italian blood and fought against the cult of the past, which, far from binding the race together, makes it anemic and causes it to rot.

Futurism, in its general program, presented an avant-garde atmosphere; it was a byword for all innovators or intellectual sharpshooters the world over. It stood for love of the new; for art impassioned by speed; for the systematic denigration of the ancient, the old, the slow, the erudite, and the professorial. It represented a new way of seeing the world, a new reason for loving life; a wholehearted glorification of scientific discoveries and of modern machinery; a flag for youth, for strength, for originality at all costs; a steel collar against the habit of twisting one's head around nostalgically; an inexhaustible machine gun trained on the army of the dead, the gouty, the opportunists, whom we wish to divest of their authority and make subservient to the bold, creative youth; a stick of dynamite for all time-honored ruins.

The word "Futurism" embodied the most far-reaching formula for renewal, that which was at the same time purgative and stimulant, smoothing out doubts, destroying skepticism, and bringing together all would-be effort into a formidable sense of elation. All innovators met beneath the flag of Futurism, because Futurism proclaimed the need always to go forward, and because it advocated the destruction of all bridges of which cowardice might avail itself. Futurism represented a man-made optimism to set against all the inveterate pessimisms, a continuous dynamism, a perpetual becoming, and a tireless will. Thus Futurism was not then subject to the rules of fashion nor to the ravages of time, nor was it a *petty religion* or a *school*, but rather a great, united movement of intellectual heroism, in which individual pride counted for nothing, while the will to renewal was all.[4]

Italian Futurism, the prophet of our war, the disseminator and exerciser of Italian courage and pride, eleven years ago inaugurated its very first artistic gathering with the cry: "*Long live Asinari di Bernezzo! Down with Austria!*"[5]

The Futurists organized *the first two demonstrations* against Austria in September 1914, in Milan, during the period of absolute neutrality, burned eight Austrian flags in the piazzas, and were imprisoned in San Vittore.[6]

They desired war, they struggled to bring it about, and they fought in it.

FUTURISTS

THOSE WHO DIED ON THE FRONT LINE

Cantucci (silver medal); Stojanovich; Sant'Elia (silver medal); Carlo Erba; Athos Casarini; Luca Labozzetta; Luigi Peron-Cabus; Visone; Occhinegro; Angelo Della Santa; Annunzio Cervi (silver medal); Ugo Tommei

THOSE WHO WERE WOUNDED ON THE FRONT LINE

Guizzi Doro; Nino Zuccarello; F. T. Marinetti; Nino Formoso; Jamar 14; Bolongaro (bronze medal); Racchella (5 wounds—disabled—bronze medal); Raffaele Merola (disabled); Berr (4 wounds—2 silver medals); Piero Bolzon; Gennari (disabled—3 silver medals); Soffici (bronze medal); Russolo (disabled—silver medal); Vann'Antò; Dessy; Olao Gaggioli (4 medals); Steiner (disabled); Mario Carli; Marcello Manni; Ugo Piatti; Ottone Rosai (silver medal); Enrico Rocca; Cerati; Astarita (silver medal); Morpurgo; Catapano (bronze medal); Paolo Rubio; Businelli (silver medal); Raffaello Franchi; P. P. Carbonelli; Urrico Foa; Berto Ronchis (disabled—3 medals); Romano Imegli (2 medals); Renato Zamboni (disabled); Giorgio Forlai; Giovanni Brunetti; Nino Scotto (4 wounds); Corrado Giusti; G. Benasciuti; Arturo Breviglieri

DIED WHILE UNDER ARMS

Umberto Boccioni

Convinced that they had participated to the fullest in the overwhelming Italian victory by virtue of their prophetic genius, their courage, their blood, and their tenacity, the Italian Futurists feel they are today directly involved in the political organization of Italy, thrusting forward a dream of renewal that is infinitely bolder and a program of freedom that is infinitely more revolutionary.

In April 1917 the *Corriere della sera* wrote:

> Let's hope Italy is not, as she sometimes seems to be, a social organism *sui generis*, neither aristocracy nor democracy, but rather a gerontocracy, a jealous, senile republic in which—with a few very notable exceptions—the road is barred to anyone who is not so long in the tooth and enfeebled as to be utterly ineffectual, be a threat to no one.

Well, that is the case. It is absolutely the case. And it is against this vile Italy—if truth be told, supported by the *Corriere* itself—that we have been fighting these past ten years.

The Manifesto of the Italian Futurist Political Party, published and launched on February 11, 1918, declares:

> We have to bring our war to outright victory, which means the total dismemberment of the Austro-Hungarian Empire, and the security of our natural frontiers, both land and sea, without which we would not have our hands free to clear out, clean up, change, and expand Italy.

Our prophecy, like others we have made, has been fully realized. Our Futurist optimism, which has been much derided, opposed by almost everyone, has been entirely vindicated.

We have our hands free. Let us begin then, without further delay, to clear out, clean up, change, and enlarge Italy by freeing her from the dead weight of her past and from foreign influences.

The Futurist Party wants an Italy that is free and strong and no longer under the yoke of her great past or of the foreigner, who is too much wooed, or of the priests, of whom we are far too tolerant. An Italy that is answerable to no one, absolutely the mistress of all her energies and straining forward toward her great future.

The Futurist Political Party will be entirely separate from the Futurist Art Movement.[6] This latter will continue in its modernization and strengthening of the creative Italian genius. The Futurist Art Movement, the avant-garde of Italian artistic sensibility, is of course always some way ahead of the slowly changing sensibilities of the people. It is, therefore, an avant-garde that is often misunderstood and often opposed by the majority, who cannot understand its amazing discoveries, the brutal directness of its polemical expression, and the fearless leaps of its intuitions.

The Futurist Political Party, on the other hand, senses present needs and interprets the frame of mind of the entire race very precisely in its purgative revolutionary impulse. All Italians can belong to the Futurist Political Party, men and women of all classes and ages, regardless of whether or not they have any notions whatsoever about art or literature.

The hostility that has been stirred up by artistic Futurism need not worry new members of the Futurist Political Party.

The artworks of the Futurist Movement may well appear too programmatical and violent in their eyes, too full of theory and of foregone conclusions.

That is only natural.

The faces of those who are digging a tunnel are bound to be tense with their violent exertions and tenacity.

The faces of those who enter a tunnel, lounging in a luxurious, speeding train, are calm, relaxed, contented, satisfied, and without any signs of tension.

Our Political Party wishes to create a free Futurist democracy which, in its scorn for pacifist, namby-pamby utopias, draws its power to develop from the typically vigorous qualities of all the Italian people.

These Italianate qualities, which were put to the test and glorified in their bloody victories by the humblest infantrymen, must be transformed tomorrow, in that humblest of infantrymen (workers and peasants), into an unshakable pride in feeling themselves Italian.

All daring, all progress, and all freedoms are present in this great light that is called Italy.

Italy, sovereign and indivisible.

Everything, everything for the freedom, the well-being, the physical and intellectual improvement, the strength, the progress, the greatness, and the Italian pride of even the humblest, the most insignificant of Italians.

Being Italian today means possessing the highest nobility, a great right, something of inestimable value.

Therefore, we Futurists urge in all Italians a renewed, heroic effort, because in overcoming all the weaknesses of our race, trampling over and killing off all cowardice and every habit of mind, heart, and sinew, let them break brutally with all their past and appear, at long last, manly, *completely remade and wholly Italian.*

The Futurist Political Party therefore declares itself to be decidedly antimonarchical,[7] but not being content with the stale, spineless republican ideal, wishes to arrive at a form of technocratic government made up of thirty or forty young, able directors who are invested with authority without parliament and who are elected by all the people through their trade unions.

The Futurist Party, whose objective is *maximum* freedom, *maximum* well-being, and the *maximum* power of production of all Italians, all being brought to their maximum value, calls for the gradual abolition of marriage through facilitating divorce, giving the vote to women, and ensuring their participation in national life. Moreover, we wish to abolish the existing system of policing and public order, reducing to a minimum the present complicated yet ineffectual protection of the citizen, who must—*above all else*—be responsible for protecting himself.

The Futurist Party desires, above all else, with its policy of absolute intransigent anticlericalism, to liberate Italy from churches, priests, friars, nuns, candles, and church bells.

The Party's only religion is the Italy of tomorrow, and admitting of no half measures, it urges unequivocally the expulsion of the Papacy.

In February 1918, the Futurist Political Party's Manifesto proclaimed the need

> to maintain the army and the navy in full operational order until the Austro-Hungarian Empire had been dismantled. After which, the reduction of the number of personnel to a bare minimum, while training a large number of officer cadres through a system of rapid instruction. By way of examples, 200,000 men with 60,000 officers, whose training could be divided into four three-month courses each year. Then, the provision of military and sports education in schools. Preparation for a total mobilization of industry (arms and munitions) to come into effect in the event of war and at the same time as military mobilization takes place. In short, everything ready at minimum cost in the event of war or revolution.

As the dismemberment of the Austro-Hungarian Empire has, in fact, been accomplished, we think we can now go beyond this provision by campaigning for the complete abolition of conscription, the creation of a small army of volunteers which will organize our colonies and constitute the starting point for a necessary general mobilization of a large army in the event of war.

This text served as an introduction to the book *Democrazia futurista* (1919), which presented two independent yet closely related branches of the Futurist movement, one political and one artistic.

47

Branches of the Futurist Political Party, the Arditi, and the Legionnaires of Fiume[1]

The Rome Group: Mario Carli, Fabbri, Calderini, Businelli, Scaparro, Bolzon, Enrico Rocca, Volt, Beer, Rachella, Calcaprina, Balla, Bottai, Crescenzio Fornari, Verderame, Formoso, Scambelluri, Auro d'Alba, Marchesani, Giacobbe, Santa Maria, Gino Galli, Silvio Galli, Remo Chiti.
The Milan Group: Marinetti, Mazza, Buzzi, Natali, Pinna, Cerati, Somenzi, Macchi, Luigi Freddi, Bontempelli, Gigli.
The Florence Group: Nannetti, Settimelli, Spina, Rosai, Marasco, Gorrieri, Mainardi, Manni.
The Perugia Group: P. P. Carbonelli, Madia, Dottori, Presenzini-Mattoli.
The Turin Group: Azari.
The Bologna Group: Nanni Leone Castelli.
The Messina Group: Jannelli, Nicastro, Carrozza.
The Palermo Group: Alioto, Sortino-Bona.
The Genoa Group: De Gasperi, Depero, Alessandro Forti, Sciaccaluga, Ferraris, Santamaria, Pellizzari, Tami, Gigli, Carlo Bruno, Guglielmino, Cavagnetto.
The Ferrara Group: Crepas, Gaggioli.
The Naples Group: P. P. Carbonelli.
The Piacenza Group: Giuseppe Steiner.
The Stradella Group: Masnata.

The Futurist Mario Carli established the first Association of Arditi[2] in Rome.[3]

In the retreat from Caporetto,[4] with heavy heart, though by no means vanquished, I led my bombardiers in perfect order, as far as the river Piave. On the shores of that river I was then in command of a company of bombardiers that had been transformed into riflemen at Nervesa.[5]

In the trenches at Capo Sile I was in command of a battery of Stokes mortars.[6]

On June 15, once again with the mortars, supporting the Casale Brigade in Assa Valley.

I then moved to the corps of armored machine-gun carriers[7] and, as commandant of my Seventy-fourth Corps, at the battle of Vittorio Veneto,[8] I pursued the Austrians and was first into Aviano and Tolmezzo. I captured two Hungarian regiments at Amaro, and took part, in the Eighth Squadron, in the most important capture of the commandant of an Austrian Army Corps.

On my return to Milan,[9] I again took up the Futurist struggle through speeches, fistfights, and thrashings, in the cause of Dalmatia.[10] Along with Ferruccio Vecchi, I forced the first celebration of Vittorio Veneto to take place in the Cathedral Square, speaking from the top of the monument while others were doling out the beatings, or handing out the beatings myself while others were making the speeches. I was in Rome, Milan, Naples, Genoa, and Turin, and wherever the Futurist cause needed promoting.

The Milanese Section of the Association of Arditi was actually founded (1919) at my apartment (The Red House, 61 Corso Venezia) in Milan.

The Futurist pilot Azari invented the Futurist Theater of the Skies with his first attempts at flight dialogues and dances in the air in the skies over Busto Arsizio.[11]

This text appeared in *Marinetti e il futurismo* (1929).

48

‿⚬‿

A Meeting with the Duce

I meet the editor of *Il popolo d'Italia*, who invites me to go and see Mussolini.[1] I find him in the editorial office. He is seated at his table, which has a dramatic backdrop, a great black flag covering the wall—the flag of the Arditi—with the skull and crossbones. He's in quite a temper, with his bulging eyes flashing fire at every word spat out against the Yugoslavs.[2] He's ranting about the fleet that should have been handed over to us![3]

He's in the process of writing an inflammatory article. He leaps up on his chair, waves his arms about, fills the tiny room, and makes it burst at the seams. He tells one of his editors to go and get a Caproni[4] because he absolutely must go by plane to Livorno to deliver a lecture. He shows me a list of names of the great number of our officers who have died in this offensive, which he's going to publish, in response to foreign innuendoes seeking to devalue our victory.

He talks to me about the Florentine branch of the Futurist Political Party.

"However," he says very forcefully, "I will oppose any calamitous move toward rebellion before peace is signed."

I agree with him. But I don't open up to him.

He says, "The republic is a sort of crowning ideal we all dream about. But I could well go beyond the republic to arrive at a monarchy."

I sense the reactionary in the making in this violent, agitated temperament, so full of Napoleonic authoritarianism and a nascent, aristocratic scorn for the masses.

He comes from the people but no longer cares about them. He tends toward aristocratic thought and notions of the heroic will. He's certainly no great intellect. He didn't see the need for war. He was originally an antimilitaristic demagogue without a country.[5] Out of this inevitable eruption of hostilities against the autocratic empires, he is now extracting a need for, and will toward, discipline at all costs. But it has a decidedly reactionary cast and smacks of militarism for its own sake.

He doesn't see things clearly. He is propelled by his predisposition toward heroic struggle and his Napoleonic ideal. He also aspires, I think, to riches.

He can't take his big eyes off my expensive raincoat. He bids me goodbye in a very friendly manner and is insistent I come back to see him again.

This text is taken from Marinetti's diary and can be dated December 4, 1918.

49

⌒

The Founding of the Fasci di Combattimento

We met together on the morning of March 23 in a great hall belonging to the Industrial and Commercial Circle, in Piazza San Sepolcro.[1]

When the Duce's frame appeared before me (wearing a dark overcoat with the collar turned up, a bowler hat pushed back on his head a little, and a truncheon in his pocket, like a light-cavalryman's sword on the march),[2] I felt mixed sensations of joy, artistic admiration, and hopeful confidence.[3] Seeing this man, I believed ever more tenaciously in Italy. I read his destiny in his face, so closely linked to that of the great Nation in which we have always believed, but which had not yet found its interpreter. Now the interpreter had come. The commander had arrived. How could we any longer doubt our victory?

The meeting began at ten o'clock. Benito Mussolini, with one of his generous, unprejudiced gestures as a good judge of merit, conferred the presidency of the assembly on Ferruccio Vecchi, captain of the Arditi. Vecchi spoke briefly and enthusiastically. Then discussion began. Up on the president's platform, very fine figures among the combatants were lined up, and among these, the pale, proud face of Major Baseggio[4] stood out. We Futurists preferred to remain down in the hall, mixing with the various groups, but keenly aware of everything that was going on. Mussolini listened to the different speakers who came, one after the other, to the rostrum. He listened to them in that very nice, very personal way of his, his arm resting on the table, his head against his hand, his face turned fully toward the speaker, his large eyes half closed in such a way as to perturb rather than encourage whoever was speaking.[5]

This account of the foundation of the Fasci di Combattimento was given by Marinetti in *Futurismo e fascismo* (1924). It is fairly accurate, which cannot be said of his later, poetic evocation of the meeting in the sixteen-page brochure *Il poema dei Sansepolcristi* (1939).

50

Fascism and the Milan Speech

Thanks to the editorial involvement of that inspired, persistent patriot Umberto Notari, the Ardito newspaper was founded. It was directed by Ferruccio Vecchi and the Futurist Mario Carli.[1] Together with Settimelli and some other Futurist friends, I whistled like a train at the ridiculous apotheosis of cowardly pacifism at La Scala Theater, and that same evening, I personally scuppered the whining speech of Bissolati, with my ironical Aaaaamen! which sabotaged the speaker's performance and threw everything into chaos, ending up in an Italian free-for-all.[2]

The Futurist Armando Mazza founded in Milan the first anti-Bolshevik newspaper, *The Enemies of Italy*.[3] The Bolognese Futurists established their paper, *The Assault*.[4]

Fascism, which was born immediately after Vittorio Veneto,[5] had right at its core the original, strong Interventionist minority, which had desired and then imposed the war. This nucleus was made up of very disparate revolutionary elements: patriotic ex-Socialists, Futurist poets and artists, trade unionists, anarchists, republicans, and young monarchists.

This minority was reconstituted after the victory, and with renewed vigor, in order to defend the victorious army and the victory itself against the attacks made against them by the Socialists. The latter, infuriated at not having been able to prevent the war and seeing that it had been brought to its glorious conclusion, sought to exploit the inevitable feelings of disillusionment and unrest of the postwar period, for their own electoral purposes. Therefore, they unleashed a ferocious campaign, throughout the country, against the Interventionists, accusing them of being responsible for all the ills that Italy was suffering. This campaign, which was supported by the ambitious demagoguery of Nitti,[6] reached such a level of impudence as to make life extremely difficult and undignified for ex-combatants, those who had been decorated, the injured and all manner of volunteers. Things reached a point where any sort of celebration of the Victory[7] became well-nigh impossible. At the same time, in Italy, there was a tremendous mania for strikes, which bit by bit destroyed the best of the Italian industries. There were constant threats of revolution and continuous, excessive wage increases.

Fascism, with its action squads, led by Mussolini, fought violently against all this. —Within Fascism at that time, the Futurists Marinetti, Mario Carli, Settimelli, Nannetti,[8] Gorrieri,[9] Armando Mazza, and the captain of the Arditi, Ferruccio Vecchi, also fought.

At the foundation meeting of the Fasci di Combattimento,[10] F. T. Marinetti took stock of the situation and warned against getting bogged down in pointless academic disputes. He said that we have to confront the situation in the country as it is, since it can change from one moment to the next. The Socialist Party, exploiting all the grievances of the working masses, is trying to launch an attack upon the rest of the nation. What sort of attitude will we have to assume toward them, knowing them to be fundamentally good and having, many times, felt gratitude toward them in the trenches?[11] Can we take on the task of containing or arresting this movement, which, even though it is directed toward unclear objectives and is led by despicable men, is determined by a desire for greater social justice?

Can we take upon ourselves the responsibilities and the mistakes of the ruling classes? No! Absolutely not!

The speaker, having received applause, asserts it is the duty of all men who are not afraid of the word "revolution" to identify with the masses and extricate them from the hands of their vile shepherds and lead them toward new forms of government that are freer and more modern.

After some remarks on Bolshevism, whose words hold no fears for him, and under which the masses experience all their sufferings and delusions all over again, he finishes on a forceful note, inviting Italians of spirit and faith to dare all. (*Tremendous applause*)

Captain Carli, from Rome, makes an excellent speech in support of everything that F. T. Marinetti has said, and brings with him the affiliation of eleven Italian Futurist groups.

What we wanted was to force a patriotic revolution of ex-combatants.

And therefore, in the Cathedral Square in Milan, on the April 15, 1919, we opposed with pistol shots the Socialists' first attempt at insurrection.[12]

This summary of events surrounding the founding meeting of the Fasci di Combattimento in Piazza San Sepolcro, Milan, appeared in *Marinetti e il futurismo* (1929).

51

⌘

The Battle of Via Mercanti

April 15 [1919]

Milan. General Strike.[1] Panic in the city is increasing by the hour. Yesterday, we found the time to arm us all. Many of us have three revolvers. The *Popolo d'Italia*[2] is well guarded. The streets are calm. Groups of boys and young workers go by, trying—though not too seriously—to mock the officers.

At twelve o'clock, Balla[3] arrives from Rome. He eats at my house. Then we leave. There's a huge crush of people in the Victor Emmanuel Arcade.[4] A lot of officers and Arditi. We arranged with Mussolini the previous evening that we wouldn't stage a counterdemonstration straightaway. We shall wait until we are provoked.

We talk about it with Ponzone[5] and some others who would like a counterdemonstration. I go with Balla, Russolo, Vecchi, and Mazza[6] into the cake shop in the Arcade while outside a spontaneous patriotic demonstration is taking place.

I call Vecchi over and together we organize the march. We set off for the Polytechnic. There are three hundred of us. But the column gets bigger and bigger. At the Polytechnic, we find about five hundred officers from all of the services. Leading them is the injured Alpine soldier Chiesa.[7]

We go around by Corso Victor Emmanuel. We attract into our midst both people who are applauding and others who are just curious. We come up against a cordon of carabinieri. Everyone feels that the forthcoming clash with the Bolsheviks is inevitable. We enter the Arcade in force. The Arditi are at the front. Yet again, we have to break through a cordon of carabinieri.

All of us—about a thousand ardent officers, from all of the services, plus citizens—on the Victor Emmanuel Monument, in the Cathedral Square.

A long snake of soldiers emerges from the Arcade.

A lead-colored outpouring that coils and spreads about the Monument.

Orators who seem superfluous. Candiani.[8] Nobody is listening. Everyone senses that the attack is near.

"Here they come! Here they come!"

False alarm. Ferrari[9] starts speaking again. Nobody is listening.

"Here they are! Here they come!"

Everyone gets down, pulling out their revolvers.

The carabinieri have already blocked off the entrance to via Mercanti. Here comes the march, with women in front, holding high a picture of Lenin and carrying the red flag. —A defiant column, with confident, rapid steps moves forward. It comes to a halt behind the line of carabinieri.

We are on one side, they are on the other.

A club flies and just grazes my head. —Then a hail of stones and revolver shots. Then everybody moves forward, breaking through the line of carabinieri, who give way, withdrawing to the right and the left. —We are on our feet, in open order. —Decorated officers, defiant, fearless, in the thick of it, with the zing of bullets, we fire into the air, then into the column, which, seized by panic, immediately disintegrates. Our enemies—there are around two thousand of them—throw themselves on the ground, against the steps of the Loggia dei Mercanti.

Their cries of "Down with Italy! Long live Lenin!" cease.

They're lying on the ground, terrorized by our advance of Officers, in open order, with revolvers in their hands, nonchalantly reloading them.

Then forward!

The gangs of terrified Bolsheviks are then given a good beating with our walking sticks. I discover blood on the ground and am seized by a deep sense of anguish at seeing these boys, these hired, irresponsible babies, getting beaten to death. We find 100 lire in one boy's pocket. German money. German espionage operates very efficiently from Zurich.

Forward then. Pursuit. In the piazza, a strong, thickset workman hurls himself upon me and tries twice to stab me. I fend off the two lunges and aim a blow at his head with my club. —The blow lands on his shoulder.

He staggers, then flees. —I pursue him at top speed and we both end up in a porter's lodge, with windows smashing around us, and the pair of us in the arms of a terrified concierge. —He cries out, and I stop the Arditi from beating him to death.

Everybody with guns in their hands, shooting upward, down via Dante, running along the walls, to the right and the left. I see Corridoni's brother,[10] wounded in the arm, coming back, covered in blood. He is with us. One of the Arditi sets off at full speed, like a bullet, along the empty street, and leaps up onto the Garibaldi Monument, which is densely packed with people.

He climbs up and stabs a speaker, who cries, Long live Lenin.

In the twinkling of an eye, the Monument is empty. The dark crowd that bedecked it melts away, fleeing right and left. Gradually, down there in front of the Castle, on the right, and down on the left, two hundred meters away, into the Bonaparte Forum.

Sparrows fleeing. Frenzy of dead leaves that the wind whips off the trees.

We turn back, the Arditi flag out in front. Balconies open up and everyone applauds. —We whistle at the women and we invite the gutless bourgeoisie to come down and join us.

When we were coming out of the Victor Emmanuel Arcade, desperately trying to increase the strength of our column before the imminent confrontation, I screamed and shouted frantically at the applauding onlookers, to our right and left, to join the column; *In you come! In you come! Join us! In you come!* Come on! Come on in!

So furious was my gesticulating that one of the applauding onlookers ran away from me, frightened out of his wits by my face!

Everybody up on the Victor Emmanuel Monument. Speeches from Vecchi, in his Arditi uniform. They implore me to speak. I'm dead tired. One of my feet has been injured with a blow from a cudgel, and my chest is hurting from a punch or a club.

I go off with Mazza and Vecchi and our column, to the *Avanti* offices.[11]

We come to a halt in front of the Eden Theater.[12] We have won. The battle had lasted an hour. We get our column together and half an hour later, after having routed several other cordons of policemen, it arrives in via San Damiano, attacks and sets fire to the offices of *Avanti!*,[13] throwing the furniture out of the window, but does not locate the director, Serrati,[14] who, as usual, is nowhere near the action. Among the first to enter the building was the Futurist Pinna,[15] who was wounded in the hand by a revolver shot. Many others were wounded, too. But the column, by now master of reconquered Milan, returns to Piazza del Duomo, marching to the beat of the cry: "*Avanti!* is no more!" At the head of the procession they bear the wooden sign of the burned-down newspaper office, which was given to Mussolini at the offices of *Il popolo d'Italia.*

Next day, the following manifesto appeared on walls all over Milan:

Italians!

On April 15 we had come to an absolute decision, with Mussolini, not to stage a counterdemonstration, for we had foreseen the trouble and we are horrified at the thought of spilling Italian blood. —Our counterdemonstration arose spontaneously, through the determined will of the people.

We had no choice but to react against the premeditated provocations of the army deserters, who are still in the pay of the Germans, exploiting the gullibility of the masses, to the sole advantage of Germany.

Despite our action, we have no intention of strengthening or pardoning all that is rotten, corrupt, and doomed in Italy.

With that action, we intend to assert the absolute right of four million victorious combatants, who alone should lead and, come what may, will be in charge of the new Italy.

We shall provoke no one, but if we are provoked, then we shall add a few more months' service to our four years of war, so as to annihilate the brazen-faced criminality of those notorious shirkers and hirelings, who have no right to start a revolution.

We shall respond without carabinieri, policemen, or firemen, and without the collaboration of the army. Let them witness the spectacle, and thus become increasingly aware that the strikes of *Avanti!* are the sole cause of the slowness of the demobilization.

Ferruccio Vecchi
Association of Arditi and the Fasci di Combattimento.

F. T. Marinetti
The Futurist Political Party and the Fasci di Combattimento.

Milan, April 16, 1919

Michele Bianchi, secretary of the Milanese Branch of the Fasci di Combattimento, sent a telegram to Rome, announcing the victory to the Futurist Mario Carli, President of the Association of Arditi.

Bolshevik attempt definitely foiled. Italian Milan on top of situation.

On April 16, General Caviglia[16] arrived in Milan and called me to the Hotel Continental, where, together with Ferruccio Vecchi, I explained the situation.

The victor of Vittorio Veneto, with his quick intuition, declared: "Your battle yesterday, in Piazza Mercanti, was in my view decisive."[17]

Marinetti wrote several descriptions of the battle in via Mercanti that, with increasing distance from the events, became more and more stylized and mythologized. Several versions, preserved in his paste-up albums (*libroni*) and a variety of manuscripts in the Beinecke Library, show that he recycled notes made in 1919 and the "official" version printed in *Futurismo e fascismo* (1924). The most authentic and reliable one is preserved in his diaries, which provided the source for document 51. As the actual sacking of the office is not described in the diaries, I have added a section from *Futurismo e fascismo* (1924).

52

❧

Old Ideas That Go Hand in Glove but Need to Be Separated

Before we came along, politics always lived by commonplaces or, better still, according to ideas that went stupidly hand in glove, ever linked by an illusory kinship which, in reality, doesn't exist.

Whenever you say "Monarchy," you immediately think of the army, of war, of the Nation, and of patriotism. And this is fine. Yet it is absurd, when, for example, you say the words "Nation," "patriotism," "war," and "dedicated army," you should necessarily associate them with a reactionary monarchy.

Whenever you say "nationalism," you immediately think of a conservative spirit, of a systematically greedy imperialism, of a spirit of tradition and reaction, of police repression, militarism, emblazoned nobility, and clericalism.

Ideas that go hand in glove but must be ruthlessly separated.

Whenever you say "democracy," you immediately think of unwarlike, humanitarian, pacifist ideas, of pietism and quietism, of renunciation, anticolonialism, humility, internationalism, absence of racial pride, or refusal to recognize race.

Ideas that go hand in glove but must be ruthlessly separated.

Whenever you say "revolution," you immediately think of antipatriotism, of internationalism, and of pacifism.

Ideas that go hand in glove but must be ruthlessly separated.

Whenever you say "sporting education," "impulse," "courage," "boldness," "muscular strength," "obsession with records," you immediately think of imperialistic or clerical monarchy.

Ideas that go hand in glove but must be ruthlessly separated.

Whenever you speak of justice, of equality, of freedom, of the rights of the proletariat, of peasants, and of the have-nots, of the struggle against parasitism, you immediately think of antipatriotism, of a pacifist internationalism, of Marxism and collectivism.

Ideas that go hand in glove but must be ruthlessly separated.

The realm of these commonplaces, eternally and absurdly linked together, accounts for the fact that one of the sentences of the first Futurist manifesto, which was published eleven years ago and glorified both patriotism and the destructive action of libertarians,[1] seemed like madness or a mere joke to the political establishment.

Everyone found it ridiculous and comical that, for the first time, the anarchist idea should go hand in glove with that of patriotism. Why on earth was the word "patriotism" not accompanied on that occasion by its friend, monarchy of order and reaction?

Why on earth was the idea of *the destructive action of libertarians* not accompanied on that occasion by its inseparable friend, *antipatriotism*?

Utter astonishment in the minds of so-called politicians, who feed on commonplaces and bookish ideologies, in their absolute inability to understand life, race, masses of people, and individuals.

But their astonishment grew out of all proportion when, in the radiant May of 1915,[2] they saw at a glance, in the tumultuous piazzas of Milan and Rome, this strange couple walking out together yet again—Destructive Action of Libertarians and Patriotism, with their new names: Mussolini, Corridoni, Corradini, Garibaldi, and Marinetti, all united in their call for *War or Revolution*.[3]

Nowadays, we separate the idea of the Nation from that of the reactionary, priest-ridden Monarchy. We link the idea of Nation with those of bold Progress and revolutionary, antireactionary democracy.[4]

Yet we still have to prize apart another of these cretinous couplings, one which is much more serious, the two ideas that go hand in glove in many Italian and European newspapers, namely, the League of Nations and pacification of the desire for revenge on the part of the defeated.[5]

And there are these other ideas going arm in arm: Concessions to inferior peoples and the Preservation of Peace.

Absurd ideas going hand in glove.

During the Great War, to sustain the forces of the Entente,[6] it was necessary to connect the idea of war with that of *the war to end all wars*; the idea of victory with that of victory without winners or losers.

There were vague thoughts about a compromise Peace, yet we fought fiercely to defeat the enemy.

How on earth could we hope that, once beaten, this enemy would immediately be at peace in his heart and not harbor an overwhelming desire for revenge?

The idea of total victory was strangely wedded to that of a Germany which was happy to have been thoroughly beaten. And the idea of a victorious Entente was bizarrely wedded to that of an Entente that was almost mortified by its victory.

Those who opposed us are up in arms about the swindle; indeed they are calling it the European-style swindle. How come! They shout in our faces: will the conflict not then serve to establish a never-ending Peace? Hurry then! Hurry! Let's set up a League of Nations, at whatever cost, to prevent the possibility of new wars. In their precious League of Nations they would have to put in seats around the one pacifying table, the victors who had been attacked and who had not wanted the war; the defeated who had so criminally brought it about; the neutrals who, in cowardly fashion, had viewed it from the balcony; and both the healthy, newly sprung nations and the decrepit, with their putrid, rickety-limbed peoples.

It would be necessary, moreover, for everyone to leave their typifying characteristics outside the door, that is, the understandable pride of the victors, the understandable desire for revenge of the defeated; the healthy appetites of the strong, newly born peoples, and the neuroses of the doomed, newly spawned peoples, with their decrepit old man's crafty pig-headedness, etc.

Life itself creates, controls, and shapes ideologies. Every political idea is a living organism. Political parties are almost always destined to become illustrious corpses.

The parties that had a glorious past are precisely those which, today, are lacking in vitality. That's a Futurist law. Today, the Republicans are reduced to an impotent doctrinarism which contents itself by invoking the shade of Mazzini. In reality, Mazzini is alive in the same way that Cavour is alive, while Cappa and Comandini are among the dead, just like Salandra.[7]

This essay appeared in different forms in *L'ardito* on May 11, 1919, and *Roma futurista* on November 12, 1919. This translation follows the version in *Democrazia futurista* (1919), excluding the last section, written by Volt (Vincenzo Fani-Ciotti, 1888–1927).

53

Futurist Democracy

Italian pride must not be, and is not, an imperialism whose goal is to impose industries, to corner markets, to effect massive increases in agrarian production.

We have a lack of raw materials, and we are a nation whose agrarian output is very modest indeed.

Our pride, as Italians, rests on our superiority as an enormous number of talented individuals.

We therefore wish to create a true democracy, conscious and bold, which will be a frank recognition and exaltation of *number*, since it will include the greatest number of talented individuals.

In this world, Italy represents a sort of extremely talented minority, entirely consisting of individuals who are superior to the average human being by virtue of their creative, innovative, and inventive powers.

This democracy will, of course, enter into competition with the majority, made up of all other nations for which, to the contrary, number signifies more or less blind masses—in other words, unconscious democracy.

In any thousand Slavs there are only two or three individuals.

Our recent, lightning victory[1] has shown that every group of Italians (of twenty, thirty, or forty) contains at least ten or fifteen individuals with personal initiative and a flair for leadership.

We still have to get rid of the papacy, the monarchy, parliament, the senate, and the bureaucracy, as well as to reclaim the deadlands of illiteracy.

This task, which was extremely difficult with a ravening enemy at the gates, is easy today, and devoid of all danger, as a result of our national unity and independence.

A nation rich in individual talent, a democracy of great intelligence. A fair number of characteristic personalities, a mass of unique types, a democracy which has no desire to dominate in the spheres of banking, industry, or colonies, but which can and must dominate the world and direct it with its greater potential and towering light.

We believe that the time has come to bring about every kind of revolution, so as to liberate the Italian people from all their ponderous weights and shackles (marriage and the suffocating Catholic family, pedantic academicism, electoralism, a pessimistic outlook, provincialism, mediocrity, and a laissez-faire attitude).

Freed from the yoke of the old, traditional family, from the dogma of reverence for old age, from parliamentarianism, from the senate, the papacy, and the monarchy, Italy will at last show forth the power of its forty million Italian individuals, all of them intelligent and capable of autonomous action.

This conception is opposed absolutely to that utterly idiotic, Germanophile vision which sought to devalue forty million Italian individuals so as to be able to organize them mechanistically.

On the stage set for the Italian race, we have to turn the spotlight on forty million different roles because it is only in such light that each individual's particular value can be perfectly realized.

Now that the Austro-Hungarian Empire has been dismantled,[2] the Italian people must not fear even disastrous strokes (sexual promiscuity, the destruction of wealth) brought about by a far-reaching revolution.

They will be short-lived. From such a revolution, today the Italian people will rise up again more alive and powerful, richer still in talented individuals, more agile, more dynamic.

We do not suffer from the congenital idleness, the torpor, the mysticism, the Byzantine obsession with ideology, the obsession with theory, of the Russians.

We are full of pragmatism, of a constructive tenacity, of an inexhaustible ingenuity, of heroism put to good purpose.

We can therefore safely entrust every right to do and to undo *to number, to quantity, to the mass*, since, in our case, *number, quantity, and mass* will not be, as they are in Germany and Russia, number, quantity, and mass of mediocre, inept, or feckless beings.

Arturo Labriola defines democracy as "a sense of the material rights of the masses over the State and the Economy."[3]

We Futurists do not think of democracy in the abstract but rather of "Italian democracy."

Talking about democracy in the *abstract* is merely rhetoric. There are very many democracies; every people has its own democracy, just as every people has its own feminism.

We think of Italian democracy as a mass of talented individuals who have readily become conscious of their rights and have naturally played their part in molding their own emergent State.

Its strength is derived from this acquired right, multiplied by its quantity value, less the weight of dead cells (tradition) and that of diseased cells (those lacking in consciousness, the illiterate).

For us, Italian democracy is a human body that needs freedom, to shed its fetters and its burdens, so as to be able to accelerate the speed of its development and increase its output a hundredfold.

Italian democracy today finds itself in a situation that is more favorable to its development. That of war-revolution,[4] in which it is compelled to resolve its contingent problems, among the thousand pains of other, unresolved problems, whose solutions can have an influence on its future. Its health requires a continuous, transforming, inventive agility.

Today, the government is alarmed when it sees innumerable ex-combatant associations being formed.[5] If it were not a government of shortsighted reactionaries, shaking with fear, it would look favorably on this rebirth of Italian vitality.

The war has simply unveiled the consciousness of four or five million Italians, now returning from the war, enriched with a political personality.

It is the first time in history that more than four million citizens of any nation have been fortunate enough to experience, in a mere four years, a complete, intensive education, with lessons in gunfire, heroism, and death.

It is a marvelous spectacle: a whole army that left for the war with virtually no political awareness, returning now politicized and worthy to govern.[6]

Futurist democracy is now ready for action, for it feels all its living cells aquiver.

Naturally, it feels an urgent need to throw the doors wide open and to step out into the open air. The government is alarmed, it represses, and it trembles, like the proverbial grandmother who is afraid her grandson will catch a cold.

Outside, the air is bracing and wholesome. The sun, fully out, drinks up the liquid from the sea, solid almost, full of zest, sky blue, all fizzing with rays, everything to be drunk to the very last drop.

This text appeared in *Roma futurista* on May 11, 1919, and in the volumes *Democrazia futurista* (1919) and *Futurismo e fascismo* (1924).

54

⌘

The Proletariat of Talented People

There can be no doubt that our race outstrips all others in the extraordinary number of geniuses it produces.

In even the smallest group of Italians, in the tiniest of villages, there are *always* seven or eight young people in their twenties, who are all atremble with their intense desire to create and who are full of ambitious pride, which is revealed in volumes of unpublished verse and in their outbursts of eloquence at political meetings in the piazzas.

Some of them really are deluding themselves, but *not many*. They might never arrive at true genius. Yet they have a basic talent, by which I mean they are open to suggestion and serve the useful purpose of increasing the overall intellectual level of a Country.

In that selfsame group or small Italian village, it is easy to find seven or eight mature men who, in the course of their little lives as clerks or professional men, in their local cafés, or in their family homes, bear the melancholy signs of failed genius. They represent broken scraps of talent who never found themselves in the right circumstances and were thus crushed by economic necessity or family obligations.

The Futurist artistic movement, which we started eleven years ago, aimed specifically at a radical modernization of the worlds of art and literature by curtailing the power of their vested authorities, at rooting out and destroying the gerontocracy, cutting down to size the critics and pedantic professors, and encouraging the daring leaps made by talented young people, so as to create a healthy atmosphere, full of oxygen, and to give encouragement and assistance to all the talented young people of Italy.

There are, without doubt, two or three hundred thousand of them throughout the country.

Encourage them all, increase their self-esteem a hundredfold, open all roads to them and, as quickly as possible, reduce the number of failed and repressed geniuses in Italy.

I have explained, in many of my earlier works, how three-quarters of the obstructions which hinder the rapid progress of Italy—psychological defects, weaknesses, errors, failures of courage, inertia—had their origin in what we call Traditionalism. It is manifested in an obsessive cult of the past and of past glories, in a stubborn aversion to all that is new, in pessimistic attitudes toward the abilities of our race, in scholastic academicism and literary purism, in a cult of imitation and aping the ancient, in the passion for museums, in the exaltation of the plodders, and so on.

Traditionalism was, for a long time, the basic philosophy of the education system and of parental upbringing. It was fostered by many absurd ideologies that were, to a greater or lesser extent, imports and were typically anti-Italian.

A despicable, socialistic kind of intellectualism predominated, it was antipatriotic, internationalist, and separated the body from the spirit. It idealized a stupid hypertrophy of the brain, it taught forgiveness for offenses committed, it proclaimed universal peace and the abolition of war, whose *horrors* would be replaced by a war of ideas. It was an intellectualism of Germanic origins, an obsession with books, the worship of books, an extreme pedantry. It manifested itself through scorn for gymnastics, the brutalization of boys in closed, foul-smelling classrooms, a total lack of attention to health and muscular strength.

An enfeebled youth stagnated in this musty atmosphere, deprived of the freshness of spring, deprived of their manhood.

How many young men have we seen coming out of schools, downcast, stooping, weak, hardly ever speaking or taking action, pale, shriveled up, always shortsighted and wearing thick lenses, clutching under their arms, with a sort of fearful, pitiable pride, their *Promessi sposi*,[1] just like Don Rodrigo clutching his plague-induced sores.

Their bubonic plague was a Teutonic culture worship.

People went about preaching that Italian youth was ignorant and that their minds were in need of a solid, serious, methodical culture. What they were preaching, in all truth, was a hatred of intellectualism. Read, study, meditate, shut yourselves up in libraries, consult your manuscripts, study the ancients! Live in museums! Copy pictures and statues! You must learn to write, to paint, to sculpt by imitating the works of the great! The Italian language is extremely difficult, one has to decide, only after *serious* meditation, who are the masters one should prefer, and which are the dictionaries one should consult. Bartoli, Boccaccio, Machiavelli, Tommaseo, Rigutini, Fanfani . . . they have to be annotated.[2] This one shows genius but he uses Gallicisms. "This business of Gallicisms is a plague that manifests itself in all sorts of ways . . ."[3]

In this web of prohibitions, of nonexistent hurdles to be cleared and false gods to be respected, to be avoided, not to be offended, the gifted young man loses touch with his true driving instinct and suppresses his proud courage. All his strengths remain knotted up inside him as, in a state of grievous anguish, he confronts the endless road without aid or comfort.

Beneath the menacing storm cloud of the futile examinations he has to pass or the incessant rain of idiotic exercises he must write, the student trains his mind and spirit to accept fear and pedantry.

Every evening, among his family, he finds a typical narrow-mindedness and mediocrity, a hatred of all forms of adventure and daring, a petty priestly moralizing, the grotesque struggle between a grasping miserliness and a provincial desire for luxury, the morbid, overprotective, and suffocating affection of his mother, and the harsh, overbearing behavior of a languid father who believes, nonetheless, that it is his duty to put his son down, at all costs, *in whatever he dreams of, aspires to, or desires.*

This talented young man senses a violent, mysterious force playing on his nerves. He will become a poet, a painter, an actor, a builder of bridges over American rivers, a contractor on far-off lands that are to be reclaimed, a member of parliament, or whatever; but he can't say exactly what.

He would gladly risk all that is dear and pleasurable to him, affections, friendships, his first sexual bliss or student pranks, for immediate, firsthand experience and demonstration of this power of his.

Instead, he is surrounded by the deepest, blackest pessimism and overwhelming denials. He inhales a poisonous skepticism and he hasn't a cent in his pocket.

If he has enormous pluck or the spirit of rebellion, he will succeed in breaking down and overturning all obstacles. Yet a total lack of money, the final, insurmountable snare, holds him back and nails him to the absolute impossibility of making a break and chancing all.

This sort of failure, in talented youth, is very common and typical of certain areas of Italy, such as Tuscany. Even though these areas are, indisputably, the most intelligent of all, they are the least active in and least useful to the development of the nation.

Florence is full of young genius, stagnating, having no sense of direction, which pours forth the most wonderful tangle of thoughts and poetry beneath the electric suns of its cafés, without ever having the slightest hope of being appreciated, noticed, or used.[4]

Write? What's the use of that? Who'll publish it? They won't pay for it, that's for sure! In fact, it'll be they who'll want paying! For the newspapers? What, when the director is chosen from among the four or five most cretinous people in the city? Institutionalized obstructionism. So, far better to lay to rest his downward-spiraling, melancholy song beneath the antique moonlight, whose golden sheen is cast upon the banks of the Arno or the Ponte Vecchio, or take his pleasure with one of the girls from the Cascine,[5] someone offering furnished rooms at a knockdown price.

I have known very many talented young men in Florence, Tuscany, Naples, and Sicily. Virtually all of them were embittered; their hearts already imprisoned in a dull rancor against society; many of them poisoned by a premature envy, which muddies the pure wellsprings of genuine inspiration and joyous, creative fervor.

Sometimes it is very difficult to recognize, appreciate, and encourage young people of talent. For, instead of embracing Italy spiritually, as a huge flexible mass to be molded, they see her as a ridiculous network of abuses of power, of camorras, of sponging authorities, of idiotic prohibitions. And they're right. Wherever you go, in our land, talent is underrated, ridiculed, and restrained. Those who take the crown, who are revered, are the mediocre opportunists or the geniuses of yesteryear, now in their dotage.

Futurism discovered, unveiled, reanimated, and gathered together many of these young men of talent, the best of them without a doubt, though by no means all of them. In the vast revolution of tempestuous *serate*, which it instigated throughout the Peninsula, Futurism came in contact with almost all of them. Yet a more systematic operation by the country's authorities is needed if this widespread proletariat of the creative imagination is to be saved, given new heart, and put to good use.

I propose that in every town premises be set up which will be called something like: "Open Exhibitions of Creative Talent."

1. Paintings, sculptures, all kinds of art, architectural designs, blueprints for machines and proposals for inventions will be on display for a month.

2. Large or small musical compositions, for piano or orchestra, of any sort whatsoever, will be performed there.
3. Poetry, prose, writings on all the sciences, of all types and lengths, will be read, displayed, and performed.
4. Anyone at all will have the right to exhibit there, free of charge.
5. Works of all types and qualities will be exhibited or read without being formally judged, no matter how absurd, idiotic, mad, or immoral they may appear to be.

Marinetti published this short text in *Dinamo* no. 5 (June 1919) and presented it again in a speech given in Genoa on July 5, 1919 (see Marinetti, *Taccuini*, p. 419). It became a key topic in his address to the First Fascist Congress on October 10, 1919, with sections of this text quoted verbatim (see document 62). The ideas were further elaborated in the long essay "Beyond Communism" (1920; see document 63). The text translated here is taken from the volume *Democrazia futurista* (1919). In *Futurismo e fascismo* (1924) it is dated May 1919.

55

cℐ⌀

Against Marriage

The family, governed as it is at present by marriage, without the possibility of divorce, is absurd, harmful, and antediluvian.[1] Almost always it constitutes a form of imprisonment. Frequently, it is like the tents of the Bedouin, with their loose mix of aged invalids, women, children, pigs, donkeys, camels, chickens, and shit.

The family dining room is the twice-daily repository of bile, bad temper, prejudice, and tittle-tattle.

In this grotesque constriction of nerves and spirit, we can see that continuous boredom and pointless irritations systematically constrict and corrode all personal enthusiasms, all youthful initiative, all practical, effective decisions.

The most energetic and outstanding characters are worn down by this relentless chafing of elbows.

A contagion emerges, or sometimes a real epidemic of idiocies that are larger than life, of catastrophic manias, of nervous tics that are converted into the goose steps of a troop of Germans or a ragbag of emigrants in the hold of a ship.

The whims of the womenfolk and the excesses of spoiled brats are causes of hard, uncontrollable anger in ungenerous fathers.

Spring faces are drained of color in the presence of an agony that goes on for ten years. One victim, two victims, three martyrs, an executioner, an absolute madman, a tyrant who forfeits his power.

Everyone suffers, becomes depressed, exhausted, imbecilic, under the dictate of a fearful deity that must be overthrown: namely, Sentimentalism.

Corridors full of ridiculous quarrels, whole litanies of condemnation, the impossibility of thinking, of creating by oneself. It comes to
grief in the daily grind of domestic economic sweat and banal vulgar-
ities.

If the family works badly, it is an inferno of plots, quarrels, betrayals,
pique, meanness, and a concomitant desire for escape and revolt in all
concerned. There is cutthroat jealousy between elegant and beautiful
mother and daughter; a duel of miserliness and profligacy between
conservative father and free-living son. Everywhere in Italy, the sad
spectacle of the rich, egotistical father who wishes to impose the traditional "serious profession" on his poetical or artistic son, and so on.

If the family works well, it is a quagmire of sentimentalism, a grave-
stone of maternal care. A day school of fear. Physical and moral cowardice when faced with a cold in the head, some new situation or new
idea.

The family which, so far as the woman is concerned, is born out of a
buying and selling of body and soul becomes a masquerade of hypocrisies
or else a facade of good sense, behind which a legalized prostitution,
with a dusting of moralism, is played out.

All of this takes place in the name of a terrifying divinity that must
needs be overturned—Sentimentalism.

We declare that Sentimentalism is a characteristic typical of a vege-
tating, parasitical, static way of life. In animals it becomes a vice,
among men a crime, since it fatally curbs their dynamism and the
speed of their evolution.

To say "my woman" is to utter a childish piece of foolishness or an
expression of the slaver. The woman is "mine" in the same degree that
I am hers, today, in this moment, for an hour, a month, a couple of
years, according to the flight of her fancy and the power of my animal
magnetism or my intellectual influence.

The family, with its "my wife," "my husband," clearly establishes the
norm of adultery at all costs or of a veiled prostitution at all costs. It
gives birth to a school of hypocrisy, betrayal, and ambivalence.

We want to destroy not only the ownership of the land but also that
of women. Those who do not know how to work the land should be dis-
possessed of it. Those who cannot give joy and strength to women
should not impose their embrace or their presence upon them.

Woman does not belong to man but rather to the future and to the
development of the human race.

We want a woman to love a man and to give herself to him only for
as long as she wishes; and then, unfettered by any contract or moraliz-

ing tribunal, give birth to a creature that society must educate physically and intellectually up to the high concept of Italian freedom.

A single teacher is all that is required to facilitate and defend, without constraints, the early development of one hundred infants, whose first dominant precept will be the need to build up their own courage, the urgency to resolve by themselves, and as quickly as possible, the intricate problems of balance and nutrition. That atmosphere of endless sniveling and clinging to skirts and obsessive kissing which is the stuff of early childhood will be abolished entirely.

And that mixing of males with females at a very early age, which is the cause of a harmful effeminacy in the male, will be abolished once and for all.

Male children—in our opinion—must develop separately from little girls, so that their early games are unequivocally masculine, which is to say, totally devoid of all cloying affections, of all womanish refinements. They must be lively, combative, muscular, and violently dynamic. Male and female children living in the same environment is always the cause of retarded development in the character of the male, who invariably falls prey to the charm and compelling seductiveness of the young female, like tiny gallants or foolish little slaves.

The abject hunt for a husband will finally be abolished, along with the ridiculous ordeal of frantic mothers who bring their eligible daughters up to every ball or to seaside resorts, like so many heavy crosses, to be driven into the ludicrous Golgotha of a good marriage.

"We have to get them settled"—in the bed of some consumptive or other, controlled by the tongue of some old man or other or the fists of some neurasthenic, between the pages of a dictionary, like a dried leaf, in a tomb, in a safe or a sewer—but "they have to be settled."

A violent constriction of the heart and of the senses of a virgin who, with fatal consequences, looks upon the legalized prostitution of marriage as an indispensable condition, if she is to attain the semi-freedom of adultery and regain her ego through betrayal.

The widespread participation of women in the national labor force, brought about by the war, has created a typical piece of matrimonial grotesquerie. The husband used to hold the money or used to earn it, but now he has lost it and is struggling to start earning it again.

His wife works and finds the means of earning a substantial wage at a time when the cost of living is very high.

The wife, because of that selfsame job, has no need to be a housewife, while her husband, not having a job, concentrates all his energies on an absurd concern with domestic order.

The complete overturning of the family, in which the husband has become a useless woman, with bullying masculine ways, and the wife has doubled her human and social value.

An inevitable clash between the two partners, conflict and the defeat of the male.

This essay was first published in *Roma futurista* on May 25, 1919, and reprinted in *Democrazia futurista* (1919).

56

⟡

Synthesis of Marx's Thought

1. *The theory of value.*[1] In Karl Marx's opinion, the function of capital, in the production process, is sterile. Only the object of labor is fertile.

The highest value of the product is therefore exclusively the result of labor, and to this it *must* belong. Instead, it passes unfairly to the capitalists, in the form of profits. Profit is the *surplus value*[2] not paid for by the entrepreneur. Society thus divides into exploiters and exploited. The exploitation becoming ever more intense, by virtue of the needs of production, while the class of the exploited increases, and that of the exploiters decreases.

The increasing proletarianization of society is the consequence.

When the capital is eventually concentrated in few hands, it will be easy for the mass of the unconsciously exploited to expropriate the few capitalists and reorganize the system of production in such a way as to award the whole of society's income to the workers.

Now, the *premise* that the function of capital is sterile in the production process is *false*.

If the productive function of capital were sterile, the industries in which salary-capital (labor) prevailed over fixed capital would have to provide higher revenue than those industries in which fixed capital prevailed over salary-capital (labor).[3]

But that doesn't happen in reality!

2. *The theory of economic determinism or historical materialism* of Karl Marx,[4] who attributes a causal value to the economic factor, has al-

most failed. Science and human thought have demonstrated the impossibility of establishing a causal relationship *among factors*, which are very numerous, of varying power, all of them active, dynamic, and *devoid* of logic. There is a relationship of flexible interdependence and not one of causality among the numerous elements that make up the complex social phenomenon. Let us not forget either the enormous importance of moral factors, which are particularly volatile and determinative.

3. *The concept of union among workers of all countries*. The world war has violently demonstrated the absurdity of this concept of union among workers who are very different from one another, often opposing and hostile out of self-interest, by virtue of social status or differing conditions of labor.

The beginning of this essay can be found in Marinetti's diary entry for May 7, 1918. These notes were then expanded for an article in *Roma futurista*, May 11, 1919, reprinted soon after in *Democrazia futurista*.

57

$\mathcal{C\!\mathscr{D}}$

Synthesis of Mazzini's Thought on Property and Its Transformation

Property, as it exists today, is totally without justification.[1]

The value of any property is the product of society. The legitimacy of possession must derive from its usefulness to society. The legitimate ownership of property can only be the concern of the collective whole.

Labor, together with the freedom of association, must become master of the soil and of capital in Italy.

The worker must not pass from receiving a wage from the private individual to receiving it from the State (collectivism), but he must make use of the State to construct the new economic order which will free him from exploitation.

We must compel the State to recognize the character and the social function of Property and so to intervene to ensure an evermore just distribution of it. We must aim at the nationalization of the land, of water, and of the subsoil.

We have to distinguish between ownership of property and the ways in which it is used.

Property has to be taken out of the hands of the individual. But it should not become a charge of the State.

The State must affirm the social right to property in the name of the collective.

Management must be entrusted to individuals, groups, and associations.

When the State has accepted the principle that *the value and function of property are social*, it will be necessary to arrange things in such a way that every piece of land yields maximum output and every laborer has enough work. The uncultivated lands on the big estates, as well as all unprofitable lands, must pass out of the hands of their present owners into those of the workers, on *long-term lease* or collective leasings.

The transfer can be achieved through expropriation or as a matter of course; much better, in fact, through the abolition of the rights of succession.

The beginning of this essay can be found in Marinetti's diary entry for May 10, 1918, that is, the period of his reflections on an Italian revolution and a Futurist democracy. Like the previous document, *Synthesis of Marx's Thought*, these notes may have been intended for an article in *Roma futurista*, but were only published in *Democrazia futurista* (1919).

58

cℐ∾

Technocratic Government Without Parliament or Senate, but with a Board of Initiatives

In the aftermath of war, the problems besetting a country like ours that is far from wealthy will, I think, overwhelm any regime's ability to govern and will thus perforce admit of none other than a revolutionary solution.[1]

There can be no doubt, however, that parliamentary government, which is bogged down in endless bureaucracy, is—of all possible types of government—the least able to resolve them.

Let us look at the situation from the point of view of the producers.

The government has earmarked three billion lire for public works, yet no one has been charged with overseeing them or with ensuring that they are carried out swiftly. Work on the railways, for example, which should reduce the problem of unemployment, as well as heading off a very grave transport crisis.

The government argues that we must produce and go on producing and producing! Yet how can we produce if every factory is today a creditor of the State? And what raw materials are they to use (if they are not yet guaranteed)? What will be the cost of these raw materials?

The State has shown itself to be inept both in acquiring them and distributing them.

The government should instead allow industries the greatest possible freedom by removing all obstacles and shackles.

The involvement of the State needs to be replaced by that of the trade unions and industrial consortia, which, under the tutelage of the State, will be responsible for providing such raw materials.

We must escape from this state of affairs, which inhibits personal initiative, and abolish our truly outdated taxation systems.

Admittedly, we have to pay close attention to our monetary needs and ensure that revenue from taxation is high enough *to cover all our debts.*

But we must not stand in the way of the production of wealth.

We will accept new taxes as long as they facilitate the production of wealth and only as long as they become due when something has actually been produced.

Monopolies that strike at raw materials increase the costs of internal production and make it extremely difficult to import those things that are necessary for the economic reconstruction of the country.

Embargoes on exports are absurd. It is argued that we cannot be allowed to export because internal prices are already too high and would increase even further, while by prohibiting exports such prices must inevitably fall because the raw materials *divested* in this way will end up coming onto the market.

This is a mistake. This sort of provision, which should only strike at hoarders, will in fact cripple production and bring it to a standstill.

We are therefore in danger of losing our foreign markets.

An intelligent government would instead allow exportation within reasonable limits and put a ceiling on internal prices.

In this way, a revitalized industry would be able to take on a large part of the workforce now being laid off by the industries that produced weapons during wartime.

However, our parliamentary government is typically lacking in intelligence.

Let's now look at the situation from the point of view of the merchant shipping industry.

The war brought seafarers' cooperatives into being, with the purpose both of owning and of operating ships. This most significant development must definitely be supported by Italian law.

If it is indeed supported without any mistrust, it will constitute one of the best sorts of social pacification.

Articles 9 and 10 of the Villa decree[2] must be radically altered, because Article 10 prevents the State from owning ships to be leased to the seafarers' cooperatives.

Since the beginning of the war, the hire charges paid out to foreign ships amount to more than nine billion lire. The charter costs paid out to Italian ships, since the start of the war, come to one and a half billion lire.

To avoid this flight of capital abroad, we would have to buy cheap transport ships immediately. This proved possible even in 1915 and 1916. When we realized that it was our duty to buy gold in order to retrieve all the gold handed over to foreign arms suppliers, the price of the ships was unbelievably high.

The nation sensed the danger and thought about limiting the damage.

New shipyards started up, established shipyards expanded, and hundreds of thousands of tons of the very best steamships were launched.

To its shame, the Villa decree cut short this magnificent development and thus we went back to squandering our wealth and to granting charters to foreign companies.

To build transport ships quickly, we had to turn to specialized industries. Private companies, not usually concerned with shipbuilding, were nevertheless able to manufacture essential parts for ships and to produce work of comparable quality. Boilermakers, for example, were competent in making ships' furnaces. And so they went ahead and constructed them. Thousands of specialized industries signed up, with Futuristic speed, to collaborate in the building of ships. And this marvelous enterprise happened without even minimal assistance from the government.

This very rapid and not too costly assembly-line construction should have been generously supported and championed by the government.

Prefabricated ships[3] have very few curves. Every part has its assembly number. The fitter, on receiving individual parts, consults the plans and follows their instructions. Nothing could be simpler.

This is undoubtedly a wartime method and largely precludes any sort of development in construction. All the ships are identical and none is any better than the others. However, this defect can easily be avoided, and there can be no doubt that assembly-line production should be championed and supported by the government, by virtue of its practicality and its immunity from bureaucracy.

But parliamentary government is typically opposed to practicalities.

We Futurists consider the State to be a human reality. The State must be the administrator of the great company that belongs to that great association, the Nation.

Patriotism is nothing but a sublimation of the respectful attitude that good companies instill in their employees.[4]

This two-part essay was published in *L'ardito* on July 13 and 20, 1919, and reprinted in *Democrazia futurista* (1919). In *Futurismo e fascismo*

(1924), it is dated May 1919. I have omitted here two long excerpts from proposals made by the Futurist Volt (i.e., Vincenzo Fani-Ciotti, 1888–1927) which seek to demonstrate how the concept of a "technocratic government" can be given concrete shape. Marinetti does not offer any exact citation for this quote, but Volt's suggestions can be found in his essays "Aboliamo il parlamento," *Roma futurista*, December 30, 1918, p. 2, and "Come sostituire il senato," *Roma futurista*, January 5–12, 1919, p. 1. The last section of Marinetti's text, dealing with the anarchists' adherence to traditionalist attitudes, was previously published in the chapter "War, the Sole Cleanser of the World" (see document 9) in *Le Futurisme* (1911) and *Guerra sola igiene del mondo* (1915).

59

✍

Futurist Patriotism

In our view, the idea of the Nation by no means represents an extension of the sentimental ideal of the family.[1]

Family feeling is an inferior, animal-like fear of the great, free-ranging
beasts and of the darkness so full of snares and misadventures. It arrives
with the first signs of old age, making cracks in the metal of youth,
those first signs of quiescence, of a tempering prudence, of a need for
rest, for hauling down one's sails in some calm, comfortable harbor.

The warm glow of the family is that of the hen brooding over the rotten eggs of cowardice. The ludicrous, petty squabbles between the father, the mother, the grandmother, the aunt, and the children always
end up with a closing of ranks against sacred dangers and hopeless
heroism. And their steaming soup bowl is the censer in that temple of
Monotony.

The idea of the Nation, on the other hand, is altogether superior. It
represents the furthest individual extension of human generosity, flowing outward to encompass all like-minded, compatible comrades. It
embodies the most far-reaching, most solid sense of unity among agrarian, maritime, commercial, and industrial interests, bound together in
a single geographical unit, and by a similar combination of background
and outlook. In fact, it represents the destruction of the self-centered,
restrictive attachment to family that is now outmoded or harmful to
the individual.

Some people say that the Nation is our great family. Others may argue that the family is a small nation. We, however, proclaim that the

human heart, in its ever-widening expansion, crushes and destroys the small, suffocating family circle to arrive at the furthest extremities of the Nation, where it becomes aware of the beating heart of its fellow nationals, as if they were the very nerves at the extremities of its body.

The idea of the Nation nullifies that of the family. It is generous, heroic, dynamic, and Futurist, while that of the family is small-minded, fearful, static, conservative, and is bound by tradition.

The true conception of the Nation comes into being only now, out of the Futurist perception of the World. Until now it has been a hodge-podge of parochialism, classical rhetoric, ceremonial eloquence, and a subconscious urge toward heroism. Rather stupidly, this idea has been based on a commemoration of dead heroes, on a lack of confidence in the living, on a fear of war, and on a conservative rehabilitation of everything that is dead.

On the other hand, Futurist patriotism is a fierce passion; it is both violent and dogged in its pursuit of the progressive, revolutionary development of its own race, hell-bent on conquering the most distant goals. As the individual's most powerful emotional driving force, Futurist patriotism, though essentially selfless, metamorphoses into useful practicalities aiding the continuity and development of whatever race it is focused on. Instead of laboring for its sons of today, Italian patriotism strives, fights, and dies for the Italians of tomorrow. The most powerful paternal love feels for not just four or five sons but for forty million.

The emotional charge of my Italian heart reaches out boundlessly to embrace the Nation, the greatest possible number of my own and of our shared ideals, interests, and needs, which are bound up together and in no way opposed to one another.

Because of the geographical makeup of our God-given peninsula, the pleasing range of our climate, and the unusually varied qualities of our blood that is unique to, and characteristic of, our race, that aforementioned greatest possible number of common interests and ideals extends perforce as far as the Trentino, Istria, Dalmatia, Vallona, Rhodes, Smyrna, Benghazi, and Tripoli.[2]

Let us end by affirming that the Nation represents the furthest possible extension of the individual being or, perhaps better, it is the biggest of all living beings, which can endure for an inordinate length of time, and can control, keep in check, and defend every part of its body.

This essay appeared in *Roma futurista* on June 1, 1919, and was reprinted in the collection *Democrazia futurista* (1919).

60

⚭

Against the Papacy and the Catholic Mentality, Repositories of Every Kind of Traditionalism

It is a waste of time listing all the political reasons which make it absolutely essential for a victorious Italy to free herself from the Papacy, as soon as possible.[1]

Cavour, Crispi,[2] and a hundred other Italians have shown how the Papacy is, in time of peace, a millstone around our necks, and in turbulent times or in wartime, an enemy under our own roof or, at the very least, an enemy informer.

I demand the expulsion of the Papacy so as to rid Italy of the Catholic mentality.

The concept of the family or the legal concept of matrimony cannot be touched as long as the power of the priest persists.

This power is behind the absurd, life-denying idea of the eternal, which weighs so heavily on life itself.

Eternity of spiritual values, eternity of joy in an extraterrestrial heaven, and therefore the absurd eternity of love on Earth.

A man who loves a woman *must* love her for the whole of his life.

If he stops loving her after three years, there is a moral uproar, great alarm, and fear.

If he stops loving her after three months, it is a diabolical scandal, an infamous crime, which demands infernal punishment.

Priests have created the most absurd prison of all—indissoluble marriage.

So, to make sure that the law of eternal love is not broken, priests have imprisoned the hearts and the sensibilities of women, compelling them to pretend they are in love, to prostitute themselves, every night, to a man they loathe, thereby necessitating a vile, unending hypocrisy to flourish within and around them and—even worse—for their children.

Eternal love and the artificial conservation of sexual attraction are ludicrous concepts—yet the priests, not content with these noxious poisons, set themselves against the courageous instinct for adventure and risk-taking and the wonderful spirit of improvisation that drives strong individuals and the most vigorous temperaments.

Priests loathe whatever is temporary, instantaneous, fast, impetuous, or passionate. And in this they violently extinguish the fiery, precious essence of Christ's morality, which accorded all rights, all forgiveness, and every sympathy to the burning passions, to the inconstant flame of the heart. Priests forget Christ's words to Mary Magdalene: Many things will be forgiven in one who has loved much. And these too: Let he who is without sin among you cast the first stone. Both of these sayings glorify free love and give a kick up the backside to the indissolubility of marriage.

If a woman, as sometimes happens, has been desired, taken, and carelessly made pregnant by a man, a priest will demand that the woman be not exposed to further risk, to any new adventure. She will be propelled immediately into the prison of marriage with a man who no longer wants her, who detests her as an obstacle. They will be like two daggers locked together, neither of which can be used, though they dream of fighting each other, and each will blunt the other and end up injuring the child. The latter is born rosy as an apple but soon becomes a ball and chain shackling the two convicts.

These absurd concepts of eternal love and indissoluble ties between soul-bodies that detest each other are the hypocritical rules and demonstrations of hatred that are handed on each day, by way of education, to the child. But still the priest isn't satisfied. He says: Are you not happy? You will be in Heaven! Wither away, both of you! Wear yourselves out! Renounce all tenderness, beauty, bodily strength, and nervous energy; postpone your adultery until you are in Heaven.

Thus, marriage is the common purgatory of all exuberant, forceful temperaments. A Purgatory for sins not committed, the wearing down of one's youthfulness, humoring an absurd, negative, bullying, and depressing view of life, which will not acknowledge the triumphant extension of physical pleasure or of the freedom to take risks, to be reckless.

The priest requires, and imposes, the foul laws of renunciation and indolence.

So that wherever we go in this strong and healthy Italy of ours, we find so many souls in agony, worn out; women who didn't know how to make up their minds, who loved one man but gave themselves to another, who have hopes for a third but will give themselves to a fourth. Always making the wrong decision, always waiting expectantly, yet having an idiotic, pessimistic view of life. Men and women condemned, incapable of granting themselves the rapid absolution, the happy release of the tempest, the rain, and of suicide.

In order that we may arrive at the Futurist precepts of the ephemeral, of speed, and of continuous, heroic struggle, we must burn the priests' black robes—symbols of inertia—and melt down all the church bells to turn them into wheels for new superfast trains.

This plodding inertia, this daily preparation for a distant and wholly uncertain joy which, willingly or not, the imagination will then consign to an afterlife in paradise, this patient, mystical, institutionalized Catholic preparation is not unlike the military preparation of the Germans, which, fortunately, has recently collapsed in their huge defeat.

Our lightning Italian victory, after an offensive lasting only ten days, which saw all our lands retaken;[3] the political dreams of our fathers plucked out of the air, realized, and secured—all these glories of ours are anti-Catholic in spirit. At long last the inertia imposed upon us by the priests has been overturned. The tempestuous speed of Italian genius is freeing us from all that petty medievalism based on sacrifice, on ecstatic dreams, on beggars' hands, on hassocks, on diplomacy, on Platonic irredentisms, and academic nostalgia.

At long last, we are no longer looking back at the far-off processions of Roman heroes. We look at ourselves in the mirror, and what we see is ourselves, for we are ourselves. Today's fast-moving Italians have—in a matter of ten days, and gaily, like schoolboys—shattered the great Austro-Hungarian army, which even in our dreams seemed invincible, yet which, in reality, proved to be nothing more than a plaything in our powerful hands. And this took place despite all the cautions imposed by history, by pessimism, by being the progeny of Catholic families, by being suffocated beneath ancient ruins, and by being subjected to the miserable little electoralism of the provinces and the narrow-mindedness of our government jobs.

This provincial family with its hypocritical marriage and with its lurid priest as custodian, with the scorpions of moralism in all the nooks and crannies of the walls, must be burned to cinders as quickly as possible.

And after the fire, a swift salvo of spit to extinguish it completely.

The priest is the brother of the policeman. The prison of indissoluble matrimony. *Divorce* and *free love* are a couple of perilous *assault troops*.[4] They sing while others are sleeping and often break windows—squaring up to the traditionalists. The traditionalist is one who is afraid, who takes cover, who doesn't face up to his responsibilities, who remembers wistfully, who takes his ideas from the most prudent daily papers, who doesn't dare question his son about his obvious gonorrhea, who thinks he can curb the sprightly sexuality of his sixteen-year-old daughter by locking her inside the house with the heavy chains of his paternal doting.

While he goes off—hypocritically—to smoke his pipe in a brothel and tell the Homeric tale of his wife's failings upon the pillow of some prostitute or other, his daughter, shut in the house, throws the window and her legs[5] wide open to the student who, from the window opposite, explains to her what Latin *virtue* really means.[6]

The Italian life of tomorrow must be nothing less than a series of grenades tossed between the legs of these two irksome, lugubrious enemies of ours, the priest and the carabiniere. The spring is full of laughter, is exploding despite the laws, the prohibitions, the confessionals, and the council of elders, and it will win, it will *always* win. Yet how much more splendid its fruits would be if, one day, we were at last to hear a voice joyously filling the air with the news that the Papacy is gone, is cast out of Italy, together with the last few priests and policemen!

Our victorious war has uncovered a fierce antagonism between combatants and carabinieri,[7] as it has between Interventionists and priests of any sort—clerical, academic, and socialist.

Our shock troops hate the carabinieri, who have dreamed of shackling these Heroes.[8]

In their view, Heroes have to be quiet people who never shout, who are circumspect, who fear and tread warily, who don't use their elbows in a crowd, and who wait patiently at the window where the uncouth employee of the State does everything at his leisure and doles out indolence.

The Arditi despise networks and military discipline, those shackles imposed by academic strategy and Teutonic science.

Everything they do is spontaneous, especially their dedication to a final victory. They are Futurists,[9] for they have no truck with the Roman "reinforcements" deployed throughout history, nor do they require scientifically planned preparatory bombardments.

They take the enemy trench (shaped like a potbellied banker) by surprise; they break through it, empty it, and then, with one bound, head for Trieste.[10]

During the war, the carabinieri had the job of carefully checking passports so as to catch the great number of spies who were on the move. They allowed many to get through, and it took them four years to learn how to do their job, and now, at last, they know how to do it so well that they are still checking the passports of the victors!

The priests are still priests, guardians of inertia and bureaucracy, obnoxious medieval jailors of the quick and burgeoning spring, bursting with revolutionary energy!

In conclusion, we have to:

Replace our present rhetorical, inactive anticlericalism with something that is full of action, of violence, and more resolute, to rid Italy and Rome of their theocratic medievalism, which can go and find some more appropriate country in which to wither away and die.

Our totally uncompromising anticlericalism provides the basis for our political program; it will admit of no half measures nor double-dealing, for it urges clear and simple expulsion.

Our anticlericalism wishes to free Italy from churches, priests, friars, and nuns, from madonnas, candles, and church bells.

The only admissible religion is the Italy of tomorrow. For her we have fought without regard to the kind of government we have, for that is inevitably bound to follow the theocratic medievalism of religion in its final fall.

This essay appeared in *L'ardito* on June 8, 1919, and was reprinted, with a few textual variations, in *Democrazia futurista* (1919) and *Futurismo e fascismo* (1924).

61

⁂

Speech in Parliament

On July 11, 1919, I received an invitation from Bevione[1] to visit the public gallery at Montecitorio Palace.[2] With Ferruccio Vecchi,[3] I waited for the right moment.

Faces displaying intensified idiocy.[4]

Open mouths in cliff faces, awaiting the foaming spittle of the sea of people.

Fear of bombs making their bellies wobble even harder.

Suction seats: every cardinal's seat holding fast a deputy sitting on its knees.[5]

High up on the circular wall, the horses of Sartorius[6] dripping with sweat.

Roof of stained church glass, filtering a feeble light.

The dominant tones: dark red stains of vomited wine dotted with pale pink peas of blotting paper.

Marcora,[7] a skeleton in a frock coat, with huge, deep-sunken eye sockets.

In other sections of that funnel-shaped sewer, monstrous bones emerge, fragments of mammoths.

A deputy struggles his way up the steps and goes to sniff at a flabby body that quivers oddly, like worms wriggling. Dead maybe? Not yet. But not long. Why does it smell so bad? The stench of corpses mingles with the voices of eunuchs, or comes from ancient, rusted medieval portals.

A flash of excitement among the gasping red socialist fish, all attentive, listening to a pettifogging whale.

The deputies who are still alive wander about, wearily, sleepily, like guides or ushers in a mausoleum not mentioned in Baedeker.

To be pelted as befits you, you mammoths, you walruses, you biblical whales, you toothless sharks, you swamp eels, you certainly don't need one of my speeches!

You deserve one of those ferocious, inundating streams of phlegm hawked up by an infantryman after an August offensive on the scorching Carso, awash with tears!

When the defeatist speech by the Socialist deputy the Hon. Lucci[8] was finished, I broke the silence with these words:

"In the name of the Fasci di Combattimento, the Futurists, and the intellectuals . . ."

A deputy: "Who's that?"

Marinetti: "I'm Marinetti."

Another deputy: "Let's hear him!" (*Commotion, murmurings: then, miraculously, an absolute silence fell.*)

Marinetti (*speaking very loudly*): "I protest against your politics and I shout at you: Away with Nitti![9] I say that the ministry of saboteurs of our Victory can continue no longer, with its humiliations of our officers, this ministry that defends itself with carabinieri and policemen! Your cowardice is the most grotesque mockery of the sacrifice made by our soldiers who despise you and categorically reject your right to represent them any longer. Shame on you! The young people of Italy, whose mouthpiece I am, cry out at you: You are disgusting! Disgusting!"

I was arrested in the corridors of the Chamber. As soon as I was released, I received the following letter from D'Annunzio:

My dear Marinetti,
Well done for your protest of yesterday! As courageous as all of your actions.
I should like to see you.
If you can, please come.

Yours
Gabriele D'Annunzio

Marinetti published three accounts of the event: in *Roma futurista*, July 13, 1919; in *Futurismo e fascismo* (1924); and in *Marinetti e il futurismo* (1929). Our translation is based on the 1929 version.

62

Address to the Fascist Congress of Florence

Dear Fascists, Futurists, and Arditi!

I invite you to applaud a courageous Fascist, who is not with us, though he would have been, had not the anti-Italian government of Nitti[1] condemned him to three months in prison: MARIO CARLI.[2] (*Unanimous cries of "Long live Mario Carli!" And applause*)

The Futurist Mario Carli escaped from Albricci's[3] police and is basking in the salubrious air of Italian Fiume.[4] The typically Futurist flexibility of this poet, who is well acquainted with the most perilous journeys of the spirit, the subtlest of psychological analyses, the most colorful races and even the best strategy to adopt with streets in an uproar, as well as the management of popular gatherings, has shone forth yet again.

We owe the foundation of the Roman branch of the Fasci di Combattimento to Mario Carli, the poet of *Notti filtrate*,[5] together with Settimelli of the Futurist Political Party and *Roma futurista*.[6] He led all the violent demonstrations in defense of our victory against the red and black Bolsheviks, the Nittian defeatists.[7] I invite you to cry again: Long live the Futurist Mario Carli! (*Ovation, applause*)

Getting rid of the Vatican.[8] In the name of Futurism and of the Italian Futurists, I approve wholeheartedly the program of the Fasci di Combattimento, as explained by my friend Fabbri.[9] However, I find in the program certain grave omissions, and I draw your attention to them.

Fascists! There is no greater danger to Italy than the black peril. The

Italian people, who have had the courage to dare, to desire, and to bring to completion the immensely heroic and victorious war effort, and with their victory to ensure that of an open-minded, gifted Futurism over a rigid and pedantic Teutonic conservatism, would fail in their mission if they did not strive to liberate our peninsula, which is so dynamic and throbbing with life, from the filthy plague of the papacy. We must desire, demand, and carry out the expulsion of the papacy, or put more precisely, we must "devaticanize" Italy. (*Applause, ovation*)

The "Board of Initiatives."[10] Going on with my analysis of the program of the Fasci di Combattimento, I find there is a proposal to replace the Senate with a National Technocratic Council. Well then, I have to say to you that while the technical idea is very important, it is not sufficient by itself. In the history of any people, the Senate represents a deferential nod in the direction of the wisdom of the old, who are called upon to act as a check on the executive body, to refine its proposals and to channel its decisions. This notion of the Senate is like that of the chorus in Greek tragedy, and has had the effect of weighing down, cluttering, bureaucratizing, and delaying the spiritual and material progress of mankind.

All legislators and philosophers whose sole concern has been to preserve, perfect, and consolidate the status quo have seen in the Senate an ideal guarantor of order and tradition, the powerful curb of lived experience imposed on the potential follies of governments.

Those people who have not prostrated themselves before this institution have pushed audacity to the limits by seeking to "perfect" the Senate by ensuring that it was an elected body. But you who wish to abolish the Senate, does it not occur to you that the Technocratic Council, designed to take its place, will inevitably be sick with senility, with cowardly prudence, bureaucratic pedantry, with decrepitude and persistent hatred of innovation and youthful daring? Instead, the Technocratic Council should be a body of very young men and, in my opinion, it should act and be known as the Board of Initiatives.

Legislators have always dreamed of curbing the powers of government. They were clearly ignorant of the fact that the power is synonymous with the curbing. They were not aware that a government is always, to a greater or lesser degree, a policeman. Nothing would seem more absurd than setting one policeman to watch another. Let us place a subversive, a rebel, or an agitator at his side. And in that way we shall give birth to the Board of Initiatives, a stimulating, simplifying, and accelerating body, which in a race such as ours will be fired with youthful flair, and will provide the best defense for the young, will be the strongest guarantor of progress and vitality of spirit. For Italy, I dream of a government of technical experts, spurred on by a council of very young men, who will take the place of our present parliament, with its incompetent prattlers and irrelevant pedants, which permits itself to be overruled by a Senate composed of men who already have one foot in the grave.

The Technocratic Council, which will replace the Senate, should therefore be made up of very young men, men who have not yet reached thirty. And I insist on this because in Italy we're in the habit of calling the "young" to power, albeit, with the understanding that a man of fifty-five is very young and still in his prime. Salandra[11] cries out, "Let youth advance!" Yet all of those with him fear the young—they put a forty-year-old in quarantine as if he were afflicted with cholera, a fifty-year-old as if he were a dynamiter, and they think of a sixty-year-old as daring and almost mature enough for the government of Italy! . . .

We must avoid this new peril—a Technocratic Council of old men who, having failed to put their technical talents to any use for so long, are now technically capable of nothing better than dying.

Italian life remains degraded by the dismal coexistence of a variety of boards of ancestors that are without authority or reputation, yet which cast a heavy shadow all about them, of pessimism, dogmatism, professorial austerity, patriotic verbiage, and the dust of ancient Rome. And grubbing around in the midst of all of this, tightfisted, provincial, and slatternly, is an unkempt serving wench who does everything badly, keeps house badly, improves nothing, and who wastes whole days poring over the accounts, always afraid to spend anything for fear of becoming penniless,[12] and who thinks making cheap vegetable soup, with not much salt, a culinary triumph.[13]

The senile gerontocracy mumbles away: "Remember the Roman legions, the *Urbs*[14] . . . the city fathers conversing beside the Sacred River[15] . . ."

The serving woman explains breathlessly how, when gossiping with tradesmen and by virtue of her brusque obstinacy, she upholds the high renown of her master, maintains good relations with the family doctor, and so on.

She sings her own praises as a courageous freethinker because she mocks the priest behind his back, but nevertheless she goes to mass every Sunday. She is on friendly terms with her parliamentary representative, and she's really very adept at keeping a close check on the *dreadfully* high cost of living. The servants and the moribund master are up in arms at any suggestion of moving house. They are even in full agreement about preserving the dust, the woodworms, the mice, the mildew, the prefects, and what have you.

The men behind those ancestral portraits are Boselli[16] and Salandra; the serving wench is called Giolitti or Nitti. (*Ovation*)

To counter the effects of the gerontocrats and the slattern, we propose a *Board of Initiatives*, made up of students and Futurist Arditi.[17]

Spirit of the Arditi—the School for physical courage and patriotism. A third omission I find in the program of the Fasci di Combattimento is concerned with education. Our Futurist friend Fabbri has wisely directed our attention to the absolutely necessary, far-reaching reform of education.

I believe, however, that we could gain all we desire, and a wonderful future surpassing even our wildest dreams, by insisting on an absolutely rigid, no, better, an utterly merciless regime of physical exercise in all our schools.

In addition to all kinds of practical and technical instruction, both in factories and on farms, we have to establish traveling schools as soon as possible, or better still, educational trips, as well as actual courses in or schools for physical courage and patriotism.

Every day, in the joy of life in the open air, with games taking absolute precedence over books, we have to talk about the divinity of Italy to the children of Italy, to persist in teaching them about physical courage and scorn for danger, always rewarding fearless daring and heroism.

The schools for physical courage and patriotism must replace the courses in Greek and Latin, which are suitable only for prehistoric cavemen.

We Futurists are convinced that this is the only way to breed that kind of heroic citizen who will be able to take care of himself, who can really be liberal in his thoughts and with his fists, and who will make the existence of the police, police stations, carabinieri, and priests wholly superfluous.

My Futurist friend Mario Carli, a captain in the Arditi, and Captain Vecchi, the head of the Association of Arditi,[18] have, like me, both understood how *Arditismo*, that new sensitivity to heroic, revolutionary patriotism, arose out of Futurism and the Great War. *L'ardito*, the newspaper directed by Captain Vecchi, the destroyer of *Avanti!*,[19] is a forthright paper and we must recommend it to all young Italians. (*Ovation*)

Perhaps a day will come when we shall have, in Italy, those *schools for danger* that I was recommending ten years ago in the first Futurist manifestos[20] and which came into being during the war in the everyday training routines of the Arditi (advancing on all fours under the withering fire of machine guns; waiting, without batting an eyelid, for the close passage of a girder hanging just above their heads, and so on).

The proletariat of talented people. And now I want to fill another gap in the program, telling you about the only proletariat that is truly forgotten and oppressed—that singularly important proletariat of talented people.[21]

There can be no doubt that our race outstrips all others in the extraordinary number of geniuses it produces.[22] In even the smallest group of Italians, in the tiniest village, there are always seven or eight young people in their twenties, who are all atremble with their intense desire to create, who are full of ambitious pride which is revealed in volumes of unpublished verse and outbursts of eloquence at political gatherings in the piazzas. Naturally, some of them really are deluding themselves, but not many. They could never achieve true genius. Yet they have a basic talent, by which I mean they are open to suggestion and serve the useful purpose of raising the overall intellectual level of a country.

In that selfsame group or small Italian village, it is easy to find seven or eight mature men who, in the course of their little lives as clerks or professional men, in their local cafés or in their family homes, bear the melancholy signs of failed genius. They represent broken scraps of talent who never found themselves in the right circumstances and were thus crushed by economic necessity or family obligations.

The Futurist artistic movement, which we started eleven years ago, aimed specifically at a radical modernization of the worlds of art and literature by curtailing the power of their vested authorities, at rooting out and destroying the geriatric hegemony, cutting down to size the critics and pedantic professors, and encouraging the daring leaps made by talented young people, so as to create a healthy atmosphere, full of oxygen, and to give encouragement and assistance to all the talented young people of Italy. To encourage them all, to increase their pride a hundredfold, to open up before them every possible outlet, thereby reducing, as quickly as possible, the number of failed and isolated geniuses.

Sometimes it is very difficult to recognize, appreciate, and encourage young people of talent. For, instead of embracing Italy spiritually, as a huge flexible mass to be molded, they see her as a ridiculous network of abuses of power, of camorras, of sponging authorities, of idiotic prohibitions. And they're right. Wherever you go in our land, talent is underrated, ridiculed, and restrained. Those who take the crown, who are revered, are the mediocre opportunists or the geniuses of yesteryear, now in their dotage.

Futurism assembled many of these young, talented people. In the white heat of Futurism, many among them grew in stature and shone: Boccioni, Russolo, Buzzi, Balla, Mazza, Sant'Elia, Pratella, Folgore, Cangiullo, Mario Carli, Mario Dessy, Vieri, De Nardis, Pasqualino, Funi, Sironi, Chiti, Jannelli, Nannetti, Cantarelli, Rosai, Baldessari, Galli, Depero, Dudreville, and Primo Conti; the talented creators of the Theater of Essential Brevity, Bruno Corra and Settimelli; and the courageous Futurist editors of *Roma futurista*, Rocca, Bottai, Federico Pinna, Volt, and Bolzon, the high-flying flag of Italian culture in America.[23]

With their wonderful flexibility in passing from art to political action, these young men were with me everywhere during our earliest demonstrations against Austria, during the Battle of the Marne,[24] in prisons for the Interventionist cause, and on the fields of battle.

Other young men are continually swelling the Futurist ranks, dynamic, impetuous, drunk with spiritual heroism and revolutionary patriotism. Yet many of them remain unacknowledged, depressed, and suffocated in an atmosphere of small-town ultraconservatism. In the long series of *serate*[25] and tempestuous demonstrations that spread throughout the peninsula, Futurism came into contact with almost all of them. Nevertheless, a much better coordinated effort, by all the political forces in the Country, will be needed to save, revitalize, and harness this huge proletarian army of talent.

I propose that in every town, premises be set up that will be called something like *Open Exhibitions of Creative Talent*. And on these premises:

1. Paintings, sculptures, all kinds of art, architectural designs, blueprints for machines and proposals for inventions will be on display for a month.
2. Large or small musical compositions, for piano or orchestra, of any sort whatsoever, will be performed there.
3. Poetry, prose, writings on all the sciences, of all types and lengths, will be read, displayed, and performed.
4. Anyone at all will have the right to exhibit there, free of charge.
5. Works of all types and qualities will be exhibited or read without being formally judged, no matter how absurd, idiotic, mad, or immoral they may appear to be.[26]

With these open exhibitions of creative talent, which will be entirely free of charge, we Futurists oppose the grave danger of the creative spirit foundering in a flood tide of ideologies, in the squabbles surrounding the proposals of Communism and the dictatorship of the proletariat. Let us defend the mind! Everywhere one encounters signs of weariness caused by the war, by the mania for plagiarism, by provincial shortsightedness, verbose journalism, or the vile abominations of conservatism. Wherever you look, attempts are being made to deify the manual worker and to raise him up above the labors of the intellect.

I am absolutely convinced that Messieurs Anatole France and Barbusse are in complete bad faith when, descending from the highest peaks of irony and skepticism, from the gilded peaks of their successful novels, they put their signatures to manifestos addressed to *the Manual and Intellectual classes.*[27]

Italians! Rest assured that political Futurism will be violently opposed to any attempt at such leveling. Everything—and I mean everything—can be conceded to the manual workers, but not this sacrifice of the spirit, of genius, of the great, guiding light.

All the parasitic plutocracies in the world can be sacrificed to the toiling workers, to the oppressed classes.

However, let the intellectuals and intuitive creators emerge organically from among the manual workers, as they alone are capable of inventing, discovering, renewing, as they alone are capable of increasing the sum total of earthly happiness.

You Interventionist Fascists know that our great revolutionary war was ventured, desired, brought about, and tenaciously carried forward to final victory by a minority of intellectuals. They were the best, the least imbued by tradition, the most Futurist. While the whole population was still immersed in the inertia of pacifism, they understood the need for war, they brutally cut their ties with other intellectuals who possessed only the negative, pedantic, cultural, reactionary, and quietist attributes of the spirit. Challenging and soaring above the old, leaden intellectualism of academics and cowards such as Benedetto Croce and Barzellotti,[28] and against the quibbling, legalistic intellectualism of those like Treves and Turati,[29] the absolutely pure, lyrical, creative spirits hurled themselves into battle and pointed out the road which had to be taken.

Among these was Gabriele D'Annunzio, who flew over Vienna and who made a gift of Fiume to Italy.[30] There was also Benito Mussolini, the great Italian Futurist, who, from the redoubt of his *Popolo d'Italia*, fearlessly covered our backs as combatants at the front against a succession of internal enemies, thus leading the cities of Italy from the grim episode of Caporetto to the ideal glory of Vittorio Veneto.[31] (*Applause*)

Therefore, glory be to the Italian people who fought and won the war, but glory too to the geniuses who inspired them. In June 1910 I delivered a sensational speech, which was brimful of Futurism, on the need for, and the beauty of, Violence, at the Labor Exchange in Naples, the Workers' Association in Parma, and at the Teatro d' Arte Moderna in Milan. On those occasions I looked forward to the vigorous and decisive intervention of artists in Italian public life.[32] This prediction has today been brilliantly fulfilled in an Italian Fiume, under the command of Gabriele D'Annunzio.

The artists will at last turn government into a disinterested art, in place of the narrow-minded system of thievery and cowardice it is at the moment.

But I hear you talking already about our lack of experience.

Don't be ridiculous! . . . Don't forget that the Italian race knows very well how to produce great artists and great poets.

It is my belief that our parliamentary institutions are fatally destined to perish. I also believe that Italian politics are inevitably bound to fail unless this life-giving strength of the creative talents of Italy is nurtured, and unless we rid ourselves of those two particularly Italian scourges, the lawyers and the professors.

Once Italy has been liberated, through the dynamic force of the Board of Initiatives, the patriotic blast of the Arditi mentality, the schools for physical courage and heroism, the open exhibitions of creative talent, and the proletariat of talented young Italians, it will at last illuminate the world with Italian brilliance.

Creative genius, artistic flexibility, a talent for concentrating on the practical and essential aspects of life, speed of improvisation, and flashes of enthusiasm are the vital forces which explain the victory of June 15 on the Piave[33] and that of Vittorio Veneto. (*Applause*)

Improvising with studentlike high spirits and artistic, creative genius, the Arditi got themselves killed on Mount Grappa so as to mislead the old Austrian bull with their bloody demise, luring it with its horns to a place where it should not have broken through. A gigantic game of chess. Thousands of dagger-wielding Casanovas on the footbridges of the Piave, below the daring swoops of the *Cagliostro del cielo*,[34] masters of the winds. Along the semicircular front that curved around from Astico to the sea, the arrow sped from the center, Montello, toward Vittorio Veneto. Neither to the left on Mount Grappa, nor to the right toward Cervignano, but to the center! The most audacious of targets, the least expected. Against that target, twenty-two divisions! With bloody wings, breasts surging forward, bursting with blood and fire, they won through.

Artistically improvising everything, the swiftly moving troops, the cavalry, the cyclist marksmen, and those in armored vehicles played a very clever trick on the Austrian army and strangled it as it retreated.

Improvising everything artistically, and with truly creative genius, my beautiful armored car of the eighth squadron, under the command of Captain Raby,[35] forded the raging torrents like a torpedo boat. Then it hurtled down from the Carnic Alps with the frantic, lightning thrust of the Ardito's dagger, into the endless dropsical belly of the defeated Austrian army, and shot out from behind it toward Vienna.

The creative genius of D'Annunzio conquered Fiume in an artistic manner. Recently, in Italian Fiume, I experienced the sharpest spasm of joy of my whole life, crumpling up a wad of Austrian kronas, whose value had been reduced to a few cents by our victory.[36]

At long last, the wild joy of crushing the financial, military, and traditionalist heart of our hereditary enemy, in this way, between my fingers, that were still trembling with the vibration of my machine gun at Vittorio Veneto! (*Ovation*)

> **The address was given on October 10, 1919, at the First Fascist Congress, which had an audience of ex-combatants, members of the recently founded Fasci di Combattimento, the Arditi, and many Futurists. The cooperation among these groups of ex-combatants began during the Great War and led to the foundation of the Futurist Political Party (see above, documents 45–47) and the Fasci di Combattimento (see above, documents 49–50). The speech was published in *I nemici d'Italia* (October 23, 1919), *L'ardito* (October 26, 1919), *Roma futurista* (November 2, 1919), and *Futurismo e fascismo* (1924).**

63

❦

Beyond Communism

The heroic citizen—Schools for courage

Artists in power

Centers of genius—Life as celebration

We Futurists have abolished all ideologies and instead introduced everywhere our own new concept of life, our formulas for spiritual health, our social and aesthetic impetus, the true expression of our temperaments as creative, revolutionary Italians.

After struggling for ten years to bring about the modernization of Italy, after destroying the ultraconservative Austro-Hungarian Empire at Vittorio Veneto,[1] we were thrown into prison, accused of having threatened the security of the State,[2] when, in reality, we were guilty of Italian Futurism.

And yet, we are more indefatigable, bolder, and richer in our ideas than ever before. We have already made many of them public and we shall create even more. Therefore, we Italian creators are ill-disposed to taking orders from anyone, or to aping the Russian Lenin, disciple of the German Marx.

Humanity is marching toward an anarchic individualism, the dream and the goal of all strong spirits. Communism, on the other hand, is an outdated exponent of mediocrity, which the exhaustion and terror caused by the war have today given a new lease of life and turned into an intellectual fashion.

Communism is the extreme expression of that cancer of bureaucracy that has always gnawed away at mankind. It is a German cancer, a typical product of over-meticulous German planning. All pedantic schematizations are inhuman and incapable of reacting to unforeseen events. History, life itself, the world, belong to the Improvisers. We loathe, in equal measure, the military and the Communist barracks. The true spirit of anarchism despises and breaks out of the Communist prison.

For us, the Nation[3] is tantamount to the greatest possible extension of the generosity of the individual, spreading out in a circle to envelop all human beings with whom he feels an affinity. It signifies the most extensive, concrete solidarity between the interests of the spirit, the land, the rivers and ports, the industries, all bound together by geography, by similar climates and horizons of a similar hue.

In its ever widening circle, the human heart breaks out of the small, suffocating circle of the family, to touch the furthest bounds of the Nation, where it senses the beating hearts of its fellows on the very frontiers, like the nerve ends of its own body. The concept of the Nation obliterates that of the family. It is a generous concept, heroic, dynamic, Futuristic, whereas the notion of the family is narrow, fear-ridden, static, conservative, and traditionalist. It is only now, for the very first time, and owing to our Futurist ideas, that a powerful awareness of the Nation is beginning to emerge. Until now it has been a chaotic mixture of parochialism, Greco-Roman rhetoric, commemorative eloquence, unconscious, instinctive heroism, glorification of the heroic dead, mistrust of living heroes, and fear of war.

Futurist patriotism, however, is an unstinting passion for the unfolding revolutionary progress of our race.

As the most powerful form of individual love, Futurist patriotism, though devoid of self-interest, creates the most favorable environment for the continuity and progress of the Italian race.

The ever widening circle of love of our Italian hearts embraces the Nation, which represents the greatest possible number of our practicable ideals, interests, and needs, harmoniously bound together.

The Nation is the greatest extension of the individual, or better, perhaps, the broadest possible individual who is capable of living fully extended, directing, controlling, and defending every part of his body.

The Nation represents the psychological and geographical awareness of the individual's urge toward self-improvement.

The idea of the Nation can only disappear if one takes refuge in egotistical isolation. To say, for example, "I am not Italian, I am a citizen of the world," has the same meaning as "I don't give a damn about Italy, Europe, or Humanity. All I care about is myself."

The concept of the Nation is as indestructible as that of the political party.

The Nation is nothing other than a vast political party.

Rejection of the Nation is tantamount to isolating, castrating, belittling, disparaging, or killing oneself.

The workers, who today march beneath their fluttering red flags, are demonstrating—after four years of triumphant war—their dimly perceived need to fight their own heroic and glorious war.[4]

It is absurd to undermine our victory with cries of "Long live Lenin! Down with war!," for after having urged the Russian people to renounce one war, Lenin forced them into another against Kolchak, Denikin, and the Poles.[5]

Thus, quite involuntarily, Russian Bolshevism is generating patriotism, which is born out of the need for a defensive war.

It is impossible to get away from these two concept-feelings: *patriotism*, by which we mean the practice of developing the individual and the race; and *heroism*, which is the all-embracing necessity of progressing beyond human strengths, and the upward urge of the race.

All of those people who are exhausted by the tempestuous, ever changing variety of life hanker after the passive, ever constant uniformity that Communism promises. They wish for a life without surprises, a world smoothed out like a billiard ball.

However, pressure on space has not yet leveled the mountains of the earth, and life—which is an art form—is composed (as is any work of art) of peaks and troughs.

Human progress, the essence of which is accelerating speeds, acknowledges, as does all speed, that there are obstacles to be overturned, which means revolutionary wars.

The lives of insects show us that everything is reduced to reproduction at all costs, and to purposeless destruction.

Humanity dreams in vain of escaping these two laws, which stimulate and weary it by turns. Humanity dreams of establishing peace through a unique, universal kind of man who, however, should then be immediately castrated lest his aggressive virility generates other, new wars.

A unique kind of human being should live in a world that is perfectly flat. Every mountain represents a challenge to every Napoleon and every Lenin. Every leaf protests against the warlike will of the wind.

The unchanging number of needs for and means of human transport is an affront to the Communist dream.

The necessity of traveling by tram, then by train, then by boat over a lake, then by train again, and finally by boat so as to reach the liner on the sea which, if it were merely a little yacht, would not take you to America, is tragically anti-Communist.

After the most multifaceted and tumultuous of wars, it is only logical that mankind pulls out its old Communist ideal of a lasting peace.

Communism perhaps finds its realization in the graveyard. However, given that there are many who are buried alive, and given the overall, uncontrollable death toll of mankind, as well as the fact that some intuitively perceptive people survive and die at different times, the graveyards play host to the most turbulent meetings, holding rebels in captivity as well as vaulting ambitions. There will be many different attempts to establish Communism, counterrevolutionaries who will make war, and revolutions that will defend themselves by having recourse to war.

Relative peace is nothing more than a breathing space to get over the exhaustion of the last war or the last revolution. Absolute peace will prevail perhaps only after the human race has disappeared altogether. If I were a Communist, I should be worrying about the next war between homosexuals and lesbians, who will then join forces against normal men.

I would begin making propaganda against the interplanetary wars of the future.

In Russia, there are some revolutionaries who are semi-egalitarian and who defend their power, which is being assailed by other revolutionaries who don't believe in equality and who would like to reduce the amount of equality or to reintroduce inequalities all over again.

Bolshevism has been, first and foremost, a violent, revengeful antidote to Tsarism.

Now it has become a warlike defense by those social physicians who are being transformed into masters of a sick people.

In some places, there isn't enough bread for everyone, in others, not enough comfort for all.

Everywhere you go, they cry out that everyone will have enough bread, that everybody will be well off.

We would prefer to shout that everyone will be healthy, strong, and clever!

Communism experienced in Italy will immediately provoke an anti-egalitarian counterrevolution, or itself give birth to a new kind of inequality.

Let's not waste any time glorifying the Russian pseudo-communism, as if it were definitive, or some kind of earthly paradise.

Our spirit should reach beyond that.

. . .

In all countries, and in Italy in particular, it is misleading to make any distinction between the bourgeoisie and the proletariat. There isn't any bourgeoisie that is entirely rotten and moribund, nor is there a proletariat that is all health and energy. What there is are rich and poor—poor because of misfortune, illness, lack of ability or even honesty; rich through fraud, astuteness, miserliness, or intelligence. Exploited and exploiters. Stupid and intelligent. False and genuine. So-called rich bourgeois, who work harder than the workers. Workers who work as little as possible, trying to do absolutely nothing at all. The swift and the slow. The victorious and the defeated.

It is absurd to call that redoubtable mass of intelligent, hardworking, young middle-class men a rotten, moribund bourgeoisie. Students, clerks, and farmers, businessmen and industrialists, engineers, notaries, lawyers, and so on, all of them are sons of the people, all of them intent on going beyond the modest well-being of their fathers, by dint of their unstinting labors.

During the war, they were the subalterns and the captains, and today, though completely exhausted, they are heroically ready to take up life's new challenges.

They are not intellectuals, but they are workers gifted with intelligence, foresight, a spirit of self-sacrifice, and determination. They represent the best part of our race. The war was fought by these energetic young men, always at the head of the infantries, made up of peasants and manual workers.

The peasants and workers who fought the war, as yet lacking any national consciousness, would not have been victorious without the example and the intelligence of these heroic petit bourgeois lieutenants. What's more, there can be no doubt that the strivings of Communism are, and always will be, guided by thrusting, ambitious young men from the middle classes.

On the other hand, it is absurd to describe all workers with the word "proletariat," promising an equal glory and dictatorship to the peasant infantrymen who are today again taking up their tireless work on the land and the manual workers who say they are utterly exhausted.

We have to destroy the tendency to look to the past, cowardice, passiveness, traditionalism, self-serving materialism, the refusal of modernization, fear of responsibility, and provincial mimicry.

It is provincial mimicry that cries out, "Long live Lenin, down with Italy; long live the Russian Revolution!" Far better to shout, "Long live the Italy of tomorrow! Long live the Italian Revolution! Long live Italian Futurism!"

The Russian Revolution has its own justification in Russia and can only be judged by Russians; it cannot be imported into Italy.

There are endless differences between the Russian and the Italian peoples, in addition to those which are typical of conquered and victorious races.

Their needs are different and diametrically opposed.

When a conquered people feels its patriotism dying within, it renews itself through revolution or apes the revolution of a neighboring people. A victorious people, such as ours, desires to make its revolution by emulating the pilot who jettisons ballast so as to climb ever higher.

We should not forget that the Italian people, with their abundance of keen individualisms, are the most anticommunist of all, hankering always after an anarchic individualism.

As there is no anti-Semitism in Italy, we have no Jews to emancipate, consider, or pursue.[6]

The Italian people can be compared to a fine wrestler who wanted to fight without doing any training or without having even the means of such training at his disposal. Circumstances dictated that he would either win or fade away. The Italian people came out of the war as glorious victors. Yet the effort required was too much for them, so that now, gasping, at the end of their tether, almost incapable of enjoying their great victory, they malign us, their trainers, and open their arms to those who counseled them against fighting.

Between these partisans of the quiet life, who want to keep the wrestler down on the ground, and we who want to restore him to health, to raise him up at all costs, a quarrel has erupted which, unfortunately, is being carried on over the weary body of the wrestler himself.

The tremendous tangle of difficulties, obstacles, and miseries that every war leaves in its wake, the frustrations of the returning troops who sink into an immense quagmire of bureaucracy, the delayed vigorous taxation of excessive war profits, are added to the still unresolved question of the Adriatic, to that of the Brenner not turned to our advantage, and so forth.[7]

We have been governed by an incurable neutralist who did everything in his power to minimize the moral strength of our victory.[8]

This government favored the Socialists who, flaunting the Communist flag of a conquered people such as the Russians are, took possession of the tired, discontented, yet victorious Italian people in the elections.

We are not talking about a struggle between a bourgeoisie and a proletariat but rather one between those who, like us, have the right to
initiate an Italian revolution and those who must accept both its conception and its realization.

I know the Russian people. Six months before the outbreak of the world
war, I was invited by the Society for Important Lectures to deliver eight
lectures on Futurism in Moscow and Petrograd.[9] The triumphal, far-
reaching, ideological effects of these lectures and my personal success
as a Futurist orator have become legendary in Russia. I want to make
all that clear so that my judgment on the Russian Futurists may appear
absolutely and objectively fair. I am pleased to learn that the Russian
Futurists are all Bolsheviks and that Futurist art was, for some time,
State art in Russia. The Russian cities were decorated by Futurist
painters for the last festival in May.[10]

Lenin's trains were painted on the outside with forceful colored designs that were very reminiscent of those of Boccioni, Balla, and Russolo. This was an honor for Lenin and cheers us, being one of our
victories. All the Futurisms in the world are children of Italian Futurism, which we created in Milan a dozen years ago. However, all Futurist
movements are autonomous. All races had or still have a traditionalism
of their own to overturn. We are not Bolsheviks because we have to
bring about our own revolution.

We are not able to accept the subtleties of official socialism:[11]

1. They declare that the war should have been avoided at all costs, yet
   recognize (in lowered voices) that the development of revolutionary socialism is one of the fruits of war.
2. They declare that German tyranny was absolutely preferable to the
   mass spilling of heroic blood.
3. They praise the malingerer and despise the hero as if he were a
   bloody brigand.
4. They consider the deserter to be a worthy representative of the
   people.
5. They accuse and reject the Interventionist, revolutionary socialists
   as being responsible for the "pointless slaughter."
6. They pour scorn on the officer class in a country in which there is
   no militaristic tradition.

7. They urge the masses toward revolution and then they hold them back, saying that the spoils to be divided up would be too poor.

8. They hold back from the struggle against traditionalism and make common cause with the priests to target us alone, the Interventionist revolutionaries.

9. They devalue our victory, ignoring the fact that it lifts everyone morally, rich and poor alike.

We ask the official socialists:

1. Are you ready—as we are—to liberate Italy from the Papacy?
2. Are you willing to sell off our artistic heritage to fund the poorer classes and, in particular, proletarian artists?
3. Are you ready to abolish, once and for all, the tribunals, the police, police stations, and prisons?

If you do not have these three revolutionary aims, you are conservatives, reactionary police-State clerical archaeologists beneath your veneer of red communism.

We desire to liberate Italy from the Papacy, from the Monarchy, from the Senate, from marriage, and from Parliament. We desire a technocratic government without any parliament, supported by a council or Board of Initiatives, composed of very young men.[12] We desire the abolition of standing armies, of tribunals, of the police, and of prisons, so that our talented race can realize to the full the potential of its free, strong, hardworking, innovative, and quick-thinking individuals.

All of this we desire under the auspices of the great, loving sense of togetherness of our perfect race, in our perfect peninsula, within the compact circle of our borders, which were won and deserved through our great, utterly perfect victory.

Not only are we more revolutionary than you, the official socialists, but we have gone way beyond your revolution.

Against your immense system of egalitarian, communicating bellies,[13] your tedious ticketed refectories, we oppose our wonderful anarchic paradise of total freedom, art, ingenuity, progress, heroism, fantasy, enthusiasm, gaiety, variety, novelty, speed, and new records.

We shall have to let you first try out another experiment, which I call headlessness.

"Everybody being imbeciles so as not to suffer nor desire" is, in reality, a more egalitarian and calming ideal than the one you proclaim: "Everybody work as little as possible so that everybody can eat a little."

We have to leave you to get on with trying to destroy human intelligence, since intelligence is the primary source of inequality and of oppression. We do hope that your attempts at communism will at least have the result of destroying the new forms of inequality, which have been produced by exploitation of the war and by the principle of heredity, which we oppose just as much as you do.

We dream of a Futurist Italy, which is free, manly, flexible, expansive, drunk on progress, ready for anything—which means taking on unforeseen wars or revolutions, without standing armies, but with the maximum number of those citizens we call heroic.

We prepare these citizens through our comprehensive propaganda about intellectual freedom, sport, art, heroism, and Futurist originality.

In the name of our Futurist originality, we reject the common notion that the words "democracy," "freedom," "justice," "feminism," and so on, are formulas that can simply be applied universally.

Every country has its own particular concept of democracy. In a country overflowing with individuality and genius, such as Italy, democracy signifies quality and not quantity.

We are strongly optimistic.

The Italian blood that was spilled at Tripoli was better than that spilled at Abba Garima.[14] That spilled on the Carso was even better; that spilled on the Piave and at Vittorio Veneto, even better still.[15]

Employing the schools for physical courage,[16] which we are proposing, we want to increase the strength of Italian blood, predisposing it to every bold enterprise and an ever greater propensity for artistic creation, inventiveness, and spiritual satisfaction.

We have to heal every sort of cowardice and weakness and shape the spiritual elegance of our race, for it is the peak of its spiritual elegance—its generosity and heroism—which is the best that is to be found in a crowd in ferment.

We need to increase mankind's ability to live the ideal life of lines, of forms, of colors, of rhythms, of noises, and of sound, all combined by genius.

We might even be able to satisfy the hunger of the stomach. There will always be *some* who know how to gain for themselves the most sophisticated, privileged meals.

We need to stimulate spiritual hunger that finds satiation in great, stupendous, and joyous art.

Art is revolution, improvisation, impulse, enthusiasm, flexibility, elegance, generosity, a superabundance of kindness, being lost in the Absolute, the struggle against chains, a carefree dance upon the burning peaks of passion, the destruction of old ruins before the gods of speed, openings to be made, hunger and thirst for the sky . . . joyous airplanes greedy for the infinite . . .

There are human masses lost in darkness, spineless, blind, without light, hope, or will.

We shall drag them along with us.

There are some souls who fight with no sense of generosity, but rather to win a place on a pedestal, a laurel crown, or rank and status.

We shall convert these petty souls to aspiring to an elevated spiritual elegance.

We have to inspire everyone to think, to create, to awaken, to renew, and we have to discourage in everyone the tendency to endure, to conserve, or to plagiarize.

While the last remaining religions are in their death throes, Art must become the ideal nourishment to console and reanimate the most restless races, dissatisfied and deluded as they are by the eventual collapse of so many ideal yet insufficient banquets.

Nothing but the heady alcohol of art can finally eliminate and take the place of the tedious, vulgar, and destructive alcohol of the proletariat's Sunday taverns.

Thus, in my hilarious tragedy *King Guzzle,* the artistically innovatory dynamism of the Idiot-Poet, who is scorned by the mob, is fused with the revolutionary dynamism of the libertarian Big-Guts, so as to propose, as a unique solution to mankind's universal problem, all power to Art and to revolutionary Artists.[17]

Yes! Artists in power! The vast proletariat of talented people will rule.[18]

The most ignored yet the most worthy of all proletariats. Everybody is exhausted and disillusioned. But the Artist does not give up. Before long, his genius will cause huge roses of cheerful, purifying, and calming artistic power to blossom forth over Italy and the world.

In government, the proletariat of talented people will make free theater for all a reality as well as the great Futurist Theater of the Skies.[19] Music will reign throughout the world. Every square will have its orchestra and its choir. Everywhere, therefore, there will be fountains of harmony that, day and night, will sparkle with musical genius and embellish the sky, thus bringing color and refinement, vitality and freshness to the harsh, dark, stale, and brutal rhythm of daily life. In place of night work we shall have night art. Groups of musicians will perform, one after another, so as to increase a hundredfold the splendor of the days and the sweetness of the nights.

The proletariat of talented people will alone have the expertise to undertake the gradual, worldwide sale of our artistic heritage, in accordance with the bill outlined by us nine years ago.[20] This spiritual grain and fuel will generate admiration for us, even among the coarsest of peoples.

Our museums, when sold to the world, will become powerful reminders overseas of our Italian genius.

The proletariat of talented people, with the help of industrial technology, will arrive at that optimum salary and that minimum of manual labor which, without decreasing production, will permit all intelligences the freedom to think, to create, and to enjoy the arts.

In every town, a Palace or House of Talent will be constructed for *Open Exhibitions of Creative Talent*.[21]

1. Paintings, sculptures, all kinds of art, architectural designs, blueprints for machines and proposals for inventions will be on display for a month.
2. Large or small musical compositions, for piano or orchestra, of any sort whatsoever, will be performed there.
3. Poetry, prose, writings on all the sciences, of all types and lengths, will be read, displayed, and performed.
4. Works of all types and qualities will be exhibited or read, free of charge and without being formally judged, no matter how absurd, idiotic, mad, or immoral they may appear to be.

The Futurist revolution that will bring artists to power promises no earthly paradise. It will certainly not be able to suppress human torment, which is the upward-driving force of the race. The artists who are the untiring ventilators of this restless toil will succeed in reducing the pain.

They will resolve the problem of well-being in the only way possible, which is spiritually.

Art must not be a balm but an alcohol.[22] But not the alcohol that brings oblivion; rather that of uplifting optimism, which turns young men into gods, increases maturity a hundredfold, and rejuvenates old age.

This intellectual art-alcohol must be in profuse supply for all. In this way, we shall multiply the number of creative artists. We shall have a perfect race made up almost entirely of artists. In Italy, we shall have a million intuitive prophets, hell-bent on solving the problem of collective human happiness. An assault as awe-inspiring as this can only end in victory. We shall have an artistic solution to the social problem.

In the meantime, we are intent on greatly extending the people's propensity for dreaming and to shape it in an entirely practical sense.

Satisfying every need gives pleasure. Yet every pleasure has its limits.

At the limits of pleasure, dreams begin. What we are concerned with is regulating dreams and preventing them from becoming nostalgia for the infinite or a hatred of what is finite. The dream has to envelop and caress pleasure, to perfect and idealize it.

Each mind must have its own palette and its own instrument, to color and accompany everything with music, even the most humble acts in life.

The daily round is too burdensome, austere, monotonous, materialistic, stifling, and, if not quite choking, then at very least congested.

While we await the completion of our Futurist Theater of the Skies, we propose a huge program of free daily concerts, to be given in every part of the city, as well as cinemas, reading rooms, books, and newspapers, all absolutely free. We shall expand the spiritual life of the people and increase a hundredfold their capacity for dreaming.

Thanks to us, a time will come in which life will not be simply a matter of bread and toil, nor of idle existence, but *a work of art*.

Every man will live out the best possible vision he has in him. The most talented spirits will live out their best possible poem. There will be no competitions catering for greedy or status-seeking individuals. Men will vie with one another in lyrical inspiration, originality, musical refinement, surprise, happiness, and spiritual openness.

We shall not have a paradise on Earth, but the economic inferno will be made more cheerful, less stressful, by an unending number of art festivals.

In this manifesto I have condensed some of the ideas I expounded in my essay *Futurist Democracy*, which was published a year ago, and in my lecture "The Necessity and Beauty of Violence," which I delivered on June 26, 1910, at the Labor Exchange in Naples and subsequently published in *La propaganda* in Naples and in *L'internazionale* in Parma,[23] because today I feel there is an urgent need for their resolute and effective diffusion.

This essay was written during the twenty-one days of Marinetti's incarceration in the San Vittore prison in Milan, following his arrest (together with that of Benito Mussolini, Ferruccio Vecchi, and Piero Bolzon) on November 20, 1919, for their "attack on State security and organization of armed bands." It appeared in the newspaper *La testa di ferro* of August 15, 1920, and as a brochure published by the same journal. It was reprinted, with some textual variations, in *Futurismo e facismo* (1924) and *Marinetti e il futurismo* (1929).

64

❦

To Every Man, a New Task Every Day!: Inequality and the Artocracy

I wished to consult my favorite counselor, the Sea,[1] about the extremely complex knot of social and political problems that trouble the world.

First I spoke to her from high above, standing against the parapet of a serene, floating terrace, seeming almost to be flying, so far did it protrude above the turbulent swell.

I dominated my counselor, an immense, blue arc of sea, a third of the Earth's circumference. Agave trees, cactuses, palm trees, and Camerus leaned out with me to embrace that expanse of sea, with its plowed furrows, a desert furrowed by the trails of caravanners.

The sea answered me by giving birth to speeding motorboats, resembling flatirons amid liquid laces and embroidered waves. Steamboats, bristling with metal cranes, like jetties come adrift and voyaging. Servile sails begging the wind. Fishing boats belegged with oars, sweating and dripping.

Not very satisfied with these sibylline answers, I went down among the rocks and leapt into the seething foam of the sea, feeling like a drunken man's thoughts bobbing about in a glass of champagne.

Going in headfirst, I became aware of the dissimilarities between fishes, crabs, jellyfish, and algae, the artistic games of the sun's rays and reflections, the childish seesawing of the current's undertow, the untiring pumping of water on the veins and muscles of my darting body, and all the keen smells—sour fresh bitter—that wrangle with the velvety bittersweet of figs cooked by the sun.

The wind excites my palate and, as I swim, mouth open, I have a foretaste of a splendid cluster of a sailing ship with swelling sails on the horizon. I swim on. It gets bigger. I swim faster. The sailing ship becomes gigantic and dominates, with the solemnity of a cathedral, the communism of waves that compose the arc of the sea.

A deceptive communism with very few binding ideas that weigh heavily on the tortured and torturing quibbling of thousands upon thousands of new ideas about to be born.[2]

I reach the ship, clamber up its swaying mainmast, then like an acrobatic cabin boy amid the topmost sails, I check the copper rings, the groaning pulleys, and the folds of coarse canvas. I look down from on high at the swollen-sail people, at nurses' breasts, at bellies going mad, at bundles of parachutes. Ambitions, dropsies, pregnancies?

I don't know. I couldn't care less, as I whistle above this seaquake, earthquake of sails, domes of a thousand crumbling religions.

A flash of lightning, Gothic monk of the last embers, kneels before them on the sea.

But the winds buffet the ship, playing with the rounded sails, ivory balls on a very wobbly green billiard table.

I sing like a carefree cabin boy:

> *Away with equality!*
> *Away with justice!*
> *Away with fraternity!*
> *Whores they are, O Freedom,*
> *Leave them and rise with me!*

I shall not go down to swab the decks. The waves sweep and swill them better than I. I have better things to do!

I have no sense of fraternity with the waves. There is no justice between us! I'm just a simple cabin boy, it's true; but let the captain try—if he wants—to order me to furl the highest sails.[3] They are putting the balance of the ship in jeopardy, I know! But I want them full and swelling! What joy, what joy, what joy it is rolling to the right, then to the left, in danger, down, down!

Away with equality! Indeed, I am the equal of no man. I am unique. An inimitable model. Don't you copy me! Plagiarizing clouds! That's enough! I know every one of your shapes. I have catalogued them all. Originality! Fantasy!

Away with justice! I am the only inattentive judge of the unbounded tribunal of the sea. Do you perhaps want me to condemn the waves to being slaves of the Winds, or the Waves to playing master over them? No. No. I swing back and forth on the mast like Injustice.

Look, I've already seduced the dripping, salty Winds. Spluttering their enthusiastic choruses, they yell out my song.

I sing:

> *Away with equality!*
> *Away with justice!*
> *Away with fraternity!*
> *Whores they are, O Freedom,*
> *Leave them and rise with me!*

The Winds reply:

> *Long live elegance!*
> *Long live originality!*
> *Long live exaggeration!*

I sing:

> *Away with democracy!*
> *Away with universal suffrage!*
> *Away with the Masses!*
> *Whores they are, O Liberty,*
> *Leave them and rise with me!*

The Winds reply:

> *Long live disproportion!*
> *Long live quality!*
> *Long live poetry rare!*

I sing:

> *Away with politics!*
> *Away with parliament!*
> *Away with communism!*
> *Whores they are, O Liberty,*
> *Leave them and rise with me!*

The Winds reply:

All glory to Difference! Long live Distinction! Be atypical! Unique! The strongest! The fastest! The most colorful! Hold the record for fire! Hold the record for color! The record for enthusiasm!

I would set fire to the sails to compete with the scarlet fires of the sunset.

The sunset is a painter gone mad, I know, I know!

And the sea is his crazy palette, I know, I know.

The sunset pretends, paints, deludes, I know, I know.

Long live art that deludes, which differentiates and evaluates the world! Art, our only treasure, only queen of all Variety! The only divinity!

Death to the commonplace! Death to monotony! Variety, variety, variety! Long live Inequalities, divine nectar of the Earth, the orange which I, fledgling cabin boy, hanging from the highest sail's only hook, hurl, hurl, and hurl again at the fledgling Stars.

Meanwhile, the Winds were tearing the sails to shreds, and with the skill of the windmill, turned them into paper, so that they flew up, innumerable newspapers printed in red, with large block capitals.

And in this way it finally became possible to read the new truths from one pole to the other:

Increase inequality among mankind.

Encourage originality in the individual, everywhere, and push it to the extreme.

Distinguish, evaluate, and make everything disproportionate.

Insist on variety in work.

A new task for every man, every day.[4]

Liberate workers from the soul-destroying monotony of their habitual gray toil and their usual boozy Sundays.

Humanity is dying from the leveling force of its day-to-day living.

Only inequality, by multiplying differences, light and shade, volumes, caprice, heat, and color, can save Art, Love, Poetry, the Plastic Arts, Architecture, Music, and an indispensable joie de vivre.

Destroy, indeed annihilate, politics, which clouds everything. It is an extremely stubborn leprosy-cholera-syphilis.

Quarantine, as soon as possible, all those who are infected.

Burn and bury the old, outworn, grubby ideas of Equality, Justice, Fraternity, Communism, and Internationalism.

Impose Inequality everywhere, so as to set every individual part free by separating it from the huge, heavy, muddy whole!

The ship was rocking, bearing its authoritative, parchmentlike sails, and the Winds spread everywhere and at full speed a dynamic Inequality that will bring the world to an unfailing Artocracy ere long.

This essay was published in *Il resto del Carlino* on November 1, 1922, and with the title *Inegualismo* in *Il futurismo: Rivista sintetica illustrata* on May 1, 1923. A French version appeared in *Noi* in August 1923. The Italian text was reprinted in *Futurismo e fascismo* (1924).

65

cℐ℘

Artistic Rights Defended by the Italian Futurists

MANIFESTO TO THE ITALIAN GOVERNMENT

Vittorio Veneto[1] and Fascism's rise to power[2] signal the realization of the minimal Futurist program (the maximal program is yet to be achieved) launched around fourteen years ago by a group of courageous young men who, with their persuasive arguments, challenged the entire Nation, which was humiliated by a senility and a mediocrity that lived in dread of foreigners.

This minimal program stood up for Italian pride, for a boundless faith in the future of Italians, for the destruction of the Austro-Hungarian Empire, for day-to-day heroism, for the love of danger, for the vindication of violence as a decisive argument, for the glorification of war as the sole cleanser of the world, for the religion of speed, for novelty, for optimism and originality, for our youth to rise to power and to oppose the bureaucratic, academic, and pessimistic parliamentary spirit.

Our influence in Italy and throughout the world has been—and still is—enormous. Italian Futurism, which is epitomized by its patriotism and which has generated numberless Futurisms abroad, does not necessarily share their political beliefs, e.g., the Bolshevik politics of Futurism in Russia, where Futurism has become State art.[3] Futurism is unequivocally an artistic and ideological movement. It becomes involved in politics only in time of grave peril for the Nation.[4]

We were the first among the first of the Interventionists. We were imprisoned for our Interventionism in Milan, at the time of the Battle of the Marne.[5] We were imprisoned with Mussolini for our Interventionism in Rome, on April 12, 1915.[6] We were imprisoned with Mussolini in Milan in 1919 for the Fascist attack on the security of the State and for the organization of armed bands.[7]

We set up the first Associations of Arditi and many of the early Fasci di Combattimento.[8]

Prophets and pioneers of the great Italy of today, we Futurists are only too happy to applaud in our not yet forty-year-old prime minister, a wonderful Futurist temperament.[9]

As a Futurist, Mussolini had this to say to foreign journalists:

> We are a young people who desire to create, and must create, and we refuse to be a Syndicate of hotel keepers and museum curators. Our artistic past is to be admired. But, speaking personally, I've been in a museum probably no more than a couple of times.

Recently Mussolini made this typically Futurist speech:

> The Government I have the honor to lead is a Government of speed, in the sense that we curtail everything that is redolent of stagnation in our National life. At one time, the bureaucracy slumbered over outmoded practices. Now everything has to move along at top speed. If we all maintain this same rhythm of strength, will, and cheerfulness, we shall overcome the crisis which, when all's said and done, has already been overcome in some measure. I am also happy to see the regeneration of this Rome of ours, which can show us workplaces such as this. I have absolutely no doubts that Rome can become a center of industry. The Romans must be the first to reject outright living only on their memories. The Colosseum and the Forum are glories of the past; but we must create glories for the present, and for tomorrow. Ours is the generation of builders who, with our work and the discipline of our hands and our intellects, desire to reach that far-off point, that longed-for goal of the greatness of the Nation of tomorrow, which will be the Nation of all producers, not a nation of parasites.

With Mussolini, Fascism has rejuvenated Italy. It is his task to help us bring new life to the world of art, which is still dominated by obnoxious people and organizations.

The political revolution must support the artistic revolution, which means Futurism and all other avant-gardes.

WE ASK FOR:

1. **Certain safeguards for young, innovative Italian artists** in all artistic events promoted by the State, by city councils, and by private individuals. For example:

   (a) Foreign Futurists and avant-gardists (Archipenko, Kokoschka, Campendonk)[10] were invited to the Venice Biennale, while Italian Futurists (the creators of all other Futurisms) received no such invitation. We have to root out this systematic and ignoble anti-Italianism![11]

   (b) Foreign Futurists and avant-gardists (Stravinsky, Ravel, Schoenberg, Scriabin, Schreker) are welcomed with open arms at the Augusteo,[12] while Italian Futurists and avant-gardists are ignored or turned down. We have to root out this systematic and ignoble anti-Italianism!

   (c) At La Scala (which is vouchsafed the task of presenting and glorifying new Italian musicians), they put on two of Wagner's operas every year, but none (or very very few) by young Italians. Foreign singers, who are inferior to our own, are preferred. We have to root out this systematic and ignoble anti-Italianism![13]

   (d) The Theater at Syracuse cannot be used exclusively for the glory of the Greek classics![14] We demand that, as an alternative to the presentation of classical works, a competition be mounted there to find a colorful modern drama, suitable for open-air production, by a young Sicilian, who will receive his prize and be solemnly crowned in the theater itself. (*Proposed by: Marinetti, Prampolini, Jannelli, Nicastro, Carrozza, Russolo, Mario Carli, Depero, Cangiullo, Giuseppe Steiner, Volt, Somenzi, Azari, Marasco, Dottori, Pannaggi, Tato, Caviglioni, Paladini, Raciti, Mario Shrapnel, Raimondi, G. Etna, Sortino-Bona, Cimino, Soggetti, Rognoni, Masnata, Mortari, Piero Illari, Rizzo, Soldi, Leskovic, Buzzi, [Caprile, Clerici, Casavola, Scirocco, Vasari]*).[15]

2. **Loans banks for artists** for the exclusive benefit of Italian creative artists.[16]

   Just as credit Banks are set up to aid industry and commerce, similar institutions must be created to underwrite artistic events or Institutes for Industrial Art, or to loan money to artists to assist them in their work (manuscripts, paintings, sculptures, etc.), in their educational or promotional travels.

These credit Institutions can be either privately owned (joint stock companies) or government owned (agencies and foundations). With the first option, the creation of this sort of Institution depends, to a greater or lesser extent, on the goodwill and number of participants. In the second case, the necessary capital could be guaranteed only if the State were to levy even a small yet wideranging tax on war profits, inherited wealth, and so on, or by means of a national subscription organized by the State.

The Institution would act like a bank for artists: it would accept deposits of works of art, and, on the basis of their real value, would forward subventions or make credit available.

The work of art thus deposited would have advantages for both the depositor and for the Institution itself, in that it would stimulate artistic initiatives, sales, and so on. In this way, the artist and the work of art would have a recognized value.

These Institutions could authorize loans for artistic industries and secure the use of apartment blocks as halls of residence for Art Colleges or for temporary exhibitions. (*Proposed by Prampolini, Marinetti, Russolo, Cangiullo, Depero, Settimelli, Mario Carli, Buzzi, Marasco, [Casavola].*)

3. **Defense of Italianism**

   (a) Immediate and obligatory Italianization of hotels (all captions, signs, menus, accounts, and so on, *to be written in Italian*), shops, and business correspondence. Automatic means for spreading the Italian language at no cost. (*Proposed by Marinetti, Russolo, Buzzi, Folgore, Mario Carli, Settimelli, Depero, Cangiullo, Somenzi, Marasco, Rognoni, [Casavola].*)
   (b) Italianization of the new architecture in contrast to the systematic plagiarism of foreign architectures. Begin this Italianization in all State buildings and especially in the liberated territories. (*Proposed by Virgilio Marchi, Depero, Russolo, Buzzi, Somenzi, Azari, Marasco, Prampolini, Folgore, Volt.*)[17]
   (c) Obligatory Italianization of publications and typographical characters. (*Proposed by Frassinelli, Rampa-Rossi.*)[18]

4. **Abolition of the Academies** (Art Colleges and Professional Schools).

The current teaching systems are out of step with the aesthetic requirements of an art that is in a constant process of evolution. Art cannot be taught. Those who currently receive diplomas are neither competent technicians nor artists.

All the academies will therefore be replaced by:

(a) *Free Institutes for artistic techniques* to teach the qualities of materials in relation to their different applications in art and in manual techniques, so as to produce capable workers. This is to be combined with a free choice of curricula, courses, and teachers.

(b) *Institutes for aesthetic experience* in order to spread widely a love of art, theoretically, practically, and popularly, by means of lectures, theatrical performances, recitations, exhibitions, and concerts. In the light of the justifiable decline in collecting, develop interior and exterior decorative arts in particular, through national competitions and sales exhibitions in major State buildings. (*Proposed by Prampolini, Marinetti, Russolo, Buzzi, Somenzi, and Piero Illari.*)

(c) *Abolition of the Academies* of Fine and Professional Arts with nothing replacing them. (*Proposed by Marasco.*)

5. **Italian Artistic Propaganda Abroad** *through the auspices of a National Institute for Artistic Propaganda Abroad,* which will oversee the artistic and economic interests of Italian artists.

This Institute must be directed by young artists who have an international reputation and who will promote innovative Italian talent in a true Italian manner. It will have *permanent commissions relating to the various arts* and offices in all the major art centers abroad. It will operate through lectures, concerts, exhibitions, and journals dedicated to such propaganda. (*Proposed by Prampolini, Russolo, Buzzi, Volt, and Marasco.*)

6. **Free Art Competitions.** Use some of the funds the State currently spends on art in establishing competitions for poetry, the plastic arts, architecture, and music, to be reserved for young people under twenty-five and to be judged by means of popular referendums. (*Proposed by Balla, Marinetti, and Marasco.*)

7. **Assign the Organization of National and Local Celebrations** (parades, sports competitions, etc.) to groups of avant-garde Italian

artists who have already demonstrated their undoubted innovative talents, the source of that optimism which is indispensable to the country's health. (*Proposed by Depero, Azari, Marinetti, and Marasco.*)

8. Financial Assistance for Artists:

(a) Legal recognition, by the government, of *authors' copyright* for people working in the fine arts, *based on the highest price reached by their work, in successive sales*, managed by an institution similar to the Society for Authors.

(b) A single tariff for transportation abroad, established not in relation to weight but rather on the length of the journey. Fix a *maximum weight* and on this basis regulate the cost.

(c) A reduction of 75 percent for *the transport of works of art* and on *the cost of the journey for the artist*.

(d) Abolition of international customs duties for the import and export of works of modern art. (*Proposed by Prampolini, Depero, Azari, Marasco, Marinetti, and Volt.*)

(e) Arrange for *notes of hand* and *insurance* to be the responsibility of the carrier of works of art (railways, shipping lines, and so on), otherwise only the artist who can afford it makes use of such guarantees. (*Proposed by Prampolini and Marasco.*)

9. **Advisory Technical Councils** made up of artists and elected by artists, a proportionate number with avant-garde tendencies. These Advisory Technical Councils will be entrusted with looking after artists' interests in their dealings with State and local institutions, private organizations, and the artists themselves. (*Proposed by Prampolini, Marasco, and Volt.*)

10. **Proportionate Representation.** The Italian artistic avant-garde must be invited to participate, with proportionate representation, in all State, local, and private artistic events and responsibilities. (*Proposed by Prampolini, Marasco, Marinetti, and Volt.*)

11. **An International Consortium** to safeguard the artistic and economic interests of avant-garde artists. This Consortium should think about the centralization of the best avant-garde artistic institutes, thereby serving the interests of solidarity and protection,

as well as artistic and economic publicity. (*Proposed by Prampolini, Marasco, Marinetti, and Volt.*)

FOR THE DIRECTORATE OF THE FUTURIST MOVEMENT

AND FOR ALL ITALIAN FUTURIST GROUPS.[19]

F. T. MARINETTI

A first version of this manifesto originates from 1919, when the Futurists were in close alliance with the Fascists and were making plans for the time when their coalition would form the new Italian government. The key proposals were subsequently presented by Enrico Prampolini at the Düsseldorf Congress of Avant-garde Art in May 1922. The version translated here was first published in *Il futurismo: Rivista sintetica illustrata mensile* (March 1, 1923); then in the Futurist-Fascist newspaper *L'impero* on March 11, 1923; in Prampolini's art magazine, *Noi* (April 1923), and in Marinetti's *Futurismo e fascismo* (1924). The version in *Il futurismo* and *L'impero* contained a P.S.: "This program was personally put forward by Marinetti to the President of the Council, who approved it fully." The later editions were introduced with a letter from Mussolini: "My dear Marinetti, I wholeheartedly approve your initiative regarding the creation of a Credit Bank set up specially for Artists. I am sure you'll find a way around the objections the habitual stick-in-the-muds are likely to raise. Anyhow, with this letter comes my blessing. Cheers, in friendship, Mussolini."

THE RETURN TO THE ARTISTIC
DOMAIN (1920–33)

After the end of hostilities and the return of most soldiers from the war, Italy was plunged into a two-year crisis. Yet despite the political turmoil and the social unrest, people had a desperate need for entertainment. The Futurists re-presented themselves to the country in an artistic capacity in a national exhibition held at the Cova Gallery in Milan (March–April 1919) and also began to publicize their latest works in the fields of literature, theater, music, and so on. At that time, Marinetti's prime focus was on political matters, but other Futurists set up some memorable ventures, such as the Bal Tic-Tac and the Cabaret Diavolo.

After the disappointing results of the November elections, and after twenty-one days spent in prison, Marinetti decided to withdraw from politics and to concentrate again on his artistic career. It was not only disappointment with his Fascist comrades that made him want to "[d]estroy, indeed annihilate politics, which clouds everything. It is an extremely stubborn leprosy-cholera-syphilis" (see document 64). He also discovered—at the age of forty—the power of love. In 1919, he made the acquaintance of Benedetta Cappa, and by 1920 this love affair was changing his life. During a summer holiday in Antignano, he felt like Amerigo Vespucci on the verge of discovering new continents—in his private life as well as in artistic matters.

Marinetti's writings suddenly abound with words such as "pleasure," "joie de vivre," and "sensuality." He rekindled the old discussion on the relationship between art and life and developed a program for organizing Futurist creativity in the everyday sphere. And in autumn 1920 it seemed as if his old dream of an Italian Revolution was at last going to come true. The occupation of the factories, which started in September 1920, appeared to ring in a new era. For the next two years, Marinetti located new coalition partners in the recently founded Communist Party and worked with them towards a union of political and artistic revolutionaries. Many of the younger members of the Futurist movement cooperated with the young socialists and communists in joint initiatives that had much in common with the KOMFUTS (Communist Futurists) in Russia. But after Gramsci's departure from Italy in summer 1922, the hard-line supporters of Amadeo Bordiga clamped down on these initiatives and imposed a political aesthetic that left no space for avant-garde experiments.

Marinetti's political disillusionment became even more acute after the Fascists' March on Rome and Mussolini's appointment to the post of Prime Minister on October 30, 1922. A new brand of Fascism that had only the name in common with the movement Marinetti had supported in 1919 established law and order in the political and artistic spheres. Marinetti, who had resigned from the Fasci di Combattimento on May 29, 1920, was extremely worried about the new developments and even more so when it became clear that Mussolini was actively obliterating the memory of his former alliance with the Futurists. The Duce's artistic preferences became public when, in 1923, he opened the first exhibition of the conservative Novecento group in Rome. From then on, traditionalists were given positions of honor while Futurists were pushed to the margins. Marinetti's artistic policies of the years 1923 to 1930 were characterized by an often desperate desire to gain recognition by the new regime. He undertook several attempts to present himself as a major figure in the Italian cultural landscape. In 1924, he issued a manifesto, *Le futurisme mondiale*, that portrayed Futurism as a movement of significant influence on the international avant-garde. A national congress in his honor, the *Onoranze a F. T. Marinetti animatore d' italianità* of November 23, 1924, propagated his role in the Interventionist movement, the Great War, and the postwar revitalization of Italian culture. And a collection of essays, *Futurismo e fascismo*, presented Futurism as an integral element of Fascism's rise to power. The Duce responded with granting Marinetti formal favors, such as appointing him secretary of the Writers' Union (1928) and member of the Italian Academy (1929), but otherwise, Futurists were given scant consideration in the allocation of posts and emoluments and were forced to exploit the niches in the Italian art market to sell their wares and make a living.

Compared to the international avant-garde, Futurism was no longer truly original and innovative, but in the increasingly stifling political climate of the peninsula, many of its products still offered a rare breath of fresh air. Consequently, as far as the Fascist leaders and bureaucrats were concerned, the Futurists were "as welcome in the Fascist temples of art as dogs in a church" (Enzo Benedetto).

The 1930s was the period of Aero-Futurism and found a fairly sympathetic response from the art-interested population. But after Mussolini's alliance with Nazi Germany, the most traditionalist and reactionary *gerarchi* gained the upper hand in the Fascist cultural bureaucracy. Marinetti fought against the concept of degenerate art, against the burning of books and works of art, against political censorship and anti-Semitism. But the support he received from other artists made little impression on the Fascist hard-liners. In January 1939 they shut down the Futurist paper *Artecrazia* and, with it, Futurism as a viable artistic movement.

66

❧

What Is Futurism?: Elementary Lessons

IN LIFE, A FUTURIST IS:

1. Anyone who loves life, energy, joy, freedom, progress, courage, novelty, practicality, and speed.
2. Anyone who acts quickly, energetically, and does not hesitate out of cowardice.
3. Anyone who, caught between two possible decisions, prefers the more generous, the bolder one, provided it offers a greater perfection and development of the individual and his people.
4. Anyone who acts joyously, with his eye always on tomorrow, without remorse, splitting hairs, false modesty, rejecting all mysticisms and melancholy.
5. Anyone who is flexible enough to move, in a carefree manner, from the most serious matters to the most pleasurable pastimes.
6. Anyone who loves the open-air life, sport, and gymnastics, and pays close attention to the strength and agility of his own body, every day.
7. Anyone capable of delivering a punch or a knockout blow, at just the right moment, and who admires the Arditi[1] and emulates them in his actions.

IN POLITICS, A FUTURIST IS:

1. Anyone who cares for the progress of Italy more than for himself.
2. Anyone who wishes to abolish the papacy, parliamentarianism, the senate, and the bureaucracy.
3. Anyone who desires the abolition of conscription and the standing army, replacing them with a voluntary force,[2] and the creation of a strong, vigorous, industrious, entirely free democracy, empty of all utopias and senile attitudes, and which is equally capable of staging a war or purging itself through revolution.
4. Anyone who through the abolition of the present police force wishes to modernize and improve all public-order institutions and encourage citizens to take charge of their own personal defense.
5. Anyone who wishes to hand over the government of Italy to the young soldiers who secured our tremendous victory.
6. Anyone who wishes to expropriate all uncultivated or badly cultivated land, bit by bit, thereby preparing for the distribution of land to its workers.
7. Anyone who wants to abolish every kind of industrial and capitalistic exploitation.
8. Anyone who wishes to ensure that all workers are adequately recompensed for their productive efforts.
9. Anyone who loves and desires every kind of freedom, apart from the freedom to be a coward, an exploiter, or anti-Italian.

IN ART, A FUTURIST IS:

1. Anyone who thinks and expresses himself with originality, strength, liveliness, enthusiasm, clarity, simplicity, agility, and concision.
2. Anyone who loathes ruins, museums, cemeteries, libraries, cultural snobbery, the authority of professors, academicism, imitation of the past, purisms, matters long drawn out, and punctiliousness.
3. Anyone who rejects tragedies and plays performed in a hushed atmosphere and instead prefers the café-concert, where the audience smokes, laughs, and joins in with the actors, lightheartedly, free of dreariness and boredom.
4. Anyone who wants to modernize, revive, and brighten up Italian art, freeing it from imitation of the past, from traditionalism and

academicism, and encouraging all the most audacious creations of the young artist.[3]

Marinetti wrote several definitions of Futurism. A first version of this text, arranged in a discursive rather than bullet-point format, appeared with the same title on the leaflet *Il futurismo: Supplemento alla rassegna internazionale "Poesia"* (1910), which announced the *serata* at the Fenice Theater in Venice. The 1919 version, translated here, updates the *Manifesto of the Futurist Political Party* (document 45) for the changed realities of postwar Italy. The text was printed on the back page of most issues of *Roma futurista*, nos. 7–42 (February 14 to October 12, 1919), in *Dimamo* no. 1 (February 1919), and as a leaflet in 1920. A 1921 edition of the leaflet reduced the second section from nine to six points and eliminated the list of branches of the Futurist Political Party in the Postscript not translated here. Another version, consisting of Sections 1 and 3, can be found in the exhibition catalogs *Bologna: Teatro Modernissimo*, January 1922, and *Turin: Winter Club*, March–April 1922. An English translation of Section 3 followed by Section 1 was published in the first (and only) number of the New York journal *Futurist Aristocracy*, dated April 1923.

67

☙

Tactilism: A Futurist Manifesto

Full stop. New paragraph.[1]

Futurism, founded by us in Milan in 1909, gave the world a hatred of Museums, of Academies, and of Sentimentalism; and in their place it proposed Action-Art; defense of youth against every kind of senility; the glorification of illogical, crazy, innovative talent; artistic sensibility for machines and speed, for the Variety Theater,[2] and for the simultaneous intermingling of modern life experiences;[3] Words-in-Freedom;[4] plastic dynamism;[5] the Noise Machines;[6] and the Theater of Essential Brevity.[7] Today Futurism is redoubling its creative efforts.

Last summer, at Antignano, at the point where via Amerigo Vespucci—named after the discoverer of the Americas[8]—curves along the coastline, I invented Tactilism.[9] In the workshops, which were occupied by their workers, the red flags were fluttering.[10]

I was naked in the silken waters lacerated by foaming rocks, sharp-edged like scissors knives razors, swimming among beds of seaweed saturated with iodine. I was naked in a sea of flexible steel, rippling against my body in an animated, manly, fertile fashion. I drank from the sea's cup, which was filled to the very brim with genius. The sun, with its long blistering flames, vulcanized my body and bolted the keel of my brow, in full sail.

A girl from the common people, who smelled of salt and hot stones, smiled when she looked at my first tactile panels: "You're enjoying yourself making your little boats, aren't you!"

I answered her:

"Yes, I'm building a boat that will bear the human spirit toward unknown regions."

These were my reflections as I swam in the waters:

The simple, untutored majority came out of the Great War with only one thing on their minds—how to achieve greater material well-being for themselves.

However, the minority, made up of artists and thinkers, who are sensitive and refined, show signs of a deep, inexplicable unease, which is probably a consequence of the huge, tragic exertion that the war demanded of humanity.

The symptoms of this malady are a depressing lassitude, a womanish hysteria, a hopeless pessimism, a nervous lack of decision, of instincts all awry, and a total lack of willpower.

The simple, untutored majority throws itself impulsively into the revolutionary conquest of a communist paradise, and makes a final assault on the problem of happiness, convinced it will solve it by satisfying all material needs and appetites.[11]

The intellectual minority ironically scorns this tiresome endeavor, and having lost its taste for Religion, Art, and Love, which at one time were its privilege and refuge, is now attacking life itself, which it can no longer enjoy, and is indulging in the most rarefied sorts of pessimism, in homosexuality and artificial paradises[12] such as cocaine, opium, ether, and so on.

The majority and the minority turn their backs on Progress, Civilization, the mechanical Power of Speed, Comfort, Health—in short, on Futurism, believing them to be responsible for all their past, present, and future misfortunes.

Almost all of them are calling for a return to a primitive, contemplative, slow, solitary life, far away from the accursed cities.

However, we Futurists are valiantly facing up to the heartrending dramas of these postwar years,[13] we support all the revolutionary insurrections the majority will attempt. But to the minority of artists and thinkers, we cry out in a loud voice:

"Life is always right! The illusory paradises that you believe will eradicate all hardship are a waste of time. Stop this absurd dreaming about a return to the primitive life. Be on your guard against condemning the higher forces in society and the wonders of speed. Rather, you should be trying to cure this postwar malaise,[14] by giving humanity new, nourishing pleasures. Instead of destroying everything man has created, you should be perfecting it. Intensify communication and association among human beings. Break down the distances and barriers that separate them in love and friendship. Give fullness and total beauty to these two vital aspects of life, Love and Friendship."

From my careful, unconventional observations of all the erotic and sentimental factors that unite the two sexes, and of the no less complex features of friendship, I have realized that human beings speak to one another with their mouths and their eyes, but that they never quite manage to be totally sincere, because of the insensibility of skin, which is ever a poor conductor of thoughts.

While two individuals can communicate their most intimate selves by means of eyes and voices, the sense of touch conveys almost nothing when they bump into each other, wrap themselves around, or stroke one another.

From this it follows that we need to transform the handshake, the kiss, the coupling into a continuous communication of thoughts.

I have begun by subjecting my own sense of touch to an intensive education, pinpointing vague notions of will and thought at different places on my body and especially the palms of my hands. This kind of education is slow, but easy, and through such tutoring all healthy bodies can attain surprising and precise results.

Underdeveloped sensibilities, on the other hand, which draw their excitability and their apparent fulfillment from the very weakness of their bodies, will arrive at the great tactile power less readily, spasmodically, and hesitantly.

I have created an initial learning scale for touch, which is at the same time a scale of tactile values for Tactilism, or the Art of Touch.

FIRST LEVEL OF THE LEARNING SCALE, USING FOUR CATEGORIES OF TOUCH

First category: very sure, abstract, cold touch.
Sandpaper
Silver paper

Second category: touch without heat, persuasive, reasoning.
Smooth silk
Crimped silk (crêpe)

Third category: exciting, luke-warm, nostalgic.
Velvet
Pyrenean wool
Wool
Silk-wool crêpe

Fourth category: almost irritating, warm, willful.
Granular silk
Woven silk
Spongy material

SECOND LEVEL OF LEARNING SCALE, USING VOLUMES

Fifth category: soft, warm, human.
Suede
Horse or dog hair
Human hair and body hair
Maribou (soft, fluffy material)

Sixth category: warm, sensual, light-hearted, affectionate. This category has two divisions:

Coarse iron	Plush (*Peluche*)
Soft brush	Fluffy body hair or peach bloom
Sponge	Eider down
Wire brush	

By means of these distinctions between tactile values, I have created:

1. THE SIMPLE TACTILE PANELS

These I shall present to the public in conferences, or, rather, *contactilations,* on the Art of Touch.

I have organized the previously listed tactile categories into carefully classified harmonious or antithetical combinations.

2. ABSTRACT OR EVOCATIVE TACTILE PANELS (JOURNEYS WITH THE HANDS)

The tactile qualities of these panels have been arranged in a manner that will allow the hands to wander along colored tracks, thus making the user conscious of a succession of suggestive sensations, whose finely tuned rhythms are by turns languid, modulated, or tumultuous.

One of these abstract tactile panels, which I have devised and named *Sudan-Paris,*[15] contains, in the *Sudan* section, coarse, oily, rough, prickly, stinging tactile qualities (absorbent materials, sponge, sandpaper, wool, brushes, wire brushes). In the *Sea* section it has tactile values such as slippery, metallic, cool (silver paper), while in the *Paris* section, its tactile attributes are soft, very delicate, caressing, warm, and cold at the same time (silk, velvet, feathers, and goose down).

3. TACTILE PANELS FOR THE DIFFERENT SEXES

In these tactile panels, the arrangement of tactile qualities allows the hands of a man and a woman, moving in harmony, to pursue and evaluate their tactile journey together.

These tactile panels are extremely varied. The pleasure they provide is enhanced by the unexpected, just as with two rival sensibilities that will make a great effort to feel more keenly, and explain more clearly, their competing sensations.

These tactile panels are destined to take the place of the mind-deadening game of chess.

4. TACTILE CUSHIONS

5. TACTILE SOFAS

6. TACTILE BEDS

7. TACTILE SHIRTS AND CLOTHES

8. TACTILE ROOMS

In these tactile rooms we shall have floors and walls made from great tactile panels. Tactile qualities for mirrors, running water, stones, metals, brushes, low-voltage wires, marble, velvet, and carpets will afford different sensations to barefooted dancers of both sexes.

9. TACTILE STREETS

10. TACTILE THEATERS

We shall have theaters specifically designed for Tactilism.[16] The audience will place their hands on long, tactile conveyor belts which will produce tactile sensations that have different rhythms. One will also be able to mount these panels on turntables and operate them to the accompaniment of music and lights.

11. TACTILE PANELS FOR IMPROVISED WORDS-IN-FREEDOM

The Tactilist will announce the different tactile sensations that he experiences during the journey made by his hands. His improvisation will take the form of Words-in-Freedom, which have no fixed rhythms, prosody, or syntax. These improvisations will be succinct and to the point, and as nonhuman[17] as possible.

The improvising Tactilist can be blindfolded, but it would be better if he were submerged in the light of a projector. The eyes of members of the audience, who are new to Tactilism and have not yet had any tactile training, will be blindfolded.

As far as experienced Tactilists are concerned, the bright light of a projector is preferable, since complete darkness has the disadvantage of concentrating the sensibilities unduly on superfluous abstractions.

Tactile Education

1. One should wear gloves for many days, and in that time the brain will focus one's desires on different tactile sensations in the hands.
2. Swim underwater, in the sea, trying to distinguish by touch the mingling currents and different temperatures.
3. Every night, in total darkness, count and be aware of all the objects in your bedroom. It was precisely through this exercise, in the subterranean darkness of a trench in Gorizia, in 1917,[18] that I first experimented with Tactilism.

I have never claimed to have invented tactile sensibility, which was already present in extremely imaginative forms in *La Jongleuse* and *Hors nature* by Rachilde.[19] Other writers and artists have previously been vaguely aware of Tactilism.[20] Moreover, plastic art of touch has been in existence for a long time. My great friend Boccioni, the Futurist painter and sculptor, was effectively a Tactilist when, in 1911, he created his assemblage *Fusion of a Head and a Window* with materials that were totally different as regards weight and tactile value: iron, porcelain, and female hair.[21]

The Tactilism that I have created is an art that is totally distinct from the plastic arts. It has nothing to do with, and nothing to gain from, painting or sculpture, but has everything to lose by being associated with them.

We must avoid, as much as possible, the use of any color on the tactile panels, as this would create impressions more in keeping with the plastic arts. Painters and sculptors, who naturally enough tend to subordinate tactile values to visual ones, are unlikely to have the gift for creating tactile panels of any significance. Tactilism seems to me to be particularly suited to young poets, pianists, typists, and all those with sophisticated and forceful erotic temperaments.

Nevertheless, Tactilism must avoid any sort of collaboration with the plastic arts, as well as any association with pathological erotomania. It must strive toward nothing but tactile harmonies, contributing only indirectly to the perfect spiritual communication between human beings through the epidermis. Distinguishing only five senses is purely arbitrary. One day we shall undoubtedly be able to discover and record many others. Tactilism will encourage such discoveries.

The ideas contained in this manifesto were first communicated in a speech given at the Théâtre de l'Œuvre on January 15, 1921, and published in *Commœdia* on January 16, 1921. An Italian version, dated January 11, 1921, was published as a four-page leaflet on April 20, 1921. The flier *Italian Futurism in 1921* mentions as subsequent venues for the speech Geneva, Rome, Milan, Genoa, Palermo, Messina, Cagliari, Sassari, and others.

68

_❧_

Tactilism:
Toward the Discovery of New Senses

I

In January 1921 I presented my first tactile panels to an intellectual public, at the Théâtre de l'Œuvre in Paris.[1] These panels, which represented my first forays into tactile art, which I invented, were premised on a harmonious combination of tactile values. Since the resounding success of that lecture,[2] I have intensified my research and my endeavors.

Before revealing my findings to my readers, I think it would be a good idea if I explained the origins of my invention.

In both literature and the plastic arts, a sense of the tactile has been in existence for a very long time. My great friend Boccioni, the Futurist painter and sculptor, had tactile sensations when, in 1911, he created his assemblage _Fusion of a Head and a Window_, with materials that were absolute tactile opposites in terms of weight and other qualities: iron, porcelain, and female hair. This assemblage, he told me, was made not only to be seen but to be touched as well. One night during the winter of 1917, without a candle, I felt my way down into the subterranean darkness of the trench where my battalion was billeted, to get to my pallet. I was trying not to bump into things, but I tripped against bayonets, mess tins, and the heads of sleeping soldiers. I lay down, but I couldn't sleep, for I was preoccupied by the tactile sensations I had just experienced and logged in my mind. That night was the first time I thought in terms of a tactile art.[3]

II

Just suppose the Sun leaves its orbit and forgets about the Earth! Utter darkness. Men blundering into one another. Utter terror. Then, the beginnings of a vague sense of security settling in. Caution from the epidermis. Life feeling its way. Having attempted to create artificial lights, men become used to the darkness. They feel a respect for the nocturnal animals. Dilation of human pupils, which react to the tiny amount of light present in the darkness. The attentive powers of the optic nerve are built up.

A visual sense is born at the tips of fingers.

An intervisionary sense develops, and some people can already see inside their bodies. Others dimly perceive the interiors of nearby bodies. Everyone feels that sight, smell, hearing, touch, and taste are but modifications of one very active sense, namely that of touch, split in different ways and localized at different points.

Other localizations are necessary. And here they are. The center of the abdomen can see. The knees can see. Elbows can see. Everyone admires the variations in speed that differentiate light from sound.

The new art form could thus be born spontaneously—the Tactilism which it seems we have created with an act of Futurist whim-faith-will.

We are convinced that Tactilism will have many practical uses, in the training of surgeons with hands that see and by offering new means of educating the mentally retarded.

The Futurist Balla maintains that through Tactilism everyone can enjoy the sensations of his past life all over again, with total freshness and sense of surprise, in a way that would not be quite possible through music or painting.[4]

Exactly. Yet we are going much further.

We are familiar with the hypotheses about the essence of matter. Through that extremely convincing hypothesis, which posits that matter resembles electronic systems operating in harmony, we have come to reject any distinction between spirit and matter.

When feeling a piece of iron, we say, "This is iron," and we are satisfied with a word, and ask for nothing more. Yet between the iron and the hand, there is a conflict involving less than conscious force-thoughts-feelings. Maybe there is more thought at the tips of the fingers and in the iron than in the brain that arrogantly observes the phenomenon.

With Tactilism, we intend to penetrate better the true essence of matter without having recourse to scientific methods.

Senses not yet defined

The five senses that are already known, defined, and studied, more or less scholastically, are more or less arbitrary, localized phenomena belonging to that confusion of interlacing senses that constitute the characteristic, driving forces of the human machine.

I believe that these forces can be better observed at the epidermic frontiers of our bodies. It is for this reason that I give the name "Tactilism" to that knot of senses that has yet to be determined.

It is my intention to identify a few of them:

1. *The sense of absurd equilibrium.* In addition to the sense of mechanical equilibrium, which is a characteristic of the human body and which is to be explained through the laws of mechanics, there is also a mysterious absurd equilibrium—by which we mean an unconscious reserve of equilibrium which is manifested when the mechanical equilibrium breaks down.

   Runners, soccer players, boxers, and wrestlers are well acquainted with this absurd equilibrium that can intervene and save them from a fall which, in mechanical terms, would be entirely logical. This absurd equilibrium is to be observed in the tremendous straining of a cart horse.

2. *The sense of orientation when airborne.* This sense is beginning to emerge with the development of aviation. There are airmen who are able to pinpoint their whereabouts without a compass, and even in the thickest of fogs.

3. *Tactile sense at a distance.* This goes by the name of presentiment. It would be better called pre-sensation: to speak about someone or something, then to see them appear not long after, or to cry out before having bumped into some resistant object in the dark.

4. *Shoulder sense.* This tactile sense, at a distance, is undoubtedly centered in the shoulders. Human beings who are very well protected at the front of the body (eyes, hands, nails) have, in the shoulders, a more or less developed sense that warns them of the approach of friend or foe. This sense is particularly well developed in thieves and, in general, among all those who are threatened by arrest or death.

   In animals, and especially the cat family, it becomes a sensation in their backs. This can be observed in a cat in a darkened room.

5. *Tactile sense of physical identity.* This sense may only be observed in

rare moments, when it reveals itself as a result of extreme physical tiredness or lethargy brought on by sleep.

6. *Target sense.* Or sights of the human rifle. The end point of an ideal line that is followed by our striking fists in a fight.

7. *Musical sense* or physiological sense of timing. The point of contact between our skin and the infinite-time-space that enfolds us. It could also be called sense of bodily rhythm. This sense seeks to harmonize our bodies with the earth's rhythms and the rhythms of the planets. Sometimes one becomes aware of this sense of timing in a fight when, quite illogically, we feel the moment has arrived to deliver our punch. The same sense is also experienced during a swift descent from a high mountain.

8. *Sense of a strength beyond fatigue.* Excessive work generates a new strength. Creative artists are aware of it in moments of extreme mental stress.

9. *The physical sense of speed.* A bodily sense which measures the different ruptures of the air we pass through.

10. *The tactile sense of height.* This is manifested in an uncomfortable feeling a speaker sometimes experiences in his legs or feet when walking on a platform that is too high.

11. *A surgical sense of touch.* Sometimes, when examining a patient for the first time and discovering he has a high temperature, a doctor isn't too worried because he feels that this temperature is normal for that patient.

12. *Maternal bodily sense.* The drama of positive forces, which comes into play in the space between the hands of a mother and the cheeks of her child, who has been declared to be beyond the help of medical science.

New tactile panels
A physio-psychic-tactile portrait of Marinetti

Central generating block. Roughness in part, roundness without being coarse, strength, and softness at the center revealing the sensibility of the person. (A warm brush = aspirations in life. A block of rock and wood = the highest potential. Sponge = sensitivity to the environment.)

Movements with a smooth rhythm. Secure creations. (Silver-plated laminates.) On the surface, signs of anguish, coarseness, brute strength. Can't be brought to a halt. (Paper-glass-coarse body hair.)

Vitality. Bare, rippling muscles (natural rubber). Slackened muscles (soft rubber). Human muscles (rubber covered with skin). Muscles tensed as far as possible (rubber wrapped in silver).

Incisive will of the innovator. (Element that harms in order to make itself distinctive = pointed stone.)

Creation. Bridges in the sky and leaps into space. Softness on wires and curves that enfold the space (metal laminate covered intermittently, in zigzags).

Cast down in sadness. (Violent cutting of the laminate, writhing in descent, and attraction.)

Giving oneself up to tenderness, love, humanity, sweetness. (Zones made warm with cloth—leather of increasingly finer quality—velvet—in concentric circles around a warm nucleus of feathers [*pause*].)

Leap toward the infinite with a vertical force. (Steel laminate covered with silver in its final section.)

Tactile panel of an arid landscape

Starting out from a fairly arid, high plain (normal brush), we come down into a rough area that is alive with a lacerating intensity (cluster pines and brambles), then a harsh region (hard brush), a vegetal-human area that is almost dead, and dank with the grayness of the atmosphere (dried algae and cork).

A sudden irritation (a grater), after which everything falls back into the previous set of sensations, which have become almost abstract, ever more imprecise (on sandpaper of different grades, straw, and coarse grasses laid out in symmetrical bundles).

Abstract tactile panel of Nostalgia for Warm Softness

The foregoing tactile panel is linked to this one through sandpaper which, from its set of imprecise, abstract sensations passes over into boredom (wide zone of sandpapers over which the hands should linger).

Rebellion of sensibility (hard brush and smooth rock) which creates roughness that is softened (a grater covered with silk spongy material), sliding (leather) into an increasing nostalgia for voluminous softness (padded silk and wool, thick leather), waves of warm wool to end up in zones of maternal warmth (Pyrenean wool), warmth of love (satin wool and silk), tenderness (velvety silk feathers), and finally an *abstract repose*, smooth and cold.

Abstract tactile panel of Aggressive, Dynamic Will

From repose we move on to a consolidated will concentrated at the center (twisted leather—a wooden cylinder—a wooden parallelepiped—a small cylinder of polished stone), then with increasing speed and leaping over obstacles and frictions, with and without lines (a large cone, octagonal blocks of wood, a cork bridge).

Waves also of very slow speed, slightly faster speed, of wind speed (metal deck, revolving wooden balls, smooth cylinder of wood, cloth-covered metal bridge slung over a void).

Smooth aerial level for flying (silver paper).

New tactile experiences

The Futurist Maga makes the following suggestions for tactile experience:[5]

1. a box with many different-sized compartments, to be filled with different materials in different colors.
2. a rosary made up of beads of different materials, strung at irregular intervals. The hands would then be trained to recognize things in the dark, such as marble, iron, coral, polenta, pasta, tobacco, and so on.
3. portraits of people composed of materials that are representative of their different temperaments. A hard, cynical man, made from elephant hide. A strong, intelligent man, made from ox's nerve strings. A good-looking, seductive man, with silk velvet on his cheeks and rose leaves in his eyes.

All of this research takes us further and further, without ever pausing to rest. At the first Italian Futurist Congress in Milan,[6] on November 23, I shall be presenting the research into Touch of Charles Henry, the director of the Laboratory for the Physiology of Sensations at the Sorbonne.[7]

This sequel to the previous document, *Tactilism: A Futurist Manifesto,* first appeared, without the introductory section "I," in an English translation in the New York journal *Futurist Aristocracy,* no. 1, April 1923. Extracts of the sections "Senses not yet defined" and "A physio-psychic-tactile portrait of Marinetti" were printed in *L'impero* of February 17, 1925. The full text appeared in *L'ambrosiano* on November 8 and 10, 1924.

69

❧

The Theater of Surprises

(Theater of Essential Brevity[1]—zany physical comedy[2]—Words-in-Freedom[3] on stage—Dynamic and Multichanneled Recitation[4]—News-Theater[5]—Gallery Theater[6]—improvised conversations among different musical instruments, and so on)

Manifesto

We have brought glory to the *Variety Theater*[7] and given it a new lease on life. In the *Theater of Essential Brevity*[8] we have destroyed the overriding concerns with technique, verisimilitude, logical development, and step-by-step exposition.

In this *Theater of Essential Brevity*, we have established a brand-new mix of the serious and the comic, of unreal as well as of believable characters, the interweaving and coexistence of time and space,[9] the drama of objects[10] and discords,[11] the visual, structured flow of images,[12] shop windows[13] of ideas and actions. If today there exists a young Italian theater with different combinations of serious, comic, and grotesque, with fantastic characters in everyday settings, with a sense of the interpenetrating yet coexistential nature of time and space, then it is thanks to our *Theater of Essential Brevity*.[14]

Today, we are compelling the theater to take yet another leap forward.[15] Our *Theater of Surprises* is designed to stimulate enjoyment through surprise, with all the stock-in-trade of actions, ideas, and contrarieties that we have not yet brought to the stage, entertaining assortments of things that we haven't yet made use of but that have the power to move human sensibilities through delight.

Many a time we have declared that surprise is an essential component of art, that the work of art is autonomous and can only be compared to itself and thus it takes on the appearance of the miraculous.

Indeed, Botticelli's *Primavera*—like many other masterpieces—when it first appeared had, over and above its different virtues of composition, rhythm, depth, and color, that essential attribute of its surprising originality. Our familiarity with this picture, and with the illicit reproductions and imitations it gave rise to, has destroyed that element of surprise for us. And this demonstrates how the cult of works of art of the past—admired, plagiarized, and imitated—is, quite apart from being injurious to new creative ingenuity, both futile and absurd, considering that today we can admire, imitate, or plagiarize only a few of those works.

Raphael, having decided on a particular wall in a room in the Vatican for one of his frescoes—a wall already painted, some years before, by the brush of Sodoma—had the latter's wonderful work scraped off. He then painted his fresco, in homage to his own creative pride, thinking that the chief value of a work of art lay precisely in that aspect of surprise.[16]

This being so, we set an absolute value on the aspect of surprise. The more so since, after so many centuries that had a superabundance of works of genius which, as they appeared, caused their own particular sensation, it is now extremely difficult to astound in the same way.

In the *Theater of Surprises*, the *novelty* unleashed by the author must be capable of:

1. Shaking an audience's sensibilities utterly, through pleasurable surprise.
2. Suggesting a continuous stream of other hilarious ideas, just like a jet of water spurting a great distance, or like circles rippling outward on water, or echoes resounding.
3. Stimulating in an audience words and behavior that are quite unforeseen, so that each *surprise* spawns new surprises in the stalls, in the box circle, throughout the entire city the selfsame evening, the day after, and so on ad infinitum.

By bringing the Italian spirit into full play, with all its spiritual, a-logical gymnastics, the *Theater of Surprises* hopes to tear young Italians away from the current monotonous, funereal, repulsive obsession with politics.[17]

In conclusion: in addition to all the zany physical comedy typical of a Futurist *Caffè concerto*,[18] with its gymnasts, athletes, magicians, conjurors, and its crazy characters, and in addition to the *Theater of Essential Brevity*, the *Theater of Surprises* also contains a *News-Theater* of the Futurist movement and a *Gallery Theater* of the plastic arts,[19] as well as Dynamic and Multichanneled Recitations of Words-in-Freedom, interspersed with dances, poems in the style of the Words-in-Freedom, improvised musical conversations between pianos, between pianos and songs, free orchestral improvisations, and so on.

The *Theater of Essential Brevity* (created by Marinetti, Settimelli, Cangiullo, Buzzi, Mari Carli, Folgore, Pratella, Jannelli, Nannetti, Remo Chiti, Mario Dessy, Balla, Volt, Depero, Rognoni, Soggetti, Masnata, Vasari, Alfonso Dolce) has triumphantly made its presence felt in Italy by the companies Berti, Ninchi, Zoncada, Tumiati, Mateldi, Petrolini, Luciano Molinari; in Paris and Geneva by the avant-garde theater group Art et Liberté; and in Prague by the Czechoslovakian Company of the Švanda Theater.[20]

Our *Theater of Surprises* has been brought to the public's attention and staged by the De Angelis Futurist Company for audiences in Naples, Palermo, Rome, Florence, Genoa, Turin, and Milan, all of which were—in the words of one newspaper, *Il giorno*, that was not very favorably disposed to it—"wildly enthusiastic."[21] In Rome, the worshipers of the past were extremely insolent and were given a drubbing by Marinetti, Cangiullo, and the Fornari brothers. The kick up the backside that the painter, Totò Fornari, meted out to one stick-in-the-mud, who had gone up onto the stage to press his stolid arguments, has become legendary. With that surprise kick, the painter Fornari sent the aforesaid traditionalist flying into the circle.[22]

In Naples, the *Theater of Surprises* exhibited the pictures of the Futurist artist Pasqualino Cangiullo;[23] in Rome, those of the Futurist painter Totò Fornari, which were presented from the stage by the painter Balla; while the pictures of the Futurist painters Marasco and Bernini were shown in Florence and Milan, respectively.[24]

The *Theater of Surprises* staged conversations between improvising pianos and between a piano and a cello, these being the creations of the Futurist musicians Aldo Mantia, Mario Bartoccini, Vittorio Mortari, and Franco Baldi.[25]

This manifesto was written jointly by F. T. Marinetti and Francesco Cangiullo and published in a French and in an Italian version in *Il futurismo* on January 11, 1922, accompanied by five examples of the new dramatic genre, as well as four pieces from the Theater of Essential Brevity. It was dated October 11, 1921, and thus related to the first tour of the De Angelis company with a program of "Surprises" (September 30, 1921, to February 6, 1922).

70

ℐ

Memorandum on Stage Presence and the Style of Theater

1. Essential, condensed, geometrical expression with geometrical and arithmetical actions.
2. A multichanneled and dynamic form of recitation.[1]
3. Swift, condensed, epistolary[2] style (3 uncertainties, 1 kiss, 7 expressions of foreboding).
4. Ordered yet a-logical intonation.
5. Invented gestures and movements and facial expressions.
6. Important parts of the human body (a braided arm, eyes beneath a helmet) made to stand out against the darkness through the use of a spotlight.
7. Typical and significant parts of the characters spotlighted.
8. Transitions to segments of landscape or parts of the human body before the eyes of the audience.
9. Painted scenery expressed and suggested through music.
10. Small loudspeakers carried by every actor and actress.
11. Abolition of characters' exits and entrances.

This list of instructions was related to the second tour of the Theater of Surprises, set up in November 1923. Marinetti possessed complete artistic control over the enterprise, which allowed him to engage two Futurist musicians, Franco Casavola and Silvio Mix, and to commission scene paintings from Prampolini and Depero. Rodolfo de Angelis was given the task of finding a well-known star performer, two dancers, and three actors from the variety circuit. This brief text instructed them in the key components of a Futurist style of theater. It remained in the Salimbeni Archive and was published by Luciano Caruso and Giuliani Longone in *Il teatro futurista a sorpresa: Documenti* (Florence: Salimbeni, 1979).

71

✑

The Abstract Antipsychological Theater of Pure Elements and the Tactile Theater

The whole of contemporary young Italian theater,[1] which has justifiably swept away the Naturalistic theater[2] and the theater of D'Annunzio, which would be Futurist if it were not cluttered up with psychology and philosophy. This young Italian theater would never have had the audacity that led to the mingling of reality and unreality, of the serious and the grotesque, the simultaneous presentation of reality and vision and scenes of inanimate objects, if our Futurist Theater of Essential Brevity had not forced them all on Italian audiences.

The audiences that are now applauding the new drama of Pirandello[3] are also applauding the theatrical ploy of making the audience participate in the action of the play. Audiences may remember that this particular feature was the brainchild of the Futurists.

This trailblazing in theatrical invention, in operetta, and in the musichall was noted by critics in Paris, England, Berlin, America, and recently in a lead article in the Parisian *Comœdia*, in which Gustave Fréjaville wrote: "Speaking from up on the mountain, ten years ago, F. T. Marinetti made us listen to many truths that today are being imposed by dint of overwhelming evidence."

The *Futurist Theater of Essential Brevity* (created by Marinetti and Settimelli)[4] has been triumphantly imposed in Italy by companies such as the Berti, Ninchi, Zoncada, Tumiati, Mateldi, Petrolini, and Luciano Molinari;[5] in Paris and Geneva by the avant-garde company "Art and Action";[6] in Prague by the Czech Company of the Švanda Theater.[7]

The *Theater of Surprises*, created by Marinetti and Cangiullo, has been pressed on audiences in Naples, Palermo, Rome, Florence, Genoa, Turin, Milan, and so on, by the Futurist De Angelis Company.[8]

The *Futurist Theater of Essential Brevity* and the *Theater of Surprises*, performed and published in every language and commented on in innumerable newspapers, have had an influence on all theatrical actors and environments.[9]

The success of *Six Characters in Search of an Author* by Pirandello (which, along with long-winded, ultratraditionalist psychological and philosophical rigmarole, contains typically Futurist scenes with inanimate objects), demonstrates that audiences are enthusiastically accepting Futurism in its more moderate forms.[10] Besides this, the revolution in stage and set design in the Russian theater is owed entirely to Italian Futurism and to the Futurists Balla, Prampolini, and Depero. This is noted by Luigi Chiarelli in an article in *Corriere italiano*:

> The Russian stage and set designers have taken virtually everything from our Futurists, because in Russia, the name of Marinetti is always held in high esteem. The spiritual interpretation of works, insofar as it involves an ambience, is often influenced by the bold attempts at shedding a psychological light, carried out by Anton Giulio Bragaglia, who, for quite a few years, even though starved of adequate funds, has been working in Italy toward a renaissance in theatrical staging. Echoes of even the Theater of Color of the late lamented Ricciardi are quite noticeable in Russia. Tairov, of the Kamerny Theater, inspired by the staging of Alexander Exter, is trying to make theatricality popular, yet he too is following the manifestos of the Italian Futurists. His scenes dance with actors, just like the ballet *Epileptic Cabaret* by Bragaglia and Marinetti.[11]

In 1911 Emilio Settimelli and I worked out a total theatrical revolution.[12] Our ideas, which were absolutely opposed to those currently dominating the stage in Italy and abroad, urged us toward the destruction of all canons and all prohibitions so as to arrive at a theater which was free and open, at last, to all new forms of spiritual freedom.

Everybody was working to perfect staging, but nothing at all was being done to modernize the themes of drama.

The writers who wanted to revitalize the theater (Ibsen, Maeterlinck, Andreyev, Claudel, Shaw) never gave a thought to freeing themselves from a technique characterized by prolixity, detailed analysis, and lengthy exposition, and of creating a truly pithy form of theater. When confronted by the works of these authors, an audience feels as resentful as a group of bystanders who indulge their fear and pity as they watch the lingering agony of a horse that has collapsed on the pavement. The sighs and applause that break out at the end relieve the audience's stomachs of all the undigested time they have swallowed. Each act is exactly like having to wait patiently in some antechamber for a minister to receive you (*coup de théâtre*: a kiss, a shot, a word that reveals all, etc.). All of this traditional or semi-Futuristic theater, instead of concentrating action and ideas into the smallest number of words and gestures, totally destroyed the multiplicity of locations (a source of great interest and dynamism) by shoving lots of landscapes, piazzas, and streets into the one sausage of a single room.[13]

In the *Futurist Theater of Essential Brevity*, we have dispensed with worries about technique, verisimilitude, sequential logic, and step-by-step exposition.[14]

In the *Futurist Theater of Essential Brevity*, we have found new dramatic themes, creating the very latest combinations of the serious and the comic, of real and unreal characters, the interweaving and simultaneous presentation of time and space, the drama of objects, discords, dramatized images, and window displays[15] of ideas and actions. If a new Italian theater has come into existence—with a mixture of the serious-comic-grotesque, unreal characters in real settings, simultaneity of action, and interpenetration of time and space—this is owing entirely to our *Theater of Essential Brevity*.

Our *Theater of Surprises* is designed to exhilarate through surprise, with all the means, actions, ideas, and antitheses that we have not yet brought to the stage, entertaining assortments of things that we haven't yet made use of but which have the power to move human sensibilities through delight.[16]

Now, I regard as a matter of urgency the need to combat the predominance of psychologism, in its different forms, in the theater:

1. Traditional scientific-documentary psychologism.
2. The Parisian sort of semi-Futurist, fragmentary, effeminate, and ambiguous psychologism (Proust).[17]
3. Italian psychologism, which dresses up its enormous, pettifogging, ponderous, funereal, moralistic, academic, pedantic analyses as Futurism, with their associated decrepit Hamletisms: "To be or not

to be; live, dream" and philosophical dialogues which have no tangible concern or dramatic pacing.

All three of these psychologisms are equally analytical, long, opaque, without lyrical qualities, monotonous, tedious, depressing, and anti-Italian—that is, contrary to the fine lyrical, fun-loving, explosive, extemporizing, sublime, and highly colorful qualities of our race.

Therefore, we have created two new kinds of theater (which have been staged during the tour of the New Futurist Theater in eighteen Italian cities):[18]

1. An abstract and a-logical condensed drama of pure elements which, without any psychology, presents the forces of life in movement to an audience. The abstract synthesis is an a-logical and surprising combination of blocs of typical sensations.[19]
2. A tactile, muscular, sporting, and mechanical condensed drama devoid of psychology.[20]

This manifesto was written for the second tour of the *Theater of Surprises* by the De Angelis company in January–February 1924, but only published a month later in a special issue of *Noi* (March 1924) printed for the International Exhibition of Theater Technology in Vienna. The manifesto also appeared in Lajos Kassák's journal *MA* (in the *Musik und Theaternummer* of 1924 printed in Vienna). A later reprint can be found in *L'ambrosiano* of November 19, 1924.

72

Futurist Photography

F. T. MARINETTI, TATO

Photographing a landscape, a person, or a group of people, achieving harmony, a profusion of fine detail, and a likeness such as elicits the comment "It looks like a picture" is for us utterly passé.

Following on from the photodynamism and photography of moving bodies created by Anton Giulio Bragaglia, together with his brother Arturo,[1] and presented by me, in 1912, at the Pichetti Hall in Rome,[2] and imitated thereafter by all the avant-garde photographers in the world,[3] we must achieve these new photographic goals:

1. The drama of moving and immobile objects; the dramatic intermingling of moving and immobile objects.[4]
2. The drama of the shadows of contrasting objects, isolated by the objects themselves.[5]
3. The drama of humanized objects, turned to stone, crystallized or made plantlike by means of camouflage or special lighting.
4. Diffracted images[6] of some parts of human or animal bodies, either in isolation or joined together[7] again in the wrong order.
5. The fusion of aerial, oceanic, and terrestrial perspectives.
6. The fusion of images taken from below with those taken from above.
7. Moving or static views of objects or human and animal bodies.
8. The moving or static suspension of objects and their state of equilibrium.
9. The dramatic disproportioning[8] of moving and static objects.
10. The desired or violent interpenetration of moving and static objects.

11. Transparent and semitransparent images of people and concrete objects with their semiabstract phantoms superimposed on them with the simultaneous effect of dream memories.[9]

12. Hugely exaggerated magnification of some tiny, almost invisible object in a landscape.[10]

13. Tragic or satirical interpretation of life by means of a symbolism of disguised objects.

14. Composition of totally extraterrestrial, astral, or mediumistic landscapes by manipulating the negative's density, elasticity, depth of focus, transparency, and mathematical and geometrical value, without using any human, vegetal, or geological features.[11]

15. Organic composition of a person's different states of mind[12] through the intensified expression of the parts of his body that best characterize him.

16. The art of photographing camouflaged objects, with the intention of developing the art of wartime camouflage, the aim of which is to deceive aerial reconnaissance.

All of these studies aim at extending the possibilities of the science of photography into pure art and at automatically assisting its development in the fields of physics, chemistry, and war.

This manifesto is dated April 11, 1930, and was written for the occasion of a national photography competition held in Rome in September 1930. Parts of it were published under the titles "La fotografia dell'avvenire" and "La fotografia futurista" in *Gazzetta del popolo* (November 9 and 15, 1930). The final version translated here was published in *Il futurismo: Rivista sintetica illustrata* on January 11, 1931. Points 1–15 and the concluding paragraph were reprinted with the title *Il grande manifesto della fotografia futurista di S. E. F. T. Marinetti accademico d'Italia* in the catalog, *1ª Mostra Sperimentale di Fotografia Futurista*, held in Turin from March 15 to April 10, 1931.

73

✑

Manifesto of Futurist Cuisine

Italian Futurism, which has sired numerous Futurisms and avant-garde movements abroad, is by no means the prisoner of worldwide victories it has won "over twenty years of great artistic and political battles that have often been consecrated by the spilling of blood," as Benito Mussolini has suggested. Yet again, Futurism risks unpopularity with its scheme for a complete rethinking of what we eat.

Of all artistic-literary movements, it is the only one that is essentially reckless and without fear. The Novecento movement[1] in painting and literature is, in reality, two very moderate, practical Futurisms of the political Right. Bound by tradition, they feel their way carefully toward the new by taking full advantage of what each has to offer.

AGAINST PASTA

Futurism has been defined by philosophers as "mysticism in action,"[2] by Benedetto Croce[3] as "antihistoricism," by Graça Aranha[4] as "liberation from aesthetic terror," and by us as "innovative Italian pride," being the formula for "original life and art," "the religion of speed," "humanity's maximum drive toward synthesis," "health of the spirit," "a method for continuous creativity," "fast-moving geometrical splendor," and "aesthetics of the machine."

Contrary to established practice therefore, we Futurists disregard the example and cautiousness of tradition so that, at all costs, we can invent something *new*, even though it may be judged by all as madness.

Though we recognize that great things have been achieved in the past by men who were poorly fed or who survived on coarse victuals, we assert this truth: What we think or dream or do is determined by what we eat and what we drink.

On this subject, let us consult our lips, our tongue, our palate, our taste buds, our gastric juices, and let us enter—in a spirit of originality—the world of gastric chemistry.

We Futurists sense that for the male, the pleasure of love is found in plumbing the depths from top to bottom, whereas for the female it is fanned out horizontally. Gastronomic pleasure, on the other hand, for both the male and the female is always upward, from the bottom to the top of the human body. And furthermore, we think it necessary to prevent Italian men from becoming stolid, leaden hunks, dull and insensitive. They need to be more in tune with the Italian female, who is a slender, spiraling transparency of passion, tenderness, light, strong will, impulsiveness, and heroic tenacity. We must make the Italian body agile, in keeping with the super-lightweight aluminum trains that will take the place of the heavy iron, wood, and steel trains currently in use.

We Futurists are convinced that in the likely event of future wars, it will be the most lithe, agile peoples who will be victorious. To this end we have greatly enlivened the literatures of the world with Words-in-Freedom and the technique of simultaneity. We have turned boredom out of the theaters, with our concentrated, a-logical *Theater of Surprises* and dramas of inanimate objects,[5] and have greatly extended the range of the plastic arts through our antirealism. We have also created an architecture of geometrical splendor, devoid of ornamentation, as well as abstract cinema and photography. And now, after all of this, we are establishing a diet in keeping with an increasingly airborne, faster pace of life.

Above all, we believe it is necessary:

a) to be rid of pasta, that idiotic gastronomic fetish of the Italians.

It may well be that cod, roast beef, and puddings are good for the English, and that the same goes for the Dutch with their meat cooked with cheese, or the Germans with their *Sauerkraut*, smoked *Speck*, and *Kotelett*; but pasta is not good for the Italians. It contradicts, for example, the lively spirit and the passionate, generous, intuitive nature of the Neapolitans. They have been heroic fighters, inspired artists, powerful orators, sharp-witted lawyers, and industrious farmers in spite of their mountains of pasta every day. By eating it, they develop their characteristic ironical, emotional skepticism, which often crushes their exuberance.

A very intelligent Neapolitan professor, Dr. Signorelli, has written, "Unlike bread and rice, pasta is a food that is swallowed and not chewed. This starchy food, for the most part, is digested by the saliva in the mouth and the task of conversion is carried out by the pancreas and the liver. This leads to an imbalance and, consequently, has negative effects on these organs. It induces sluggishness, depression, inertia brought on by nostalgia, and neutralism."

AN INVITATION TO THE CHEMISTS

Pasta, which is 40 percent less nutritious than meat, fish, and vegetables, binds the Italians of today, with its knotty strands, to the languid looms of Penelope[6] and to somnolent sails waiting for a wind. What is the point of continuing to let its heavy bulk stand against that immense network of long and short waves that Italian genius has flung over the oceans and continents, against those landscapes of color, form, and sound with which radio-television circumnavigates the Earth? The apologists for pasta carry its leaden ball, its ruins, in their stomachs, like prisoners serving a life sentence, or archaeologists. Bear in mind too that the abolition of pasta will liberate Italy from the costly burden of foreign grain and will work in favor of the Italian rice industry.

    b) The abolition of volume and weight in the way we understand and evaluate nutrition.

    c) Abolition of all the traditional recipes in order to try out all the new, seemingly ridiculous combinations recommended by Jarro, Maincave, and other Futurist chefs.[7]

    d) Abolition of the routine daily insipidities from the pleasures of the palate.

We invite the chemical industry to do its duty and, very soon, provide the body with all the calories it needs by means of nutritional equivalents, supplied free of charge by the State, in the form of pills or powders, albuminous compounds,[8] synthetic fats, and vitamins.[9] We shall thus arrive at a real reduction in the cost of living and of wages, with a corresponding reduction in the number of working hours. Today, the production of 2,000 kilowatts requires only one workman. Machines will soon constitute an obedient workforce of iron, steel, and aluminum at the service of mankind, which will be relieved, almost entirely, of manual labor.[10] This being reduced to two or three hours, will allow the refinement and the exaltation of the other hours through thought, the arts, and the anticipation of perfect meals.

For all social classes, meals will be a thing of the past, yet the daily round of nourishing equivalents will nevertheless be perfect.

The perfect meal requires:

1. An inventive harmony between the table setting (glassware, crockery, and decoration) and the tastes and colors of the food.
2. Absolute originality in the choice of foods.

"SCULPTED MEAT"

Example: To prepare *Alaska salmon baked in the rays of the sun, with a Martian sauce*, you take an Alaska salmon, you slice it, season it with pepper, salt, and fine oil, and place it under the grill until it is a golden brown. Add tomatoes (sliced in two and grilled beforehand), parsley, and garlic.

When ready to serve, place several anchovy fillets on the slices to form a chessboard pattern. Top each slice with capers and a thin slice of lemon. The sauce will be made from anchovies, the yolk of hard-boiled eggs, basil, olive oil, a small glass of Italian Aurum liqueur,[11] all passed through a sieve. (Recipe by Bulgheroni, head chef of the Goose Quill restaurant.)[12]

Example: To prepare *Woodcock Mount Rosa with Venus sauce*, you take a fine woodcock, clean it, cover the breast with slices of ham and fatty bacon, place it in a casserole with some butter, salt, pepper, and juniper berries, and cook it in a very hot oven for fifteen minutes, basting it with cognac. Take it out of the casserole and place it immediately on a large square of toasted bread, soaked in rum and cognac, then cover it with puff pastry. Return it to the oven until the pastry is well cooked. Serve it with the following sauce: half a glass of Marsala and white wine, four spoonfuls of huckleberries, and some finely chopped orange peel, the mixture having been boiled for ten minutes. Pour the sauce into a sauceboat and serve it very hot. (Recipe by Bulgheroni, head chef of the Goose Quill restaurant.)

3. Invention of appetizing food sculptures, whose novel harmony of shape and color feeds the eyes and titillates the imagination before tempting the lips.

Example: *Sculpted meat*, created by the Futurist painter Fillìa[13] as a snapshot interpretation of Italian landscapes, is made from a large cylindrical rissole of minced veal, stuffed and roasted with eleven different kinds of cooked vegetables. This cylinder, placed vertically in the center of the plate, is crowned with thick honey and supported at its base with a ring of sausage set on three spherical pieces of golden brown chicken.

EQUATOR + NORTH POLE

Example: The edible plastic composition *Equator + North Pole*, created by the Futurist painter Enrico Prampolini,[14] is made from an equatorial sea of egg yolks with oysters and salt, pepper, and lemon juice. From the center, a cone of solid egg white emerges, decorated with orange segments that resemble succulent pieces of the sun. The top of the cone is strewn with pieces of black truffle, shaped like black airplanes soaring triumphantly to their zenith.

These appetizing, sculpted, colored, scented, and tactile compositions will provide perfect simultaneous meals.

4. Banishment of the knife and fork when eating these sculptures, so that they give tactile pleasure before ever reaching the lips.
5. Use of the art of scents to enhance the taste of food. Each dish should be heralded by a perfume that will be expunged from the table by means of ventilators.
6. The use of music must be limited to the intervals between one course and the next, so as not to distract the sensibilities of the tongue and palate, yet having the effect of nullifying the tastes already enjoyed and returning the taste buds to a virginal state.
7. Banishment of speeches and political discussion from the table.
8. Measured use of poetry and music as impromptu ingredients, to kindle up the flavors of a particular dish through their sensual intensity.
9. Between courses, a rapid presentation to the nostrils and eyes of the diners of some dishes they will be eating and of others they will not, to generate curiosity, surprise, and fantasy.
10. The creation of simultaneously eaten, continually changing appetizers that contain ten or twenty flavors, to be sampled in just a few moments. These canapés will have the same magnifying, analogical function in Futurist cuisine as images have in literature. A particular appetizer will have the power to sum up a whole area of life, the development of a passionate affair, or an entire voyage to the Far East.
11. The kitchen to be equipped with scientific instruments: *ozonizers*, to lend the scent of ozone to liquids and foodstuffs; *ultraviolet lamps*, since many foodstuffs, when irradiated with ultraviolet light, acquire

active properties, become more digestible, prevent rickets in young children, etc.; *electrolyzers*, to alter the composition of extracted juices, etc., so as to obtain a new product, with new properties, from a known product; *colloid blenders*, to facilitate the milling of flour, the pulverization of nuts and spices, etc.; *distillers and vacuum stills, sterilizers, dialyzers*, the use of which must be well informed, avoiding the error, for example, of cooking foodstuffs in steam pressure cookers, which destroys active ingredients (vitamins etc.) owing to the high temperatures. *Chemical indicators* will register the acid and alkaline content of sauces and will have the effect of correcting errors such as lack of salt, too much vinegar, too much pepper, and too much sweetness.

This manifesto was first published in the *Gazzetta del popolo* (Turin) on December 28, 1930, and in a French version in *Comœdia* (Paris), January 20, 1931. It also appeared in the advertising brochure of the first Futurist restaurant, the Taverna del Santopalato, inaugurated on March 8, 1931, in Turin, and in the Futurist cookbook, *La cucina futurista*, edited by Marinetti and Fillìa in 1932.

74

⟡

Total Theater: Its Architecture and Technology

Multiple stages—cinematographic—simultaneous—radiophonic—
televisionic—tactile—olfactory—gymnastic—multisensational

The stage, whether of the fixed or rotating sort, is always more or less like the toy theaters they give to children. More suited to marionettes than to human actors, it reminds one of a highly decorated fireplace, or of a cage for performing blackbirds, imprisoned by the wings and the backdrop, and giving an appearance of freedom only on the side opening out toward the audience.

This is why we Futurists, with our fund of inventive genius, have already outlined a blueprint for total theater.[1] With no thought of personal gain, we offer it to the world at large, which is by now used to benefiting from our spiritual gifts and to feeding on them, improving them in its turn and flourishing as a result.

The inevitable, sickening monotony of traditionalist theater results from the unities of place and action,[2] as well as from the unvarying position of the spectator, who remains always outside the action.

In our view, this isolation must cease, for in real life, any given episode takes place at the same time as many others, all of which contribute to its importance and meaning in relation to life as a whole, perceived and thought of as the field of human actions. The same must hold true for the actor as well.

We therefore shall place the spectator at the center of a multilayered scene or, to put it more precisely, at the center of a number of simultaneously operating scenes, most of which will add to the effect and the significance of the main and the principal scenes. Different lines of action will develop contemporaneously; one or two of them will be of capital importance, whereas the other three or four or five will be secondary. These will have the effect of increasing the symbolic significance of the former, by enveloping them in an atmosphere that is true to life and in such a way that they will not remain absurdly isolated from the world they seek to represent, as happens currently in conventional theater.

Architecture and Technology of the Total Theater

Synthetic—multisensational—simultaneous—multiple stages—

aeropoetic—aeropictorial—cinematographic—radiophonic—

tactile —olfactory—sound-producing

The ground plan of the great Futurist theater will be round.[3] There will be several stages: one will be very big and circular, about two meters high, surrounding the whole of the stalls area—like a circular platform. This, in its turn, will be surrounded by a trench filled with water deep enough to swim in (sea or river). From this trench, film projectors will throw a succession of lively images onto a great tilted cyclorama, which will rise up to form a theater dome.[4] Animated aeropaintings and aeropoems[5] will be projected onto it.

A second stage will be placed in the middle of the stalls; it will be round and about one meter high. Around this central stage, every member of the audience will have a revolving seat and a little table made from shatterproof glass to eat off. Each group of spectators will have a radio and television screen to get close-up views, and will be able to move about, becoming part of the action at will, on the wide, circular, mobile walkway which will be set beside the great circular stage.[6] This will be separated from the stage by a tactile and odoriferous moving belt, also circular, which will be pleasurable to the touch.

The great circular stage will be divided into lots of smaller stages that can be separated one from another by movable perpendicular walls. The different complementary and contradictory actions of a single Futurist drama will take place on these various stages all at the same time. This drama will be conceived as an expression of all the simultaneously occurring events in human life.

Thus, for example, a spectator will watch a happy event—for instance, a student party in a tavern on one of the smaller stages, then, effortlessly swiveling his seat around, witnessing a poignant conversation between a husband and wife, while behind him, on the other two or three or four stages, black, gray, or rose-tinted actions will be taking place, in different and contrasting settings. Thus a Futurist dramatist, enjoying unlimited freedom in the structuring of his play—after presenting, for example, the stirrings of a great revolution in a modern capital on those four or five smaller stages—will be able to develop his play extensively on the circular stage and, by making the dividing walls disappear in an instant, flood the stage with rushing crowds, with scuffles and barricades, as he pleases. As the action unfolds and the space gets more and more crowded, the play will finally command the magnificent resource of the central stage and reach its climax. It will be there that, by means of trapdoors and other devices, the characters who must determine the culminating scene and pronounce the final words of the play will appear.

The spectator will no longer be outside the action and will feel himself bound up in the contending passions of the characters, caught between their shouts and their aggressive behavior, or in the swirl of their excitement. He will no longer be watching a brawl from up in a balcony but down there, among the crowd, he will, in a sense, almost feel the physical sensations of the play.

High up in the theater, an electric sun and moon will move on metal tracks through the orbit of the cupola, complemented by a careful simulation of starlight.[7] There will be neon lights and colored smoke. Airplanes, actors, and so on will be involved. It will be a real electric sun, a great yellow globe, which will be raised from one side, climbing toward its zenith, to then gradually set on the other side of the theater, in accordance with the movement of time in the drama. Plays set at nighttime, or in the countryside, will be illuminated by the slow, curving passage of an electric moon, veiled in cloud, according to circumstances. This sun and electric moon will travel, as the plays require, shedding light over forests or the sea, which film projectors will produce, as in the cinema, on the fixed cyclorama.

Alternatively, they will shine on the riotous silhouettes of cities that are brightly lit or languishing under fog or the fumes of ports or blinding street lights. Each small stage, whose function it is to represent an interior, will be illuminated only by the great electric sun (if the action takes place during the daytime), giving an absolute illusion of daylight.[8]

In nighttime scenes for such an interior, we will, of course, use lanterns suited to the particular scene, though without footlights, which we have abolished.

[It is our opinion that the recent innovation, already tried out in many theaters, of illuminating actors with differently colored lights, according to the degree and color of their emotions, is a system that is somewhat crude and primitive.][9] In our simultaneous, multiscenic theater, the spectator assumes greater importance, becoming almost a collaborator of the actor. Having thus moved to the center of the dramatic action, he must be personally predisposed to the development of emotions through the suggestive influence of light and color. That is, the spectator must be immersed in rose-tinted light if he is really to feel a sense of joy, for seeing this light playing on the actor should, in fact, have the inevitable effect of stimulating in him a contrary emotion by virtue of a law of the most natural contradiction.

Given that from time to time we shall want to immerse the spectator in happy or tedious, dark or enthusiastic, rose-, violet-, green-, or red-colored lights, we shall arrange the seats on a glass floor, beneath which there will be a whole battery of multicolored lanterns.[10]

The spectator, who will be turned toward a small Stage A, on which, perhaps, uproarious, thrilling, and glorious events will be taking place, will feel himself warmed by red light flooding him from below. He will experience involuntary stirrings of elation and heroic exhilaration, perfectly in keeping with the tumultuous events unfolding on the small stage. Then imagine that the stage reverts to a single one, and that the heroic red drama washes over the whole theater, right up to the central stage, like a red liquid contained in many interconnecting vessels. Then again, imagine that between the actors on the center stage, and those whom they are applauding on the outer circular stage, there are the spectators who feel the deep red light, coming up through the glass floor, washing over them. Imagine that and you will easily understand the tremendous pitch of emotion at which the spectator will arrive. In this way, the sad, bitter ending of a play will be accompanied by the green pangs of the entire glass floor.

The purpose of the stages into which the great circular stage will be divided is, first and foremost, that of presenting at one and the same time many different, coincident facets of life, the parallel movements of a drama that, in the traditional theater, are of course narrated, causing differing degrees of boredom in the spectator and a slowing down of the action. For example, on one of the small stages, we shall have a gaming house where in the space of one night, a prosperous factory owner ruins an old nobleman, the father of his own young wife's lover. On another stage, the wife in question gives herself up to the kisses of the young man in a moonlit garden.

On a third stage, the workers will destroy the factory of the owner who was lucky at the gaming table. On another stage, a girl who has been betrayed and abandoned by the nobleman's son will kill herself.

On a fifth stage, the General Confederation of Workers decides to expropriate all the workshops and to burn down all gaming houses.

Along the circular road of the stage, which has become one again, the sudden spread of the revolt will destroy gamblers, lovers, capitalists, nobles, workers, the dying girl, and the scantily clad adulteress by interrupting and connecting everything. Divided stages have the additional function of allowing the actors to see—or not—the various actions that take place on the other stages, thereby producing a host of new dramatic effects, such as hallucination, telepathy, and presentiment.

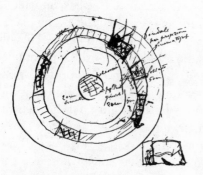   

1) **Inscriptions from left to right:**
   20 m diameter; stage; revolving armchairs 20 m; corridor; moat 50 m; backdrop for film projections.

2) **Inscriptions from left to right: moat, corridor, corridor, armchairs.**

The manuscript is accompanied by ten drawings. The two ground plans reproduced here are the most helpful for understanding the descriptions in the first section of the manifesto.

Action in Futurist plays will be continuous and not divided into acts. It will be divided instead into different locations in different cities that are far apart. In this latter case, it will be possible to give a sense of enormous distance between the smaller stages by projecting film sequences of the countryside, the sea, the mountains, and the progress of trains, enveloped in smoke, all skillfully released.

The much-publicized and -researched use of film in the theater has at last been realized.[11]

A great array of film projectors positioned beneath the auditorium will cast all possible combinations of the fantastic or the realistic upwards, from different angles, onto the single cyclorama—all possible illusions of speed, the deep chasms of populous cities constantly in motion, swarming crowds, great sea-storms, the flight of airplanes, the docking of great steamers and cruisers, sea-battles, and so on.

Presented in this way, with the illusion of the speed of the great international communication networks, the spectator in this simultaneous, all-embracing theater will witness not only the dramatic synthesis of a city but sometimes even a dramatic synthesis of the whole world.

On one of the stages, there will be Japanese actors presenting a stormy session with the Mikado[12] or the departure of the Japanese army from the port of Yokohama,[13] while on another, there will be Russian generals gorging themselves at a club in Port Arthur.[14] On the backdrop above both of these stages, film projections will show the voyage of the Japanese fleet and a naval battle, if it is appropriate.

On the second stage, the carousing of the Russian generals will then be violently interrupted by a shell, which will blow a gaping hole in the wall, while in the main Japanese war port, the anarchists will be exploiting the war by urging the people to revolt.

On the second stage, Russian actors will be taking action, while some British actors will be engaged in a violent parliamentary debate about the pros and cons of a declaration of war against Japan, which is threatening Europe. The actions unfolding on the various small stages must be totally different in character—indeed, the very opposite in terms of color and intensity.

Futurist theater will be able to give expression to contemporary life, which has undergone essential changes as a result of great scientific discoveries and the great speeds attained by land and sea, as well as to our expanded sensibilities and the sensitivity of our nerves, which have become clairvoyant. Futurist theater will synthesize the world. Some will object that it isn't possible to give one's attention to a dramatic action if one is already deeply involved in another such action. Such an objection might well be true of peasants and hermits but not of the inhabitants of the modern metropolis, where a man thinks, argues, meditates, loves, sells, buys, provides, destroys, lifts up, sings, laughs, and cries in a whirlwind of other contradictory and parallel lives, which also compound their own activities in a thousand different ways. These days, nothing is done in absolute silence; the vigor of the cities impresses its vibrations into the walls of even the remotest of rooms, which are all aquiver with premonitions, with unnatural silences and barely noticeable resonances, and which ever anxiously await or remember a voice, a shout, or a thought.

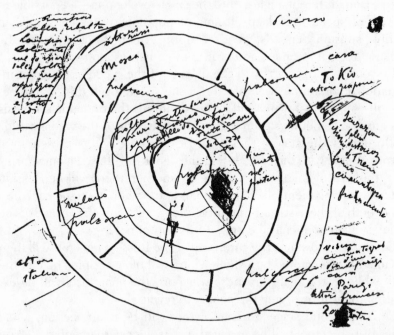

The drawing indicates, on the outer stage, four locations: Moscow (Russian actors), Tokyo (Japanese actors), Milan (Italian actors), and France (French actors); in the text, this final location has been replaced by London (British actors). On the central stage is indicated: Dark-colored seats. Everything should be pale in color so that other colors stand out. In the top left-hand corner, he states that the lights at the side of the stage, at the back of the seats, on the armrests, and under the seats should be brightly colored. Right of the Tokyo section he notes: Sensations of distance; vision of trains; smoke, cinematographically. In the bottom right-hand corner is written: Cinematographic visions of a street in Paris. 20 meters.

The productions in this Futurist theater will command the double interest of actors and audiences, the latter forever changing their opinions and their sentiments like miraculous chameleons as they sit in their revolving seats. They will laugh until they are fit to burst, seeing Novelli,[15] the very funny, carousing, prodigal son, before their eyes on one stage, then they will weep immediately afterward at the sight of Zacconi,[16] his emaciated, abandoned, and grieving father.

The stages into which the great circular stage is divided will present us not only with apartment interiors but also with sections of houses and sometimes with their facades, from whose balconies we shall see besieged anarchists shooting at the police, whom we shall see falling wounded on the main stage.

The spectator will thus find himself in the midst of a true revolt, beneath a hail of missiles, in a total illusion of reality.

This sort of Futurist theater is naturally constructed not only by means of prose but also from music, and the great, dramatic, musical poem of the future will also, perforce, evolve on the great circular stage and the main stage, beneath which a full orchestra will be gathered.

A Futurist production will only last for an hour and will be given four or five times a day. It will present modern life without dragging the monotonous aspects of life into the enclosed space of the theater.

Futurist theater abolishes at a stroke the accumulated history of theatrical production and forbids every ludicrous attempt at reviving them. It will even furnish the dullest, most sterile playwrights with some imagination.

[A company has already been set up in Milan, for the construction of the great Futurist theater, with capital amounting to 500,000 lire.][17]

A first version of the text was first published in *Futurismo*, January 15, 1933, and in the *Almanacco letterario per l'anno 1933*, published by Bompiani in Milan. A longer and more detailed manuscript version was published by Mario Verdone and Luce Marinetti in *Teatro contemporaneo* 5, no. 9 (February–May 1985): 373–84. The translation here is based on the original manuscript and offers a number of variants to the 1985 transcription. Several of the drawings contained in the manuscript have been reproduced by Claudia Salaris in her biography *F. T. Marinetti*, p. 241.

75

✐

A Futurist Theater of the Skies
Enhanced by Radio and Television

During the First Aerosports Day,[1] which he organized in Rome in November 1930, the Futurist aeropainter Mino Somenzi[2] suddenly discerned a dramatic use of the radio to add to Azari's Theater of the Skies. Personally, I think it would be useful to perfect his conception by the following means:

1. Special loudspeakers mounted on vehicles that are camouflaged in a novel way, thus transforming them from tragic to comic. These loudspeakers will argue and bicker in their support for one or other of the planes acting up in the sky. When one section of the gambling crowd has placed its bets on the outcome of the aerial drama, the loudspeakers will announce details of the bets to the gamblers at the other end of that vast arena.
2. Huge panels of aeropoetry[3] and screens for television[4] which, hung from special airplanes, will be moved around so as to give all the spectators the opportunity of seeing that part of the aerial play which is very high up and therefore hardly visible.
3. A totally dynamic, aerial spectacle of aircraft moving, swiftly or slowly, from one altitude to another or from one cloud to the next.
4. A special dynamic, aerial spectacle in which a machine displays its changing, very particular, marvelous display of colored smokes.[5]

Perfected in this way, the chief characteristics of the Theater Enhanced by Radio and Television will be:

a) The most unusual, suggestive power of dramatic actions performed the right way up, upside down, and in all directions.
b) A continuing suspense maintained by the constant danger of every artistic or acrobatic maneuver of the planes. In the Theater of the Skies, every kiss is fatal!
c) Total surprise, given that no other theater can offer entrances or exits of actors at 200 or 300 kilometers per hour. We shall have competitions of speed feelings, ideas, and instincts. We shall have emotional championships between weight, lightness, flexibility, and darting.

It will be the first real, open-air theater that is all-embracing, light, and extremely entertaining.

This manifesto is part of a longer text published under the title *Il teatro aereo radiotelevisivo* on January 15, 1932, in the *Gazzetta del popolo*, on the same date in *L'aviazione*, and on January 16, 1932, in *Il telegrafo* (Livorno). It was reprinted in *Il teatro futurista sintetico* (Naples: CLET, 1941). The first section, omitted here, is an enlarged and partly rephrased reissue of Fedele Azari's manifesto "Il teatro aero futurista," first launched in a propaganda flight over Milan in April 1919.

76

The Radio

F. T. MARINETTI AND PINO MASNATA[1]

Futurism has radically transformed literature with its Words-in-Freedom, aeropoetry,[2] and its swift, simultaneous, free-word style; it has removed boredom from the theater, using a-logical surprise syntheses[3] and the drama of objects.[4] It has enriched the plastic arts with antirealism, plastic dynamism, and aeropaintings; created the geometric splendor of a dynamic architecture, which, lyrically and without adornment, makes use of new building materials; and invented abstract cinema and photography. At its second National Congress,[5] Futurism decided on the following program of future conquests.

Going beyond love for women "by means of a more intense love for women, in opposition to the erotico-sentimental distractions promoted by many foreign avant-gardes, whose artistic expression has foundered in the fragmentary and nihilistic."

Going beyond patriotism "by means of a more fervid patriotism, transformed in this way into an authentic religion of the Nation; a warning to the Semites that they should identify themselves with specific countries or risk expulsion."

Going beyond the machine "by means of man's close identification with the machine itself, destined, as it is, to free him from hard physical labor and extend his mind."

Going beyond Sant'Elia's "victorious architecture of today by means of a Sant'Elia architecture that is even more explosive with lyrical color and original innovations."

Going beyond painting "by means of a more vital aeropainting and more versatile techniques, employing many tactile materials."

Going beyond the Earth "by imagining the means necessary for journeying to the Moon."

Going beyond death "with the metallization of the human body and seizing hold of the spirit of life as a driving force."

Going beyond war and revolution "with a ten- or twenty-year artistic-literary war and revolution, which will fit in your pocket like an essential revolver."

Going beyond chemistry "with a free-to-all nutrition, enhanced with vitamins and calories."[6]

We already have television at a resolution of 50,000 dots for every large image on a big screen.[7] While we are waiting for the invention of tele-touch, telesmell, and teletaste, we Futurists are perfecting the radio,[8] which is destined to increase the creative genius of the Italian race a hundredfold, to abolish the ancient, tormenting nostalgia for faraway places, and to impose Words-in-Freedom everywhere as its logical, natural mode of expression.

Radia, the name which we Futurists give to the great radio events, is STILL TODAY (a) realistic, (b) studio-bound, (c) trivialized by music which, instead of developing in a variety of original ways, is in a repulsive state of languid, negro monotony, (d) a wishy-washy imitation, by avant-garde writers, of the Futurist Theater of Essential Brevity and Words-in-Freedom.

Alfred Goldsmith of the New York Radio City[9] has said: "Marinetti has imagined the electric theater. Though very different in conception, the two types of theater have a point of contact in that their realization necessarily involves active participation and intellectual effort by their audiences. The electric theater will require a huge imaginative effort, firstly by its authors, but then also by actors and audiences."

Even the French, Belgian, and German avant-garde theorists and actors of radio drama (Paul Reboux, Théo Fleischman, Jacques Rece, Alex Surchamp, Tristan Bernard, F. W. Bischoff, Victor Heinz Fuchs, Friedrich Wolf, and M. Felix Mendelssohn, among others)[10] praise and imitate our Futurist Theater of Essential Brevity and our Words-in-

Freedom, yet almost all of them continue to be obsessed with a realism which can, nonetheless, be quickly left behind.

THE RADIA MUST NOT BE

1. theater, because radio has killed off the theater, which had already been defeated by the talking cinema.
2. cinema, because the cinema is in its death throes (a) from the stale sentimentalism of its subject matter; (b) from realism, which envelops even some of the simultaneous and compressed dramas;[11] (c) from endless technical complications; (d) from a fatal desire for coproductions, which always lead to banality; (e) from reflected light that is inferior in quality to that emitted by the television screen.
3. books, because the book, which is to be blamed for having made mankind shortsighted, implies something heavy, strangled, suffocating, fossilized, and stodgy (only the great, luminous billboards of Words-in-Freedom will live on, for they are the only poetry which needs to be seen).[12]

THE RADIA ABOLISHES

1. the space or stage necessary for the theater, including the *Futurist Theater of Essential Brevity* (actions unfolding on a fixed and unchanging stage) and the cinema (with scenes that change very quickly, are extremely varied, take place simultaneously, and are always realistic).
2. time.
3. the unity of action.
4. the theatrical character.
5. the audience, in the sense of a judgmental mass—self-electing, systematically hostile and servile, always antiprogressive and backward-looking.

THE RADIA WILL BE

1. Freedom from all contact with literary and artistic traditions. Any attempt to reconnect radia with tradition is grotesque.[13]
2. A new art form that starts where theater, cinema, and narration break off.
3. Immensity of space. Being no longer visible nor confined to a frame, the scene becomes universal and cosmic.
4. Reception, amplification, and transformation of vibrations[14] released by living or dead beings, dramas of states of mind, full of sound effects but without words.

5. Reception, amplification, and transformation of vibrations emitted by matter. Just as today we listen to the song of the woods and of the sea, tomorrow we shall be seduced by vibrations from a diamond or a flower.

6. Pure organism of radiophonic sensations.[15]

7. An art without time or space, without yesterday or tomorrow. The possibility of picking up radio broadcasts from stations in different time zones,[16] together with the absence of light, destroys the hours, the day, and the night. Reception and amplification, by means of thermoionic valves, of light and of voices from the past, will destroy the concept of time.

8. Compressed dramas comprising an infinite number of simultaneous actions.

9. Human art, which is cosmic and universal, as a voice with a true psychology and spirituality of sounds, of voices and silences.

10. Characteristic life of every sound, with an endless variety of concrete versus abstract, of real versus imagined, through a community of sounds.[17]

11. Tussle between sounds and varying distances, that is, a spatial drama in addition to the temporal drama.

12. Words-in-Freedom. The word has been gradually developing into a collaborator with mime and gesture.[18] The word needs to be recharged with all its power, thereby becoming the essential, totalitarian word, that which, in Futurist theory, goes by the name of word-atmosphere.[19] Words-in-Freedom, daughters of the aesthetics of the machine, contain a whole orchestra of sounds and sound harmonies (realistic and abstract) which, single-handedly, can assist the colorful and pliable word in its flash representation of that which cannot be seen.[20] If the broadcaster does not wish to have recourse to Words-in-Freedom, he must express himself in that free-word style (which is a derivative of our Words-in-Freedom) which is already present in avant-garde novels and in newspapers, that free-word style which, typically, is rapid, snappy, compact, and simultaneous.

13. The isolated word, repetition of verbs ad infinitum.[21]

14. Essentialist art.[22]

15. Gastronomic, amorous, gymnastic, etc. music.[23]

16. Utilization of sounds, noises, harmonies, simultaneous music or sound, of silences,[24] all with different gradations of harshness, of loudness and softness, which will become a strange kind of brush for painting, defining, and coloring the infinite darkness of the radia,

giving the broadcasts cubic, round, or spherical—essentially, geometrical—shape.

17. Utilization of the interferences between stations and of the intensification and fading of sounds.

18. Geometric definition and construction of silence.[25]

19. Utilization of all the different resonances of a voice or sound to
indicate the size of the location from which the voice is speaking.
Characterization of the silent or semisilent atmosphere which surrounds and colors a given voice, noise, or sound.[26]

20. Elimination of the concept or importance of the audience, which
has always, even for the book, had a distorting or harmful influence.

**This text was published with the title *La radia: Manifesto futurista* in the
Gazzetta del popolo on September 22, 1933, and as *Manifesto della radio*
in *Futurismo*, October 1, 1933. A French version appeared in *Comœdia*
(December 15, 1933) and *Stile futurista* (December 1934). In 1941 it was
republished with the title *Il teatro futurista radiofonico* in the collection
Il teatro futurista sintetico and the journal *Autori e scrittori* (August 1941),
both edited by Marinetti, with an appendix of fourteen short radio
plays. The main author of this manifesto was Pino Masnata (1901–68).**

APPENDIX
Manuscript Version of Document 11
The Necessity and Beauty of Violence

I

Part of the manuscript, preserved in the Beinecke Rare Books and Manuscript Library, has been corrected with a different pen and in a smaller handwriting. Some of the large-lettered text, which is typical of Marinetti's speech manuscripts, has been crossed out, often in a manner that makes the original text illegible. Two full pages in that smaller handwriting, with two pasted-in excerpts from the *Comœdia* interview (document 3) in an unidentified Italian translation, have been added. I presume that the corrections in Marinetti's hand were done in 1910 to recast the speech for a publication, which in the end did not materialize. Part of that corrected text, with a number of additions and alterations, was then printed in *L'ardito* on June 15, 1919.

My lecture, as advertised, is on "The Necessity and Beauty of Violence." This topic, however, will form only the final part of my address. First of all, I shall be talking to you about our new Futurist ethic—the ethics of danger, of courage, and of day-to-day heroism—and about our only obdurate antagonists: mediocrity and cowardice.

This change in topic arises naturally out of a clear need to explain, above all else, the passion that courses through our veins and those ideals which, more than any others, illuminate our minds.

I shall then demonstrate how from a clear love of danger, from habitual courage, and from everyday heroism spring precisely—and naturally—an urgent need for, and recognition of, the beauty of violence.

All of this is entirely free of any political agenda; something you'll not be very used to. I am revealing my thoughts to you in this very straightforward manner so that in them you will easily recognize a proposal for action or merely look upon them as something entertaining.

I am well aware of the reservations you have built up against us Futurists, as a result of the more or less amusing gossip of mercenary newspapers, those emasculated custodians of Italian mediocrity and enemies of any sort of novelty. And it may well be that you don't yet have any clear notion of what we are and what we stand for.

Just imagine, in the doleful, stagnating republic of letters and arts, a group of young men who are utterly rebellious and destructive, who are fed up with adoring the past, sick of academic pedantry, bursting with the desire for fearless originality, and positively gasping for a life that is free, full of adventure, vitality, and a habitual heroism, and who want to liberate the Italian spirit from that heap of prejudices, banalities, deference, and veneration that we call *traditionalism*. In short: we Futurists are a group of anarchists operating in the field of art.

As artist and poet I shall therefore abstain from giving you any advice on political matters, or on how best to defend your economic interests. People like Arturo Labriola, Paolo Orano, and Enrico Leone can do that much better than I can.

I shall dangle a few general concepts before your eyes and then some fiery sentiments that blaze more fiercely and are more devastating than any onslaught by Garibaldian red shirts.

In our Futurist Manifesto, published one year ago in the Parisian *Le Figaro,* we extolled the whole gamut of Patriotism, War—the sole cleanser of the world—, the destructive acts of the anarchists, and the beautiful ideas that are worth dying for, gloriously contrasted with the vile ideas people currently live for.

Certainly, these principles and these words have never, until now, had any contact with each other. You have been accustomed to thinking of patriotism and war as being totally opposed to anarchism, which caused so many lives to erupt, in the struggle for greater freedom.

Without getting bogged down in lengthy and tedious discussions of a more or less philosophical nature, let us simply acknowledge that the seemingly contradictory ideas—the collective and the individual—are, in reality, very closely related. For does not the development of the collective depend on the exertions and initiatives of individuals? And what's more, the prosperity of a nation has its origins in hostility toward, yet imitation of, the multiple elements of which it is composed. In just the same way, the industrial and military rivalry that arises between nations is an essential factor in the progress of mankind. A strong nation can contain, at one and the same time, masses of people intoxicated by patriotic enthusiasm and reactionaries who are panic-stricken at any sign of revolt! Here we see two quite different directions for the very same instinctive courage, strength, and energy.

Do not the destructive acts of the anarchist perhaps represent an absurd yet beautiful hankering after the ideal of a justice that can never be realized? Are they not perhaps a barrier erected to oppose the invasive arrogance of the dominant, victorious classes? Speaking personally, I much prefer the bomb of a Vaillant to the cringing attitude of the bourgeois who hides away in a moment of danger, or to the loathsome selfishness of the peasant who deliberately maims himself rather than serve his country.

As for our glorification of war, which we shall never tire of repeating, it does not constitute a contradiction of our ideals, as some people think, nor does it point to regression to a barbaric age. Our position is that the vital questions of physical and moral well-being ought, of necessity, to be resolved precisely by having recourse to war, in preference to all other solutions. Is not the life of the nation rather like that of the individual who fights against infection and high blood pressure by means of the shower and of bloodletting? In the same way Nations, in our view, have to observe a constant, healthy regime of heroism, and indulge themselves in glorious bloodbaths!

And the consequences? You will tell me . . . We know them well enough! We know that a period of misery inevitably follows a war, whatever its outcome. Yet it is quite a short period when a war has been won, and not as long as you might think, when it has been lost. True enough, but don't we have such periods of misery—and without any glorifying light—as a result of a simple crisis in the stock market or the dirty game of stock-jobbing?

Off with you! Away with this sort of self-interest! Will you then accept no other ideals than those of your own comfort and a quiet life? And furthermore, just remember that the logical and necessary purpose of great armies on land and on sea is war. It is better therefore to embrace it as a soldier than to endure it like a sheep.

To your shame, you have adopted Giolitti's reformist blueprint, the cause of our present decline, that inauspicious, indeed, idiotic prescription of a greedy, profiteering peace settlement. We, on the other hand, promote and support the dual preparation for war and revolution, under the auspices of a more intense patriotism, in the divine name of Italy, blazoned across our skies in the fiery vapors of a revitalized Italian courage. We believe that only an aesthetic of blood and an ethic of danger and heroism can purify and regenerate our nation.

Those among you who are more loyal to tradition will object that that sort of intellectual program will inevitably remain at the level of utopianism and vain paradox.

Arturo Labriola in his recent article in *Il pungolo* censured in us Futurist poets and painters our tendency to mix art and politics, so as to defend our national pride and encourage the expanding working-class movement.

This famous sociologist, and our dear friend, seems to me to have succumbed, not unnaturally, to a prejudice, given the historical novelty of our point of view.

Indeed, try and answer my question:

From the moment we realized we owe the fearful state of corruption, opportunism, and easygoing commercial cynicism into which the Italian parliamentary system has gradually sunk, to several generations of politicians, we poets and artists (by virtue of what I would say is a total absence of any profitable market) have been the only ones to keep alive the flame of an absolute selflessness, in the blinding light of an ideal of unattainable beauty. Have we not, therefore, we who only write verse or paint pictures, without any hope of adequate remuneration, have we not perhaps the right to teach selflessness? Are we not allowed, then, to chase the merchants from the temple and to offer our strength and our hearts to Italy, in the name of art? Do you maybe think we are incapable of practical politics because of our excessive imagination? Certainly, regardless of all our artistic shortcomings, we shall do no worse than our predecessors. And besides, we believe that history awaits us. Undoubtedly, you will have observed that in the unfolding of human events, a period of idealistic, self-sacrificing violence is inevitably followed by one of self-centered, avaricious mercantilism, such as that in which we now find ourselves.

Now, we wish to revive the bold, passionate endeavor of the race that knew how to bring about Italian independence, and we shall do it without the exciting stimuli of unfurling flags and military bands, we poets and artists; without having recourse to new political systems, and spreading only the fire of an inextinguishable enthusiasm throughout this Italy that is plagued with skeptics and cynics, by simply electrifying this vile and deluded Italy! Would it really seem absurd to you if one day our parliament were to embrace five hundred artists instead of the usual five hundred profiteers?

You will tell me, in obedience to the teachings of our great Georges Sorel, that nothing is more harmful to the interests of the revolutionary proletariat than intellectuals. And you'll be right, for in this present day, intellectualism and culture are synonymous with egotistical ambition and a backward-looking obscurantism.

But we artists are not intellectuals of that sort. Above all else, we are fast-beating hearts, bundles of electrified nerves, instinctive beings who are ruled only by a divine, intoxicating intuition, and we believe ourselves to be, or indeed are, all ablaze with the proverbial sacred flame.

Without stopping, we have passed through the catacombs of pedantic erudition. We know enough to walk without stumbling, and we won't stumble, we wouldn't even if we were less cultured, for we have the sure instincts of youth.

We wish to snatch violently away from the old, the dying, and the dead all the rights and the authority and instead grant these to youth.

Futurism therefore proclaims the necessary intervention of artists in public affairs, so as *to turn government into a selfless art*, at last, in place of what it is now, robbery become a pedantic science.

But I can already hear you mumbling about our technical inexperience. What of it? Away with you! . . . Don't forget that the Italian race is only capable of producing great artists and great poets, whom it should not be entirely impossible to instruct quickly, after a few months' observation of parliamentary mechanisms.

I believe that parliamentarianism, which was devised to give the majority a say in the running of the country, is destined to perish if artists are not permitted to replace the lawyer class which, until now, has had a monopoly of the seats, demonstrating beyond all measure their sole function, that of selling and skillfully exploiting their knowledge and their words.

Therefore, it is especially from these habitual practices of the lawyers that we wish to liberate Italian political life. And it is for this reason that we vigorously oppose the people's lawyers, and generally every sort of intermediary, such as brokers and middlemen, all the great cooks of universal happiness, and most particularly those who wish to slow down with every means at their disposal the advent of a glorious future, especially the enemies of all violence, the ignoble masters of low diplomacy, whom we deem harmful to, and obstacles in the way of, the rise of the human spirit in its conquest of a greater freedom.

Their presence has by now become ridiculous, laughable, in the midst of this violent, inflexible life of ours, which is intoxicated by a frenzied ambition, and over which there towers the new, terrible god of danger.

The dark forces of Nature, ensnared in the nets and traps of chemical and mechanical formulas, and therefore enslaved by mankind, wreak a terrible revenge, leaping at our throats, with all the impetuous savagery of mad dogs. But you know all about this, you who labor in the arsenals, you stokers on ocean liners, you submariners, you steelworkers and laborers at the gasworks!

II

Part II of the speech is heavily corrected and the resulting version is printed, with only minor changes, in *La giovane Italia* on July 10, 1910, and *L'internazionale* on July 16, 1910. The last section ("This facile, discouraging, and destructive irony" to "not of a dead worker this time, but of the Revolution!"), translated in document 11, is not included in the manuscript. Instead, it contains the following paragraphs:

But is Italian patriotism really dead? No, it isn't, but it has been doused down and submerged in the murky sea of pacifist and internationalist rhetoric. But it will be rekindled—not like some excavated ancient monument but as a steadying influence in our blood, one of life's essential components. Love of our nation is nothing more than an extension of the love we feel for our mother. To those who see me as backward-looking and conservative because I revere the love of country, I declare that nothing can bridge the enormous gap between my mother, whom I adore, and all other women, to whom I remain indifferent. Nothing can cast down the invisible barriers that separate our native land from those other lands that surround it.

I am well acquainted with your past objections and can predict those yet to come. Your corrosive logic is also quite capable of reducing the present arrangement of separate countries into a simpler separation of races. But this will only come about hundreds of years from now, certainly no sooner, despite our quick-as-lightning ability to get anywhere, made possible by the railways and their innumerable tunnels.

Give the human heart time to grow over two or three centuries and it may get used to being proud of belonging to the Latin race and of loving Latin blood.

In the meantime, it can only be proud of being Italian and of loving only Italian blood.

So I'm telling you that the twin ideas of the nation and of revolution blossom forth from the loftiest, most complex intellects. Do you honestly believe that those who abandoned their native land to go abroad created internationalism and destroyed the idea of the nation?

In their wanderings, those emigrants, thirsting for adventure and conquest, like burning brands shot out of the fire, have borne the Italian flame to foreign hearths, without in any way dousing that original flame back home. You don't need me to tell you that *Patriotism* means above all else fortifying national industry and commerce and intensifying the development of our intrinsic qualities as a race in the forward march of our victory over competing races.

France may serve as a warning against excessive intellectualism and loss of habitual courage, ever-increasing personal freedom, and a mercurial susceptibility toward revolution, not to mention her magnificent combative patriotism. But don't mistake me for a starry-eyed optimist. I have long studied the defects of our great Latin sister and am thus perfectly aware of them: her incurable alcoholism—albeit limited almost exclusively to Paris; her diminishing population—not brought about by alcoholism itself, or by an excessively erotic culture, or indeed by a lack of religious feelings, as many have claimed, but more, rather, by a spirit of parsimony and niggardliness, as Professor Richet clearly demonstrated in his study, *Documents of Progress*. Thus it is that in France too we find traces of that same money-minded mediocrity that plagues the Italians. Nonetheless, we have to admire the intense, fervid, prolific activity of that nation, where the antimilitarism of Gustave Hervé flourishes alongside the latest Orléanist revolt, both of which beat against and wear down the crumbling walls of a radical-socialist parliamentarianism, which is stolidly defended by the shrewd resolve of Georges Clemenceau and Aristide Briand. And all of this unfolds in the immense glow of a single word: France! Just ask any French worker, who is not involved in an antimilitarist union and not fired up by an immediate desire to make propaganda, and he will reply in the magniloquent tones of an Emperor: I am a Frenchman.

This is what we want for every single Italian. If we are to revive and defend the worn-out idea of freedom and rekindle the faded notion of justice, we need, above all else, to have a proud and strong sense of our own identity. To have a sense of our own identity means, for us, being proud of being Italian. This we desire with all our heart. We are independent, patriotic Italians, steadfast in our courage, thirsting for the freedom and heroism to make war or revolution, and not be a flock of starving sheep.

III

The manuscript of part III of the speech is preserved in three different drafts. The large-lettered text will have been Marinetti's speech manuscript. Sections of it are heavily corrected and some of the new text is identical with the version printed in *La propaganda* of July 16–17, 1910. For one long passage ("And it is for this reason that we would exile all priests from schools" to "imposing figures such as Napoleon, Crispi, Ferrer, and Blériot"), there is no equivalent in the manuscript. One must assume that Marinetti added these new passages to the speech when he gave it in Milan or Padua, or that he wrote them specially for the printed version.

NOTES

INTRODUCTION: F. T. MARINETTI (1876–1944): A LIFE BETWEEN ART AND POLITICS

1. F. T. Marinetti, "Le Mouvement poétique en Italie," *La Vogue*, April 1899, p. 61.
2. Carlo Carrà, "La mia vita," *Tutti gli scritti*, ed. M. Carrà (Milan: Feltrinelli, 1978), p. 655.
3. "Prime battaglie futuriste," *Guerra sola igiene del mondo*, in *Teoria e invenzione futurista*, 1st ed. p. 201, 2nd ed. p. 235; see document 25, *Futurism's First Battles*.
4. Quoted in David D. Roberts, *The Syndicalist Tradition and Italian Fascism* (Chapel Hill, N.C.: University of North Carolina Press, 1979), pp. 103–104.
5. For a survey of these attitudes, see Klaus Vondung, ed., *Kriegserlebnis: Der erste Weltkrieg in der literarischen Gestalt und symbolischen Deutung der Nationen* (Göttingen: Vandenhoeck und Ruprecht, 1980); Elizabeth A. Marsland, *The Nation's Cause: French, English, and German Poetry of the First World War* (London: Routledge, 1991); Richard Cork, *A Bitter Truth: Avant-garde Art and the Great War* (New Haven, Conn.: Yale University Press, 1994); Philippe Dagen, *Le Silence des peintres: Les artistes face à la Grande Guerre* (Paris: Fayard, 1996); Frédéric Lacaille, *La Première Guerre mondiale vue par les peintres* (Paris: Citédis, 1998); Uwe Schneider and Andreas Schumann, eds., *Krieg der Geister: Erster Weltkrieg und literarische Moderne* (Würzburg: Königshausen & Neumann, 2000); and Ugo Leonzio, *La grande guerra vista dagli artisti* (Rome: Canesi, n.d.). The Italian scene has been illuminated by Mario Isnenghi, *Il mito della grande guerra da Marinetti a Malaparte* (Bari: Laterza, 1970), and Fabio Todero, *Pagine della grande guerra: Scrittori in grigioverde* (Milan: Mursia, 1999).
6. See document 26, *The Battle of Trieste*.
7. Carlo Carrà, *Guerrapittura* (Milan: Edizioni futuriste di "Poesia," 1915), p. 47.
8. Giovanni Antonucci, *Lo spettacolo futurista in Italia* (Rome: Studium, 1974), p. 47.
9. For a detailed analysis of these performances, see Günter Berghaus, *Italian Futurist Theater, 1909–1944* (Oxford: Clarendon Press, 1998), pp. 197–201.
10. This is what he called it in the manifesto *Dynamic and Multichanneled Recitation*, *Teoria e invenzione futurista*, 1st ed. p. 105, 2nd ed. p. 123; see in this volume p. 193.

11. The history of the party, its activities, and its political program has been analyzed in Günter Berghaus, *Futurism and Politics: Between Anarchist Rebellion and Fascist Reaction, 1909–1944* (Oxford: Berghahn, 1996), pp. 97–155.

12. Marinetti, *Taccuini*, p. 409.

13. Ibid., p. 405. A longer character portrait of the Duce can be found in document 48.

14. All relevant documents from the Italian State Archives have been published in Berghaus, *Futurism and Politics*, pp. 112–17, 162–63. As to the three Futurists mentioned here: Ferruccio Vecchi (1894–1957?) was a leading figure in the Futurist Political Party, coeditor of *Roma futurista*, and chairman of the Milanese section of the Association of Arditi. In 1921, he was expelled from the Arditi and Fasci because of his intransigent ideological attitudes. Mario Carli (1889–1935) was a noted Futurist writer, coeditor of *L'Italia futurista* and *Roma futurista*, and founder of the Association of Arditi. He had strong Bolshevik leanings and left the Fasci in June 1920 in protest against Mussolini's move to the Right. Vittorio Ambrosini (1893–1971) was a journalist and founding member of the Arditi, and later joined the Communist and anti-Fascist Arditi Rossi. See also note 1 to document 50, *Fascism and the Milan Speech*.

15. Marinetti, *Taccuini*, p. 448.

16. See the speeches in Piazza Belgioioso, in Monza, and in Piazza Sant'Alessandro, printed in *Teoria e invenzione futurista*, 1st ed. pp. 471–76, 2nd ed. pp. 541–46.

17. Marinetti, *Taccuini*, p. 487. Literally translated, he wrote, "We have not come down from the Karst . . ." The Battle of the Karst (Carso) in July 1915 brought Italy a major victory.

18. For a survey of Futurists engaged in anti-Fascist activities, see Berghaus, *Futurism and Politics*, pp. 173–217.

19. Mario Carli and F. T. Marinetti, *Lettere futuriste tra arte e politica*, ed. Claudia Salaris (Rome: Officina, 1989), p. 52.

20. Letter of February 1, 1919, in Francesco Cangiullo and F. T. Marinetti, *Lettere, 1910–1943*, ed. Ernestina Pellegrini (Florence: Vallecchi, 1989), p. 125.

21. Ibid., pp. 134–35.

22. Letter of February 2, 1920, in the private archive of Massimo Carli, quoted by E. Gentile, "Il futurismo e la politica," in Renzo de Felice, ed., *Futurismo, cultura e politica* (Turin: Agnelli, 1988), pp. 105–59, quotation on p. 139.

23. See Marinetti's introduction to *Futurismo e fascismo* (1924), in *Teoria e invenzione futurista*, 1st ed., pp. 430, 432; 2nd ed., pp. 494, 496–97.

24. Most of them participated in the dozens of local groups sprinkled across the peninsula, some operating as "independent Futurists." The number of "over one thousand" is given by Tullio Crali in Ervino Pocar, *Il mio fratello Sofronio* (Gorizia: Cassa di Risparmio, 1976), p. 193, and confirmed by the journal *Futurismo*, which reported on October 15, 1933, that "more than one thousand artists participate in the First National Exhibition of Futurism."

25. Although several thousand German artists fled into exile, many more chose to remain in Germany and work in fields deemed "unpolitical," thus earning a livelihood and surviving under conditions of what is usually referred to as *innere Emigration*.

26. Corrado Govoni, "Facciamo i conti," *Futurismo* 2, no. 28 (March 19, 1933).

27. Enzo Benedetto, *Futurismo cento x 100* (Rome: Arte-Viva, 1975), p. 88.

28. See Tullio Crali's testimony in Pocar, *Il mio fratello Sofronio*, p. 193.

29. Stefano Tuscano, "Eroismo e pagliaccismo nell'arte e nella vita," *Il perseo* 8, no. 10 (May 15, 1937): 1–2.

30. See Y. de Begnac, *Taccuini mussoliniani*, ed. F. Perfetti (Bologna: Il Mulino, 1990), p. 325.

31. The spies of the Ministry of Popular Culture monitored not only Marinetti's statements against the new race laws but also the positive echo his protestations found in the Jewish press. See Archivio Centrale dello Stato, *Ministero di Cultura Popolare*, busta 6, fasc. 57, fol. 10.

32. Relevant papers in the Central State Archive in Rome, documenting "an unmitigated hostility towards the Ministero della Cultura Popolare" have been discussed in Berghaus, *Futurism and Politics*, pp. 254, 274–75, 281–90, 303–306.

33. Osvaldo Licini in a letter to Giuseppe Marchiori, dated February 1, 1939, in O. Licini, *Errante, erotico, eretico: Gli scritti letterari e tutte le lettere* (Milan: Feltrinelli, 1947), p. 140.

34. The journal was edited by Mino Somenzi, who was regularly attacked because of his Jewish origins. In Renzo de Felice's view, the last issues of *Artecrazia* were among the most forceful attacks on Fascist anti-Semitism, hypocrisy, and corruption to be mounted by Italian intellectuals. See his *Storia degli ebrei italiani sotto il fascismo*, 3rd ed. (Turin: Einaudi, 1977), vol. 1, pp. 368–75.

35. F. T. Marinetti, "Collaudio," Carlo Belloli, *Testi-poemi murali* (Milan: Edizioni Erre, 1944).

THE PRE-FUTURIST YEARS (1876–1908)

I SELF-PORTRAIT

1. Enrico Marinetti (1838–1907) went to Egypt in 1865 to offer legal advice to the parties involved in the construction of the Suez Canal (1859–69). He set up a lawyer's office in Alexandria, with branches in Cairo and Khartoum, and became a rich and highly respected member of the large expatriate community in Egypt. But in the 1890s the rising tide of Muslim and Egyptian nationalism and the political unrest directed against corruption in the Khedival government made the life of European businessmen ever more precarious. In 1895 Marinetti senior decided that it was time to enjoy the fruits of his years of expatriate labor and returned to Milan, where he acquired the elegant house in via Senato 2, referred to in document 2, *The Foundation and Manifesto of Futurism*.

2. Amalia Grolli (1842–1902) was the daughter of a professor of literature at the University of Milan and a trained musician, with a degree from the conservatory in Milan. She did much to encourage her son's love of poetry and music.

3. Although there were several Italian schools in Alexandria, a strict and thorough French education was deemed to be more advantageous in an upper-class family.

4. This streak of mysticism, as opposed to conventional Catholic religiosity, continued

throughout his life. In the 1910s it revealed itself in his interest in parapsychology and occult sciences, and in the 1930s in the spiritual dimensions of aero-Futurism. It was only in his last years that the former propagandist for "de-Vaticanization" returned to the bosom of the Church.

5. This is not entirely true. As a letter of the rector to Marinetti senior of June 15, 1891, indicates, the fifteen-year-old boy was found reading books that were deemed "contrary to Catholic morality," publicly praising the authors of novels "whose titles he should not even know," and propagating ideas deemed "intolerable." One can imagine how the upright lawyer reacted to this revelation. Consequently, Marinetti junior threatened to leave school, but was persuaded otherwise by the rector, who liked the boy because of "the quality of his mind and heart." Marinetti expressed his great esteem for Zola in an essay in *Le Papyrus*, "Le Mouvement littéraire contemporain."

6. Twenty-one numbers in all appeared between February 1894 and January 1895. After issue 17 (October 10, 1894), the editorship passed into other hands. It was the anticlerical tone of the publication that caused Marinetti's final rupture with his school and his decision to take his final exams in Paris.

7. He enrolled at the Sorbonne in April 1894 and took his baccalaureate there in July 1894.

8. John Stuart Mill (1806–73) was a major philosopher and political scientist. He was considered in his time to be a radical and a socialist because of his positive views on public ownership of natural resources, equality for women, compulsory education, and birth control. Marinetti's early enthusiasm for Mill is likely to have been prompted by *On Liberty* (1859), translated into French in 1860 as *La Liberté*, but he would also have studied *Thoughts on Parliamentary Reform* (1859) and *Considerations on Representative Government* (1861), especially when he wrote his doctoral thesis on parliamentary democracy.

9. In November 1895 Marinetti enrolled at the University of Pavia to study law. After the death of his brother Leone, he continued his studies in Genoa (1897) and took his doctorate on July 14, 1899, with a thesis titled "The Role of the Crown in Parliamentary Government."

10. From 1898 Marinetti functioned as *sécrétaire général* of *Anthologie-Revue de France et d'Italie: Recueil mensuel de littérature et d'art*, a poetry magazine founded in 1897 by Edward Sansot-Orland and dedicated to popularizing French Symbolism in Italy and making the Italian Symbolist poets known in France. "Les Vieux Marins" was published in *Anthologie-Revue* 1, no. 12 (December 1898). Gustave Kahn's *Samedis populaires* were a regular series of matinee poetry readings and performances of plays written by young poets and playwrights. Kahn made a conscious attempt, with his *samedis*, to return poetry to its true domain, that of public recitation, where voice and gesture transformed the printed word into live acts of the highest intensity.

11. In the early 1900s Marinetti presented the latest Italian poets in France and toured Italy with an equally modern French repertoire, stocked with many of his own poems. This experience furnished him with the virtuosity and adroitness he would later draw on when, in 1910, he commenced his Futurist *serate*.

12. Between 1905 and 1909 Marinetti published thirty-one numbers of *Poesia*.

13. These are only some of the Futurist poets. The journal was truly international in orientation and published poems by French, German, English, Spanish, and Russian authors.

14. Although the germs of Futurism can be found in Marinetti's early publications, the journal *Poesia* only became the official organ of the Futurist movement in 1909.

15. This collection of poems was published in 1902 by the Éditions de la Plume.

16. Marinetti's first play, *Le Roi Bombance: Tragédie satirique en 4 actes, en prose*, published in 1905 by the Société du Mercure de France, was a veiled satire on the reformist Socialist Filippo Turati, the intransigent Socialist Enrico Ferri, and the Revolutionary Syndicalist Arturo Labriola.

17. The production was organized by the Théâtre de l'Œuvre, directed by Aurélien-François Lugné-Poë, and was performed April 3–5, 1909, at the Théâtre Marigny in Paris. For a detailed analysis of the play and its production, see Günter Berghaus, *The Genesis of Futurism* (Leeds: Society for Italian Studies, 1995).

18. Charles-Henri Hirsch had written a derogatory review of *Le Roi Bombance* and suggested that its author had had an affair with Jane Catulle-Mendès, which caused Marinetti to box his ears at the Théâtre des Arts on April 14, 1909. The next day, Hirsch sent his second, and on April 16, 1909, the duel took place at the Parc des Princes. In the ninth reprise, Hirsch's sword broke; in the eleventh reprise, Marinetti injured Hirsch's forearm and caused a hemorrhage. Hirsch was attended to by a doctor, but he was adamant about going on with the duel. However, after the twelfth reprise, everybody agreed that he was unable to carry on, and the duel was suspended, giving Marinetti another proof that eleven was his lucky number.

19. The text continues with a report on the first *serate*, which I have omitted here as it is presented more fully in the texts translated in documents 25–29.

THE FOUNDATION OF FUTURISM (1909)

2 THE FOUNDATION AND MANIFESTO OF FUTURISM

1. The first part of this text is an epic account of the foundation of the Futurist movement, written a few months after the manifesto itself (which can be dated October to December 1908), and continued in document 4, *Second Futurist Proclamation: Let's Kill Off the Moonlight*. The famous *Figaro* version of February 20, 1909, consisting of introduction and manifesto, was issued with a "health warning" by the editors: "Mr. Marinetti, the young Italian and French poet, a remarkable, hot-blooded talent known throughout the Latin countries by virtue of his resounding public appearances, . . . is solely responsible for the ideas [expressed in this manifesto], which are singularly audacious and exaggerated to the point of being unjust to certain eminently respectable and—luckily—generally respected matters. However, we thought it interesting to offer to our readers the first edition of this publication, whatever opinion they may form on it."

2. The introduction to the manifesto is highly autobiographical: Marinetti often sat with his friends Buzzi, Cavacchioli, Notari, and Lucini in his salon filled with Oriental

clutter, which had been brought back from Alexandria in Egypt, where his family had lived for thirty years. Following his student years and the death of his mother (1902), Marinetti moved into this apartment and shared it with his father. After the latter's death in 1907 it became the headquarters for Marinetti's publishing enterprise.

3. The roaring automobiles and screeching double-decker trams ran down Corso Venezia, only a few steps away from the via Senato, where Marinetti was living.

4. The Naviglio canal ran close by Marinetti's house and was lined with old villas and patrician houses.

5. Death was an important trope in Marinetti's early poetry, linked to Nietzsche and anarchism, both referred to often in the iconoclastic poetry of his pre-Futurist days. For example, in his cycle of poems *Destruction* (1904), death was described as a positive "life" force, which gives energy and dynamism to the universe. Death releases the creative potential of human beings and fuels the metamorphoses of existence. Marinetti cultivated the image of the rebel through his publications, public lectures, poetry recitations, and cultural activities. With *The Foundation and Manifesto of Futurism*, he cast a poetic grenade into the world, which appears to have been inspired by a passage in Nietzsche's *Gay Science*: "The desire to destroy, to change, to create something new, can be the expression of an abundant force, pregnant with Future. My term for this is, as everyone knows, 'Dionysian'" (*Fröhliche Wissenschaft*, §370).

6. Marinetti was born in Egypt to middle-class parents who had their two children looked after by local wet nurses. Filippo Tommaso's affection for his Sudanese nurse is also mentioned in document 1.

7. Marinetti's evocation of the birth of Futurism as a dangerous journey resembles several of his early poems, such as "Le Démon de la vitesse," "A Mon Pégase," or "La Mort tient le volant." Marinetti himself was the proud owner of an automobile and nearly lost his life in an accident, which was described in a note in *Corriere della sera* on October 15, 1908: "This morning, shortly before twelve o'clock, F. T. Marinetti drove in his automobile along via Domodossola. The owner of the car was himself at the steering wheel. He was accompanied by the mechanic Ettore Angelini, 23. For unknown reasons, but probably in order to avoid a cyclist, the automobile ended up in a ditch." The experience did not lessen Marinetti's love of cars. He hailed the automobile as a symbol of modern life and saw in the racing car a modern equivalent to the Winged Victory of Samothrace (see note 8 below). Just as the ancients had sung their dithyrambs to honor the god Dionysus, he dedicated several odes to this modern demigod. Both were friends and benefactors of the human race and provided it with the means of achieving *ivresse*. What for the ancients was wine, for his modern contemporaries is speed. Marinetti saw these gifts as elixirs of life that could inspire man to the poetic expression of his vitality.

8. A famous marble sculpture commissioned around 190 B.C. by the citizens of Rhodes to commemorate their naval victory over the Seleucid king, Antiochus III. It portrays Nike, the Greek goddess of victory, standing on a ship's prow, with her wings spread and her clinging garments rippling in the wind. The sculpture was discovered in 1863 on the Aegean island of Samothrace and given a new home in the Louvre.

9. This is a reference to recent inventions and technologies that allowed human beings to overcome the age-old limitations imposed by time and space, for example, high-speed travel (steam trains, bicycles, automobiles, airplanes) and the use of new means of communication (telegraph, telephone).

10. On Marinetti's concept of health and hygiene see document 9, *War, the Sole Cleanser of the World.*

11. This is a reference to the spectacular assassinations of Tsar Alexander II (1881) and King Umberto I of Savoy (1900) and the anarchist bomb attacks that shook Paris in 1892–94. When Marinetti was studying in Paris, he had plenty of opportunity for acquainting himself with the doctrines of Anarchism. After his return to Italy he became friends with the Revolutionary Syndicalist Walter Mocchi and the anarchist poets Gian Pietro Lucini and Umberto Notari. Together they frequented the anarchist and syndicalist circles in Lombardy and recruited there some of the early supporters of the Futurist movement. The iconoclastic mentality of the artists Marinetti gathered around himself was also reflected in his own writing, which often celebrated the anarchists' *beaux gestes libertaires.* It has even been suggested that Marinetti's early poetry was influenced by the style and tone of anarchist magazines, brochures, and posters. See Fanette Roche-Pézard, "Marinetti et l'anarchie," in Jean-Claude Marcadé, ed., *Présence de F. T. Marinetti* (Lausanne: L'Âge d'Homme, 1982), pp. 67–85; and Giovanni Lista, "Marinetti et les anarcho-syndicalistes," ibid., pp. 127–33.

12. The phrase "scorn for women" caused considerable discussion and forced Marinetti to clarify the issue in the preface to *Mafarka* (see document 5) and in *Against Sentimentalized Love and Parliamentarianism* (see document 10).

13. As Marinetti elucidated in his interview with *Comœdia* (see document 3), he made a distinction between a feminist movement "as it triumphs in France today, thanks to a magnificent elite of intellectual women," and its variant in Italy, "where it is confined to unbridled and small-minded careerism and oratory ambitions." See also his comments on the English suffragettes in *Against Sentimentalized Love and Parliamentarianism* (document 10) and in *Lecture to the English on Futurism* (document 16).

14. Marinetti was familiar with and influenced by Gustave Le Bon's analysis of the burgeoning mass society.

15. This is a reference to Leonardo da Vinci's *Mona Lisa* painting in the Louvre.

16. Marinetti was only speaking metaphorically here, as he made clear in his interview with the French theater magazine, *Comœdia.* See p. 19.

17. On Marinetti's understanding of the concept of violence see document 11, *The Necessity and Beauty of Violence.*

3 FUTURISM: AN INTERVIEW WITH MR. MARINETTI IN COMŒDIA

1. The first production of *Le Roi Bombance*, organized by the Théâtre de l'Œuvre, was directed by Lugné-Poë and was performed between April 3 and 5, 1909, at the Théâtre Marigny in Paris.

2. Auguste Vaillant (1861–94) was an anarchist who, on December 9, 1893, threw a nail bomb from the second row of the public gallery in the Palais Bourbon into the Chamber of Deputies. This protest action against the repressive policies of the gov-

ernment of Casimir Périer injured twenty deputies. He was subsequently condemned to death and guillotined on February 3, 1894.

3. Salomon August Andrée (1854–97) was a Swedish aeronautical engineer and a pioneer of manned and dirigible balloon flights; Wilbur Wright (1867–1912) and his
younger brother Orville (1871–1948) invented and flew the first practical airplanes.

4 SECOND FUTURIST PROCLAMATION: LET'S KILL OFF THE MOONLIGHT

1. The list of the Futurist brothers-in-arms varies from edition to edition, depending on
who recently joined or left the movement, or in some cases *promised* to become part
of it. When the manifesto was first published (in August 1909 but dated April 1909),
the *actual* membership was certainly much smaller than indicated here. Neither
Boccioni, Carrà, Russolo, Severini, nor Balla had yet become members of the movement. However, the list makes it clear that Marinetti intended his "school" to extend
beyond the confines of literature into the fine arts and music.

2. In 1915 Marinetti published extracts of this manifesto as a broadsheet, *Discorso futurista agli abitanti di Podagra (Roma) e di Paralisi (Milano)*, which indicated unmistakably
that he had Rome and Milan in mind with the inhabitants of Goutville and Paralysis.

3. The structural device of portraying Futurism as a journey—already employed in *The
Foundation and Manifesto of Futurism*—was a metaphor Marinetti had used repeatedly in his early poetry, although at that time the anarchist rebellion was not yet
called Futurism. See Berghaus, *Genesis of Futurism*, pp. 45–55. Given Marinetti's
humanist education, he may also have drawn parallels with Prometheus's challenge
to the gods, Ulysses' travels, the flight of Icarus, the Battle of the Centaurs, etc. The
message behind the incendiary rhetoric is that the future can only be erected on the
ruins of the past.

4. Marinetti alludes here to Nietzsche's concept of death as a midwife of the New
Man. Marinetti saw himself as a Messianic leader in the mold of Zarathustra, and
his followers as a race of "Supermen" crossing the bridge between past and future.

5. Marinetti made the "pleasure of being booed" a fundamental principle of his Futurist *serate* and theater performances. However, the violent confrontation with the
forces of tradition was also a common feature of his recitations of anarchist poetry
in the years preceding 1909.

6. Marinetti's love of madness draws heavily on Nietzsche, who portrayed the *Übermensch* as a man who also used the "bolt of lightning that is madness" against the
"mumblers and mollycoddlers" who live in "a city of pusillanimous souls and frail
bodies," and against "the old academies, where self-conceit and arrogance reigned."
The copious parallels between Marinetti's Futurists and Zarathustra's army of "pro-
creators and cultivators and sowers of the future" have been discussed in Berghaus,
Genesis of Futurism, pp. 65–72.

7. Marinetti harks back here to his early poetry, where moon and stars were symbols of
sentimentality, nostalgia, and lethargy. He pitched the sun as the life force against
the hypnotizing *claire de lune*, or sought to disarm this "accursed sorceress" by
means of the electric light.

8. Marinetti had already dealt with this theme in his playlet *Dans les cafés de nuit* (1904).

It also featured in a painting by Balla, depicting Volta's first arc lamp, which had been erected in front of Rome's main railway station. Balla himself claimed that "I wanted to show that romantic 'moonlight' had been defeated by the light of the modern electric lamp. In other words, it was the end of romanticism in art: the phrase 'Let's kill off the moonlight' came from my painting." See Berghaus on this claim, *Italian Futurist Theatre*, p. 260, note 3.

9. The Indian Ocean, Arabian Sea, and Bay of Bengal meet at Cape Cormorin, the southernmost tip of India.

10. As Simone Cigliana has shown in *Futurismo esoterico* (Rome: La Fenice, 1996), pp. 158–60, Marinetti is drawing here on the mythological fight of Ardjuna against the sons of the Moon, the Kauravas, as it was related in the Mahabharata and Bhagavad-Gita and interpreted by Edouard Schuré in *Les Grands Initiés* (Paris: Perrin, 1889).

11. Disciples of the historical Buddha Shakyamuni were known to wear blue robes.

5 PREFACE TO *MAFARKA THE FUTURIST*

1. This list gives an adequate idea of the size of the Futurist "brotherhood" in its initial phase, whereas the names mentioned in the second manifesto, *Let's Kill Off the Moonlight*, indicate Marinetti's "target group."

2. The novel *Mafarka the Futurist* caused considerable uproar at the time and became the subject of a drawn-out court case, which itself became the topic of a Futurist publication (*I processi al futurismo per oltraggio al pudore*, 1918). Its controversial nature has not diminished over the years, as the copious critical literature shows; however, as Carol Diethe, in the foreword to her recent English translation, emphasized, there are still many aspects of the novel that need further exploration.

3. In §9 of *The Foundation and Manifesto of Futurism* (document 2), Marinetti declared his scorn for women as a complementary measure to the hygienic value of war. This led to an extended discussion on the women's question in the pages of *L'Italia futurista*. Many of these articles showed that the Futurist war against sentimentalized *amore* and old-fashioned *donnine* went hand in hand with an active support for a liberated sexuality and the idea of a modern woman unencumbered by the forces of tradition. See also document 10, *Against Sentimentalized Love and Parliamentarianism*, and document 55, *Against Marriage*, and the legislative measures proposed in document 45, *Manifesto of the Futurist Political Party*.

4. In Marinetti's early poetry, the tyranny of the stars and the moon were symbolic of the crushing force of nostalgia and melodramatic sentimentality. The Futurist insurrection was only a politicized and more encompassing rebellion against this general Italian malaise.

5. Marinetti's rhetoric is modeled on the language of prophets and messiahs in the best tradition of Catholic *propaganda fidei*. This complements the style of bardic hymns adopted for *Let's Kill Off the Moonlight*, the medical vocabulary of Futurism as a cure for sclerosis of body and mind, and his anarchist war cries against the establishment.

6. This is Chapter 9 of the novel *Mafarka the Futurist*.

7. This is an oft-repeated metaphor in Marinetti's Futurist writings, referring to the view that the avant-garde can only serve its function for a short while. In *The Foundation*

and Manifesto of Futurism (document 2, p. 16) he writes, "Our successors will rise up against us, from far away, from every part of the world, dancing on the winged cadenzas of their first songs, flexing their hooked, predatory claws, sniffing like dogs at the doors of our academies, at the delicious scent of our decaying minds, already destined for the catacombs of libraries."

8. The word used here by Marinetti, *dura*, refers to the sorghum grain, a staple of the Arabian and North African diet, where it is commonly known as *dhurra*. It is used for making porridge, flat bread, beer, syrup, and molasses.

9. Many of Marinetti's metaphors seem to have received inspiration from Nietzsche's *Thus Spake Zarathustra*. Mafarka's railing against the forces of tradition is very similar to Zarathustra's vituperation of the pusillanimous souls and frail bodies living in a "city of shopkeepers, where floweth all blood putridly and tepidly and frothily through all veins." See Book III, Chapters 51 ("On Passing By") and 52 ("The Apostates").

10. The myth of Icarus serves as a parallel to the myths of Prometheus and of the Centaurs, alluded to in *Let's Kill Off the Moonlight*. Challenging the stars and reaching out to infinity is also a prominent topos in Marinetti's early poetry. See Berghaus, *Genesis of Futurism*, pp. 45–55.

11. As Emilio Gentile has demonstrated in his studies of nineteenth- and twentieth-century salvation movements with a political bent, a great number of secular religions arose out of the crisis of civilization that followed the Industrial Revolution and occupied a place that had formerly been filled by the Church and its dogmas. Marinetti was the Messiah of just such a quasi-religious project for restoring health to the modern psyche.

12. A few years later, when Futurism reached its second phase, this became the guiding principle for the "Futurist re-fashioning of the universe," a Utopian program based on abstract, absolute, and universal principles. The aim of the artists and innovative thinkers involved in this enterprise, inspired by Marinetti's earlier formulation of this task, was to replace the "given" nature with a newly created nature.

13. A zumhara is a long, obliquely held flute, popular among nomads of the Sudan.

14. This glorification of death as a force for fecundation, taken principally from Nietzsche and various anarchist theorists, was expressed in similar form in *Le Roi Bombance*. See Berghaus, *Genesis of Futurism*, pp. 69–71.

15. Such treacherous dallying in the arms of a beautiful woman was a prominent feature of the heroic journeys depicted in Marinetti's early poetry. Some of these were dedicated to "Térésah," Marinetti's girlfriend, the poet Teresa Corinna Ubertis.

16. Saint Putrefaction was an allegorical character in *Le Roi Bombance*, who exhales "the vivifying and destructive breath of metempsychosis" (p. 238) and explains the eternal cycle of "Creation, Destruction, Regeneration" thus: "What you call death is nothing but one of many mutations, which in their succession constitute life" (p. 247). This philosophy of life is, of course, derived from Nietzsche's Law of Eternal Return.

17. Marinetti repeatedly portrayed death as a midwife to life, who "from a dying womb pulls forth the future, a radiant baby" (*Le Roi Bombance*, p. 111). This is largely based on Zarathustra's doctrine of Voluntary Death, which sees dying not as "going down" into an abyss but as "going over" a bridge poised between two states of existence.

6 WE RENOUNCE OUR SYMBOLIST MASTERS, THE LAST OF ALL LOVERS OF THE MOONLIGHT

1. Symbolism was a French school of literature and fine art, flourishing approximately from 1885 to 1905. Marinetti considered one of its masters, Gustave Kahn, his "mentor" (see *La Grande Milano*, p. 243), and much of his early poetry was written in late-Symbolist style. The "moonlight" in the title stands for romanticism, i.e., a culture to be overcome by modernism. This manifesto was therefore an act of literary patricide.

2. ". . . a former heaven where beauty blossomed." The line is quoted from the poem "Les Fenêtres" (1863) by Stéphane Mallarmé.

3. In Poe's eerie poem "The Raven" (1845), the sleepless narrator, who has been mourning the death of his lover, is visited by a prophetic bird of death, who responds to all questions with the ominous refrain "Nevermore."

4. See document 15, *Extended Man and the Kingdom of the Machine*.

5. The *esthétique du paysage* refers to "given Nature" as opposed to created Nature. A few years later, Balla and Depero wrote a manifesto on this Futuristically refashioned universe.

6. There was a long-standing enmity between Marinetti and D'Annunzio, who, like the French Symbolists, had a profound influence on him. Marinetti settled his account with his former hero in *Les Dieux s'en vont, d'Annunzio reste* (Paris: S. Sansot, 1908).

7. Giovanni Pascoli (1855–1912), one of Italy's best-loved poets, was regarded as a latter-day Virgil because of his bucolic *Myricae* (1891) and *Canti di Castelvecchio* (1903).

8. Antonio Fogazzaro (1842–1911) was a poet and novelist whose deeply religious spirit animated his literary works, which were primarily concerned with moral issues. Marinetti wrote an excoriating diatribe against him, "Antonio Fogazzaro poeta degl'imbecilli," *Poesia* 5, nos. 3–6 (April–July 1909): 62–65.

9. Marinetti singled out these authors primarily because they focused on modern city life and the role of the new collectives in an industrial civilization. Émile Zola (1840–1902), founder of the French Naturalist school, was Marinetti's favorite author during his student years in Egypt. The American bard Walt Whitman (1819–92), author of zestful hymns celebrating freedom, democracy, and modern man, also interested him because of his use of Free Verse. J. H. Rosny-Aîné, pseudonym of Joseph-Henri-Honoré Boex (1856–1940), was a popular science fiction author who wrote, among other things, *Le Bilatéral: Mœurs révolutionnaires parisiennes* (1887) and *La Vague rouge: Roman de mœurs révolutionnaires* (1910). Paul Adam (1862–1920), an anarchist friend of Marinetti's, was author of over forty socially critical novels portraying mass man, modern industry, capitalism, and so on, including *Le Trust* (1910). Gustave Kahn (1859–1936) was a major representative of French late-Symbolist poetry and a great influence on Marinetti. *Les Villes tentaculaires* (1895), by the Belgian author Émile Verhaeren (1855–1916), described how the great industrial centers devoured the surrounding countryside. In the 1911 version of the manifesto, Marinetti adds to this list the anarchist author Octave Mirbeau (1850–1917) and his satirical depiction of business life in the drama *Les Affaires sont les affaires* (1903).

10. In the 1911 version of the manifesto, this paragraph starts with "Futurism, with the

great poets Gian Pietro Lucini and Paolo Buzzi at its helm, launches Free Verse in Italy. The dynamism of Free Verse, which is essentially fluid . . ."

11. Cf. document 20, *Technical Manifesto of Futurist Literature*, §§10 and 11.

12. As in the previous paragraph, "Futurist lyricism" replaces the "Futurist Free Verse" of the 1911 version of the manifesto.

13. The Parnassians were a late-nineteenth-century French school of poetry that thought of the "I" as resulting from a creative tension between selfhood and exterior reality.

14. Marinetti was engaged in a long-standing debate on abstract art with the Florentine Futurists, especially Arnaldo Ginna. After 1912, the Roman Futurists Balla and Prampolini also carried out significant research in the field of abstract art. Marinetti's position wavered between partial acceptance and global rejection of abstract art. See Giovanni Lista, *Futurisme: Abstraction et modernité* (Paris: édition trans/form, 1982).

15. This is an excerpted quote from document 2, *The Foundation and Manifesto of Futurism*.

16. The same passage is quoted in document 20, *Technical Manifesto of Futurist Literature*.

THE FUTURIST POLITICAL PROGRAM (1909–13)

7 First Futurist Political Manifesto

1. The Associazione Nazionalista Italiana (ANI) was founded in 1910 by Enrico Corradini (1865–1931).

2. Marinetti's political engagement on the side of both nationalism and anarchism caused considerable consternation at the time and forced him to clarify his position in several essays and interviews. See Berghaus, *Futurism and Politics*, pp. 59–62.

3. Marinetti's patriotic sentiments made him a fervent advocate of irredentism, the political movement seeking to "redeem" the territories claimed by Italy but then still governed by Austria. The political status of Trieste was a key focus in this debate, hence Marinetti's attempts at stirring up unrest in that city by means of political demonstrations, articles in the local press, and theater evenings of a political character. See Berghaus, *Futurism and Politics*, pp. 48–52, and *The Battles of Trieste*, document 26.

4. The *serata* (plural: *serate*) was a theatrical genre invented by the Futurists, characterized by the violent audience reactions it provoked. See documents 25–30.

5. This *serata* has been analyzed in Berghaus, *Italian Futurist Theatre*, pp. 86–91.

6. This *serata* has also been analyzed in Berghaus, *Italian Futurist Theatre*, pp. 91–97.

7. General Vittorio Asinari di Bernezzo (1842–1923) was forced to take early retirement, in 1909, following some anti-Austrian and irredentist pronouncements made to his soldiers. See note 10 to document 25, *Futurism's First Battles*.

8 Our Common Enemies

1. Ottavio Dinale, editor of *Demolition: An International Review of Battle*, had taken a serious interest in Marinetti's movement and had printed, in the issue of March 15, 1909, *The Foundation and Manifesto of Futurism*. It found a controversial reception

in anarchist circles and prompted a lively dialogue between the most radical subversives of the artistic and political spheres, leading, in May 1910, to the foundation of a Union of Revolutionary Forces. Marinetti's essay was introduced with the following editorial note: "We are neither so sectarian nor so stupid as to set narrow, specific limits on our beliefs. And that's what we made clear to F. T. Marinetti when he launched his courageous journal *Poesia*, and even more so when we read his Futurist proclamations. So, when F. T. Marinetti, in his aspirations for a great future, hurls anathema at a past that is clogged up with mummies and prejudice, and throbs for every manifestation of life and revolt—from the frissons felt at a rally to the hurricane of a strike or an act of assassination by a libertarian—we say 'Bravo!' And we don't give a damn if the audience at the Teatro Lirico in Milan hoots and whistles, or if the hirelings of subversive factions protest and hurl their insults at us."

2. In medieval theology, the empyrean was the seventh and highest heaven.

9 War, the Sole Cleanser of the World

1. It appears that the relationship between Futurism and the anarchist movement deteriorated in 1911. Marinetti continued to operate with the (anarchist) concept of a (revolutionary) war, although at the time of the War in Tripoli and of the First World War, it took on other dimensions too. This was also the case for the anarchists, who largely supported the national war. The heated debates between anarchists and Futurists in 1910–11 have been documented in Umberto Carpi, *L'estrema avanguardia del Novecento* (Rome: Editori Rinuniti, 1985), and Alberto Ciampi, *Futuristi e anarchisti: Quali rapporti?* (Pistoia: Archivio Famiglia Berneri, 1989).

2. The concept of health occupied a central role in Marinetti's writings. "Dr. F. T. Marinetti," as he proudly signed many of his early essays and theoretical reflections, conducted his surgical strikes against the perceived illnesses of the body politic, and earned himself a reputation for being *il Poeta Pink*, named after a popular medicine advertised as a means "of restoring a weak organism and providing the best cure against anemia, sclerosis, and general fatigue." Marinetti considered Futurism, war, and revolution to be purgatives that could cleanse the political system constipated with bile and dead matter.

10 Against Sentimentalized Love and Parliamentarianism

1. See *The Foundation and Manifesto of Futurism*, document 2. The text bears many similarities to the ideas of Valentine de Saint-Point, an intimate friend of Marinetti's, who was given responsibility for "Women's Action" in the directorate of the Futurist movement and had been solicited to write *The Manifesto of Futurist Women* and *The Futurist Manifesto of Lust*.

2. Although Marinetti's wording is rather ambiguous, he does not refer here to the female sex per se, but to the idealized myth of "eternal femininity." In fact, Marinetti's use of the sign "Woman" (a symbolic embodiment of an outmoded aesthetic and a reactionary social practice) was markedly different from the actual support he gave to female artists, causing the French journal *Femina* to comment: "May I express a certain doubt about M. Marinetti's scorn for women? It appears that his pen is more

brutal than his thinking." Marinetti's disdain for the traditional woman's role in Italian society and the conventional life model of "kitchen, children, church" received enthusiastic responses from many women, especially young ones. A large number of their letters and essays on the women's question were published in *L'Italia futurista*, the only Italian newspaper published by a woman, and in the "Woman and Futurism" section of *Roma futurista*.

3. This translation follows Marinetti's usage of lowercase *amore* and capitalized *Amore*, although he never establishes clear semantic boundaries between the two.

4. Marinetti gave three lectures to suffragettes in London in 1910 (see document 16, *Lecture to the English on Futurism*), and participated in the window-smashing suffragette march through the London Docklands in 1912, causing "many Suffragettes to convert to Futurism . . . and to come to the station with a sudden show of friendship, to see us off" (*La Grande Milano*, p. 292). Consequently, the London press viewed Futurism and the suffragette movement as two faces of the same coin, labeled "the output of a lunatic asylum," "the source of the plague," "demented and maniacal creatures," and so on. See Janet Lyon, "Militant Discourse, Strange Bedfellows: Suffragettes and Vorticists Before the War," *Differences: A Journal of Feminist Cultural Studies* 4, no. 2 (1992): 100–33.

5. The reference here is to vote-buying from poor, uneducated women.

6. Particularly in France and Italy there was a growing opposition to the deceitfulness and dishonesty of the governing classes and the corrupt state of liberal democracy, causing many intellectuals to advocate a clean break with the parliamentary system.

7. Leo Tolstoy (1828–1910) preached the doctrine of Christian love, nonviolence, and nonresistance to evil.

8. The French queen, Cathérine de Medici, ordered the killing of Huguenot nobles, many of whom were assembled on the occasion of her daughter Marguérite's wedding to the future King Henry IV, on St. Bartholomew's Day (August 24, 1572). It caused the death of some two thousand Protestants in and around Paris and an estimated eight thousand to ten thousand throughout France.

9. Louis Blériot (1872–1936) was an inventor, aircraft designer, and pilot, best known for his flight over the English Channel on July 25, 1909. Many of his early constructions crashed, but his Blériot V was the world's first successful monoplane.

10. In *Mafarka the Futurist* (1910) Marinetti tells the story of the creation of an artificial being, Gazurmah, by the African king Mafarka. See document 5, *Preface to Mafarka the Futurist*.

II The Necessity and Beauty of Violence

1. For Part I of the speech, I follow the version printed in *L'ardito* on June 15, 1919, headed: *Abolition of the Police*. It contains a number of textual changes not found in the original speech of 1910. Most significantly, the first column of the *L'ardito* version is entirely related to the political situation of 1919 and has been omitted here. A translation of the original manuscript of Part I (*L'amore del pericolo e l'eroismo quotidiano*, Beinecke Library, Box 18, Folder 1180) can be found in the Appendix.

2. Marinetti's concept of violence is based on Georges Sorel's writings, which were

highly influential in Italy, especially in the Revolutionary Syndicalist movement. Sorel's "violence" was not an appeal to terrorist bloodshed, but rather a metaphysical principle that resembled Bergson's *élan vital*. Without this positive life force, there would be no evolution or progress. For a detailed examination of these concepts and their influence on Marinetti, see Berghaus, *Genesis of Futurism*, pp. 17–27.

3. See document 2, *The Foundation and Manifesto of Futurism*, §9.

4. See Marinetti's interview with the French theater magazine *Comœdia*, on March 26, 1909, translated as document 3.

5. In Marinetti's anthropology, class struggle and the struggle between nations—revolution and war—were two sides of the same coin, called *élan vital*.

6. Giovanni Giolitti (1842–1928), parliamentary representative since 1882 and five times prime minister. Leonida Bissolati (1857–1920), right-wing Socialist leader, who cooperated with the bourgeois government and was expelled from the PSI in 1912. On January 11, 1919, Marinetti participated in a protest action against Bissolati's willingness to cede Dalmatia to Yugoslavia. This passage in the 1919 edition of the speech would have been formulated differently in 1910.

7. Arturo Labriola (1873–1959), a militant socialist who left the PSI in 1907 and became a leader of the Revolutionary Syndicalist movement. He was an important point of reference in Marinetti's early career. Labriola took a sustained interest in the Futurist movement and wrote several articles about their activities.

8. Cf. Luke 20: 45–46: "And he went into the temple, and began to cast out them that sold therein, and them that bought; saying unto them, It is written, My house is the house of prayer: but ye have made it a den of thieves."

9. Georges Sorel (1847–1922), a leading theoretician of the Revolutionary Syndicalist movement, whose principal work was *Reflections on Violence* (1908). He was one of the most significant influences on Marinetti's political concepts.

10. The three Cooks of Universal Happiness in Marinetti's play *Le Roi Bombance* were the reformist Socialist Filippo Turati, the intransigent Socialist Enrico Ferri, and the Revolutionary Syndicalist Arturo Labriola.

11. Part II is taken from the article "La necessità della violenza," in *La giovane Italia*, no. 43 (July 10, 1910), reprinted in *L'internazionale* 4, no. 307 (July 16, 1910).

12. Francisco Ferrer ý Guardia (1859–1909), anarchist and educator, was accused of masterminding the riots and rebellion in Barcelona during what came to be known as the Tragic Week (*Setmana Tràgica*, July 26–31, 1909). These events were the culmination of the long struggle against the Catholic Church and Castilian domination, and served as a model for the Spanish Civil War (1936–39). Protestors burned down eighty churches and blew up railroads, but were eventually defeated by Spanish soldiers, who killed over six hundred workers; 1,725 individuals were indicted by military courts and five of them were sentenced to death. The case against Ferrer was almost completely without legal foundation. He had been abroad between March and June 1909 and spent most of the Tragic Week on his farm, some fifteen miles outside of Barcelona. However, he was much hated by the government and clerics, who were intent on destroying him. An international protest movement, in which Marinetti also participated, tried to save his life, but he was executed by a firing

squad in Montjuich prison, on October 13, 1909. The judicial murder of Ferrer was an act of gross injustice that led to demonstrations throughout Europe.

13. In Greek mythology, Tithonus, son of the king of Troy, was such a beautiful mortal that Eos, the goddess of the dawn, became enamored of him and implored the gods to grant him immortality. Zeus assented to the request, and the couple lived peacefully in her palace. But as Eos had forgotten to have eternal youth included in the gift, her consort withered as he grew older, until in the end he was no longer able to move his limbs.

14. In 1909 Marinetti fought a well-publicized duel with the novelist Charles-Henri Hirsch (see p. 419, note 18), and in 1911 challenged the publisher Tito Ricordi, who declined, however, to participate in such barbaric acts of violence.

15. This paragraph bears some resemblance to *Le Roi Bombance*, where Saint Putrefaction, like a bird of prey, hovers over the Pools of the Past.

16. Calatafimi, in the Sicilian province of Trapani, is connected with Garibaldi's victorious battle against the Bourbons, on May 15, 1860.

17. The Julian Alps stretch from northeastern Italy to Slovenia, where they rise to 2,864 meters at Mount Triglav. They are named, like the province of Venezia Giulia, after Julius Caesar. The region was contested between Italy and Austria during the period of the Risorgimento, and was one of the focal points of the irredentist struggle up to the First World War.

18. A system of philosophy based upon the teachings of Epicurus (c. 340–c. 270 B.C.). In its popular sense, the word stands for a desire to lead a life of refined pleasures of the senses, particularly of the palate.

19. The Cimitero Monumentale is an evocative artistic necropolis, built between 1863 and 1866 by the architect Carlo Maciachini. It contains an astonishing array of works which make it a major museum of both modern and classical Italian sculpture.

20. Marinetti makes reference here to an event that occurred during the General Strike of 1904. On September 15, in via Carlo Farini, Angelo Galli, an Italian anarchist, was killed by the police. As his funeral was going to be used as a political demonstration, the police forbade holding the service in the cemetery. Determined to bury their comrade, the anarchists gathered in a square in front of the cemetery, where they were attacked by the police, mounted on horseback, who nearly knocked the coffin to the ground. The Futurist Carlo Carrà, an active member of the anarchist movement, recorded the event in his autobiography and in a famous painting, *Funeral of the Anarchist Galli*.

21. Marinetti repeatedly chastened the workers for their materialistic preoccupations ("the reign of the belly"): "The masses still love street demonstrations and noisy colorful processions more than anything else. I believe that our race, more than any other, would love to have these violent and tragic, but also revolutionary demonstrations, as well as bloody battles, *on a permanent basis* and always *on the streets* (because after the spectacle—crush punch thrash police arrest fisticuffs revolver shots—people can go and have dinner and recount what they have seen and done, and then go *to bed* to have a good fuck!)—Revolution is an intermittent war, with the

evening spent in the bosom of the family and in bed with the wife." Marinetti, *Taccuini*, p. 418.

22. Part III of the speech is taken from "Necessità e bellezza della violenza," *La propaganda: Giornale sindacalista* 12, no. 878 (July 16–17, 1910).

23. See document 10, *Against Sentimentalized Love and Parliamentarianism*.

24. Per Henrik Ling (1776–1839), Swedish medical-gymnastic practitioner, suffered much from rheumatism and developed a set of daily exercises that completely restored his bodily health. He believed in a unifying relationship of mind and body and that health was based on a harmony among the nervous, circulatory, and respiratory systems.

25. D'Annunzio's novels were notoriously considered to be erotic and scandalous at the time of their publication.

26. Francesco Crispi (1819–1901), Italian statesman, leading figure in the struggle for national unity and a key architect of the young Italian State. Louis Blériot (1872–1936), inventor, aircraft designer and pilot, who built the world's first successful monoplane.

27. The next paragraphs repeat, with a few minor textual variations, the text at the end of Part II, from "This facile, discouraging, and destructive irony" to "not of a dead worker this time, but of the Revolution!"

12 SECOND FUTURIST POLITICAL MANIFESTO

1. Soon after the unification of Italy, attempts were made at colonialist expansion, especially in North and Northeast Africa. The occupation of Libya (then a part of the ailing Ottoman Empire) in October 1911 was contested by Turkey and led to war. The peace treaty of Ouchy (October 18, 1912) granted Italy sovereignty over Tripolitania and Cyrenaica.

2. The Peace Palace in The Hague was set up to house the Permanent Court of Arbitration, established by the Convention for the Pacific Settlement of International Disputes, concluded at The Hague in 1899 during the first Hague Peace Conference.

3. The dreadnought was a powerful, much-feared, big-gun battleship, developed by Britain after Japan's victory over the Russian navy at the 1905 Battle of Tsushima, in which long-range fire decided the outcome.

13 THIRD FUTURIST POLITICAL MANIFESTO

1. The manifesto was published on the occasion of the 1913 national election campaign. The street actions that accompanied the distribution of this program have been documented in Berghaus, *Futurism and Politics*, pp. 70–71. Rumor had it that Marinetti was going to run as a candidate against Bissolati, a rumor which he scotched in an interview with *Giornale d'Italia* on October 30, 1913. Nonetheless, he declared that he intended to lead Futurism into the political battlefield, with a program that "fused the ideas of the Nation and war with the concepts of progress and liberty." Asked whether his manifesto converged with the program of the Nationalists, he emphasized again their diverging attitudes toward tradition and the cultural values of the past.

THE FUTURIST COMBAT IN THE ARTISTIC ARENA (1910–15)

14 AGAINST ACADEMIC TEACHERS

1. The German philosopher Nietzsche was one of the foremost influences on Marinetti's ideology and weltanschauung, as is evident in his early notebooks, poems, and essays. See Berghaus, *Genesis of Futurism*, pp. 65–72.
2. Italian translations of Nietzsche's works began to appear in 1898, and in the years preceding the First World War Nietzschean thinking was rapidly disseminated in Italy, although generally only its more superficial aspects, such as the doctrine of the *Übermensch* and the *Wille zur Macht*, were cultivated. See Manuela Angela Stefani, *Nietzsche in Italia: Rassegna bibliografica, 1893–1970* (Assisi: Carucci, 1975). On Marinetti and the Superman myth see notes 4 and 6 to document 4, *Second Futurist Proclamation: Let's Kill Off the Moonlight.*
3. The shooting of Camillo Ghelli, a teacher of literature at the Lycée Vittorio Emanuele II in Palermo, by his pupil Riccardo Li Donni, took place on May 18, 1910, and probably gave rise to this manifesto.
4. The Futurist method of slaps and punches was used in the protest actions at Rome University in December 1914. See Berghaus, *Italian Futurist Theatre*, pp. 74–77.
5. See note 9 to *Against Sentimentalized Love and Parliamentarianism*, document 10.
6. I have quoted one of the police files on Marinetti in Berghaus, *Futurism and Politics*, p. 52.

15 EXTENDED MAN AND THE KINGDOM OF THE MACHINE

1. The foregoing chapter was "Against Sentimentalized Love and Parliamentarianism" (document 10).
2. In later editions, the preceding paragraphs are omitted and the manifesto starts with the sentence, "We are developing and promoting a great new idea . . ."
3. Marinetti is probably referring to the great rail strike of 1906, during Clemenceau's first term as prime minister.
4. However, in the *Technical Manifesto of Futurist Literature* (document 20), Marinetti warned against any superficial projection of human feelings onto the machine: "Be careful not to force human feelings onto matter. Instead, divine its different governing impulses . . . Through intuition we will conquer the seemingly unconquerable hostility that separates out human flesh from the metal of motors." For a detailed discussion of the Futurist machine cult and its main proponents, see Berghaus, *Italian Futurist Theatre*, pp. 396–494.
5. Jean-Baptiste Lamarck (1744–1829) was a biologist whose theory of evolution had a great influence on Darwin. He believed that adaptive changes in lines of descent, over long periods of time, were ultimately driven by environmental change, causing the mutation of species through the formation and modification of organs according to need.
6. The Futurists, like many scientists of the period, took a great interest in paranormal phenomena. Marinetti, Balla, Boccioni, Russolo, Bragaglia, Severini, Ginna, Corra, and others attended spiritualist events, studied hypnotism and psychokinesis, and

explored clairvoyance and telepathy. See Germano Celant, "Futurism and the Occult," *Artforum* 19, no. 5 (July 1981): 36–42.

7. Arthur Schopenhauer (1788–1860) saw in love the manifestation of a biological necessity and a powerful impulse toward "the will-to-life." In his dissertation "The
Metaphysics of the Love of the Sexes," in the second book of *The World as Will and
Idea* (1818), he quoted Spinoza's definition, "*Amor est titillatio, concomitante idea
causae externae*" (Love is an erotic stimulation accompanied by the idea of an outer
cause; *Ethica* iv., propos. 44, *demonstr.*), and held that "love, however ethereally it may
bear itself, is rooted in the sexual impulse alone." Nonetheless, it causes emotional
upheavals and "the pathetic and sublime elements in affairs of love, which for thousands of years poets have never wearied of representing in innumerable examples." In
his view, works of art and philosophy offer consolation from the pain of a broken heart.

8. See document 4, *Second Futurist Proclamation: Let's Kill Off the Moonlight.*

16 LECTURE TO THE ENGLISH ON FUTURISM

1. Marinetti went to London in late March 1910 to discuss the possibility of a Futurist
serata with an English impresario. He used the occasion to give a lecture, in French,
at the Lyceum, a women's club with a large suffragette membership. Pratella's
chronicle, "Futurism and War" (*Teoria e invenzione futurista*, 1st ed. pp. 482ff, 2nd
ed. pp. 554ff), mentions another lecture in London, in April 1910. These speeches
were repeated, at least in substance, in December 1910. According to Luciano Folgore, "In November [1910], Marinetti gave six lectures in six days, founded an English group of Futurist painters, and took part in two banquets given in his honor"
(*Negli hangars del futurismo*, in C. Salaris, *Luciano Folgore e le avanguardie*, p. 153).
The month given here is likely to be wrong, as on December 3, 1910, Marinetti
wrote to Pratella: "I leave for London today and shall be back on the 15th or 16th"
(Lugaresi, *Lettere ruggenti a F. Balilla Pratella*, pp. 18–19). The lecture was attended
by quite a few suffragettes and reviewed by Margaret Wynne Nevinson (the mother
of the painter C.R.W. Nevinson, coauthor of *The Futurist Manifesto against English
Art*), under the title "Futurism and Woman," in *The Vote*, December 31, 1910. *Futurismo e fascismo* mentions as the date for the text of this lecture June 1910, but this
probably refers to the Italian version of the speech. Soon after his return to Italy,
Marinetti edited a broadsheet, *Il futurismo trionfa a Londra*, in which he described a
recitation given at the Poets' Society, and the response his lecture received at the
Lyceum Club. According to Marinetti's testimony of 1929, the "Speech to the English" was complemented by readings of manifestos dedicated to Futurist literature,
drama, painting, and music. His presentation of *The Founding and Manifesto of Futurism*, with its provocative statement about "scorn for women," caused "the plentiful
Suffragettes, present in the hall, to instigate violent pandemonium and interruption"
(*Teoria e invenzione futurista*, 1st ed. p. 514, 2nd ed. p. 590). It seems that Marinetti's views on the English did not change over the years, as parts of this manifesto
were still reprinted in the volume *Inghilterra fogna di passatismo* by Gaetano Patta-
rozzi (Rome: Unione Editoriale d'Italia, 1941).

2. See note 3 to document 12, *Second Futurist Political Manifesto.*

3. Although Oscar Wilde was a successful author, his literary attacks on the manners and double standards of the English upper classes also earned him many enemies. His relationship with Lord Alfred Bruce Douglas, or Bosie, the third son of the eighth Marquess of Queensberry, was not tolerated by London high society, as homosexual acts were illegal in England at that time. When Bosie's father accused him of being a sodomite, Wilde took legal action against him. At the Old Bailey, Queensberry was acquitted of libel, and instead Wilde was put on trial. He was convicted of indecent behavior and sentenced to two years of hard labor.

4. A first attempt at introducing a sanitary "necessary" came in 1596, when Sir John Harrington, godson to Queen Elizabeth I, set about making a water closet fitted with a flushing toilet bowl. In the 1770s, Alexander Cummings, Samuel Prosser, and Joseph Bramah perfected the design. Thomas Twyford revolutionized the water closet business in 1885, when he built the first trapless toilet in a one-piece, all-china design. Milan's transformation into a modern city, around the turn of the twentieth century, brought to its citizens unprecedented sanitary comforts, such as drinking water running directly into apartment blocks, drains connecting every house to an underground sewage system, and water closets fitted into every modern building.

5. This sentence ends Chapter 2 of *Le Futurisme*. The next passages form part of Chapter 3, "Ce deplorable Ruskin."

6. John Ruskin (1819–1900) was Slade Professor of Art at Oxford University and one of the greatest British art critics of the Victorian age. He fiercely attacked the worst aspects of industrialization and helped to start the environmental movement. He was a painstaking antiquarian and a champion of the Gothic Revival style, which drew its inspiration from medieval architecture in Europe. In *The Stones of Venice*, a three-volume study of Venetian art and architecture (1851–53), he sought to prove that the city's Gothic architecture reflected national and domestic virtue, whereas everything afterward was a sign of corruption and decadence. He was particularly concerned with Venice's abused and neglected treasury of buildings and started the first "Venice in Peril" campaign. This stood in total contrast to Marinetti's desire to raze the rotting buildings to the ground, abolish the tourist trade, and turn Venice into a great industrial city (see document 27, *The Battles of Venice*).

7. This may be a reference to *The Odyssey* IV, lines 113–154, where Helen spinning yarn in the presence of Telemachus is characterized as "Artemis of the Golden Spindle." The material from which wool was made (flax or similar) was rolled into a ball and laid into a basket. The fibers were then drawn out, twisted into a thread, and wound around a whirling spindle. In Book 6 of *The Odyssey* it is described in the following manner: "The queen her hours bestowed / In curious works; the whirling spindle glow'd / With crimson threads, while busy damsels call / The snowy fleece, or twist the purpled wool. / . . . / Her royal hand a wondrous work designs, / Around a circle of bright damsels shines; / Part twist the threads, and part the wool dispose, / While with the purple orb the spindle glows."

17 THE FUTURIST MANIFESTO AGAINST ENGLISH ART

1. Christopher Nevinson (1889–1946) was a relatively minor painter who became a Futurist after meeting Severini in Paris in 1912. He exhibited in the "Post-Impressionist and Futurist Exhibition" in October 1913 and in the 1915 Vorticism show, both at the Doré Gallery in London. Vorticism was the first avant-garde art movement in England, launched in 1914 by the writer and artist Wyndham Lewis. He published a journal, *Blast: Review of the Great English Vortex,* which bore many traces of Futurist influence. Nevinson was the only orthodox Futurist in England, unlike the other Vorticists, who guarded their independence and were indebted to other avant-garde movements, too.

2. He is probably referring to Stanley Spencer (1891–1959), who was often considered to be a primitivist. However, in prewar London, a great deal of modernist art was considered to be primitivist.

3. Parisian modernism in its chic, rather than avant-garde, variant, dictated many of the London fashions of the period. In the years before the First World War, Roger Fry, the *arbiter elegantiarum* of the period, introduced an innocuous and elegant form of Post-Impressionism to English high society.

4. The School of Barbizon, active between 1830 and 1870, went against the academic tradition of producing landscape paintings in the studio, and instead worked in direct contact with nature. In their *paysages intimes,* in their realistic representation of simple areas of nature imbued with a special sense for light and atmosphere, these artists became precursors of the Impressionists.

5. James Watt was the inventor of the steam engine; George Stephenson pioneered the building of the first railways in Britain and the locomotives to run on them; Charles Darwin established the concept of the organic evolution of species, known as Darwinism.

6. Founded in 1886 as an exhibition society, this club of British artists felt that the official jurors of the Royal Academy neglected innovative and modern works and set up a kind of *salon des refusés* in order to make such works known to the British public. They looked principally to France for their inspiration and fostered the growth of a London Impressionist group of painters.

7. Followers of Dante Gabriel Rossetti, the Pre-Raphaelite painter.

8. The comparison of art and creativity with a drug is of capital importance in the 1920 essay *Beyond Communism* (document 63).

18 FUTURIST PROCLAMATION TO THE SPANIARDS

1. The first paragraphs of the manifesto refer to Spain's Golden Age, in the sixteenth and seventeenth centuries, when the country's exploration of the New World made it the most powerful nation in Europe. The story of this conquest is told in the form of a journey (cf. documents 2, 4, and 5) that was eventually brought to a halt by the forces of traditionalism.

2. The passage may possibly refer to some darker episodes in the history of Spain, with the suppression of Muslim resistance in the south and the activities of the Inquisition.

3. See notes 6 and 7 to document 4, *Second Futurist Proclamation: Let's Kill Off the Moonlight*.

4. On May 5, 1808, the Spanish king surrendered his crown to Napoleon, opening the way to a constitutional monarchy, proclaimed four years later. However, Catholicism remained a dominant political and economic force in the country. Different attitudes toward clericalism among the middle classes separated conservatives from radicals. Both republicans and liberals had an influential anti-Catholic faction, but the strongest supporters of a lay state were the socialists and anarchists.

5. This reference to the dark rock of the Sierra Nevada, Sierra de Gredos, Sierra de Guadarrama, etc., may have an associative connection with the black habit of the monks mentioned earlier in the manifesto.

6. The *bandiere dell'aurora* (flags of the dawn) were a symbol of the progressive political movements of the period.

7. Spanish political movement of traditionalist character that originated in the 1820s. The Carlists supported the conservative Don Carlos rather than his enlightened brother, Ferdinando VII, and advocated clerical absolutism, the restoration of the Inquisition, and military opposition to parliamentary liberalism. Ferdinando VII's death, in 1833, unleashed a Seven Years' War between supporters of Don Carlos and the successor to the throne, Isabella II. This conflict between reactionaries and liberals was one of the most significant forces in Spanish politics in the nineteenth and early twentieth centuries and caused no fewer than three civil wars.

8. After the brief First Republic of 1873–74, Spain returned to monarchical rule, by turns presided over by conservative and liberal ministries.

9. José Canalejas y Mendez (1854–1912) was a liberal monarchist who, after holding several cabinet posts, became premier in March 1910. He sought to curb the power of the religious orders and of large estate owners, but his measures against labor unrest alienated many of his left-wing supporters. He was assassinated by an anarchist.

10. The Republican Socialist Conjunction, of 1909, was a hopeful union of liberal, anticlerical, and modernist forces, led by Lerroux and Iglesias. In the local elections of December 1909, the Conjunctión Republicano-Socialista gained a large share of the vote and took control in nine provincial capitals. Alejandro Lerroux y García (1864–1949) first won prominence as a radical and virulently anticlerical demagogue, in Barcelona. In January 1908, he founded the Radical Party, which remained under his direction until the Civil War. Pablo Iglesias Posse (1850–1925) was one of the most influential leaders of the Spanish socialist movement. In 1879 he founded the Spanish Socialist Workers Party; in 1886 he became the director of *El Socialista*, and in 1889 was elected president of the UGT (Workers' General Union). In 1910 he became the first socialist deputy in the Spanish Parliament.

11. The pernicious effect of the tourist industry was also a central charge in the manifesto *Against Traditionalist Venice* (document 27).

19 AN OPEN LETTER TO THE FUTURIST MAC DELMARLE

1. Aimé-Félix Delmarle (1889–1952) arrived in Paris in 1912 and shared a studio with Severini, who introduced him to Futurism. As a result, he changed his Cubist style

of painting and became the only avowedly Futurist painter in France. He signed his manifesto *A bas Montmartre* as "A. F. Mac Delmarle Peintre Futuriste." An English translation can be found in the catalogue *Futurism & Futurisms* (Venice: Palazzo Grassi, 1986), pp. 463–64. For a recent study on the painter see Patricia Belbachir, *Félix del Marle: Itineraire d'une liberté* (Ponte-sur-Sambre: Association Connaissance Locale, 1996).

2. Marinetti arrived in Paris in June 1913 to open Boccioni's first exhibition in France, at the Galerie La Boëtie, and to give a lecture there on June 22 titled "Untrammeled Imagination and Words-in-Freedom."

3. "Mimi Pinson est une blonde / Une blonde que l'on connaît" was a song by Alfred de Musset on "a tart with a heart," immortalized by Puccini in his opera *La Bohème.*

4. The Severini-Delmarle dispute, of July 1913 (see below, note 6), was the first occasion for Marinetti to present himself not as a "Pope of Futurism" but as the leader of a "broad Church" that could accommodate both dogmatists and dissidents. Delmarle denied Severini (whom he called a "lesser chieftain of Futurism") the right to enforce the rules of a "Futurist Party" and declared himself pleased not to belong to a regiment or sect with a code of behavior and sacred hierarchies. Instead of prostrating himself before a Futurist directorate in Milan he wished to belong to "a broad and nonofficial Futurist movement, devoid of troop detachments or inner circles," i.e., a Futurism "which is virgin territory, not belonging to anyone and accessible to all those who wish to develop their individuality freely; a Futurism, that is, which represents a united, sincere attempt to create a flourishing art in tune with our civilization" ("Les Futuristes se mangent entre eux," *Comœdia*, July 23, 1913).

5. In fact, there were two battles in this Roman theater, on February 21, and March 9, 1913. Both have been described in detail by Berghaus, *Italian Futurist Theatre*, pp. 111–18.

6. This acrimonious and publicly conducted dispute was the ultimate reason for this open letter by Marinetti. Severini saw himself as the official representative of Futurism in France and was justifiably piqued to see Delmarle publish a Futurist manifesto to the French, which had not been approved by the headquarters in Milan or by him in Paris. In a letter to Marinetti on July 17, 1913, he called Delmarle a nullity, a fake, a plagiarist, a beast, and an idiot, "who feigns admiration and sympathy simply to take advantage of the celebrity of the 'Futurist' name." A. C. Hanson, *Severini futurista* (New Haven, Conn.: Yale University Press, 1995), p. 152. In an open letter to *Comœdia* and *Gil Blas* (July 19, 1913), Severini denied Delmarle the right to speak for Futurism and called the manifesto "a plagiarism penned by someone who wants to make publicity for himself, with the help of Futurism. Judging by the clichés this colleague of yours has published [in his manifesto], it is blatantly obvious that he is an absolute artistic nullity and quite unknown to the Futurist group." This caused a flurry of articles in various papers and created a great deal of confusion among journalists as to who was a "true" and who was a "false" Futurist, who belonged to the "official" school and who was a dissident. See P. A. Jannini, *La Fortuna del futurismo in Francia* (Rome: Bulzoni, 1979), pp. 255–57, and G. Lista, ed., *Futurisme: Manifestes, proclamations, documents* (Lausanne: L'Age d'Homme, 1973), pp. 390–94.

20 TECHNICAL MANIFESTO OF FUTURIST LITERATURE

1. *La battaglia di Tripoli (26 ottobre 1911) vissuta e cantata da F. T. Marinetti* (Padua: Tipografia Elzeviriana, 1912; 2nd ed. Milan: Edizioni futuriste di "Poesia," 1912).

2. The typesetting in both the French and Italian broadsheet version of this text does not indicate clearly where the "propeller speech" ends and the author takes up the thread again. After the first paragraph of §11, the text continues with a 16-mm space, just like the first two paragraphs before §§1–11. This seems to indicate that the propeller speech finishes with "—something that neither physicists nor chemists will ever accomplish." However, such an arrangement is not dictated by the meaning of the text, but follows the layout of the original.

3. Many of the proto-Surrealist devices mentioned in this manifesto come close to Breton's concept of *le merveilleux*. The Futurists repeatedly presented dramas of objects and automata with a life of their own in their Theater of Essential Brevity and Theater of Surprise shows. Such techniques were also an important feature of Futurist cinema.

4. See *The Futurist Cinema* (document 43) and *Some Parts of the Film* Futurist Life (document 44).

5. The leaflet edition renders the points 1–3 in the following manner: "It is furthermore necessary to capture the weight (ability to fly) and smell (ability to scatter) of objects, a thing which up until now one has neglected in literature."

6. Marinetti experimented with this idea in his poem "Ritratto olfattivo di una donna" (Olfactive Portrait of a Woman).

7. Marinetti describes here the origins of *Aeropittura*, officially inaugurated with a manifesto in the *Giornale della domenica* of February 1–2, 1931.

8. This address can only be found in the introduction to the collection *I poeti futuristi*. The leaflet edition says simply "voi tutti" (all you who have loved me . . . .).

9. Marinetti is not quite right here. The Königsberg philosopher and successor to Emmanuel Kant, Karl Rosenkranz, published the first systematic investigation of the aesthetics of ugliness in his treatise *Ästhetik des Häßlichen* (Königsberg: Bornträger, 1853).

10. Free Verse is a style of unrhymed poetry, which retains the rhythmic cadences of traditional poetic meter without adhering to traditional poetic forms. It was promoted by Marinetti's mentor, Gustave Kahn, a leading representative and theoretician of this type of poetry. See Clive Scott, *Vers Libre: The Emergence of Free Verse in France 1886–1914* (Oxford: Clarendon Press, 1990). Marinetti adopted the technique in his early poetry and developed from it the *parole in libertà* (Words-in-Freedom) as a Futurist invention.

11. The metaphors of hygiene and purging were central to Marinetti's thinking. See note 2 to document 9, *War, the Sole Cleanser of the World*.

12. Marinetti expands here on ideas expressed in *Extended Man and the Kingdom of the Machine*, document 15, and anticipates the advent of the Futurist mechanical art of the 1920s.

13. In other editions, this section is entitled "Supplement to the Technical Manifesto of

Futurist Literature," printed originally as a broadsheet in which the emphasized words were set in italics rather than bold.

14. Marinetti's debt to Bergson has been analyzed by Berghaus, *Genesis of Futurism*, pp. 17–20.

15. Marinetti describes here the Dadaist/Surrealist technique of automatic writing *avant la lettre*. I have discussed some of these precursor functions of Futurism in Berghaus, "Futurism, Dada, and Surrealism: Some Cross-Fertilisations Among the Historical Avant-gardes," in Berghaus, *International Futurism in Arts and Literature* (New York: De Gruyter, 2000), pp. 271–304.

21 DESTRUCTION OF SYNTAX—UNTRAMMELED IMAGINATION—WORDS-IN-FREEDOM

1. The Chinese Republican Revolt of 1911 made the founder of the Kuomintang, Sun Yat-sen (1866–1925), provisional president of the new Chinese republic (January 1, 1912). On February 12, 1912, the last Manchu emperor abdicated.

2. Alexis Carrel (1873–1944) was an innovative surgeon whose experimental transplants of body parts led to advances in the field of surgery. In 1912 he was awarded the Nobel Prize in Medicine and Physiology for his methods of transplanting blood vessels and keeping tissues artificially alive in the laboratory. His work on tissue culture first raised the possibility of growing organs outside the human body. In 1912–13 newspapers reported widely on his experiments with a chicken embryo, inaccurately depicting it as a growing, throbbing chicken heart kept artificially alive.

3. In 1909 Robert E. Peary traveled to the North Pole. The South Pole was reached first by Roald Amundsen (December 14, 1911) and almost immediately thereafter (January 18, 1912) by Robert Falcon Scott.

4. Enrico Caruso (1873–1921) and Eugenia Burzio (1879–1922) were among the most successful opera singers of their time. Their voices were immortalized on hundreds of records.

5. Marinetti refers here to the Battle of Tripoli, a central event in the Libyan War of 1911–12. The Italian army landed at Tripoli on October 5, 1911, and eventually ended Ottoman occupation of North Africa. Marinetti described the events in his book *La Bataille de Tripoli (26 Octobre 1911)* (Milan: Edizioni futuriste di "Poesia," 1912).

6. The anarchist Jules Bonnot is credited with having said: "To be an anarchist means to cherish liberty and equality; to be independent of all social, economic, political, and cultural guardianship; to be alive; to live one's life and not to jettison it for the sake of making money; to declare the end of the reign of lords and masters who deprive us of our livelihood; to advocate the abolition of the State, of the bosses, of the wage system, of the borders, of the clergy, and of all similar stupidities."

7. A later edition of the manifesto interpolates here passages from the manifesto *Extended Man and the Kingdom of the Machine* (document 15).

8. See the *Technical Manifesto of Futurist Painting* (1910) in Apollonio, *Futurist Manifestos*, pp. 27–31.

9. See Francesco Balilla Pratella's manifesto *Contro il "grazioso" in musica*, published in *Lacerba* on May 15, 1913, and on p. 466, note 5 to document 43.

10. See Luigi Russolo's manifesto *L'arte dei rumori* (March 11, 1913).

11. See document 20, *Technical Manifesto of Futurist Literature*.

12. This paragraph was published in *Lacerba* on November 15, 1913.

13. See note 10 to document 20, *Technical Manifesto of Futurist Literature*.

14. Cf. §4 of document 33, *Dynamic, Multichanneled Recitation*, and see document 20, *Technical Manifesto of Futurist Literature*. ("We are not concerned with producing spectacles of humanized matter"; "take care not to bestow human feelings on matter.")

15. This and the following section were published in *Lacerba* on November 15, 1913.

16. Brownian motion refers to the random motion of small particles suspended in a fluid, owing to bombardment by molecules. It was first observed by Jan Ingenhousz in 1785 and subsequently rediscovered by the botanist Robert Brown in 1828, when he examined under a microscope pollen immersed in water. The phenomenon was later explained by Maxwell and Einstein as invisible water molecules hitting the visible particles and moving them slightly. Modern physics calls this a stochastic process.

17. The following three paragraphs are taken from the version printed in *I manifesti del futurismo*.

18. See document 20, *Technical Manifesto of Futurist Literature*.

19. Although Marinetti was not antireligious, he had a deep-seated aversion to the Catholic Church and its clerics, regarding them as one of the most reactionary forces in the country and a key factor in Italy's backwardness in many fields.

20. Marinetti participated in the military operation during the Bulgarian-Turkish conflict and observed the assault on Adrianopolis (Hadrianopolis, or Edirne) in October 1912. The polyphonic spectacle of sounds and smells inspired him to write *Zang Tumb Tumb. Adrianopoli, ottobre 1912. Parole in libertà* (Milan: Edizioni futuriste di "Poesia," 1914). The last chapter, "Bombardment of Adrianopolis," became a *pièce de résistance* in many of Marinetti's poetry recitations and was also preserved on disk.

21. This section, taken from *Lacerba*, November 15, 1913, is an extended version of the one printed in *Lacerba*, June 15, 1913.

22. Here, for a change, Marinetti's claim is not exaggerated. On the Futurist typographical revolution, see Giovanni Lista, *Le Livre futuriste: De la libération du mot au poème tactile* (Modena: Edizioni Panini, 1984); and Mirella Bentivoglio, "Innovative Artist's Books of Italian Futurism," in Berghaus, *International Futurism in Arts and Literature*, pp. 473–86.

23. The following three paragraphs are taken from *I manifesti del futurismo*.

24. This is again a complete reversal of Marinetti's pre-Futurist views, as in 1908 he had translated Mallarmé's works, published in 1916 as *Mallarmé: Versi e prose. Prima traduzione italiana* (Milan: Istituto Editoriale Italiano, n.d.). Mallarmé's *Un coup de dés jamais n' abolira le hasard* (1897) predates not only Marinetti's attempt at abolishing punctuation but also the graphic organization of words on the page.

25. This section is taken from *Lacerba*, November 15, 1913.

26. *A Fortnightly Paper for Culture and the Arts.*

27. The Futurist artists thus transmogrified were Paolo Buzzi, Luciano Folgore, Carlo Carrà, Giovanni Papini, Ardengo Soffici, Umberto Boccioni, Francesco B. Pratella, Armando Mazza, Corrado Govoni, Luigi Russolo, Aldo Palazzeschi, Giacomo Balla, Gino Severini, Francesco Cangiullo, Auro d'Alba, Dinamo Correnti, Libero Altomare, Gesualdo Manzella Frontini, Enrico Cavacchioli, F. T. Marinetti.

28. Marinetti's career as a verse speaker began in 1898, at Gustave Kahn's *samedies populaires.* He regularly toured France and Italy with a recitation program and developed a special aesthetic, which he taught his fellow Futurists when they introduced such recitatations to the Futurist *serate.* See Berghaus, *Genesis of Futurism,* pp. 36–38, and *Italian Futurist Theatre,* pp. 172–75.

22 Down with the Tango and *Parsifal*!

1. The tango, originally a Gypsy dance, was brought to America by the Spaniards, where it mixed with influences from other immigrant cultures. In the 1880s a modern version of the tango came into existence in Buenos Aires. It was mainly danced in bars, gambling houses, and brothels, where concepts of social etiquette, taste, and propriety were markedly different from those of the middle classes. When, in the early 1900s, the tango arrived in Europe, it was thought to embody lewdness and obscenity, just as the waltz was in the early 1800s. The first dance to allow body contact and a "close-hold" technique, it soon found a home in the venues of popular entertainment, where professional dancers embraced its risqué nature. By 1914, when the tango had become an exotic social dance in the cafés, cabarets, and dance halls of Paris, Berlin, London, Madrid, and Rome, it had lost the overt sexuality of its South American prototype.

2. Marinetti refers to works which abound with Spanish local color, such as Victor Hugo's *Hernani* (1830) and *Ruy Blas* (1838), Alfred de Musset's *Les Contes d'Espagne et d'Italie* (1828–30), and Théophile Gautier's *Tras los montes* (1843), *Voyage en Espagne* (1845), and *España* (1845). In a more general sense, he criticizes French authors of a Romantic or Symbolist pedigree who popularized a certain hackneyed type of exoticism and Orientalism.

3. Jean Lorrain (1855–1906, pseudonym of Paul Duval) was a Symbolist poet, novelist, and dandy par excellence; Joris-Karl Huysmans (1848–1907), a French writer, much admired by the young Marinetti, wrote two of the best-known Decadent novels, *A Rebours* (1884) and *Là Bas* (1891); Oscar Wilde's public appearances as a homosexual dandy made him a scandalous figure in his own time. The three authors elaborated on some of the decadent themes in Baudelaire's *Les Fleurs du mal* (1857).

4. Marinetti refers here to the conversion of a fiery, erotic Latin American dance into a schematized and stereotyped dance-hall fashion, popularized by the nascent record industry in Berlin and London.

5. The passage ". . . or staring at the toes of your shoes" to the end of the paragraph was added in the second version of the text, published in *I manifesti del futurismo* of 1919.

6. Here, Marinetti seems to be following Nietzsche, who in his book *The Case of Wagner* presented Wagner as a symbol of decadence and neurasthenia (*névrosé* in the

French edition of 1910) that plagued German culture and from which Nietzsche sought to liberate his country. Marinetti set himself similar aims with regard to Italy, and for this reason forsook his youthful infatuation with Wagner, who in 1900 had still stirred up "the delirious heat in my blood and is such a friend of my nerves that willingly, out of love, I would lay myself down with him on a bed of clouds, so much am I enamored of him, right down to the most hidden heart strings of my very being" (*La Grande Milano*, p. 21).

7. Maxim's de Paris was a legendary restaurant of the Belle Époque, opened in 1893 on rue Royale by Maxime Gaillard.

8. In Wagner's opera, Kundry is a mysterious heathen sorceress who brings a phial of balm to treat Amfortas's festering lesions, which have not closed since Klingsor wounded him in a magical garden.

9. These views stand in marked contrast to Marinetti's early appreciation of Wagner as "the most appropriate artist for our modern souls." See Berghaus, *Genesis of Futurism*, pp. 42–43.

10. Here, again, Marinetti reverses his views of fifteen years earlier, when, as a critic for the journal *L'Art dramatique et musical,* he judged Wagnerian composition techniques to be superior to Debussy's Impressionist orchestration.

23 GEOMETRICAL AND MECHANICAL SPLENDOR AND SENSITIVITY TOWARD NUMBERS

1. In the *Lacerba* version of March 15, 1914, this paragraph is worded: "Its essential characteristics are: unbridled strength, speed, intense light, the happy precision of well-oiled gears; a concise bundling of forces; the molecular cohesion of metals which gather velocity in the infinite reaches of speed; the harmony of simultaneous but diverse rhythms; the fusion of independent enterprises and energies converging in one victorious path."

2. See note 3 to document 12, *Second Futurist Political Manifesto.*

3. In the *Lacerba* version he writes "gymnasts, jugglers, and clowns."

4. Cf. the proposition in document 20, *Technical Manifesto of Futurist Literature*: "In literature, eradicate the 'I,' which means all psychology" and "replace [it] with a lyrical obsession with matter."

5. During the war with Turkey in Tunisia, the Italians were entrenched near Tripoli, between Sidi-Messri and Bu-Meliana. On October 26, 1911, they were nearly wiped out by the superior cannons of the Turks.

6. The Parnassians were a late-nineteenth-century French school of poetry, which derived its name from the journal *Le Parnasse contemporain* (1866–76). The members confessed a rigorous formalism, sophisticated workmanship, and emotional detachment. Their works had traits similar to the "l'art pour l'art" aesthetics of the Decadents, and they exercised a profound influence on the Symbolists.

7. Omero Vecchi (1888–1966), a Futurist poet who replaced his old-fashioned name ("Homer Old") with the pseudonym Luciano Folgore ("Lightning"), published the poem "Salone d'albergo" (Hotel Lounge) in *Ponti sull'oceano* (Milan: Edizioni futuriste di "Poesia," 1914). It describes the hustle and bustle in a cosmopolitan hotel with its "confluence of life," "fusion of races," "amalgamation of brains," and so on.

8. Marinetti repeats here concepts already discussed in the section " The Signal Adjective, Beacon Adjective, or Atmospheric Adjective" in the manifesto *Destruction of Syntax—Untrammeled Imagination—Words-in-Freedom* (document 21).
9. This poem was printed in *Lacerba* on February 1, 1914.
10. The poem in the *Lacerba* of January 1, 1914, used graphically arranged words to imitate the shape of a train carriage, of people standing in corridors, and of a man leaning on a bench making smoke rings.
11. The words "Restrained Turkish Balloon" on p. 120 are shaped like a balloon and surrounded by shrapnel and cannon shots. In a preparatory drawing, the image is called "Embuscade de TSF bulgare." The TSF (transmitteur sans fils) was the radio-directed gunfire shot from a tank turret.

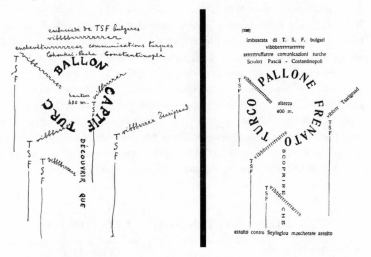

12. The poem, printed in the *Lacerba* of February 1, 1914, summarizes—in a satirical manner—the general characteristics of Italian traditionalism and eulogizes four years of Futurist battle against the forces of the past.
13. This was first published in the *Lacerba* of February 15, 1914.
14. This was Marinetti's first major book publication and was issued by the La Plume publishing house in Paris in 1902.
15. Stéphane Mallarmé (1842–98) was greatly admired by the young Marinetti. Although he criticized him repeatedly in his Futurist years, he also translated some of his prose and verse into Italian. The passage here comes from the poem "Les Fenêtres" of 1863.

24 ON THE SUBJECT OF FUTURISM: AN INTERVIEW WITH *LA DIANA*

1. Although the journal published many contributions by Futurists, the "Lacerbiani" only partially agreed with the "Marinettisti" and on several occasions were vehemently opposed to Marinetti.
2. Giuseppe Prezzolini (1882–1982), codirector of the influential literary-political magazines *Il Leonardo* and *La voce*. He was an adversary of Marinetti and an opponent of Futurism.

3. Gaetano Salvemini (1873–1957), Italian historian and political activist, professor at the University of Messina, and founder of the socialist newspaper *L'unità* (1911–20).

4. Giovanni Papini (1881–1956) and Ardengo Soffici (1879–1964), writers, artists, critics, and editors of *Lacerba*, who for a few years joined forces with the Futurists to oppose the stifling cultural climate in Italy.

5. These two essays appeared in *Lacerba* on October 1, 1913, and September 15, 1914.

6. *Mafarka il futurista* was taken to court for pornography in 1910, and *Le Roi Bombance* was slaughtered by the critics when it was performed in Paris in 1909.

7. "Life transcends intellect." Henri Bergson in *L'Évolution créatrice* reflects on the role of the intellect: "Real duration is that duration which gnaws on things, and leaves on them the mark of its tooth . . . Intellect turns away from the vision of time. It dislikes what is fluid, and solidifies everything it touches. We do not *think* real time. But we live it, because life transcends intellect. The feeling we have of our evolution and of the evolution of all things in pure duration is there, forming around the intellectual concept properly so-called an indistinct fringe that fades off into darkness. Mechanism and finalism agree in taking account only of the bright nucleus shining in the centre. They forget that this nucleus has been formed out of the rest by condensation, and that the whole must be used, the fluid as well as and more than the condensed, in order to grasp the inner movement of life." Henri Bergson, *Creative Evolution*, trans. Arthur Mitchell (London: Macmillan, 1914), pp. 48–49.

8. The second part of this paragraph can be found nearly verbatim in the manifesto *In This Futurist Year* (document 38).

BIRTH OF A FUTURIST THEATER (1910–17)

25 Futurism's First Battles

1. This first paragraph can only be found in the first chapter of *Le Futurisme* (1911). The extraordinary battles fought between the Futurists and their adversaries during the *serate* have been described in Berghaus, *Italian Futurist Theatre*, pp. 85–155.

2. The first issue of *Poesia* appeared in 1905, not 1902! Between 1905 and 1909 Marinetti published thirty-one numbers of the magazine.

3. "Elettricismo" was another name considered for the movement. On the group of poets belonging to Marinetti's circle in 1908–1909 see note 2 to document 2, *The Foundation and Manifesto of Futurism*; and note 1 to document 5, *Preface to* Mafarka the Futurist.

4. Marinetti made various claims as to the number of adherents he gathered in the first months of the existence of his movement. But 22,000 in one month is exaggerated even by his own standards!

5. The *Manifesto of Futurist Musicians* was published on October 11, 1910. Notice the plural in the title, when, in reality, there was only one musician active in the movement.

6. In an interview with *Il giornale d'Italia* on December 18, 1913, D'Annunzio declared, "With regard to wanting a strong and dominant Italy, I too am a Futurist, and there is a lot of Futurism in my works." In September 1909 D'Annunzio—nicknamed *Il*

Wright italiano—participated in an aviation festival in Brescia, and in two interviews with the *Corriere della sera* (September 11 and 13, 1909) he declared his great passion for airplanes and the ultramodern world of Wilbur Wright and Blériot, which he was going to incorporate into his latest novel. The artistic outcome of this infatuation with aviation was *Forse che sì forse che no* (Maybe Yes, Maybe No, 1910), which has as its protagonist the pilot Paolo Tarsis, a quasi-Futurist *Übermensch* who expresses his temperament by means of aerial flights and seeks a heroic death by diving with his plane into the sea. The interview Marinetti refers to appeared in *La tribuna* of June 4, 1909, in which D'Annunzio described aviation as "the most heroic feature of modern civilization" and therefore "incompatible with love." From this he concluded: "The scorn for women is a fundamental requirement for being a modern hero."

7. Vincenzo Gemito (1852–1929) was a Neapolitan sculptor who defended the Futurists in an interview with *Don Marzio*. The text was reprinted by Marinetti and distributed as a broadsheet, entitled *Vincenzo Gemito difende il futurismo* (1910). Luigi Capuana (1839–1915) was an influential critic and writer. His views on Futurism were distributed by Marinetti in two broadsheets, *Luigi Capuana difende il futurismo* (1910) and *Luigi Capuana futurista* (1910).

8. On the *serata* at the Politeama Rossetti see document 26, *The Battles of Trieste*.

9. For a detailed description of the *serata* of February 15, 1910, compiled from a broad selection of contemporaneous sources, see Berghaus, *Italian Futurist Theatre*, pp. 91–97.

10. General Vittorio Asinari, Count of Bernezzo (1843–1923), was an ardent nationalist who in 1909 made a violently anti-Austrian speech in Brescia. As a consequence, he was suspended from his post and was forced to take early retirement. The ode composed in homage to his deed was penned by Paolo Buzzi.

11. Among them were the Revolutionary Syndicalist Filippo Corridoni and the patriotic Socialist Benito Mussolini.

12. According to a letter written by Marinetti to Cangiullo shortly after the event, they sought to stop the proceedings, as Marinetti had announced an evening of poetry, not of anti-Austrian propaganda.

13. The Triple Alliance of 1882 (and renewed at ten-yearly intervals) was concluded by Germany, Austria-Hungary, and Italy, and was greatly opposed by the irredentists in Italy.

14. For a detailed description of the *serata* at the Politeama Chiarelli, held on March 8, 1910, see Berghaus, *Italian Futurist Theatre*, pp. 97–99.

15. As early as 1430 an association of artists was established in Turin, which was subsequently turned into a guild, to which Carlo Emanuele granted the exclusive right to practice their profession. In 1652 it was reorganized as the Accademia Albertina di Belle Arti.

16. The Naples *serata* at the Mercadante Theater is dealt with in the following paragraphs. For the Venice *serata*, see document 27, *The Battles of Venice*. The Padua *serata* of August 3, 1910, more or less repeated the program presented in Venice.

17. The *serata* at the Mercadante Theatre in Naples took place on April 20, 1910. See the critical account in Berghaus, *Italian Futurist Theatre*, pp. 99–102.

18. Both the French and the Italian edition present at this point a short synopsis of the court case against *Mafarka il futurista* in 1910.

19. In spring 1911, Marinetti instituted a second series of *serate*, which started on March 25 at the Teatro Bonacossi in Ferrara and should have continued on March 27 in Parma, had it not been forbidden by the chief of police on March 23. The "other provincial cities" mentioned here were Mantua (April 6), Como (April 20), Palermo (April 26), Pesaro (May 16), Bergamo (May 23), and Treviso (June 3).

20. The *serata* was scheduled to take place on March 27, 1911, at the Teatro Reinach. To stimulate interest in the event, the young poet and student, Franco Lucio Caprilli, gave a public lecture on Futurism. It caused violent disputes and prompted the authorities to issue a warning that any repetition of such scenes would lead to the participating students' expulsion from university. Nonetheless, the following Sunday, further clashes occurred on the streets of Parma between pro- and anti-Futurist students. Consequently, the *serata* was forbidden by the police "to protect public order." The Futurist students who had been involved in the event were expelled from their school or university. When, two days later, Marinetti and his companions arrived in Parma, they organized a demonstration against the city authorities. By the afternoon, some two thousand people, rioting in the streets, had to be pacified by police. Thus, the *serata* had, in reality, been shifted from the Reinach Theater onto the streets of Parma, engaging with life in the manner that had always been the professed aim of the Futurists. See Berghaus, *Italian Futurist Theatre*, pp. 105–107.

21. The Futurist group in Parma included the young anarchist Renzo Provinciali, the poet Lucio Francesco Caprilli, the composer Spartaco Copertini and his brother Crisso, the art student Riccardo Talamassi, the theater critic Giacomo Burco, and a certain Jori.

22. This open letter was distributed as a broadsheet in Parma and appeared on March 4, 1911, in the *Gazzetta di Mantova*, serving, no doubt, as publicity material for the *serata* to be held there on April 6, 1911.

23. When Marinetti arrived in Parma on March 26, he went immediately to the police headquarters to have the interdict placed on the *serata* overturned. When this could not be achieved, he and his followers strolled to the city center and sat in the Café Marchesi. Within minutes a huge crowd had assembled outside the café and the police had to intervene to protect Marinetti and his friends. They were escorted to the railway station and guarded until the next direct train to Milan could take them out of the city.

24. Apparently it had been raining cats and dogs for days, and the street propaganda on March 25 was thoroughly spoiled by torrential rain.

25. The Bersaglieri wore green hats.

26. The forbidden *serata* eventually took place on June 21, 1911.

27. The wordplay in the Italian original is on *testi* (texts) and *teste* (heads).

26 THE BATTLES OF TRIESTE

1. The events of January 12, 1910, at the Politeama Rossetti in Trieste, analyzed by Berghaus, *Italian Futurist Theatre*, pp. 86–91, served as a blueprint for many of the following *serate*. Marinetti's previous political engagements in Trieste, related

to the irredentist cause, have been discussed in Berghaus, *Futurism and Politics,* pp. 48–49.

2. The writer Antonio Fogazzaro became a senator in 1900. See note 8 to document 6, *We Renounce Our Symbolist Masters.*

3. The border of Slovenia, at that time part of the Austro-Hungarian Empire.

4. It did indeed become a major battlefield during the First World War.

5. Cormons, Friuli's wine capital, is a beautiful medieval town near Gorizia. Miramare Castle was built between 1856 and 1860 as a residence for Maximilian of Hapsburg and his consort, Charlotte of Belgium.

6. The version printed in *I manifesti del futurismo* (1919) carries the date March 1909, but this was when Marinetti had a previous engagement in Trieste and delivered the speech *Trieste nostra bella polveriera* (*Teoria e invenzione futurista*, 1st ed. pp. 247–48, 2nd ed. pp. 289–90). The Beinecke Library holds two manuscript versions of the speech, which make reference to other *serate* of 1910. This means that Marinetti used the speech again, or part of it, in later performances.

7. Armando Mazza (1884–1964) was a poet, a journalist, and an important performer in the Futurist *serate*. He was a real Sicilian Hercules, stocky, barrel-chested, with the volatile energy of a Catherine wheel and a massive body that resembled more that of a prizefighter than that of a versifier.

8. Marinetti is exaggerating yet again, just like the posters that had announced this literary soiree ("una serata di lettura poetica"), with personal appearances by Buzzi, Cavacchioli, Palazzeschi, de Maria, Mazza, and Marinetti. The first two found it prudent to stay at home, de Maria never intended to come, and Mazza ruined his voice in the first half of the *serata*, so that Marinetti and Palazzeschi had to recite most of the poems on their own.

9. Tzambal, accordion, and violin are the typical instruments of a Gypsy orchestra. The tzambal (cembalum) is a hammered dulcimer derived from the Indian/Iranian santoor.

10. The *bora* (Venetian: *borea*; Serbian: *bura*) is a strong northeast wind in the upper Adriatic.

11. Admiral Giovanni Bettolo (1846–1916) entered the House of Deputies in 1890 and was three times minister of the Marine (1899–1900; 1903; 1909–10).

12. A suburb of Trieste, famous for its vines and its carnival, and a popular destination for weekend excursions.

27 THE BATTLES OF VENICE

1. Marinetti may be referring here to his first play, *Paolo Baglione*, a historical drama, with a romantic Venetian setting, which deals with a fifteenth-century coup d'état against the aristocratic regime of the republic.

2. The Balkan countries on the northeastern Adriatic coast formed part of the Austro-Hungarian Empire. Some of this territory was claimed by Italian irredentists as belonging to the Italian nation.

3. In a letter to *Comœdia* printed on June 17, 1910, Marinetti wrote that "tout récemment" 200,000 multicolored leaflets, with this manifesto, were thrown from the

Clock Tower. I have discussed the alleged action in Berghaus, *Italian Futurist Theatre*, pp. 69–70. The four Venetian newspapers, usually thirsting for newsworthy events in the summer months, did not mention the event after either of the two dates.

4. A shortened version of *Contro Venezia passatista*, printed in three languages under the headings *Venezia futurista, Venise futuriste*, and *Futurist Venice*, was designed to be distributed from the Clock Tower in Piazza San Marco, presumably to advertise a *serata* at the Teatro Fenice and a Boccioni exhibition at the Ca' Pesaro.

5. In the letter to *Comœdia* of June 17, 1910, Marinetti wrote that this speech was given in Piazza San Marco, to the accompaniment of the municipal orchestra. The *serata* at the Fenice was meant to rally support and to rouse interest in a Boccioni exhibition at the Ca' Pesaro, which opened on July 15, 1910. However, the Fenice had recently changed hands and was hired by a new production company for the autumn season. The *serata* took place, at rather short notice, on August 1, 1910. This being the height of summer, the publicity failed to achieve its objective and hardly anyone turned up for the event. Marinetti's claim that the fist of Armando Mazza, the gigantic athlete and Futurist poet, lent weight to his arguments, is not borne out by the newspapers. They only mention the presence of Marinetti, Boccioni, Carrà, and Russolo.

6. See the manifesto translated in document 4.

7. From the twelfth to the sixteenth century Venice was one of the richest cities in the world and the center of a mercantile network spanning virtually the whole world.

8. The sirocco is a hot, dry wind blowing sand and dust from the Sahara across Italy. As the winds pick up moisture over the Mediterranean, they become increasingly humid and are the cause of oppressively sultry weather in Venice.

9. The naval Battle of Lepanto was fought on October 7, 1571, between the Holy League and the Turkish fleet. It was the first major victory of the Christians against the Ottoman Empire.

10. The island of Philae, the ancient Pi-lak, south of the city of Aswan, in Egypt, was in ancient times the most important sanctuary of the goddess Isis. It was submerged in the waters of the Aswan Dam and reconstructed on the nearby island of Agilkia.

11. To raise water levels for irrigation, several dams were built across the Nile, the first being the Aswan Dam, near the ancient city of Syene in southern Egypt. It was designed by English engineers and completed in 1902. It created a large water reservoir and provided hydroelectric power.

12. Torcello, Burano, and San Michele are islands in the Venetian lagoon. The latter is called Isola dei Morti because, at the time of the Black Death, the dead were buried there. It now serves Venice as the city's cemetery.

13. Venice became part of the Hapsburg Empire in 1798 and was thus ruled by the emperor. It was incorporated into the Italian State in 1866. Marinetti is probably referring to Kaiser Wilhelm II's visit to Venice, on March 25, 1914, to meet King Victor Emmanuel and receive confirmation of Italy's continuing support for the Triple Alliance.

28 THE BATTLES OF ROME

1. See note 6 to document 16, *Lecture to the English on Futurism*.

2. The via Appia Antica leads out of Rome, passes the ancient tombs of Romulus and

Cecilia Metella, and leads to the underground cemeteries of the early Christian Church.

3. Originally, the Colosseum had a large temporary roof to protect the audiences against inclement weather.

4. This lecture was delivered by Marinetti at a matinee performance at the Costanzi Theater, in Rome, on February 21, 1913. The theater had recently been taken over by Marinetti's old friend Walter Mocchi, who allowed Boccioni to hold an exhibition in the foyer and to open it with a theatrical presentation before an invited audience. It was a memorable event which had, as a central item on the program, Giovanni Papini's *Speech Against Rome*. See Berghaus, *Italian Futurist Theatre*, pp. 111–15.

5. Like major classical texts of other nations, Dante's masterpiece spawned a whole library of editions, commentaries, and interpretations.

6. In the foyer of the Costanzi, Mme Carelli served tea for the visitors of the Futurist exhibition.

7. For a more objective description of the event, see Berghaus, *Italian Futurist Theatre*, pp. 115–17.

8. Prince Altieri, Prince Boncompagni, Prince Potenziani, Marchese Cappelli, and Marchese Marignoli occupied the Royal Box and bombarded the Futurists with some particularly nasty missiles. Consequently, Marinetti and Boccioni entered into fisticuffs with Prince Altieri and gave him a thrashing with an umbrella.

9. This was a café on via del Corso whose back room was much frequented by artists and writers. After the performance on March 9, it was the scene of a banquet held in honor of the Futurist performers.

10. Via delle Mercede in central Rome housed the popular café chantant Sala Umberto. In 1913, year of the "Variety Theater" manifesto, the area was of particular importance to the Futurists. Around the corner, in via due Macelli, was the Salone Margherita, the most famous of the Roman variety theaters. Very close by, too, was via del Tritone, where the Futurist art gallery of Giovanni Sprovieri was housed, and the Café Groppo, where Balla's Futurist circle used to meet.

11. The Lux bookshop in via delle Convertite, an extension of via delle Mercede, took its name from the Lux et Umbra cinema on via del Corso. At the time of the Futurist exhibition in the Foyer of Teatro Costanzi, it advertised the show by displaying a number of Futurist paintings in its window, which caused quite a stir among passersby.

12. Angelo Zanelli (1879–1942) was a sculptor, famous for his decoration of the Vittoriano monument in Rome.

13. Ivan Meštrović (1883–1962) was a Croatian sculptor who spent some twenty years in various European cities, including Rome, where he prepared the Serbian pavilion for the 1911 International Exhibition.

14. Giovanni Prini (1877–1958) was a Genoese sculptor who taught at the Academy of Fine Arts in Rome.

15. Felice Carena (1879–1966) was a Symbolist painter from Turin who had been living in Rome since 1910, where he exercised considerable influence.

16. Pieretto Bianco was the artistic pseudonym of Pietro Bortoluzzi (1875–1937), who was well known for his decorative Venetian landscape paintings.
17. Dinamo Correnti was the pseudonym of the poet Renato Santamaria (1890–1953), a member of the Florentine Futurist circle and contributor to their journal, *Lacerba*.
18. See note 7 to document 11, *The Necessity and Beauty of Violence*.
19. Giuseppe Sergi (1841–1937), historian, anthropologist, sociologist, and paleontologist, was a professor at the universities of Bologna (1880–84) and Rome (1884–1916).
20. Goffredo Bellonci (1882–1964) was a critic and journalist who, with his wife Maria, kept a famous salon in Rome called Sunday Friends (*Amici della domenica*).

29 THE BATTLE OF FLORENCE

1. The *Lacerba* report on the *serata* at the Teatro Verdi begins with a summary of the contestant parties, their arms, states of mind, allies, the number of casualties, and the final result of the skirmish. The following nine pages contain the speeches given on that occasion, including the two by Marinetti translated here. For a detailed analysis of the *serata* see Berghaus, *Italian Futurist Theatre*, pp. 122–28.
2. The Dardanelles (Turkish Çanakkale Boğazi, ancient Hellespont) is a strait between Asian Turkey and the Gallipoli Peninsula of European Turkey. They connect the Aegean and Marmara Seas and form the only water link between the Mediterranean and the Black Sea. Because of its strategic position, this waterway has been the scene of several battles, from the times of Xerxes to the First World War.
3. The text, in *Lacerba,* continues with Soffici's lecture, *Futurist Painting*, Papini's *Against Florence*, Carrà's *Against the Critics*, and Boccioni's *Plastic Dynamism*, before returning to Marinetti's speech.
4. See document 12, *Second Futurist Political Manifesto*, §2.
5. Giuseppe Garibaldi (1807–82) and Giuseppe Mazzini (1805–72) were leaders in the struggle for the unification of Italy.
6. Filippo Turati (1857–1932) and Leonida Bissolati (1857–1920) were both leaders of the reformist wing of the Socialist Party. Whereas the former took a negative view on the Libyan War, Bissolati argued in favor of it and was consequently expelled from the PSI.
7. When Germany challenged French interests in Morocco, and the Agadir crisis blew up (July 1911), Italy decided to take control of the Ottoman-ruled regions of Libya. On September 29, 1911, Italy declared war and in the following weeks seized most of Tripolitania's ports and coastal towns. In the Treaty of Lausanne (October 8, 1912), Turkey had to cede Tripolitania and Cyrenaica to Italy.
8. In 1902 Italy had signed an agreement with France to support its expansion in Morocco, and in return gained the dominant influence in Libya. Many Italian newspapers, no doubt encouraged by the government, depicted Libya as the promised land and led a campaign for the colonization of North Africa.
9. See note 5 to document 21, *Destruction of Syntax—Untrammeled Imagination—Words-in-Freedom*.

30 The Exploiters of Futurism

1. *Mondo Baldoria*, by Aldo Molinari, an independent Futurist production based on Palazzeschi's *Controdolore* manifesto, was released in February 1914 and advertised as "Primo soggetto futurista in Cinematografia" (First Futurist Scenario in the Cinema). See Lista, *La Scène futuriste*, pp. 156–57, 164. Marinetti's mistrust of the commercial cinema sector meant that several potential collaborators, such as the Bragaglia brothers, were kept out of the "inner circle" of the Futurist movement.
2. On the high box office take, see Berghaus, *Italian Futurist Theatre*, pp. 138–39.
3. The *serata* as a theatrical genre is described in documents 25–30.
4. The brawls and quarrels were a hallmark of the Futurist *serate* and set them apart from all other theatrical genres of the period. See Berghaus, *Italian Futurist Theatre*, pp. 85–155.
5. See Berghaus, *Italian Futurist Theatre*, p. 74

31 Manifesto of Futurist Playwrights: The Pleasures of Being Booed

1. Authors critical of the nineteenth-century theater industry often refer to its products as *théâtre digestif*, aids to help digest a heavy meal.
2. The Italian beauty Francesca da Rimini, daughter of Guido da Polenta of Ravenna, lived in the thirteenth century. She was married to the crippled lord of Rimini, Gianciotto Malatesta, whose handsome brother Paolo became Francesca's lover. When Gianciotto discovered their affair, he killed them both. The story is immortalized in Dante's *Divine Comedy* and many other literary and artistic works.
3. This is a rather astonishing statement, considering that in the *Technical Manifesto of Futurist Literature* (document 20) Marinetti described Free Verse as having become surpassed by the Futurist technique of Words-in-Freedom.
4. Marinetti refers to his own career as a reciter of Symbolist poetry, described in Berghaus, *Italian Futurist Theatre*, pp. 31–32. See also the comments on the literary bias of *The Manifesto of Futurist Playwrights*, ibid., pp. 156–61, and the short characterization of the theatrical conventions this manifesto was directed against, ibid., pp. 11–25.
5. Edmond Rostand (1868–1918) was a French poet and dramatist, popular for his romantic and entertaining plays, which served as an alternative to the Naturalistic theater of his time. Rostand revitalized the old romantic verse drama with *Cyrano de Bergerac* (1897), which was given a euphoric reception in 1898. Audiences loved the play's swashbuckling hero, the passionate love story, its comic elements and fast-paced action. Constant-Benoît Coquelin, who played the title role in Paris and subsequently in London's Lyceum Theatre, turned the play into one of the greatest theater events of the turn of the century.

32 The Variety Theater

1. The terminology of these popular forms of entertainment was never particularly precise, and the same genre designation could have different meaning in different countries. Marinetti was very familiar with the French format of *revue*, *variété*, and *café-concert*, and also experienced firsthand London music-halls. For an outline

of the entertainments Marinetti refers to, see Berghaus, *Italian Futurist Theatre*, pp. 161–71.

2. It was a common practice to insert short movies into Variety and music-hall performances, just as cinema screenings were often framed by dance and musical numbers executed by Variety performers. Marinetti saw in this medley of diverse and entertaining numbers a model for Futurist theater.

3. On the Futurist concept of *le merveilleux* (a wondrous invention or astounding feat), see note 2 to document 20, *Technical Manifesto of Futurist Literature*.

4. Nicholas Petrovitch-Njegos (1840–1921) was proclaimed king of Montenegro on August 28, 1910. Major Enver Bey (later Enver Pasha) (1881–1922) was the leader of the Young Turks movement, whose attempts to regain control in the Balkans lead to the Bosnian Crisis of 1909. On January 23, 1913, he directed a successful coup d'état against Kiamil Pasha and subsequently led Turkey into the First World War. Stoyan Danev (1858–1949) was the Bulgarian prime minister and minister for foreign affairs and religions. On June 29, 1913, he began the Second Balkan War by ordering an attack on the Serbs and Greeks. Eleftherios Venizelos (1864–1936) was prime minster of Greece from 1910 to 1915 and led his country throughout the First Balkan War (1912–13).

5. The *macchietta* was a specialized genre of the Italian popular stage. A *macchiettista* offered portraits of common people with eccentric but nonetheless good-natured character traits.

6. American eccentrics were clowns or comedians who used tricks and gimmicks, such as special makeup and personal idiosyncrasies, to gain effects. To distinguish them from straight performers, they were also known as funnymen. Many eccentric funnymen specialized in bizarre, nonsensical comedy acts. Circuses and vaudevilles often featured performers specializing in "legmania." They twisted their elongated forms and legs into almost unbelievable shapes, performed high kicks above their heads, and doubled up their bodies so that they could disappear into ordinary barrels. Sometimes they were dancers (also known as India rubber men) performing contortionist feats. As most of these artistes performed anonymously, it is difficult to say who, in particular, Marinetti had in mind when using this term.

7. Paul Cambon (1843–1924), French ambassador to Spain (1891–98) and Britain (1898–1920), was a chief architect of the Entente Cordiale between England and France (April 1904), and guided a diplomatic mission during the Moroccan Crisis of 1905. Alfred von Kiderlen-Wächter (1852–1912), German diplomat and foreign secretary (1908–12), initiated a German attempt at dismantling the French hegemony in North Africa. On July 1, 1911, he dispatched the German gunboat *Panther* to Agadir, which prompted an international crisis in Morocco. The German-French convention of November 4, 1911, recognized the right of France to erect a protectorate in Morocco and provided Germany with territories in Cameroon (German Congo).

8. See below, note 12.

9. The battle between moonlight and electric light was one of Marinetti's favorite metaphors for the battle between old and new. See note 7 to document 4, *Second Futurist Proclamation: Let's Kill Off the Moonlight*.

10. Marinetti was a great admirer of Wagner's operas during his early years as a music critic, but changed his mind during his Futurist years. See *Down with the Tango and Parsifal!* (document 22). During his repeated visits to London (see note 1 to document 16), he discussed the possibility of a Futurist theater production with various impresarios, but only one of these ever came to fruition: Russolo's *intonarumori* concerts at the Coliseum on June 15–20, 1914.

11. As the name indicates, French revues were initially performances that looked back at events of the previous year or season. This evolved, in the early nineteenth century, into annual productions satirizing the theatrical output of the previous season.

12. The first topical and satirical revues in Italy appeared in the 1860s and were almost exclusively produced by writers and journalists. They were eventually supplanted by the café-concert type of Variety Theater, produced by singers and actors. As Marinetti and Settimelli found out from their own experience, not even these performers were entirely free from traditionalist tendencies. See Berghaus, *Italian Futurist Theatre*, pp. 202–203.

13. Ermete Zacconi and Eleonora Duse were serious actors, widely admired for their interpretation of realistic characters, whereas Félix Mayol was a leading star of the café-concert. Sarah Bernhardt was one the greatest actresses of her time and in every respect the total opposite of Leopoldo Fregoli, a quick-change variety illusionist.

14. A great Romantic tragedy and one of Victor Hugo's most famous plays.

33 DYNAMIC, MULTICHANNELED RECITATION

1. On December 10, 1915, the Lombard Battalion of Volunteer Cyclists and Automobilists was broken up and the Futurists returned to Milan to wait for a new call-up, which came in spring 1916.

2. The exhibition *Fu Balla e Balla Futurista* opened at the Sala d'Arte A. Angelini in December 1915.

3. In 1916, the Futurists participated in a major show of modern artworks at the Institute of Fine Arts in Naples. At the opening, on January 16, Boccioni gave a lecture titled "The Evolution of Universal Plastic Arts from the Greeks to the Futurists," Marinetti recited his *Battaglia di Adrianopoli*, and Cangiullo presented examples of his own poetry.

4. The *Manifesto futurista di Boccioni ai pittori meridionali* was launched at a Futurist soiree in Naples on January 16, 1916, and was printed in *Vela latina* on February 5, 1916.

5. On February 28, 1916, Boccioni gave a lecture at the Teatro Andreani on the occasion of an exhibition of Mantuan artists.

6. On February 7, 1916, the Futurists held a matinee performance at the Institute of Fine Arts in Naples. The event was introduced by a lecture by Marinetti on "Futurist Poetry" and followed by various poetry recitations, which included Marinetti, Cangiullo, Jannelli, and Corra performing the poem for four voices, "Stornelli vocali."

7. The "Pagine futuriste" appeared in Ferdinando Russo's *Vela latina* from 1915 to 1916 and contained a mixture of Futurist poems, short stories, plays, and drawings.

8. The performances took place around Easter 1915 in the presence of Diaghilev, Stravinsky, and the director of La Scala, Visconti di Morone. They included a scenic presentation of Marinetti's *Teatro della luna spettatrice*, a kind of dramatic allegory derived from the ideas of *Let's Kill Off the Moonlight*; excerpts from Pratella's recently completed opera, *L'aviatore Dro*; sketches for a ballet version of *Piedigrotta* with music by Pratella and designs by Balla; and a concert with Russolo's *intonarumori*, which Stravinsky liked so much that he considered presenting them at his next concert in Paris.

9. See the manifesto *The Only Solution to the Financial Situation*, published as a broadsheet in December 1915, in *I manifesti del futurismo* (1919) and in *Futurismo e fascismo* (1924). It was also incorporated into the essay "Denaro ai combattenti," published in *Roma futurista* (January 9, 1919), *L'ardito* (September 7, 1919), and *Democrazia futurista* (1919).

10. On March 8, 1916, a benefit performance for the Red Cross was held at the Teatro Niccolini in Florence, which included a number of bellicose anti-German minidramas.

11. The term may have two different meanings in this context: one related to "synopsis" as a condensed summary of things (and as such related to another Futurist term, *sintesi*); the other literally derived from *opsis* (view) and *syn* (together), i.e., a combined or general view of several things happening at the same time (and as such related to the Futurist concept of simultaneity). Whereas a traditional narrative operates on a linear model, Futurist Words-in-Freedom present several actions simultaneously in a pictorial ("synoptic") manner. As the term is not very common in English, we have usually translated it as "multichanneled."

12. Setting aside Marinetti's customary hyperboles, he was indeed an important figure in modernizing the art of recitation, as it had been practiced by conventional actors and Symbolist poets. His long-term struggle to reform this theatrical genre, and the way it was taught in specialized schools, harks back to his experiences in France in the late 1890s, when he had the honor of witnessing Sarah Bernhardt recite his own verses at a Symbolist soiree. As he noted in his autobiography, he found the style of this great actress "rather monotonous owing to her usual way of reciting alexandrines" (*Una sensibilità italiana*, p. 243). On Marinetti's art of recitation see Berghaus, *Genesis of Futurism*, pp. 36–38.

13. Free Verse, which Marinetti adopted from his French mentor, the Symbolist poet Gustave Kahn, served as a precursor to the Futurist Words-in-Freedom.

14. Decadentism, like Symbolism, Aestheticism, and Parnassianism (see note 6 to document 23), was a cultural countermovement to the Realist and Naturalist schools in mid-nineteenth-century art and literature. The Decadents were active between 1880 and 1890 and published a journal, *Le Décadent*, which propagated subjectivism, the irrational, the subconscious, sensuality, and aesthetic refinement. Their interest in introspective analysis was combined with a hostility toward established religion, conventional morality, and societal values. Important representatives of Decadentism were Gabriele D'Annunzio, Joris-Karl Huysmans, and Oscar Wilde.

15. See document 23, *Geometrical and Mechanical Splendor and Sensitivity Toward Numbers*.

16. These terms and concepts are explained in document 21, *Destruction of Syntax—Untrammeled Imagination—Words-in-Freedom*.

17. Marinetti's description of this event is based on the account given by Pietro Sgabelloni in *Il giornale d'Italia* on March 31, 1914. For a detailed analysis of the event see Berghaus, *Italian Futurist Theatre*, pp. 235–44.

18. Marinetti draws a contrast here between the primitive, popular aspects of the Piedigrotta festival and the more erudite aspects in the processions, harking back to classical mythology and the ancient culture of the Bay of Naples.

19. Jan Kubelik (1880–1940) was, like Nicolò Paganini (1782–1840), an outstanding violin virtuoso.

20. Benozzo Gozzoli (1420–97) was an Italian early Renaissance painter.

21. Balla was dressed as a gravedigger, brandished a long writing pen, and from time to time hit a cowbell with it, chanting in a nasal voice: "nieeeet, nieeeeeet-nieeeeeeet . . ."

22. For Cangiullo's *Funeral of an Old-fashioned Philosopher*, a large backdrop painted by Balla functioned as stage design, and in one corner of the gallery hung a painting depicting three Crocean philosophers. The polemical effect of the performance was, of course, all the more powerful because Benedetto Croce, the high priest of idealist philosophy and aesthetics, was a native of Naples and generally regarded as the greatest living representative of his home town.

23. The siege of Adrianopolis (Hadrianopolis, or Edirne) took place in October 1912, during the Turkish-Bulgarian War. See note 20 to document 21, *Destruction of Syntax—Untrammeled Imagination—Words-in-Freedom*.

24. The painter Christopher Nevinson was coauthor of *The Futurist Manifesto against English Art* (document 17).

25. This is, as far as I am aware, the first recorded use of a telephone in a stage performance, anticipating many of the later multimedia works. A few weeks later, during another Futurist gallery performance in Naples, on May 17, 1914, Marinetti recited his latest *parole in libertà* via telephone from London.

26. There exists a recording of this scene, which native speakers tell me shows a very evocative use of the Bulgarian language.

34 A FUTURIST THEATER OF ESSENTIAL BREVITY

1. The Futurists organized a number of political demonstrations after the outbreak of the First World War (August 3, 1914). The first such events took place in Milan on August 12 and 20, 1914. In December 1914, Marinetti, Settimelli, and Corradini went on a propagandist lecture tour in Faenza and Ravenna. On February 19, 1915, when the new parliament assembled in Rome, the Futurists were in the front row of the Interventionist demonstration outside Montecitorio Palace, which led to the arrest of Marinetti, Cangiullo, Jannelli, Balla, and Auro d'Alba. On April 12, 1915, a similar demonstration was staged in Piazza di Trevi, leading to the arrest of Marinetti, Corra, Settimelli, and Mussolini. Marinetti and Mussolini were again arrested when they organized an Interventionist demonstration in Piazza della Pilotta in Milan. On December 9 and 11, 1914, the Futurists organized two protest actions at the University of Rome. See Berghaus, *Futurism and Politics*, pp. 73–80.

2. "Marciare non Marcire!" was a slogan of the antineutralist movement and can be translated as "March! Don't molder!"

3. The term *sintesi* does not have a direct equivalent in English and is usually translated as "synthetic." We have called the dramatic genre "Theater of Essential Brevity" and the plays "minidramas"; the adjective *sintetico* has been rendered as "compressed," "condensed," or "compact."

4. Marinetti refers here to the unity of place in Aristotelian aesthetics. But it is also a scathing comment on the state of Italian stage design, which had to be minimalist for troupes touring up and down the peninsula.

5. Marinetti uses an untranslatable pun here on *atti* (acts) and *attimi* (brief moments), i.e., long acts condensed into short actions.

6. For a list of such dramatic "kitchen manuals" and various aspects of "technique" Marinetti is attacking here, see the chapter "The State of Italian Theatre before the Advent of Futurism" in Berghaus, *Italian Futurist Theatre,* pp. 11–25.

7. This is a somewhat exaggerated claim. Many of the early works of Futurist authors were literary exercises, with some originality as dramas, but rather traditional in their use of theatrical conventions. It was only when they accompanied the tours of these plays that they learned about the everyday business of the stage and used these insights in their next creations.

8. The company of Gualtieri Tumiati premiered *Elettricità,* a cut-down version of *La donna è mobile* (i.e., the second act of Marinetti's pre-Futurist play, *Poupées électriques*), on September 13, 1913, at the Politeama Garibaldi in Palermo. The production was complemented by a variety of poetry recitations and readings from manifestos, and on some legs of the tour by a one-act play by Settimelli. On these performances and the more Futurist repertoire of the next tour, see Berghaus, *Italian Futurist Theatre,* pp. 187–97.

9. *Più che l'amore,* a play by D'Annunzio, was produced at the Teatro Costanzi in Rome in 1906. *La figlia d'Iorio* was premiered at the Teatro Lirico in Milan in 1904.

10. This play by Marinetti was premiered on February 1, 1915, in Ancona, as part of the first tour of the Futurist Theater of Essential Brevity by the Berti-Masi company.

11. Cerebralism was an artistic concept developed by Settimelli and Corra in their pre-Futurist days. It envisaged a theater "liberated" from the constraints of causality and logic, premeditation and rationality. It was an accumulation of fragments of reality in perpetual motion, organized to become an abstract, dynamic, and vital form of theater. This "pure" spectacle focused on its own theatricality and became a sign of itself. It did not communicate definite "meanings" but was a free and forceful expression of accumulated cerebral energy and, as such, a celebration of life, liberty, vitality, fantasy, and playfulness. In this way, theater did not imitate life, it *became* life.

12. *Vengono* (They Are Coming) is a play with a huge armchair and eight ordinary chairs playing the main roles on stage. It was first shown on February 1, 1915, in Ancona, as part of the first tour of the Futurist Theater of Essential Brevity.

13. This is an untranslatable wordplay on *parole in libertà* (Words-in-Freedom), here called *battute in libertà, battuta* being a theatrical cue or piece of stage dialogue.

14. Marinetti provides no information on what this is supposed to be, but there exists a minidrama by Corra and Settimelli entitled *Atto negativo* (A Negative Act), which consists of only one scene: an actor approaches the footlights and tells the audience: "I have absolutely nothing to tell you. Bring down the curtain."

15. This may again be a reference to a play, possibly Balla's *Discussion between Two Sudanese Critics about Futurism*.

16. This may be a reference to Paolo Buzzi's lyrical novel *L'elisse e la spirale* (The Ellipse and the Spiral), which Armando Mazza intended to produce for the theater.

17. Marinetti wrote a play called *Mani* (Hands), in which body parts were exhibited as in a Surrealist shop window display. The idea originally stemmed from Corra, who wrote several such pieces.

18. Ettore Berti ran a company that took the Futurist Theater of Essential Brevity on tour in 1915; Luigi Zoncada performed in Andrea Maggi's Compagnia Drammatica, which put on Marinetti's *La donna è mobile* in Turin in 1909. Ettore Petrolini performed this first Futurist bill, to little acclaim, in June 1916, and in an altered form in Milan in October of the same year. Therefore, his name is not mentioned in the 1915 edition of this manifesto.

19. Marinetti had to wait until 1926 before he could embark seriously on the realization of this plan. He found Mussolini sympathetic toward the construction of an ultramodern and technically advanced, permanent Futurist theater in Milan, but the minister of culture turned it down for financial reasons.

35 FUTURIST DANCE

1. Luisa Casati (1881–1957) was a rich and bewitchingly beautiful femme fatale who counted D'Annunzio among her lovers and Marinetti and Balla among her most ardent admirers. She had her portrait done by many of the leading painters and photographers of the period.

2. See document 26, *The Battles of Trieste*.

3. A river a few kilometers northeast of Gorizia and site of several battles during the First World War.

4. Lyda Borelli (1884–1959) was a queen of the theater and a diva of the silver screen. Luciano Molinari (1880–1940) was an actor, singer, and revue performer best known for his imitations of the great stars of the Italian stage.

5. This introduction is missing from the version of *Roma futurista*. Some of the phrases appear verbatim in Marinetti's war diary entry of April 12, 1917.

6. Following the discovery of the Franco-Cantabrian cave art in the late nineteenth century, there was a great deal of speculation on the function and meaning of prehistoric art. A favorite explanation was that it was used as hunting magic.

7. Marinetti appears to be mixing up half-digested information here. The dance of the spheres was a Pythagorean concept, revived in the Renaissance period by the Neoplatonists. The *ronda* Marinetti refers to were probably the *sema*, the Sufi dances of the Whirling Dervishes, which he saw in Alexandria and described in his book *Il fascino d'Egitto* (*Teoria e invenzione futurista*, 1st ed. pp. 979–80, 2nd ed. pp. 1071–72).

8. The Cambodian dances were first seen in Europe at the Marseille Exposition Coloniale in 1906. The Javanese dances appeared at the Paris Exposition Universelle of 1889.

9. Marinetti would have been familiar with these dances from his teenage years in Alexandria, Egypt. More recently, he had reviewed a show by Arabian dancers at the Milan Universal Exhibition in *Teatro illustrato* of July 1906. However, much of what passed as "Oriental" dancing in European salons and theaters was an invented, Orientalist concoction popularized by Mata Hari, Ruth St. Denis, Sent M'ahesa, and others, and in even more fantastical form by Diaghilev's first Paris seasons.

10. His reference point is the classical tradition of c. 1810 to 1870, although even during the age of Russian dominance, the Italian school possessed a major representative in Enrico Cecchetti (1850–1928).

11. There were several attempts to add new flavors to the classical tradition by drawing on "primitive" sources taken from Africa, the "Orient," or ancient Greece.

12. The Latin craze of the early 1900s affected both music and social dance, but much less so the stage dance. The *tango argentino* was danced on stage in Monmartre as early as 1909 and became extremely fashionable in Paris in 1912–13; the *maxixe*, or Parisian *brésilienne*, never became very popular in Europe and vanished from the salons in the late 1910s. The *zamacueca* originates from Peru and was called *cueca* in Chile. Like the *santafé*, they did not become much known outside their countries of origin.

13. Marinetti here refers to the early phase of the Ballets Russes. During the First World War, Diaghilev looked for a new direction and sought the collaboration of Marinetti and various designers and musicians from the Futurist movement.

14. This may seem rather astonishing to us nowadays, as Nijinsky's most geometric dance, *L'Après-midi d'un faune*, caused an enormous scandal because of its overt sexual theme and execution. However, to heterosexual audiences at the time, only the ballerina functioned as an erotic icon, and never a man. As a well-oiled muscular machine, Nijinsky offered a suitable counterimage to Isadora Duncan's expressiveness.

15. Picasso's "Cubist" ballet, *Parade*, was created in Rome during the period of the Diaghilev-Futurist collaboration.

16. It may seem astonishing that Marinetti does not make any reference here to Rudolf von Laban, who was most instrumental in freeing dance from music and who instituted, with his Expressionist dance, the most far-reaching revolution in modern dance history. But in 1917, hardly anybody in Italy had heard of Laban or knew anything about the revolution he had initiated in Munich, Zurich, and Ascona.

17. See the illustrations in Günter Berghaus, "Dance and the Futurist Woman: The Work of Valentine de Saint-Point, 1875–1953," *Dance Research* 11, no. 2 (1993): 27–42.

18. Marinetti himself introduced Saint-Point to the Futurist movement and made her one of its directors, primarily because he supported her ideological rather than aesthetic tenets. In an open letter published in the *Journal des débats* of January 7, 1914, she declared her departure from the movement, but Marinetti kept in contact with her and promoted her work in Italy. The *Métachories* were the fruit of her col-

laboration with the "cerebralist" Riciotto Canudo and were performed on April 3, 1917, at the Metropolitan Opera House in New York. Marinetti found these dances far too subjective, Symbolist, or Impressionist to be mistaken for Futurist creations.

19. Émile Jaques-Dalcroze's eurhythmic exercises had been developed to enhance the rhythmic feeling of young musicians and singers. Over time, the rhythmic training of the body became an aim in itself and turned into a dance that trained the harmonic sensibility in the widest sense. They were not used for the toning of muscles or the portrayal of rural labor.

20. Fuller's electrified dances were well known in Italy and highly appreciated in Futurist circles. Lucini sang her praises in a poem published in Marinetti's journal *Poesia* (April 1908), Ginna and Corra in the brochure *Paradosso di arte dell'avvenire* (1910). Severini was a great admirer of hers and captured her *Serpentine Dance* in an illustration for *Lacerba* (July 1, 1914). The film *Vita futurista* of 1916 contained a scene, "Danza dello splendore geometrico," that was inspired by her *Danse de l'acier*. Balla represented her dances in a stylized sculpture made from wire.

21. The cakewalk was a precursor of the ragtime and was imported into fashionable Paris in 1903.

22. See document 15, *Extended Man and the Kingdom of the Machine.*

23. Marinetti is probably imagining free-word scenarios here, which together with the placards and the dancer's onomatopoeic recitations indicate that he approached dance from the standpoint of a writer rather than of a choreographer. He also knew of Saint-Point's dances that interpreted poems recited from the wings of the stage. Many years later, he himself recited his poems for Giannina Censi. A later example of Words-in-Freedom exhibited on stage is mentioned in note 3 to document 69, *The Theater of Surprises.*

24. In the edition *I manifesti del futurismo* (1919), this passage reads: "Italian Futurist dance can have no other purpose than to magnify heroism, the master of metals, fused together with the divine engines of speed and war." In the version printed in *Roma futurista*, the last two paragraphs of the introduction, following "Words-in-Freedom," are missing. The dances are ordered (1) aviator, (2) shrapnel, (3) machine gun.

25. The martial theme may appear astonishing, if not objectionable, to modern readers, but when it was first introduced in *L'Italia futurista*, it appeared in the context of other texts focusing on war events. The dances described in the manifesto had their origin in Marinetti's experiences at the front. Several entries in his diary describe the "theater of war" in the form of Words-in-Freedom, and the choreographed movements of soldiers and canon volleys struck him as having the quality of a dance.

26. Marinetti was a member of the Alpine regiment. See document 37, *The Futurists, the First Interventionists.*

27. Although in the following text the dancer is grammatically determined as female, the subheading uses the male gender (except in the 1919 edition of *I manifesti futuristi*). This reflects Marinetti's uncritical acceptance of the ballet tradition of male roles being performed by female dancers *en travesti*. It was only after he met Giannina Censi, some thirteen years later, that he could consider the role of a female pilot or aviatrix.

28. Such billowing veils were used with great technical proficiency by Loïe Fuller.
29. We have to imagine this as some sort of floor covering painted like a map.
30. The costume designs were never exhibited and have not been preserved. The stage sets Marinetti refers to were for Stravinsky's *Feu d'artifice*, produced by Diaghilev in 1917. See Berghaus, *Italian Futurist Theatre*, pp. 253–59. A set of costume designs by Gino Galli, inspired by the *Dance of the Machine Gun*, have been reproduced in Claudia Salaris, *Filippo Tommaso Marinetti* (Scandicci: La Nuova Italia, 1988), p. 161.

FUTURISM AND THE GREAT WAR (1911–17)

36 ELECTRIC WAR: A FUTURIST VISIONARY HYPOTHESIS

1. A dielectric is a material that prevents electrical conduction while at the same time absorbing electrical charges until saturation point is reached. Oliver Joseph Lodge demonstrated in 1888 that radio frequency waves could be transmitted along electric wires, and in 1894 he devised a radiotelegraphic set with a receiver. In 1909 the Nobel Prize for physics went to Karl Ferdinand Braun and Guglielmo Marconi in recognition of their contributions to the development of wireless telegraphy.
2. In 1906 Joseph John Thomson was awarded the Nobel Prize for physics for his work on the conduction of electricity through rarefied gases.
3. Heinrich Daniel Ruhmkorff (1803–77) invented an induction coil that could be used as a portable light source and later for radio transmissions. His experiments were widely known in France and played a significant part in the novels of Jules Verne.
4. See document 4, *Second Futurist Proclamation: Let's Kill Off the Moonlight*.

37 THE FUTURISTS, THE FIRST INTERVENTIONISTS

1. Marinetti's description of the events is contradicted by the Milan police reports printed in Berghaus, *Futurism and Politics*, p. 75.
2. The painter-turned-musician Luigi Russolo was constructing his orchestra of *intonarumori*. See the photographs in Berghaus, *Italian Futurist Theatre*, pp. 121 and 133.
3. Marinetti had a particular dislike of Puccini's music and of his (conservative) role in the Italian opera business. See his scathing remarks in a review of *Tosca*, printed in Berghaus, *Genesis of Futurism*, p. 43.
4. The Victor Emmanuel Arcade in Milan is a shopping mall, shaped like a cross, with a glass dome at its center. It is usually filled with tables, which are served from the cafés on both sides of its corridors.
5. Antonio Peterno, Marquis di San Giuliano (1852–1914), served as Italy's foreign minister from 1910 until his death in 1914. During the July Crisis of 1914, he strove to preserve the Triple Alliance. It was on his recommendation that the Italian government refused to join the Central powers and declared neutrality (August 3, 1914).
6. The person in question was probably the librettist Arturo Colautti (1851–1914).
7. San Fedele is a little church next to the Cathedral and the Arcade. The city's police headquarters (*Questura centrale*) was situated in Piazza San Fedele.
8. The Futurists stayed in the San Vittore prison for six days. As Boccioni reported to

his family, the conditions of their detention were such that they could feel rather comfortable. The director of the jail paid his respects to them, "with great courtesy," and gave them preferential treatment, with "all possible privileges," including books and first-rate food brought in from outside the prison. As to the court case, no formal charges were brought against them. "The examining judge told me that it will all come to nothing and that they only want to exercise some pressure on us because of *Futurism* and because they fear that such demonstrations might be repeated" (Boccioni in a letter to his family of September 22, 1914, in *Archivi del futurismo*, vol. 1, p. 347).

9. See document 34, *A Futurist Theater of Essential Brevity*. The touring production of the Berti-Masi company, directed by Emilio Settimelli, consisted of ten to twelve *sintesi*, depending on the town and the reactions of the audience. The troupe visited eight Italian cities from February 1 to March 1, 1915. See Berghaus, *Italian Futurist Theatre*, pp. 193–97.

10. In December 1913 Balla wrote a manifesto on antineutral fashion design, and in December 1914 he provided a tailor with some drawings to have a colorful Futurist suit made as prototype. Marinetti gave the whole thing a political shading and turned it into an "antineutralist" suit resembling the Italian flag. Cangiullo wore it under a drab-looking Austrian loden coat before entering La Sapienza University. The whole action is described in Berghaus, *Italian Futurist Theatre*, pp. 74–77.

11. Balla's concept of fashion design has been documented in the well-illustrated exhibition catalogues *Il futurismo e la moda: Balla e gli altri* (Venice: Marsilio, 1986) and *Balla: Futurismo tra arte e moda. Opere della Fondazione Biagiotti Cigna* (Milan: Leonardo, 1998).

12. For an English translation of the manifesto see Apollonio, *Futurist Manifestos*, pp. 197–200.

13. The demonstration, with all participants wearing Balla's antineutralist clothes, was staged in Piazza di Trevi. A report in the *Corriere della sera* suggested that Mussolini might, by that time, have converted from socialism to Futurism. See Berghaus, *Futurism and Politics*, pp. 78–79.

14. The group reached the front on May 24, 1915, and then transferred to Peschiera, on Lake Garda. On October 12 the battalion moved to Malcesine, where they first engaged in battle (Marinetti turned the fighting on Monte Altissimo into a picture-poem in the style of the Words-in-Freedom). On December 10, 1915, the unit was broken up and the Futurists returned to Milan to wait for a new call-up.

15. The Second Alpine Regiment was formed in 1882 and was later renamed Corpo d'Armata Alpino (Mountain Corps). The Alpini fought, together with the Volunteer Cyclists and Automobilists, in the attack on Dosso Casina (October 22–24, 1915).

16. The manifesto was published in *Vela latina* on January 15, 1916, and as a two-sided broadsheet. It enlarged in a prolix manner on six key reasons for being proud to be Italian: "1. The creative genius of the Italians; 2. The flexibility, the talent for improvisation, which the Italians constantly display; 3. The physical strength, agility, and resistance of the Italians; 4. The passion, violence, and tenacity with which the Italians are capable of fighting; 5. The patience, logic, and precise calculation of

the Italians when making war; 6. The moral inspiration and nobility of the Italian Nation in nourishing the war with its blood and financial resources." See *Teoria e invenzione futurista,* 1st ed. pp. 437–40, 2nd ed. pp. 502–506.

17. The Battle of the Carso, in July 1915, brought Italy a major victory and became part of the national mythology for years to come.

18. See document 42, *The New Ethical Religion of Speed.*

19. At the tenth Battle of the Isonzo (May 12–June 8, 1917), Monte Kuk was taken. On May 14, Marinetti was badly wounded and taken to a hospital in Udine, where he stayed until June 10.

20. This event took place on June 4, 1917 (see Marinetti, *Taccuini,* p. 111).

21. The manifesto, by Pasquale Marica, appeared in *L'Italia futurista* on November 1, 1916.

22. The Battle of Caporetto took place on October 24, 1917; the first issue of *Roma futurista* appeared on September 20, 1918.

23. These groups of ex-combatants formed the power base for Mussolini, who, in the course of three years, turned the organization into the Fascist Blackshirts. Marinetti's narration of war events continues in document 47, *Branches of the Futurist Political Party.*

38 In This Futurist Year

1. See note 10 to document 25, *Futurism's First Battles.*

2. On the theme of hygiene and Marinetti's role of doctor for the ailments of Italy, see note 2 to document 46, *An Artistic Movement Creates a Political Party.*

3. *Mafarka the Futurist* (1909) was a novel by Marinetti, and *Le Roi Bombance* (1905) his first major play.

4. "Life transcends intellect." Marinetti quoted the same phrase from *L'Évolution créatrice* in his interview with *La diana.* See note 7 to document 24, *On the Subject of Futurism.*

5. The second part of this paragraph can be found nearly verbatim in his interview with *La diana.* See document 24, *On the Subject of Futurism.*

6. See note 4 to document 7, *First Futurist Political Manifesto.*

7. The term used here is *contrasto,* a type of medieval poem in which two people (often two lovers, though not necessarily) debated a topic, often heatedly. As a popular form of poetry it is represented in every age of Italian literature, right up to the early twentieth century.

8. This probably refers to treaty negotiations that led to Italy's declaration of neutrality on August 3, 1914.

9. The first lines of this paragraph repeat phrases and demands from the *Second Political Manifesto* of October 11, 1911 (see document 12).

10. Theodor Mommsen (1817–1903), German historian.

11. Benedetto Croce (1866–1952), critic, philosopher, historian, and politician. His conservative, classical taste made him the target of many Futurist diatribes.

12. Antonio Salandra (1853–1931), prime minister of Italy from 1914 to 1916, declared Italian neutrality in the first months of the First World War.

13. Cesare de Lollis (1863–1928), philologist and literary critic, secretary of the Italian Historical Institute, professor of New Latin studies, and, from 1905 to 1915, professor of French and Spanish literature at Rome University. He was the target of the Futurist protest action at La Sapienza on December 9 and 11, 1914. (See Berghaus, *Italian Futurist Theatre*, pp. 74–77.)

14. Giacomo Barzellotti (1844–1917), Neo-Kantian philosopher and, since 1896, professor of the history of philosophy at Rome University.

39 The Meaning of War for Futurism: Interview with *L'Avvenire*

1. Marinetti here lays claim to an originality which is not at all borne out by the extensive literature on Italian nationalism in the late nineteenth and early twentieth centuries.

2. Marinetti gave a detailed explanation of the *serate* as a means of propaganda and a method of militant actionism in *Futurism's First Battles* (document 25). On the patriotic, anti-German *serate*, see Berghaus, *Italian Futurist Theatre*, pp. 197–200.

3. See document 25, *Futurism's First Battles*.

4. See document 12, *Second Futurist Political Manifesto*.

5. This is a reference to the demand "The tiresome memory of the greatness of Ancient Rome must be eradicated by an Italian greatness that is a hundred times more impressive." See document 12, *Second Futurist Political Manifesto*.

6. This demand cannot be found in the manifesto.

7. On Enrico Corradini's Associazione Nazionalista Italiana (ANI), founded in 1910, see note 1 to document 7, *First Futurist Political Manifesto*.

8. In 1910 Marinetti entered into communication with the nationalist movement of Enrico Corradini, then in the process of being organized into the Associazione Nazionalista Italiana (ANI). Together with Boccioni, he visited their foundation congress in Rome in December 1910, but, as far as I am aware, he never joined the ANI.

9. See note 3 to document 7, *First Futurist Political Manifesto*.

10. Piazza delle Erbe means "fruit and vegetable market." Many Italian cities possess an ancient market with such a name. One of the most famous is the one in Verona, erected on the ruins of a Roman forum. It became the political and economic center of the city and is surrounded by palaces and ancient monuments. One of these is the Arena, which was excavated from 1834 to 1914 and inaugurated with Verdi's *Aida* on August 10, 1913.

11. This refers to the First World War, which started on August 3, 1914, without Italian participation.

12. See document 38, *In This Futurist Year*, where he repeats the same phrase verbatim.

13. No exact information is available on how, when, and where Mussolini and Marinetti became acquainted. When they participated in the Interventionist movement of 1915, Marinetti interpreted Mussolini's active advocacy of Italy's entry into the war as an indication of the latter's Futurist frame of mind. On April 12, 1915, they staged together an antineutralist demonstration in Piazza di Trevi in Rome, leading to the arrest of Marinetti, Corra, Settimelli, and Mussolini. Marinetti and Mussolini were

again arrested when they organized an Interventionist demonstration at the Piazza della Pilotta in Milan.

14. The Revolutionary Syndicalist Filippo Corridoni (1887–1915) was an outspoken advocate of a revolutionary war and supported Italy's entry into the First World War. At the second Futurist *serata,* at the Teatro Lirico in Milan (February 15, 1910), held in honor of General Vittorio Asinari di Bernezzo, Corridoni and Mussolini were reported to have taken sides with the Futurists against the conservative audience. See Marinetti, *La Grande Milano,* p. 95, and Buzzi, *Futurismo,* vol. 2, p. 207.

15. This is a reference to the Senate, whose members were appointed for life.

16. The seat of the Italian parliament. See note 2 to document 61, *Speech in Parliament.*

17. See document 10, *Against Sentimentalized Love and Parliamentarianism.*

18. The *Third Futurist Political Manifesto* (document 13) sparked a rumor that Marinetti was going to run as a candidate against Bissolati. Marinetti denied this in an interview with the *Giornale d'Italia* of October 30, 1913, and said that currently he was too busy with his artistic activities to consider the offers he had received for a political candidacy. However, in the near future he hoped to enter the political battlefield, but only on a list for a really important constituency ("un collegio di prim'ordine"). These were exactly the same words as he used in this interview with *L'avvenire.*

19. "Marciare non Marcire!" ("March! Don't molder!") was the slogan of the antineutralist movement.

20. Behind the pseudonym is hidden the Sicilian Futurist Guglielmo Jannelli Ravidà (1895–1950). He met Marinetti at the first Futurist *serata* in Palermo (April 26, 1911) and participated in the Sicilian tour of Marinetti's play *Elettricità* (1913). He was an active supporter of Italy's intervention in the Great War, organized several demonstrations for this purpose, and was three times arrested for it.

40 FUTURISM AND THE GREAT WAR

1. The term used here is *conflagrazione,* literally "the all-consuming fire." It was a common expression at that time for what we now call the First World War.

2. Garibaldi's "Red Shirts" were a volunteer army whose success in liberating large parts of Italy was due to their fervor and enthusiasm rather than to military training.

3. Giacomo Barzellotti (1844–1917) was professor of philosophy at Rome University; Benedetto Croce (1866–1952) was a critic, philosopher, and historian; Enrico Ferri (1856–1929) was editor of the Socialist daily *Avanti!*; Claudio Treves (1868–1933) was a reformist Socialist and parliamentarian.

FUTURIST ART DURING THE FIRST WORLD WAR (1916)

41 BIRTH OF A FUTURIST AESTHETIC

1. Literally, "multiplied man." As indicated in the manifesto *Extended Man and the Kingdom of the Machine* (document 15), published in the same volume of *Guerra sola igiene del mondo,* this biological body, extended by prosthetic limbs and synthetic joints and ever more powerful human–machine interfaces, gave rise to visions of conquering the physical and mental limitations of the human species.

2. In the Russo-Japanese War the Japanese invaded Manchuria—since 1900 under Russian occupation to safeguard the building of the Trans-Siberian Railway—and unleashed a war that cost more than 150,000 lives in the Battle of Mukden (Shenyang) alone.

3. The Japanese torpedoes in the Russo-Japanese War were so effective that only three of thirty-five Russian battleships managed to reach Vladivostok.

42 THE NEW ETHICAL RELIGION OF SPEED

1. A gyrocompass uses an electrically powered spinning wheel to find true north, i.e., the direction of the earth's rotational axis, as opposed to magnetic north. It has the advantage over magnetic compasses of not being affected by the metal in a ship's hull. It was patented in 1885 by Martinus Gerardus van den Bos and in an improved version in 1903 by Hermann Anschütz-Kämpfe.

2. This star, in the southern part of Ursa Major, was listed by the astronomer Stephen Groombridge (1755–1834) in his catalogue as no. 1830. In 1842 Friedrich Wilhelm August Argelander (1799–1875) noted its exceptionally high speed of rotation, now considered to be the third highest after Barnard's and Kapteyn's stars.

3. The collection of poetry in which this manifesto was reprinted contained a hymn to the motorcar entitled "A mon Pégase," originally printed in *Poesia* under the heading "A l'Automobile." It begins with the lines: "Vehement god from a race of steel / Automobile drunk with space / trampling with anguish / biting with strident teeth! / O fearsome Japanese monster with furnace eyes / nourished by fire and mineral oils / hungry for horizons and astral prey." As an epilogue to the volume, Marinetti contributed a prose piece called *La Mort tient le volant* (Death Holds the Steering Wheel), written, as the subtitle indicates, in Brescia on the day of a car race, the "Contest for the Prize of Speed."

4. On Marinetti's theory of analogy and "untrammeled imagination," see *Technical Manifesto of Futurist Literature* (document 20), and *Destruction of Syntax—Untrammeled Imagination—Words-in-Freedom* (document 21).

5. "Lyricism" meant for Marinetti a dynamic, intense, and powerful life force.

6. Juan Bielovucic (1889–1949), a Peruvian aviator, participated in many flying competitions, won the Circuit Européen in 1911, flew the Paris–Bordeaux race in 1912, and crossed the Alps in 1913. During the Great War he joined the air squadron "Les Cigognes" and received the Ordre National de la Légion d'Honneur and Croix de la Guerre.

43 THE FUTURIST CINEMA

1. See document 34, *A Futurist Theater of Essential Brevity*.

2. See document 32, *The Variety Theater*.

3. The early history of narrative cinema was strongly rooted in the tradition of melodrama. It borrowed from it the style of scenography and gestural language as well as some of its most popular actors.

4. At the same time, Marinetti's literary and theatrical manifestos advocated the use of cinematic means in order to modernize the older artistic traditions.

5. *Antigrazioso* was an important topic in the Futurist aesthetic, meaning forceful, virile, intuitive, dense, expressive. Pratella defined its opposite, the *grazioso*, as being of bourgeois origin and of feminine temper, with relations to the pure, the elegant, the vague, the refined, the dignified, and in France to *le joli* (pretty, nice). See "Contro il grazioso in musica," *Lacerba*, May 15, 1913, p. 37.

6. This seems to contradict the previous rejection of literary models for the cinema. Perhaps Marinetti thought of intertitles as being composed in the manner of Words-in-Freedom.

7. This may refer to the hand-tinting techniques employed by the Pathé company or, more likely, to the abstract symphonies of colors produced by the Corradini bothers and described in "Abstract Cinema—Chromatic Music 1912," Apollonio, *Futurist Manifestos*, pp. 66–70.

8. See Marinetti's theory of analogy in document 20, *Technical Manifesto of Futurist Literature*.

9. This is a reference to Baudelaire's symbolism: "Tout l'univers visible n'est qu'un magasin d'images et de signes auxquels l'imagination donnera une place et une valeur relative." See "Le Gouvernement de l'imagination. Salon de 1859," *Curiosités esthétiques, l'art romantique, et autres œuvres critiques* (Paris: Garnier, 1962), pp. 328–29.

10. Giolitti (1842–1928) was several times prime minister prior to the outbreak of the First World War, in which he sought to keep Italy neutral.

11. This passage of the manifesto is not simply meant to ridicule Carducci, although Marinetti made it abundantly clear in the essay *In This Futurist Year* (document 38) that he regarded his poetry as "dead and buried." As Arnaldo Ginna told Mario Verdone in 1965, the author of this passage was Emilio Settimelli, who greatly admired Carducci's neoclassical poetry. See Mario Verdone and Günter Berghaus, "'Vita futurista' and Early Futurist Cinema," in Berghaus, *Futurism in Arts and Literature*, p. 408.

12. The Scamander is a river near Troy, with its source on Mount Ida. It plays an important role in Greek mythology and is often mentioned in Homer.

13. This concept was explored in Ginna and Settimelli's play *Uno sguardo dentro di noi* (1915).

14. The idea had already been voiced in the *Technical Manifesto of Futurist Literature*, §11 (document 20), and experimented with in the Futurist Theater of Essential Brevity, e.g., Marinetti's *Vengono*. It also bears close resemblance to the mechanical theater of Balla's Futurist circle in Rome.

15. The *vetrina* was another Futurist dramatic genre, exhibiting objects and actions on stage in the manner of a shop window display, e.g., Marinetti and Corra's *Le Mani*, published in the *Teatro sintetico* collection of 1915.

16. Arnaldo Ginna wrote many fantastical short stories of this kind.

17. This idea relates to Marinetti's typographic revolution and poetic program as outlined in his literary manifestos.

18. This idea was developed by Balla and Depero in their manifesto *The Futurist Refashioning of the Universe* (1915). See Apollonio, *Futurist Manifestos*, pp. 197–200.

44 SOME PARTS OF THE FILM *FUTURIST LIFE*

1. Futurist lyricism is not related to music. Marinetti described it in *Destruction of Syntax—Untrammeled Imagination—Words-in-Freedom* (document 21) as a "capacity for inebriating oneself with life," "an area of intensified life," "a superior life that is more compressed and intense than that which we live from day to day," a "pugnacious and dynamic" experience of life. See also *We Renounce Our Symbolist Masters* (document 6).

2. The Triple Alliance of 1882 was concluded by Germany, Austria-Hungary, and Italy, leading to a rival pact between France, Britain, and Russia, known as the Triple Entente. The conflict between these alliances led to the First World War. Italy decided to renege on its moral obligation to support Germany and Austria in the war and instead entered into negotiation with the Entente powers. In 1915 Italy declared war upon its former allies, thereby dissolving the Triple Alliance.

3. At the Futurist *serata* of February 15, 1910. See document 7, *First Futurist Political Manifesto,* and document 25, *Futurism's First Battles.*

4. The film *Vita futurista* was shot during the summer of 1916, edited in the autumn, and submitted to the censors in December 1916. For a description of its contents, see Günter Berghaus and Mario Verdone, "'Vita futurista' and Early Futurist Cinema," in Berghaus, *Futurism in Arts and Literature,* pp. 398–421. *L'Italia futurista* announced on August 25, 1916, that the film would be shown *prossimamente* (soon). On October 1, 1916, the column "Attività futurista" informed its readers that the film had been completed and would be screened in the near future. On the back page, a large advertisement promised "plays with objects, experiments with lights, Futurist fantasies, new cinematographic techniques." The synopsis of the film, translated here, was first published on October 15, and printed again on November 1, November 15, and December 1, 1916. The premiere finally took place at the Teatro Niccolini in Florence on January 28, 1917.

THE POSTWAR POLITICAL BATTLE (1918–23)

45 MANIFESTO OF THE FUTURIST POLITICAL PARTY

1. The Futurist Political Party (Fasci Politici Futuristi) was one of many political organizations that grew out of the combatants' movement (among the others were the Arditi and Mussolini's Fasci di Combattimento, with which the Futurist Political Party collaborated). The party was founded during one of Marinetti's vacations in Rome (August 11–17, 1918) and had its first official meeting in Florence on December 6, 1918. Within half a year, local branches had been established in about a dozen Italian cities. The party's first political manifesto was composed by Marinetti on the basis of his earlier *Futurist Political Program* of October 1913 (document 13). See Günter Berghaus, "The Futurist Political Party," in Sascha Bru and Gunther Martens, eds., *The Invention of Politics in the European Avant-Garde, 1905–1940,* Amsterdam & New York: Rodopi, 2006, pp. 153–82.

2. This passage fell victim to censorship in the editions of both *L'Italia futurista* and *Roma futurista* and was omitted from later editions.

3. The civil status of women in Italy forbade them to manage property, to engage in trade, to enter industry or a profession, to practice an art, to hold office, and so on, without authorization of either father or husband. Marinetti demanded the abolition of this necessity for marital permission or authorization in order to undertake legally binding actions and transactions.

4. Of the three million Italians serving in the First World War, 1,400,000 were discharged by December 1918, and 500,000 followed over the next three months. The reintroduction of these masses into civilian life and the care for the legions of war victims was a charge of paramount importance to the government. However, the bureaucracy was ill-prepared for a task of such monumental proportions. With some delay, an Opera Nazionale Combattenti (National Institute for War Veterans) was created, but its work was impeded by bureaucratic slowness and the incoherent guidelines issued by the government. Given the close ties of the Futurist Political Party with the ex-combatants' and Arditi movements, and given the dominant role played by these ex-servicemen in the first postwar years, the political prospect of Futurism was closely linked to these sectors of society. The program of the Futurist Political Party found a very favorable response among ex-combatants of a left-wing orientation and served as the basis for a coalition of the three organizations of Futurists, Arditi, and Fascists.

5. See Marinetti's earlier suggestions in the speech, *Against Traditionalist Venice* (see document 27, *The Battles of Venice*).

6. The Futurist art movement was practically nonexistent in 1918–19, and its reputation was such that Marinetti deemed it necessary to separate the political party from the artistic root and branch of the movement. Critical observers suggested that Marinetti was changing tack in order to salvage the remnants of Futurism—that essentially he was flogging a dead horse.

7. For this purpose, they printed a membership form entitled "PARTITO FUTURISTA ITALIANO fondato da Marinetti—Mario Carli—Settimelli. TESSERA per l'anno 1919," on which applicants had to fill in the following data: Branch of . . . Membership card of Signor . . . Resident at . . . Street . . . Is a member of the branch . . . of the Futurist Political Party. The secretary of the branch . . . Member's signature . . .

46 AN ARTISTIC MOVEMENT CREATES A POLITICAL PARTY

1. The first branch of the Futurist Political Party was opened in Florence on November 30, 1918, soon to be followed by others in Milan, Perugia, Turin, Bologna, Messina, Palermo, Genoa, Ferrara, Naples, Piacenza, and Stradella. This, at least, is the list of *fasci* given by Marinetti in 1929 in his book *Futurismo e fascismo* (see document 47, *Branches of the Futurist Political Party*). Since at that time there was a need to boost the significance of the Futurist Political Party as a forerunner of the Fascist movement, we should be cautious when reading statements about the "rapid growth" and "immense success" of the Futurist Political Party soon after its foundation. In fact, a much more realistic assessment of the Futurist Political Party in 1918–19 can be found in the police files preserved in the Central State Archives in Rome and communicated by Berghaus, *Futurism and Politics*, pp. 104–10, 158–60.

2. In the writings of "Dr F T Marinetti," as he proudly signed many of his early essays and theoretical reflections, the concept of health occupied a central role. See note 2 to document 9, *War, the Sole Cleanser of the World*.

3. A note by Marinetti, explaining his use of the word *sozzalista* (from *sozza*: filthy, foul, repulsive) instead of *socialista*, reads: "Sozzialist instead of Socialist was a common, disparaging term in those days." Another note in *L'Italia futurista* of November 15, 1916 ("Sozzalisti e Socialisti"), reads: "Sozzialism and Sozzialists are terms used to distinguish Turati and Treves from Italian socialists like Bissolati."

4. A similar phrase is used in the introductory paragraph of document 19.

5. This was the motto of the Futurist *serata* held at the Teatro Lirico in Milan, February 15, 1910. See note 1 to document 7, *First Futurist Political Manifesto*.

6. A detailed police report on this event has been communicated by Berghaus, *Futurism and Politics*, pp. 75–76.

7. This statement appears to be a volte-face of the previous ten years of commitment to radical change, both in the arts and society at large. However, by the end of 1919 it became obvious that the Futurist Political Party and its coalition with the Fascists were a disaster. After years of working predominantly in the political field, Marinetti developed a "Surprise Program for 1920," in which he declared the Futurists' intention to "return to their impassioned creative work." See the Introduction, p. xxv.

8. This statement, as well as the one below against the papacy, highlights Marinetti's principal objection to Mussolini's conciliatory attitude toward the forces of tradition.

47 BRANCHES OF THE FUTURIST POLITICAL PARTY, THE ARDITI, AND THE LEGIONNAIRES OF FIUME

1. In the political battles of the first postwar years, Futurists, Arditi, and D'Annunzio's Fiume troops formed a coalition. See Berghaus, *Futurism and Politics*, pp. 92–143. For a critical assessment of Marinetti's list of branches of the Futurist Political Party, drawing on more reliable police reports, see ibid., pp. 104–105.

2. The name Arditi (Daring Ones) was a popular expression used for the Italian *reparti d'assalto* (assault units) during the First World War. Their function was similar to that of the German *Sturmtruppen*, on which they were, to some extent, modeled. The Arditi formed the spearhead of the Italian army and were generally regarded as a military elite. Often described as adventurous types with a streak of anarchical antiauthoritarianism, these militiamen certainly distinguished themselves from ordinary soldiers by their distaste for common morality, law, and order. They were called into existence by a special circular of the Military High Command, dated June 26, 1917, which ordered that each army corps should select a number of soldiers suited to serve in "a special battalion assigned to the most risky undertakings." Service in these units was voluntary and not everybody was accepted, which helped to create the image of the Arditi as a military elite and the "avant-garde of the battlefield." During the war, contacts were established between Futurists and Arditi, which soon went beyond the confines of informal acquaintances. The *Futurist Political Manifesto* was widely distributed among the shock troops, and the newspaper *L'Italia*

futurista, which had been founded with the aim of propagating Futurist ideas among the common soldiers, served as an important forum for discussion between Futurists and Arditi. In the summer of 1918, a formal political alliance was created between the two movements. Regular meetings took place in the offices of the newspaper *Roma futurista*, which became the official organ of Ardito-Futurism. Their political program was published in four installments in the same newspaper, leading, on January 1, 1919, to the foundation of the Association of Italian Arditi.

3. This event on January 1, 1919, was followed on January 19 by the founding of a Milan branch in the Futurist headquarters, i.e., Marinetti's apartment. Their first political pronouncements, published in *Roma futurista*, bore a close resemblance to the program of the Futurist Political Party.

4. Caporetto (Karfreit) was the site of a war of attrition between Italians and Austrians. In October 1917 the Austrians succeeded in breaking through the Italian front and penetrated deep into the Veneto, where their advance was halted on the banks of the river Piave.

5. Marinetti joined the Bombardieri di Nervesa on September 7, 1917, and was sent to the front on the Carso. He was with the 112th Gruppo Bombardieri from September 7, 1917, to October 14, 1917.

6. On February 10, 1918, Marinetti returned to the front after a two-week winter holiday. The most renowned mortar of the First World War, invented by Frederick Wilfred Scott Stokes (1860–1927), could fire as many as twenty-two shells per minute and had a maximum range of 1,200 yards.

7. On June 26, 1918, he was appointed to the Squadriglie Automitragliatrici Blindate, with which he remained until September 23. Following a short holiday in Rome, he returned to the front for the period October 1 to November 26, 1918.

8. In the collective mind of most Italians, Caporetto was a symbol of national disgrace and defeat, whereas the successful Battle of Vittorio Veneto (October 30, 1918) stood for final victory over the Austrians. On November 4, 1918, the war was ended.

9. Marinetti arrived in Milan on December 4, 1918, and was immediately invited to meet Mussolini (his negative impressions of the future Duce are described in document 48). The following day he departed for Florence to participate in the first official meeting of the local branch of the Futurist Political Party.

10. Dalmatia was another symbol of the *terre irredente*, to be "redeemed" from Austrian occupation.

11. Busto Arsizio was an air force base near Milan, where in 1916 Fedele Azari took his pilot's license and where his battalion was stationed during the First World War. Azari states in the manifesto *A Futurist Theater of the Skies* (April 1919) that in 1918 he performed elementary examples of his Aerial Theater in the skies over the camp. For a detailed description of this form of theater see Berghaus, *Italian Futurist Theatre*, pp. 485–94.

48 A MEETING WITH THE DUCE

1. Marinetti had just returned from the front. After meeting some Futurist friends (Bruno Corra, Luigi Russolo), he went to the Caffè Savini in the Victor Emmanuel

Arcade, where some military and political acquaintances were dining. Mussolini's office at the *Popolo d'Italia* was just a short walk away.

2. On December 1, 1918, the Kingdom of the Serbs, Croats, and Slovenes was formally proclaimed, which led to border disputes with six neighboring states, including Italy.

3. Following the demise of the Austro-Hungarian Empire, the former emperor Charles I gave the entire war and merchant fleets to the Kingdom of the Serbs, Croats, and Slovenes.

4. The Caproni aeronautics factory was founded in 1908–1909 and became one of Italy's largest industrial groups of the interwar years. They produced one of the most successful heavy bombers of the First World War and a series of biplanes for civil aviation.

5. The nineteen-year-old Mussolini was a bohemian revolutionary with pacifist leanings. To avoid military service, he moved to Switzerland (July 1902), where he became friendly with some Italian socialists, who taught him a great deal about Marxism, syndicalism, and anarchism. Mussolini was an effective speaker at political gatherings and published a number of inflammatory essays in the socialist press. When they organized a strike of local masons, he was deported. For a while he traveled in Germany, Austria, and France, then returned to Switzerland. In late 1904 he decided to end his status as draft dodger, departed for Italy, and in January 1905 joined a regiment of Bersaglieri near Verona.

49 THE FOUNDING OF THE FASCI DI COMBATTIMENTO

1. The famous assembly in Piazza San Sepolcro was attended by some two hundred restless revolutionaries and discharged soldiers, syndicalists, and discontented socialists, Futurists, and anarchists, who met to discuss the establishment of a new force in Italian politics, Fascism. After 1920 Mussolini began to distance himself from the revolutionary spirit of this meeting and his Futurist ex-brethren in arms. Consequently, Futurism's historic role in the event was underplayed in the official history of the Fascist movement, causing Marinetti to press the regime for recognition of their contribution to the early development of the Fasci di Combattimento.

2. This description is actually based on a diary note of January 12, 1920, following a meeting of the central committee of the Fasci, which offers a far more satirical portrait of the Duce: "He has his bowler hat pulled down over his eyes. He walks nervously, his collar turned up, like Petrolini in the Torreador."

3. This description diverges massively from Marinetti's diary notes of January 11, 1919, which characterize him as a "megalomaniac who will bit by bit turn into a reactionary" (*Taccuini*, p. 405), and of March 24, 1919, i.e., the day after the San Sepolcro meeting, when he speaks of him as "Mussolini the overbearing aristocrat, his eyes possessed, with reckless spurts of excited words. He turns ostentatiously toward each speaker and scrutinizes him very closely, his head resting on his hand, his elbow on the table. Just like an orderly or a soldier who, with powerful, unflagging energy, pugnaciously leaves none in any doubt that his beloved, much-admired captain or superior is the most obvious and preferable choice for a given office in the as-

sembly" (*Taccuini*, p. 409). After the Third Fascist Congress, he called him "this coarse, uncivil proletarian, with the huge head of a Caesar, his heart brimful of a savored revenge against his erstwhile socialist companions" (*Taccuini*, p. 511). Notwithstanding these privately voiced criticisms, after 1923, Marinetti's official line vis-à-vis the Duce became ostensibly affable.

4. Cristoforo Baseggio (1869–1959) was one of the founders of the Arditi and, being a socialist, vehemently contested Mussolini's later move to the Right. In 1921 he even challenged him to a duel.

5. At the end of the chapter there follows a list of speakers, including the Futurist Armando Mazza. Mario Carli communicated the declaration of accession from the Futurist Political Party, represented at the meeting by Piero Bolzon, Enrico Rocca, Alberto Businelli, Emilio Settimelli, Gastone Gorrieri, Ottone Rosai, Marcello Manni, Neri Nannetti, and Olao Gaggioli.

50 FASCISM AND THE MILAN SPEECH

1. The writer and publisher Umberto Notari (1879–1950) was an old friend and supporter of Marinetti's. The engineer and Ardito captain Ferruccio Vecchi (1894–1957?) was a leading figure in the Futurist Political Party, coeditor of *Roma futurista*, and chairman of the Milanese section of the Association of Arditi. In 1921 he was expelled from the Arditi and Fasci because of his intransigent ideological attitudes. Mario Carli (1889–1935) was a noted Futurist writer, coeditor of *L'Italia futurista*, and cofounder of *Roma futurista*. On September 20, and December 10, 1918, he published the two founding manifestos of the Association of Arditi and chaired its first meeting on January 1, 1919. He had strong Bolshevik leanings and left the Fasci in June 1920 in protest against Mussolini's turn to the Right. The newspaper *L'ardito* was founded on May 11, 1919, and ceased publication in 1921.

2. On January 11, 1919, Marinetti participated, together with Mussolini, in an irredentist action at La Scala, in protest against Bissolati's willingness to cede Dalmatia to Yugoslavia.

3. Armando Mazza (1884–1964) was a poet and major actor in the first Futurist *serate*. Later he turned to journalism. *I nemici d'Italia* appeared from 1918 to 1920.

4. *L' assalto: Giornale del fascismo* was published from November 1920 until 1943 by the Bologna section of the Fasci di Combattimento, under the directorship of Dino Grandi. The Futurist Leone Castelli was one of its founders.

5. Scene of the final decisive Italian victory over Austria in the First World War (October 30, 1918).

6. Francesco Saverio Nitti (1868–1953) was minister of agriculture (1911–14) and of finance (1917–19) before becoming prime minister in June 1919. In the postwar period he had to confront a grave economic, social, and political crisis. He was unable to quell the social unrest fomented by the maximalist demands of the Socialist Party and was much criticized for his indecisive foreign policy. In June 1920 he handed in his resignation.

7. November 4 was the official anniversary of the Italian victory over Austria.

8. The Florentine painter Vieri Nannetti was an active collaborator of *L'Italia futurista*

and participated in the first major postwar exhibition of Futurist art, at the Galleria Cova in Milan.

9. The journalist Gastone Gorrieri was a member of the Florentine branch of the Futurist Political Party and attended the San Sepolcro meeting of March 23, 1919.

10. This was the founding assembly of the Fasci di Combattimento, in Piazza San Sepolcro, Milan, on March 23, 1919, which made the Futurists Mario Carli, Bruno Corra, Mario Dessy, Ferruccio Vecchi, Gastone Gorrieri, and Marinetti "Fascists of the First Hour." This and the following paragraphs are taken verbatim from the front-page report "L'imponente 'Adunata' di ieri a Milano" (Yesterday's Impressive Gathering in Milan), *Il popolo d'Italia*, March 24, 1919.

11. See the extended debate in *Roma futurista* on the attempted collaboration between socialists (including some PSI members) and Futurists.

12. See document 51, *The Battle of Via Mercanti*, on the infamous assault on the *Avanti!* offices.

51 THE BATTLE OF VIA MERCANTI

1. The sacking of the *Avanti!* office in Milan, on April 15, 1919, was one of the first and most notorious examples of Fascist *squadrismo* and was no doubt supported by quite a few Futurists. Still accustomed to the violence and loss of lives in the First World War, the Futurists were not squeamish in their choice of means for bringing about the political changes they were advocating. For them and their allies, the Great War had not finished on November 11, 1918, but rather had to be seen through to its bitter end, when the enemy within would also be defeated. Seen from this perspective, *squadrismo* seems the logical concomitant of Ardito-Futurist *azionismo* (direct action), which itself transposed the military methods of the First World War into the quasi–civil war situation of 1919. The idea of *squadrismo* had been aired on November 6, when Marinetti noted in his diary: "Mussolini talks in the Fascio about the necessity of forming a true squad [*quadrato*] of Fascist forces. And he gives command of them to Vecchi and me."

At the end of February, the government had ended the ban on public meetings proclaimed during the war, and on April 13 the socialists had organized an assembly in Piazza Garigliano. The main speaker was an anarchist, Ezio Schiaroli, who attacked Mussolini and called upon the workers to take over the government. At this point the police dissolved the meeting and provoked a riot, leaving one man dead and several wounded. In response, the trade unions called a general strike for April 15 and organized a protest meeting in the Arena in Milan, causing the Interventionists to answer with a counterdemonstration. According to Marinetti's interpretation of events (in *Marinetti e il futurismo*), the situation in Milan resembled that in Petrograd in October 1917: it was intended that the strike be a full-scale insurrection, with the aim of creating a Soviet of Lombardy and, in the long run, a Soviet Republic of Italy. In an unpublished manuscript (Beinecke Gen. Mss. 130–38–1674), Marinetti wrote that the Ardito Carlo Maraviglia was passing on reliable information about the movements of the "Reds" and that the regional command of the armed forces was not intervening because they had not received appropriate orders from

Rome. In view of the "apathy of the Nittian guards" and the "danger to the Nation," the Futurists, Fascists, and Arditi decided to move into action.

2. The newspaper edited by Mussolini, the mouthpiece of the Fascists.

3. Giacomo Balla (1871–1958) was a Roman painter and leader of a Futurist circle in the city.

4. The Victor Emmanuel Arcade, next to the Cathedral, is a shopping arcade and a popular meeting place for the citizens of Milan.

5. Giovanni Ponzone (1888–1922) was a Fascist activist during the postwar period.

6. Luigi Russolo (1885–1947) was a Futurist painter and musician. Ferruccio Vecchi (1894–1957?) was an Ardito captain and a leading figure in the Futurist Political Party. His version of the events of April 15, 1919, can be found in his autobiographical novel *La tragedia del mio ardire*, pp. 88–89. Armando Mazza (1884–1964) was a Futurist poet and journalist.

7. Mario Chiesa was a Milanese student active in the Futurist Political Party.

8. Ettore Candiani was an industrialist and a liberal member of parliament.

9. Enzo Ferrari was a lawyer and member of the Fasci di Combattimento's Central Committee.

10. Baldino Corridoni, brother of the trade union leader Filippo Corridoni.

11. *Avanti!*, the foremost Socialist newspaper in Italy, had been responsible for a sustained agitation against Mussolini and the Fasci di Combattimento. In the infamous assault on April 15, the Milanese office was sacked and burned down.

At this point, Marinetti's diary stops. There are no comments on the sacking of the newspaper offices. In the version published in *Futurismo e fascismo*, the events are more or less recounted as in the diary. After a long description of the battle in via Mercanti, he ends his account in the manner translated on pp. 294–96.

12. The following text is taken from a description of the battle in via Mercanti published in *Futurismo e fascismo* (1924).

13. As Marinetti declared in an open letter to *L'ardito* of August 1, 1920, he was "in no way involved in the burning of the newspaper offices," but in the comment printed in *Futurismo e fascismo*, he reasoned that the counterdemonstration was the only way to prevent Italy from falling into the hands of "confused agitators with a foolish admiration for a fantastical Russia they had never seen." The price of the street battles of April 15 was not only a devastated city center but the loss of four lives.

14. Giacinto Menotti Serrati (1876–1926), since 1914 director of *Avanti!*

15. Federico Pinna Berchet (1898–1961) was one of the editors of *Roma futurista*.

16. Enrico Caviglia (1862–1945) was a leading general in the Italian army and played a decisive role in the victory of Vittorio Veneto. In 1919 he became a senator and minister of defense. Marinetti met him in 1918 and was told, to his astonishment, that the general had been a supporter of Futurism in the prewar *serate*. In 1922 Marinetti dedicated a pamphlet to him, entitled *I condottieri: Enrico Caviglia*.

17. According to F. Vecchi, his words were: "Captain! Signor Marinetti!, I am delighted at the action you have carried out. Captain, your Arditi have saved the Nation." For this and some other reports on the meeting, see Berghaus, *Futurism and Politics*, pp. 111 and 162, n. 71.

52 OLD IDEAS THAT GO HAND IN GLOVE BUT NEED TO BE SEPARATED

1. Libertarianism was a synonym for anarchism. The *beaux gestes libertaires* or *beaux gestes destructifs* of anarchist activists were often praised in Marinetti's writings.

2. The *radiose giornate di maggio* (the "radiant days of May"), refer to the public demonstrations in favor of Italy's entry into war, following Italy's treaty with England, France, and Russia (April 26, 1915) and the cancellation of the Triple Alliance with Austria and Germany (May 4, 1915). The declaration of war against Austria took place on May 23, 1915.

3. In December 1914, Marinetti and Enrico Corradini, leader of the Italian Nationalist Association, went on an Interventionist propaganda tour to Faenza and Ravenna. Marinetti and Mussolini joined forces in April 1915, during the Interventionist demonstrations at Piazza di Trevi, in Rome, and Piazza della Pilotta, in Milan. The Revolutionary Syndicalist Filippo Corridoni (1887–1915) was an outspoken advocate of a *guerra rivoluzionaria* and supported Italy's entry into the First World War.

4. The paragraph in *Roma futurista* is more to the point here: "Nowadays, we separate the idea of the Nation and our profound passion for a divine Italy from the idea of a Monarchy and from the old formulas of liberalism and democracy. We link the idea of Nation with those of bold Progress and Futurist democracy, which is: virile, practical, revolutionary, antipolice, and decisively anticlerical."

5. The League of Nations was a forerunner of the United Nations. A covenant for the formation of the League was part of the Versailles peace treaty, which ended the First World War. Its first meeting was held in Geneva on November 15, 1920, and one of its first tasks was to decide on the future of the vanquished states, their territories and colonies.

6. *Entente cordiale* (though established in 1904) was an expression much in use in the early part of the twentieth century to describe the amicable relations between Great Britain and France.

7. During the fight for the unification of Italy, Giuseppe Mazzini (1805–72) was the leader of the republican wing of the Risorgimento. Camillo Benso di Cavour (1810–61) was instrumental in bringing about the proclamation of the Kingdom of Italy in 1861. In the 1880s, the republicans came to terms with the monarchy and developed into a middle-of-the-road political party (PRI). Before the First World War, the Interventionists saw themselves as completing the mission of Mazzini and Cavour, by forcing Austria into "redeeming" the last provinces considered to be Italian. Ubaldo Comandini (1869–1925) was a leader of the Republican Party and a minister without portfolio, for aid and propaganda, during the First World War. The lawyer and popular orator Innocenzo Cappa (1875–1945) was a philo-Fascist Republican, who defended Marinetti during the *Mafarka* trial in 1910. In 1937 he wrote a book on Giuseppe Mazzini. Antonio Salandra (1853–1931) was a conservative Liberal, who served as prime minister from 1914 to 1916. Initially, he announced Italy's policy of neutrality, but in 1915 he campaigned for the country's entry into the war. Nonetheless, for Marinetti, he was an emblematic representative of the old regime (see document 62, *Address to the Fascist Congress in Florence*).

53 Futurist Democracy

1. The successful Battle of Vittorio Veneto (October 30, 1918) led to the demise of the Austro-Hungarian Empire.
2. The Austro-Hungarian Empire collapsed after its military defeat in the autumn of 1918 and was formally dissolved into several independent states.
3. Arturo Labriola (1873–1959), the leader of the Revolutionary Syndicalist movement in Italy, was an important point of reference in Marinetti's early career.
4. For many politicized ex-combatants, the victory over Austria at Vittorio Veneto was only the first stage of the Italian Revolution. The second phase was directed against the old political class in Italy. The so-called *biennio rosso* (two red years) of 1919–20 did indeed often verge on civil war.
5. On April 29, 1917, the National Association of War Victims (Associazione Nazionale fra Mutilati ed Invalidi di Guerra, ANMIG) was called into existence. Although the steering committee refrained from proclaiming allegiance to any political party, there were continuous efforts from politicians of the Left and Right to exercise influence on the organization. One of these politicians was Benito Mussolini, who saw the soldiers returning from the trenches as the "political avant-garde" and the "new aristocracy of the post-war period." Following the armistice, ANMIG developed into an organizational network that challenged the government's authority and threatened public order. In their newsletter, the *Bolletino*, they campaigned for a complete overhaul of the Italian political structure. The soldiers were exhorted to "shake off the yoke of the old Parties and to break the fetters of decrepit traditions"; they were asked to form a "compact band" (*fascio compatto*) and act as the country's avant-garde in the political arena.
6. On November 12, 1918, the Central Committee of the ANMIG mooted the foundation of the National Association of Ex-Servicemen (Associazione Nazionale Combattenti, ANC), which soon provided political orientation for the dozens of ex-combatant organizations that sprang up in Italy in late 1918 and early 1919, many of them with anticonstitutional, subversive aims and anarchist, communist, or socialist members. The Futurist Political Party recruited its supporters from this pool of actual or potential revolutionaries.

54 The Proletariat of Talented People

1. Manzoni's *The Betrothed* (1840–42) is a classic of Italian literature. Its protagonist, Lucia, attracts the attention of a local grandee, Don Rodrigo, who thwarts her marriage to her beloved Renzo and then seeks to abduct the girl. Later in the story he falls victim to the plague and dies of it.
2. Niccolò Tommaseo (1802–74), Pietro Fanfani (1815–79), and Giuseppe Rigutini (1829–1903) were the authors of various dictionaries of the Italian language. Matteo Giulio Bartoli (1873–1946) wrote an Italian grammar and compiled an atlas of Italian dialects. Giovanni Boccaccio (1313–75) and Niccolò Machiavelli (1469–1527) were using variations on the Tuscan dialect on which Italian was based, and were held up as models to emulate in Italian schools.

3. Censoring the widespread use of French words was common among linguistic purists, especially teachers.

4. Following the manifestos against past-loving Rome and Venice, Marinetti never penned a sequel against Florence. However, he organized a *serata* against traditionalist Florence (December 12, 1913), in which Papini delivered a vilification of "this worm-eaten tomb of the arts [. . . which] suffocates any vigorous life with its provincial narrow-mindedness and passéist bigotry."

5. The Cascine is a park outside the city gates of Florence much frequented by prostitutes.

55 AGAINST MARRIAGE

1. This essay coincided with the Futurist Political Party's demand for the gradual abolition of marriage through facilitating divorce, giving women the right to vote, and fostering their participation in national life. See *An Artistic Movement Creates a Political Party* (document 46) and also the essay *Against the Papacy and the Catholic Mentality* (document 60). A similar set of ideas was expressed in the essay "Against Marriage," in *L'ardito* on September 21, 1919, and the chapter "Revolutionary Italian Pride and Free Love" in *Democrazia futurista* (1919).

56 SYNTHESIS OF MARX'S THOUGHT

1. Marx's theory of value is principally developed in *Das Kapital*.

2. Marx developed his theory of surplus value in *Das Kapital*, where he distinguishes between the exchange value and the use value of products. It is an essential feature of capitalism that it seeks to increase the value of the money that is put into circulation. When labor becomes a commodity on the market, it is not being rewarded according to its use value, but according to its commodity price (or its exchange value). The difference between what the capitalist pays the worker and the value of what the worker produces is called surplus value.

3. Marx distinguishes between two aspects of capital: *constant capital*, which is expended on means of production (machinery, tools, raw materials, and so on), and *variable capital*, which is expended on labor. The *constant capital* never leaves the sphere of production and is therefore *fixed capital*.

4. Historical materialism is a method of explaining the progress in human society as being determined by its material, productive, and especially economic forces. It sets itself apart from idealist theories of history, which see intellectual, political, and cultural phenomena as the principal causes for historical change. Marx regarded these ideological factors as belonging to the "superstructure" of society, which is ultimately a reflection of its "basic structure," or modes of production.

57 SYNTHESIS OF MAZZINI'S THOUGHT ON PROPERTY AND ITS TRANSFORMATION

1. Giuseppe Mazzini (1805–1872) was one of the leaders of the Italian Risorgimento and a theorist of liberal nationalism. He sought to improve the relations between labor and capital in a democratic Italian State.

58 Technocratic Government Without Parliament or Senate, but with a Board of Initiatives

1. Part of that "revolutionary solution" was the institution of an *Eccitatorio*, included in the *Manifesto of the Italian Futurist Political Party* (document 45), §4: "Instead of a Parliament full of incompetent orators and irrelevant academics, moderated by a Senate full of has-beens, we shall have a government of twenty technocrats stimulated (*eccitato*) by an assembly of under-thirty-year-olds." It was taken up again in the speech given at the Florence Congress of the Fasci di Combattimento (see document 62).
2. Giovanni Villa (1862–1930) was a lawyer, a senator, and during the Orlando government (May 15, 1918–January 17, 1919) minister of transport, minister of the interior, and president of the Council of Ministers.
3. An American type of standardized ship made for fast assembly.
4. This paragraph can also be found in Marinetti's diary entry for May 8, 1918.

59 Futurist Patriotism

1. This essay was part of an extended debate on the social and political structure of Italian society conducted in the pages of *Roma futurista*. Several other texts from this period are translated in this volume. See, in particular, the manifesto *Against Marriage* and the *Manifesto of the Futurist Political Party*. Marinetti's patriotism is to be seen in conjunction with his cosmopolitan upbringing and internationalist literary career, which for a long time made him favor the French over the Italian language. See Berghaus, *Genesis of Futurism*, pp. 6–7. On his anti-Nationalist nationalism see Berghaus, *Futurism and Politics*, pp. 59–61.
2. The first four regions were considered *terrae irredentae*, i.e., lands currently occupied by Austria, which needed to be "liberated," whereas the last four occupied an important role in Italy's colonial history.

60 Against the Papacy and the Catholic Mentality, Repositories of Every Kind of Traditionalism

1. This essay needs to be seen in the context of Mussolini's turn to the Right and his overtures toward traditionalist forces such as monarchists and Catholics. Marinetti's disagreements with this policy caused him to sever his links with the Fasci di Combattimento. He was supported in this oppositional stance by other Futurists, such as Settimelli, Rosai, Chiti, and others. Settimelli's brochure *Svaticanamento: Dichiarazione agli italiani* attacked Mussolini's conciliation with the Vatican in such strong terms that it was immediately sequestered and Settimelli was taken to court. On Marinetti's anti-Catholic sentiments, see also the *Futurist Proclamation to the Spaniards* (document 18); his views on marriage were previously voiced in *Against Marriage* (document 55).
2. Camillo Benso di Cavour (1810–61) and Francesco Crispi (1819–1901) were key political architects of the unified Italy.
3. Reference is again made here to the Battle of Vittorio Veneto. The Italian offensive started on October 24, 1918. On November 3, 1918, the Austrian general, Weber von Webenau, signed the capitulation.

4. In the Italian, Marinetti uses the term *arditi*, which of course appealed to the ex-combatant readers of the journal *L'ardito*. Furthermore, it linked up with a very topical debate about the Arditi's attitude to law and order. Many Arditi had joined the Special Forces because they were not bound by the same rules and regimentation as the corps of normal soldiers. This attitude of "standing above the law" caused a great deal of friction after the war. See below, note 7.

5. In a later edition of this text in *Futurismo e fascismo* (1924), the wording is bowdlerized to "she opens her window and heart."

6. The Latin word *virtus* is derived from *vir*, "man." "Virtue" in this context means "manliness," in the sense of sexual prowess.

7. In May 1919 the Arditi regiments were reorganized by the Ministry of Defense and combined with the security forces, which caused Mario Carli to publish an article in *L'ardito* entitled "Arditi, Not Policemen," in which he condemned the minister's decision and called "the transformation of the Arditi into policemen and government constables the worst humiliation that has been inflicted upon them." M. Carli, "Arditi, non Gendarmi!," *L'ardito*, May 18, 1919.

8. The national government police force is known in Italy as polizia and carabinieri. The latter were constituted in 1814, as the Corps of Royal Carabinieri, by Victor Emmanuel I of Savoy, in imitation of the then departing French Gendarmerie Nationale. Its officers were mainly recruited from the ranks of the aristocracy, who were given authority over both the armed forces and the civilian population. In the First World War the carabinieri were often positioned behind the lines of common soldiers to keep their fighting spirit under constant observation and to prevent desertions (or in the case of the Arditi, reckless behavior).

9. Marinetti was very actively involved with making propaganda for Futurism among the Arditi. As his war diary and many articles in *L'Italia futurista* and *Roma futurista* show, he was indeed successful in recruiting new supporters from their ranks.

10. Trieste was the only Austrian seaport of any size or importance. It was captured by the Italian forces in 1918 and incorporated into the unified Italy.

61 SPEECH IN PARLIAMENT

1. Giuseppe Bevione (1879–1976) was a parliamentarian and later a senator and Accademico d'Italia.

2. An imposing palace designed by Bernini and completed by Carlo Fontana in 1697. It was originally the seat of the Roman Curia, but in 1871 it became the home of the new Italian parliament.

3. Ferruccio Vecchi published his account of the Montecitorio action in his autobiographical novel, *La tragedia del mio ardire* (1923), pp. 95–102.

4. This and many other phrases and expressions are taken verbatim from Marinetti's diary entry for July 11, 1919 (*Taccuini*, pp. 420–21).

5. Marinetti is probably referring here to the fact that originally Montecitorio housed the Curia, that the chairs formerly belonged to cardinals, that their ghosts still occupy the chairs, and that these papist structures still influence the postwar government.

6. John Nost Sartorius (1759–1828), British artist known for his equestrian paintings,

which were extremely popular and sought after from the late 1700s to the mid-1800s.

7. Giuseppe Marcora (1841–1927) fought with Garibaldi in Sicily. He was president of the Chamber of Deputies from 1904 to 1906, was reelected in 1907, and remained in that post until December 1919.

8. Arnaldo Lucci (1871–1945), trade unionist and militant socialist, became a professor of law and parliamentary deputy for Naples. When he was expelled from the Socialist Party, he sat in parliament as an independent socialist. Being a vociferous critic of Italy's entry into the Great War, he became a formidable opponent of Prime Minister Salandra.

9. On Nitti, see note 6 to document 50, *Fascism and the Milan Speech*.

62 ADDRESS TO THE FASCIST CONGRESS OF FLORENCE

1. See note 6 to document 50, *Fascism and the Milan Speech*.
2. See note 1 to document 50, *Fascism and the Milan Speech*.
3. General Alberico Albricci (1864–1936) was a military commander in the First World War.
4. In September 1919 Mario Carli joined D'Annunzio in the occupied city of Fiume, where he set up a very active Futurist cell and a newspaper, *La testa di ferro*. After the Fiume adventure, he moved the paper to Milan, where he was arrested on suspicion of having organized a terrorist attack with several anarchists.
5. *Notti filtrate* was a cycle of ten poems, published by the Edizioni futuriste de "L'Italia futurista" in 1918.
6. Emilio Settimelli (1891–1954), a writer and theater impresario, was a key member of the Florentine circle of Futurists. In 1918 he moved to Rome, where he founded, with Marinetti, the journal *Roma futurista*.
7. The Futurists, Fasci di Combattimento, and Arditi were among the most virulent agitators in the social unrest after the end of the First World War.
8. The concept and the term *svaticanamento* ("getting rid of the Vatican") came from Marinetti's friend Umberto Notari, who made this a key demand of his Associazione italiana d'avanguardia. See also Marinetti's manifesto *Against the Papacy and the Catholic Mentality* (document 60).
9. Sileno Fabbri was a founding member of the Roman branch of the Futurist Political Party, a leader of the Fasci di Combattimento, and a key architect of its political program.
10. On this institution, see document 58, *Technocratic Government Without Parliament or Senate, but with a Board of Initiatives*.
11. See note 7 to document 52, *Old Ideas That Go Hand in Glove*.
12. As Marinetti explains later in the speech, one of the models for the serving wench was Giovanni Giolitti (1842–1928), a career civil servant and economic expert who was the minister of the Treasury with Crispi, became prime minister in 1892, and headed two broad coalition governments before the war (1906–1909, 1911–14). He tried to curb the excessive spending of previous governments and was responsible for

passing a national insurance act (1911). Marinetti and many intellectuals of his generation regarded Giolitti as an emblem of a small-minded, small-scale Italy (*Italietta*).

13. The other model for the serving wench was Francesco Saverio Nitti; see note 6 to document 50, *Fascism and the Milan Speech*.

14. *Urbs* is Latin for "city," here meaning Rome (*urbs Romana*).

15. The *Flumen sanctum* is the river Tiber, in Roman times considered to be a divinity: "teque pater Tiberine tuo cum flumine sancto" (Ennius, *Annalium fragmenta* 1.54), and similarly Virgil, *Aeneas* VIII: 72: "Tuque, o Thybri, tuo genitor cum flumine sancto."

16. Paolo Boselli (1838–1932) served as minister of education and minister of the Treasury before becoming Salandra's successor (June 1916) and presiding over Italy's first wartime national coalition government.

17. It is impossible to assess how many of the Arditi were Futurists. To promote Futurist ideas among the Association and to counteract Mussolini's reactionary influence, Mario Carli published a *Manifesto of the Futurist Ardito* in November 1919.

18. On Ferruccio Vecchi see note 1 to document 50, *Fascism and the Milan Speech*.

19. Vecchi was a leader of the infamous assault on the headquarters of the Socialist newspaper *Avanti!* See document 51, *The Battle of Via Mercanti*.

20. See document 45, *Manifesto of the Futurist Political Party*, §3.

21. See document 54, *The Proletariat of Talented People*, which elaborates on the theses presented here.

22. Most of the following four paragraphs are taken verbatim from document 54, *The Proletariat of Talented People*.

23. Piero Bolzon (1883–1945) traveled widely in Latin America before the First World War. He was one of the right-wing leaders of the Arditi who followed Mussolini into the conservative camp and turned *L'ardito* into a reactionary newspaper. In fact, much of Marinetti's glowing praise of the Arditi must be seen as a tactical measure, as only a month before the Congress he had been very critical of the recent political developments in the Association. See Marinetti, *Taccuini*, p. 440.

24. The Second Battle of the Marne (July 15–September 16, 1918) marked the turning of the tide in the First World War and became the Allies' first victorious offensive of 1918.

25. See document 30, *The Exploiters of Futurism*, and documents 25–29.

26. These key points can be found verbatim in document 54, *The Proletariat of Talented People*.

27. Anatole France (1844–1924) and Henri Barbusse (1873–1935) were French novelists actively involved in the peace movement during the First World War. They signed a large number of manifestos and declarations, individually and collectively. The one Marinetti refers to here may be "Un Appel d'Anatole France et d'Henri Barbusse," published in *L'Humanité* on November 6, 1919.

28. Giacomo Barzellotti (1844–1917) was a senator and professor of philosophy at Rome University.

29. Claudio Treves (1868–1933) was a parliamentarian and director of the Socialist

papers *Il tempo* and *Avanti!* who, with Filippo Turati (1857–1932), was leader of the reformist wing of the Socialist Party.

30. On August 9, 1918, Gabriele D'Annunzio (1863–1938) flew over Vienna in a publicity stunt, distributing 390,000 leaflets exhorting the Viennese to surrender. After the signing of the armistice, President Wilson of the United States opposed Italy's annexation of Fiume, and the Paris Peace Conference ordered the Italian troops to leave the city. In the Versailles treaty of June 28, 1919, Fiume was placed under British suzerainty. In August 1919 Italian troops in Ronchi chose D'Annunzio as their Duce to liberate Fiume. On September 12 they marched toward the city, and General Pittaluga, the Commandant of the Inter-Allied Presidium in Fiume, refused to fire on Italian soldiers. While D'Annunzio fenced himself in with his soldiers and framed the Fiume Constitution, the Italian government cut off supplies to the city and began a protracted, but not particularly effective, siege.

31. *Il popolo d'Italia* was the foremost Interventionist and, later, Fascist newspaper. It was founded by Mussolini in 1914 and ran from November 15, 1914, to July 24, 1943. On the Battles of Caporetto and Vittorio Veneto see notes 4 and 8 to document 47, *Branches of the Futurist Political Party*.

32. See document 11, *The Necessity and Beauty of Violence*.

33. See note 4 to document 47, *Branches of the Futurist Political Party*.

34. On October 24, 1918, D'Annunzio supported General Diaz's offensive with his air squadron and made three sorties over the enemy armies entrenched near Vittorio Veneto.

35. Guido Raby was Marinetti's superior, who, according to his diary entries, also became a good friend and comrade.

36. Marinetti arrived in Fiume on September 15, 1918, together with Ferruccio Vecchi. He had ten meetings with D'Annunzio, whose political abilities he viewed in increasingly negative terms. On October 1 he had to leave the city, having been expelled for a variety of political and personal reasons. Thus the euphoric praise of D'Annunzio in this speech does not at all accord with his privately voiced opinions. See Berghaus, *Futurism and Politics*, pp. 135–39.

63 BEYOND COMMUNISM

1. See note 8 to document 47, *Branches of the Futurist Political Party*.

2. See note 7 to document 65, *Artistic Rights Defended by the Italian Futurists*.

3. The term *patria* has been translated here as "Nation" because "Fatherland/*Vaterland*" was, in the first half of the twentieth century, such an overwhelmingly emotive, German term.

4. The period 1919 to 1920 was often referred to as the "two red years." The increase in revolutionary spirit brought about the election of Socialist administrations in Naples, Florence, and Turin. The elections of November 1919 returned 156 Socialists to parliament. Strikes occurred in every industrial center, peasants took possession of uncultivated areas, factories were occupied by the workers. To many people it appeared only a question of time before Italy would experience a Soviet-style revolution.

5. Aleksandr Vailiyevich Kolchak (1874–1920) was a former Tsarist admiral who became minister of war and the navy in the anti-Bolshevik socialist government established at Omsk. He gained control over much of Siberia but after several defeats handed over control to General Anton Ivanovich Denikin (1872–1947), the commander of the anti-Bolshevik forces, which controlled southern Russia. Denikin's attempt to seize control of Moscow in June 1919 proved unsuccessful: in October 1919 his army was comprehensively defeated at Orel and forced back to the Crimea. In April 1920 Józef Klemens Piłsudski (1867–1935) launched a Polish invasion of the Ukraine and plunged the Bolsheviks into a new crisis.

6. In the early 1900s anti-Semitism was indeed a fringe phenomenon in Italy. Even the early Fascist movement had no anti-Semitic program. There were 5 Jews among the founders of the Fasci di Combattimento and 230 participated in the March on Rome. In 1932 Mussolini told Emil Ludwig, in the famous *Colloqui con Mussolini*, that racism was stupid and anti-Semitism did not exist in Italy. However, the situation changed markedly after 1936 with the rapid political convergence of Italy and Hitler's Germany, and the formal Italo-German alliance of 1939.

7. Italy joined the Allied nations during the First World War in the hope of acquiring territory at the expense of the Austro-Hungarian Empire. However, in the Versailles Peace Treaty (June 28, 1919), Italy's prime minister Vittorio Orlando was not granted the Dalmatian islands, the Brenner Pass, or Fiume. Italy was awarded the South Tyrol (Alto Adige), the Trentino, and Venezia Giulia (East Friuli, Trieste, Istria, and part of Carniola), but at American insistence the eastern Adriatic coast went to the new state of Yugoslavia.

8. On Nitti, see note 6 to document 50, *Fascism and the Milan Speech*.

9. Marinetti visited Russia from February 8 to 28, 1914 (January 26 to February 15 by the Russian calendar), but his stay was only a qualified success.

10. See Vladimir Tolstoy, Irina Bibikova, and Catherine Cooke, *Street Art of the Revolution: Festivals & Celebrations in Russia, 1918–33* (London: Thames and Hudson, 1990).

11. The Official Socialist Party (PUS—Partito Ufficiale Socialista) was another name for the reformist, social democratic PSI (Partito Socialista Italiano), the largest party in the Italian parliament. The derogatory expression *pussisti* was used to differentiate the social democrats from the revolutionary socialists, the anarcho-syndicalists, and other maximalist factions.

12. See document 58, *Technocratic Government Without Parliament or Senate, but with a Board of Initiatives*.

13. Communism, as a reign of the belly, was the theme of Marinetti's play *Le Roi Bombance*. The term *ventri comunicanti* is a wordplay on *vasi comunicanti* (communicating vases), where the water level is always equal.

14. After declaring war on Turkey, on September 29, 1911, the Italian army occupied Tripoli on October 6, 1911. The decisive battle of October 23, 1911, forced Turkey to cede Tripolitania and Cyrenaica to Italy. In contrast, the Battle of Abba Garima, on March 1, 1896, was a military and political disaster, leaving 42 percent of the Italian forces (or 6,600 soldiers) dead on Abyssinian soil.

15. The Battle on the Karst (Carso), on September 13, 1916, brought Italy its first major victory in the First World War. After experiencing a major defeat at Caporetto (October 24, 1917), the Italian army halted the Austrian counteroffensive on the banks of the river Piave (June 1918), leading to the successful Battle of Vittorio Veneto (October 30, 1918).

16. The idea was already expressed in *The Necessity and Beauty of Violence* (document 11) and the *Manifesto of the Futurist Political Party* (document 45), which demanded "Schools promoting courage and the Italian spirit." The idea was further elaborated upon in the essays *Aboliamo la costrizione* (*L'ardito*, May 18, 1919) and *Il cittadino eroico: L'abolizione delle polizie* (*L'ardito*, June 15, 22, and 29, 1919).

17. The action of *Le Roi Bombance* (King Guzzle) takes place in a fairy-tale kingdom called Blunder. The first act is set in the park of the Castle of Abundance, where King Guzzle reigns. A revolution has been planned by the three Scullery Boys—Syphon, Torte, and Béchamel—supported by Estomacreux (Big-Guts) and the hungry masses of the kingdom. The Scullery Boys promise Big-Guts the position of Superintendent of the Kitchens in exchange for his support in the conspiracy, and the Hungry Ones are assured that they will be liberated from the specter of Saint Putrefaction and the Ponds of the Past that surround the castle. When the three Cooks of Universal Happiness fail to feed the masses, the court idiot/poet shows them how to escape the great hunger by returning to "the land of Azure Dreams, where . . . one lives on sweet music and caressing words." Later in the play he shows Big-Guts that fulfilling the masses' material desires will never lead to a liberated society. The quest for freedom is like a never-ending ascent to the Heights of the Absolute.

18. See document 54, *The Proletariat of Talented People*.

19. Fedele Azari launched the manifesto *A Futurist Theater of the Skies* in a propaganda flight over Milan in April 1919, and published it subsequently in a number of newspapers.

20. I am not aware of this bill ever reaching parliament.

21. This idea was first mooted by Boccioni in a Free Art Exhibition in Milan in 1911. It was organized with the help of the Humanitarian Society at the Milan House of Labor and sought to demonstrate the universal language of creativity in the works of Futurists, amateur artists, children, and ordinary workers.

22. Marinetti's terms are carefully chosen here to avoid any comparison with Marx's oft-quoted phrase from *Critique of the Hegelian Philosophy of Right*, "religion is the opiate of the masses."

23. The essays mentioned here can be found in documents 53 and 11, respectively.

64 TO EVERY MAN, A NEW TASK EVERY DAY!: INEQUALITY AND THE ARTOCRACY

1. The metaphors of the sea, the waves, and the stars used throughout this essay hark back to Marinetti's Symbolist poetry. Marinetti exploits the wordplay *mer–mère* and presents the sea as the Mother of Revolution. The book *La Conquête des étoiles* (1902) takes as its theme the revolt of the fertile life forces against the debilitating reign of idealism and Romanticism. The waves are the "knights of the sea" and send

their "infernal charge" into the sky until the rule of the stars is broken. In *Destruction* (1904), he invokes "the omnipotent Sea" to deliver him from the regime of idealism. He introduces a "puerile soul," who may be a precursor of the Cabin Boy, and a "condemned sailor," who takes a boat into "the fateful port," obtains Death's "deifying power, and dies, without coming to an end!"

2. As Marinetti's diary (*Taccuini*, p. 511) indicates, the essay was written in autumn–winter 1921 while he was negotiating with the Communists about a coalition that would replace the former Futurist-Fascist alliance. Hence, the ship may represent the Communist Party and the waves the socialists who fight under its banner.

3. The final break between the Communists and Futurists came in June–July 1922, when the hard-liners around Amadeo Bordiga forced the young philo-Futurist communists to toe the party line, thus severing all links between the two worlds of political revolutionaries and artistic avant-garde.

4. The idea expressed here stems from Karl Marx and Friedrich Engels, who described in *German Ideology* a communist society liberated from the division of labor, "where nobody has one exclusive sphere of activity but each can become accomplished in any branch he wishes, society regulates the general production and thus makes it possible for me to do one thing today and another tomorrow, to hunt in the morning, fish in the afternoon, rear cattle in the evening, criticize after dinner, just as I have a mind, without ever becoming hunter, fisherman, herdsman, or critic."

65 Artistic Rights Defended by the Italian Futurists

1. See note 8 to document 47, *Branches of the Futurist Political Party*.

2. Mussolini became head of state on October 28, 1922.

3. The Russian Futurists were active supporters of the Russian Revolution. In 1918 several of them managed to occupy responsible positions in government and administrative offices, which they used for promoting modernist concepts of art and culture. In 1922 the Futurists were officially acknowledged as the Left Front for the Arts, and the Central Committee decided to support its publications. However, in the years that followed, the avant-garde was systematically marginalized and Russian Futurism went into a long period of decline.

4. This was Marinetti's official line vis-à-vis a Fascist State he could no longer fully support. In 1919 he had still maintained: "The Futurist movement pursues first of all an artistic program while at the same time indirectly influencing Italian political life" (*Le Futurisme avant, pendant, après la guerre*). In 1920, when Mussolini led the Fasci di Combattimento into the right-wing camp, most Futurists left the organization and focused again on their artistic work. The formal division between politics and art came to be repeated in later publications. See *Teoria e invenzione futurista*, 1st ed. pp. 430, 509, 2nd ed. pp. 494, 584.

5. The Futurists were imprisoned several times in 1914–15. The First Battle of the Marne took place between September 6 and 12, 1914. The imprisonment he refers to must therefore have been the six days that eleven Futurists spent in San Vittore prison, in Milan, after the Interventionist demonstration in the Victor Emmanuel Arcade on September 16, 1914.

6. On April 12, 1915, Marinetti, Corra, Settimelli, and Mussolini were imprisoned after staging a demonstration in Piazza di Trevi.

7. On November 20, 1919, Marinetti, Ferruccio Vecchi, Piero Bolzon, and Benito Mussolini were sentenced to twenty-one days of incarceration in the San Vittore prison for their "attack on State security and organization of armed bands."

8. The Association of Arditi was founded by Mario Carli on January 1, 1919, and its Milanese section was set up in Marinetti's apartment in Milan. On March 23, 1919, several Futurists participated in the founding assembly of the Fasci di Combattimento in Milan's Piazza San Sepolcro, and subsequently established local branches in various Italian cities.

9. From now on, Marinetti found it tactically opportune to remind Mussolini of his Futurist support in 1919, whereas the Duce did everything he could to distance himself from his Futurist past.

10. Marinetti's attempt to create a *Futurisme mondiale* made him inflate the number of Futurists by adding to his list a variety of avant-garde painters and composers (like those in paragraphs a and b) who had never joined the Futurist movement.

11. This exclusion from the Biennale would vex the Futurists for many years to come. At the opening by the king of the next Biennale (April 25, 1924), Marinetti caused a major scandal when, at the end of the ceremony, he shouted: "Down with the anti-Italian presidency of the exhibition because it refuses to host young Italian artists!"

12. The Augusteo was a theater created out of the ruins of the Augustus Mausoleum in Rome. From 1908 on, it became the home of the symphony orchestra of the Accademia Nazionale di Santa Cecilia. The Augusteo was demolished in 1936.

13. The case here is greatly exaggerated, with the exception that La Scala never supported experimental operas by young composers. The Futurists voiced their opposition to this "Pompeii of Italian theater" in a group manifesto of February 27, 1911: *Noi futuristi contro la Scala, Pompei del teatro italiano*, which they distributed in a protest action during a performance of Richard Strauss's *Der Rosenkavalier*.

14. Sicily possesses some of the best-preserved ancient Greek monuments, and the amphitheater at Syracuse became the center of a "Greek revival" organized and promoted by the theater critic Ettore Romagnoli. The Futurists voiced their opposition to such a cultural policy in a colorful street action and a *Futurist Manifesto on the Classical Performances at the Greek Theater in Syracuse*, distributed on the occasion of the premiere of Aeschylus's *Libation Bearers* on April 16, 1921. On April 18, Marinetti gave an "anticlassical" lecture in Syracuse at the Archimedes Café, repeated on April 19 at the Epicarmo Theater, and then in Catania, Palermo, and Messina. This provoked polemics in a large number of Sicilian newspapers and led to a second manifesto, which circulated under the titles of *Modernize the Greek Amphitheater, Against the Greek Theater*, and *Let's Utilize the Amphitheater of Syracuse* (June 11, 1921). The journal *L'imparziale* launched a referendum on the question, which had major national repercussions and found an overwhelmingly positive response. In January 1922 the magazine *La balza futurista* published a special issue titled *A Modern Drama at the Greek Theater*, which summarized the debate from a number of viewpoints.

15. The list of signatories to this and several other proposals changed in different editions of the manifesto. Those in brackets withdrew or were added at a later stage.

16. On March 16, 1923, *L'impero* ran a referendum on the issue of a credit bank set up specially for artists, and printed some of the responses over the following weeks. Marinetti pursued the idea for many years to come, repeating the demand at the Bologna Congress of Fascist Culture (March 29–30, 1925) and through the Writers' Union, after becoming national secretary of the Sindacato Autori e Scrittori (1928).

17. Marchi was the only trained architect in this group, although Volt had published a manifesto on Futurist architecture in 1919 and Prampolini would publish others in 1924 and 1926.

18. Carlo Frassinelli (1896–1983) was a typographer by profession and a contributor to the development of a Futurist book art. Like Franco Rampa Rossi, he was a Communist and highly critical of various aspects of this manifesto. See Berghaus, *Futurism and Politics*, pp. 186 and 194–95.

19. Before publishing the manifesto, Marinetti sent it to various Futurist groups for comments. Notwithstanding the dissent it incurred, Marinetti chose to ignore the objections and published it in the name of *all* groups. Subsequently some of them publicly dissociated themselves from the manifesto. See Paladini's letter in *Rovente* (March 20, 1923) and Rampa Rossi's protest note in *L'impero* (May 19, 1923).

THE RETURN TO THE ARTISTIC DOMAIN (1920–33)

66 WHAT IS FUTURISM?: ELEMENTARY LESSONS

1. See note 2 to document 47, *Branches of the Futurist Political Party*.

2. This point became the topic of an article, "Aboliamo la coscrizione," in *L'ardito* on May 18, 1919.

3. I have omitted the postscript, entitled "Futurist Actions Before, During, and After the War," which repeats text previously published in "An Artistic Movement Creates a Political Party" and "Branches of the Futurist Political Party." Part of it was used again more or less verbatim in the introduction to *Futurismo e fascismo* (1924), *Teoria e invenzione futurista*, 1st ed. pp. 430–31, 2nd ed. pp. 494–95. The last section comprises an advertisement for the Futurism exhibition at the Gallery Cova in Milan (March–April 1919).

67 TACTILISM: A FUTURIST MANIFESTO

1. This unusual beginning of a manifesto can be found in the leaflet version published by the Leadership of the Futurist Movement, dated January 11, 1921.

2. See document 32, *The Variety Theater*.

3. Dynamism, simultaneity, and interpenetration were three key aspects of Futurist art, intended to reflect "the frenetic life of our great cities" (*Manifesto of Futurist Painters*), Apollonio, *Futurist Manifestos*, p. 25.

4. See document 20, *Technical Manifesto of Futurist Literature*.

5. Boccioni wrote extensively on "plastic dynamism" as a force that extends from a piece of sculpture into its surrounding environment.

6. These are Russolo's *intonarumori*. They looked like sound boxes with large funnels attached and produced a wide array of sounds, which could be tuned and rhythmically regulated by means of mechanical manipulation. The first instruments built in 1913 made an explosive sound like an automobile engine, a crackling sound like rifle fire, humming sound like a dynamo, and different kinds of stamping noises.

7. See document 34, *A Futurist Theater of Essential Brevity.*

8. The Florentine navigator Amerigo Vespucci (1454–1512) claimed that in 1497–98 he reached the South American mainland before any other explorer. Similarly, Marinetti declares here that he himself discovered another virgin continent, called Tactilism.

9. Marinetti spent the summer holidays in 1920 with his new girlfriend, Benedetta, at Primo Conti's house in Antignano near Livorno. Marinetti is rather disingenuous in not mentioning Benedetta's contribution to the Tactilism experiments. See Lia Giachero, "Mani 'palpatrici d'orizzonti': Il contributo di Benedetta Marinetti al manifesto per il tattilismo," *Ricerche di storia dell'arte* 45 (1991): 65–67.

10. During the *biennio rosso*, the "two red years" after the First World War, many factories in Tuscany were occupied by the workers.

11. Marinetti's opposition to a form of socialism exclusively focused on material well-being ("the reign of the belly") had already been satirized in the comedy *Le Roi Bombance* of 1905.

12. Charles Baudelaire's *Les Paradis artificiels* (1860), inspired by Thomas De Quincey's memoir *Confessions of an English Opium Eater* (1821), brought the term "artificial paradise" into general circulation.

13. The Futurists were indeed fully supportive of the workers' fight for improved living standards, but highly critical of the organization that exploited this desire for its own partisan political objectives.

14. Much of this hardship was caused by the return of some two million soldiers into civilian life, for which the government was ill-prepared. Little was done to offer medical, financial, and social assistance; vocational training; and access to the labor market. In 1919–20 this led to the occupation of fields and factories, the plundering of shops and warehouses, strikes, and other forms of unrest.

15. See the illustration in *Noi e il mondo* 11, no. 4 (April 1921): 327. The panel was shown at the opening of a Futurist exhibition at the Casa d'arte Bragaglia in Rome.

16. On Marinetti's Tactile Theater see Berghaus, *Italian Futurist Theatre*, pp. 364–66, 539–40.

17. On the style of mechanical delivery see also document 33, *Dynamic, Multichanneled Recitation.*

18. In February 1917 Marinetti was sent with the Seventy-third Artillery Battalion to the Gorizia front. See document 68, *Tactilism: Toward the Discovery of New Senses.*

19. Rachilde was the pseudonym of Marguerite Eymery Vallette (1860–1953), a Symbolist author of over sixty works of fiction, drama, poetry, and criticism, among them *Les Hors nature, mœurs contemporaines* (Nature's Outcast, 1897) and *La Jongleuse* (The Juggler, 1900), both published by the Société du Mercure de France.

20. Following the publication of the lecture, *Comœdia* received several readers' letters. On January 18, Francis Picabia pointed out that Tactilism had in fact been invented

in 1916 by the American sculptor Edith Clifford Williams in New York, and that on November 13, 1918, Guillaume Apollinaire had given a lecture on the same topic at the Galerie Paul Guillaume, with excerpts published by the *Mercure de France* (February 16, 1918). Marinetti responded in *Comœdia* and *L'Esprit nouveau* (March 1921) that he was unaware of these predecessors. He pointed out that he had not produced a piece of conventional sculpture or merely a theoretical statement, but a new "technique presque définitive" and a novel masterpiece called *Soudan-Paris.* The controversy was commented on in the *New York Herald* of January 20, 1921, in an article titled "Picabia and Marinetti Disagree on 'Tactilism.'"

21. The polymaterial sculpture *Fusione di una testa e di una finestra* is known only from a photograph and is now considered lost or destroyed.

68 TACTILISM: TOWARD THE DISCOVERY OF NEW SENSES

1. See document 67, *Tactilism: A Futurist Manifesto.*
2. Nothing could be further from the truth. The lecture was seriously disturbed by a group of Dadaists and the audience could understand only a little of the text. See Michel Sanouillet, *Dada à Paris* (Paris: Pauvert, 1965), pp. 236–37. The reception of the speech was not much better in Italian theaters. See Berghaus, *Italian Futurist Theatre,* p. 365. Nonetheless, Marinetti assembled several pages of positive responses in the article "Polemiche sul Tattilismo" in *Cronache d'attualità,* May 1921, pp. 56–59.
3. The following paragraphs, omitted here, are a shortened version of the first Tactilism manifesto, with only a few textual readjustments.
4. Balla was one of several Futurists with a serious interest in paranormal phenomena, pursuing experiments of an occult and spiritualist nature. See Germano Celant, "Futurism and the Occult," *Artforum* 19, no. 5 (January 1981): 36–42.
5. Maga (Giuseppe Magagnoli) (1878–1933) was a graphic designer who in 1920 founded an advertising agency in Bologna and in 1921 opened an office in Paris. He became well known for his effective posters, some of which show a Futurist influence.
6. The event of November 23, 1924, organized by Mino Somenzi, opened in the Teatro dal Verme and included a reception at the city's council house, a triumphal procession through the streets of Milan, and a banquet at the Cova Gallery. The official proceedings, with over forty presentations, took place at the Spatenbäu and lasted until 9:00 p.m. Marinetti gave a speech titled "Tactilism—Discovery of New Senses—Antipsychological Theater—Abstract *sintesi*—Tactile *sintesi*—Inequality—The Aesthetics of the Machine." Benedetta spoke about her *Gesamtkunstwerk* concept of "plastic-polymaterial-rumoristic complexes portraying the visual, tactile, and olfactory relations between color, material, form, weight, heat, and emotionality."
7. Charles Henry (1859–1926) was the first director of the laboratory, created in 1897 at the Sorbonne, under the auspices of the department of experimental psychology.

69 THE THEATER OF SURPRISES

1. See document 34, *A Futurist Theater of Essential Brevity.*
2. Marinetti and Cangiullo probably had a type of comedy in mind that was champi-

oned by Ettore Petrolini, whose physical acting style was praised by Marinetti in an essay, "La risata italiana di Petrolini, Cangiullo, Balla, Corra," *L'Italia futurista*, July 1, 1917. The term used here, *fisicofollia* (body-madness), is not an established theatrical expression but refers to the highly physical style of acting to be found among music-hall and variety comedians. See Berghaus, *Italian Futurist Theatre*, pp. 166–72, 205–209.

3. These Words-in-Freedom were a literary device, described in documents 20 and 21, and are here applied to the theater. An example was Marinetti and Cangiullo's *Giardini pubblici* (The Public Gardens), appended to this manifesto, which contrasted a pair of lovers on one side of the stage with a wet nurse, formed by the letter *B*, suckling a baby, formed by the letter *S*.

4. See document 33, *Dynamic, Multichanneled Recitation*.

5. *Teatro-giornale* was a way of presenting current news items in an abbreviated, highly physical form of acting to illiterate audiences. In the 1920s it developed into a highly effective graphic form of agitation-propaganda utilized by working-class theater collectives.

6. On the Futurist Afternoon Performances in the Galleria Sprovieri, see Berghaus, *Italian Futurist Theatre*, pp. 232–45.

7. See document 32, *The Variety Theater*. The Futurist performances falling into this category have been described in Berghaus, *Italian Futurist Theatre*, pp. 201–209.

8. See document 34, *A Futurist Theater of Essential Brevity*. The Theater of Surprises was conceived to follow on from this but essentially became an amalgamation of all these components.

9. An example was Marinetti's *Simultaneity: A Compenetration*, appended to this manifesto, which showed the intermingling of the lives of a bourgeois family and of a coquette in a tenement block. The term "coquette" refers to a flirtatious "young thing" who seeks a sexual freedom not typically allotted to her sex. Ever since the courtesan Ninon de Lenclos defended her social behavior in the autobiographical novel, *La Coquette Vengée* (The Coquette Avenged, 1659), these young independent girls were deemed by puritans and respectable citizens to lead a dissolute and promiscuous life.

10. First announced as a "dance of objects" in the *Technical Manifesto of Futurist Literature* (document 20), this rather surreal genre became a popular component of the Futurist Theater of Essential Brevity. An example, Marinetti's *They Are Coming*, was appended to this manifesto.

11. This is an unclear term. It may refer to musical dissonances, or to plays such as Settimelli and Corra's *Dissonanza*, printed in the *Teatro futurista sintetico* collection of 1915.

12. Giacomo Balla was probably the first Futurist to turn paintings into stage performances. Such an actorless theater of images was also explored by Depero and Prampolini.

13. This new genre of a *vetrina*—actions and images presented as in a shop window display—was explored in several pieces by Bruno Corra and by Marinetti in *The Hands* (1915).

14. The liberating effect of the Futurist theater experiments of the 1910s on other playwrights and theater artists in Italy is discussed in Berghaus, *Italian Futurist Theatre*,

pp. 218–23. Marinetti enlarged on this passage in the later reworking of this manifesto, *After the Theater of Syntheses*; see document 71.

15. The Theater of Surprises Company, directed by Rodolfo de Angelis, gave its first performance on September 30, 1921, at the Mercadante Theater, in Naples, and then went on tour throughout Italy. The manifesto was written, according to Cangiullo, in a room of the Hotel de Londres on October 9, 1921.

16. When Raphael arrived in Rome, the pope appointed him to decorate the Vatican apartments, thus replacing the more conservative Sodoma. However, Marinetti is bending the truth slightly, as Sodoma had not progressed much beyond the ceiling of the Stanza della Segnatura. Raphael must have thought of himself as completing, rather than competing with, the work of his predecessor, as he portrayed himself next to Sodoma in his fresco *The School of Athens*.

17. This passage again shows Marinetti's disillusionment with politics, following the demise of the Futurist Political Party, the end of the Futurist revolution in Fiume, and Mussolini's turn to the Right. The Theater of Surprises was one of his most significant and commercially successful enterprises of the postwar years.

18. *Caffè-concerto* was an Italian equivalent to the French *café-concert* and the British music-hall. There were several successful attempts at bringing the ideas contained in the *Futurist Variety Theater* manifesto to fruition. See Berghaus, *Italian Futurist Theatre*, pp. 201–209.

19. This may be a reference to Depero's *Teatro plastico* (see Berghaus, *Italian Futurist Theatre*, pp. 316–18) or his magical box, *Panoramagico* (see ibid., p. 299). Another possibility is the dramatic sculpture of Benedetto Croce, created and destroyed in the Galleria Sprovieri as part of Cangiullo's *Funeral of a Passéist Philosopher*. See Berghaus, *Italian Futurist Theatre*, pp. 238–39.

20. Information on these performances can be found in Lista, *La Scène futuriste*; Berghaus, *Italian Futurist Theatre*; and Berghaus, *International Futurism*.

21. A collection of reviews, in Italian, can be found in Luciano Caruso and Giuliano Longone, eds., *Il teatro futurista a sorpresa: Documenti* (Florence: Salimbeni, 1979). For an English description of the performances of the first and second tour, see Berghaus, *Italian Futurist Theatre*, pp. 359–75.

22. The incident with the Futurist painter Antonio Fornari, who exhibited some of his creations on the stage of the Margherita Theater, was reported in a review in *Il popolo romano*, October 12, 1921.

23. Pasqualino Cangiullo (1900–75) was Francesco Cangiullo's younger brother.

24. Antonio Marasco (1896–1975) and Franco Bernini belonged to the Florentine group of Futurists.

25. The first tour of the Theater of Surprises had some thirty pieces in its repertoire, which were supplemented by further numbers dependent on the talent in the local Futurist circles.

70 MEMORANDUM ON STAGE PRESENCE AND THE STYLE OF THEATER

1. See document 33, *Dynamic, Multichanneled Recitation*.

2. This term was probably derived from the "telegraph" style (*Telegraphenstil*) common

in German Expressionist plays. These jerky, staccato outbursts reduced a text to its essential components and omitted articles, prepositions, etc.

71 THE ABSTRACT ANTIPSYCHOLOGICAL THEATER OF PURE ELEMENTS AND THE TACTILE THEATER

1. Marinetti is referring here, in the first instance, to the Theater of the Grotesque, which emerged during the First World War. Settimelli provides a more detailed list in "Il nuovo teatro italiano" (*Roma futurista*, January 4, 1920): Cavaccioli, Chiarelli, Pirandello, Antonelli, Rosso di San Secondo, Lopez, Praga, Niccodemi, Bracco, Benelli, Morselli.

2. Marinetti uses the term *verismo* here, coined to characterize a literary trend of the 1880s and in particular the works of Giovanni Verga. Although inspired by the French Naturalists, it never attained the radicalism of a Zola or Antoine. Together with Symbolism, it constituted a significant attempt at creating an artistic (as opposed to purely commercial) form of theater and drama.

3. Marinetti refers here to *Six Characters in Search of an Author*, which was premiered in Rome in 1921.

4. The third signatory, Bruno Corra, is not mentioned here, presumably because he had distanced himself from the Futurist movement by 1924.

5. The tours and productions are described in Berghaus, *Italian Futurist Theatre*, 193–201, 204–15.

6. See Michel Corvin, *Le Théâtre de recherche entre les deux guerres: Le Laboratoire Art et Action* (Lausanne: L'Âge d'Homme, 1976).

7. See Giovanni Lista, *La Scène futuriste*, pp. 362–67.

8. See note 16 to document 69, *The Theater of Surprises*.

9. Examples of the Futurist Theater of Essential Brevity were indeed performed in various countries but were by no means published in "every language."

10. The Futurist influence on Pirandello has been discussed in Mario Verdone, "Teatro pirandelliano e futurismo," *Teatro contemporaneo* 2, no. 4 (June–September 1983): 113–25; Umberto Mariani, "Pirandello e il futurismo," *Nemla Italian Studies* 10 (1986): 71–84; Mario Verdone, "Luigi Pirandello e i futuristi," *Canadian Journal of Italian Studies* 14, nos. 42–43 (1991): 50–59.

11. The essay was published on January 31, 1924. Both Chiarelli and Marinetti are overstating the Futurist influence on Russian stage design. The most significant influence came from the Constructivist movement, but other sources also left their mark on the theater of the Russian Revolution. See Konstantin Rudnitsky, *Russian and Soviet Theatre: Tradition and the Avant-Garde* (London: Thames and Hudson, 1988).

12. The early date given here is highly unlikely, as Settimelli's playwriting efforts of the years from 1910 to 1913 were rather conventional. It was only in 1914, following his involvement with the Futurist Theater of Essential Brevity, that he became an avant-garde author.

13. This paragraph is a quote from document 34, *A Futurist Theater of Essential Brevity*.

14. See document 34, *A Futurist Theater of Essential Brevity*, demands 1, 4, 5, 6, 7.

15. See note 17 to document 34, *A Futurist Theater of Essential Brevity.*
16. The following four paragraphs, until ". . . ad infinitum," is a quote from the manifesto *The Theater of Surprises* (document 69).
17. There is certainly a great deal of psychology in the novels of Marcel Proust, but this Parisian author can hardly be classified as "semi-Futurist." What Marinetti may have had in mind was Proust's interior monologues in *A la recherche du temps perdu* (*Remembrance of Things Past*), which bear some resemblance to the Futurist Words-in-Freedom. See his note 10 in the manifesto *The Synthetic Novel* (1939).
18. See Berghaus, *Italian Futurist Theatre*, pp. 366–69.
19. Marinetti refers here to his plays *Indecision, Fight between Backdrops, Tactile Quartet*, and *The Great Cure*, which were performed during the tour and printed in the appendix to the manifesto.
20. This passage refers to other numbers in the show, the mechanical ballets *Anihccam 3000* by Depero and Casavola, *Dance of the Propeller* by Prampolini and Casavola, and *Psychology of the Machines* by Prampolini and Mix.

72 FUTURIST PHOTOGRAPHY

1. Anton Giulio Bragaglia (1890–1960) and Arturo Bragaglia (1893–1962) took up photography at an early age and joined the film company CINES, managed by their father, Anton Giulio, who worked as a journalist and later dedicated himself to the theater, was the more intellectual of the two brothers and developed, in 1911–13, a Futurist theory of photography, culminating in a booklet on photodynamism (1913). Arturo was more practical in his outlook and specialized in the technical side of photography.
2. In March 1913 the Futurist gallery owner Giuseppe Sprovieri organized a series of Futurist events at the Sala Pichetti. One of these was a lecture by A. G. Bragaglia on photodynamism, which was presented by Marinetti, Folgore, and Altomare.
3. Needless to say, they did not. In the intervening years between Bragaglia's and Tato's manifestos, the new artistic trends in photography were determined by the Dada photo collages, the Constructivist photomontages, the oneiric photography of the Surrealists, the New Objectivity of *rapportage* photography, and so on.
4. Following the chronophotographic studies of Jules Etienne Marey and Eadweard Muybridge, photographers developed new techniques and took up new theoretical positions on how to render movement in the static medium of a photographic print. The "drama of objects" was a genre reflected upon in the manifesto *A Futurist Theater of Essential Brevity* (document 34); and in the 1920s, Tato experimented with ways of dramatizing static objects and giving them anthropomorphic connotations in form of a "photographic theater."
5. The experiments with photograms by Man Ray, László Moholy-Nagy, and others were a major influence on the Futurist photographers Veronesi and Tato. In fact, Moholy-Nagy's essay "The Future of the Photographic Process" (1929) bears many similarities to the manifesto *Futurist Photography.*
6. The term used here, *spettralizzazione*, has nothing to do with spectroscopic images, but rather denotes an array of body parts composed like a scale or spectrum of images.

7. The terms *ricongiungere*, *fusione*, *compenetrazione*, and *sovrapposizione*, used in this and the following paragraphs, all refer to the techniques of photomontage.

8. The use of distorting perspectives or optical distortions by means of concave/convex mirrors was practiced by many photographers in the 1920s.

9. Surrealist influences are particularly recognizable in the photographs of Vinicio Paladini, whose *immaginismo* was a cross between Futurism, Dada, and Surrealism.

10. Photomicrography was widely practiced ever since Fox Talbot used a solar microscope and photographed an insect's wing, magnified some fifteen times.

11. Futurist photography concerned itself not only with movement or abstract light-and-shadow play. Tato also sought to employ dematerializing effects, to go beyond the phenomenal appearances of things, and to represent the transcendental and unseen.

12. Boccioni's "States of Mind" paintings of 1911 influenced A. G. Bragaglia's attempts at dematerializing photography and using it to express passing states of mind.

73 Manifesto of Futurist Cuisine

1. Novecento was an artistic movement founded by Margharita Sarfatti in 1922 and formally launched with an exhibition in 1923, under the patronage of Benito Mussolini. From 1925 onward it also extended, under the guidance of Massimo Bontempelli, into the literary fields. It came closer to the position of State art than any of the other competing factions due to its mixture of modern and conservative aesthetics and its firm alliance with the Fascist cause. While Futurism was systematically marginalized in major shows such as the Venice Biennale, Novecento artists received the honors of a quasi-official recognition by the regime.

2. Marinetti used the term *mistici dell'azione* as a motto in his book *Futurismo e fascismo* (1924) and ascribed the term to "the Theosophists." In other writings he defined Futurist actionism in quasi-religious terms, not unlike the Christian crusaders and the warriors of an Islamic *jihad*.

3. Benedetto Croce (see note 12 to document 38) was repeatedly critized by the Futurists. He answered his adversaries with "Il futurismo come cosa estranea dell'arte," *La critica*, November 20, 1918; and "Futurismo e fascismo," *La stampa*, March 15, 1924.

4. Graça Aranha (1868–1931) was a Brazilian writer who played the role of official host during Marinetti's 1926 lecture tour in Brazil. Aranha welcomed Marinetti on May 15 in the Lírico Theater of Rio de Janeiro with a highly complementary speech and later published the collection *Futurismo: Manifesto de Marinetti e seus companheiros* (1926).

5. See the manifestos *A Futurist Theater of Essential Brevity* (document 34), *The Theater of Surprises* (document 69), *Abstract Antipsychological Theater of Pure Elements* (document 71), and *Tactilism: A Futurist Manifesto* (document 67).

6. Penelope, in Greek mythology, was the wife of Odysseus. During his twenty-year absence she was weaving, and secretly unraveling, a shroud as a ploy to ward off her suitors.

7. Jarro was the pseudonym of Giulio Piccini (1849–1915), a journalist, theater critic, and author of many volumes of fiction and popular monographs. In 1910, Marinetti

published a broadsheet, *Jarro per il futurismo*, in which he printed a telegram of the critic announcing his adherence to the Futurist movement. As founding editor of the *Almanacco gastronomico* (Florence: Bemporad, 1912 ff.), Jarro strove for a renewal of the Florentine and Tuscan cuisine and regularly cooked for the cultural elites in the hotels and restaurants of Florence. Jules Maincave (?–1916) was a French chef who in the 1910s ran a restaurant on the Left Bank. He was known for his extravagant creations, such as beef in kummel garnished with slices of banana and stuffed with Gruyère; pureed sardines with Camembert; tomatoes sprinkled with brandy and whipped cream; or sole flambéed with rum and served with a mousse of crème Chantilly. On September 1, 1913, the Parisian journal *Fantasio* published an essay on "La Cuisine futuriste," which contained a "Manifeste de la cuisine futuriste" by Maincave. It made demands for a "cuisine that is suited to the comforts of modern life and the latest concepts in science . . . Futurist cuisine aims at uniting elements of food and drink that nowadays, owing to a strange overcautiousness, are strictly separated. It seeks to provoke, by means of these encounters, unknown gustative sensations." Some fourteen years later, the text was translated into Italian as "Manifesto della cucina futurista" in *La fiera letteraria* 3, no. 21 (May 22, 1927): 3. On the other Futurist chefs Marinetti refers to and their creations, see Günter Berghaus, "The Futurist Banquet: Nouvelle Cuisine or Performance Art?," *New Theatre Quarterly* 28, no. 1 (February 2001): 3–17.

8. Albumin is a protein that can be found in animal tissues such as egg white, milk, muscle, and blood plasma; it also occurs in plants, especially in seeds.

9. The concept of artificial food runs through a number of Futurist publications of the 1920s and '30s, but Marinetti was particularly taken by Fedele Azari's concept of food engineering and artificial nutrition.

10. Marinetti draws here on Fedele Azari's vision of a mechanized world designed to iron out "the imperfection, weakness, and inconstancy of the organic world." Mass man had been replaced by a "mass of machines," which "redeem mankind from the slavery of manual labor, poverty, and class struggle." The human race lives in symbiosis with a "harmonious and elegant squadron of machines" and controls industrial production by means of robots and computers. See his manifesto "Per una società di protezione delle macchine," in *La fiera letteraria*, April 24, 1927.

11. Aurum is a brandy-based, pale-gold liqueur blended with a distillate of citrus fruits. Its golden appearance, from which its name is derived, is sometimes enhanced by saffron.

12. La Penna d'Oca was a prestigious restaurant in Milan and venue of a Futurist banquet given on November 15, 1930, for local notables, writers, and journalists.

13. Fillìa was the pseudonym of Luigi Colombo (1904–36), a painter, poet, dramatist, and leader of the Turin group of Futurists. In 1931 he decorated, together with Nicolaj Diulgheroff, the Futurist restaurant Holy Palate in Turin; in 1932, together with Marinetti, he wrote a Futurist cookbook.

14. Enrico Prampolini (1894–1956) was one of the most influential Futurist painters and theoreticians.

74 TOTAL THEATER: ITS ARCHITECTURE AND TECHNOLOGY

1. In the 1920s several artists and designers published their plans for a total theater. Moholy-Nagy's concept of a *Theater der Totalität* was disseminated in 1925, 1927, and 1929; Farkas Molnár's *U-Theater* in 1925; Andreas Weininger's *Kugeltheater* in 1927. See Günter Berghaus, *Theatre, Performance and the Historical Avant-garde* (New York: Palgrave, 2005), pp. 221–22. These essays and drawings appeared in publications of the Bauhaus, which Prampolini—Marinetti's preferred architect for the Futurist national theater—regularly received in Rome. The most famous blueprint for a total theater came from Walter Gropius, the head of the Bauhaus. It was designed for Erwin Piscator and described in the essay "Vom modernen Theaterbau, unter Berücksichtigung des Piscatortheaterneubaues in Berlin," *Berliner Tageblatt*, November 2, 1927, p. 5; and in *Die Scene* 18, no. 1 (1928): 4–6. Ivo Pannaggi's detailed and well-illustrated report on this project in the Italian theater journal *Scenario* 1, no. 6 (July 1932): 46–50, must have been known to Marinetti when he wrote this manifesto.

2. Neoclassical aesthetics demanded, in accordance with Aristotle, the unities of place, time, and action. Although by the nineteenth century these precepts had lost their binding force, most Italian theater companies could not afford to travel with more than one set for each play they were performing. Therefore, the "unity of place" remained in force until permanent theaters, with improved stage technology, became more common in Italy.

3. In the published version of this essay, Marinetti states that the theater should have a diameter of 200 meters. The outer stage should be 10 meters wide, 2 meters high, and 5 meters away from the wall of the building. The drawings in the manuscript contain more measurements: 50 meters for the trench, 5 meters for the walkway, and 20 meters for the stalls. It is easy to see that these measurements do not add up to a consistent building plan and do not always square with what is said in the manuscript. It is likely that manuscript, drawings, and published text were produced at different times and were the outcome of flashes of inspiration rather than logically developed concepts.

4. In the published version of the manifesto, Marinetti suggests the use of movable screens, positioned in the space between the outer circular stage and the theater wall, to be used for film projections and television programs.

5. The theme of flying was an important motif in Futurist paintings of the late 1920s and was given a theoretical foundation in the "Manifesto of Aeropainting" (1931). Early Futurist publications focusing on the subject of aviation were Marinetti's *L'aeroplano del Papa* (1908), *Aeroplani* by Paolo Buzzi (1909), *Ponti sull'Oceano* by Luciano Folgore (1914), and *Intervista con un Caproni* by Mario Carli (1916). Marinetti theorized on aeropoetry in a manifesto published with different titles in 1932 and 1933.

6. In the published version, Marinetti adds: "The spectators can move about on the eight-meter-wide walkway, individually or in groups, engage in the chance adventures of a journey, participate in the nautical actions unfolding in the trench. Or they can exit, using specially made elevators, into the brightly lit basement for refreshments or a moment of relaxation. Thus, having behaved and performed like actors,

and, like dispersed troupes, having speedily communicated with each other with their radio-telephones, they can return to their seats and tables. The latter have been provided with a moving belt which gives unexpected tactile sensations, complemented and enhanced by different smells. These are controlled by a keyboard and can be sucked away by special vacuum cleaners."

7. In the published version of the manifesto, he states that the cupola should be one hundred meters aboveground.

8. In the published version of the manifesto, Marinetti writes: "The enormous red ball of a magnificent sunset . . . fuses with the view of a busy street in an American city, transmitted by television."

9. The sentence set in square brackets has been crossed out in the manuscript. The reference here may be to Achille Ricciardi's *Teatro del Colore*, one of the most important Futurist theater experiments, which took place in Rome in March 1920. After 1919, colored "gels" (gelatin filters placed over the lighting source) became common in Western theaters. They allowed designers to give scenes a "wash" of any color, usually to suggest mood or atmosphere.

10. Here, as in other sections of the text, Marinetti speaks as a layman fascinated by the new stage technologies recently introduced in Germany, England, France, and the United States. Prampolini, Depero, and Pannaggi, for example, were Futurist stage designers with practical experience outside Italy; they could have furnished Marinetti with some of the information he built upon for his grand but unrealistic schemes.

11. The most sophisticated interaction between actors and screen could be observed in Erwin Piscator's productions of *Tidal Wave* (1926), *Storm over Gottland* (1927), *Hoppla, We're Still Alive* (1927), *Rasputin* (1927), *Schweijk* (1927), and *The Merchant of Berlin* (1929). Previously, Eisenstein's "montage of attractions," *The Wise Man* (1923), had incorporated a brief film specially shot for the production, entitled *Glumov's Diary*. These and many other experiments have been analyzed in Claudine Amiard-Chevrel, ed., *Théâtre et cinéma années vingt: Une quête de la modernité*, 2 vols. (Lausanne: L'Âge d'Homme, 1990); and Béatrice Picon-Vallin, ed., *Les Écrans sur la scène: Tentations et résistances de la scène face aux images* (Lausanne: L'Âge d'Homme, 1998).

12. Mikado, which literally means "exalted gate" or "sublime porte," is the archaic title for the emperor of Japan, popularized in the West by the Gilbert and Sullivan operetta of that name.

13. Yokohama began to flourish as a commercial center and leading seaport when it was opened to foreign commerce in 1859. It was almost totally destroyed by an earthquake in 1923.

14. Russia leased Port Arthur from China and made it the headquarters of her navy in the Pacific region. On February 8, 1904, the Japanese launched a surprise attack on Port Arthur and initiated the Russo-Japanese War, which ended on September 5, 1905, with the signing of the Treaty of Portsmouth.

15. Ermete Novelli (1851–1919), a great Italian actor who by 1885 had his own company. He enjoyed great success in Paris in 1898 and 1902, and established a new theater in Rome, the Casa di Goldoni, on the lines of the Comédie Française.

16. Ermete Zacconi (1857–1948), an Italian actor who established his own company in 1894 and made himself a name as a champion of modern drama and as a partner of Eleonore Duse.

17. In 1926 Marinetti began to seek public funding for the erection of an ultramodern and technically advanced, permanent Futurist theater in Milan. In 1927 he submitted a Memorandum to the Duce, in which he outlined the shortcomings of the existing theater and of the acting profession and how these could be overcome in an institution built according to plans drawn up by Prampolini, Depero, Bragaglia, Balla, and Pannaggi. To improve the state of the Italian acting profession, he proposed to attach to this playhouse a state acting school as well as a new type of conservatory for directors, stage designers, and theater technicians. (The unpublished document is preserved in the Archivio dello Stato di Roma, *Segreteria Particolare del Duce, C.O.,* fasc. 509.446.) Mussolini was sympathetically inclined toward the project and had it carefully assessed by the minister of education and the minister of finances, who eventually turned it down for financial reasons. Nonetheless, Enrico Prampolini continued to campaign for such an institution. See his essay "L'Istituto Internazionale d'Arte Teatrale" in *L'impero*, May 3, 1932.

75 A FUTURIST THEATER OF THE SKIES ENHANCED BY RADIO AND TELEVISION

1. The Futurist Aviators' Club in Milan developed, inspired by Fedele Azari's manifesto *A Futurist Theater of the Skies*, a number of theatrical projects, some of which were presented at the Prima Giornata Aerosportiva in Rome in November 1930. See the chapter on Azari in Berghaus, *Italian Futurist Theatre*, pp. 485–94. Marinetti used the event to issue this extended edition of Azari's manifesto.

2. Mino Somenzi (1899–1948), a painter, sculptor, and journalist who in 1928 developed the concept of aeropainting. He was effectively second in command in the Futurist movement, founded the newspaper *Futurismo* (1932–33), and edited its sequel, *Artecrazia,* until it was closed down by the Fascists.

3. Marinetti was probably thinking here of large-scale panels with Words-in-Freedom painted on them. He explained the concept of aeropoetry in "Manifesto to the Poets and Aviators" in *Futurismo*, October 2, 1932, which ends with the following words: "Aeropoetry finds its natural outlet in the radio. If, however, it is fixed on paper, this turns immediately into a flier and a well-aired page of the sky. It displays the purest and most condensed poems, suspended from high above and traveling in the manner of clouds."

4. On February 9, 1929, *L'impero* printed a report entitled "Progress of Television," from a correspondent in New York, which predicted that within a few years there would be as many television sets in Italy as there were already telephones and radios. On September 18, 1930, John Logie Baird conducted a widely reported experiment at the Berlin Funkausstellung: he transmitted television signals from a studio in Friedrichstrasse to the Scala theater, where a thirty-line screen, fitted with 21,000 bulbs and measuring 60 by 180 cm, showed the images. As radio and television were seen to be ultramodern technologies, they had a great allure for the Futurists and were held by Marinetti to be appropriate complements to Azari's Theater of the

Skies. For another combination of television and theater, see his manifesto of 1933, *Total Theater: Its Architecture and Technology* (document 74).

5. A by-product of Azari's Theater of the Skies was the idea of a Futurist aerial scenography, first presented by Gino Cantarelli in his manifesto *Pyrotechnics—A Means of Art* (1920).

76 THE RADIO

1. Pino Masnata (1901–68) was a close friend of Paolo Buzzi and Armando Mazza and entered the Milanese branch of the Futurist movement when he was a medical student. His dramatic concepts were very different from those of the Theater of Essential Brevity. In 1920, he published "Manifesto of a Visionic Theater" in *Roma futurista* (February 22, 1920) and *La testa di ferro* (November 14, 1920) and proposed to abolish "the borderline between the real and unreal, thought and action," to "deform and mingle the timescales, the scene actions, the personages" and to make use of "cinematographic transformations." Masnata wrote several plays for this semi-Surrealist type of theater, in which he applied Marinetti's concept of "wireless imagination" and made use of cinematographic techniques. He never became actively involved with any of the Futurist theater companies of the time, partly because of his professional career as a surgeon and partly because, as he once confessed, "I was convinced that my plays could only be fully realized in the cinema. But this medium was inaccessible to me." In the 1930s, Masnata published about a dozen radio dramas, one of which (*Il cuore di Wanda*) was broadcast by Radio Milano on December 20, 1931.

2. Futurism in its third phase, which lasted from about 1931 to 1940, presented itself under the banner of *aerovita* (airborne life), and its artistic creations as *aeropittura*, *aeromusica*, *aeropoesia*, and so on.

3. See the manifestos *A Futurist Theater of Essential Brevity* (document 34) and *The Theater of Surprises* (document 67).

4. See document 34, *A Futurist Theater of Essential Brevity*.

5. The second Futurist Congress was held on the occasion of the exhibition *Omaggio futurista a Umberto Boccioni*, held in May 1933 at the Galleria Pesaro in Milan, and had some ninety participating artists.

6. The concept of artificial nutrition, suited to an airborne and mechanized world, was first developed by the Futurist Azari, then taken up by Fillìa and Marinetti in their *Manifesto of Futurist Cuisine* (document 73).

7. After the first experiments with televised images in 1909–11, some very successful new technologies were publicly demonstrated by John Logie Baird in London (1925) and Édouard Belin in Paris (1926). In 1929 Baird Television Ltd. began operating the first TV service for the BBC. On February 9, 1929, *L'impero* printed an interesting report on "the progress of television" from a correspondent in New York and predicted that within a few years there would be as many television sets in Italy as there were now telephones and radios. This gave rise to Marinetti's manifesto *Il teatro futurista aeroradiotelevisivo*, published on January 15, 1932, in the *Gazzetta del popolo*.

8. These attempts had already begun in the 1920s, when Giuseppe Fabbri published the journal *L'antenna* (1926), Gianfranco Merli issued the first volume of his series Edizioni radiofuturiste "Electron" (1929), and Bruno Munari founded a group called Radiofuturismo in the same year. On December 20, 1931, the first Futurist radio drama, *Tum-Tum*, by Pino Masnata, was broadcast under the title *Il cuore di Wanda* (Wanda's Heart) by Radio Milano, followed, on January 19, 1933, by Marinetti's *Violetta e gli aeroplani*.

9. Alfred N. Goldsmith (1888–1974) conducted his first radio transmission tests in 1915. He became the director of research for the Marconi Wireless Telegraph Co. of America, and when that company was acquired by the newly founded Radio Corporation of America in 1919, he was made director of research for RCA. Although New York possessed some fifty-seven radio stations by 1927, none of these was called New York's Radio City. I presume that Marinetti or Masnata were mixing up some information here related to New York's Radio City Music Hall, built in 1932 as the largest indoor theater in the world.

10. This is a rather heterogeneous list of practitioners, mixing innovative with traditionalist figures in early radio history, and is rather flawed in its spelling of names. Paul Reboux (1877–1963) was a French writer of cookbooks, etiquette books, and collections of pastiches, as well as fiction. Théo Fleischman (1893–1979) was a writer and journalist as well as a radio pioneer who, in 1924, initiated a daily, half-hour "spoken newspaper" program ("le journal parlé—het gesproken dagblad") for Radio Belgique and Société Belge de Radio. Alex Surchamp was a journalist and one of the collaborators of the *Journal parlé de la Tour Eiffel*, which first went on the air on November 3, 1925. Tristan Bernard (1866–1947) was a popular French playwright, novelist, and journalist, best known for his lighthearted comedies of manners. The Silesian Expressionist poet Fritz Walther Bischoff (1896–1976) was director of Breslau Radio as well as author of several radio dramas and critical essays on the new media. His highly successful "radio symphony," *Hallo! Hier Welle Erdball!*, was broadcast on February 4, 1928, on Radio Breslau, and excerpts were preserved on two records, directed by Viktor Heinz Fuchs. Fuchs was an actor who had become first announcer and production manager of the Schlesische Funkstunde in Breslau (1926–28). Friedrich Wolf (1888–1953) was a well-known and highly productive communist playwright and theoretician of socialist-realist literature. He wrote an interesting radio play about a Russian icebreaker rescuing an Italian airplane stranded in the Antarctic, *SOS . . . rao rao . . . Foyn "Krassin" rettet "Italia,"* transmitted in Berlin (1929) and Paris (1931). M. Felix Mendelssohn and Robert Seitz created the radio opera *Malpopita* in 1931, with music by Walter Goehr. I have not been able to identify Jacques Rece, who is known to me only through an article published in the Belgian journal *Variété* in August 15, 1929.

11. This may be a criticism of some of the later *sintesi*, written after the manifesto *A Futurist Theater of Essential Brevity* (document 34).

12. The graphic design of the words on the page creates an optical effect. However, this would require transmission via television.

13. This and several of the following demands were already contained in Marinetti's re-

sponse to an inquiry into radio, published by *Il convegno* in August 1931, and in the nine-point declaration "Perchè mi piace la radio," transmitted by Radio Trieste in April 1932.

14. This refers to the technical process of transforming sound waves into electrical signals, thence into high-frequency radio waves, and then back into sound waves.

15. This emphasis on sensation rather than information, as well as the previous two demands, bear a resemblance to another Futurist manifesto, Arnaldo Ginna's *L'arte della radiofonia* published in *L'impero* January 23, 1932, which sought to "merge sensibility and technique into effects of a purely phonic essence." Ginna also published other pertinent notes and reflections on the radio in the "Spettacoli" section of *L'impero* and *Oggi e domani*.

16. The BBC's Empire Service broadcast, on December 19, 1932, was a first "radio hookup" to five time zones. It may be that Marinetti's *Dramma di distanze*, mentioned in note 17, was inspired by this event.

17. See Marinetti's radio drama *Dramma di distanze* (1933), which juxtaposes seven different sound samples recorded in Rome, Santos, Tokyo, Varese, New York, Milan, and Rio de Janeiro. This application of Russolo's theory of noise to the medium of radio predates the *musique concrète* of the 1950s. However, Pierre Schaeffer confessed (in *La Biennale*, July–December 1959, pp. 65–71) to having been unaware of his Futurist predecessors.

18. See document 33, *Dynamic and Multichanneled Recitation*.

19. See document 21, *Destruction of Syntax—Untrammeled Imagination—Words-in-Freedom*.

20. Marinetti gave an excellent demonstration of this in his radio broadcasts of his own poetry. On May 21 and 22, 1926, he read several poems on Radio Rio in Brazil; in February 1929 he transmitted on EIAR *Il bombardamento di Adrianopoli*; and on August 12, 1933, he improvised an aeropoem celebrating Italo Balbo's transatlantic flight.

21. As Marinetti explained in document 21, *Destruction of Syntax—Untrammeled Imagination—Words-in-Freedom*, the verb in the infinitive was for him the quintessence of speed in literature.

22. In Futurist theory, essentialism was a complement to dynamism, simultaneity, and compression.

23. See document 73, *Manifesto of Futurist Cuisine*, and the Futurist "sport dances," *Tennis* (Mix), *Football* (Hradil), *Vortex* (Pratella), and *Propeller* (Casavola), presented on June 22, 1928, at the Teatro delle Feste in Turin. In the 1930s Masnata collaborated with the composer Carmine Guarino on experimental operas for radio. Similarly, the Futurist composer Franco Casavola applied some of Russolo's concepts to film music. Marinetti himself collaborated with Aldo Giuntini on the writing of a *Manifesto dell'aeromusic sintetica*, published in 1934.

24. In radio technology, silence is not an absence of sound, but a recording of ambient sounds of varying quality.

25. This was probably Marinetti's most revolutionary demand, leading to his radio dramas of 1933, *The Silences Speak to Each Other* (containing seven periods of silence of up to forty seconds) and *Battle of Rhythms* (containing, in the middle, a three-

minute period of silence), which predate John Cage's 4'33" by nineteen years. Cage heard of Marinetti's *sintesi radiofoniche* through Allan Kaprow in 1958–59.

26. This refers to the studio techniques of eliminating the natural resonance of a recording space and adding artificially created resonances by means of reflecting screens, absorbing curtains, echo chambers, etc.

BIBLIOGRAPHY

This bibliography lists only those works repeatedly referred to in the Notes. For a more extensive bibliography on Futurism and the works of F. T. Marinetti, see Günter Berghaus, "Futurism: A Bibliographic Reference Shelf," in G. Berghaus, ed., *Futurism in Arts and Literature* (Berlin: De Gruyter, 2000), pp. 487–597.

Apollonio, Umbro. ed. *Futurist Manifestos*. London: Thames and Hudson, 1973.

Berghaus, Günter. *The Genesis of Futurism*. Leeds: Society for Italian Studies, 1995.

———. *Futurism and Politics: Between Anarchist Rebellion and Fascist Reaction, 1909–1944*. Oxford: Berghahn, 1996.

———. *Italian Futurist Theatre, 1909–1944*. Oxford: Clarendon Press, 1998.

Berghaus, Günter, ed. *Futurism in Arts and Literature: Interdisciplinary Studies on Futurism as an International Phenomenon*. Berlin: De Gruyter, 2000.

Caruso, Luciano, ed. *Manifesti, proclami, interventi e documenti teorici del futurismo, 1909–1944*. 4 vols. Florence: S.P.E.S., 1980.

Crispolti, Enrico. *Storia e critica del futurismo*. Rome: Bulzoni, 1986.

Lista, Giovanni. *La Scène futuriste*. Paris: C.N.R.S., 1989.

Lista, Giovanni, ed. *Futurisme: Manifestes, proclamations, documents*. Lausanne: L'Âge d'Homme, 1973.

———. *Marinetti et le futurisme*. Lausanne: L'Age d'Homme, 1977.

Lugaresi, Giovanni, ed. *Lettere ruggenti a F. Balilla Pratella*. Milan: Quaderni dell'Osservatore, 1969.

I manifesti del futurismo. Florence: Edizioni di *Lacerba*, 1914.

I manifesti del futurismo. 4 vols. Milan: Istituto Editoriale Italiano, 1919.

Marinetti, Filippo Tommaso. *Le Futurisme*. Paris: Sansot, 1911.

———. *Guerra sola igiene del mondo*. Milan: Edizioni futuriste di "Poesia," 1915.

———. *Democrazia futurista*. Milan: Facchi, 1919.

———. *Futurismo e fascismo*. Foligno: Campitelli, 1924.

———. *Marinetti e il futurismo*. Rome: Edizioni "Augustea," 1929.

———. *Teoria e invenzione futurista*. Luciano de Maria, ed. Milan: Mondadori, 1968; 2nd ed. 1983.

———. *La grande Milano tradizionale e futurista. Una sensibilità italiana nata in Egitto*. Luciano de Maria, ed. Milan: Mondadori, 1969.

———. *Taccuini, 1912–1915*. Alberto Bertoni, ed. Bologna: Il Mulino, 1987.

Noi futuristi. Milan: Quintieri, 1917.

Salaris, Claudia. *Storia del futurismo: Libri, giornali, manifesti*. Rome: Editori Riuniti, 1985; 2nd, enlarged ed., 1992.

———. *F. T. Marinetti*. Scandicci: La Nuova Italia, 1988.

———. *Luciano Folgore e le avanguardie*. Scandicci: La Nuova Italia, 1997.

Scrivo, Luigi, ed. *Sintesi del futurismo: Storia e documenti*. Roma: Bulzoni, 1968.

NAME INDEX

GEOGRAPHICAL NAMES

PERSONAL NAMES

SUBJECT INDEX

For cross-references to personal names, see the Name Index.